CONTEMPORARY TOPICS IN URBAN SOCIOLOGY

GENERAL LEARNING PRESS
250 James Street
Morristown, New Jersey 07960

Manufactured in the United States of America

Published simultaneously in Canada

Library of Congress Catalog Card Number 76-28830

ISBN 0-382-18272-3

Preface

The history of civilization is written in the city. For many years historians, sociologists, economists, geographers, and others have attempted to interpret the human urban experience. How, why, when, and where did the first cities appear? What is the link between urbanization and economic development? How have social institutions established in agricultural society adapted to large urban concentrations? What forces have led to the massive differentiation among types of cities? What forces have led to the socioeconomic differentiation within the individual metropolis? How has the residential structure of urban populations been shaped by the processes of growth and aging? How have migrants to cities been integrated into and adjusted to the collage of urban institutions and activities? How do urbanites organize themselves for provision of basic educational, security, and health services? How have cities worked to release the creative genius of individual urbanites while simultaneously fostering and encouraging ugly, brutal, vulgar, and destructive impulses as well? How may the urban environment be structured to accentuate the more human and the more humane? These and many more questions form the core of a true science of the city. The goals of this science are to describe as accurately as possible the state of urban affairs and to explain the reasons for current and past urban events. Through explanation we not only sate our inherent curiosity about our urban roots, but we also lay the foundation for sound, ameliorative programs as well.

The science of the city is and must be both a basic and an applied science. The rapid rate of world urbanization and its accompanying problems have eliminated the luxury of abstract and idle speculation about cities. The demand for sound knowledge about cities that is translatable into action programs has served to increase the tempo and quality of urban research in recent years.

No book can adequately summarize all of our knowledge about cities. Yet there are certain concepts, theoretical models, and empirically verified generalizations that can explain today's urban experience and provide a foundation for further study. The goal for this book has been to cull from the major areas of urban sociological research the most important ideas and to present them to the student in a manner that will maximize comprehension. Unfortunately, summaries of complicated matters tend to play down the emerging nature of urban knowledge and to minimize some of the intellectual conflicts that have marked the growth of this science. However, the reader who wishes to go beyond our material may, through use of each chapter's bibliography, become immersed in the mainstream of a particular topic.

This book spans the gamut of the concerns of urban sociologists. The author of each chapter is both a creative scholar on the topic covered and a concerned teacher. Each author structured the chapter to identify the main dimensions of the topic. The exposition of the material was calculated to reach and interest the student in the general undergraduate course in urban sociology.

We invite you to join us on an exciting, challenging, and important odyssey—the study of our most complex form of communal life, the city.

The authors wish to express their appreciation for the fine editorial work of Carol Z. Rothkopf. She is a rare combination of skill, persistence, and pleasantness. We are grateful for her efforts.

Kent P. Schwirian

The Ohio State University

Contents

PART THREE·PROBLEMS, POLITICS, AND PLANNING

Introduction: An Overview of Urban Sociology

Kent P. Schwirian

The purposes of this introduction are to provide a general overview of the breadth and foci of urban sociology and to present a general introduction to the specialized chapters that follow. Each of the subsequent chapters is written by an urbanist who has specialized in teaching and research on the chapter's particular topic. There is no single, common, underlying theoretical scheme binding the separate chapters of this book into a single treatise because urban sociology as a field has no such single perspective. Indeed, the sociological study of the city has included many perspectives and varied research methodologies. Collectively, urban sociological theorizing and research have amassed an enormous quantity of findings which have generated an equally large number of additional questions that await future exploration. This book is organized in terms of the major topical areas of the field since the principal audience will consist largely of beginning students in urban studies. Most of the chapters reflect the state of the art through the mid-1970's. Undoubtedly, the research agendas of urban sociologists for the rest of this decade and through the 1980s will include the issues raised in the topics covered here.

The order in which the chapters are presented roughly corresponds to the topical order of many beginning courses in urban sociology. However, since each chapter is a complete instructional unit in itself there is no reason why the chapters cannot be read and studied in some other sequence. While the chapters are largely by sociologists and thus are aimed chiefly at students in sociology courses, the study of the city is not the exclusive domain of sociologists. Geographers, planners, economists, political scientists, and others have made major contributions to our understanding of man's urban experience. Where such contributions coincide with sociological interests and concerns they have been included.

The overview of urban sociology in this chapter is divided into four main sections: 1. a brief history of the early development of urban sociology in America; 2. a survey of the variety of theoretical perspectives that have come to characterize the field; 3. an elaboration of the major foci of sociological concerns with the city; and 4. a discussion of urban sociology's data sources and ways of obtaining them.

DEVELOPMENT OF URBAN SOCIOLOGY IN AMERICA

Definitions of the field of urban sociology are many and varied. To some it is the sociological study of life in the city in its broadest terms. To others it is the comparative study of the city as a macro-social form—comparative through time and comparative across societies. Whatever definition is adopted, any serious consideration of urban sociology today must encompass the broad study of the process of urbanization, including its causes and its consequences both for organizations and individuals.

While urban sociology in America has its roots in the earliest sociological thought, it was in the late 1800s and the early 1900s that the study of the city flowered. In 1899 Adna Weber completed *The Growth of Cities in the Nineteenth Century*. In 1925 the American Sociological Society devoted its annual meeting to "Urban Sociology" as a distinctive area of endeavor from "Rural Sociology," which had been the topic of the 1916 meeting. In the 1920s separate treatments of urban sociology appeared as textbooks—Robert Park, E. W. Burgess, and R. D. McKenzie's *The City* [1925]; Scott Bedford's *Readings in Urban Sociology* [1927]; and Nels Anderson and E. C. Lindeman's *Urban Sociology* [1928]. During the 1930s many extensive works of concern to urban sociologists were published and widely circulated. Among them were Niles Carpenter's *The Sociology of City Life* [1931]; Maurice Davie's *Problems of City Life* [1932]; R. D. McKenzie's *The Metropolitan Community* [1933]; and William F. Ogburn's *Social Characteristics of Cities* [1937]. These works joined an expanding literature on cities by historians and other social scientists, including such now standard references as N. S. B. Gras, *An Introduction to Economic History* [1922]; Henri Pirenne, *Medieval Cities: Their Origins and the Revival of Trade* [1925]; J. H. Breasted, *The Conquest of Civilization* [1926]; Arthur M. Schlesinger, *The Rise of the City* [1933]; V. Gordon Child, *Man Makes Himself* [1936]; and Lewis Mumford, *The Culture of Cities* [1938].

The theorizing and research of the sociologists in the first quarter of this century established the main direction of much of the work of the following decades. Even today many questions addressed by urban researchers have their roots in the work that appeared in the 1920s and 1930s. Two major currents came to characterize urban sociology in this early period. The first, emanating from the sociologists at the University of Chicago, emphasizes the demographic and ecological structure of the city, the social disorganization and pathology of the urban normative order, and the social psychology of urban existence. The second current has come to be called "community studies." It consists of broad-gauged ethnographic studies of the social structure of individual communities and the ways of life of the inhabitants.

The Chicago School

Chicago, in the early years of this century, was a natural place for the development of urban sociology. The city was large, rapidly growing, and sprawling over the nearby agricultural plain. The city's population was very heterogeneous. Rural migrants came to seek their fortune in the midwest metropolis, as did large numbers of European immigrants to whom the city's ambience was strange and demanding, necessitating enormous individual readjustments. The Europeans, coming from a dozen different countries, brought to the city new languages, new customs, new foods, new beliefs, and new aspirations that combined to make variety the norm. This environment challenged the scientific curiosity of Robert Park, his colleagues, and students at the University of Chicago to make sense of the social processes and social change going on around them. In a 1916 essay, "The City," Park announced an agenda for urban research. Many questions were developed that served to guide numerous research activities. Among these questions were:

1. What are the sources of a city's population and how is city growth a combination of natural increase and net migration?

2. What are the city's natural areas and how is the distribution of the city's population among the neighborhoods affected by economic interests such as land values and by noneconomic factors as well?

3. What are the social rituals of various neighborhoods—what things must one do in the area to be fully socially integrated and to avoid being looked upon with suspicion or to be thought to be peculiar?

4. Who are the local leaders; how do they embody local interests; how do they attain and maintain social influence and power; and how do they exercise control?

5. Do social classes in fact become cultural groups? Do they acquire an exclusiveness and independence of race and nationality?

6. Do children in the city follow in the occupational footsteps of their fathers?

7. Do occupational differences among people become related to normative differences among them?

8. Are there pathological conditions in communities that correspond to hysteria in the individual? How are such conditions produced and how are they controlled?

9. How is social unrest generated and manifested? Are strikes and mob violence produced by the same conditions that generate financial panics, real-estate booms, and mass movements of the general population?

10. What changes have taken place in the family? In what areas of family life has change been the greatest? How has such change been induced by the urban environment?

11. How have educational and religious institutions been modified by the process of urbanization?

12. Does property ownership affect school truancy, divorce, or crime? In what areas of the city and among which groups is crime endemic?

13. Do immigrant parents live in the same "social world" as that of their children? Are differences in language, ideals, and values between immigrant parents and their children reflected in juvenile delinquency? To what extent are the home mores of a particular immigrant group responsible for criminal behavior among members of the group?

14. What community values and interests are expressed in the local political organization? What devices exist that can be used to mobilize the forces of political organizations and get them into action?

15. To what extent do the newspapers control public opinion? To what extent are the media controlled by public sentiment?

These and many other questions formed the bases for the seminal research on the city by the sociologists at the University of Chicago. Among the many classic studies to appear were Nels Anderson's *The Hobo* [1923]; Frederick Thrasher's *The Gang* [1927]; Louis Wirth's *The Ghetto* [1928]; Clifford Shaw's *Delinquency Areas* [1929]; Harvey Zorbaugh's *The Gold Coast and the Slum* [1929]; Shaw's *The Jackroller* [1930]; Walter Reckless' *Vice in Chicago* [1933]; Shaw and Henry D. McKay's *Juvenile Delinquency and Urban Areas* [1942]. These volumes provide a rich ethnography of the early twentieth-century city. Sharing the same general theoretical perspective, they have provided a picture of the city that is well summarized in Wirth's essay, "Urbanism as a Way of Life" [1938].

Claude Fisher [1972] has suggested that Wirth presented two basic arguments in his theoretical model. One dealt with social organization and the other with social psychological concerns. Essentially, according to Wirth, the large size of the city's population, its dense settlement pattern, and the extreme social heterogeneity of the residents led to structural differentiation of the system, the formalization of institutions, and anomie. Structural differentiation refers to the process by which one social organization is subdivided or reorganized into several social organizations. Such differentiation may arise in response to a change in the context in which the organization operates, or it may arise in response to some internally generated impulse. The formalization of institutions involves an increasingly greater emphasis on the formal system rather than the informal as relationships come to be based upon role rather than personality. Interactions between individuals then tend to follow formal, prescribed scenarios, and transactions between individuals become limited to concerns of their respective roles. Anomie as a characteristic of the social system refers to the condition of low normative cohesion and integration. Anomie is reflected in aggregate rates of deviance, volatile political activity, and intergroup conflict. Presumably, with urbanization (the massive redistribution of a society's population from nonurban to urban areas) the city's population grows, becomes more diverse, and more heterogeneous. The city's institutions are then characterized by a tendency to structural differentiation, as well as formalization and anomie.

Wirth suggested that the structural changes that accompany urbanization had serious consequences for the typical urbanite. Life in such a system may produce high levels of nervous stimulation, psychological overload, and social isolation for the urbanite. The urban environment was described by Wirth as being stimuli-rich. The variety of information, cues, and norms was seen as producing information overload in the individual. To cope with this overload, such mechanisms as blocking out, filtering, and reducing general attention levels were employed by the city dweller. Individual isolation was seen as the inevitable consequence of living in the highly differentiated, stimuli-rich, anomic city. Wirth, and others, envisioned a kind of model personality for the urbanite. This personality is probably best described as showing detachment, selective inattention, impersonality, lack of broad concerns, limited horizons, alienation, potential deviance, and as being somewhat unhappy!

Do cities today display the social organizational characteristics described by Wirth? Are urbanites the dour, glum, and individuated actors he described? Two generations of urban researchers have focused much attention on Wirth's ideas and the best net answer to date is "In some ways, yes, and in some ways, no." The response is not very satisfying, yet it is a more accurate description of today's city dweller than either a simple "yes" or "no." We must remember that Wirth was writing about the structural and individual changes in a great city at one point in its development and growth. Many of Wirth's observations and those of the other Chicago sociologists are limited to this period that witnessed the massive readjustment of institutions and people. Since several of the following chapters in this book touch evaluatively on many of the contributions of the Chicago sociologists we, therefore, leave them at this point.

Community Studies

The second mainstream of urban sociology in this century is often referred to as "community studies." A community study focuses on the interrelationships of social institutions and groups in a single locality—presumably a natural, comprehensive setting [Bell & Newly 1974]. Community studies attempt to view social organization and human behavior within the sociologically rich context of a communal system. While community studies may tend to focus on one institution—such as the political or the family—they trace out the links and interdependencies with other institutions. While the focus of community studies tend to be on interdependencies within the locale, many studies do assess the impact of nonlocal change upon local institutions. In recent years the local-nonlocal aspects of community structure have come to be called the vertical and horizontal patterns of organization [Warren 1972].

The vertical patterns of relationship are those that exist among various institutions and groups within the local community and the social systems outside the community. Many local bodies have important ties to nonlocal organizations. The decision-making center that affects the very existence of the local outpost often may be very far removed. Yet decisions made elsewhere may be more critical to the local institutions than any of those that are made by other local bodies. This is clear in the case of branch plants that must constantly look to the distant main office or in military bases whose fate is decided in Washington. But, we see it in other local groups, too—the link between the parish and the removed diocesan office, the tie between local and national labor unions, the regulation of the local school by the state legislature. Some sociologists have argued that one hallmark of the highly developed society is the emergent importance of the vertical pattern of relationships in defining the scope and shape of local organizations, and the ebb and flow of local life [Greer 1962].

The horizontal patterns of relationship consist of all those ties among local bodies. The relationships among schools, churches, families, business, voluntary associations, governmental agencies, labor groups, and health care organizations make up the bulk of the horizontal system. Traditionally, community studies have concentrated on the structure and functioning of the horizontal system. The particular configuration of horizontal relationships has been used to distinguish between types of communities. One major theme that has come out of American community studies is the increasingly inconsequential nature of the horizontal system as the major shaper of local life. As the vertical system has been strengthened, the local community has become less protected from outside influences and impulses for change. It is enormously difficult in the study of a single community to strike a net balance of the importance of vertical and horizontal systems. Suffice it to say that both dimensions of community organization shape the lives of residents and both require much attention to understand the direction of local life.

Just as institutions and groups are oriented both vertically and horizontally, so too are individuals within the local community. Community studies frequently center on individuals as interesting characters in the local drama. Some individuals are more concerned with extra-local matters than they are with the local scene. They have come to be called "cosmopolitans" since their significant world lies elsewhere [Merton 1957]. The cosmopolitan "resides" in the local community but he "lives" in the larger world. "Localites," on the other hand, may be aware 'or even concerned with outside matters, but they confine their main interests and significant relationships to the local scene. The localite both resides and lives in the local community. The localite's wins and losses are scored locally. The horizontal system is the localite's sphere of operation.

Given the amount of interest in community studies and the amount of effort invested in detailed analyses of individual communities, it is somewhat perplexing that there is so much disagreement about the definition of the theoretical construct "community" itself. In an analysis of more than ninety various definitions of community, George Hillery [1955] has identified marked areas of disagreement and little specific consensus. Many definitions, however, seem to include the elements of area, population, common ties, and social interaction. Thus a community could well be defined as a network of relationships among the population residing in a common area through which they provide for their physical, social, and mental needs. The probable elements of the relationship network would be the familiar institutions and groups that link local residents together.

Many of the roots of American community studies can be found in the writings of the classic sociological scholars. For example, the rural-urban continuum concept, which is often an implicit theme in community studies, has its roots in the distinction drawn by Ferdinand Tönnies between social relationships that he called *Gemeinschaft* and *Gesellschaft*, and in Emile Durkheim's *mechanical* and *organic* social solidarity. Tönnies' dichotomy is between the traditional, intimate, personalized system of the community (Gemeinschaft) in which family, neighborhood and friendship systems were paramount organizing foci for local life and the more formal, contractual and rational system (Gesellschaft) of the society in which intimate associations are replaced by the formal, impersonal, large-scale organizations. Durkheim's mechanical solidarity is seen in social systems that manifest cohesion based upon common sentiments, while organic social solidarity is reflected in an integration based upon complementary functions—as in the interdependence of specialized parts. The conceptual distinctions made by Tonnies and Durkheim were taken by many community researchers as "ideal types" against which to gauge community social structure and social integration, as well as changes in structure and integration.

The classic American community studies include: Robert and Helen Lynd's study of *Middletown* [1929] and *Middletown in Transition* [1937]; Lloyd Warner's mammoth Yankee City series [1941]; A. B. Davis and M. Gardner's *Deep South* [1941], and many others. In a reassessment of American community studies, Maurice Stein [1960] has identified three major perspectives on the community that have characterized much of the past and current community studies research. These three perspectives are anthropological, sociological, and psychoanalytic. The anthropological perspective is seen in many concepts employed by community sociologists, as well as in techniques that are used for gathering data. The concepts of culture, subcommunity, folk society, and ritual appear in many community studies. Many community sociologists employ the full range of observational techniques that characterize basic ethnographic research—those for studying community life from the detached position of the outside observer to those of the inner perspective of the participant in the community's life.

The psychoanalytic perspective in many of the community studies is shown in the emphasis on the stresses and strains of urban life, as well as the mental health of the urbanites themselves. Psychoanalytic concepts enable the community sociologist to explore the parameters of local psychopathology and to study the emotional consequences of normal behavior. Focus is thus upon the whole spectrum of the human life cycle and the quest for identity and emotional maturity.

The sociological perspective primarily deals with the community as a social system and the macro-processes that bring about change in the local community system. Stein identifies three key processes that are reshaping community structure today. They are urbanization, industrialization, and bureaucratization. Urbanization involves the influx of large numbers of heterogeneous individuals who make an impact on local urban institutions, and who must face an adjustment process as they work out their new lives. Industrialization as a process of change involves the reorganization of work activities. Industrialization brings increasing specialization of work, more elaborate integrative mechanisms, and the elimination of the old craft and guild production systems. Bureaucratization involves the reorganization of ownership patterns and decision-making structures, as well as recruitment and advancement criteria within organizations. One major consequence of societal bureaucratization is the loss of local community autonomy. All American communities—large cities and small hamlets—according to Stein are, to some extent, being reshaped as urbanization, industrialization, and bureaucratization proceed on a society-wide basis.

THEORETICAL PERSPECTIVES

The studies by the early Chicago sociologists and those of the students of the local community have been joined in the last thirty years by an enormous body of studies and speculations reflecting a very wide range of theoretical perspectives. Gideon Sjoberg [1965] has classified these different approaches to urbanization and the city into several major schools of thought. The first he calls the *urbanization* school. It is well-exemplified in Wirth's writings. According to such researchers as Wirth, the city is characterized by role segmentation, secondary relationships, secularization of values, and ambiguity of the normative order. A critical question for the urbanization school of thought concerns how the usual social mechanisms work as the agrarian way of life gives way to the urban.

A second major theoretical perspective is named the *subsocial* school by Sjoberg. The subsocial perspective represents, to some extent, a merger of Social Darwinism and classical economics. The spatial and temporal patterns of man and society are viewed against a backdrop of natural, unplanned processes. Man is viewed as one element of nature and, as such, responds to impelled biosubsocial pressures and motivations. Human behavior reflects a marriage between these subsocial pressures and motivations whose source are in the social normative order.

The *sustenance* school and the *ecological complex* perspectives are rather similar. The sustenance school is mainly concerned with how a population organizes itself to provide for its sustenance needs. Urbanization is viewed as one of the mechanisms that is used by the population to create the type of organization necessary to support large numbers. According to the sustenance school, urbanization varies directly with the degree of division of labor of sustenance activities. This, in turn, varies in response to the society's level of technological development. The ecological complex consists of four macro-variables and their interrelationships. Those macro-variables are population, social organization, technology, and environment. Substantive problems from this perspective are analyzed in terms of variables representing organizational, environmental, technological, and population dimensions. It can be assumed that a change in any one of the ecological variables would cause a change in the others.

The *economic* school of urban sociology is made up of those who give primacy to economic explanations of urbanization and urban affairs. Sjoberg has included in this group the Marxist social historians who write of socialist cities, capitalist cities, feudal cities, and slave-owning cities. He has also included other approaches to the city that view urbanization as a progressive reorganization of markets and economic activities from primary to secondary to tertiary. As the economy changes, so too does the whole society, particularly the social organization of cities.

The *environmental* approach to the city frequently reflects more of a spirit of social reform than of scientific detachment. Here the city represents man's mode of adaptation in his struggle for survival. As long as the form of the city is in harmony with the rest of nature all is well.

Many environmentalists think that the industrial city as we know it has grown out of harmony and its pollution threatens to destroy the vital and fragile web of life. Environmentalists frequently become visionaries calling for a complete reorganization of urban structure so that it will be more in harmony with nature. Many of the basic ideas of urban planning and redevelopment come from the environmentalist perspective.

According to Sjoberg's catagorization, the *technological* school accords primacy to technological variables—such as modes of transportation—in explaining the location of cities, the interdependencies among cities, and the spatial patterning of the city's population and economic activities. While the technological school tends to ignore the impact upon urbanization and urbanism of nontechnological factors, the *value orientation* school stresses the role that noneconomic values play in urban-structure and urban land-use patterns. The sociocultural system of society is used as the explanatory factor in accounting for urban patterns. Differences between pairs of cities and differences through time in individual cities are explained by value and sentiment differences between the local populations. The *social power* school concentrates on the ability of various special interest groups in the city to achieve their goals as they compete with other groups. Power and politics affecting the city may be studied exclusively at the local level or it may be analyzed at state and national levels as decisions made at those levels affect the organization of local life.

Although several different theoretical perspectives may be identified, in practice we may find in the work of a single investigator more than one perspective being drawn upon in the formulation of hypotheses or in explanation of observed data regularities. And, in the study of single topics, such as urban land-use patterns or the growth and development of cities, contributions to our understanding have been made by more than one of these theoretical perspectives. Observation of the variety of these perspectives is one way to see the scope of urban sociology; another way is through a discussion of principal topics that have been investigated with some intensity in recent years.

MAJOR FOCI OF URBAN RESEARCH

One of the first topics to receive attention in the study of urban communities is the meaning of the concept of community. How does the community differ as a unique unit of social organization from other units studied by sociologists? What are the unique properties of communities as systems that make them different from societies, institutions, groups, or regions? How may the geographical expanse of the community be delineated, and how may we draw distinctions among the community's primary, secondary, and tertiary components?

As noted earlier, a very important question of urban research deals with the social characteristics of the city. What are the unique systemic properties that differentiate the urban community from the folk or rural community? What is unique to the "urban way of life"? Are communities either "urban" or "rural," or are there gradations in between? If so, along what dimensions does community differentiation occur and how may we best measure it? What are the links between community and society? As societies change and develop, what role do cities play in such change?

The Emergence and Rise of Cities

The nature of the community as a system and the unique characteristics of urban communities have received much attention by sociologists, but the whole topic of urbanization and human settlement patterns also has been of interest to historians, economists, and geographers. The emergence and rise of cities has been a central topic. Where did the first cities appear? What conditions were necessary for the development of the first cities? What role did environmental, technological, demographic, and social organizational factors play in early urbanization? Cities are not randomly scattered across the face of the earth; there are systematic patterns of cities' location. What factors explain why cities develop where they do—transportation, accessibility to agricultural hinterlands, the presence of unique geographical features, or resource fields? Why is it that some cities become specialized in one or a few economic functions while others specialize in different activities? What are the consequences of differential economic specialization for the social mix of the city's population and for the whole organization of local life?

Some societies have developed what has been called a "primate city" pattern of urban concentration. Within such a society there is only one large urban concentration whose population is much greater than that of any other communities. The "primate city" contains all of the key institutions that dominate the life of the whole society. Other societies have several large cities that are functionally differentiated from each other but are integrated into what has been called an "urban hierarchy." One serious area of research has been the attempt to discover the factors that account for why some societies have the primate city pattern while others approximate an urban hierarchy. An important question for researchers here has been the identification of the consequences for societal development given primacy rather than urban hierarchy. Some researchers have argued that the primate city pattern retards economic development across the whole society. However, some societies with the primate pattern of urban concentration are found in the most economically developed regions of the world. The nature of primacy, its causes and its impact are important topics in the study of societal settlement patterns.

In the Western nations urbanization has been a long-term process that has accompanied industrialization and demographic transition from high to low levels of both fertility and mortality [Weinstein 1976]. Much of the recent attention of urban sociologists has been directed toward the analysis of urbanization in developing countries. Will the developing countries replicate the pattern of the historic West? The best current answer to this question seems to be "no." Thus, much effort is being directed to describing and explaining a new kind of urbanization in Asia, Africa, and Latin America. Comparative urbanization studies in the emerging countries are concentrating on the process of migration and assimilation. What causes people from the agricultural regions to leave their homes and seek employment in crowded, large cities? How do the migrants adjust to the change in life and in work? What are the long-run consequences of this migration—for the place of origin, the city of destination, and for the migrants themselves?

The Metropolitan Community

The concept of metropolitan community has been used to describe the functional interdependencies between the city and the surrounding dependent population. Much research has centered on the functional differentiation of the city and the fringe, and on the differential social characteristics of city and fringe dwellers. Indeed, the massive literature on suburbia has had as one of its foci the process by which residential and industrial suburbs have come to differ in function, population composition, and life styles of residents. Another concern has been the impact of political fragmentation on the metropolitan community that has resulted from each major city being ringed with functionally interdependent but politically independent suburbs and special districts.

Some investigators feel that the metropolitan community may be just an intermediate level of community organization. The concept of "megalopolis" is sometimes used to describe urban regions in which there are large numbers of adjacent metropolitan communities such as those found on the east coast of the United States [Gottmann 1961]. The urban pattern stretching from New England through Washington, D.C. is viewed as the prototype megalopolis. Proponents of this concept argue that within a megalopolis there is actually a functional differentiation among the various metropolitan communities, as well as an economic specialization of each that is formally integrated so that the region, which was once characterized by formerly separate metropolitan communities, is now one superconstellation. It is frequently argued that this pattern or organization may also come to characterize the California coast and the Great Lakes region of the Midwest.

Another general area of urban research deals with the residential pattern of the city's population. Studies have shown that population density peaks near the city's center and declines rather sharply with increasing distance from the center. This pattern is found in cities in both the developed and the developing countries. Much research has been directed toward the study of locational factors that make for this characteristic pattern. Longitudinal studies have shown that in the developed countries the relationship between distance and density declines through time; that is, density does not seem to vary as systematically with distance as it did in the past. Aggregate density patterns have interested many researchers, but in recent years an increasing number of studies have attempted to ascertain the effects of high-density living on individuals and families. The essential question that has been posed is, "Does living under differing density conditions differentially affect human behavior over and above the effect of basic social characteristics such as social status and race?" Social scientists soon should be able to make firmer statements in response to this question than they have in the past.

In addition to aggregate density patterns, sociologists have been interested in the geometry of urban spatial patterns. A number of models have been developed to describe the differential distribution of social status and racial groups, industrial and residential land uses, and single homes and apartment areas. Various theories have suggested that cities display concentric zonal patterns, sectors, or multiple nuclei. Others have attempted to identify the basic dimensions along which urban subareas become differentiated from each other through the application of factor analysis techniques. In a more general and encompassing way, the neighborhood life-cycle model has attempted to describe and explain the general patterns of change displayed by a typical urban neighborhood as it passes from initial development through maturity into old age.

Residential Segregation

One of the most important areas of all of urban research is that which deals with the residential segregation of race and ethnic groups. The segregation of blacks in American cities has been stubbornly maintained in the face of more than 20 years of legislation to the contrary. Studies have shown that only a very small fraction of the segregation level of blacks can be explained by differences in aggregate social status between the black and white populations. Increasingly, racial segregation studies are coming to define the urban housing market as two distinct submarkets, one for the black population and one for the white population.

Studies of residential segregation have not dealt exclusively with blacks. The various incoming nationality ethnic groups also have been studied. Attempts have been made to find out what factors accounted for the original segregated patterns of the ethnics and then led to their cultural assimilation and residential dispersion. It seems that the physical distance in urban residential space among the ethnic groups reflects the degree of social distance between them as indicated by language and customs. As the social distance diminishes, so does the physical distance. While the European ethnics have been studied frequently in the past, the Puerto Ricans and Cubans now are coming under empirical scrutiny more often as their numbers expand in the large cities of the United States. The basic question asked by students of these groups is, "Will the same patterns and processes that characterized the residential experiences of the Europeans also come to characterize that of the Puerto Ricans and Cubans?"

Students of the city have also been interested in the general question, "Who runs things?" How are important decisions that affect the city's population in significant ways made? Is there a single group of influentials that call most of the shots or are there a variety of groups that compete in influence-wielding—the particular mix of groups in any one issue depending upon the particular problem at hand. Power and politics in the city have received much attention, as has the study of the social involvement of individual urbanites. While Wirth's view of city life led to the expectation that most urbanites are isolated and generally uninvolved, much empirical research has indicated just the opposite. Voluntary associations, neighborhood cliques, relatives, and work associates provide urbanites with a wide variety and change of contacts and relationships. While rates and forms of participation vary by social class, age, sex, and other social characteristics, participation and involvement seems to be more the norm than the exception.

Urban Problems

The analysis of urban problems has come to be centered on several problems unique to large cities. While crime, mental illness, and drug addiction are problems found in cities, they are not systemic urban problems. Problems that are fundamentally unique to the city as a social system include the resources and obligations of urban administrations; the quantity and quality of transportation and housing; and institutional inadequacy, especially in the areas of education, health care, and welfare. The specter of ever-expanding problems has prompted increasing concern with the sociology of the solutions to problems. Urban planning analysis inevitably leads back to discussions of power and politics. Who can solve the city's problems? What are the appropriate roles for planners, politicians, administrators, and the general public? Are architectural changes enough or must people be changed as well? Can the local community cope with its own problems by itself, or must there be intervention by outside agencies or higher levels of government? How can we best organize ourselves to promote harmony, peace, and self-fulfillment?

It can be seen from this brief overview, that the number and expanse of topics falling within the domain of urban sociology is great and varied. Sociologists are concerned with the social structure of cities current and past, in the developed and the developing nations. Also of interest are the ways men cope with urban life through their institutions and social groups. This broad study of the city demands a variety of data sources and research methodologies. The following section reviews some of the main elements of urban research.

RESEARCH IN URBAN SOCIOLOGY

The goals of scientific research frequently are listed as description, explanation, prediction, and control. *Description* refers to those activities in which one's aim is to characterize as completely as possible the phenomenon or object of interest. However, we are seldom satisfied only to describe the world. Our intellectual curiosity leads us to demand more of our research. Description by itself is usually insufficient to sate our curiosity. We then move from simple description to explanation as we try to account for why things are the way they are. *Explanation* involves the identification of the factors or variables that we think affect the object of interest; the formulation of hypotheses that state how the independent variables (causes) influence the dependent variables (effects); the testing of the hypotheses with relevant data; and the integration of our findings into the broader explanations or generalizations we call theories. *Prediction* is a logical consequence of explanation. If we can explain a phenomenon, we should be able to predict future events. As astute observers we sometimes find ourselves in the curious position of being able to predict the outcome of an event without being able to explain it to our own satisfaction. In such a situation our prediction usually flows from having observed a repeated statistical regularity without ever really coming to grips with the underlying "why." *Control* essentially involves those efforts of bringing scientific knowledge to bear upon some problematic condition that may be ameliorated through programmatic efforts. This is the "applied" aspect of science where we try to control real-world phenomena to produce a better life for ourselves and our fellow human beings.

The efforts of researchers in urban sociology are directed toward those scientific goals. To achieve these goals, urban sociologists strive to produce an accurate description of urban structure and urban life; to develop general explanations of urban phenomena; to predict significant events in our evolving urbanism; and to try to lay a foundation of knowledge that is sufficient for the task of reconstruction and humanization of the urban environment. It is hoped that the more we learn about our urban environment, the better able we will be—collectively and individually—to cope with the problems and dislocations so evident in our cities today. The bottom line of science reads "to improve mankind's lot." Yet, science can be a guessing game to some extent. We seldom fully anticipate the programmatic payoff of specific lines of investigation. We are much like the traveler to an unknown destination—we really don't know what's there until we arrive. Some lines of investigation will have immediate and direct payoff in the solution of social problems; others will have long-run contributions that are not immediately evident; and still others will have slight value in a programmatic context but they will enable us to fill in a little more of the picture of our nature and of our relationship to the world around us. The scientists' payoff mainly comes in *knowing*—the intellectual satisfaction of the end of the chase— and in seeing their work assist in making the world a little better place in which to live.

The data for urban studies usually comes from one of two general sources. The first is official statistics collected and published by government agencies. Many urban research projects involve the secondary analysis of U.S. census reports or vital statistics on births, and deaths. Comparative studies frequently utilize the reports issued by population agencies of various nations. For international data, the United Nations in its *Demographic Yearbook* and in reports of separate divisions have provided data on urbanization, urbanism, economic development, and living conditions whose collection by an individual researcher would be prohibitive in terms of both money and time. However, sociologists conducting the secondary analysis of such public statistics must continually face problems of validity, reliability, and comparability of data [Schwirian 1974].

When the official statistics do not include the type of information required the urban researcher must collect data through any one or more of a variety of observational techniques. These originally generated data are the second major source for the student of urban affairs. Sample surveys of urbanites, organizations, and of behaviors are very common methods of collecting data. The object of such studies is to obtain uniform observations that may be quantified and analyzed through various statistical procedures. Increasingly, urban sociologists are turning toward more ethnographic and unobtrusive means of data collection. One such approach that is gaining popularity is participant observation of urban groups and activities in which the social scientist takes an actual role. Such methodologies of observation have produced their own problems of validity and reliability, yet they have provided rich detail on the nature of urban life that is not available in the more rigid and statistical analyses of official statistics. Conspicuously absent from the urban researchers' bag of research designs is the experimental. Experimental designs demand that the researcher is able, at least to some extent, to control the operation of an experimental stimulus so that he or she may see that some of the subjects receive it while others do not. By comparison of the performances of the experimental subjects and the control subjects some inference may be made about the importance of the stimulus as a causal agent. Most of the phenomena studied by the urban sociologist are not amenable to such experimental manipulation. Thus nonexperimental research designs predominate in this field.

With the increasing capabilities of computers available to social scien-

tists, the advent of simulations and gaming for both instructional and research purposes in urban studies have been evident. Instructional gaming aims to involve the student in "real" world situations found in the city. The purpose is to have students gain some insight into specific events, problems, or issues by having them face the types of decisions that must be handled in such situations. In this context the computer is usually used as a record keeper, a provider of information needed for decision making, and/or as a generator of parameters affecting problem solutions. The computer frequently is used in simulation research to assimilate vast quantities of objective data and provide output in accordance with prescribed formulas. Through manipulation of the formulas that are, in effect, the researcher's hypotheses of how things work, he or she is able to see how alternative formulations affect the results, or to test how accurate formulations are by comparing predicted results with actual empirical situations.

Urban research can be very expensive. The money costs are great, as are the costs of time and energy of the researcher. Sources of research support are found in both the public and private sectors. The United States government through such agencies as the National Science Foundation, Office of Education, Department of Labor, and National Institute of Health make available millions of dollars for social research, some of which supports research directly related to urban phenomena. Private foundations such as Ford and Rockefeller periodically develop programs that fund research on cities, urban problems, and administrative matters. More and more research funds are coming to urban sociologists in the form of contracts for applied problems rather than grants for the more basic research questions. The movement toward greater support for applied problems reflects a growing sense of urgency among funding agencies that specific problems need immediate attention. The tendency to move toward research contracts rather than grants reflects the increasing desire of research-funding bodies to maintain greater control over the work that is done to insure that the problem they fund gets the type of attention the agency feels it requires [Baker 1975]. As a result, the role of the funding agency in shaping urban research is becoming more prominent. Since research is costly, few researchers can rely on their own resources or those that can be generated locally, and they must look to the granting agencies for their support. An important skill for contemporary researchers to cultivate is that of effecting a marriage between their own professional interests and those topics that the funding agencies will support.

SUMMARY

The purpose of this introduction has been to provide a general overview of urban sociology. To do so the field has been approached from several directions. First, we focused upon the early development of urban sociology and identified many of the substantive concerns that have shaped much of urban sociology in the ensuing decades. We then surveyed some of the variety of perspectives that characterize much of the work being done on today's cities. Then, taking a topical approach, we gained some sense of the scope of the field in terms of questions asked and areas explored. Finally, we saw that urban research is a complex field in which differing data sources and research strategies come in to play. Research funding is not always easy to come by. Funding agencies increasingly are supporting research for applied problems through issuing contracts to urban researchers working for private firms, public agencies, and colleges and universities.

The chapters of this book are organized topically in order that most of the major areas of urban research may be surveyed. While it was not possible to touch on every area of urban investigation, the student should find ample material to provide an excellent grounding in the sociology of cities.

BIBLIOGRAPHY

Nels Anderson, *The Hobo.* University of Chicago Press, 1923.

Nels Anderson and E. C. Lindeman, *Urban Sociology: An Introduction to the Study of Urban Communities.* Crofts, 1928.

Keith Baker, "A New Grantsmanship." *American Sociologist,* 1975, 10(4):206–218.

Scott E. W. Bedford, *Readings in Urban Sociology.* Appleton, 1927.

Colin Bell and Howard Newley, *Community Studies.* Praeger, 1974.

J. H. Breasted, *The Conquest of Civilization.* Harper, 1926.

Niles Carpenter, *The Sociology of City Life.* Longmans, Green, 1931.

V. Gordon Child, *Man Makes Himself.* London: Watts, 1937.

Maurice R. Davie, *Problems of City Life.* John Wiley and Sons, 1932.

A. B. Davis and M. Gardner, *Deep South.* University of Chicago Press, 1941.

Claude S. Fischer, "Urbanism as a Way of Life: A Review and an Agenda." *Sociological Methods and Research,* 1972, 1(2):187–242.

Jean Gottmann, *Megalopolis: The Urbanized Northeastern Seaboard of the United States.* Twentieth Century Fund, 1961.

N. S. B. Gras, *An Introduction to Economic History.* Harper, 1922.

Scott Greer, *The Emerging City.* Free Press of Glencoe, 1962.

George A. Hillery, "Definitions of Community: Area of Agreement." *Rural Sociology,* 1955, 20:111–123.

Robert Lynd and Helen Lynd, *Middletown.* Harcourt Brace Jovanovich, 1929.

Robert Lynd and Helen Lynd, *Middletown in Transition.* Harcourt Brace Jovanovich, 1937.

R. D. McKenzie, *The Metropolitan Community.* McGraw-Hill, 1933.

Robert Merton, "Patterns of Influence: Local and Cosmopolitan Influentials," *Social Theory and Social Structure.* Free Press of Glencoe, 1957, pp. 387–420.

Lewis Mumford, *The Culture of Cities.* Harcourt Brace Jovanovich, 1938.

William F. Ogburn, *Social Characteristics of Cities.* International City Managers Association, 1937.

Robert E. Park, "The City : Suggestions for the Investigation of Human Behavior in the Urban Environment," *American Journal of Sociology,* 1916, 20:577–612.

Robert E. Park, E. W. Burgess, and R. D. McKenzie, *The City.* University of Chicago Press, 1925.

Henri Pirenne, *Medieval Cities: Their Origins and the Revival of Trade.* Princeton University Press, 1925.

Walter Reckless, *Vice in Chicago.* University of Chicago Press, 1933.

Arthur M. Schlesinger, *The Rise of the City, 1878-1898.* Macmillan, 1933.

Kent P. Schwirian, *Comparative Urban Structure: Studies in the Ecology of Cities.* D. C. Heath, 1974.

Clifford Shaw, Henry D. McKay, Leonard Cottrell, Frederick Thrasher, and Harvey M. Zorbaugh, *Delinquency Areas.* University of Chicago Press, 1929.

Clifford Shaw, *The Jackroller.* University of Chicago Press, 1930.

Clifford Shaw, and Henry D. McKay, *Juvenile Delinquency and Urban Areas.* University of Chicago Press, 1942.

Gideon Sjoberg, "Theory and Research in Urban Sociology." In Philip M. Hauser and Leo F. Schnore, eds., *The Study of Urbanization.* John Wiley and Sons, 1965, pp. 157–189.

Maurice R. Stein, *The Eclipse of Community.* Harper, 1960.

Frederick Thrasher, *The Gang.* University of Chicago Press, 1927.

Lloyd Warner and Paul S. Lunt, *The Social Life of a Modern Community.* Yale University Press, 1941.

Roland Warren, *The Community in America.* Rand McNally, 1972.

Adna F. Weber, *The Growth of Cities in the 19th Century.* Columbia University Studies in History, Economics, and Public Law, 1899.

Jay A. Weinstein, *Demographic Transition and Social Change.* General Learning Press, 1976.

Louis Wirth, *The Ghetto.* University of Chicago Press, 1928.

Louis Wirth, "Urbanism as a Way of Life." *American Journal of Sociology,* 1938, 44:1–24.

Harvey Zorbaugh, *The Gold Coast and the Slum.* University of Chicago Press, 1929.

Part One

The Emerging Metropolis

1.

URBANIZATION: A WORLDWIDE PERSPECTIVE

Anthony J. La Greca

Urbanization is a word that is synonymous with the United States, a nation that is now almost 75 percent urbanized. The litany of America's cities reads like a catalogue of one's old friends—Atlanta, Denver, Cleveland, Houston, New Orleans, Seattle, Milwaukee—all are names that every American has heard since he or she can remember. But what about such places as Accra, Abidjan, Addis Ababa, Harbin, Kirin, Medellín, Sapporo, and Surabaja? These are the Atlantas and Denvers of other nations throughout the world. They represent just a small fraction of the many cities of the world that have so much importance for their particular nation but are relatively unknown to most Americans. The average American has studied the world's cities only during the years of grade- and high-school education. Yet, the impact that these cities have on the average American is becoming more and more pronounced. Nuclear research and testing in Bombay, fighting in Beirut, unrest in Djakarta, starvation in Karachi—all these events and many, many more are taking place in cities that were almost unknown to American newspaper readers 50 years ago. Now one needs a world atlas to understand the evening news on television.

Cities, whether they are familiar or not, are the centers of a nation's culture and government. And today, perhaps more than ever, they are also the centers of ideological, political, and economic maneuvers that tug at the fragile threads that hold the world back from all-out conflict. As the developing nations industrialize, urbanization is increasing at such a phenomenal rate that problems of administration, housing, health care, and other related urban ills increasingly preoccupy world leaders. The rapid increase of industrialization und urbanization in the developing nations has led to battles about how their economies should be developed. In addition, the migration of hundreds of thousands of people to cities is severely straining their social and economic institutions of those cities.

This chapter seeks to introduce the world's cities and to outline some of the dynamics that have meshed industrialization, urbanization, and economic development into a union that is having a widespread impact on every phase of modern life. First, the rise of early cities and the appearance of preindustrial cities are reviewed. Urbanization then is discussed from the time of the Industrial Revolution to modern times. Included is a discussion on the disparate effects of modern industrialization in various countries and how this disparity influences a country's economic development. Finally, the important role migration plays in the modern urbanization process is examined.

CITIES FROM ANCIENT TIMES TO THE INDUSTRIAL REVOLUTION

As a general guideline, it is helpful to think of two broad categories that are related to the definition of "city." One deals with the rise of cities and their appearance up to the time of the Industrial Revolution. For this extensive time period, a city can be viewed as "a community of substantial size and population density that shelters a variety of nonagricultural specialists, including a literate elite "[Sjoberg 1973, pp. 19–20]. For the period from the Industrial Revolution to the present rise of the megalopolis, a city may be described as having the following components: 1. a large population; 2. sufficient population density to permit compact settlement; 3. social heterogeneity so that a cross-section of a given society is represented; 4. a means of political and social control and administration. Later, when urbanization per se is discussed, other characteristics will be noted.

The Earliest Cities

"Where" and "when" cities first appeared is not known exactly. Breakthroughs in carbon-dating techniques, other sophisticated archaeological instrumentation, and a keener understanding of the ability of ancient civilizations to consolidate large populations all lend credibility to the estimate that cities may have existed since 10,000–8000 B.C. Although these ancient dates have not been verified beyond dispute, it is certain that cities existed by between 5000–3500 B.C. in Mesopotamia, as the area between the Tigris and the Euphrates rivers is called. Cities in this area exhibited Gideon Sjoberg's three necessary conditions for the rise of cities [1973]: 1. technological advancement beyond a mere folk society; 2. an environment conducive to agricultural productivity; 3. a social structure that could coordinate agricultural production, as well as administer the new specialties of division of labor (the sum total of a society's tasks and occupations). The labor force was used to construct buildings, build irrigation systems, form an army, and the like, but the urban social organization also needed a ruling elite, as well as a basis of beliefs (usually religious), which was strong enough to ensure the rural populace's willingness to provide food for city inhabitants.

In terms of administration and coordination, both technology and social organization had to evolve in a parallel manner for cities to emerge and to be maintained. The cycle of this evolution can be summarized as follows. As the use of more efficient agriculture tools increased, enough food was produced so that a larger and larger proportion of the populace—although miniscule by today's standards—could engage in nonagricultural activity. The division of labor in a society increased as a city's population took up the increasingly diverse activities that were related to political administration, military protection and expansion, commerce and trade, and religious and social activities. As this division of labor increased, even more complex means of political control were needed to keep both rural and urban populations in check. As the political and social structure of a society expanded, the society itself was able to implement and coordinate an ever-increasing range of activities that further advanced technological progress. These advances in technology allowed both for more and more of a population to be freed from agricultural activity, as well as for the expansion of cities and empires. In fact, "empire building" became so nearly synonymous with urban expansion that history can truly be depicted as "the study of urban graveyards" [Sjoberg 1973, p. 24]. Such names as Thebes, Knossos, Nineveh, Ecbatana, and Memphis are now only shadowy reminders of once great and powerful empires. Nevertheless, from the bureaucratic structure of ancient Egypt down to the bureaucracies of today, social organization and technology have maintained their parallel influence on the rise and maintenance of cities.

This parallel evolution was not limited to the Old World. Recent archaeological findings show that the Tehuacán Valley of Mexico also experienced new advances in technology so that by the time the Purron culture emerged (2300–850 B.C.), larger and larger settlements appeared. Unlike their counterparts in the Old World, however, these early inhabitants of the Americas relied heavily on plant production and did not domesticate the variety of herd animals that helped account for the faster rate of urbanization in the Old World [Macneish 1973]. The Mayans, Aztecs, and Incas had empires centered in cities but none of these societies reached a magnitude or level of urban development equal to that of Europe, Asia, or Northern Africa.

The development of the cities of Europe was sharply set back in the fifth and sixth centuries A.D., however, when barbarian tribes from the north and east overran "civilized" western Europe and eventually dominated it. With the fall of the Western Roman Empire in A.D. 476, European urbanization declined rapidly. By A.D. 622 Constantinople and Teotihuacán (Mexico) were the only two western cities among the twenty-five largest cities in the world [Chandler & Fox 1974, p. 305). By A.D.

800 Constantinople had fallen from being the world's largest city to the third largest, and Cordoba (Spain) replaced Teotihuacan as the only other western city among the twenty-five largest cities of the world [Chandler & Fox 1974, p. 306]. This lack of representation of western cities among the world's largest remained relatively constant until modern times. Nevertheless, Europe did experience, especially in the Middle Ages, the rise of small- and middle-size cities. It was these cities that contributed to the West's overall domination of urbanization in general. That is, although the western world may have had only a few of the largest cities of the world, it still had a larger proportion of its population living in cities than did other parts of the world. In spite of this difference in overall levels of urbanization, Sjoberg [1960] maintains that although preindustrial cities were found in a variety of cultural contexts, they displayed "strikingly similar social and ecological structures" [1960, p. 5].

The Preindustrial City

As one might expect, the preindustrial city usually had a small population, although a few of the later ones did eventually grow to fairly substantial size. The dominant functions of these cities were administrative and/or military. In both instances the factor of power (and also religion) was the dominant characteristic of the city. As a result, many of the leading preindustrial cities were built near or within a walled fortress. For example, the historic walled core of Moscow is the Kremlin with its palaces, churches, government buildings, and marketplace.

A wall surrounded nearly all preindustrial cities. The area enclosed by the wall often was itself further compartmentalized by other walls that left little areas or cells as "subcommunities, as worlds unto themselves" [Sjoberg 1960, p. 91]. The walls, or various other ingenious devices such as moats, served as a means (although often an ineffective one) of protecting the city from its enemies and as a means of regulating merchant exchanges, as well as of controlling undesirables. In addition to the controls at the outer gates and entrances to the city, the individual cells within the city could also close their entrance ways, thus further sealing their little worlds off from thieves, marauders, and anyone else that had no legitimate basis for being let in to the area.

A lack of space and transportation accounted for the fact that buildings were placed close together. People frequently lived and worked in the same structure. Except for a few main thoroughfares, the streets were winding, narrow, unpaved passages. These passages usually had little or no drainage and became mere mudways whenever it rained or snowed.

The specific land-use configuration of the inner parts of the city was determined by three considerations:

1. the pre-eminence of the "central" area over the periphery, especially as portrayed in the distribution of social classes. . .

2. certain finer spatial differences according to ethnic, occupational, and family ties. . .

3. the low incidence of functional differentiation in other land use patterns [Sjoberg 1960, pp. 95–96].

The city's central area, which usually was also its physical center, was dominated by governmental and religious structures, and as Sjoberg states, "Both physically and symbolically, the central governmental and religious structures dominate the urban horizon" [1960, p. 96]. Interestingly, the main market—so important to later cities—had a prestige position below that of the religious and the political sectors. As one would expect, the chief economic activities of the preindustrial city were based on individual crafts and trade.

In terms of the class structure that occupied these preindustrial cities, Sjoberg stresses two points: 1. the preindustrial city had an all-pervasive, rigid class system; 2. the upper class of preindustrial civilized cities was urban in nature [1960, p. 113]. The residential and work land-use patterns of the preindustrial city reflected the class structure. The elite lived in and near the center of the city where political and religious activity were paramount. The urban poor were crowded into the remainder of the city or lived outside its walls. The city, therefore, was clearly divided along class (including racial and ethnic) lines, as well as along occupational lines that were associated almost exclusively with one's place of residence.

The preindustrial cities of the Middle Ages were beset with a multitude of problems, chief among them the many plagues and pestilences that threatened the lives of the population. Basically, plagues can be divided into three types, all of which are usually fatal: "pneumonic (attacking primarily the lungs), bubonic (producing buboes, or swellings of the lymph glands), and septicemic (killing of victim rapidly by poisoning the blood)" [Langer 1973, p. 106]. The most terrible of all medieval plagues was the Black Death, which takes its name from the dark blotches caused by hemorrhaging. The disease, which was transmitted by fleas that lived on diseased rats, reflected the generally low standard of hygiene and sanitation that were prevalent. The most virulent outbreak of the Black Plague occurred during the mid-fourteenth century and has been estimated to have killed three-quarters of the population of Europe and Asia.

The physical proximity of the population and poor sanitation combined to increase the likelihood of plague outbreaks in Europe's crowded cities. Once someone was infected, the chances of surviving beyond 3 days were less than 1 in 5. Given this estimated mortality rate of over 80 percent, by 1400 the population of Florence declined from 90,000 to 45,000; Siena lost 27,000 people with only 15,000 people surviving; and almost two-thirds of Hamburg's population was destroyed [Langer 1973, pp. 106–107]. The Black Death continued to take its toll in later centuries. It took the lives of almost 30 percent of the inhabitants of Venice in 1576–1577; almost 45 percent of the population of Marseilles in 1720, and about one-half of the citizens of Messina in 1720 [Langer 1973, p. 107]. The plague was of such ferocity that nations and individual cities were forced to use extreme tactics to prevent the spread of infection:

> In an epidemic in 1563 Queen Elizabeth took refuge in Windsor Castle and had a gallows erected on which to hang anyone who had the temerity to come out to Windsor from plague-ridden London. . . . In the afflicted cities, entire streets were closed off by chains, the sick were quarantined in their houses and gallows were installed in the squares as a warning agains the violation of regulations [Langer 1973, p. 108].

The Black Death destroyed populations and sunk Europe into an economic depression. The inhabitants of rural areas lost a market for their crops since so many consumers in the cities had died. As the need for crops decreased, farmers moved in large numbers to nearby towns in search of employment as artisans [Langer 1973, p. 110]. The Black Death, which depleted cities of their populations then, ironically became the cause of the growth of towns, many of which were to be the cities of a later Europe freed from the threat of the plague.

The Cities Survive—and Grow

Somehow, however, the preindustrial city managed to survive the plagues and wars that dominated Europe's Middle Ages. The gradual disappearance of feudalism with its scattered settlements and self-sufficient economic units led Europe, unlike most of the rest of the world, to grow more and more dependent on its cities. By the end of the eighteenth century, newer sanitation and medical procedures had begun to check outbreaks of the plague. The artisan and merchant populations of cities began to make major improvements in the quality, quantity, and efficiency involved in the production and delivery of goods. These improvements provided a major impetus for the rapid urbanization of Europe: the Industrial Revolution.

By the beginning of the nineteenth century, when the Industrial Revolution was just beginning to gain momentum, London had become the largest city in the world and had the distinction of being the United Kingdom's only city with over 100,000 people. Nevertheless, the United Kingdom, in 1800 was still the most urbanized nation in the world [Davis 1973, p. 100]. By 1850, there were 11 cities besides London that had populations of over 100,000 people. What caused this rapid increase in urbanization?

The answer is found in the two-fold process: a rise in agricultural technology and a decrease in the number of people needed to tend the farms. The Industrial Revolution left its permanent imprint on the history of man by drastically altering human settlement patterns. There was little to stop urbanization once a nation became involved in developing its technology. Furthermore, demographic changes began to occur that helped the urbanization process: the mortality rate was exceeded by the birth rate [Weinstein 1976]. This demographic change supplied urbanizing nations with the population necessary to maintain the advance of technology. In non-western nations these increases in population did not have the same effect as they did in the West. Non-western nations did not keep pace with the West in improvements in agricultural production and manufacturing. In addition, many of these countries came under the colonial rule of European nations, which hindered the development of trends toward urbanization since, as will be discussed in more detail later, it was more advantageous for a colonial power to rule from one central city than to try to keep several areas of large population concentration under control.

In the United States after the colonists had won their independence, they first devoted their attention to establishing a stable government rather than to settling cities. In 1790, the new United States of America had almost 4 million people but only 5.1 percent of them were living in cities—settlements of over 2,500 [Ward 1973, p. 21]. Most of this urban population lived in the five largest cities: Boston, New York, Philadelphia, Baltimore, and Charleston. Although many of America's early leaders, such as Thomas Jefferson, disdained the increasing importance of American cities, the bountiful amount of natural resources, and a relative lack of outside interference allowed the United States in the nineteenth century to participate in the Industrial Revolution without restraint. Initially, the location of cities in America followed the "break-in-transportation" scheme. Hence, until the twentieth century, most of America's leading cities were established as trade centers where water transportation (the oceans, the Great Lakes, and key rivers) met with the land. As trade between America and Europe (especially the United Kingdom) increased, New York City rose in prominence as the principal city of the United States.

As steam power became more efficient, northeastern cities continued their growth as trade and industrial centers. In the South, the rate of urbanization was checked both by the plantation system (and its concomittant dependence on an agricultural economy), as well as by the severe toll taken by the Civil War. As recently as 1910, less than one out of five southerners lived in cities [Ward 1973, p. 45]. Nevertheless, by the twentieth century the United States ranked as the most industrialized nation in the world. By the end of the first decade of the twentieth century, America had 109 cities with populations of over 50,000.

INDUSTRIALIZATION, ECONOMIC DEVELOPMENT, AND URBANIZATION

The urbanization that took place in Europe and the United States was not equalled in other parts of the world. Later, we shall look at these other areas in greater detail. At this point it is sufficient to recall that Asia, Africa, and South America did not follow the parallel pattern of industrialization and economic development that is necessary for urbanization.

It must be emphasized at the outset that any discussion of these processes is hindered by a lack of agreement regarding the real meaning and measurement of these three processes. Kent Schwirian and John Prehn [1962], for example, looked at urbanization by placing it in an axiomatic theoretical framework. Others look at it from what is, for the layman, a rather technical operational definition based on various formulae and measuring procedures [Arriaga 1970]. Leo Schnore [1964] argues that urbanization can be seen as playing three roles in the process of economic development: **1.** changing the behavior of a population as it adopts urbanism as its way of life;   2. altering the social and economic structure of a society from one geared to agriculture to one geared to industrialization; and   3. changing the distribution of population concentration in two ways—by increasing the proportion of a nation's population found in urban areas and by the more rapid rate of growth of urban as opposed to rural population. In the context of this section, urbanization is best seen from Schnore's latter two perspectives. First, urbanization parallels a change in the complexity of the division of labor of a society as it moves deeper and deeper into industrialization. Second, urbanization is best measured by looking at the proportion of a nation's population that lives in cities. (The social-psychological dimensions of the city are not reviewed here since they are better understood in the context of urbanism as a style of life as a population changes its values, mores, and customs from a rural to an urban basis.)

Although scholars' definitions of urbanization vary, one thing is certain: a high level of urbanization (proportion of a nation's population living in cities) cannot be achieved without an increase in economic development, which is itself part of a nation's evolution from dependency on an agricultural economy to dependency on an industrial economy. Economic development is usually measured by increases in per capita income or by increases in real income per capita. Per capita income is the total earnings of a nation's work force divided by a nation's total population. Real income is these same earnings adjusted (from a previous base year) to take into account inflation, devaluation, and any other event that lessened or strengthened the purchasing power of income.

Levels of Economic Development

A country is thought to be "underdeveloped" or "undeveloped" if its per capita income (or per capita real income) falls below that of more modernized, technologically advanced nations. A nation is developed if its level of economic development falls within a range of per capita income that best describes these modern, technologically advanced nations. Just what this range is varies from study to study. David Kamerschen [1969], for example, used $586 in per capita income as his cut-off point to distinguish between the two levels of economic development. Other researchers use different cut-off points. The nations described here as developing or underdeveloped and those described as developed are so identified on the basis of a variety of studies and measurements that are too numerous to mention. Nevertheless, it is generally agreed that as of 1970, "there were 55 countries all told that could be considered developed; these, on the average, had 67.2 per cent of their population living in places defined as urban and 43 percent living in cities of 100,000 or more" [Davis 1973, p. 100]. Most of these fifty-five countries are in the West.

A further word of caution, however, must be included. The terms "developed" "undeveloped," and "underdeveloped" are often criticized as being value-ladened terms that reflect a western bias. In this chapter, these terms are not used in a judgmental fashion to compliment or criticize a nation's level of economic development. There is neither an implicit assumption that a certain level of economic development is "right" nor that any level below it is "wrong." This does not, however, lessen the importance of the fact that the day-to-day well being of a people is, in part, determined by a country's level of economic development, nor can one ignore the parallel process of the rise in economic development that is associated with increased urbanization.

Some authors, however, take exception to an implication of a one-to-one correspondence between industrialization and economic development with urbanization. Gerald Breese [1966], for example, claims that, "it would be extremely difficult to find a more detailed, intensive and comprehensive division of labor than is involved in the caste system which persisted over thousands of years in the absence of any significant degree of urbanization and industrialization" [p. 52]. However, countries with an entrenched caste or class system (for example, India) failed to develop the "climate" of entrepreneurship necessary for industrialization and economic development [Hoselitz 1960]. Colonial rule, established nonpliable traditional patterns, and an often basic lack of natural resources impeded a nation's establishing the social and economic institutions conducive to individual enterprise. The development of national and international markets went little beyond the boundaries of an essentially agricultural economy based primarily on the sustenance of the national population. Higher standards of living were reserved for those in the upper castes and classes who manipulated social and economic institutions to maintain the status quo. In spite of the objections of some, a large body of literature supports the concept of a relationship between industrialization and economic development with urbanization [Greer 1962; Hoselitz 1957, 1960; Mabogunje 1965; Morrissett 1958; Nixon & Gerhardt 1964; Roberts & McBree 1968].

Jack Gibbs and Walter Martin [1958] studied the relationship between the degree of urbanization in a society and the spatial dispersion of objects consumed by the population of that society. They found that as the size of cities increased, the degree of urbanization in the country varied directly with the dispersion of objects of consumption. Therefore, nations with a wide dispersion of goods had many cities. In a later paper, Gibbs and Martin offered the following hypotheses relating urbanization with economic development:

IA. The degree of urbanization in a society varies directly with the division of labor;

IB. The division of labor in a society varies directly with the dispersion of objects of consumption;

IIA. The degree of urbanization in a society varies directly with technological development;

IIB. Technological development in a society varies directly with the dispersion of objects of consumption [1962, p. 669].

Basically, they found support for all four hypotheses. They felt that further research, with better data, should be undertaken to explain the few exceptions and deviant cases that did not conform to these four hypotheses. They were, however, emphatic in rejecting the notion that a nation's level of urbanization is mainly determined by sociocultural values and ideologies;

> We reject such an interpretation and emphasize that a high degree of urbanization depends on the division of labor, technology, and organization to requisition dispersed materials. The value systems of some societies may in fact favor a high degree of urbanization, but there is no particular set of values that is a sufficient condition for a high degree of urbanization. It makes no great difference whether the population professes socialism or capitalism, liberalism or conservatism, Buddhism or Free Methodism; for if a high degree of urbanization is to be maintained, widely dispersed materials must be requisitioned, and this can be accomplished only through the division of labor and technological efficiency [Gibbs & Martin 1962, p. 677].

Gibbs' and Martin's emphatic tone underscores the paramount relationship between economic development (which is dependent upon industrialization) and urbanization. A look at the following tables will help us to better understand this relationship.

Table 1 shows the per capita income for twenty-seven countries for 1960 and 1970. Looking at this and the following tables, bear in mind that the quality of data varies since some nations use more sophisticated data-gathering techniques and more representative samples than do others. With this caveat in mind, table 1 shows that, for 1970, 19 of the 27 countries listed have per capita national incomes below $1,000, and 13 of these countries have per capita incomes below $500. The developed nations—Australia, Canada, France, Israel, Japan, the United Kingdom, and the United States—have per capita incomes above $1,600. Puerto Rico, usually seen as a country in the gray area of development versus underdevelopment, has a per capita income of $1,671 primarily due to the domination that San Juan has over Puerto Rico, plus the nation's close link with the United States. As one would expect, the United States is far and away the world's leader in per capita income for large nations.

TABLE 1. Per Capita National Income (in U.S. dollars)

Country	1960	1970
Australia	1,438	2,629
Barbados	330	621
Brazil	196	379
Canada	1,909	3,246
Chile	245	678
Cyprus	494	829
Ecuador	200	250
Egypt	127	197[2]
France	1,202	2,606
Greece	399	998
Honduras	197	264
India	70	86[2]
Iraq	192	278[2]
Israel	857	1,636
Japan	421	1,658
Kenya	91[1]	131
Republic of Korea	132[1]	250
Mexico	315	632
Pakistan	78	132[2]
Paraguay	149	530
Philippines	226	241
Puerto Rico	717	1,671
South Africa	387	699
Tunisia	204	224
Turkey	197	348
United Kingdom	1,276	1,986
U.S.A.	2,559	4,294

Source: *Statistical Yearbook, 1972.* New York: Statistical Office, Department of Economic and Social Affairs, United Nations, 1973.

1. Per capita income for these nations is based on 1963 data.
2. Per capita income for these nations is based on 1969 data.

TABLE 2. Percent Urban Population 1950, 1960, 1970

Country	1950	1960	1970
Algeria	23.6	32.5	39.0
Australia	68.9	83.3	85.5
Brazil	36.2	45.1	55.9
Bulgaria	24.6	33.6	52.3
Canada	61.6	69.6	76.0
Chile	59.9	67.2	75.9
Ecuador	82.5	36.1	38.2
Egypt	30.1	37.7	42.0
France	53.0	63.4	69.9
Greece	36.8	43.3	64.8
Honduras	29.0	30.5	32.2
India	17.3	18.0	19.9
Iraq	33.8	39.2	57.8
Israel	83.9	77.9	82.1
Japan	37.5	56.3	72.2
Mexico	42.6	50.7	58.7
Pakistan	11.4	13.1	13.1
Paraguay	34.6	35.8	35.7
Puerto Rico	40.5	44.2	56.5
Tunisia	29.9	35.6	40.1
United Kingdom	80.8	80.0	78.2
U.S.S.R.	—	47.9	56.2
U.S.A.	64.0	69.9	73.5

Source: *Demographic Yearbook.* New York: Statistical Office, Department of Economics and Social Affairs, United Nations, 1955, 1962, 1971, 1972.

Table 2 gives the percentage of urban population for 23 countries from 1950 to 1970. With the exception of Chile and Mexico, table 2 shows that those nations considered to be underdeveloped nations all have urban populations that are less than 50 percent. These nations are Algeria, Ecuador, Egypt, Honduras, India, Iraq, Pakistan, Paraguay, and Tunisia. Pakistan, with one of the lowest levels of economic development and standards of living in the world, had only 13.1 percent of its population living in urban areas as of 1970. The more developed nations, such as America, Japan, France, and the United Kingdom, all have over 50 percent urban populations. Further study of table 2 shows that the all the developed nations, except for Israel, showed a consistent rise in urbanization from 1960 to 1970. Brazil and Puerto Rico, which are considered to be in a highly transitory stage towards development, both have now more than 50 percent of their population living in cities.

TABLE 3. Economically Active Population by Country

	Total economically active	*Agriculture (percent)*	*Industrial (percent)*	*Activities not adequately defined (percent)*
Algeria (c. 1966)	2,564,663	50.4	35.2	14.4
Australia (c. 1971)	5,240,428	7.4	88.4	4.2
Brazil (c. 1970)	29,545,293	44.2	50.7	5.1
Bulgaria (c. 1965)	4,267,798	44.3	44.1	11.6
Chile (c. 1970)	2,607,360	21.2	70.1	8.7
France (c. 1968)	20,002,240	15.7	84.2	0.1
Greece (c. 1971)	3,282,880	40.5	57.5	2.0
Japan (c. 1970)	52,235,264	19.3	80.6	0.1
Korea (c. 1966)	7,963,060	57.1	42.8	0.1
Mexico (c. 1970)	12,955,057	39.4	54.8	5.8
Puerto Rico (c. 1970)	679,745	7.0	87.0	6.0
South Africa (c. 1970)	2,361,910	9.6	86.7	3.7
Tunisia (c. 1966)	1,052,891	42.6	50.2	7.2
Turkey (c. 1970)	14,533,725	67.0	32.0	1.0
United Kingdom (c. 1971)	21,523,600	3.0	96.0	1.0
U.S.A. (c. 1970)	82,048,781	3.5	92.2	4.3
Zanzibar (c. 1967)	171,047	81.6	17.9	0.5

Source: *Demographic Yearbook 1972.* New York: Statistical Office, Department of Economic and Social Affairs, United Nations, 1973. Data is based on various sample sizes.

Table 3 shows the percentages of population of selected nations that is engaged in agriculture and industrial activities. As one might anticipate, such highly developed nations as Australia, France, Japan, the United Kingdom, and the U.S.A. have over 80 percent of their population engaged in industrial activities. The less developed nations of Algeria, Turkey, and Zanzibar have less than 36 percent of their population engaged in industrial activity. Unfortunately, systematic comparison for underdeveloped nations and nations in a state of transition are difficult to make with table 2 because, as mentioned earlier, there is a wide variation in the way nations define industrial activity and the sample size involved in data collection. Inspite of the data collection problems, table 3, when looked at in conjunction with tables 1 and 2, does show a relative degree of consistency for the relationship between industrialization (percent of the labor force employment in industry), economic development (per capita income), and level of urbanization.

What are the consequences of this relationship between these three variables? The answer lies in the following areas: **1.** developed nations are more likely to exhibit an urban hierarchy pattern while underdeveloped nations are more likely to exhibit a primate pattern; **2.** underdeveloped nations are often viewed as being economically and technologically incapable of coping with massive influxes into their few cities; hence, these nations are often termed "overurbanized"; 3. the impact of the world's rapid population growth is hardest felt in underdeveloped nations.

Urban Hierarchies

It is generally held that cities in most highly developed, large nations can be arranged in a type of urban hierarchy in which one city ranks above another. This ranking is usually best established by looking at a city's function, as well as its input to the national economy. To illustrate this, all one needs to do is to examine American cities. New York, Chicago, and Los Angeles, for example, are seen as *national* capitals since they have a great deal of influence over the economic and social life of all other American cities. In fact, much of the recent concern over New York City's possible default was related to the conceivably disastrous national ramifications of such a step by the city. Each time default was mentioned in the news, the stock market took severe plunges because national and international investors appeared to fear that the collapse of New York City would be detrimental for the many cities that are dependent on New York for their survival. Cities like Detroit, Atlanta, and Houston are seen as *regional* capitals since they are so vital to the economic and social future to the cities that are affected by their economic well being. For example, auto plants across America, as well as plants associated with the auto industry, close down within days after Detroit's auto industry is hit by strikes or cutbacks. This hierarchy of cities can be established all the way down to the smallest Standard Metropolitan Statistical Areas (SMSAs) in the United States. An urban hierarchy in developed nations is, therefore, a system of cities arranged in order of national importance and impact.

The Primate Pattern

Unfortunately, the notion of "hierarchy" is a difficult concept to prove empirically, and what is more, an actual one-to-one correspondence between an urban hierarchy and its national ramifications is even more difficult to establish. Where the hierarchial pattern does not appear, however, one often sees its opposite: the primate pattern. This pattern, which is typical of many underdeveloped nations, is often viewed as detrimental to a nation's future economic development and urbanization.

The concept of the primate city was developed by Mark Jefferson in 1939. The state of research at the time was not as systematic as it is today, hence, he did not present a full complement of hypotheses to account for the existence of primate cities. Although there are a variety of reasons why one city might become larger than its national counterparts, Jefferson felt that once a city became the largest city in the country, it had the impetus to grow at the expense of all other cities. For those exceptions when the primate pattern did not occur, for example in the Soviet Union and Italy, Jefferson cited various historical or idiosyncratic circumstances to account for this lack of a primate pattern. Jefferson's notion of the primate city received little attention until the mid-1960s when urban researchers began to realize the impact that primate cities had on a nation's level of economic development and urbanization.

Primate cities are often viewed as being "parasitic" [Hoselitz 1955]. That is, they develop and grow at the expense of a nation's overall level of economic development and urbanization. Inherent in the view that primate cities are parasitic is a belief that they exploit the hinterland and are the prime beneficiary of a country's production of goods and services. To maintain a level of exploitation, a primate city becomes the political, social, and administrative center of a nation. This consolidation of key activities is often self-perpetuating since members of a society realize that the real road to mobility and a higher standard of living is equated with living in the primate city. When a country is occupied by a colonial power, the primate pattern is more pronounced since the primate city allows a colonial ruling power to have a centralized locus of economic and political power. Arnold Linsky lists six key hypotheses that help describe the impact of the primate city:

1. the areal extent of dense population in a country will be negatively associated with the degree of primacy of the leading city. . .

2. average per capita income in a country will be negatively associated with the degree of primacy of the leading city. . .

3. dependence of the economy of a country on exports will be positively associated with the degree of primacy of the leading city. . .

4. the ex-colonial status of a country will be either positively or negatively associated with the degree of primacy of the leading city. . .

5. the proportion of a nation's work force engaged in agriculture will be positively associated with the degree of primacy of the leading city. . .

6. a rapid rate of national population growth will be positively associated with high primacy of the leading city [1969, pp. 287–288].

Linsky went on to test these hypotheses for 39 countries that had at least one metropolitan area with 1 million inhabitants. In general, his findings supported the presence of the primate city pattern in underdeveloped countries.

> The overall pattern which emerges is that high primacy is precluded in large countries but is not characteristic of all small countries. However, primacy is characteristic of those small countries which have low per capita income, are highly dependent upon exports, have a colonial history, an agricultural economy, and a fast rate of population growth. These are all attributes of underdeveloped countries, particularly those in the transitional or emergent phase of social and economic development [1969, pp. 292].

Countries like France, Denmark, and Austria did not exhibit a primate pattern because of their lack of a recent colonial history, their dependence on an industrial economy, and their established history of national policies geared towards economic development.

In a discussion of Mexico City as a primate city, Clyde Browning, states that the dominance of one city in a nation was in fact a hindrance for both national economic development and urbanization. Browning felt that this dominance of one city grossly impeded the development of provincial and regional capitals:

> It is the overwhelming dominance that is disturbing. Mexico City's attraction is powerful not only quantitatively but qualitatively as well, for it attracts the best brains and talent in the country. Consequently, it is extremely difficult for an individual to make a name for himself in virtually any field without journeying to Mexico City. Considering the dominance of the capital, it is easy to understand why so many provincial capitals are unable to provide necessary services and facilities [1962, pp. 17–18].

Browning attributes the primate pattern in Mexico to a lack of local entrepreneurship. The rise in economic development for western nations was usually led by a type of basic middle-class elite who were true business entrepreneurs who gave primary emphasis to industrial expansion [Chodak 1973]. This industrial expansion, as was noted above, is closely tied with an increase in a nation's division of labor and its level of urbanization.

The primate pattern, therefore, is often found in underdeveloped nations that do not have an established class of entrepreneurs.

Primate cities, therefore, are not always parasitic, especially over a long period of time [Hoselitz 1955]. Even in the underdeveloped nations of modern times, there are those who feel that the primate city eventually can have positive effects on the economic development and urbanization of a nation. Surinder Mehta [1964] lists four ways in which the primate pattern may be beneficial, which can be summarized as follows:

1. Once a nation gains its independence from a colonial power, it already has a "ready-made" administrative trade, cultural, and educational center that can pursue a focused and centralized policy for developing the hinterland.

2. Since a primate city is usually located at the center of transportation lines, it is more efficient for a government to keep investing in a primate city than to develop its cities.

3. Inhabitants of a primate city, unlike their rural counterparts, are already used to an urban life and can face the problems of the city better than those in the hinterland.

4. Finally, a primate city can be generative since, as a cultural and economic center, its innovations and values can be more easily diffused into the hinterland than would be true if there were a series of less developed cities.

Inspite of these beneficial aspects of the primate city one is still hard pressed to argue against the fact that high economic and social costs are involved. Although Mehta feels that there is not absolute certainty that the "balance sheets" will always show the cost to be too great for a nation's economic development, the modern presence of primate cities in underdeveloped nations does, in fact, seem to be a negative economic factor for those countries as a whole. The primate pattern also can be shown to be associated, in part, with a more general consequence of a nation's lack of economic development: overurbanization.

Overurbanization

With at least 65 percent of the world's population living in developing countries, there is a difference of opinion about consequences of overurbanization to these countries. Developing nations are often termed overurbanized if they have a larger proportion of their population living in cities than can realistically be supported by their level of economic development. The standard measure of overurbanization is made by comparing the percentage of the economically active males not engaged in agriculture to the percentage of population living in cities of a 100,000 or more [Davis & Golden 1954].

N. V. Sovani [1964] criticizes this measure of overurbanization because it does not adequately take into account the pace of urbanization in underdeveloped countries, nor does it take into account the fact that underdeveloped nations are a highly heterogeneous group. Sovani notes that "the correlation worked out by Davis and Golden varies at different stages of industrialization and is not stable through time" [1964, p. 116]. Sovani also feels that there is no justification for using developed nations such as the U.S.A., France, Germany, and Canada as the criterion group for overurbanization. He also notes that most analyses of overurbanization do not take into account the historical pattern of developed nations. Switzerland, for example, in 1888 had 16 percent of its labor force in nonagricultural occupations but it did not have a single city of 100,000 or more. Sovani also criticizes the notion of overurbanization when it is explained by "push" factors: that is, the belief that unemployment and the poor conditions of the countryside "push" migrants to the city rather than having the benefits of the city lure or "pull" migrants into urban areas. He maintains that although new migrants to cities in an underdeveloped country usually find themselves either unemployed or in low-productive jobs, they are still much better off economically than in rural areas. As a result, the city might well be attracting migrants who hope to increase their incomes—the traditional attraction of cities for people in the developed nations. Sovani maintains that rural urban migration is a complex matter that cannot be understood solely in terms of "push" factors and overurbanization.

Kamerschen [1969] carried Sovani's criticisms even further. As noted earlier, he looked at 80 countries and classified those countries that had a per capita income of $586 or more as developed nations; those below $586 were classified as underdeveloped nations. He found that the notion of overurbanization did not provide an adequate explanation for the varying amount of urbanization found between developed and underdeveloped countries. Whether or not the concept of overurbanization is a viable rationale for explaining an underdeveloped nation's slow rate of economic development is also highly debatable according to Kamerschen. This debate over the utility of using the concept of overurbanization in comparing developed and underdeveloped nations is an ongoing one. However, the migration of predominantly poor, rural populations to cities in undeveloped nations is an historical fact. This migration will be discussed in greater detail in the closing section of this chapter.

The Rank-Size Rule

Do overurbanization, the primate pattern, and urban hierarchies have other effects on economic development and urbanization? A partial answer to this question can be ascertained by looking at the population size of a nation's cities. Researchers have developed and empirically tested the "rank-size rule" that says that any given region (a country, a province, an American state),

> will likely contain many small cities, a lesser number of medium-size cities, and but few large cities. This pattern of city sizes has been observed to be quite regular from one area to another. That is, when the frequency of occurrence of city sizes in any area is compared with the frequency of occurence of sizes in another area, the two frequencies are very much alike [Berry & Garrison 1958, p. 83].

Generally, rank-size regularities have been associated with a system of urban hierarchy while the primate pattern has been associated with overurbanization and a lack of a consistent rank-size pattern [Berry 1961]. In his study of thirty-eight countries, Brian Berry [1961] found that there was no relationship between city-size distribution and a nation's level of economic development and urbanization. However, he does stress the basic conclusion presented in this chapter: economic development and urbanization are highly associated [1961, p. 587]. Berry's findings regarding the rank-size rule per se are, however, in contrast to other research including his own [Beckman 1958; Berry & Garrison 1958]. Given the recent pressing problem of population growth in underdeveloped nations, the important consideration may not so much be the size of cities, but rather the size of a nation and the effects of increased size on economic development and urbanization.

Table 4 gives an indication of the rapid natural increase of population for developing nations. Chile, Ecuador, Egypt, Honduras, India, Iraq, Mexico, Pakistan, Paraguay, and Tunisia have rates of natural increase of over 20 percent. Mexico, with the highest rate, 34.3 percent, is experiencing a natural increase of population (without taking migration into account) of 3.43 percent each year. Brazil, a nation that is experiencing

T A B L E 4 . **Natural Increase of Population 1950, 1960, 1970**

Country	1950	1960	1970
Australia	13.7	13.5	12.0
Brazil	22.4	31.0	28.3
Bulgaria	10.6	9.5	5.5
Canada	18.1	17.9	9.5
Chile	19.0	22.8	20.2
Ecuador	29.6	35.0	33.5
Egypt	25.3	—	21.5
France	7.9	6.3	6.3
Honduras	28.4	33.0	31.9
India	8.8	19.3	26.1
Iraq	3.7	13.9	33.8
Israel	27.4	16.5	19.7
Japan	17.3	9.5	12.6
Mexico	29.3	34.3	34.3
Pakistan	6.8	30.0	32.5
Paraguay	16.7	30.0	33.8
Puerto Rico	29.1	24.7	19.1
Tunisia	23.1	32.5	30.3
United Kingdom	4.6	6.4	3.0
U.S.S.R.	—	16.6	9.5
U.S.A.	13.9	12.9	6.2

Source: *Demographic Yearbook.* New York: Statistical Office, Department of Economics and Social Affairs, United Nations, 1955, 1962, 1972.

increasing economic growth, still suffers from a high natural growth of 28.3 percent. In contrast such highly developed nations as Canada, France, the United Kingdom, and the U.S.A. have rates of natural increase below 10 percent. Table 4 clearly shows that the "population bomb," which is often referred to in popular writing [Ehrlich 1968], is a real factor that developing nations must face.

This tremendous increase in population is underscored when it is placed in the context of all recorded history. According to Shirley Hartley:

> It took all of human reproductive history up to the Birth of Christ for human numbers to reach about one-third of a billion. It took another 1850 years for the human population to reach one billion. Then it took about 75 years to add a second billion, 35 years to add a third billion and it is presently taking about 15 years to add the fourth billion [1973, pp. 191–192].

This increase in world population is considered especially detrimental to the economic development of underdeveloped nations. As these nations grow and grow, the mere survival of their expanding population necessitates using resources that could have gone into increasing productivity. Furthermore, as underdeveloped countries grow in population, the pool of unskilled laborers increases and the difficulty of raising the level of the labor force's skill becomes more pronounced:

> There is no way that increasing the number of needy persons in the less developed nations will increase their productivity. If need (in contrast to effective demand) were the prerequisite for national production, India and China would already be the most productive instead of among the least productive nations of the world [Hartley 1973, p. 199].

Hartley goes on to emphasize the fact that Canada, with a population of only 20 million, has a level of productivity greater than India's with 550 million people and a level of productivity almost equal to that of China with over 800 million people! Joseph Spengler emphasizes this relationship between population growth, economic development, and urbanization. He notes that by the year 2000, only 41 percent of the population of developing nations is expected to be urban. Developed nations, meanwhile, will have 8 out of 10 people living in urban areas [Spengler 1973, p. 578]. Unless the underdeveloped nations can radically increase their economic development, the outlook for their urbanization is not sanguine.

Research Needs

The foregoing is, of course, only a brief sketch of the complex interrelationship between industrialization, economic development, and urbanization. Our understanding of these processes, however, will always be lacking as long as needed research is not undertaken. Leo Schnore succinctly stated the challenges that exist for the modern researcher seeking to unravel the complexities of these three processes:

> Further research is vitally needed in both Western and non-Western settings. In the developing countries of the world, the example, it is of the first order of importance to learn the extent to which efficient large scale production and distribution systems absolutely require a concentrated labor force and market, or whether modern means of power generation, transportation and communications have minimized the need for the huge agglomerations of population that were created during nineteenth century industrialization in the West [Schnore 1964, pp. 47–48].

To meet these research challenges, the following steps must be taken:

1. The development of precise and concise definitions of industrialization, economic development, and urbanization. These definitions must be applicable to cross-cultural studies.

2. An agreement must be reached regarding the establishment of true empirical indicators for the actual measurement of these processes.

3. A systematic gathering of reliable data on the national level for both developed and undeveloped nations must be undertaken.

4. A conceptual framework or scheme to explain the *dynamics* that link these processes together must be developed.

5. An all-out effort by interdisciplinary teams of researchers from different cultural backgrounds must be implemented to investigate the complex interrelationship between industrialization, economic development, and urbanization.

Until these five goals are achieved, our understanding of these three processes will remain sketchy and speculative. The next section of this chapter reviews the available research and examines the present level of urbanization around the world.

WORLD URBANIZATION

Africa

Because none of the areas of the world is as unique in regard to urbanization as Africa, it will receive the majority of our attention. Africa is characterized by an increasing number of new nations and of varying national approaches to political, economic, and social problems. Of all the inhabited continents of the world, Africa is the least urbanized [Hance 1970]. Yet, it would still take volumes of literature to cover African urbanization since there are many different "Africas" on that large continent, as well as many different types of urban areas. However, one general, geographical demarcation that can be utilized in regard to Africa is the Sahara Desert. Sub-Sahara Africa is a different world from the northern area. Egypt, which is discussed later, is an excellent unit to look at to understand northern African urbanization. Sub-Saharan African urbanization, on the other hand, is more difficult to study because of the vast differences between the eastern, western, and the extreme southern parts of the continent.

Africa South of the Sahara

The two white-dominated nations—Rhodesia and the Republic of South Africa—are atypical of sub-Saharan countries since they represent a continuation of what many native Africans continue to call "colonial rule." The Republic of South Africa is both the most industrialized and most urbanized nation on the continent. Almost one-half of its population lives in urban areas. As a nation it more closely resembles the countries of the West than it does its neighbors. Rhodesia, which is much more rural than the Republic of South Africa, is administratively dominated by the white government centered in Salisbury. Both these nations have been the object of both internal and external pressures to allow greater participation of the indigenous population. The exact future of these two countries is unclear, as is the picture regarding their future urbanization if the present ruling structure is altered.

East and West Africa have cities that are characterized by three basic historical periods: 1. the precolonial period; 2. the colonial period; and 3. the postcolonial period. The precolonial period existed before the nineteenth-century invasion by European powers. Timbuktu, Mombasa, Segou, Kumasi, and other cities all were prestigious and influential centers, even if for short periods. Most were centers of Muslim power and their fates were tied to the strength of their respective rulers. These cities have long since lost their importance for present-day East and West Africa, but their appearance early in the history of the continent shows that Africa was partly urbanized before European colonization began.

The colonial period extends from the nineteenth century until the multitude of revolutions and declarations of independence that have occurred since the end of World War II. The cities established during the era of foreign rule were mostly trade centers that were controlled by colonial powers. The colonial imprint is still evident in the dominance of the primate city pattern. As we have seen, primate cities, at least until the disappearance of the colonial governments, tended to impede national urbanization. Therefore, cities were used as a tool to maintain the class structure dictated by the European nations, that controlled individual African countries. This class structure existed at the expense of the economic advancement of the indigenous African population. Nevertheless, many of the modern, important cities of East and West Africa were founded in the colonial period. Such cities as Accra (Ghana), Port Harcourt (Nigeria), Kampala (Uganda), and Nairobi (Kenya) owe their early development to European administrators. And, with independence, these cities continue to serve as the administrative and cultural centers for the new African nations.

Postcolonial African cities, although still mostly primate, have grown to larger and larger sizes [Hance 1970]. In the last three decades these cities have experienced tremendous growth while, at the same time, their new national governments have tried to increase both the economic and urbanization levels of the country as a whole. These attempts, however, are not always as vigorous as they should be. Since 1960 alone, over thirty nations that were formerly colonies have gained their independence. The new governments of these nations might realize that overall urbanization and economic development go hand-in-hand, yet they also recognize that a primate city allows them to keep tight administrative control over nations that are still experiencing internal struggles for power. These primate cities, such as Lagos (Nigeria) and Dakar (Senegal), control the social, political, and economic life of a nation. One can expect that both East and West Africa will continue in this primate pattern until the control and direction of national governments are stabilized. The continuance of the primate pattern not only hinders urbanization but also stunts the level of economic development needed for large-scale urbanization. African nations are among the least developed economically. The increases in population, coupled with poor agricultural output, have hindered the attempt to release large numbers of people from food-producing activity. What is more, many nations are unable to raise enough food to feed their own populations and must pay high costs for imported food. With some exceptions, such as Nigeria, the eastern and western African nations have not been able to use their natural resources (such as people, oil deposits, unmined ores) to offset their economic stagnation or the lack of marked economic advancement. At present, the future of industrial expansion, and the resulting urban expansion, do not appear to be great for East and West Africa.

Urbanization is also lessened in the Sub-Saharan regions by the traditional importance of tribes and clan. Although an African may leave both the tribe and countryside, the new city-dweller does not always forget them, nor cut off relationships with them. It has been pointed out that "The urbanized African is outside the tribe, but not beyond the influence of the tribe. Correspondingly, when a man returns from the towns into the political area of his tribe he is tribalized again—de-urbanized—though not beyond the influence of the towns" [Gluckman, quoted in Southall 1961, p. 70].

The urban African may depend upon the city for wages but is still culturally tied to the tribe or clan community. The urban African often does not become reconciled to town life, so wives are sent home at the time of childbirth. "Almost all men state that they wish to return to their home communities before their death so that they may be buried in their traditional compounds" [Lloyd 1968, p. 124].

It is debatable, however, whether or not an actual "detribalization" process [Molohan 1957], must take place for urbanization to succeed. It can be argued that as African cities gain in importance, the urban milieu, and not tribalism, will become the cultural niche for new arrivals to African cities. Yet, it is very common to see actual tribal neighborhoods in African cities. These are areas of a city that are settled by certain tribal members where the new African urbanite is initially introduced to city life by means of urban tribal associations. Even these associations become less important, however, as trips back to the tribal hinterland become less frequent. Perhaps this tribal influence will follow the fate of ethnic influences for immigrants to American cities. That is, urban tribal associations will serve as an initial source of support while the new urbanite seeks occupational and social mobility in his new urban world [Gutkind 1965]. The future of urbanization in East and West Africa is, therefore, a highly complex matter. Not only must economic development increase, but the actual impact of historic tribal influences must be understood and dealt with.

Africa North of the Sahara: Egypt

Northern Africa is more urbanized than the nations south of the Sahara taken as a whole. Recalling the ancient empires that were dominated by Carthage and Alexandria, it is not difficult to perceive that the attributes that made these cities ancient cultural and trade centers are still present. Africa's Mediterranean nations have urban populations of at least 20 percent with Egypt's 42 percent being the highest. Most of the population lives along the coast and in the Nile River valley because the interior is arid and mountainous. Yet, although more urbanized than the South, these northern nations are still predominantly rural, have a relatively low level of economic development, and have a low standard of living compared to the West. A nation such as Algeria, for example, went through a colonial period somewhat similar to that of the nations south of the Sahara, but Northern Africa is an altogether different social world. Muslim dominance coupled with rich oil deposits, provide cultural and economic distinctions from the Sub-Saharan countries. The two regions, however, are quite similar in regard to the importance of the primate city. Of all the nations of North Africa, Egypt maintains the best census and has been researched the most extensively. It is discussed here as the dominant nation of the region and as one that is fairly typically North African.

Egypt is an excellent example of the scholarly disagreement that exists regarding the concept of overurbanization. Although Egypt is often cited as an example of overurbanization, Janet Abu-Lughod [1965] makes a strong argument that the country is not overurbanized. In her view, it is, rather, overconcentrated. Abu-Lughod bases here position on four points: 1. since Egypt's occupational figures include all males over the age of 6, the proportion of males in nonagricultural jobs is not properly represented; 2. the physical boundaries for Egyptian cities are "overly generous" and include communities that have densities far below those that should be classified as urban; these concentrations represent sprawling rural areas rather than cities; 3. the Egyptian cultural preference for these concentrated rural settlements rather than a scattering of farm sites has created a statistical fiction of overurbanization; 4. the concentration of over 52 percent of its urban population in Cairo and Alexandria has also distorted the true picture of Egypt's overconcentration as opposed to its overurbanization.

Whether or not Abu-Lughod is correct in her argument regarding overconcentration is not as important here as is the fact that Egypt does typify the consequences of a primate urban development pattern. Without a doubt, Alexandria and, especially, Cairo have grown at the expense of both the smaller cities and the hinterland. These two cities have impeded general urbanization for Egypt in the past and can be readily viewed as deterrents to future overall urbanization since it is, at least in the short run, both expedient and efficient for a nation to expand its economic growth in primate cities rather than in smaller cities. In fact, of the three types of Egyptian middle-size cities (100,000 to 500,000 inhabitants), Cairo and Alexandria's satellite cities are nothing more than vehicles of primate expansion. The second type of middle-size cities are canal cities that are essentially outside of the mainstream of Egyptian urbanization since most are surrounded by desert lands. Of Egypt's three types of middle-size cities only those termed "regional capitals" offer Egypt any real hope for breaking the primate pattern. It is these cities "whose growth must be encouraged and stimulated if the existing overconcentration is to be reduced and if Egypt is to achieve the full complement of urbanization necessary to mature and decentralize industrial development" [Abu-Lughod 1965, p. 329]. Since these regional capitals have been less parasitic on the rural hinterland than Cairo or Alexandria, it is anticipated that the development of these cities is a prerequisite for both social change and economic development.

Asia

Asia, like Africa, is a region made up of nations with different histories and traditions. As a result, it is difficult to talk about any one type of Asian urbanization. According to Tertius Chandler and Gerald Fox [1974] Asia's domination of the world urbanization picture dates to the eleventh century. By 1102, Kaifeng, the capital of most of China, had a population of 442,000 and was the largest city in the world. Although Constantinople resumed its position as the world's largest city in 1150, it was again replaced by a Chinese city, Hangchow, in 1200. Except for Cairo (1350) and Constantinople (1650 and 1700), either Nanking (1400–1500) or Peking was the largest city in the world until London's population reached 2.3 million in 1850 [Chandler & Fox 1974, pp. 310–328]. By 1968 Asia, excluding Soviet Asia, had nine of the world's largest cities. If one views Soviet Asia as a part of the Asian continent, this total rises to eleven cities. In fact, even excluding Soviet Asia, fully one-third of the present world's urban population lives in Asian cities.

Yet, both Europe and America are much more urbanized than Asia when one looks at the percentage of the population living in cities. Unfortunately, much of our contemporary understanding of Asian urbanization is hindered by a lack of verifiable data regarding population size and the level of economic development of Asian countries. Despite deténte and the opening of communications between East and West, China, with over 800 million people, still remains a great mystery to urban scholars in the West. However, Asia has two countries, India and Japan, which offer a striking contrast regarding urbanization, and considerable research has been done on both these countries. Each country represents a different dimension of the development/urbanization continuum. India is still, overall, an underdeveloped nation while Japan parallels, and even exceeds, the levels for both development and urbanization of some western nations.

India

As with most developing nations, India's proportion of city dwellers has increased slowly in contrast to the United States. The effect of British rule has left India with fewer large cities than the size of its population would seem to dictate. Furthermore, most large cities created by the British were either administrative or trade centers. The long-time, stable population of India's cities tends to be made up of bureaucrats employed in administrative or professional positions. The influx of urban migrants is characterized by an overrepresentation of males over the age of 20 who leave rural areas to earn money in the city to send back to rural areas. A consequence of the predominance of males in cities has been to "generally create problems of adjustment and behavior" [Gist 1968, p. 26]. Today, India represents a nation that is caught between two worlds: the modern urban world of technology and the historically dominant rural village.

Calcutta is a classic example of the struggle between old world traditions and contemporary values. Its population of over 7 million makes it India's largest city. Physically, it is a dramatic example of a lack of planning. Parts of Calcutta are actually under water and the rest of the city's proximity to water threatens Calcutta with flooding whenever its inadequate drainage system is taxed. Although Calcutta is India's cultural and economic capital, the allegiance of many of the city's inhabitants still belongs to the countryside. Many of the people who come to work and live in Calcutta continue to send the bulk of their limited income to relatives in rural areas.

In addition, the economy of Calcutta reflects the relatively nonindustrial economy of India. As a city, it possesses no more than the "rudiments of the technological apparatus that makes life possible for the comparable population and population density of London . . . or New York" [Bose 1970, p. 60]. With fully three-fourths of its population living in slums, Nirmal Bose has labeled Calcutta a "premature metropolis" since it cannot adequately support its large population. With the caste system still fairly firmly entrenched, much of Calcutta's populace cling to the occupation of their particular caste or ethnic groups. Since competition between castes is culturally discouraged, an economy based on agriculture and handicraft further impedes the marked division of labor that is conducive to the development of a strong urban economy. This cultural handicap to a developed urban economy is accompanied by poor urban transportation, sanitation, and health conditions. To offset some of these problems, the Calcutta Metropolitan Planning Organization was established in 1961. Although it has met with only limited success so far, the Planning Organization hopes to implement plans to alleviate many of Calcutta's problems by the late 1980s. The realization of this goal depends, of course, on the degree that India itself can experience an upswing in its overall economic development, as well as India's ability to reshape or reform some of its culturally entrenched caste values.

Whether or not Calcutta or the other cities of India will follow the spatial structure of western cities is still debatable. However, a study by Mehta [1968] suggests that at least the Indian city of Poona is beginning to show just such a tendency toward following the spatial patterns of western cities. However, it will be some time before Poona or any major city of India begins to decentralize. As with Calcutta, this lack of decentralization can be traced both to the caste system, which favors the centralization of the upper castes, as well as to Poona's lack of modern transport system.

Japan

Of all the countries of Asia, Japan most closely resembles western nations both in terms of its level of economic development and in terms of its overall urbanization. Its 1970 per capita national income of $1,658 makes it one of the most economically developed nations outside of the western world. In fact, Japan is even more urbanized and industrialized than some western nations. Tokyo, the economic and cultural capital of Japan, is one of the largest cities of the world. The urban area made up of Tokyo-Yokohama is the largest metropolitan area of the entire world.

As with other Asian cities, the traditional role of the city in Japan goes back to the Middle Ages. Unlike other Asian countries, however, Japan was forced to open its doors to the world in the nineteenth century and began to establish itself as a world trade and industrial center. Japan, at the same time, became subjected to a variety of competing western traditions that helped to foster a strong anti-West attitude in the twentieth century, culminating in Japan's initiation of the World War II conflict in the Pacific. The subsequent defeat of Japan, its occupation by Allied forces, and its impressive post-World War II reconstruction have placed Japan in the ranks of the world's industrial leaders.

The problems of overcrowding, pollution, and an ever-increasing crime rate are, unfortunately, clear signs that Japanese cities are becoming more and more like western cities each day. The rapid postwar industrial and urban expansion did not keep pace with the demand by city dwellers for adequate transportation, sewage, and other services. Consequently, the physical level of comfort for Japanese urbanites is below that of a country like the United States. Although Japan has its great industrial base to work from, its strong dependence on exported goods and its high level of inflation both lessen the chances of Japan's dealing with its lack of adequate urban services in the immediate future.

Of course, India and Japan do not represent all of Asia. In general, the future of urbanization in Asia rests on its ability to achieve an expanded pace of industrial development. Some scholars feel that this pace has been seriously impeded bacause of western colonization. Many believe that westerners exploited Asian cities, especially Asian trade and port cities [Murphey 1969]. As nationalism increases in Asia, the individual countries will pursue paths toward urbanization that cannot, as yet, be fully predicted. Nevertheless, demographic trends suggest that Asia by the beginning of the twenty-first century will have more urban dwellers than any other continent in the world, although its rate of urbanization and its level of economic development probably will still lag behind the West.

Europe

Only four European countries have populations of over 50 million. They are West Germany, the United Kingdom, Italy, and France. Curiously, although none of the ten largest countries of the world are found in Europe, it has two of the ten largest cities in the world (1970): London and Paris. If Soviet Europe is included Moscow would be the third European city on the list of the world's largest cities.

Europe represents two sides of the urbanization picture. On the one hand, there is Western Europe, most of whose countries (with the exception of Spain and Portugal) have experienced urbanization levels similar to those of North America. On the other hand there is Eastern Europe which has few countries with a high level of urbanization. Because of this discrepancy in development and because of the wide variety of countries, and their ethnic and cultural heritages, it is impossible to treat all countries of Europe with any great depth in these pages. Instead, urbanization in Europe will be examined by way of nations that are illustrative of the relationship between industrialization and urbanization. In Western Europe these nations are the United Kingdom and West Germany:

> The chief feature common to the development of urban communities in Britain and Germany is that the transformation of our towns bears the stamp of industrialization . . . . With the advent of industrialization, the growth of the towns and cities of Western and Central Europe was predominantly stimulated by decisions taken in the economy, and no longer by the decisions of those in authority in local government. Wherever industry invested, wherever business developed, wherever service industries were concentrated, the fate of the town's further development was decided for it [Koschnick 1974, p. 209].

West Germany and the United Kingdom

Since the end of World War II West Germany has experienced a phenomenal rate of growth and industrial expansion. According to Ulrich Pfeiffer [1974], there has been a strong relationship between the expansion of West German cities and national market forces. This relationship can be seen by the fact that almost six out of ten homes in West Germany have been built since 1945, that there has been great industrial development in the cities at the expense of rural industrial development, and finally, that West Germany, like most of the developed western nations, has experienced a very high rate of rural migration to the more job-promising, industrial cities. Such cities as Munich, West Berlin, Stuttgart, and Frankfort on the main have grown rapidly since the war. Today, Hamburg has a population of over 1 million people and West Berlin has over 2 million people. As a result, most of the urban problems found in other developed countries also are found in West Germany [Koschnick 1974].

The Industrial Revolution began in the United Kingdom and developed there with greater intensity than it did on the continent. By the 1870s the urban consequence of the Industrial Revolution was far more apparent in the United Kingdom, which even that early had over 60 percent of its population living in towns and cities of over 2,000 inhabitants. At the same time, the comparable figure for Germany was 36 percent and for France, 31 percent [Trewartha 1969, p. 66]. As was noted, London has been among the ten largest cities in the world since 1650, and throughout the twentieth century it has consistently ranked as one of the three largest cities in the entire world. As table 2 shows, 78.2 percent of the United Kingdom's population was classified as urban in 1970. Furthermore, in 1970, Birmingham, Leeds, and Manchester had urban area populations of over 1 million. Since it has been a world leader in urbanization, one would expect the present British urban trends to be following those of another urban leader, North America. This is exactly the case in regard to the population movement out of the city and into suburbs and outlying areas. Alan Evans [1974], attributes this exodus of people and industries from the central city to the increased use of privately owned means of transportation, especially the automobile. Evans feels that the increased use of automobiles is a leading reason for the rapid and consistent growth of small and medium-sized British cities:

> The very large cities have usually inherited an extensive suburban railway system, and are densely built up. Any significant shift to motorized transport, particularly for commuting, is prevented by traffic congestion. In the medium-sized cities, on the other hand, a lower density allows a much larger number of people to use the motor car before increased use is prevented by congestion. As a result there is a significant incentive for both plants and households to locate in the medium-sized cities, losing the benefits of location in a larger city but gaining increased mobility [Evans 1974, pp. 74–75].

There is another factor in contemporary British urbanization trends. As in the United States where many people are moving into the "sun-belt" area of the South and Southwest, so many Britons are moving to the more appealing southern area of England. This movement is not into London but rather into the small and medium-sized cities that are in more appealing settings than the older northern industrial areas. Southern England is therefore enjoying an increase in economic activity. However, the United Kingdom, like many other Western European nations, is beset with economic difficulties. It remains to be seen how the present economic situation will influence future urbanization in Western Europe.

East Europe

The urbanization of East Europe has advanced rapidly since the end of World War II. Much of this urbanization can be explained by the "push" factor that drove the unemployed rural inhabitants to seek employment in the cities, which "pulled" these people by creating new jobs to staff the area's industrial development. This industrialization was a distinguishing characteristic of post-World War II East Europe and greatly facilitated the urbanization process [Mihailovic 1972]. Of the eight Eastern European countries studied by Kosta Mihailovic, East Germany and Czechoslovakia were the most urbanized with 72.9 percent of the German Democratic Republic's population living in cities in 1965 and 61.0 percent for Czechoslovakia for the same year. In 1965 the percentages of urban population for five other East European countries were as follows: Poland, 49.7 percent; Bulgaria, 45.8 percent; Hungary, 42.6 percent; Romania, 33.9 percent; Yugoslavia, 31.0 percent. Albania, in 1964, had a 33.2 percent urban population [Mihailovic 1972, p. 194].

Established rural values and the traditional role of craftsmen in the economy have been detrimental to the urbanization process of most East European nations. This has been true particularly for the filtering down of industrialization into smaller settlements for where traditional patterns of production and the predominance of rural-oriented values and policies have blocked economic development. According to Mihailovic, the economic development of small- and medium-sized settlements is best achieved by a national policy that disperses industrial activity and administrative functions across the entire country. "All the countries under consideration lacked vital attributes of the policy of urbanization, such as the division of functions among various types of towns, proper hierarchial relations and coordination with regional development and through this with socioeconomic development [p. 100].

As a hierarchial pattern is established through a general diffusion of industrial activity and urban institutions, Mihailovic expects East Europe to proceed even more rapidly into urbanization.

North and South America

If West and East Europe represent two different pictures of urbanization on the same continent, then most assuredly, North and South America represent two extremes between continents. As table 2 shows, in 1970, 76 percent of Canada's population was considered urban, as was 73.5 percent of the population of the United States. Central and South America (collectively referred to here as Latin America) are not nearly as urbanized. South America, however is now believed to have just about the same percentage (53 percent) of its population living in cities as is true of

Europe. The real difference between North American and Latin America is that North America is much more industrially developed and its cities follow the hierarchial pattern while most Latin American countries have relatively low levels of economic development and follow the primate urban pattern.

Canada and the United States

Unlike the United States with New York, Chicago, and Los Angeles, Canada has no city among the forty largest cities of the world [Chandler & Fox 1974, p. 372]. However, Montreal, Toronto, and Vancouver all have urban area populations of over 1 million people, and Montreal is rapidly moving closer to the ranks of the world's forty largest cities. With a total national population of only about 22 million people, it is not all that surprising to learn that, based on 1975 population estimates, only one out of every four Canadians lives in one of the three largest cities. Thus, in spite of its colonial history, Canada has been able to achieve a high rate of industrial development, which provides it with one of the highest per capita incomes of any nation in the world.

In many ways, both the present level of Canadian economic development and urbanization run fairly parallel to Canada's southern neighbor, the United States. Although not quite as urbanized as Canada in terms of the percentage of its population living in cities, the United States has eight of the world's largest cities: New York, Los Angeles, Chicago, Philadelphia, Detroit, San Francisco, Boston, and Washington, D.C. [Chandler & Fox 1974, p. 372]. The only states that are less than 50 percent urbanized are Alaska, Mississippi, North Carolina, North Dakota, South Carolina, South Dakota, Vermont, and West Virginia (see table 5). The five most urbanized states are California (90.9 percent), New Jersey (88.9 percent), Rhode Island (87.1 percent), New York (85.6 percent), and Massachusetts (84.6 percent). Of course, individual states vary greatly in the number of large cities that each contains. Nebraska, for example, has 61.5 percent of its population classified as urban yet only Omaha has more than 350,000 people and Lincoln is the only other city in the state that has over 150,000 inhabitants. The next largest city in Nebraska is Grand Island with less than 40,000 people. Ohio, on the other hand, has Cleveland, Columbus, and Cincinnati all with SMSA populations of 1 million or more.

TABLE 5. Percent Urban Population By State, 1970

1970 State	Percent Urban Population
Alaska	48.4
Alabama	58.4
Arizona	79.6
Arkansas	50.0
California	90.9
Colorado	78.5
Connecticut	77.4
Delaware	72.2
Florida	80.5
Georgia	60.3
Hawaii	83.1
Idaho	54.1
Illinois	83.0
Indiana	64.9
Iowa	57.2
Kansas	66.1
Kentucky	52.3
Louisiana	66.1
Maine	50.8
Maryland	76.6
Massachusetts	84.6
Michigan	73.8
Minnesota	66.4
Mississippi	44.5
Missouri	70.1
Montana	53.4
Nebraska	61.5
Nevada	80.9
New Hampshire	56.4
New Jersey	88.9
New Mexico	69.8
New York	85.6
North Carolina	45.0
North Dakota	44.3
Ohio	75.3
Oklahoma	68.0
Oregon	67.1
Pennsylvania	71.5
Rhode Island	87.1
South Carolina	47.6
South Dakota	44.6
Tennessee	58.8
Texas	79.7
Utah	80.4
Vermont	32.2
Virginia	63.1
Washington	72.6
West Virginia	39.0
Wisconsin	65.9
Wyoming	60.5

Source: U.S. Bureau of the Census, *Statistical Abstract of the U.S., 1972.* Washington, D.C.: U.S. Government Printing Office, 1972.

The United States has long been known for its cities and modern American culture has become synonymous with its urban culture. Unfortunately, America's urban culture has also developed its own monstrous image of congestion, unemployment, and crime. Since these topics are all taken up elsewhere in this book, they will not be discussed here. (See the chapters on "Critical Urban Problems" and "Violence in Urban Society.") No cities of the world are studied or dissected as much as American cities. Classifying schemes for American cities abound [see Atchley 1967; Hadden & Borgatta 1965] and researchers and scholars are constantly trying to "understand" the cities of the United States. A principal key to this understanding lies, of course, in the fact that the United States is the most industrially and economically advanced nation in the world. Since its beginning as a nation, cities have played a pivotal role in trade and commercial development.

As a nation of cities, virtually all aspects of American life are dominated by the urban complexes that have grown from river and seaport towns to the largest megapolitan areas in the world. It is estimated that by the year 2000, about 85 percent of all Americans will live in cities [Commission on Population Growth and the American Future 1972]. Large megapolitan areas, it is estimated, will touch all of the contiguous states except Idaho, Iowa, Montana, Nebraska, Nevada, North and South Dakota, Vermont, and Wyoming.

Latin America

No one knows what the optimal level of urbanization for a nation is. The eyes of scholars and policymakers are on the United States of the future to judge just how far industrialization and urbanization can go in a nation. In much of Latin America, however, the concern is not so much with how far industrialization and urbanization can go but rather with how to get industrialization going at a level that is high enough to promote economic development and urbanization.

Although some Latin American nations do, in fact, have populations that are over 50 percent urban, many others are still struggling to overcome past colonial influences and primate city patterns. Numerous Latin American cities were designed by the Spanish who saw the city center as the focal point of civic, religious, and social life. Even in the earlier Aztec and Mayan cultures the city center was seen as the area of residence of elites [Schnore 1965]. Thus, to this day, many Latin American cities still exhibit an inverse gradient pattern with the wealthy living near the city center and the poor living on the city's periphery. The legacy of Spanish rule can also still be seen in the national domination of single cities. As noted earlier, these primate cities were the economic and administrative nucleii for colonial rulers. Although such a primate pattern was advantageous for colonial powers, its effect on postcolonial Latin American industrialization and urbanization has been negative in the long run:

> To evaluate the size of primate cities and the effects of primacy on modernization, short-run versus long-run considerations once again become relevant. Even in the largest countries it is probable that during the initial stages of industrialization and modernization the country will benefit more than it suffers from the high-primacy situations. Over the long run . . . . high primacy becomes increasingly a negative factor for several reasons. For one thing, the centralization it represents may serve to handicap the development of other regions of the country [Browning 1967].

Finally, Spanish rule had, as part of its imperialistic policy, regulations limiting the production and consumption of goods in its colonies. These limitations proved to be a grievous impediment to future Latin American urbanization.

All of this is not to say that Spanish (and, in some areas, Portuguese) rule totally impeded urbanization. As table 2 showed, in 1970 Brazil had 55.9 percent of its population classified as urban; Chile had 75.9 percent; and Mexico had 58.7 percent. Yet, all three of these nations have had a highly focused national policy aimed at economic development and industrialization. Furthermore, all three, at least at present, have governments that are backed by a strong military—a kind of stabilization that further intensifies the ability of these nations to pursue economic development. Still, as seen in table 1, the per capita income levels of the inhabitants of these countries are at the lower level of the per capita income continuum. Many other Latin American nations have both low levels of urbanization and low per capita incomes. Ecuador's population is only 38.2 percent urban, Paraguay, 35.7 percent, Honduras, 32.2 percent, and Bolivia, 25.3 percent. All of these nations have among the lowest per capita incomes in the world.

However, although most Latin American nations have some stated program for national and regional development, most lack the technology and natural resources to implement such programs. In addition, political instability in many Latin American countries makes long-run economic planning and development unfeasible. There is, however, a most unique attempt by several Latin American nations to bring industrialization and economic development to depressed regions by literally bringing cities to these areas. Venezuela, for example, is building the industrial city of Ciudad Guayana in its economically undeveloped eastern region, and Brazil has built the world's most famous implanted city, Brasília, as the new national capital. In the late 1950s, Brasília had fewer than 20,000 residents. Today, it has over 500,000 people. However, the city has been criticized by leftist political activists as being a haven and refuge for the powerful and wealthy of Brazil while the poor still live in squalor. In fact, aerial photos of such cities as Brasília, São Paulo, and Lima, show them to be modern-looking cities of skyscrapers and concrete. However, on closer examination, all major Latin American cities are seen to contain extensive areas of dismal poverty. This urban poverty is not only indicative of a low level of national economic development, but it is also a visible manifestation of one of the most pressing problems facing cities of underdeveloped nations: squatter or migrant settlements. The next and final section takes a look at the general topic of migration and the extremely poor living conditions that many migrants confront in large cities.

THE ROLE OF MIGRATION IN URBANIZATION

There are many different types of migration. One can speak of migration within regions, within countries, from city to city, from city to countryside, and from countryside to city. It is this latter rural to urban migration that is the subject of this section.

The decision to migrate essentially involves weighing the perceived benefits of moving against the perceived costs of moving. Even when migration is forced upon a population, such as the recent expulsion of citizens from the cities of China and Cambodia, the notions of costs and benefits are still there. In these extreme cases, the decision not to move would result in imprisonment. In most cases, the situation is not so extreme. Rather, for every decision to migrate, there will be certain costs involved. Essentially, these costs can be grouped into the following categories: **1.** the economic cost of actual money and related resources spent to relocate;   **2.** social costs (to an individual) regarding leaving familiar social settings; and   **3.** psychological costs to the individual who, perhaps, sees moving as a traumatic experience. The benefits of moving can be grouped in a similar manner: **1.** the economic and living-condition benefits of moving to a better job; **2.** the social benefits of moving into a more compatible social world (e.g., less crime); and **3.** the psychological benefits of seeing a move as being a new beginning. For the middle-class American, these three cost/benefit dimensions may also include such factors as a better climate or a chance to live in a golf condominium. For the rural populations of most developing nations, however, these three factors basically revolve around simply providing sustenance for oneself and one's family.

Migration in the Developed Nations

In the United States and in most other developed nations, the end of World War II saw an acceleration of rural to urban migration. Initially, this migration was attributed mostly to people wanting to find a better job and a better standard of living in the city. Some policy makers have contended that the recent movement to American cities is not only attributable to job opportunities in the city but also to migrants seeking the more accessible welfare payments and programs of the city. However, recent research seems to refute this welfare "pull" contention [DeJong & Donnelly 1973; Pack 1973]. Of course, other factors such as ethnicity [Segal 1973], kinship [Tilly & Brown 1974], religion [Toney 1973], and a variety of other variables also influence migration.

That migrants tend to maximize benefits derived from moving is, however, a well-supported fact. Richard Cebula and Richard Vedder [1973] studied 39 Standard Metropolitan Statistical Areas in 1968, which contained 38 percent of the entire American population and over 65 percent of the population living in SMSAs of more than 250,000 people. They looked at the net migration for these SMSAs from 1960 to 1968 and concluded that their study

> tends to confirm the theoretical notion that migrants are interested in long-run, not merely short-run, benefits from migration. . . . We would conclude that migrants, at least in the 1960–1968 period, behaved in a manner consistent with the predictions of economic theory, attempting to maximize the net positive benefits of migration [pp. 209–210].

Today, in the most economically advanced nations, however, other factors are operating besides the quest to improve one's economic life. In such nations as the United States, the United Kingdom, and Canada, both rural to urban and urban to urban migration is due, to an extent, to the climate and amenities of a given area. In its December 1974 *Current Population Report,* the U.S. Census Bureau listed the twenty fastest growing SMSAs in America. Of these twenty, sixteen are in the American "sun-belt." Eight of the twenty fastest growing SMSAs are in Florida; four are in Texas; two are in Arizona; and California and North Carolina each have one. The explanation for the extraordinary growth of these cities, of course, lies in the large numbers migrating to these cities. It would seem, therefore, that once a nation obtains a certain high level of economic development, the decision to migrate, at least for some members of the population, may be based on more than purely economic reasons.

Migration in the Developing Nations

Basically, however, it is argued that rural migrants to a city generally are employed at occupational levels lower than the natives of that city [Blau & Duncan 1967; Sjoberg 1966]. Wilbur Bock and Sugiyama Iutaka [1969] give an excellent summary of the factors that one must take into account in determining the disadvantaged position of rural migrants to the city. The factors to be considered can be summarized as follows:

1. Being "disadvantaged" is a relative phenomenon based on the population group to which the "disadvantaged" are compared. That is, rural migrants to cities might be disadvantaged compared to urban natives but much better off than their rural counterparts who stayed in the country.

2. Age at the time of migration is important. Younger migrants to the city are more likely to be more upwardly mobile than are older migrants.

3. The more time a migrant spends in the city, the greater the chances for upward mobility.

4. Early socialization appears to be just as important as age and length of time spent in the city. The longer one is socialized into a rural environment, the lower are the chances for upward mobility in the urban environment.

5. If migrants are knowledgable about a city before they migrate to it and if they obtain assistance upon arriving in the city, their chances for upward mobility increase.

6. Finally, people from rural backgrounds who migrate to smaller cities have a greater chance for upward mobility than people who migrate to larger cities.

After studying migration to cities in Argentina, Brazil, and Chile, however, Bock and Iutaka reached a somewhat startling conclusion. They found, in general, that the six factors were of limited applicability or none at all to the cities and countries studied. They concluded that although level of education played a part in effecting upward mobility,

> The formation of an industrial occupational structure in the developing societies may be far more complex than previous studies indicate. The migrants have as good a chance to climb or descend socially as the natives, and the rural migrant does not differ from the urban migrant. The process of migration appears to be related to the formation of the structure itself: in other words, the migrants do not enter into a structure but help to form it . . . once the structure is established, rural-urban background may be an important variable [1969, p. 353].

Bock and Iutaka maintain that Latin America, with all its developing nations, is still in the stage of developing its industrial occupational structure.

Bock and Iutaka also were researching social mobility. New migrants to a city generally have a status lower than urban natives, hence, their chances of social mobility are better than that of the indigenous population. What is important here is that the Bock and Iutaka study revealed the complexity of the key considerations that must be closely scrutinized when studied in the context of developing nations. The complexity of the entire migration process is most evident, however, in the problems arising from the large urban migrant settlements in many of the major cities of the world.

In the past two decades the tendency for people to move to improve their lot has become most pronounced among those millions of people who have migrated to the major cities of the developing nations. In Cairo they are simply called the "have nots"; in Lima, their residential area is labeled *pueblos jóvenes;* in Rio de Janeiro, they live in the *favelas.* The "they" represent one of the major social problems of modern man— the new migrants to the cities of the developing nations. Most agree that these migrants end up living in some of the worst slums imaginable, and most also recognize that they have a most difficult time in gaining steady employment and income. Many of the migrants' shantytowns are on the periphery of the city, which makes the delivery of water and sanitation services most difficult. As noted earlier, many of the migrants to these squatter settlements return to the countryside to bring their city-earned wages to their families in the country. Over time, however, these trips become more and more infrequent and soon the family joins the chief male urban migrant in a permanent move to the city.

Curiously, some of these squatter settlements are actually consequences of planned invasions that are often actually supported by the government. The *pueblos jovenes* of Lima, Peru, are prime examples of squalid living areas that came into being and continue to exist in three stages: 1. through informal contacts with friends and relatives, a group of people learn of a planned invasion of empty land in Lima; 2. on a planned day, often a holiday, the invaders invade the land and hastily build shacks or huts for immediate occupancy; usually, the invaders have notified the media in Lima so that the presence of representatives from the media will mitigate the possibility of law-enforcement officials stopping the invasion; and 3. finally, the squatters form a quasi-legal association to gain final control of the land. Of course, these invasions are not always successful. Such invasions are likely to meet with failure if the squatters try to invade privately owned land. Consequently, most of the land that is invaded is owned by the government, which often actually coordinates the establishment of the *pueblos jóvenes* [Delgado 1969; Mangin 1967, 1970]. Nevertheless, the new residents of the *pueblos jóvenes* and similar squatter settlements in other cities of the developing nations face an uncertain future of poverty and squalid living conditions. Unless these nations succeed in improving their level of economic development, there is no reason to believe that these squatter settlements will disappear in this or the next generation.

The Maori Migration

However, not all migration to the city need be traumatic or pathological. The Maori of New Zealand represent a relatively poor, rural population that successfully migrated to New Zealand cities with a minimum of adjustment problems. Their migration represents the benefits of a nation's having an expanding economy that can cope with migration. The Maori were indigenous to New Zealand long before the European (Pakeha) colonists came to that country. After their defeat at the hands of the Pakeha colonists in the 1860s, the Maori withdrew from the Pakeha settlements and remained in the outlying rural areas. By the turn of the twentieth century, the New Zealand government thought the Maori were dying off and began a national policy of benevolence and cultural independence for the Maori. This policy, coupled with New Zealand's strong sense of equality, facilitated the future urbanization of the Maori. This urbanization came during World War II when severe manpower shortages in major industries occurred in New Zealand. Approximately one-fourth of the adult Maori population was moved to the cities to work in industry. An even greater number were assigned work duties in rural agriculture production. Although many of the Maoris left the cities after the end of the war, the forcible movement of some of them to the cities had exposed a significant number of Maori to urban culture and experiences. The post-World War II Maori who returned to their rural village not only brought some urban experience back but were again living on incomes much lower than those of the Pakeha landowners.

By 1959 the New Zealand government had firmly set itself on a course of bringing the Maori into the cities. The wartime experience had exposed the Maori to the fact that there were greater incomes awaiting them in the city than in rural areas. This fact, coupled with the government's program to urbanize the Maori, led many of them to New Zealand's cities in search of the "better life." In terms of physical artifacts, the Maori adjusted to their new urban life rapidly. They eventually were at the forefront of trying to acquire material goods and amenities. In fact, "When a desirable and new (to New Zealand) artifact of Western technology was introduced it was adopted more quickly by urban Maoris than by urban non-Maoris" [Collette & O'Malley 1974, p. 151]. Yet, unlike most migratory experiences, the urban Maori were able to acquire material possessions without losing their cultural heritage. Probably because of the racial differences between the Maori and the Pakeha populations, and because of their cultural history, the Maori have established strong organizations and associations that aim to preserve their culture. The open social climate in New Zealand serves as a fertile environment for the urban Maori to advance economically without losing their historical identity. Perhaps if more nations were able to follow the example of New Zealand, the squatter settlements of large cities would soon be things of the past.

The importance of urban migration, whether it be in New Zealand, Chile, or India, lies in the strong relationship between migration and economic development. Earlier in this chapter, it was noted that there was a close relationship between industrialization, economic development, and urbanization. Gustav Ranis [1963] postulates that: **1.** to be successful, a country's economic development must absorb people into the industrial labor force at a rate faster than its population growth; 2. the actual heart of the entire development process "lies in the gradual shifting of the economy's center of gravity from the agricultural to the industrial sector through labor reallocation" [Fei & Ranis 1963, p. 283]. For this reallocation to occur, a population must either somehow have industry brought to it or must bring itself to that industry. In developing nations, the latter alternative is the most feasible. As a result, unless overurbanization occurs, migration to the city—the center of industrial activity— becomes an essential element of ensuring sufficient growth in the industrial labor force [Hance 1970; Kuper 1965; Lowry 1966; Morrill 1965]. Without this expansion of the industrial labor force, a nation can hardly expect to reach the level of economic development that is necessary for expanded urbanization.

CONCLUSION

This chapter began with a discussion of the early rise of cities. Most notable in this early rise of cities was the development of an ever-increasing division of labor. In more recent times this division of labor has reached its greatest level of complexity in industrially advanced nations. It was noted that industrialization was a necessary corollary both to economic development and to urbanization. The relationship between these factors was examined for developed versus underdeveloped nations, and, then, a short description of urbanization in the major continents of the world was given. Finally, recent migration to cities, especially those in underdeveloped nations, was discussed.

Obviously, this chapter dealt with a variety of complicated and intricate topics that could not be treated in detail. The undeniable point to be stressed, however, is this: the present and, at least immediate, future of urbanization rests squarely on industrialization and economic development. Any nation that does not fully realize the interplay between these three variables cannot be expected to excel in any of them.

BIBLIOGRAPHY

Janet L. Abu-Lughod, "Urbanization in Egypt: Present State and Future Prospects." *Economic Development and Cultural Change,* 1965, 13:313–343.

Eduardo E. Arriaga, "New Approach to the Measurement of Urbanization." *Economic Development and Cultural Change,* 1970, 18:206–218.

Robert C. Atchley, "A Size-Function Typology of Cities." *Demography,* 1967, 4:721–733.

Martin J. Beckman, "City Hierarchies and the Distribution of City Size." *Economic Development and Cultural Change,* 1958, 6:243–248.

Brian J. L. Berry, "City Size Distributions and Economic Development." *Economic Development and Cultural Change,* 1961, 9:573–588.

Brian, J. L. Berry and William L. Garrison, "Alternate Explanations of Urban Rank-Size Relationships." *Annals of the Association of American Geographers,* 1958, 48:83–91.

Peter M. Blau and Otis Dudley Duncan, *The American Occupational Structure.* Wiley, 1967.

Wilbur E. Bock and Sugiyama Iutaka, "Rural-Urban Migration and Social Mobility: The Controversy on Latin America." *Rural Sociology,* 1969, 34:343–355.

Nirmal K. Bose, "Calcutta: A Premature Metropolis." *Cities: A Scientific American Book.* Alfred A. Knopf, 1970, pp. 59–74.

Gerald Breese, *Urbanization in Newly Developing Countries.* Prentice-Hall, 1966.

Clyde E. Browning, "Primate Cities and Related Concepts." In Forrest R. Pitts, ed., *Urban Systems and Economic Development.* University of Oregon Press.

Harley L. Browning, "Urbanization and Modernization in Latin America: The Demographic Perspective." In Glenn H. Beyer, ed., *The Urban Explosion in Latin America.* Cornell University Press, 1967.

Richard J. Cebula and Richard K. Vedder, "A Note on Migration, Economic Opportunity, and the Quality of Life." *Journal of Regional Science,* 1973, 13:205–211.

Tertius Chandler and Gerald Fox, *3000 Years of Urban Growth.* Academic Press, 1974.

Szymon Chodak, *Societal Development.* Oxford University Press, 1973.

John Collette and Pat O'Malley, "Urban Migration and Selective Acculturation: The Case of the Maori." *Human Organization,* 1974, 33:147–153.

Commission on Population Growth and the American Future, *Population and the American Future.* U.S. Government Printing Office, 1972.

Kingsley Davis, "Introduction: The Evolution of Western Industrial Cities." *Cities: Their Origins, Growth and Human Impact.* W. H. Freeman, 1973.

Kingsley Davis and Hilda H. Golden, "Urbanization and the Development of Pre-Industrial Areas." *Economic Development and Cultural Change,* 1954, 3:6–26.

Gordon F. DeJong and William L. Donnelly, "Public Welfare and Migration." *Social Science Quarterly,* 1973, 54:329–344.

Carlos Delgado, "Three Proposals Regarding Accelerated Urbanization Problems in Areas: The Lima Case." *American Behavioral Scientist,* 1969, 12:34–44.

Alan W. Evans, "Market Forces and Urban Change in Britain." In Richard Rose, ed., *The Management of Urban Change in Britain and Germany.* Sage Publications, 1974.

John C. H. Fei and Gustav Ranus, "Capital Accumulation, and Economic Development." *American Economic Review,* 1963, 53:283–313.

Jack P. Gibbs and Walter T. Martin, "Urbanization and Natural Resources: A Study In Organizational Ecology." *American Sociological Review,* 1958, 23:266–277.

Jack P. Gibbs and Walter T. Martin, "Urbanization, Technology, and the Division of Labor: International Patterns." *American Sociological Review,* 1962, 27: 667–677.

Norman P. Gist, "Urbanism in India." In Sylvia Fleis Fava, ed., *Urbanism in World Perspective.* Thomas Y. Crowell, 1968.

Scott Greer, *The Emerging City.* Free Press, 1962.

Peter C. W. Gutkind, "Network Analysis and Urbanism in Africa: The Use of Micro and Macro Analysis." *The Canadian Review of Sociology,* 1965, 2:123–131.

Jeffrey K. Hadden and Edgar F. Borgatta, *American Cities: Their Social Characteristics.* Rand McNally, 1965.

William A. Hance, *Population, Migration and Urbanization in Africa,* Columbia University Press, 1970.

Shirley F. Hartley, "Our Growing Problem: Population." *Social Problems,* 1973, 21:190–206.

Bert F. Hoselitz, "Generative and Parasitic Cities." *Economic Development and Culture Change,* 1955, 3:278–294.

Bert F. Hoselitz, "Urbanization and Economic Growth in Asia." *Economic Development and Cultural Change.* 1957, 6:42–54.

Bert F. Hoselitz, *Sociological Aspects of Economic Growth.* Free Press, 1960.

Mark Jefferson, "The Law of the Primate City." *Geographical Review,* 1939, 29:226–232.

David R. Kamerschen, "Further Analysis of Overurbanization." *Economic Development and Cultural Change.* 1969, 17:235–253.

Hans Koschnick, "Politics and Urban Change." In Richard Rose, ed., *The Management of Urban Change in Britain and Germany.* Sage Publications, 1974.

Hilda Kuper, *Urbanization and Migration in West Africa.* University of California Press, 1965.

William L. Langer, "The Black Death." *Cities: Their Origin, Growth and Human Impact.* W. H. Freeman, 1973.

Arnold S. Linsky, "Some Generalizations Concerning Primate Cities." In Gerald Breese, ed., *The City in Newly Developing Countries.* Prentice-Hall, 1969.

P. C. Lloyd, *Africa in Social Change.* Praeger, 1968.

Ira S. Lowry, *Migration and Metropolitan Growth: Two Analytical Models.* Chandler, 1966.

Akin L. Mabogunje, "Urbanization in Nigeria—A Constraint on Economic Development." *Economic Development and Cultural Change,* 1965, 13:413–438.

Richard S. Macneish, "The Origins of New World Civilization." *Cities: Their Origin, Growth and Human Impact.* W. H. Freeman, 1973.

William Mangin, "Latin American Squatter Settlements: A Problem and a Solution." *Latin America Research Review,* 1967, 11:65–98.

William Mangin, "Two Types of Peruvian Communities." In William Mangin, ed., *Peasants in Cities.* Houghton Mifflin, 1970.

Surinder K. Mehta, "Some Demographic and Economic Correlates of Primate Cities: A Case for Revaluation." *Demography,* 1964, 1:136–147.

Surinder K. Mehta, "Patterns of Residence in Poona (India) by Income, Education and Occupation." *American Journal of Sociology,* 1968, 73:496–508.

Kosta Mihailovic, *Regional Development Experiences and Prospects in Eastern Europe.* The Hague, Netherlands: Mouton, 1972.

M. J. B. Molahan, *Detribalization.* Dar es Salaam Tanzania: Government Printer, 1957.

Richard L. Morrill, *Migration and the Spread and Growth of Urban Settlements.* Lund, Sweden: C.W.K. Gleerup, 1965.

Irving Morrissett, "The Economic Structure of American Cities." *Papers and Proceedings of the Regional Science Association,* 1958, 4:239–256.

Rhoads Murphey, "Urbanization in Asia." In Gerald Breese, ed., *The City in Newly Developing Countries.* Prentice-Hall, 1969.

John H. Nixon and Paul H. Gerhardt, "Urban Economic Development." *The Annals of the American Academy of Political and Social Science,* 1964, 352:39–47.

Janet Rothenberg Pack, "Determinants of Migration to Central Cities." *Journal of Regional Science,* 1973, 13:249–260.

Ulrich Pfeiffer, "Market Forces and Urban Change in Germany." In Richard Rose, ed., *The Management of Urban Change in Britain and Germany,* Sage Publications, 1974.

Gustav Ranis, "Allocation Criteria and Population Growth." *American Economic Review,* 1963, 53:619–633.

Robert E. Roberts and George W. McBee, "Modernization and Economic Development in Mexico: A Factor Analytic Approach." *Economic Development and Cultural Change,* 1968, 16:603–612.

Leo Schnore, "Urbanization and Economic Development: The Demographic

Contribution." *American Journal of Economics and Sociology,* 1964, 23:37–48.

Leo F. Schnore, "On the Spatial Structure of Cities in the Americas." In Philip M. Hauser and Leo F. Schnore, eds., *The Study of Urbanization.* John Wiley & Sons, 1965.

Kent P. Schwirian and John W. Prehn, "An Axiomatic Theory of Urbanization." *American Sociological Review,* 1962, 27:812–825.

Edwin S. Segal, "Ethnic Variables in East African Urban Migration." *Urban Anthropology,* 1973, 2:194–204.

Gideon Sjoberg, *The Preindustrial City.* Free Press, 1960.

Gideon Sjoberg, "Rural-Urban Balance and Models of Economic Development." In Neil Smelser and Seymour M. Lipset, eds., *Social Structure and Mobility in Economic Development.* Aldine, 1966.

Gideon Sjoberg, "The Origin and Evolution of Cities." *Cities: Their Origin, Growth and Human Impact,* W. H. Freeman, 1973.

Aidan Southall, *Social Change in Modern Africa.* London: Oxford University Press, 1961.

N. V. Sovani, "The Analysis of 'Over-Urbanization.' " *Economic Development and Cultural Change,* 1964, 12:113–122.

Joseph J. Spengler, "Economic Development and Population Growth." *International Journal of Health Services,* 1973, 3:577–581.

Edward G. Stockwell, "The Relationship Between Population Growth and Economic Development." *American Sociological Review,* 1962, 27:250–252.

Charles Tilly and Harold C. Brown, "On Uprooting, Kinship, and the Auspices of Migration." In Charles Tilly, ed., *An Urban World,* Little, Brown, 1974.

Michael B. Toney, "Religious Preference and Migration." *International Migration Review,* 1973, 7:281–288.

Glenn T. Trewartha, *A Geography of Population: World Patterns.* John Wiley & Sons, 1969.

U.S. Bureau of the Census, Current Population Report. U.S. Government Printing Office, December 1974.

David Ward, *Cities and Immigrants.* Oxford University Press, 1973.

Jay A. Weinstein, *Demographic Transition and Social Change.* General Learning Press, 1976.

ANTHONY J. LA GRECA · 75

2.

GROWTH AND STRUCTURE OF THE METROPOLITAN COMMUNITY

Richard A. Smith

Robert H. Weller

Cities are diverse as well as similar phenomena. Their diversity can be seen in their wide range of sizes, types, and characteristics. For example, in the United States in 1970 the sizes of urban places ranged from 2,500 (the minimum size necessary to qualify as an urban place according to the U.S. Bureau of the Census) to 7.9 million persons, with the average city's population being 21,000. Moreover, there is a great deal of variation around this average city size. For instance, only 4.5 percent of all urban places are in the 20,000- to 25,000-size class. In addition, the social, economic, and political differences that exist between cities of various sizes are sufficiently great to make the notion of an (average) city unrealistic. Can one really compare Marianna, Florida, Ithaca, New York, and Chicago, Illinois, three cities existing at the lower, average, and high ends of the city-size scale?

On another level, however, significant similarities do exist between cities. These are similarities in process rather than in manifest characteristics. All urban places can be viewed as belonging to a particular class of ecological organization whose existence and growth can be accounted for by the same set of hypotheses and the same theories of urban development. Although cities often show marked differences in overt characteristics, their processes of growth are strikingly similar. It is necessary to appreciate these basic growth factors in order to understand and grasp the significance of the differences in manifest characteristics that exist. Accordingly, our purposes in this unit are two-fold: **1.** to portray the factors influencing growth and development, indicating the processes by which urban areas have grown from small population centers to major metropolitan communities, **2.** to discuss the effects of these processes upon selected aspects of the community structure. We shall be concerned particularly with the structure of metropolitan areas and the processes of growth that affect this structure.

THE CONCEPT OF THE METROPOLITAN COMMUNITY

The Ecological Frame of Reference

Two early and comprehensive treatments of the growth and structure of metropolitan communities were provided by Norman Gras [1922] and R. D. McKenzie [1933]. Both illustrate the basic ecological approach to the study of the metropolitan community. Gras utilizes a neo-evolutionary approach in which he posits a relationship between successive stages of technological development and the emergence of complex forms of community organization. According to Gras, the form of settlement is a response to new possibilities for securing a livelihood from the natural environment. Thus, particular technological improvements have decreased people's reliance upon the immediate environment, have allowed some control and even exploitation of this environment, and have simultaneously facilitated the development of more complex systems of production, trade, and community organization extending over increasingly wider spatial areas. Gras identifies five stages or types of community organization that correspond to these technological improvements. These are: **1.** the collectional economy, **2.** the cultural nomadic economy, **3.** the settled village economy, **4.** the town economy, and **5.** the metropolitan economy. This last stage, organized around the metropolitan community, is identified by Gras as the new, emergent form of organization, characterized by a high degree of specialization and a division of labor between community units.

A similar theme emerges from McKenzie's study of the metropolitan community in which the development of urban areas in general, and the metropolitan community in particular, is seen as a function of three successive stages in the improvement of communication and transportation technology. Each successive technological improvement is associated with a new kind of urban organization, ranging from the small, independent settlement to the large, complex metropolitan region. Thus, McKenzie divides the history of American settlement into three periods as follows: **1.** the prerailway era extending from colonial times to about 1850, **2.** the railway era from 1850 to about 1900, and **3.** the motor transportation era, which began in about 1900. The major characteristics of this third settlement phase are similar to those given by Gras, that is, there is a territorial division of labor organized around the dominance of the central, major city identified as a metropolitan community.

The large center has been able to extend the radius of its influence; its population and many of its institutions, freed from the dominance of rail transportation, have become widely dispersed throughout surrounding territory. Moreover, formerly independent towns and villages and also rural territory have become part of this enlarged city complex. This new type of super community, organized around a dominant focal point and comprising a multitude of differentiated centers of activity differs from the metropolitanism established by rail transportation in the complexity of its institutional division of labor and the mobility of its population. Its territorial scope is defined in terms of motor transportation and competition with other regions [McKenzie 1933, pp. 6–7].[1]

Three features of Gras's and McKenzie's discussion of the development of the metropolitan community are important. First is the view of community organization adopted by human ecologists: cities are a form of collective organization developed in response to a population's need to adapt to an environment given the conditions of life presented by that environment. The environment consists of the social, economic, and political, as well as the physical, milieu of a population. Adaptation may consist either of modification of the environment or of passive adjustment to the environment. A primary reason for the existence of cities is that they are an effective means of increasing this adaptation.

A second vital feature of Gras's and McKenzie's analysis is the emphasis upon the variable nature of this adaptation. The particular type of community organization that is developed is viewed as a dependent variable, affected by the type and level of resources available to the population for exploiting the environment and wresting a livelihood from it. Both Gras and McKenzie emphasize the role of technology in the development of new forms of community organization, particularly transportation and communication technologies. The development of increasingly efficient and extensive means for shipping goods and products, as well as for non-face-to-face communication over space brings wider areas of population settlement into contact with one another. This widened network of communication results in an increase of the range and diversity of environmental resources, ideas, and production facilities that are available to each community. Through the development of a system of trade, new forms of specialization and a more extensive division of labor at both the intra- and inter-community levels are made possible. Community organization is thereby elaborated.

In addition to technological improvements, other resources or conditions are recognized by human ecologists as affecting the development of the community. Population itself may be one such resource, according to the types and levels of skills associated with it and with its size. Skills affect the kinds of tasks that can be developed and performed within the population group, and size limits the extent to which a system of differentiated roles can emerge. Environmental resources are also important. Among other conditions, fertile soil, favorable climate, and the

---

1. From *The Metropolitan Community* by R. D. McKenzie. Copyright 1933 McGraw-Hill. Used with the permission of McGraw-Hill Book Company.

presence of mineral deposits, water, and food supplies will significantly affect the productivity of a population, its ability to sustain itself and grow in size within a given setting, and the types of goods and services it is best suited to produce. Particular types of social organizational conditions also have an impact upon the development of different settlement patterns. Systems of control embodied in an explicit legal code and administered by central governments, mechanisms for the integration and coordination of functions, and arrangements for the distribution and allocation of community products will have a bearing upon the extent to which a more complex division of labor can exist and function.

Ecologists have generally recognized these four factors—population, organization, environment, and technology—under the heading of the ecological complex and have used this concept to explain the particular form of community organization existing at any given time and place. When the community is seen as a dependent variable, changes in its form can be explained by reference to corresponding changes in one or more of these four conditions and the interaction between them. Hence the growth of the metropolitan community is not uniform but variable, and must be understood in terms of the ecological complex as a form of collective adaptation.

A third common feature of the work of Gras and McKenzie is that they introduce the particular form that this adaptation has taken. Community development is seen as proceeding in terms of an increasing complexity of organization, a greater level of specialization between parts of the community, and a more extensive division of labor involving reciprocal trade and exchange relationships. The metropolitan community thus represents a breakdown of the insularity of the small, independent community and its replacement by an extensive system of interdependence among communities organized under a territorial division of labor. The metropolitan community is thus a system of socially and economically integrated communities, organized under the dominance of a large central city, and extending to the limits of daily commuting patterns.

Census Versus Ecological Definitions

Although refined somewhat by later writers on this topic, this ecological approach to the essential nature of the metropolis continues to be accepted. Thus, Amos Hawley writes that the metropolitan community "is delineated by the frequency with which outlying residents and institutions transact their affairs in the metropolis, whether through direct visitation or through indirect means of communication" [1971, p. 149].

Measuring such interaction is difficult, however, because its boundaries usually do not correspond to visible objects or to political borders or jurisdictions. It is necessary, therefore, to utilize an operational definition of a metropolitan community, incorporating those identifiable areas that seem to belong in a metropolis and excluding those that do not. The U.S. Bureau of the Census has operationalized this definition and currently recognizes 243 places as Standard Metropolitan Statistical Areas (SMSAs). Each of these SMSAs consists of the following characteristics:

1. One or more contiguous counties that contain at least one city with a minimum of 50,000 population. If there are "twin cities" with a combined population of at least 50,000 inhabitants, these may be used in the absence of a single larger city.

2. Any other contiguous counties that are socially and economically integrated with the large, central city. The criteria of social and economic integration include such factors as residence and employment patterns, the extent to which the labor force consists of nonagricultural workers, and per-capita telephone calls between the county and the central city, newspaper circulation reports, official traffic counts, and the extent of retail trade in the central city by residents of the contiguous county.

Thus, SMSAs consist of one or more contiguous counties that contain a large city and are socially and economically integrated. The persons residing within an SMSA are referred to as the metropolitan population. This population is divided into two parts. People living in the large city are classified as central city residents, and all other persons are classified as noncentral city residents. Conceptually, this latter group corresponds to suburbanites, although not all of them live in suburbs. Many of the people in this second group live in smaller cities located within the metropolitan area, and a minority of them live on farms that are located within the outlying areas of the SMSA.

Each SMSA is assigned the name of the central city. Thus there is the Harrisburg SMSA, the Tallahassee SMSA, and so forth. When there is more than one central city within an SMSA, their names are used jointly, with the largest being first and the smallest being last, as in the Albany-Schenectady-Troy and the Newport News-Hampton

SMSAs. Sometimes an SMSA contains counties in two or more states. For instance, the Fort Smith SMSA consists of Sebastian County (where Fort Smith, the central city, is located) and Crawford County in Arkansas and LeFlore and Sequoyah Counties in Oklahoma.

Approximately 50 percent of the SMSAs consist of only one county, and only 18 (about 7 percent) consist of 5 or more. On the basis of the number of political jurisdictions involved, the Washington SMSA is the largest, containing the District of Columbia, two counties in Maryland, and seven counties in Virginia. In 1970, with an absolute population size of 11,528,649 inhabitants, the New York SMSA was the largest. The Meriden, Connecticut SMSA was the smallest in 1970, having only 55,809 inhabitants [U.S. Bureau of the Census 1971, pp. 34–46].

Most discussion and research on metropolitan areas makes use of the U.S. Bureau of the Census definition. For ecological purposes, however, using political jurisdictions to construct SMSAs is partially inadequate because the area of social and economic interdependency that constitutes the metropolitan community may not conform to these political boundaries. If we imagine that the boundaries of the "real" or ecological metropolitan community could be established and compared with those boundaries established using the Bureau of the Census's operational definition, there would be three possible outcomes. In the ideal situation, the real boundaries would coincide with those employed by the Census Bureau, and we would have "truebounded" metropolitan areas. However, the statistical area defined by the Census Bureau could be smaller than the "real" community boundaries, in which case we would have an "underbounded" metropolitan community. Similarly the statistically defined boundaries could be larger than the "real" ones, and we would have an example of an "overbounded" area.

Of the few studies of the adequacy of the Census Bureau's approach to delimiting metropolitan areas, the most systematic analysis has been conducted by Allan Feldt [1965]. He examined 1950 census data and concluded that 47 percent of the Standard Metropolitan Areas (the name used in 1950) were underbounded. Only about 20 percent were overbounded. Examples of underbounded metropolitan areas (in 1950) included Indianapolis and San Francisco-Oakland. Examples of overbounded metropolitan areas included Pittsburgh and Ogden, Utah. Since 1950, the Census Bureau has altered its definition of metropolitan areas somewhat, has shifted to the nomenclature Standard Metropolitan Statistical Area, and has expanded the areal boundaries of a substantial number of metropolitan areas. However, given that areas of ecological interaction rarely correspond exactly to political boundaries, we suspect that some similar situations of under- and overboundedness still exist. The reader should remember these distinctions. While we are generally forced to employ the census delineations of metropolitan areas because of convenience and data availability, in some cases these will be partially inaccurate from an ecological perspective.

Alternative Classifications

In addition to SMSAs there are other types of statistical aggregates that are recognized by the U.S. Census Bureau, and one should be aware of the extent and nature of the differences between each of these and the SMSA. In general, these other classifications are not based upon an assessment of interdependence to the same extent as SMSAs.

Urban places—These are places with a minimum population of 2,500 and may be either incorporated or unincorporated.

Cities—These are places that are incorporated as cities and have been granted certain powers, as defined in their charters, by the state in which they are located. By definition, cities are smaller than SMSAs.

Urbanized areas—The major objective of defining urbanized areas is to separate the urban and rural population in the vicinity of the larger cities. An urbanized area consists of a central city of 50,000 or more inhabitants (or twin cities within contiguous boundaries with that combined population) and surrounding closely settled territory. The U.S. Bureau of the Census has defined "closely settled" as a population density of around 2,000 persons per square mile or a housing density of approximately 500 houses per square mile [Hawley 1971, p. 152].

Generally there is only one urbanized area in each SMSA. However, there may be more than one in cases where there is more than one city with 50,000 or more inhabitants whose boundaries are not contiguous and whose densely settled portions are physically separated. For instance, the Chicago SMSA has three urbanized areas within it. In other cases, a single urbanized area may include portions of two or more SMSAs. The New London-Groton-Norwich SMSA is the only one without an urbanized area within its boundaries.

Standard Consolidated Areas—Because of the special importance of the metropolitan complexes around New York and Chicago, several contiguous SMSAs and additional counties that appear to have strong social and economic interrelationships have been combined into Standard

Consolidated Areas. These are called the New York-Northeastern New Jersey and the Chicago-Northwestern Indiana Standard Consolidated Areas [U.S. Bureau of the Census 1972, pp. 1–4].

HISTORICAL OVERVIEW: THE GROWTH OF METROPOLITAN AREAS IN THE UNITED STATES

The U.S. Bureau of the Census first attempted to delineate places as metropolitan in 1910, when the term "metropolitan district" was used to refer to urban units that had an aggregate population of at least 100,-000 persons and contained one or more central cities of 50,000 or more persons. In 1950, the Census Bureau officially adopted the Standard Metropolitan Area (SMA) to replace the designation Metropolitan District and, in the 1960 and 1970 censuses, changed the nomenclature to Standard Metropolitan Statistical Area (SMSA), although the criteria for inclusion remain similar to those used in 1950.

Because the criteria for designating metropolitan areas have changed over time, it is advisable to use some constant definition. In 1900 there were sixty-one areas that would have qualified as SMAs under the 1950 definition. By 1960, the number of such areas had roughly tripled to 189. During this same interval, the proportion of the U.S. population living in areas classifiable as SMAs increased from about one-third in 1900 to two-thirds in 1960. Metropolitan population growth during this period was due both to the expansion of the population within existing metropolitan areas and to the growth of other areas and their subsequent reclassification as "metropolitan." Since 1950 an increasingly important source of growth has been the addition of adjacent counties to preexisting metropolitan areas [Hawley, Duncan, & Goldberg 1964]. Consequently, the number of SMSAs in the United States increased from 212 to 243, and the total population living in metropolitan areas increased by 20 million persons. However, the proportion of the national population—about two-thirds—living in metropolitan areas remained fairly constant.

Distribution within the United States

The U.S. Bureau of the Census delineates nine census divisions within the United States. Of these, the East North Central (Illinois, Indiana,

Michigan, Ohio, and Wisconsin) has the most SMSAs (forty-eight) and
the Mountain Division (Arizona, Colorado, Idaho, Montana, Nevada,
New Mexico, Utah, and Wyoming) has the least (fourteen). The number
of SMSAs and the 1970 metropolitan population for each division are
presented in table 1.

T A B L E 1. Number of SMSAs and 1970 Metropolitan Population for Each Census Division

Division	Number of SMSAs	Metropolitan Population
New England	24	8,540,254
Middle Atlantic	27	31,385,131
East North Central	48	29,738,301
West North Central	19	7,919,972
South Atlantic	38	17,691,880
East South Central	19	5,400,302
West South Central	31	12,107,170
Mountain	14	4,714,148
Pacific	23	22,658,710

Source: U.S. Bureau of the Census 1971, pp. 25, 105–114.

International Distribution
of Metropolitan Areas

There is little uniformity in the ways countries identify areas as metropolitan. Many countries attempt to designate a larger unit than the city
proper, and normally these units are defined in terms of existing political
boundaries around areas that are contiguous to a central city. Most of
these foreign definitions correspond roughly to SMSAs in the United
States, although the exact criteria that define them are different. As
a result, extreme care must be taken in making international comparisons. Kingsley Davis [1969, 1972] has compiled data from the various
countries and has attempted to control for differences in definition. Figure 1 presents the number of places with 100,000 inhabitants classified
by size of place according to Davis's data. The approximately 834 million
persons living in these places in 1970 represent 23.1 percent of the
world's population. In 1950, only about 16 percent of the world's population lived in places of 100,000+ population.

In 1970 the median city size was about 225,000 persons. Although
the number of large cities is small, these contain such very large populations that the average city size is considerably smaller than the size of
the city in which the average city-dweller lives. Indeed, Davis [1972,
pp 24–30] estimates that the median city dweller lives in a place with
1.1 million inhabitants.

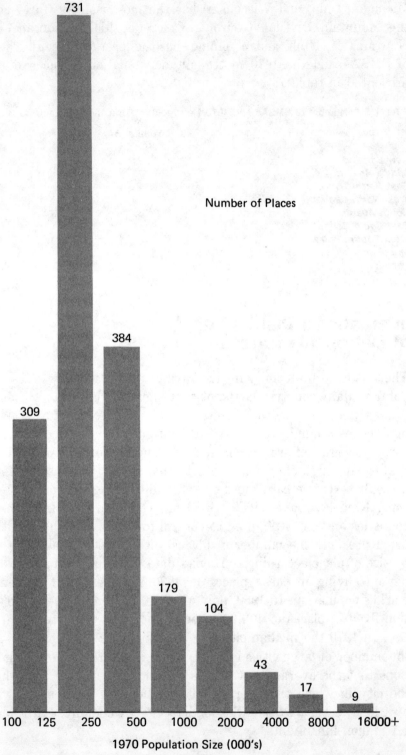

Number of Places

731

384

309

179

104

43

17

9

100   125   250   500   1000   2000   4000   8000   16000+

1970 Population Size (000's)

Fig. 1. Number of Urban Places with 100,000 + Inhabitants, Classified According to Size of Place in 1970. (Source: Adapted from Davis 1972, p. 38.)

The New York and Tokyo urban agglomerations ranked as the world's largest in 1970, the latter replacing London, which previously had ranked second for some time. In terms of proportion of the population living in cities, the four top-ranking areas in 1970 were Australia-New Zealand (61 percent), Northern Europe (58 percent), Northern America (57 percent), and Japan (55 percent). One region, Oceania, consists of small islands and has no places with 100,000 or more inhabitants. Regions with less than 10 percent of the population living in cities include most of Africa and South Central Asia. The correlation between a region's rank in 1970 and its rank in 1950 in proportion of its population living in cities is 0.98. Thus, rankings have been very stable through time. This stability has been most marked in the largest city-size category.

In general, the larger the size of place category, the greater is its concentration in economically developed countries. Thus, in 1970 only 36 percent of the world's population living in cities of 1 million or more inhabitants were in less developed countries, although these countries contained about two-thirds of the world's population. However, there has been a decline in the degree of such concentration since 1950 [Davis 1972, pp. 269–275].

Projected Trends

Predictions are hazardous, especially for longer time horizons. Therefore we have confined ourselves to projecting some general tendencies that should be present during the 1970s and perhaps even the 1980s.

1. Most of the population growth that takes place in the United States will occur within areas already designated as SMSAs. Before the reader congratulates us on our incisive foresight, he should be reminded that two-thirds of the population already lives in such areas and that we are merely projecting a statistical phenomenon.

2. Most of this growth will be caused by two factors. One is the inclusion of previously nonmetropolitan counties (and population) into already existing SMSAs as transportation and communications networks become even more encompassing. The second is the demographic factor of reproductive change. Although migration will remain predominant as a component of change in selected SMSAs, it will assume less im-

portance as a source of metropolitan growth in the United States. This is because of the high proportion of the population that is already in metropolitan areas and because migration has become increasingly *inter*metropolitan in character. Thus, there will continue to be a massive circulation of population between SMSAs, but relatively little growth will accrue to the metropolitan population of the United States as a result of net in-migration from nonmetropolitan areas.

3. If the national birth rate continues to be low, metropolitan growth will become even slower than it has been. However, because of its younger age composition, the metropolitan population will continue to grow faster than the national population. The larger SMSAs will experience much slower growth (indeed, often decline in absolute population size) than the smaller SMSAs.

4. Because net in-migration to the metropolitan areas from nonmetropolitan areas will diminish in magnitude, and because the rate of reproductive change among the metropolitan population of the United States will not be much higher than among the nonmetropolitan population, the proportion of the total population of the United States that lives in SMSAs will increase but slightly during the immediate future.

5. The central cities will lose population at accelerating rates because of the massive out-migration of whites, and because nonwhites will increasingly settle in the noncentral city portions of the metropolitan areas as their socioeconomic positions improve and as previously inaccessible markets become available.

APPROACHES TO URBAN LOCATION

Given the general conceptual approach to the metropolitan community that we have advanced in the first section of this unit, we shall now turn our attention to a consideration of the factors that influence the location and distribution of metropolitan communities. Because the metropolitan community is organized around a dominant central city, we shall begin with a consideration of the location and growth of cities, up to and through the growth of the metropolitan community. Thus, in this section we shall discuss the theories of city location, in the following section the pattern of interdependence between metropolitan areas and the relationship between metropolitan functions and location, and in the fourth section we shall discuss the process of metropolitan growth and expansion.

Throughout these three sections we attempt to emphasize the major factors influencing location and development, and to point out parallel processes that operate at different stages in urban and metropolitan growth. Because our frame of reference is derived from human ecology, many of the concepts central to this field are present in our treatment of the various issues. The themes set forth in our introduction are of central and critical importance:

- Cities represent an organizational response on the part of a population to the problems of adaption to a social, economic, and physical environment.

- Development proceeds in terms of increasing the complexity of organization, involving greater levels of specialization and a more extensive division of labor both within and between communities.

- The growth of this increasingly complex organization is significantly affected by environmental, organizational, population, and technological factors, and their changes and interrelationships.

Three Theories of Urban Location

The reasons for cities being located where they are can be understood by reference to the concept of adaptation. Although some locations are the result of historical accidents or chance, most patterns of urban location can be explained by the potential that exists at various sites for a population to exploit the environment and provide for the more efficient production and distribution of sustenance goods. Economic activity, representing a sustenance-producing activity, will locate in space according to the particular attractions that alternative locations have for that activity. Because some types of activities are better suited to particular types of locations than others, analytically distinct cities, based on different forms of economic-sustenance activity, will emerge at various kinds of locations. Through the agglomeration and concentration of population and activities at these sites, cities of varying sizes are formed.

The three theories that are generally recognized as explanations of the location of different types of economic activities are   1. break-of-bulk,   2. central place, and   3. industrial location. They correspond to three analytically separate urban types: 1. cities as transportation foci, or break-of-bulk points;   2. cities as central places in trading areas; and 3. cities as concentration points for industry and special services. In addition, some cities do not have their basis in this tripartite distinction but have been established for other, noneconomic reasons. Washington, D.C. is a good example of a city whose location was decided upon the basis of political considerations.

Break-of-Bulk Theory

The break-of-bulk theory of urban location is traced to C. H. Cooley, who suggested that "population and wealth tend to collect wherever there is a break in transportation" [1894, p.313]. This refers to an interruption in the movement of goods that might be caused by the necessity of transferring materials from one mode of transportation to another. Such transfers typically take place at the juncture of land and water transportation routes, or at points where highways and railroads meet, where deep waterways turn into shallow rivers, or perhaps in places where mountainous terrain forces a change from one type of conveyance to another. However, these mere physical interruptions in shipment—termed mechanical breaks—may not be sufficient in themselves to cause the location and concentration of economic activities. Numerous mechanical breaks exist at which are located nothing but a small service depot, loading and unloading equipment, and perhaps a restaurant. What is also necessary is a commercial break, that is, a change in the ownership of the transported goods. Where a mechanical break is accompanied by a commercial break, major trading and service facilities that are necessary for effecting the transactions may be found.

A commercial break-of-bulk greatly increases the importance of a mechanical break. At these sites there are likely to develop groups of merchants, banking and lending institutions, warehouse, legal, accounting and insurance firms, and so on, as well as the loading and unloading, repair and transportation facilities necessary for the physical transfer of the goods. In addition to these "primary" trading activities, a wide range of "secondary," population-serving activities also arise. These are not directly involved in the main economic activity of the site, which is trade; but these secondary activities do provide the wide range of services necessary for supporting the local population and include such undertakings as construction and retail, recreational, and personal services. Clearly, the type of city that is likely to develop at break-of-bulk points is a commercial city whose main activities are in trading and service relationships. We will see later, however, that manufacturing activities may also find this type of location attractive, which increases the growth and development potential of these sites and adds to the economic diversity of the city.

Many of the world's major metropolitan areas have developed, at least in part, because of the existence of a commercial break in transportation. For example, New York owes most of its prominence to its deep-water harbor and ready access to the midwestern region via the Hudson River and Mohawk Valley. Similarly, London is situated at the most inland point on the Thames that is navigable by large ships. Cairo, Bremen, Quebec, New Orleans, and other cities are all well located with respect to the juncture of riverways and land or ocean transportation. Most of the early large metropolitan areas within the United States owe their growth to location on some navigable water route. Thus, data reported by O. D. Duncan et al. [1960, table 1] show that forty-one out of fifty-nine [69 percent] SMSAs with central city populations of 100,000 or more, which attained that size in the period 1820–1920, were located on a seacoast, lake coast, or navigable river [see also Schnore & Varley 1955].

Central Place Theory

In addition to the type of commercial and mechanical break-in-bulk noted above, Cooley also recognized another important relationship between function and transportation in which a city may serve as a central collection and distribution point servicing a surrounding region. Small shipments from various parts of the region are collected at this central point and organized for long-distance shipping, and incoming shipments are disaggregated and distributed to the smaller localities of the region. Cities specializing in these collection and distribution functions for a tributary region are likely to be located at points convenient to the smaller settlements scattered about the region and, under conditions of uniform geography and accessibility, this location will be at the center of the area. Cities of this type are called central places, and their location is explained by central place theory.

The initial systematic formulation of central place theory was performed by Walter Christaller [1933], who sought a "general deductive theory . . . to explain the size, number, and distribution of towns." This theory can be best understood by reference to a few basic principles.

1. Cities exist to supply a range of services to a surrounding region and its population.

2. The services so supplied operate under certain economic constraints that define the minimum and maximum market size necessary for the continued provision of that service.

3. Consumers of these services order their buying patterns according to a frequency of use-travel relationship, so that longer distances are traveled to purchase more costly and less frequently used goods and services.

The principle that cities exist to provide services to some tributary area may also be stated in the reverse fashion: a certain amount of productive land will support an urban center of a particular size. Both formulations emphasize that the primary function for central place cities is as a service center for a region. This service principle differs markedly from the assumptions involved in other major theories of location, in which urban location is predicated on the existence of some specialized location factor or site advantage. Therefore, central place theory is more likely to apply only to those cities whose major economic activity is the provision of tertiary goods and services, ranging from retail services for the provision of clothing and food items to major wholesaling and professional services. Some central places, termed "Sunday towns," act only as centers for religious and recreational activities on holidays for the surrounding rural population. The city's central location functions to minimize the time and costs of travel to this point and of distribution of goods and services from this point to the surrounding region.

The conditions that define the minimum and maximum market area for particular goods and services and the shopping patterns of consumers combine to create not just one central place within a region, but many of them, all related to each other in a system of differentiated size, specialization, and importance. Many goods and services require relatively large market areas if they are to draw a sufficient number of consumers to remain economically viable. These goods and services are fairly specialized in nature, that is, they may not be demanded by most persons, or if used by all persons or households, they are not purchased at frequent intervals. Diamond rings and heart specialists illustrate the former type, while refrigerators, automobiles, and furniture may belong to the latter category. Other services, such as wholesaling and administration are best provided in large central locations where the demand from smaller centers can be aggregated to make these activities worth providing. At the same time consumers of these goods and services are more willing to travel larger distances to shop for these items and may demand a number of different outlets for each item so that comparison shopping is possible. Goods and services with these characteristics are thus most likely to locate in larger centers and with maximum access to the largest potential market.

Purveyors of relatively unspecialized goods, on the other hand, for which there is continual and frequent demand, may subsist on smaller potential markets and therefore will locate in closer proximity to smaller groups of population. Ubiquitous items such as common hardware goods, groceries, general medical services, gas stations, and the like, fall into this category. Between the two extremes of highly specialized and unspecialized goods are a large number of other items whose market areas also vary in size.

The effect of these conditions is to create a spatial distribution of service centers or central places that systematically vary in both the range of central goods provided and in the frequency with which centers of different sizes occur. Low-order central places, such as the "Sunday towns," provide relatively frequently purchased items, are not located very far from small groups of population, and will be the most numerous type of center throughout the region. Successively higher order central places will service larger market areas, will contain more specialized goods and services, and will be less numerous. The highest order central place, of which there will be only one, will tend to be located at the center of the region, will contain the most specialized items, and will draw upon the entire region for its market. However, each successively higher order place will also contain the functions of lower order centers in addition to their more specialized items. Because of this, the trade areas of higher order places, even for low-order goods, is likely to be large, as consumers tend to combine a number of different shopping purposes on a single trip.

A greater appreciation for this ordering principle may be had by inspecting table 2, which shows the market entry conditions in terms of population size for particular types of goods and services as found by Brian Berry and William Garrison [1958] in Snohomish County,

Washington. Particular types of establishments and services, such as department stores, public accountants, photographers, and health practitioners, first appear only in the larger centers. Lower order goods and services, such as filling stations and food stores are more ubiquitous and show a lower threshold population necessary for provision of that service.

TABLE 2. Threshold Populations for Selected Services and Percentage of Places Containing these Services for Snohomish County, Washington, circa 1958

Service	Threshold Population	Percentage of Places (N=33)
Filling Stations	196	91
Food Stores	254	61
Restaurants	276	58
Physicians	380	30
Real Estate Agencies	384	27
Insurance Agencies	409	24
Beauticians	480	30
Lawyers	528	27
Electric Repair Shops	693	24
Dry Cleaners	754	27
Jewelry Stores	827	24
Sporting Goods Stores	928	18
Department Stores	1,083	24
Optometrists	1,140	15
Photographers	1,243	12
Public Accountants	1,300	9
Health Practitioners	1,424	9

Source: Adapted from Berry & Garrison 1958, table 2.

Allied with this "nesting" pattern of goods and services is a nested spatial pattern with an inverse relationship existing between the order of a center and its frequency of occurrence. Under ideal conditions of uniform topography and accessibility throughout the region, the spatial patterning of central places will tend to approximate that shown in figure l. In this figure the more common circle shape used to denote a market area is replaced by hexagons formed out of the intersections of these circles. Two orders of centers are shown, a lower order, c, whose trade areas are represented by solid lines, and a next higher order center, B, with larger market areas (dotted lines) overlapping those of the c's.

Since numerous factors can affect the actual pattern of central places, the distribution shown in figure 2 is not frequently observed. In fact, this type of distribution seems to occur mostly in thinly settled farm districts, which are relatively self-contained. Variations in topography, accessibility, distances from other metropolitan areas, social and cultural differences in shopping patterns and behaviors, and political

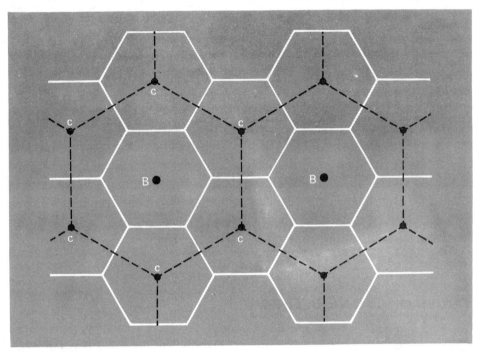

Fig. 2. Theoretical Distribution of Two Orders of Central Places and Their Market Areas.

boundaries all significantly distort the scheme. A major amount of distortion is also introduced by the location of economic activities that do not follow central place principles. Industrial concentrations, responding to factors that influence the costs of production and distribution of products, will be interspersed with central places or, more likely, create the nucleus of a city to which central place functions may be appended. Many cities, therefore, while performing some central place functions may not be solely or even primarily central place type cities. Nevertheless, the central place function of numerous metropolitan areas can be clearly recognized. Chicago, as we have already noted, is a major service center for the Midwest, specializing in the collection and distribution of grain and livestock commodities. The twin cities of Minneapolis-St. Paul are primarily grain markets servicing the western-central region, Memphis serves the cotton market for the southern cotton-producing region, and Louisville is the regional service center for the tobacco-producing areas of the middle South. If cities serve more than central place functions, such measures as population size or levels of economic activity cannot be used as indicators of central place importance. A large suburban community may serve only a few central place functions, while cities with considerably smaller populations, located in a thinly settled agricultural region, may provide important service functions for an extensive area. Measures of central place importance must take account of the levels and range of services provided. Edward Ullman [1941] has suggested one such means, based upon determining the average number of customers required to support various services in different regions. The excess of these functions over that required by the urban population alone would then serve as an index of centrality. Without making this distinction, others have attempted to measure central place importance by reference to the existence of banks, Woolworth stores, secondary schools, movie theaters, newspapers, and hospitals [Smailes 1944], the frequency of bus service [Green 1950], and shopping and travel patterns for clothing, dentists, hardware, and other items [Bracey 1953].

Industrial Location Theory

A third explanation of the location and distribution of cities concentrates more closely upon the location of industrial activities and seeks to explicate those factors that weigh most heavily in the industrial location decision. Numerous factors have been suggested as having an effect upon the location of industry. They include such considerations as the prior existence and size of markets, the availability of an appropriately skilled labor force, the location of raw materials and power sources, the availability and cost of transportation facilities, land, and capital. Other influential elements are wage and tax rates, the existence and adequacy of governmental services, linkages to other industries, and the existence of other industrial and commercial concentrations [Hunker & Wright 1963; White, Foscue, & McKnight 1964].

All of the factors that can be listed are not necessarily of equal importance. The relative impact of each factor varies considerably according to the particular character of the industry and its requirements for procuring raw materials, processing them, and distributing the finished product. Moreover, in some types of industry, factors such as the existence of raw materials or markets may be particularly important in influencing the choice of a region in which to locate, while other factors such as tax structures, government services, and land availability and costs influence the choice of a particular site within that region [Friedrich 1929; Frank 1971].

At one extreme we can point to industries that are almost totally tied to one dominant locational factor. Recreational industries, such as those contributing to the growth and development of Miami Beach, illustrate the case of industries wholly tied to natural resources located at particular sites. Wheeling, West Virginia is dependent on the location of coal deposits. At the other extreme, some resources are so ubiquitous that the location of industry relying upon them is more intimately tied to market factors and population concentrations. For example, soda bottling plants, one of whose main raw materials is water, usually are located with respect to population distribution.

Between these two extremes, most industrial activities are faced with the necessity of evaluating the costs of doing business at alternative locations, selecting that location that allows for maximum profit. These alternative locations may be at the site of raw materials, in proximity to markets, or at points in between these two poles. An appreciation of the effect of the costs of doing business at these sites is basic to understanding the choice of a location for most industries. An important component of these costs is the cost of transporting both the raw materials used in the production process and the finished products. By considering these transfer costs, we can readily understand the extreme cases of the recreation and soda bottling industries noted above. In the case of recreation, transportation of such raw materials as climate, beaches, and so forth is clearly impossible so that the industry must locate at the site. For the bottling plants, location at points other than a market would involve paying the transfer costs of a material (water) that is available everywhere. The simplest illustration of the effects of transfer costs is the case of an industry that utilizes only one raw material and sells its product to only one market located at some point other than the site of materials. [Parts of the following treatment of this topic are based on Hoover 1963.] Clearly, the industry can locate at the source of materials and thereby minimize the costs of procurement (but increase the costs of distribution), or locate at its market and minimize the costs of distribution (but increase the costs of procurement). The industry that seeks to minimize these transfer costs will consider both simultaneously and look for the location that will keep total transfer costs at a minimum.

Figures 3A-C depict three simple resolutions of the locational problem for this industry when only the transfer costs are considered. Figure 3A represents a situation in which the costs of collecting raw materials are greater per unit of distance than the costs of distributing the finished product (when comparing the amount of raw material necessary for producing one unit of product). By adding the values of each cost gradient at all points between the market and site of materials, a curve expressing total transfer costs is generated. This latter curve indicates that total transfer costs are minimized for this industry by locating at the source of materials. Figure 3B is simply the opposite: distribution costs increase more rapidly with distance from the market than procurement costs with distance from the material site. The gradient of total transfer costs indicates that a location at the market would be best.

Some particular types of goods readily correspond to the general situations represented in figures 3A and B, with some materials clearly costing more to transport while in their raw, unprocessed state and some types of finished products involving higher transfer costs than the raw materials used to make them. Generally, industrial processes that involve a large loss of weight or bulk during processing are likely to have steeper procurement than distribution gradients, for many units of the raw material will be necessary to manufacture one unit of finished product. In those instances the industry is more attracted to locations near the source of materials, where waste can be removed prior to shipment. Examples include smelting processes, the crushing of sugar cane and processing of sugar beets, the ginning of cotton, as well as the initial processing of most raw materials. In addition, where large quantities of fuel are required in the industrial process, an orientation towards fuel materials may exist because such large amounts of fuel are dissipated during production.

Industries oriented toward markets, on the other hand, show the reverse characteristics. Some products may involve a weight or bulk increase in manufacture so that transfer costs may be at a minimum near markets. Soft drinks and beer are primary examples because they have high water contents. Similarly, more bulk and greater fragility are characteristic of many products in the later stages of production, and such products may be more cumbersome to pack and handle. Furthermore, the time spent in delivery may be critical, as in the case of fashion goods and perishable products (bread, ice cream), so that a market orientation is preferred.

In many instances the structure of transfer costs may cause producers to locate at some intermediate point. Figure 3C represents this possibility, which generally occurs when both procurement and distribution involve a transshipment point or break-of-bulk. This transshipment may involve a change from water to rail transportation, which will undoubtedly increase the costs of transportation (note the large vertical

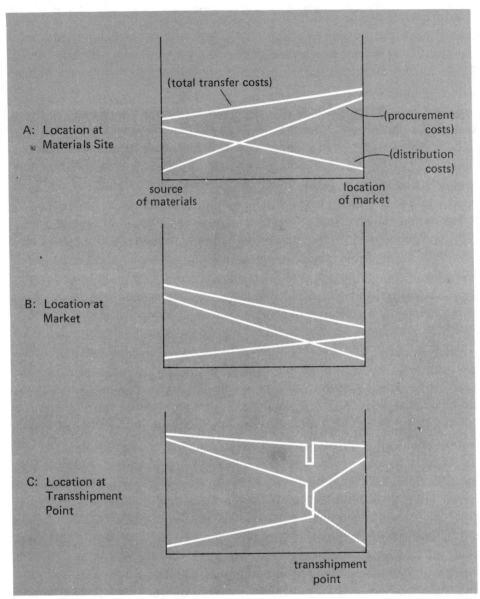

A: Location at Materials Site

(total transfer costs)

(procurement costs)

(distribution costs)

source of materials

location of market

B: Location at Market

C: Location at Transshipment Point

transshipment point

Fig. 3. Gradients of Procurement, Distribution and Total Transfer Costs for a Hypothetical Industry with One Source of Materials and One Market. (Source: Adapted from Hoover 1963, pp. 30, 39.)

rise in each gradient at the transshipment point). If a processing plant is located at the transshipment point, there may be considerable savings since materials and products need to be unloaded and loaded only once. The gradient of total transfer costs indicates that this point is the least costly location. This type of location becomes even more advantageous to an industry as the bulk and weight of materials and finished product are large in proportion to their value, and where transshipment costs are high. In this way we can see that cities which develop break-of-bulk functions and a commercial economy are also likely to develop an industrial economic base.

Our examples are simple ones because they involve only one material and one market site. More realistically, industrial products are likely to be manufactured from a number of raw materials located at different sites, and to be distributed to a number of different markets. While more complex, the basic principle of minimizing total transfer costs will still apply. In these cases, however, the configuration of the transportation network and the structure of rates as it relates to the location of materials, markets, and intermediate points, is likely to have a more complicating effect. As a result, plants of the same industry, with similar procurement, processing, and distribution characteristics, are likely to select different types of locations. What becomes important then is a recognition of the principles that apply to the locational decision rather than a recognition of characteristically market-, material-, or other-oriented industries. Generally, the preferred site will be one whose attracting forces are greater than the sum of forces of all other market and material locations. If no single location is so clearly preferable as a point of minimum transfer costs, the best location may be at any one of the material or market points or at some intermediate site dictated by the costs of transferring materials and products on any given transportation network.

Edgar Hoover [1963, pp. 42–44] has illustrated these points by noting the variety of locations chosen by individual iron and steel plants. Given slightly different proportions in the ingredients used to make steel, and the differing transportation systems and rate structures existing in the various regions, steel plants can be found at widely different types of locations. Blast furnaces at or near sources of coking coal are located in Pittsburgh, Pueblo, Birmingham, and the Ruhr. The Lorraine and Duluth plants are located near a supply of iron ore. Cleveland and Buffalo steel industries are located at transshipment points where ore and coal can be readily collected. The Ford steel plant in Dearborn is located at its market.

In addition to considering the costs of procuring and distributing material, industries must also consider the costs of processing materials at alternative locations. These processing costs may vary considerably because of the difference in the costs of the factors of production (land, labor, capital) in various regions or at specific sites. For some types of industries, moreover, processing costs may be the most important factor in influencing choice of locations, especially when transfer costs vary little between alternative sites as compared to the spatial variations in these processing costs. This will also be true of industries processing high value, compact products where transfer costs are small in relation to the value of the product. Parts of the electronic and apparel industries are strongly oriented towards processing costs. Many electronic components manufactured in the United States are shipped to Japan for fabrication and many California swimsuit companies have their cut fabrics sewn in Mexico. In both cases the lower costs of assembly outside of the United States appear to outweigh the additional costs of transportation.

The producer, of course, may be able to vary the combinations of land, labor, and capital that go into the production process, and therefore have available to him a relatively large number of locations from which to choose. Locating with an eye toward processing economies, however, will cause the producer to seek that location where an acceptable combination of these production factors can be had at a minimum cost. Industries for which neither procurement nor distribution costs are an overriding consideration and for which a number of acceptable processing locations exist are usually termed "foot-loose." These industries will tend to display the least consistent locational patterns and respond to numerous noneconomic forces, such as climate, levels of amenity, and so on. There are also other processing economies that may accrue to industrial activities at particular locations that go beyond an initial accounting of cost differences in the factors of production. One such economy may occur through a concentration of productive facilities, for example, by constructing one large plant as opposed to a number of smaller and more widely scattered plants. These economies of scale may allow for a fuller utilization of machinery, a smaller stockpiling of reserve equipment, materials, and supplies, and reductions in the purchase price of these supplies, fuel, and other services. Concentration, however, is likely to have an upper limit beyond which it is no longer profitable to increase in scale. One limiting effect may be transfer costs, particularly when the firm tends toward a market orientation and distributes to many, widely scattered markets.

Economies of concentration are another type of saving that may accrue to industries at particular locations. Economies of concentration are reductions that may occur when either similar or dissimilar economic activities are located in close proximity to each other and thus can increase their aggregate demands for certain facilities and services. The provision of better transfer services and facilities, and a larger, more flexible and diversified labor supply are examples. Additionally, services such as banks, employment agencies, utilities, fire and police protection, accounting and law firms, and others may become more readily available to service a larger group of industries, and a greater degree of specialization of functions can develop. Thus, certain operations which the industry, if located in a smaller place, would have to provide for itself can now be supplied by specialized agencies that can operate less expensively and more efficiently. At a concentrated location the industrial firm may also be able to operate with smaller material reserves, with these being more readily available at short notice than at more isolated locations. Similarly, large-scale transfer and terminal facilities may be possible, as are the sharing of rail sidings or port facilities, all of which help to create economies in transfer costs.

In sum, the location of the industrial firm is by no means haphazard. The costs of doing business and the goal of realizing profits necessarily force the firm to weigh the cost consequences of alternative locations. For some types of industries this decision is a complex one but still subject to rational calculation. By assessing the structure of the transportation network and the schedule of rates by distance, direction, and by various types of carriers with respect to the location of materials and markets, and by accounting for the differences in processing costs and potential economies at alternative locations, some reasonable indications of appropriate locations can be obtained. On the other hand, complete and perfect knowledge of all of these conditions may not be available to the individual producer, and changes in transportation networks, production processes, labor supplies, the availability of materials, and so on, may also cause new locations to become more profitable. However, the marginal costs involved in maintaining a less than optimal location must then be weighed against the costs involved in moving; moreover, these changes may not be perceived. The result is that the industry may currently be located in a less than optimal site. Nevertheless, as Hoover notes, the locational patterns of particular *types* of industries are less haphazard and more responsive to changing conditions than is the case with *individual* firms. Competition between individual producers tends to reward those that are well located and penalize those that are located more poorly, so that the former are more likely to survive through time, and some semblance of an ordered pattern of rational location is likely to emerge.

Other Factors in Urban Location

As stated earlier, noneconomic factors may also play major roles in urban location. Cities have been located for religious purposes throughout history, usually to venerate some great religious phenomenon at a particular site, or because some location was thought to be particularly sacred. Moreover, many religious groups have established urban centers as points from which they can engage in missionary activities or practice their religious rituals without interference from other groups. Military considerations have also been common factors in determining urban location. Forts were established at strategic sites to control a region's population (or to control the trade in which it engages) or to protect and administer colonial empires. Moreover, the need for protection and defense was an important consideration in the location of many urban settlements both before and during the medieval period. Lately, the development of nuclear weapons with their vast destructive potential has caused some discussion of the desirability of breaking up major urban concentrations into smaller, more scattered units.

Political reasons for urban location and development have been regularly considered in the establishment of political and administrative centers, such as national, state, and county capitals. Social reasons predominated as a major cause for the founding of many nineteenth-century communities, and are a major consideration in current efforts to establish new towns. Finally, personal reasons may contribute to urban location and growth through the migration of people seeking particular types of climates and amenities (e.g., retirement communities) and the location of economic activities caused by the personal wishes of the individual entrepreneur.

THE GROWTH AND SPECIALIZATION OF THE METROPOLITAN ECONOMY

In the preceding section we discussed a number of analytically distinct types of cities and the role of various factors in their location. The three most general types of cities—central places, transportation and trade centers, and industrial/special resource cities—are distributed in space according to the needs of various types of sustenance-producing activities and the extent to which these needs are met at particular locations. In this sense the sustenance activities of a population are adapted to the conditions for survival as presented by particular environments and thus form the basis for the growth and development of the urban community.

These environments, however, may be appropriate locations for a number of different types of economic activities so that our characterization of cities as belonging to one of three general types is an abstraction. In reality, these three analytical types of cities are not necessarily distinct since most cities, especially most larger ones, serve a variety of economic functions. Thus, at the same time a city may be an industrial and trade center, supply central-place services to a surrounding region, and act as a political, administrative, or military center.

The reasons for the multifunctional nature of most cities are fairly easy to discern. Many different types of industrial and commercial activities initially are dependent upon similar locational influences. Similarly, conditions may be created in the process of growth that make existing concentrations of economic activity attractive to other types. Thus, industrial or transportation cities may attract numerous personal and retail services that can provide expanded central-place services to a region. An initial concentration of industry or commerce may attract other economic units because of the development of existing markets, the concentration of a labor supply, successive improvements in transportation and terminal facilities, the development of business and personal services, and the elaboration of certain economies that are associated with increased concentration.

The process of urban growth thus involves an elaboration of the economic structure of cities. Cities still may tend to specialize in particular types of sustenance activities but frequently these specializations are in a number of different areas. In the present section we will discuss this process of growth and elaboration of the urban economy, stressing those factors that appear to be particularly important in affecting urban development: population, basic economic activities, accessibility, and trade. An understanding of the process of growth will then permit us to discuss the concept of functional specialization of cities and briefly note the relationship between functional specialization and location.

A Model of Urban Growth

Urban growth is a relatively complex phenomenon, involving a number of reciprocal cause-and-effect relationships. Some of the conditions for growth, such as an expanding population base to create a labor force, are also a consequence of growth, so that it becomes difficult to unravel the system of relationships by which development occurs. Bearing this complexity in mind, we can construct a relatively abstract and simple model of growth processes that highlights some of the important relationships involved. This model incorporates the important factors of population, economic base, accessibility, and trade, along with a small number of secondary concepts, and is shown diagrammatically in figure 4. This simplified model has been adapted from the one suggested by

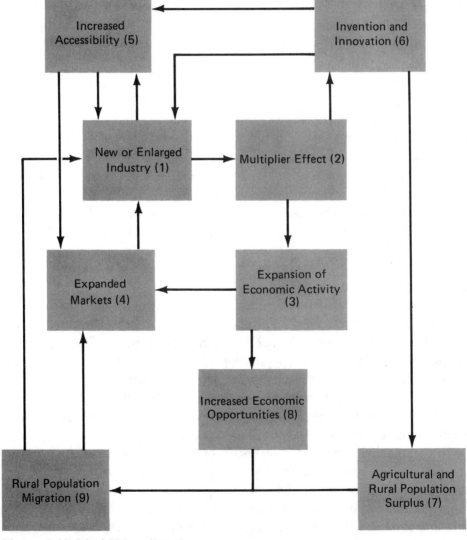

Fig. 4. A Model of Urban Growth.

Allen Pred [1966, pp. 24–41] and is intended to explain the rudiments of urban development in the United States from the latter half of the nineteenth century to the first quarter of the twentieth century—a period of relatively rapid industrial expansion and urbanization.

The model begins by positing the existence of a small commercial town located in space and unfettered by competition from other urban centers. The town is relatively self-sufficient and only minimally involved in import and export activity, servicing a local tributary area with a number of basic goods and services (e.g., a central place). Into this small town there are introduced a number of large scale factories in one or more manufacturing categories (step 1 in figure 4). The reasons for choosing this particular place for the location of these activities may be some localized resource, or the location of the community on an interregional transportation network such as a major waterway. The introduction of these new activities into the town creates a number of circular reaction chains, the first of which involves the generation of a multiplier effect (2), created by industry's demands for goods and services and the increased purchasing power of their employees. This will result in the attraction and generation of a wide range of new economic activities and services, such as a construction trade, retail stores, government utilities, services and transportation, and so on (3). As a result of this expansion of economic activity and the increase in the size of the labor force associated with it, an enlarged local market (4) for locally produced goods is created. If favorable access to other regions and communities (5) also exists, this will also increase the market available for locally produced goods, thereby stimulating an expansion of the manufacturing sector (1), and another round of growth is initiated.

At the same time, another circular sequence of reactions may occur, which reinforce and compound the first chain of effects. The expansion of manufacturing activity, population, and general economic activity tends to induce a more complex set of communications and a multiplication of interactions within the community, thereby increasing the chances for new inventions, technological improvements, and innovative organizational arrangements (6). These inventions and innovations may further expand the productive capacity of existing manufacturing plants and provide the opportunities, through changing industrial processes, for the development of related industries (1). Similarly, in time, these inventions and innovations may have an effect on the productivity of agriculture and the need for farm laborers (7). The development, manufacture, and increased availability of farm implements and machinery will generally increase agricultural output at the same time that it reduces the manpower needed in rural areas. In light of the expanding opportunities in the growing city (8), this excess rural population is attracted to urban areas (9), supplying the expanding economic base with a labor force (1), as well as increasing the size of local markets (4).

Last, the increasing growth of local industry and the local economic base (1), along with increased technological improvements in communications and transportation (6), may increase the accessibility of the local community to other population centers (5), again expanding the potential market for locally produced goods (4).

We recognize that this model of urban growth omits substantial details and can be greatly elaborated. One serious omission is any consideration of the limitations on growth in successive iterations of the model. Some of these limitations such as those that may be imposed by limited accessibility and the consequent effect on markets, are implied. Other limitations may involve competition from other urban centers, changes in industrial processes that change the comparative advantages of particular locations, the depletion of mineral deposits and the discovery of new deposits in other locations, changes in sources of power, its availability and transportability, shifts in consumer preferences, and growing diseconomies associated with increased concentration that may produce rising land costs and congestion, and so forth. In its simplified form, however, the model does highlight the effects of population growth, the growth-inducing effects of initial economic units, and the importance of accessibility and trade for urban growth. We can consider each of these three major aspects in further detail.

Basic and Nonbasic Functions

Our model of the process of urban growth is based heavily on the growth-inducing effects of manufacturing activity. But it is not entirely true that the stimulus for growth must derive from manufacturing and the associated multiplier effect. Generally, what is important is that some activity exists within the community that finds some part of its market beyond the local area, that is, an export activity is necessary. While cities may grow by increasing their production through a more extensive division of labor, typically such growth does not occur when all economic activities within the community serve only each other and the local population—a situation aptly characterized as "taking in each other's wash." In these cases a limited supply of sustenance goods, for example, money, is simply redistributed within a closed system, and a larger population can be supported only by reducing the amount of these finite resources distributed to each person.

Economic growth depends upon increasing the product of the community, as when local industries find extracommunal markets and thereby serve to import additional money into the local economy. This increment in wealth can then be used to expand productive facilities and support additional services and populations as induced by the multiplier effect. The exported product may be manufactured goods, or it may be one or many of a variety of types, including educational services; political and administrative services, as in a state capital; or storage and distribution services, as in a community servicing an agricultural region. Thus, an important distinction can be made between types of economic activities. Some are primary or basic in the sense that they are the initial city-building activities, they form the economic foundation of the community, engage in export activity, and create the demand and conditions for the growth of the service sector. The service sector, on the other hand, may be considered secondary, or nonbasic, in the sense that its growth is induced by a community's basic activities, and it exists primarily to service the needs of other community units. Nonbasic activities do not generate *new* capital because they are not engaged in export activity, although they can avoid the necessity of exporting existing capital to other communities in exchange for needed services.

This distinction between basic and nonbasic activities cuts across the distinction between activities by economic type, because it is based upon an export- versus internal-service paradigm. Manufacturing activities, for example, may be considered wholly basic when all of their products are sold to markets beyond the community. Usually, however, some proportion of a manufacturer's sales will be made within the local community, and to the extent that this occurs, some portion of its activities can be considered as nonbasic. The same holds true for personal service and retail functions. While they may serve primarily the local population, services exported to a surrounding region in the form of central-place services would be considered basic activity. Hence, department stores filling mail-order purchases or attracting customers from a surrounding region are also engaged, to a limited degree, in basic export activities. All such activities, because they import capital into the community, should contribute to the inducement of nonbasic services through the multiplier effect, although the scale of this effect will undoubtedly vary considerably according to the type of basic activity, in addition to its size. It should be recognized, however, that the basic/nonbasic distinction is relative to the areal definition used in making the distinction. If regions are taken as the unit of analysis, then more of the trade relationships of economic activities will be contained within this larger area, with the consequence that fewer activities are regarded as basic. At the national level, only those activities that are involved in international trade are basic; at the world level the distinction is meaningless.

A commonly used method of distinguishing between the basic and nonbasic components of a community's economy is to categorize the employees of each industry into each class in proportion to the percentage of income or sales of that industry derived from internal and external markets [Tiebout 1962]. When this is done for each major industrial category within a community we get a more detailed and accurate view of the community's economic structure than if we only studied total employment. The detailing of activities by type may then contribute to more accurate projections of future employment growth based upon growth assumptions in the basic sector. This detailing also provides a means for classifying towns by dominant economic functions and assessing the economic stability of the community, as well as the potential ramifications to the local economy should certain basic activities suffer an economic depression [see Cottrell 1951].

An illustration of some of these insights is provided by John Alexander's economic base studies of Oshkosh [1951] and Madison [1953], Wisconsin. Table 3 shows the total employment of each community and the percentages associated with each of five major industrial groups. At first inspection the economy of Oshkosh appears to be based most heavily in manufacturing, with services and then trade ranking second and third, respectively. Madison's economy, on the other hand, is based mainly in services and government, with manufacturing ranking third. When the local, population-serving components of these employment figures are removed, a slightly different view of the two economies emerges. Oshkosh continues to show a heavy reliance on manufacturing, but now basic employment in trade appears slightly greater than in services. Neither, however, reaches the predominance of manufacturing. Madison's basic economy rests most heavily on government employment and secondarily on manufacturing. Service activities, which rank first when total employment is considered, are shown to be substantially a nonbasic activity.

T A B L E 3. Total, Basic, and Nonbasic Employment by Major Industries, Oshkosh and Madison, Wisconsin

	Oshkosh	Madison
1950 population	42,000	110,000
Total employment	16,000	53,500
Percent employed in:		
services	19.4	27.1
government	7.5	26.7
manufacturing	51.3	22.6
trade	16.9	19.1
other	5.0	4.5
Basic employment (as a Percent of total employment) in:		
services	5.6	8.4
government	0.8	21.1
manufacturing	49.3	18.9
trade	5.9	5.6
other	1.6	0.6
Nonbasic employment (as a percent of total employment) in:		
services	13.8	18.7
government	6.8	5.6
manufacturing	2.0	3.7
trade	10.9	13.1
other	3.4	3.9

Source: Adapted from Alexander 1954.

A ratio of basic to nonbasic employment can be computed, which expresses the multiplier effect of primary economic activities in creating new employment opportunities in the secondary sector. For Oshkosh the basic/nonbasic ratio is 100:60 and for Madison, 100:82. Hence, for every 100 jobs in basic industries that are created, an increment of 60 additional jobs in Oshkosh and 82 in Madison can be expected. This ratio is frequently used as a planning tool for projecting total employment increases under assumptions of increases in basic activity. The ratio is apt to vary considerably among different cities according to income, population size, and levels of demand for services. In general, one would expect larger cities to show a greater level of nonbasic relative to basic employment because, as previously noted, larger cities can support a wider variety of services by virtue of incorporating a larger market within them. Thus, the ratio for the New York metropolitan area, as computed by Homer Hoyt for the Regional Plan Association of New York [1944] is 100:215; more than two new nonbasic jobs tend to be induced by each unit increase in basic activities.

While substantially more powerful and detailed methods for the analysis of urban economies exist (e.g., input-output analysis), the basic/

nonbasic concept is valuable because it most clearly illustrates the multiplier effect and growth-inducing influences of the primary economic activities. However, although this distinction is useful in making certain statements concerning increases in employment as a result of growth in the basic sector, it provides no basis for predicting future basic sector growth. Prediction of the latter is dependent upon our knowledge of the factors influencing the location of economic activity, which have been discussed previously.

Trade and Accessibility

If the stimulus to growth depends upon export activity, then a matter of prime importance to urban growth is the availability of extracommunal markets and, by implication, some degree of access to these markets. Trade can obviously occur only where the means for transporting goods are available. Under conditions of low accessibility and primitive means of transportation between distant population settlements, the volume of goods shipped is necessarily limited and only those items that can bear the high costs of transportation and the substantial amount of time involved will be shipped. As accessibility between distant centers increases, the volume of trade can also increase, as can the variety of items being transported. Therefore, an understanding of urban growth must take into consideration the role of accessibility and transportation improvements in facilitating the intercommunity flow of goods.

The importance of accessibility in urban growth is widely recognized. Extending transportation routes and facilities between isolated communities makes possible the development of mutual trade relationships. This benefits each community participating in the trade because each has access to a much larger population of consumers and producers than it contains within its own boundaries. In effect, the result of these trade relationships made possible by conditions of accessibility is the establishment of an intercommunity division of labor, with each community trading with others according to the differential distribution of needs and productive advantages. Community A, which might be particularly adept at making cloth, may then specialize in this activity and trade its surplus to community B for shoes, or community C for agricultural machinery, and so on. Through this process of specialization, the productive efficiency of each community is increased and the net product available to the partners in the trade is increased. Thus the demand for a particular community's products expands at the same time as does the total amount of product available to support increased investment in productive facilities and increased populations and services.

The dependence on accessibility to these other markets means that it is highly unlikely that all communities will grow at similar rates. Those communities more favorably located on the interregional transportation network will participate more readily in the trade process and have access to larger export markets. During the period in which water transportation was the chief means for long-distance hauling, cities favorably situated on navigable waterways were the ones most likely to develop to major size. During the period following the Civil War, a major change in the condition of accessibility between communities occurred with the development of an interregional rail network. The initial stages of development of this new network closely followed the existing pattern of settlement as established by the water transportation system, and the early railroads supplemented, rather than competed with, these water routes. In time, however, the greater speed, regularity, and convenience of the railroads for both passenger and freight traffic had the effect of diverting shipments from the system of waterways, and from the period of 1860-1870 onward, successive improvements in terminal facilities, rate reductions, and the extension and interconnection of rail lines increased the competitive advantage of the railroads over water routes [McKenzie 1933, pp. 129-143].

The effect of this shift in means of transportation was to increase the prospects for interregional trade by making the movement of goods cheaper, faster, and easier, as well as by opening up new areas in the interior of the country that were previously inaccessible by water routes. The growth of the railroad lines thus reinforced the competitive positions of cities that had already grown due to water trade, and encouraged the rise of smaller settlements and towns along the rail network. Having been built in an east-west pattern, the railroads also were able to redirect the prevailing flow of goods from a predominantly north-south pattern determined by the Mississippi water system. Cities lying along this east-west orientation thus received an added stimulus to growth over others.

The growth of Chicago during this period of 1860-1910 clearly illustrates the importance for growth of a favorable location on these interregional transportation networks. Given its strategic position on the Great Lakes and its transportation networks to the Midwest and to the East, Chicago slowly grew in prominence until 1860, when it ranked eighth in population size among all U.S. cities. This growth was accelerated by the development of extensive rail terminals and connections, and by 1910 Chicago was the second largest U.S. city. The magnitude of this development can perhaps be best illustrated by observing that the number of industrial employees in Chicago doubled between 1884 and 1890 and that between 1870 and 1890 the total mileage of railroads entering Chicago increased by 370 percent, and the tonnage shipped increased by 490 percent [Hoyt 1933; Pred 1966, pp. 54–55].

Population and Urban Growth

The third major component of our model of growth is the population factor. Population is important to the expansion and differentiation of the urban system in at least three ways.   1. Growing population is necessary for creating the labor force to man the expanding urban economy; 2. the expanded population creates part of the market for locally produced goods, thereby affecting outcomes of the multiplier effect;   3. population growth is also a response to urban development because expanding economic opportunities have the effect of attracting larger populations. Increasing population concentration is therefore both a cause and consequence of urban growth.

The potential sources of population increase in urban areas can be illustrated by reference to the "demographic equation." The equation is a formalization of the notion that a population can increase in size if, and only if, more people enter than leave it. There are two methods of entrance into a population: birth and in-migration. Likewise the two methods of exiting are death and out-migration. Thus,

$$P_2 - P_1 = (B - D) + (I - O),$$

where P_2 and P_1 are the enumerated populations at time 2 and time 1 and B, D, I, and O are the number of births, deaths, in-migrants, and out-migrants respectively during the time period. The parentheses are an attempt to combine related processes. (B − D) refers to the number of births minus the number of deaths, and this difference is referred to as "reproductive change." Many writers also term it natural increase, but this is a misnomer because the net effect of births and deaths is not necessarily to increase the population. (I − O) refers to the number of in-migrants minus the number of out-migrants, and this difference is called net migration. If it is positive, one speaks of net in-migration; if it is negative, one speaks of net out-migration. The important thing to realize when considering metropolitan population growth is that a population can grow if, and only if, the combined effects of reproductive change and net migration are positive. Thus, if there is net in-migration and the number of births exactly equals the number of deaths, the population will increase in size, although not as rapidly as if there were the same amount of net in-migration and if the number of births also exceeded the number of deaths in that population. Similarly, if net migration (or reproductive change) is negative, the population size can increase if, and only if, the amount of reproductive change (or net migration) is positive by a sufficiently large amount to outweigh the population loss that is otherwise incurred.

Historically, a significant proportion of local population growth in metropolitan areas has been the result of in-migration. Until recently, the relative amount of reproductive change (births minus deaths) in cities has been small. Moreover, growth through reproductive change creates a considerable time lag between birth and entry into the labor force and thus does not respond as quickly as desirable to an imbalance between population size and demand for labor created by rapidly expanding industrial opportunities.

In general, migration is seen as a response on the part of a population to perceived social and economic opportunities for living at different locations. Areas in which economic opportunities are scarce relative to the size of the population (hence producing high unemployment) will usually experience an out-migration to other areas of high economic opportunity relative to population size. In this way, migration acts as one means for effecting some adjustment between the conditions for life and population size in different areas. The growth of cities has been intimately bound up in and dependent upon this process. The higher level of economic opportunity offered by cities has encouraged population flow from the rural areas in which opportunities were declining. However, this surplus of population in rural areas also has been due partially to increasing urbanization and industrialization. Whereas high rates of positive reproductive change were once necessary in rural areas for supplying the manpower for a labor intensive industry, increased technological inventions, and the production of mechanized farming equipment by industries located in cities resulted in a change in the manpower needs of agricultural regions. The mechanization of agriculture resulted in both an increase in production, thus allowing for the support of a greater nonagricultural population, and the freeing of large numbers of workers from the soil, making them available for urban industrial employment.

The dependence of urban growth and economic development on adequate population numbers is illustrated in three cases—Australian migration policies, the development of the new Brazilian city, Brasilia, and the British new towns efforts. The Australian government has, for years, been encouraging migration from the western countries as a necessary prerequisite for development. Similarly, encouragement of the economic development of the region was part of the rationale given for the location of Brasilia, a new political and governmental center for the nation in the heart of the Brazilian jungle. Without the "captive" migrants employed in government service to settle this area, development was not foreseeable. On the whole, however, the stimulating effects of the new city on regional development appear to have been less than expected because of difficulties in inducing other people to relocate there. Much the same problem seems to have occurred in many of the British new towns.

The Concept
of Functional Specialization

We have seen that the process of urban growth involves an elaboration of the economic structure of cities: basic, or city building, activities locate in space according to particular sets of economic needs, and as a result nonbasic activities are introduced; favorable access to interregional markets stimulates the expansion of basic activity along particular lines and according to the productive advantages of communities; and interregional productivity is increased, which allows for the support of further service activities and larger populations. An important step in this process is the growth of an intercommunity division of labor and the increasing specialization of communities participating in this trade system. The process of growth involves the transformation of relatively independent and homogeneous groups of cities into a heterogeneous, interdependent set, with the relationship between community function and the productive advantage of particular locations becoming more articulated.

Given these transformations, researchers have frequently attempted to measure the relative specializations of cities, noting the essential differences between their economies and contributing to a clarification of the location-function relationship. Another value of these classifications is in their potential use for studying differences in social organization and social processes according to variation in economic structure. Little systematic work has been done in this regard, employing a standard classification of cities by dominant functions, except on a relatively unstructured and minor basis [see Bergel 1955, pp. 152–165; Reiss 1957]. Recognizing that the economic structure of a community has an important effect on social and political institutions [Marx & Engels, n.d.; Schulze 1961; Davis & Moore 1945], the use of functional typologies, both cross-sectionally and over time, are of considerable value.

One means of creating these functional typologies, based upon the distinction between basic and nonbasic activities, has already been discussed. Unfortunately, economic base studies frequently require data that are not readily available (and too time consuming to collect) for a large number of cities. As a result, a number of independently initiated base studies have been done, but no comparative study, over a large number of cities and utilizing consistent methods, exists. Large studies of urban specialization have taken other forms—less accurate and less theoretically satisfying—ranging from qualitative description to quantitative-statistical analysis.

Quantitative analyses have usually specified some minimum percentage of workers in various industrial and service categories as an indicator of the community's specialization. Thus, one might specify that a minimum of 60 percent of employment within a community be in manufacturing before that community could be classified as specializing in that function [Harris 1943]. In a more sophisticated approach the percentage of workers in a category, taken for a large number of cities, may be placed in a distribution from which a mean percentage of employment and standard deviation may be computed. Relative specialization of a community in a particular function can then be measured by the number of standard deviation units above the mean. This method has been used by Howard Nelson [1955] who finds, for example, that the percentage of workers employed in public administration activities in Washington, D.C., lies three standard deviation units above the mean percentage employed in public administration for all cities. In this way, Washington is shown to be very specialized in this function.

Most quantitative analyses of functional specializations have attempted to maintain the basic-nonbasic distinction by recognizing a minimum level of employment in each category as necessary for local consumption. Only relatively high levels of employment in a category imply basic, export activity. Nevertheless, these quantitative distinctions often neglect important community activities that give a community a particular character, although they employ relatively few persons. Thus, in both the Nelson and Harris typologies the city of Boston is not recognized as specializing in higher education, although it is the seat of many of the nation's leading universities. These qualitative distinctions have been given greater recognition by E. E. Bergel [1955]. Bergel's typology is noteworthy for its comprehensiveness and recognition of small, but culturally important, activities. For example, he recognizes religious centers, museum cities, and retirement cities, among others, although he fails to reconcile the dilemma between quantitative and qualitative criteria and their joint use in classifying functional specializations.

Functional Specialization and Location

Assuming that these classifications are at least partially valid, can they be related to the locational patterns of economic activities, and hence urban development, that were discussed earlier? Nelson [1955] has plotted the distribution of cities by functional type across the United States, and these spatial distributions do correspond to our expectations. Central place cities, specializing in retail, wholesale, and service functions, tend to be distributed in relation to regional populations. In sparsely settled regions, central places are more numerous, reflecting the difficulty of servicing widely scattered populations. Where population density is greater a smaller number of central places tends to exist because each has relatively good access to the population. In the aggregate, central place services are located at irregular intervals across the entire country.

Mining cities tend to be clustered in a few scattered regions, which is to be expected given the locations of the extractive materials and the need for mining related activities to be located near the site of the raw material. Manufacturing activity, which responds to a number of locational forces, tends to be concentrated at points of great accessibility to other regions (along waterways and rail facilities), near supplies of labor, near other industries to which it is linked, and close to points of industrial concentration. Most of these conditions are best realized in the eastern portion of the country, where larger markets and a higher density of transfer facilities tend to exist and where early industrial concentrations occurred.

Finally, cities specializing in transportation and communication services tend to be distributed in relation to the interregional transportation network. Because in the United States interregional transportation has been predominantly by rail, it is not surprising to observe that seven-eighths of the cities classified in the transportation category are railroad centers, with the remainder of the cities distributed along major water-routes.

GROWTH AND STRUCTURE
OF THE METROPOLITAN COMMUNITY

The Role of Transportation

In our discussion of the growth and differentiation of the metropolitan economy we have placed considerable emphasis on the effects of transportation improvements and increased accessibility between cities. These increases in accessibility allowed for the expansion of local markets and the extension of an interregional division of labor, resulting in the further growth and specialization of these major centers. The growth-inducing effects of these transportation improvements, however, were limited. A number of cities that were favorably located on the expanding interregional transportation network were able to participate in interregional trade and the expanding division of labor between cities. Thus, large, specialized regional centers developed. These transportation improvements, however, did not significantly improve accessibility and the potential for interaction within regions. Many smaller settlements that were not so favorably located on the growing transportation network remained relatively homogeneous and independent. They did not participate, to any great extent, in trade and export activities with other communities. As a result of this partial isolation, there was selective urban development on an interregional basis, rather than internal regional development.

The reasons for this selective development are bound up in the particular characteristics of water and rail transportation. Both modes are relatively linear and fixed, providing ready access between spatially disparate points that lie along their routes, but not providing service to wider, more general areas. Communities lying some distance from water or rail facilities, and dependent upon crude overland means of transportation to reach rail and port facilities, are significantly disadvantaged relative to those with easy access to these terminals. Moreover, the high costs of these terminal facilities, combined with the relatively low costs of movement of goods and the economies associated with full carload shipments, have operated to encourage full-cargo, long-distance hauling. Thus, smaller settlements, even if near rail and water lines, could not receive the full advantage of these transportation facilities since trade between larger but more distant cities was more profitable than the extension of markets to smaller, spatially closer settlements. Under these conditions, local, intraregional trade was restricted to a relatively small area surrounding a city. Smaller towns located in the hinterland of growing cities remained relatively isolated, producing mainly for local consumption. Many of the growing range and variety of goods now available in the larger cities remained inaccessible to the populations of these smaller, outlying towns. While some items did find their way to these populations, the high costs of overland transportation severely restricted these trade relationships. Interaction, then, decreased rapidly with distance and the costs of transport.

The development of extensive intraregional ties between communities was, as with those at the interregional level, dependent upon technological changes that increased accessibility and reduced the costs of interaction. A number of such technological advances occurred at the beginning of this century, the most significant ones being the development of the telephone and the development of the motor vehicle. The telephone vastly increased the possibilities for communication at a distance. The motor vehicle provided the conditions necessary for the increased transportation of goods and population at the local level, which was necessary for increased trade and expansion of the area of economic interdependence.

Unlike water and rail transportation, the motor vehicle is well suited to circuitous routings, does not operate on fixed time schedules, requires no extensive terminal facilities, is ideal for transporting small cargoes, and can do so over short distances at a speed and cost that cannot be matched by water and rail. Up to a distance of about 35 miles, the motor vehicle's operating costs are lower than either barge or railroad. But even with increased costs beyond this 35-mile limit, the truck still maintains an advantage over the railroad because of savings in transportation time. For distances of up to 300 miles, shipments by highway involve less than one half the time taken by rail. Thus Hawley [1950] has noted that within a radius of up to 250 miles the motor truck maintains a clear competitive advantage over the railway. This is aptly illustrated in the following example:

> If a Sioux Falls jobber could sell a bill of goods to a merchant in Brookings, S. D., to be shipped from Sioux Falls by rail, it would be best to go via the North Western, and the route taken would be west from Sioux Falls to Salem, S. D., a distance of 40 miles, then north to Huron, a distance of 68.3 miles, and then east to Brookings, a distance of 72 miles, making a total haul of 180.3 miles, and the time consumed would require second morning delivery at Brookings. The total distance from Sioux Falls due north to Brookings by truck is 58 miles and the schedule now in effect by truck is a departure from Sioux Falls at 11:00 a.m., and delivery at Brookings at 3:00 p.m. the same day [Armour's Livestock Bureau, 1930, p. 9].

The result of these reductions in the time and cost of trade *within* the region parallels the process of growth and development at the interregional level. Accessibility to new markets within the region increases the amount of trade between places and encourages the development of an intraregional division of labor. The various places participating in this process begin to specialize in those activities for which they are best suited and/or maintain a competitive advantage. As a result the net product of the region is increased, allowing for further growth of these places and the regional economy as a whole. *It is this new organization of functions and their integration through the dominant central city that constitutes the metropolitan community.*

The Redistribution of Functions

The process of internal specialization involves a redistribution of functions within the metropolitan region that follows two dominant tendencies—one centrifugal, the other centripetal. Generally, manufacturing activities, population, and the less specialized retail and personal service functions follow a centrifugal orientation, spreading outward through the region, while administrative, finance, and the more specialized retail and service activities become more centralized. The net result is that there is a very definite distribution of functions between the central city and noncentral city portions of the metropolitan area, all of which are integrated in the functional organization under the auspices of the central city.

Centrifugal Forces and the Outlying Areas

Centrifugal movements of people and activities take place in response to the particular advantages of various locations within the region and the new locational alternatives made available by increased accessibility as a result of improvements in transportation and communication. Because the spatial distribution of community units is highly dependent upon the ability to interact and communicate with each other, their spatial distribution under conditions of relatively low accessibility are somewhat restricted: residences cannot be located at very great physical distances from work places, and business and personal services are constrained by their needs to be readily accessible to business and population. Under these conditions, the territorial expansion of the city is severely limited, and a dense, fairly compact community is formed. However, as a result of the increased ease of local transportation, which reduces the time and costs of travel, the potential number of locational alternatives for population and for a variety of economic activities increases significantly. For example, when the dominant mode of local transportation was by animal, the radial limits of the area of daily commuting and interaction was about 6 miles (based upon a 60-minute travel time), which resulted in a theoretical areal limit of 100 square miles for the city. However, in the same commuting time, a person in a motor vehicle may travel 40 to 50 miles, thus expanding the area of potential development from 100 to 8000 square miles. Much of this new area for development can include the small, outlying places that previously were beyond the reach and influence of the central city.

In conjunction with the increasing size of the area in which settlement may occur, increasing diseconomies of concentration at the center of the metropolitan community, particularly for many types of manufacturing activity, have created incentives for their redistribution to outlying areas. Three general factors in particular have been instrumental in this deconcentration of industry.

1. Changes in space requirements of manufacturing due to technological changes in productive processes, combined with the relative unavailability of undeveloped inner city land;

2. Improvements in short-distance transportation and communications facilities;

3. Other technological improvements that have changed the comparative advantages of alternative locations.

The industries that have moved outward have tended to be those which require a great deal of space and specially designed buildings. Most industries now employ a continuous, assembly-line mode of production, which is faster, more efficient, and less expensive in a single-story building than in a multistory, loft-type structure. However, these new buildings require more space and the cost and efforts involved in acquiring such space in the central city would be prohibitive as compared to the suburbs. In turn, suburban land has become more accessible because of changes in short-distance transportation, particularly the automobile and increased reliance upon the motor truck for short-haul transfers of freight. Recent technological innovations in freight handling methods, such as "piggy-back" and containerized shipping have also decreased the reliances of many manufacturers on location near central city rail terminals and sidings, since goods can now be quickly and efficiently moved by truck from these rail depots to outlying locations.

Similarly, numerous other technological innovations have changed the attractiveness of central city locations in favor of suburban ones. With the development of the interstate highway system and a set of circumferential highways around cities, intercity transportation for many types of industries (especially where small distances are involved) can increasingly be by truck. Many other industries are relying more heavily on air transport and again, with air terminals located outside of the central city, the locational advantages of the suburbs have increased. Other communications improvements, such as the direct line telephone and WATS (Wide Area Telephone Service) lines have facilitated the separation of production, administration, and marketing functions, allowing administrative units to remain in the central city, close to financial, legal, and other essential services, while production facilities become suburbanized. In addition, note should be taken of the effect of the development of electronic data processing on the suburbanization of many "bookkeeping" industries, such as insurance firms and components of banking operations [Meyer, Kain, & Wohl 1965, p. 15]. Technological changes in data processing have reduced the reliance of these industries on an unskilled army of female clerical labor. In the past this force of unskilled workers could only be readily collected at central city locations via public transportation. The need for a more specialized labor force and the increased mobility afforded by the automobile has now made it possible for these industries to relocate outside of the central city.

The outward movement of certain industries has been paralleled by a similar shift in the locational preference of population. Numerous factors account for this shift, including increasing central city congestion; noise and pollution; the presence of racial minorities in the central city, which some people perceive as threatening; the desire for new housing and living environments; the availability of mortgage financing for new suburban residences; and expanding economic opportunities in the suburbs. As a result, the metropolitan population has spread outward from the center. In the early years of this century, most metropolitan growth occurred within central cities, but by 1950 the growth rates of the outlying portions of metropolitan areas averaged five times higher than central city rates. Indeed, some central cities have actually declined in absolute population size during the 1950–1960 and 1960–1970 decades.

Most of the growth in central cities that did occur during the 1950–1960 period was attributable to the annexation of land (and population) by the central cities. When this factor is controlled, the population of central cities within all 1950 SMAs increased by less than 1 percent by 1960 [Hawley 1971, pp. 159–164]. The same tendencies continued to occur in the 1960–1970 period, with almost all of the growth in the metropolitan population occurring in the noncentral city portions of the SMSAs. Even including the effects of changes in central city boundaries due to annexation, the metropolitan ring of all SMSAs taken together continued to increase about five times as rapidly as the central city population.

With respect to the components of these changes, about 75 percent of the total metropolitan population increase between 1960 and 1970 has been attributable to an excess of births over deaths. When we examine the components of population change within central cities and their rings separately, the relative importance of each demographic component differs. Any growth that occurred in the central city population took place in spite of net migration rather than because of it. This is particularly true with respect to the white population. For instance, in the SMSAs for which the proper data are available by race, the white population decreased by 1.9 million persons between 1960 and 1970. This loss would have been even greater if the amount of reproductive change (+2.2 million persons) had not partially compensated for the massive net out-migration (4.1 million) that occurred. By contrast, the nonwhite population living in central cities of SMSAs increased by about one-third, and this change was about equally divided between net in-migration and positive reproductive change.

Equally interesting is the role of reproductive change as a component of population growth in the noncentral city portions of SMSAs. Historically, net in-migration has been of major importance in the development of the surburban population. Indeed, between 1940 and 1950 about two-thirds of the growth in the suburban population was the direct result of net in-migration. However, during the 1960s reproductive change and net in-migration were of approximately equal importance as components of population change in the the rings. However, this only considers direct effects and does not consider the indirect effect of migration by which children born to their parents after their arrival in the suburbs are attributed to reproductive change. Such indirect effects can be very important. Considering the racial characteristics seemingly does not alter the relative importance of each demographic component of change in the noncentral city population.

Following close behind these population shifts has been the development of the retail and service sectors in the suburbs. This has occurred mainly for relatively unspecialized and market-oriented goods and services. Such activities tend to follow population movements and markets. The growth of these activities at suburban locations has also been amplified by increases in the purchasing power of suburban populations, the increased mobility of suburban residents due to the automobile, and the economies that accrue to businesses by concentrating in one location. Combined, these factors have resulted in the rise of large-scale shopping centers, replete with many such amenities and conveniences as parking, air-conditioned malls, landscaping, community rooms, and special events, all of which have further served to attract a considerable portion of shopping activity away from the central city.

From the human ecological perspective, the centrifugal movement of population and some economic activities from the central area to the rings of the metropolitan area is viewed as a growth in the functional specialization of the outlying areas according to the one major factor in which they have a particular advantage—that is, land, its ready accessibility, and comparatively low costs. In competition with the central city, the outlying areas have a decided advantage for those activities and population needing and/or desiring relatively inexpensive land and less congestion. By virtue of these, suburban areas may come to specialize in manufacturing, certain retail and personal services, and population, the latter being a dominant factor when viewed as a labor force supply for the central city.

Centripetal Forces and the Central City

At the same time that population and many economic activities are being attracted to the outer areas of the metropolitan community, other economic activities are being attracted to its center because of its special advantages for them. In general, the competitive advantage of the central area is found in its ready access to the population of the region through the confluence of radial transportation routes at the center, its access to other regions by way of the interregional transportation network, the economies of concentration that it can still provide for many types of economic activities, the prestige value of many central addresses, its concentration of a low-wage labor force, and the ease of face-to-face communication made possible by the density of central city activities.

As a result of these attractions, the central city has continued to contain a disproportionate share of the metropolitan community's employment. Part of this is attributable to the higher population density in that area, but the center still contains a disproportionate share of the area's employment even when this factor is controlled. Thus, one function of the center of the metropolitan community is to provide employment for a number of persons who reside in the outer areas, and one function of these outer areas is to provide a portion of the labor force for the economic activities that are most advantageously located in the center of the city.

Because only certain types of economic activities tend to be concentrated in the central city, much of the employment located there is relatively specialized. The central city also contains those highly specialized persons and institutions that control the market activities of the community and region. Examples of such activities include advertising agencies, federal reserve banks, head offices of insurance companies, investment houses, and stock and commodity exchanges. Similarly, many administrative offices of manufacturing firms, which have moved to suburban locations, are retained in the central city. This physical separation has been made possible, as noted earlier, by improvements in communication. Many of the offices and showrooms of fashion goods manufacturers—clothing, jewelry, furniture, and others—also continue to find central city locations attractive as a means of displaying their goods to the largest number of potential buyers, as well as keeping in close contact with their industry and competitors.

Many wholesaling functions that disaggregate large shipments and distribute them in smaller lots throughout the entire region may also continue to find central city locations attractive, although many other wholesaling activities, especially those servicing decentralizing manufacturing industries, have located in the suburbs. Some manufacturing activities have also continued within the central city. These may be very large industries whose products or raw materials are bulky and that are still dependent upon central city rail and water connections. Similarly numerous smaller, light manufacturers that can adapt their processing requirements to the older loft facilities continue to locate in central areas. These firms may also depend upon a large pool of relatively unskilled low-wage labor, and certain high-skill services not maintained "in-house" that are available at central locations.

The central city also functions as an entertainment center. It is here that the large hotels are located and the conventions are held, and where the major theaters, art galleries, and museums are located. Despite the abundance of shopping malls in the suburbs, the central city also has retained a disproportionately large share of the unstandardized goods and services offered to the metropolitan population. Other highly specialized services, such as medical and legal specialities that are less commonly used by the general public, continue to be strongly represented at central locations.

In general, then, the central city has continued to maintain a relative specialization in administrative functions and specialized services whose dominant locational requirement derives from an overriding need to communicate on a face-to-face basis with persons outside the firm, to maintain a close surveillance of the activities and ideas of their competitors, and to draw on relatively short notice upon a common pool of rentable space, labor, skilled contractors, services, and the like [Hoover & Vernon 1959, pp. 10–11]. Thus, it has been generally accepted that the future of the central city lies in its ability to retain and attract "control activities," that is, administration, and such associated specialized services as law, finance, and advertising. In contrast, suburban locations are increasingly becoming centers for manufacturing and residential use, as well as growing in the less specialized services associated with local populations.

Documentation of these shifts for the many types of activities involved has been difficult because of the general unavailability of appropriate data. Some gross indications do exist, however, as shown in table 4. These figures reflect both the absolute and percentage changes, on a mean annual basis, of population and employment shifts by major employment categories for the thirty-nine largest metropolitan areas (as of 1950, excluding New York). By their level of aggregation, they fail to capture the separation of administration and manufacturing and the separate locational distributions of each. Similarly, the service category incorporates types with many different locational preferences. In spite of these shortcomings, the figures do indicate the extensive postwar shifts in manufacturing and retail employment that have occurred. In each case, central cities are losing jobs, absolutely, to the suburbs. Wholesaling activity is also shown to have grown rapidly within the suburbs, but a small growth rate in the central cities also indicates that these central locations are continuing to hold attractions for certain types of wholesaling activities. The largest growth rates for the central cities are in service activities, and in spite of the relatively large rate of growth for services within the suburbs, the absolute increase in central city service employment is high. Again, the indication is that service activities (and particularly specialized services) are continuing to grow at the center.

These shifts in employment have not occurred evenly across all metropolitan areas. In the thirteen most rapidly growing metropolitan areas, central cities have managed to add to their employment in retailing, manufacturing, and wholesaling over the postwar period, although the corresponding growth rates in the suburbs for these same activities are significantly higher. Conversely, the twenty-six metropolitan areas classified as having only moderately low population growth during this period have generally experienced declines in central city retail, manufacturing, and wholesaling employment. The strength of the central city in service employment is again noted, however, by the fact that jobs in this category have grown in all central cities irrespective of the overall rates of metropolitan growth [Meyer, Kain, & Wohl 1965, tables 2 and 3]. Recent projections of employment trends for central city and suburban areas indicate a continuation of the patterns shown in table 4.

TABLE 4. Mean Annual Absolute and Percentage Changes in Population and Employment for 39 Central Cities and Metropolitan Rings (Corrected for Annexation)

Item	Central City		Metropolitan Area	
	1948–1958	1954–1958	1948–1958	1954–1958
Manufacturing	−809 (−0.6%)	−2502 (−1.7%)	1821 (15.0%)	1214 (7.0%)
Wholesaling	51(0.7%)	2(0.2%)	544(29.4%)	739(16.8%)
Retailing	−285(−0.4%)	6(0.1%)	1427(16.0%)	2110(13.6%)
Services	583(2.7%)	786(3.9%)	618(24.4%)	827(16.8%)
Population	297(0.2%)	308(0.1%)	31,672(9.4%)	34,462(6.4%)

Source: Meyer, Kain, & Wohl 1965, tables 2 and 3.[2]

2. From *The Urban Transportation Problem* by J. R. Meyer, J. F. Kain, and M. Wohl. 1965. Used with the permission of the Harvard University Press.

Dominance

The ecological view of the metropolitan community is one of interdependence. The central city is dependent upon the outer areas of the metropolis, and these are dependent upon the center. Together, they have engaged in a division of labor and specialization that enables the entire community to compete effectively in the regional—and national—economy and thus provides levels of living and services to its inhabitants that otherwise would not have been possible. To view the metropolitan community as less than this interdependent entity is to distort reality. At the same time, one must also realize that to a large extent the central city is the dominant force in the metropolitan community by virtue of its specialization in control activities, in the same way that the metropolitan community is the dominant force in the regional and national economies.

A dominant city is one that controls many aspects and conditions of life of the communities within its region. The concept of metropolitan dominance is based upon three assumptions.

1. There is a system of interdependency among cities;

2. There are considerable differences between the activities of individual cities;

3. The organizing agent, and one of the forces causing this intercity differentiation, is the metropolis [Bogue 1950, p. 6].

The metropolis can control the conditions of life in the areas surrounding it because it has a higher average degree of specialization in essential functions such as finances, services, and wholesaling, and because it has the ability to encourage industrial development in its immediate vicinity by providing favorable combinations of the factors of production. The other places within its area of influence *must* accept these conditions of life by specializing in other activities, which only heightens their dependence upon the metropolis for goods and services they cannot provide efficiently for their residents or for their economic endeavors. Thus, the metropolitan market center mediates a fairly complex exchange of goods and services between communities and thereby integrates the activities of the outlying areas with each other, as well as with those of the metropolitan center.

The most systematic study of metropolitan dominance to date has been performed by Donald Bogue [1950], who analyzed data from the 1940 U.S. census in an effort to verify the existence of metropolitan dominance by demonstrating that nonrandom and patterned sets of differences exist in the areal distribution of population and sustenance activities and that these conditions are attributable to the metropolitan center. Bogue relied heavily upon the gradient principle, which is that the extent of metropolitan influence over an area varies inversely with the distance between that area and the metropolitan center and varies directly with the size of the metropolitan city. Thus, in general, as distance from the center increases the population density of an area decreases and each unit of land accordingly supports a steadily decreasing amount of retail trade, services, wholesale trade, and manufacturing activity. Similarly, metropolitan communities with large central cities have a higher population density (per square mile) and extend their influence over a larger area, with the degree of specialization in retail, service, and wholesale activities inversely related to distance from the metropolitan center [see also Kish 1954].

Of course the range of dominance of a metropolitan center varies with the type of activity under consideration. High-frequency activities such as daily commuting to work or shopping trips for household necessities such as food usually occur within a 2- to 30-mile radius. Consequently, the gradient for these activities is short and fairly steep, and beyond that radius small centers may be quite effective competitors in satisfying these frequently occurring individual needs. The activities that occur less frequently, such as those between wholesalers and retailers or interinstitutional relations, may be spread over an area with a radius of 150 miles or more; and the gradient of influence of the metropolitan center in these activities tapers off more gradually as distance from the center is lengthened. A third type of range of dominance can be delimited by using the export function of the center. Normally the products of such activities are distributed over an area of interregional scope [Hawley 1971, p. 220; also see Duncan et al., 1960].

Dominance is not an absolute attribute but a variable and a typology can be constructed for classifying populations in terms of the range or area of their dominance and the number of functions over which dominance is exerted. In decreasing degrees of dominance, populations may be classified as dominant, subdominant, influent, or subinfluent [Bogue 1950]. Thus, a metropolitan community is an organization of many subdominant, influent, and subinfluent communities distributed in a definite pattern about a dominant city and bound together in a territorial division of labor through dependence upon the activities of the dominant city.

Although Bogue's study of metropolitan dominance was performed using data from the 1940 census, there is little real reason to doubt the general applicability of his major conclusions to the present situation in the United States and the other industrialized countries of the world. The proportion of the population living in metropolitan areas has increased dramatically since then. There also has been a trend toward the consolidation of the various forms of economic activity into corporate conglomerates that are operated from head offices located in the major metropolitan areas and that greatly influence the forms and prices of the goods and services available to the public. Moreover, the vast improvements in transportation and communication that have occurred since 1940 could only have served to extend the range of the sphere of influence of the metropolitan community.

Megalopolis—A Super Metropolis?

Considerable attention has been devoted recently to the possible emergence of a new community form, presumably representing a stage of urban development that follows extensive metropolitanization of the population. This new community form has been labeled "megalopolis," and its most publicized example has been the vast metropolitan complex that extends from southern New Hampshire to northern Virginia and goes inland 30 to 100 miles from the Atlantic to the foothills of the Appalachian Mountains [Gottmann 1961]. Megalopolis is viewed as a chain of contiguous and interrelated metropolitan areas, whose major feature is a vast concentration of people, goods, and functions, and which serves as the economic hinge of the United States, linking the North American continent with the foreign markets accessible via the Atlantic Ocean. It is conceptualized as a sort of super-metropolis, a functional entity whose parts are interdependent and whose activities dominate the American economy.

In standard ecological usage, the community has several essential characteristics. One is a common geographic area that is relatively bounded, that is, it is conceptually and/or empirically distinguishable from other areas. It is clear that megalopolis possesses this characteristic. Also essential is a system of interrelationships between the population units of that area sufficient to satisfy the minimal basic and acquired needs of the inhabitants of the area. This system of interrelationships is called the "organization" of that population, and its central feature is a division of labor and a pattern of functional interdependence between portions of the population.

Thus, if megalopolis does indeed represent an emergent form of community, it should be characterized by an interdependence between the metropolitan areas around which the area was organized previously. There should be a pattern of complementary functional specialization among the various metropolitan units. Moreover, any such pattern should have increased through time as the result of the process of differentiation of economic activity and the continued development of the intermetropolitan division of labor. Unless such a pattern exists among the metropolitan areas of megalopolis and unless the intensity of this pattern has increased through time, it is difficult to conceive of megalopolis as anything other than a grouping of continuous metropolitan areas sharing a common geographic identity.

To date, the most systematic test of the extent to which megalopolis represents an emergent community form has been performed by Robert Weller [1967] using data from the 1950 and 1960 censuses. The analysis uses location quotients to determine whether or not a given metropolitan area is functionally specialized in a particular type of economic activity, for example, durable processing. Location quotients are the ratio p_i/P_i, where p_i is the proportion of the local labor force engaged in a particular type of activity and P_i is the proportion of some base or standard population that is engaged in that activity. In this case, the collective labor force of the units of analysis is used as the standard. The usual inference drawn is that a ratio equal to 1 means that local production and local consumption coincide, so that the community neither imports nor exports the products of that particular activity. Similarly, a ratio greater than 1 indicates export of the particular commodity (or service), and a ratio less than 1 indicates that the community cannot satisfy local consumption demands and must import the product (or service) to meet this deficiency.

Thus, if an intermetropolitan division of labor has occurred, then the variation of these location quotients should be greater through time, indicating increased trade between functionally differentiated metropolitan areas.

When the labor forces of the various metropolitan areas are examined in this manner, it is found that the economic activity of metropolitan areas has become more alike rather than more differentiated. The only areas in which substantial increases in differentiation have occurred are "nondurable fabricating," "trucking," "utilities and sanitary services," and "business services."

Does this mean that megalopolis is a myth? Not necessarily. It does mean that on the basis of the available evidence there is no reason to accept the megalopolitan hypothesis. There are several reasons for qualifying any outright rejection of the hypothesis. One is the fact that there is considerable cross-sectional evidence of intermetropolitan interdependence in most of the types of economic activity that are considered. What is lacking is evidence of *increasing* differentiation—and hence interdependence—through time. As argued earlier in this unit, such differentiation has occurred in metropolitan communities and is facilitated by improvements in transportation and communications technology. Thus, if megalopolis is a valid community form, it must have evolved fully *before* 1950. Although the data are inappropriate for testing this possibility, it seems unlikely. Thus, the concept of megalopolis as an emergent community form, a super-metropolis, must be viewed with extreme skepticism.

A NOTE
ON METROPOLITAN PROBLEMS

The term "urban problems" is commonly used to evoke a long list of conditions associated with urban areas and with the transition from a largely rural to an urban, largely metropolitan society. This list includes such problems as crime, environmental pollution, poverty, inadequate health care systems, large-scale tracts of substandard housing, congested transportation facilities, an overcrowded and unimaginative educational system, corruption in government, and so forth. However, the term "urban" problems is misleading: not all of the problems that we usually identify with urban areas are truly urban in character, or are even aggravated by urban conditions. Most of the problems listed above are national in scope and incidence. They occur in rural as well as in urban areas. Some, particularly poverty and inferior transportation facilities, are probably worse in rural areas, especially for the young, the elderly, and the handicapped. These phenomena may be more visible in urban areas because of the concentration of population; but to deny the dimensions of the same problems for nonurban areas, to perceive rural poverty as less important or less prevalent than urban poverty and to look for the causes of poverty in factors indigenous to living in cities would be foolish.

However, there are some problems that can be more closely associated with metropolitan areas than with other types of settlement patterns. These are problems whose dimensions have been increased by some particular characteristic associated with metropolitan growth and whose potential solution has been made more difficult by some of the characteristics of metropolitan structure. In general, these problems may be divided into two closely related types that arise from   1. the redistribution of functions and population in metropolitan areas,   2. the increasing ecological interdependence between persons and places within the metropolitan community. The problems caused by these conditions may best be understood by reference to the unique structure of government within these areas.

The Structure of Government in Metropolitan Areas

The growth of the metropolitan community as an integrated social and economic unit has not been matched by a corresponding integration of government functions within the area. On the contrary, there has been a proliferation of governmental units, each with its own authority to formulate laws and regulations, enter into contracts and agreements, and impose taxes. These include municipal governments (cities and incorporated towns), school boards, county, town, and township governments, as well as a variety of special districts and authorities designed to plan and administer specialized functions and services. These may include health districts, housing authorities, transportation authorities, renewal authorities, and others. Consequently, any one local community within the metropolitan area may contain or be serviced by a number of different governmental units. Moreover, the jurisdictions of these governments may not coincide with each other or be coterminus with municipal boundaries. School districts and special authorities, in particular, may overlap other units of government, with part of a city being in one school district, part in another, and each such district including territory outside of the municipal boundaries.

Some idea of the number of governments within metropolitan areas and their tendency to increase in number according to the size of the metropolitan community is shown by the figures in table 5. On the average, all metropolitan areas (as defined by the Bureau of the Census) contained about 91 different local governments in 1967. This varies considerably from an average of 25 governments in the smallest SMSAs, to over 300 in the largest SMSAs. However, many metropolitan areas contain considerably more than these average numbers of governments. Chicago is reported to have 1,113 separate governments within the metropolitan area, Philadelphia has 876, Pittsburgh has 704, and New York has 551.

TABLE 5. Total and Average Number of Local Governments by Size Class of SMSA, 1967

SMSA Population (1960)	Number of SMSAs	Number of Local Governments	Average Number of Local Governments
All SMSAs	227	20,703	91.2
1,000,000 or more	24	7,367	307.0
500,000-1,000,000	32	3,878	121.2
300,000-500,000	30	2,734	91.1
200,000-300,000	40	2,919	73.0
100,000-200,000	74	3,123	42.2
50,000-100,000	27	682	25.3

Source: U.S. Bureau of the Census 1969.

The result of this multiplicity of governments has been a relative difficulty in governing metropolitan areas. Each government, concerned primarily with the interests of its own community or specialized functions, frequently undertakes actions harmful to other communities, as when one jurisdiction zones land on its periphery as industrial, while adjacent land in another jurisdiction has been developed as residential land. Other actions may result in a waste of resources, a duplication of efforts and a lack of coordination between governmental units, as when adjoining districts fail to share some major capital facility that could service both. Perhaps most important, however, has been the inability of the many local governments to organize, plan, and effectively implement programs aimed at solving metropolitan-wide problems. Problems in land use, health, transportation, pollution, and housing are primary examples. Federal requirements for region-wide planning in many of these areas has recently forced many of the separate jurisdictions within the metropolis to cooperate and coordinate their plans, but this has remained only minimally effective with most region-wide organizations lacking the power to enforce agreements over the entire region. It is against this background of political fragmentation that a number of other metropolitan problems can be understood.

Problems Associated with the Redistribution of Population and Economic Activity in Metropolitan Areas

We have seen that the growth of the metropolitan community involves a structural redistribution of population and economic activities. Particular types of economic activities, principally manufacturing, as well as numerous retail and personal services have moved to, or subsequently developed in, suburban locations. Population also has both migrated to and grown more rapidly outside central cities, and for many central cities there has been an absolute, as well as a relative, decline in population. However, many of the summary changes cited in previous sections failed to relate the detailed social and economic characteristics of central city and suburban residents and to demonstrate the significant changes in population characteristics that have occurred in this process of redistribution. Principally, these changes have involved the replacement of the out-migrating white middle-class population of central cities with a greater percentage of blacks and other minority groups, and a greater percentage of female-headed households, families below the poverty level, and elderly citizens. The data shown in table 6 attempt to portray these differences by considering the disparities between central city and suburban areas on selected social, economic, and demographic characteristics. In all cases, central cities are shown to contain a disproportionately larger percentage of the disadvantaged populations of urbanized areas.

Central cities thus appear to be the repository of a good part of the poverty and dependent populations of urban areas. While central cities by no means have a monopoly on these populations, the relative disparity is clear. Moreover, we would expect that were data available they would show that these poverty populations, even to the extent that they reside in noncentral city locations, would be relatively concentrated in particular suburban districts.

Not all suburbs, however, would contain an equal representation of the poor, the disadvantaged, the undereducated, and the unemployed. In effect, then, the growth of specialization among components of the metropolitan community has involved more than a specialization in economic functions; this specialization extends to types of population, with some parts of the metropolitan area having a greater concentration of poverty and problem populations than others.

T A B L E 6. Percent of Persons Having Selected Social Welfare Characteristics, by Central City and Fringe Residence: Urbanized Areas, 1970

Item	Number of persons Urbanized area	Central city (Percent)	Urban fringe (Percent)
Families with income less than poverty level	2,475,315	70.6	29.4
Persons receiving public assistance income	1,606,695	70.8	29.2
Families with female head	3,665,172	66.8	33.2
Persons 16 years and over, unemployed	2,082,025	60.2	39.8
Persons, 25 years and over, completing only 6 years of school	3,360,306	67.0	33.0
Persons, 65, years and over	11,136,116	61.6	38.4
Median family income	10,618	9,519	11,771

Source: U.S. Bureau of the Census 1972.

The significance of this concentration of poverty in central cities is two-fold. First, the increasing proportion of poor and aged has meant a parallel increase in the demands for poverty related social services, in such areas as housing, health, and welfare assistance. At the same time, the ability of the central city government to support these increased expenditures has declined, due both to these poorer resident populations and the loss of industry and business activity, and a consequent loss in resources taxable through the property tax. Hence, central cities have been faced with a fiscal crisis. In comparison to most suburban jurisdictions, the central city is relatively poor, with increasing demands for services occurring at the same time that taxable resources have been contracting.

Four important points can be made concerning the extensiveness of the fiscal disparities between central cities and suburbs. John Riew's study [1970] of the Milwaukee urbanized area illustrates the dimensions of the resulting financial dilemma. The first aspect relates to differences in property values. Table 7 shows the mean per-capita property values (including personal and real property) for the Milwaukee central city and 28 urban area suburbs classified by functional types. In all cases, property values in suburbs are higher than for the city of Milwaukee, with low-income suburbs having slightly greater per-capita resources to over 400 percent greater resources in industrial suburbs. Moreover, between the period 1960–1966 increases in per-capita valuation have been greater in all classes of suburbs than in the central city. The token gain of 3.8 percent for Milwaukee is matched against gains of over 13 percent for each residential suburb.

T A B L E 7. Mean Per-Capita Property Values Among Municipalities in the Milwaukee Urban Area, 1966

	Per-capita property values		Percent change, 1960-66
	dollars	*index*	
Milwaukee central city	5,454	100.0	3.8
urban area suburbs	9,219	169.0	
balanced suburb	8,982	164.7	9.0
industrial suburb	25,239	462.8	7.0
residential			
high income	10,937	200.5	16.0
medium income	7,180	131.6	15.0
low income	5,799	106.3	13.0

Source: Riew 1970, table 4.[3]

The second part of this fiscal crisis concerns tax rates. Faced with greater demands for expenditures and lower taxable per-capita resources, the central city has been forced to markedly increase the rates at which properties are taxed. Thus, as Riew's data show, central Milwaukee tax rates are at least 50 percent higher than the rates of all types of suburbs, and have increased at a much faster rate during the 1957–1966 period.

Third, if the Milwaukee experience is a valid illustration, these higher tax rates have not resulted in higher levels of per-capita tax revenues for central cities. With the exception of industrial suburbs, central city income returns are the lowest of all groups. The low return to industrial suburbs can, of course, be accounted for by their relatively low tax rates. Hence, industrial suburbs, as the others, can readily improve their income positions by increasing their rates and still not approach the tax burden felt by central city properties.

The fourth aspect of this fiscal crisis concerns expenditures. In general, central city expenditures have been higher than those of the suburbs, even given lower income returns. Suburban expenditures appear to be higher than those of the central city in the areas of highways and

3. This table from "Metropolitan Disparities and Fiscal Federalism," by John Riew in John P. Crecine's (ed.) "Financing the Metropolis," *Urban Affairs Annual Reviews,* Vol. 4 (1970), p. 142, by permission of the Publisher, Sage Publications, Inc.

education. Rapid population growth in the suburbs, requiring extensive capital outlays for school buildings and equipment would account for much of this difference in educational expenditures. Central cities, however, generally lead in expenditures for welfare, police and fire protection, health and hospitals, public housing and urban renewal, and sanitation. These higher expenditures in central cities can be related to two conditions: 1. their higher density levels, concentration of people, property and business and nonresident commuters, all of which impose additional burdens for such services as police, fire, and sanitation; and, as previously noted, 2. the greater concentration of low income and aged, increasing demands for health, welfare, housing expenditures. While particular suburban jurisdictions may show higher levels of spending than the central city in one or more of these categories (e.g., Riew's data show that high income suburbs in Milwaukee spend more per-capita for police, health, and sanitation services than the central city), it is important to realize that these particular suburbs spend more with both higher levels of taxable resources and lower tax rates, thereby, in a sense, having their cake and eating it too. Central cities spend more than all suburbs considered together, when total expenditures are considered relative to income [see Advisory Commision on Intergovernmental Relations 1965].

It is clear, then, that one of the major problems of metropolitan areas related to their patterns of growth is the existing and increasing disparity between local political units, especially suburbs and central cities, in the location of revenues and the demands for community services. Some jurisdictions can manage to provide their residents with high levels of service with only minimal strain on community resources, while others are more severely strained in meeting their obligations. The importance of these disparities is increased when we recognize that they are artificial. The distribution of taxable resources and populations within the metropolitan area is an ecological phenomenon, while the pattern of government in these areas is superimposed upon these ecological distributions. Concentrations of poverty and concentrations of high-valued property are, in ecological terms, the problems and resources of the metropolitan community as a whole, to be shared by all places within the area. The pattern of governments, however, mitigates against this sharing by confining problems and resources within separate political jurisdictions.

The inequities that have been produced by this lack of congruence between resources and needs have been maintained and magnified both by the competition between local governments for taxable resources that make minimum demands on the community for service expenditures, and by local desires to preserve particular levels of social status. One means of more equitably distributing problems and resources across the metropolitan area would be to decrease the concentration of low-income populations in the central city through the dispersal of low-income housing into the suburbs. Most suburban areas, however, have effectively resisted these incursions. Low-income housing represents a fiscal drain on communities by returning few tax dollars while the service demands on the part of low-income populations may be relatively high. Hence, this type of housing is not profitable. Suburban communities thus seek high-valued housing, "clean" industry, and commercial services that tend to yield more tax value relative to expenditures. Combined with these fiscal realities, social snobbery and racial discrimination have effectively limited the movement of low-income and black populations into these suburban areas.

The most common means for imposing these limitations has been through "fiscal zoning"; that is, through requiring large lot sizes for building, specifying minimum house sizes, and prohibiting multifamily dwellings, unless of the luxury variety. Additional devices, such as overly stringent building codes and extensive subdivision regulations also increase the costs of construction and thereby effectively discriminate against lower class and lower-middle class groups. Reinforcing these discriminations are the practices of many local real estate, building, and financial institutions that, while nominally regulated by federal and state laws, may still follow local practices and values in distributing housing within the community.

Other significant consequences also have stemmed from these disparities and the impact of suburban exclusionary practices. While the main effects of these practices have been felt by lower income groups in general, they have had a significant impact on the pattern of residential segregation by race within metropolitan areas, for a greater percentage of blacks than whites within metropolitan areas earn less than $5,000 per year (32.3 percent vs. 13.7 percent of families, respectively, 1970). Fiscal zoning and other discriminatory techniques are, in fact, frequently related more to local community attempts to exclude racial minorities than to exclude lower-income groups in general. These exclusions have had a secondary effect on levels of employment and, ultimately, on income levels of the black population since the expansion of industrial employment opportunities in suburban locations has remained relatively inaccessible to central city blacks. This is because the transportation system in most major cities is organized to service the central city; transportation from the center to remote suburban locations is difficult, time consuming, and costly, and almost invariably necessitates the use of private automobiles. The relative remoteness of these suburban job locations also means that many potential employment opportunities go unrecognized. Hence, J. F. Kain [1968] has estimated that as of the mid-1950s approximately 30,000 jobs had been lost to the central city black populations of Chicago and Detroit because of housing segregation. At the same time, the expansion of employment opportunities in central cities is frequently in low-paying service jobs, in marginal industries requiring cheap labor, or in clerical and administrative positions for which the low-skilled, undereducated black worker may be unsuited. As a result, many central city blacks are locked into low-paying, dead-end jobs, which, in turn, contributes to low levels of median income in the black population and high rates of unemployment.

Problems Associated with Increasing Ecological Interdependence

Another problem that is created by the interdependence of the communities within the metropolis, and by an inadequate governmental structure, is that of external costs and benefits, or "spillover" effects. These externalities occur when indirect consequences of actions taken by individual producers or governments spill over to some other individual or community not involved in the initial action. Such externalities may be beneficial, as when an individual entrepreneur builds a supermarket at a particular location, thereby increasing the value of surrounding land parcels for other commercial uses. The benefits in increased value may then accrue to the owners of these other parcels. Similarly, the provision of a public park in a neighborhood may result in increasing residential land values in that area, such increases again being external to the initial action and yielding benefits to second parties. But these externalities may also be unfavorable, as when the supermarket induces increased traffic flow, noise, and congestion, adversely affecting nearby residential properties.

Favorable spillovers can frequently be internalized, that is, recaptured by the units producing them. The builder of the supermarket can internalize the increased value of other commercial properties if he also owns them; the city can recapture some of the benefits produced through building a park by taxing the increased value of nearby residential properties. The supermarket builder, however, generally manages not to internalize the negative spillovers created by downgrading the adjacent residential environment, for it would not be to his advantage to do so. In this way he manages to impose some of the costs of his actions on others. Obviously, it would be in the interests of these others to force the builder to absorb external costs as well as external benefits.

Many spillover effects are relatively minor, but as urban areas grow, become more complex and more interdependent, and people live closer together, as they do in metropolitan areas, the likelihood of significant externalities occurring increases. The externalities are frequently of two types: 1. those involving individual producers or governments that create negative spillovers that they fail to internalize, and 2. those involving local governments that supply services but fail to internalize many of the external benefits produced by their services. In the former case high social and monetary costs may accrue to the metropolitan population in general, while in the latter case the local government concerned may be motivated to reduce levels of service provided. In both cases issues of equity arise that have been difficult to solve under the existing structure of government in metropolitan areas.

One of the clearest examples of actions by individual producers or local governments that produce negative spillovers for the remainder of the metropolitan population is the uncontrolled emission of noxious gases, chemicals, or inadequately treated sewage into the air and water. These untreated emissions represent a savings to the actor involved, since adequate treatment would increase the costs of industrial production or waste-disposal services. At the same time the fouling of the air and water imposes heavy costs on other local communities who must tolerate poor and dirty air, increased health hazards and costs, increased cleaning costs, decreased opportunities for recreation, and additional costs for the treatment of water for public consumption. A reduction in these public costs, that is, internalization of costs by the unit producing them, can be achieved either by forcing the responsible producer to pay the costs of cleaning the air and water or, more effectively, by having these emissions adequately treated or controlled as part of the industrial process. In either case, however, some public authority is necessary to legislate and enforce these regulations, and this is unlikely to be the government that produces the pollution or that has jurisdiction over the polluting industry. Where local government is the polluter and where this government can still draw off clean water from upstream sources while discharging dirty water downstream, the motivation for self-correction is minimal. Local governments are also reluctant to take unilateral action against industries within their jurisdictions since these controls would place them in a less competitive position vis-a-vis other communities for attracting new industry and taxable resources. Therefore, it is generally recognized that some metropolitan or region-wide authority is necessary that is capable of establishing and enforcing environmental legislation for the entire affected area.

The second situation, in which local governments provide services and facilities to their population that have substantial positive spillovers to other populations and governments, is also fairly common, particularly because the ecological interdependence between communities within the metropolitan area involves a high degree of daily movement of persons across the area. Where these external benefits are relatively large in relation to internal benefits to the local population, adequate levels of service may not be provided by any one jurisdiction since the voters of one community will be less likely to tax themselves heavily for services and facilities benefitting others. As this situation multiplies across a region, levels of service and the provision of special facilities may, in the aggregate, be abnormally low.

There are two main classes of locally provided services with heavy spillovers that may follow the above pattern [Netzer 1970, pp. 176–181]. One set is the range of services that are made available to populations of local communities and whose benefits substantially inhere in the individuals concerned. These are the services involved in human resource development, such as education, health, welfare, and manpower training. In these cases the spillovers come from population migration. Locally trained and educated persons may leave the local community; and, at the same time, unskilled, undereducated, "problem" populations may enter the local community from other areas, thereby compounding the externalities produced (positive "spill-outs" and negative "spill-ins"). This, of course, is what has happened in many of the central cities of metropolitan areas.

The second class of services involving heavy spillover effects are those for which the technology of providing the service makes it difficult to confine benefits to small areas. Examples are environmental control, transportation, major parks and recreation facilities, research and development activities, crime control, and public health programs. Environmental control, crime control, and public health programs will, for example, improve conditions over wide areas by cleaning the air and water or reducing the criminal and rat population. Conversely, the failure of any government to provide these programs affects wide areas and results in negative spillovers. The provision of major parks and roads also carries high positive spillover effects since it is difficult to regulate the use of these facilities by nonlocal residents. Improvements in highways and mass-transit facilities also creates spillovers through their effects on increased accessibility and land values. Thus, particular suburban locations may become more desirable for residential purposes as the central city improves its transportation system and eases the daily suburb-to-central-city journey to work. Other services and facilities, such as police protection, museums and libraries, sanitation services, on-street parking, are also readily available to nonresidents at no cost, and are utilized by the suburban commuter to the central city. Where the daily interchanges between populations of different political jurisdictions are bidirectional, these externalities are of little concern and tend to even out over time. In the case of the central city, however, few such reciprocal changes take place in the daily work force. Hence, an already aggravated fiscal situation is made worse.

A Note on the Reorganization of Government in Metropolitan Areas

Given the above, what appears to be needed in metropolitan areas is a reorganization of political responsibilities, bringing them into closer alignment with the ecological structure of the community. This does not necessarily mean that one government for the entire metropolitan community is necessary, although this alternative would undoubtedly satisfy the need for congruence between ecological and political borders. Less complete and drastic steps that have a greater political feasibility are possible, such as a redistribution of responsibilities between many levels of government to the point where fiscal disparities are eliminated and the distribution of costs and benefits across the region are more equitably distributed.

The Advisory Commission on Intergovernmental Relations (ACIR) [1963, p. 86] has suggested seven criteria by which the distribution of functions between levels of government can be evaluated. These may be delineated as follows:

1. The governmental jurisdiction responsible for providing any service should be large enough to enable the benefits from that service to be consumed primarily within the jurisdiction. Neither the benefits from the service nor the social costs of failing to provide it should "spill over" into other jurisdictions. For example, the central city should not be expected to pay all of the very high capital costs of constructing a subway system which primarily benefits the suburban commuter.

2. The unit of government should be large enough to permit realization of the economies of scale. For example, it costs $58 per million gallons to provide primary sewage treatment in a million gallon capacity facility, but less than half this amount in a ten million gallon capacity facility.

3. The unit of government carrying on a function should have a geographic area of jurisdiction adequate for effective performance, as illustrated by the desirability of a sewage disposal system's conforming to a natural drainage basin.

4. The unit of government should have the legal and administrative ability to perform services assigned to it. If it is going to provide modern health protection, for example, it needs to have both adequate regulatory authority and the ability to attract and hold a trained staff capable of administering a public health program.

5. Every unit of government should be responsible for a sufficient number of functions so that its governing processes involve a resolution of conflicting interests, with significant responsibility for balancing government needs and resources. Thus, in the jurisdictional allocation of individual functions, there is an ever present danger of creating so many separate entities as to result in undemocratic, inequitable, and inadequate assignment of priorities. Elected officials should be responsible and held accountable for balancing governmental needs and resources.

6. The performance of functions by a unit of government should remain controllable by and accessible to its residents. This is an essential condition of responsible government and one that is too often violated by creation of special districts whose decision-making power and purse strings are not susceptible to direct control by the voters.

7. Functions should be assigned to that level of government which maxi-

mizes the conditions and opportunities for active citizen participation and still permits adequate performance. This is another guarantee for keeping government sensitive to the citizens, as well as a way of assuring attraction of the community's best talent into positions of leadership.

Through the application of these criteria the Advisory Commission has suggested that some governmental functions are best performed at a metropolitan level, others at the local community level, and still others at levels intermediate to both. The *least* local types of functions are given as air-pollution control, water supply and sewage disposal, planning, and transportation. In descending order the most local functions are: hospitals and medical care facilities, public welfare, parks and recreation, housing, urban renewal, health, police, libraries, refuse collection and disposal, public education, and fire protection. While not considered in the report, it is conceivable that some of these local functions, or their subfunctions, could even be provided on a uniquely local level, the neighborhood.

By focusing on the optimum scale of operation for each major type of function, without reference to particular models of governmental structure, the ACIR approach illuminates the varying types of governmental accommodations that may be necessary for adequate and equitable provision of basic services. One of the implications of this evaluation is that a single, multipurpose government in metropolitan areas is not a practical necessity because only some functions require area-wide political integration. Financing, however, may still be necessary on a metropolitan basis in order to eliminate local tax disparities. These taxes, levied across the entire area, could then be distributed to local communities on the basis of need, thereby preserving local initiatives and discretions in allocating expenditures over a variety of local responsibilities. Alternatively, both area-wide and local taxing powers could be established in a manner appropriate to the distribution of functions and the costs of provision. The higher level of government could then be responsible for setting minimum service standards to insure that each lower unit of government did provide adequate levels of service to its local population.

This type of metropolitan political organization is most closely approached in the two-tier models existing in Metropolitan Dade County (Florida) and Metropolitan Toronto (Canada). In the former, the county has been charged with expanded responsibilities, while in Toronto a new federated government has been created and given area-wide functions.

Dade County, for example, exercises responsibility in the areas of expressway construction, traffic regulation, operation of mass-transit facilities, training and communication for police and fire protection, provision of hospitals and uniform health and welfare programs, provision of parks and recreational areas, establishment and administration of housing, urban renewal and air pollution control programs, establishment of minimum service standards for local communities, plus other functions under its own taxing powers [Bollens & Schmandt 1970, p. 328]. Local communities within the county perform other functions with appropriate taxing powers.

While the two-tier form of reorganization has remained appealing to metropolitan government reformers, it has been the least used approach to political integration. This has occurred principally because of the difficulties involved in enlisting the cooperation of local communities, which are jealous of their prerogatives and generally unwilling to relinquish their decision making powers over a broad variety of functions, to another government. As a result, other organizational alternatives have been more frequently adopted, such as the creation of specialized, one function metropolitan districts or limited voluntary cooperative agreements between local communities. [For a comprehensive review of these alternatives and their strengths and weaknesses, see Bollens & Schmandt 1970 and Advisory Commission on Intergovernmental Relations 1962].

While some forms of reorganization are potentially more effective than others, it should be recognized that all have limited value. They cannot and are not expected to solve all of the problems that exist within urban areas. Progress may be made in some areas, however, particularly in those instances where problem solving has been hampered by a lack of coordination between local governments, or where disparities in available tax resources have led to inadequate provision of basic services and protective reactions on the part of local governments against bearing their fair share of problems and costs.

Bibliography

Advisory Commission on Intergovernmental Relations, *Alternative Approaches to Governmental Reorganization in Metropolitan Areas.* Government Printing Office, 1962.

Advisory Commission on Intergovernmental Relations, *Performance of Urban Functions: Local and Area-wide.* Government Printing Office, 1963.

Advisory Commission on Intergovernmental Relations, *Metropolitan Social and Economic Disparities: Implications for Governmental Relations in Central Cities and Suburbs.* Government Printing Office, 1965.

John W. Alexander, *Oshkosh, Wisconsin: An Economic Base Study.* Bureau of Business Research, School of Commerce, University of Wisconsin, 1951.

John W. Alexander, *An Economic Base Study of Madison, Wisconsin.* Bureau of Business Research, School of Commerce, University of Wisconsin, 1953.

John W. Alexander, "The Basic-Nonbasic Concept of Urban Economic Functions." *Economic Geography,* 1954, 30 (July): 246-261.

Armour's Livestock Bureau, "The Motor Truck in the Food Industry." *Monthly Letter to Animal Husbandmen,* 1930, 11 (November): 8-12.

E. E. Bergel, *Urban Society.* McGraw-Hill, 1955.

Brian Berry and William Garrison, "The Functional Basis of the Central Place Hierarchy." *Economic Geography,* 1958, 34 (April): 145–154.

Donald J. Bogue, *The Structure of the Metropolitan Community.* University of Michigan Press, 1950.

John C. Bollens and Henry J. Schmandt, *The Metropolis,* rev. ed. Harper & Row, 1970.

H. E. Bracey, "Towns as Rural Service Centres: An Index of Centrality with Special Reference to Somerset." *Transactions and Papers of the Institute of British Geographers,* 1953, Publication 19:95–105.

W. Christaller, *Die Zentralen Orte in Suddeutschland.* Jena, Germany: Gustav Fisher Verlag, 1933.

C. H. Cooley, "The Theory of Transportation." *Publications of the American Economic Association,* 1894, 9 (May):312–322.

W. F. Cottrell, "Death By Dieselization: A Case Study in the Reaction to Technological Change." *American Sociological Review,* 1951, 16 (June):358–365.

Kingsley Davis, *World Urbanization 1950–1970, Volume I.* Institute of International Studies, University of California, Berkeley, 1969.

Kingsley Davis, *World Urbanization 1950–1970, Volume II, Analysis of Trends, Relationships, and Development.* Institute of International Studies, University of California, Berkeley, 1972.

Kingsley Davis and Wilbert E. Moore, "Some Principles of Stratification." *American Sociological Review,* 1945, 10 (April):242–249.

Otis Dudley Duncan et al., *Metropolis and Region.* Johns Hopkins Press, 1960.

Allan G. Feldt, "The Metropolitan Area Concept: An Evaluation of the 1950 SMA's." *Journal of the American Statistical Association,* 1965, 60 (June):617–636.

James E. Frank, "Locational Effects of Local Revenue Systems: The Case of the Property Tax." Ph.D. dissertation, Graduate School of Public Administration, New York University, 1971.

C. J. Friedrich, *Alfred Weber's Theory of the Location of Industries.* University of Chicago Press, 1929.

Jean Gottmann, *Megalopolis: The Urbanized Northeastern Seaboard of the United States.* Twentieth Century Fund, 1961.

Norman S. B. Gras, *An Introduction to Economic History.* Harper, 1922.

F. H. W. Green, "Urban Hinterlands in England and Wales: An Analysis of Bus Services." *Geographical Journal,* 1950, 116 (June-December):64–81.

Chauncey Harris, "A Functional Classification of Cities in the United States." *Geographical Review,* 1943, 33 (January):86–99.

Amos H. Hawley, *Human Ecology: A Theory of Community Structure.* Ronald Press, 1950.

Amos H. Hawley, *Urban Society.* Ronald Press, 1971.

Amos H. Hawley, Beverly Duncan, and David Goldberg, "Some Observations of Changes in Metropolitan Population in the United States." *Demography,* 1964, 1:148–155.

Edgar M. Hoover and Raymond Vernon, *Anatomy of a Metropolis.* Doubleday, 1959.

Edgar M. Hoover, *The Location of Economic Activity.* McGraw-Hill, 1963.

Homer Hoyt, *One Hundred Years of Land Values in Chicago: The Relationship of the Growth of Chicago to the Rise of its Land Value, 1830-1933.* University of Chicago Press, 1933.

Henry L. Hunker and Alfred J. Wright, *Factors of Industrial Location in Ohio.* Bureau of Business Research, College of Commerce and Administration, Ohio State University, 1963.

J. F. Kain, "Housing Segregation, Negro Employment and Metropolitan Decentralization." *Quarterly Journal of Economics,* 1968, 82 (May):175–197.

Leslie Kish, "Differentiation in Metropolitan Areas." *American Sociological Review,* 1954, 19 (August):388–398.

Karl Marx and Friedrich Engels, *The Communist Manifesto.* International Publishers, n.d.

J. R. Meyer, J. F. Kain, and M. Wohl, *The Urban Transportation Problem.* Harvard University Press, 1965.

R. D. McKenzie, *The Metropolitan Community.* McGraw-Hill, 1933.

Howard J. Nelson, "A Service Classification of American Cities." *Economic Geography*, 1955, 31 (July):189–210.

Dick Netzer, *Economies and Urban Problems*. Basic Books, 1970.

J. H. Niedercorn and J. F. Kain, *Suburbanization of Employment and Population, 1948–1975*. Santa Monica, California: The Rand Corporation, P-2641, 1963.

Allen R. Pred, *The Spatial Dynamics of U.S. Urban Industrial Growth, 1800–1914*. M.I.T. Press, 1966.

Regional Plan Association of New York, *The Economic Status of the New York Metropolitan Region in 1944*. Regional Plan Association, 1944.

Albert J. Reiss, "Functional Specialization of Cities." In Paul K. Hatt and Albert J. Reiss, eds., *Cities and Society*, rev. ed. Free Press, 1957, pp. 555–575.

John Riew, "Metropolitan Disparities and Fiscal Federalism." In John P. Creeme, ed., *Financing the Metropolis*, Sage Publications, 1970, pp. 137–161.

Leo Schnore and David W. Varley, "Some Concomitants of Metropolitan Size." *American Sociological Review*, 1955, 20 (August):408–414.

Robert O. Schulze, "The Bifurcation of Power in a Satellite City." In Morris Janowitz, ed., *Community Political Systems*. Free Press, 1961, pp. 19–80.

Arthur E. Smailes, "The Urban Hierarchy in England and Wales." *Geography*, 1944, 29:41–51.

Charles H. Tiebout, *The Community Economic Base Study*. New York: Committee for Economic Development, Supplementary Paper no. 16, 1962.

Edward L. Ullman, "A Theory for Location of Cities." *American Journal of Sociology*, 1941, 46:835–864.

U.S. Bureau of the Census, *Census of Local Governments, 1967. Volume 5, Local Government in Metropolitan Areas*. Government Printing Office, 1969.

U.S. Bureau of the Census, *Census of Population and Housing: 1970, General Demographic Trends for Metropolitan Areas, 1960 to 1970*. Final Report PHC(2)–1, "United States." Government Printing Office, 1971.

U.S. Bureau of the Census, *Census of Population and Housing: 1970, General Social and Economic Characteristics*. Final Report PC(1)–C1, "United States Summary." Government Printing Office, 1972.

Robert H. Weller, "An Empirical Examination of Megalopolitan Structure." *Demography*, 1967, 4:734–743.

C. Langdon White, Edwin J. Foscue, and Tom L. McKnight, *Regional Geography of Anglo-America*. Prentice-Hall, 1964.

Part Two

Organization of the City

3.

INTERNAL STRUCTURE OF THE METROPOLIS

Kent P. Schwirian

For many decades sociologists have been fascinated with the patterns of life, behavior, and organization found in the metropolis. Robert Park, one of the founding fathers of urban sociology, wrote in 1929, "For the city and the urban environment represent man's most consistent and, on the whole, his most successful attempt to remake the world he lives in more after his heart's desire. But if the city is the world which man created, it is the world in which he is henceforth condemned to live. Thus, indirectly and without any clear sense of the nature of his task, in making the city man has remade himself" [Park 1952, p. 73]. Prompted by Park's urging and motivated by his example, numerous sociologists, geographers, and economists have roamed cities around the globe in an attempt to describe and explain man's urban environment and his urban experience. In this chapter the focus is on some of the major, recent findings about the internal structure of the metropolis.

Urban density patterns as reflected in congestion and deconcentration are our starting point as we seek to discover how neighborhoods are established and how they change through time. Suburbanization, one of the most striking organizational trends of the twentieth century, is discussed in terms of the broad processes of metropolitan expansion and neighborhood change. A long-standing interest of students of the city has been the particular spatial geometry and regularity of land use and population distribution. Our discussion of urban spatial patterns is tied closely to the topic of social area analysis, in which empirical attempts to identify the basic dimensions of urban areal differentiations have focused on cities in developing and developed countries. Urban neighborhood structure is another topic of interest today as many social planners and critics of the city lament the "passing" of allegedly intimate, supportive neighborhood environments. The discussion concludes with a side glance at the urban land market. Usually viewed in terms of the impersonal processes of supply and demand, I suggest that from the sociological standpoint the land market really consists of established categories of groups and organizations that regularly interact in such a way as to determine the very form of the metropolis itself. Guided by differing value orientations these groups engage in competition, conflict, collusion, and cooperation to set the broad parameters within which individuals—you and I—must make their choice of housing as best they can to maximize their personal aspirations.

Much of the discussion focuses on data for cities in the developed world. While we may speculate on trends in developing societies, the available data are insufficient to permit a firm statement about patterns in such places. But it must be kept in mind that there is no guarantee that the traces of cities in the developing countries will be identical with those in the developed countries. We have come to know that there is no monolithic process of modernization that will make the Calcutta of today a Chicago of tomorrow. Different times, different technologies, and different cultural contacts and configurations give each city a unique history and future. Yet there are enough similarities for some general statements to be made and I do so where appropriate.

This chapter's topics are so intertwined that we could start anywhere in covering our ground. But we will start with congestion and deconcentration, which are two simple concepts that are really just tips of large icebergs that form the core of the internal structure of the metropolis.

CONGESTION AND DECONCENTRATION

There are two major sources of metropolitan population growth. One is net in-migration and the other is natural increase, which refers to the difference between the number of births and deaths in the community's population per year. Historically, metropolitan areas have grown principally by net in-migration, but in recent years a larger proportion of their growth has been a result of natural increase. Regardless of its source, community population growth must be accommodated by changes in the existing residential structure. Two basic dimensions of residential structure in which the accommodation of population growth is manifest are *congestion* and *deconcentration* [Winsborough 1963]. Congestion refers to the average number of persons per square mile in the urban core whereas deconcentration refers to the rate at which density falls off with increasing distance from the city's center. Deconcentration measures how compact the population distribution is. Congestion and deconcentration may be derived from the distance-density curve for a city.

In figure 1 a fairly typical density curve for a major metropolitan area is shown. On the vertical axis the number of persons per square mile is plotted, on the horizontal axis the distance from the city's center is plotted. Each neighborhood in the city is plotted by its distance and its density. The curve in figure 1 represents a general summary of how the neighborhoods are distributed by these two characteristics. The curve tells us that the areas in the center of the city have much higher density than those at the periphery. The J-shape of the curve tells us that while

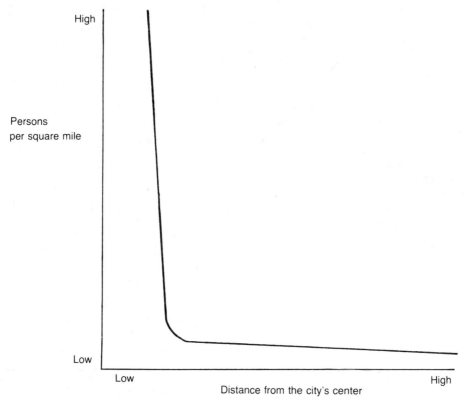

Fig. 1. Population Density and Distance from the Center of the City

for neighborhoods in the urban core density declines very rapidly with increasing distance, the picture is somewhat different at the city's edge where increasing distance is accompanied by very little decline in density. The shape of this curve is called a negative exponential. It is *negative* because it tells us that distance and density are inversely related; that is, as one increases the other decreases. Thus, the greater the distance, the less the density. It is *exponential* because of the nature of the mathematical function relating density to distance. The formula for this curve is

$$D_x = D_o e^{-bx}$$

where D_x is the density at distance x miles; D_o is the central density of the city extrapolated from the curve; b is the change in density per change in mile distance; and e is the natural logarithmic base. The value of D_o is an index of the degree of congestion, while the b measures deconcentration. This may more easily be seen if the density-distance

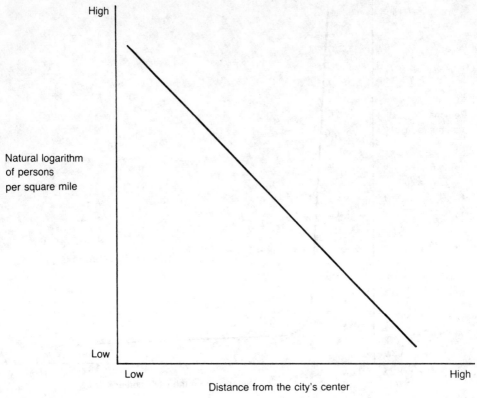

Fig. 2. Population Density in Natural Logs and Distance from the City's Center

curve is expressed in a linear form. The conversion from the negative exponential curve to a linear form is accomplished by plotting the neighborhood density values in their natural log form. Thus the curve is transformed as shown in figure 2. It is now described by the formula

$$lnD_x = lnD_o + bx$$

The lnD_o gives us the Y axis intercept of the curve and is an indication of central congestion, or the expected number of persons at ground zero, the urban core. The b gives us the slope of the curve and an index of deconcentration, which tells us how rapidly density declines with distance. As D_o values increase, congestion increases. As the b values decrease, the curve becomes flatter and deconcentration increases. Compare cities A and B in figure 3. City A is both more congested and more concentrated than city B. In city A the central density is fairly high, while the curve is very steep. Its high density is fairly well contained over a short distance. In city B the central congestion is fairly low and there seem to be only minor decreases in density moving from the center to the periphery.

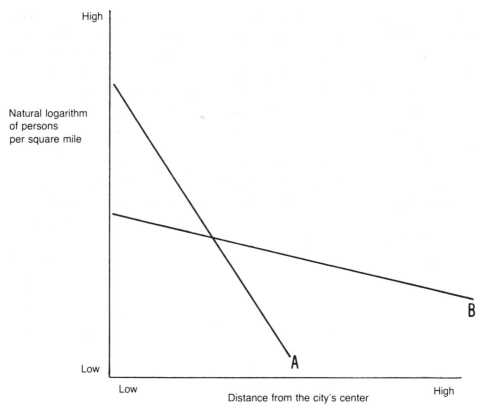

Fig. 3. Density-Distance Curves for Two Cities

The form (negative exponential) of the density-distance curve seems to hold for cities in both developed and developing societies [Berry, Simmons, & Tennant 1963]. However *absolute levels* of congestion and deconcentration vary considerably between cities at any one point in time. For example, in 1960 Los Angeles had a central density of 7,900 people per mile while New Orleans' congestion was almost four times greater— over 30,000 persons per square mile. Also, the degree of concentration of New Orleans' population was about thirteen times greater than that of Los Angeles. Thus, in 1960 New Orleans was much more congested and concentrated than Los Angeles.

A number of studies have tried to discover the factors associated with differences among cities in congestion and deconcentration. There seems to be agreement that one very important factor explaining differences among cities is age of city; or, in effect, the period in which the cities grew rapidly in population [Berry, Simmons, & Tennant 1963; Guest 1973; Muth 1969]. Cities that grew early—before 1880—had very inefficient transportation systems, which precluded the spread of the population in very low density patterns. They absorbed their growing populations by increasing both congestion and concentration. More recent urban growth has been altered by the development of the streetcar, rapid train, and automobile, which have stimulated accelerated deconcentration in both the old and new cities. Consequently the older cities reached higher congestion and concentration levels than did the newer.

While congestion and concentration vary among cities at any one point in time, congestion and deconcentration levels for individual cities vary through time as well. The residential structure of the metropolis is constantly responding to new housing demands generated by population changes. Changes in both congestion and deconcentration reflect this response. However, congestion and deconcentration need not change together. Each is a separate response to a number of factors impinging on the urban land market. For example, in a study of Chicago's development, Hal Winsborough [1963] reports that the population growth of the city has been accommodated by a continued deconcentration since 1860. Congestion increased steadily between 1860 and 1900. However, since 1920 congestion has declined continuously.

TABLE 1. Population Congestion* and Concentration in Selected U.S. Metropolitan Areas

COMMUNITY	1950		1960		Change 1960/1950	
	Congestion	Concen-tration	Congestion	Concen-tration	Congestion	Concen-tration
Boston	33.6	−.23	24.2	−.18	.72	.78
Chicago	74.1	−.15	56.0	−.12	.76	.80
Cleveland	28.4	−.30	18.2	−.20	.64	.67
Detroit	40.2	−.20	18.8	−.10	.47	.50
Fort Worth	8.4	−.25	5.5	−.13	.65	.52
Los Angeles	11.8	−.07	7.9	−.02	.67	.28
New Orleans	42.7	−.56	30.1	−.38	.70	.68
Richmond	18.8	−.40	12.5	−.26	.66	.65
San Diego	10.0	−.13	9.8	−.10	.98	.77
Washington	12.8	−.18	6.6	−.06	.52	.33

*Congestion values are in 1,000 of persons per square mile.
Source: Guest 1973, p. 65.

More recent changes in congestion and deconcentration for several U.S. cities may be seen in table 1. For all of the key metropolises congestion decreased between 1950 and 1960. Indeed the 1960 levels of congestion for most of the cities were only about two-thirds to three-fourths of what they were in 1950. Similarly, all of the communities deconcentrated in the ten-year period. Levels of concentration for most cities in 1960 were only between one-half and three-quarters of their 1950 levels.

Three major factors seem to govern the rates at which congestion and concentration levels change for cities. They are   1. the general growth context,   2. the spatial configuration of the metropolis, and   3. the prevailing modes of transportation. The general growth context refers to two major components—population growth per se and the rate of construction of new dwelling units. Rapid deconcentration requires a growing population that increases the demand for housing. Unless new housing is constructed at a pace comparable to that of population growth, much of the incremental population must be housed in the existing housing stock. The net result implies an increase in congestion. However, fast-paced construction of additional dwelling units, most of which are located in the newly developing fringe areas of the metropolis, permit and actually encourage deconcentration of metropolitan populations. Periods in which construction of new dwellings were at a low point, as during the first half of the 1940s, were also periods of residential piling-up in our growing metropolises [Duncan, Sabagh, & Van Arsdol 1962].

The spatial configuration of the metropolis in terms of its overall population size and aggregate density seems to exert effects on changes in concentration and congestion over and above those of the general growth context. High-density central cities are those with the more rapid deconcentration. It seems that such places are residentially saturated and, therefore, additional population find the preponderance of housing opportunities at the periphery. Large cities have somewhat lower rates of deconcentration. Residence at the periphery in such agglomerations means much higher travel costs in time and money than it does in smaller metropolitan complexes.

The role of transportation in deconcentration is critical. Extensive deconcentration is possible only when the transit mode is efficient enough to move large numbers of people reliably over long distances in comparatively short times. In developed societies the streetcar, the train, the automobile, and the limited-access highway have each made it possible for metropolitan population growth to be channeled into the expanding fringe. Each development in urban transportation mode has made continued deconcentration a reality. However, as our freeways become clogged and as automobile fuel becomes less available and more costly, we may see a decline in the rates of deconcentration of our largest communities. On the other hand, if employment activities, services, shopping, and important institutions continue to deconcentrate themselves, we may see a lessened need for the metropolitanite to be close to the actual urban core, which could result in another spurt in deconcentration. Some students of the city see this increased nucleation and decentralization of activity centers as a very likely accompaniment of future metropolitan development.

While the long-run trend in the developed societies has been toward decongestion and deconcentration, the pattern seems to be somewhat different in the newly developing societies. Large metropolitan centers in the developing countries annually experience large population increases but, by and large, housing construction has been inadequate to meet the increasing demand. Furthermore, the transportation system has not been sufficiently adequate to make rapid deconcentration possible. Inadequate mass transit, low rates of automobile ownership, poor highway systems, and insufficient housing construction have resulted in continuously increasing central density, a constant density-distance gradient, and a low rate of peripheral expansion [Berry, Simmons, & Tennant 1963]. Thus the long-run trend in the developing countries has been increasing metropolitan congestion and fairly constant residential concentration. These trends are likely to continue in the absence of any radical change in the growth context or transportation systems of these countries.

The broad picture that emerges from analyses of changing congestion and concentration both in the developed and developing societies is that, in the long run, metropolitan population growth is residentially accommodated by outward expansion into the fringe until such deconcentration begins to interfere significantly with internal transportation and communication. When this disruption becomes sufficiently dysfunctional for normal, necessary activities, further population growth is accommodated by increasing congestion of the existing settlement. Further deconcentration must await improvements in the transportation system and accelerated rates of new housing construction.

The characteristic J or negative exponential form of the density-distance curve results from the interplay of supply and demand in the urban land market. Explanations of density patterns usually focus on the concepts of *accessibility, competition, costs,* and *equilibrium.* Every parcel of land in the city can be assigned an accessibility rating in terms of its distance from the center of the city. Obviously, land that is close-in is highly accessible, whereas land that is at a great distance is highly inaccessible. Accessible land is highly valued since it allows the user to minimize his transportation costs in both time and money. Since transportation costs are minimized by central location, there is an enormous demand among land users for accessible parcels. However, the amount of highly accessible land is limited. For example, within a one mile diameter of the urban core there is 0.8 square miles of land. Between one and two miles there is 2.4 square miles and between two and three miles there is 3.9 miles. Thus greater quantities of land are available as distance from the city's center increases. The stiff *competition* for the highly accessible limited land means that costs for large parcels run very high. Only by intensive use of this accessible land can the costs per individual user be economically feasible. High-intensity use of core land means high central densities. The lesser competition for the fringe land means a much less intensive use, which results in lower density.

Each land user, whether a family seeking a residence or a firm seeking an office, must balance space needs against transportation costs. The intensive competition for central land raises space costs but minimizes transportation costs; at the periphery space costs are reduced but transportation costs are elevated. Each individual user must combine the two costs into a *total cost* factor. Some users are willing to incur high space costs and others are more willing to trade transportation costs for space. The density-distance pattern for a city is an aggregate result of the attempts of users to minimize both space and transportation costs. The result is frequently referred to as a *spatial equilibrium*.

DENSITY AND SOCIAL CLASS

While variations in neighborhood gross density levels are associated with distance from the metropolitan core, distance by itself in most communities explains only a minor part of the variation among neighborhoods in their density levels. In a study of thirty-seven major U.S. metropolitan areas, Avery Guest [1973] has shown that distance explained one-quarter or less of the variation in density in the majority of the cities. In only five communities was 50 percent or more of the variation in density among neighborhoods a function of distance. Clearly, then, other factors must help explain differences in neighborhood densities. One of these factors is the social status of the area's population.

In a study of four major Latin American cities—Bogotá, Quito, Lima, and Santiago—Peter Amato [1970] has shown that, in general, there is a tendency for the middle classes to live under the highest densities. However, once distance from the city's center is taken into account a fairly negative linear association results. In each city the highest class lives under the lowest density and the lowest class lives under some of the highest density. In a distance-controlled study of U.S. cities Anthony La Greca and Kent Schwirian [1974] also reported a significant negative relationship between people per acre and social status for Buffalo, Milwaukee, San Diego, and Portland. Thus, for some cities at least, social status does seem to be related to density independently of neighborhood location.

The number of people per unit area (gross density) may be viewed as a function of two major components. The first is the intensity of dwelling units. Areas of the city cluttered with high-rise apartment buildings record very large numbers of dwelling units per acre. Areas settled with single-family homes on large lots usually have comparatively few dwellings per acre. The second component is the intensity with which dwellings are used. Measures of this include household size and number of persons per room. At comparable levels of number of dwelling units per acre, those neighborhoods with larger household sizes and more people per room record higher gross densities than do those with smaller households and fewer persons per room. Variations in gross densities among urban areas, then, reflect differences in the number of dwelling units per acre, dwelling unit vacancy rates, average household size, and rates of crowding (more than 1.01 persons per room). Changes in density through time for individual areas reflect change in one or more of these factors.

Explanations for the decreasing congestion, or central density, for cities in developed societies must answer the following questions: 1. To what extent has a decline in the total number of dwelling units taken place as a result of demolitions and recombinations of formerly separate dwelling units once subdivided? 2. To what extent has higher vacancy rates contributed to a decline in gross density in the older, run-down areas? 3. To what extent has declining household size contributed to a lessening congestion as families pass into the later stages of their life cycle and the children leave home? 4. To what extent has crowding decreased by either or both a decrease in average household size or an increase in the average size of dwelling unit?

In analyzing the recent change in these components for several metropolitan areas, Roy Treadway [1969] has concluded that the loosening of the housing market along with an increasing family size has meant that population decline in the city's center took place through demolition or consolidation of existing units, increased rates of dwelling vacancy, and smaller household size. The demand for poor quality, centralized housing declined and more smaller households were formed by people who had previously lived in other households. In the fringe areas, population increase was promoted primarily by the construction of large quantities of new housing units. The net effect of these changes was accelerated deconcentration.

Since both neighborhood distance from the city's center and the social status of the local population are related to gross density we would expect them to be related to the components of density as well. Treadway [1969] has reported that: **1.** Distance is negatively related to single-unit density; **2.** vacancies are not consistently related to distance—in some metropolitan areas high vacancy rates are reported in the declining inner sections as well as in the rapidly expanding fringe where housing construction is proceeding at a faster pace than population growth; **3.** distance is positively related to household size. Thus the further out an area is, the larger the average size of the household but the fewer the number of households per unit area.

In another study with the effect of distance controlled La Greca and Schwirian [1974] report that for several cities social status is negatively related to the number of dwelling units per area. Thus at any given distance from the city's center, the higher the population's social status the fewer the number of dwelling units per acre. They also report that with distance controlled, the higher the social status the fewer people there are per room. Thus, over and above the effect of distance it seems that higher social class is associated with less intensive dwelling unit density and lower intensity of use of individual dwelling units. Undoubtedly a key factor in the differences among social status groups in their crowding rates is the ability of the middle- and upper-status groups to acquire larger (in terms of number of rooms) dwelling units.

NEIGHBORHOOD LIFE CYCLE

In addition to its distance from the city's center and the social status of its population, the age of a neighborhood is also related to density patterns. Neighborhoods seldom remain stable in terms of population, housing, and social composition of the residents. Change in these factors for individual areas is much more the rule than the exception. Edgar Hoover and Raymond Vernon [1962] have suggested that there is a general life-cycle process that may be used to characterize patterns of neighborhood change. The stages in the life cycle are: *residential development, transition, downgrading, thinning-out,* and *renewal.*

Residential development is the earliest stage. New residential con-

struction is begun on previously undeveloped land. For many urban neighborhoods the initial development of an area takes the form of construction
of single-family dwellings. However, some areas initially develop in multifamily units. Very rapid population growth is associated with this first
stage. Vacancies may be above the average because the rate of dwelling
construction necessarily runs ahead of population growth. Vacancies are
usually of short duration.

The *transition* stage is characterized by both substantial new construction and population growth, the net effect of which is to increase
the gross density over what it was during residential development. Much
of the new housing construction is in the form of multiple dwelling units.
In fact, these new units appear on previously undeveloped lots or as
replacements for some of the older single-family homes. Thus the neighborhood shifts from a single-family to an apartment-housing pattern. The
more intensive land use of such areas is frequently a result of change
in the neighborhood's ecological niche in the city. Perhaps the area was
located at the fringe in the period of residential development, but through
continued deconcentration and building beyond it the area may now have
become comparatively much more accessible to the urban core; or it could
be that the neighborhood is located close to a large, expanding institution
such as a major university or medical complex. It could be also, that
a modification of the city's road or rail transportation system has opened
the area to greater commuting potentials. Thus the demand for local
housing is greatly increased and a more intensive use of land results.

The prospect of a neighborhood moving from its initial stage of development into the transition stage can sometimes be quite alarming to some
residents, who see the prospect of such change as destructive to the
essential character of the area. Sometimes the fears of the residents
can be galvanized into collective social action aimed at prohibiting the
incursion of the multiple dwellings. In a study of Boston's Beacon Hill,
Walter Firey [1947] details the long-run pattern of resistance to transition. Located near the heart of central Boston's retailing, the area has
been maintained as an upper-class residential center while most of the
areas around it have declined or been radically redeveloped. The area
was residentially developed in the early 1800s as an upper-class neighborhood. Through the years the area has come to symbolize an ambiance
that is highly prized, even idealized, in some circles. The dogged attachment of the residents to its maintenance in the face of constant pressure
of invasion by business or apartment and hotel activities has resulted
in an atypical degree of collective social actions by its residents. In 1922

the Beacon Hill Association was formed to be the guardians of the status quo. Since then the association and other groups have been sufficiently influential in local zoning matters to preserve the essential character of the area. Thus while neighborhood transition would be of considerable economic gain to certain interests the local residents in this instance have been able to blunt serious attempts to change the area radically. It should certainly be noted that not all neighborhoods have resisted transition as successfully as Beacon Hill, and of those that have had some success, it seldom has reached the degree attained by the socially prominent Bostonians.

Downgrading is the third stage of the neighborhood life cycle. In this period the neighborhood may actually lose a number of dwelling units through demolition, accidental destruction, abandonment, or conversion to business uses. Other older housing units—both single family and multiple dwelling—are converted to greater use than was originally intended for them. Very little new construction takes place and much of the area may experience a "slum invasion," since the physical conditions of the dwellings become deteriorated or dilapidated. Unfortunately most financial inducements tend to encourage slum development. Many slum owners enjoy a financial advantage for maintaining deteriorated housing through tax write-offs, low taxes on the deteriorated structures, almost no improvement expenditures, and high income return from the large number of renters in the crowded structures. Attempts by the renters to achieve redress of their grievances usually are met with frustration and failure. Sometimes it is impossible for renters actually to identify the property owners [Hough 1970]. Such slum landlords are masters at hiding behind jungles of rental agents, amorphous corporate structures, and red tape that serve to discourage even the most dogged attempts to pressure them into fulfilling their legal obligations to maintain decent housing standards. Attempts to form effective tenant organizations and neighborhood collective-action groups have met with only limited success in some cities. Such groups require energetic, capable leaders. All too often, these leaders, because of their personal competence, become socially mobile and move from the area, leaving behind them an organization in the hands of the less capable. Of those who stay, many are defeated by the protracted war of attrition waged by the slumlords. With little real help from city hall and the federal agencies, frustration, fatigue, and defeat are the usual "rewards" for their backbreaking efforts.

Neighborhood density usually peaks during the downgrading stage. The subdivision of existing structures produces greatly inflated numbers of housing units per structure. During downgrading the average number of persons per housing unit usually rises as well. This results from the larger households that arrive and take up residence in the area. Many of the newcomers are fresh migrants to the city. They typically have low income, poor knowledge of the city's housing market, uncertain employment prospects, and may be members of minority groups discriminated against in the housing market. Typically the newcomers are also fairly young couples with growing families. It is not uncommon for them to take in relatives or lodgers who are seeking to become established in the city. Thus the large numbers of young families with sundry additional household members serve to elevate local densities to all-time highs. Through their intensive use of the poorly maintained rental structures they exacerbate the problem of local physical deterioration.

Thinning-out is the next stage in the neighborhood life cycle. Both population density and dwelling occupancy decline in this period. The major mechanism by which the decline occurs is reduction in household size. The families in the area have reached the later phases of their own life cycle. The children have left or are leaving home. Higher mortality rates characterize this somewhat older population; and formerly subdivided dwellings are being merged as vacancy rates begin to rise. Building abandonment spreads and dangerous structures are demolished. Some abandoned blocks become DMZs—no-man's-lands—inhabited only by rats, roaches, drifters, and furtive subterranean denizens.

Renewal is the final life-cycle stage. Renewal involves the massive rebuilding of deteriorated areas. Old structures are leveled and new ones take their place. Most typically, renewal involves the rebuilding of the neighborhood in multifamily structures. While the housing quality is improved, the neighborhood density may remain what it was prior to renewal or it may increase somewhat. However, whatever density gain results, it usually does not reach the level recorded during downgrading.

The history of renewal has been tempestuous. While it has made positive gains in upgrading the face of the city a number of critics have argued that renewal has not helped in solving the housing problems of the needy and the large urban minorities. Both groups are caught in the crunch of our housing inadequacies. The housing problem for them is one of both quantity and quality. Not enough housing is available; that which is available needs upgrading desperately. In what ways has renewal failed these people? First, many critics point out that too much of the redeveloped area is put into nonresidential uses. The original redevelopment plan was to permit only 10 percent of the redeveloped areas to be converted into nonresidential development, but over the years this figure has risen to 40 percent. Urban renewal land is frequently cluttered with motels, freeways, commercial buildings, and civic structures. Another criticism is that renewal subtracts from the city's stock of the low-income housing while adding housing for middle- and upper-income groups. Swank apartments and condominiums dot the sites where the poor, the black, and the Spanish-speaking previously had huddled. But what of renewal's low-income housing, which frequently take the form of massive apartment projects? Some argue that all that has resulted is the piling-up of the poor into aesthetically sterile, vapid, dreary towers that have done little to improve the human condition. One of the best known failures of public housing has been St. Louis's Pruitt-Igoe development. The project, which was first occupied in 1954, was to be the lodestar of urban redevelopment. On a 57-acre tract, 33 eleven-story buildings with over 2,700 apartments were to have a variety of black and white families [Rainwater 1970]. However, a combination of physical oversights and failures and social traumas resulted in the abandonment and demolition of much of the development in less than 20 years. The project had become a professional embarrassment for those who planned the project and a personal tragedy for those residents scarred by their tenure there. The initial construction produced elevators that stopped only at the fourth, seventh, and tenth floors, exposed elevator shafts, and exposed steam pipes. Through its history there was inadequate maintenance so that broken glass, garbage, and other refuse littered the site. Inadequate security resulted in unsafe halls, elevators, and laundry rooms, where muggings, rapes, and molestings were not uncommon. Halls and elevators were used for bodily elimination; and the pathologies of many individuals lacking personal resources to cope with the pressures of poverty, broken families, and a threatening environment went unchecked. The project became a collage of the downtrodden and the desperate. Its demolition may have removed Prutt-Igoe's failure from view but it did not solve the very human problems of its former residents.

The neighborhood life-cycle concept posits that density, dwellings, and the local population of urban areas regularly change through time as areas age and move from stage to stage. Even a casual acquaintance with urban areas makes one realize that not all neighborhoods pass through all of the life-cycle stages. Some, for various reasons, may pass through a few of the stages and then become fixed. Others may pass through more stages. Furthermore, the rates at which areas pass through the various stages vary considerably. Several major factors are influential in dictating the life-cycle process. One of these is *housing supply*. The city's housing stock changes at different rates in different time periods and these rates of change directly affect the manner in which metropolitan population growth is accommodated. Thus, pressures for neighborhood change are, to some extent, affected by the relative rates of growth of new housing to population gain.

Access is another factor affecting the operation of the life cycle. Access involves both the proximity of employment opportunities and the mode of transportation. A change in either transportation or employment opportunities will be felt across the whole city. Some areas will become relatively more accessible to jobs through such changes and will become the objects of fierce competition in the urban land and housing market. The third major factor is the social characteristics of the residents in terms of income, age, leisure activities, prejudice against or acceptance of specific minorities, and degree of local attachments. As we saw in the Beacon Hill case, the extent to which people mobilize responses in order to maintain or direct neighborhood change can have a profound effect on life-cycle operation.

The concept of the life cycle does not represent an ironclad law describing how all neighborhoods change and specifying the stages through which they will pass. Rather, it provides us with a refracting prism to help us reasonably sort out the seemingly diverse and chaotic patterns of neighborhood change. Not all neighborhoods change in the manner predicted by the life-cycle model, but all neighborhoods are subject to the forces that lead to temporal transition. A most challenging area for research today is the process of neighborhood change, and many investigators find it intellectually profitable to start with the life-cycle model.

SUBURBANIZATION

The deconcentration of activities and population from the city to the adjacent fringe areas is called suburbanization. Among the most dramatic results of urban sprawl are the conversion of once agricultural land into residential villages and industrial uses and the transformation of established agricultural villages into metropolitan suburban centers. The term *suburb* is used in a number of ways, but in this chapter we will restrict its use to refer to settlements of urban density located near a very large metropolitan center. Suburbs may be politically incorporated units or unincorporated developments. All suburban communities are socially and economically interdependent with the nearby city. Their populations are urban and not rural in character; their economies are nonagricultural; their social structures reflect their interdependency with the adjacent city; and their residents usually identify with both their suburb and the city.

Although suburbanization is not a new phenomenon for American metropolitan areas, fringe growth since the end of World War II has been most striking. We use the term *fringe growth* here to refer to those portions of the metropolitan population residentially located outside of the city. In 1950, 13.9 percent of the U.S. population lived in the fringe of our Urbanized Areas. By 1970 this figure had risen to 26.8 percent. In the same period the percentage of the U.S. population that was classified as rural declined from 36.0 to 26.5 percent. Thus, we have slightly more people in the fringe of our Urbanized Areas than we do in our rural areas. Also by 1970, 31.4 percent of the U.S. population was in the central cities of our Urbanized Areas while 15.1 percent was located in our remaining urban settlements. The term *Urbanized Area* has been discussed thoroughly in other chapters of this book [Gibbs; Smith & Weller] but basically it refers to at least one central city of 50,000 or more population plus all of the nearby urban, densely settled area with at least 1,000 persons per square mile. *Urbanized Area* is not to be confused with *Standard Metropolitan Statistical Area* (SMSA), which is an alternative operationalization of the concept of metropolitan community. The SMSAs consist of entire counties and groups of counties. A SMSA has at least one central city of 50,000 or more inhabitants, plus all of its county, plus all of the surrounding counties that are socially and economically interdependent with the central city. Using total counties, the SMSA usually includes some agricultural and nonsuburban small town population in addition to the city and the suburban components. For the purposes of this chapter we shall focus on the Urbanized Area rather than the SMSA since the fringe population of the Urbanized Area is unambiguously suburban while that is not true of the SMSA. Thus when we talk of suburban growth we refer to the growth that takes place in the fringe adjacent to the central city.

The growth of our suburban population has been accompanied by a *net redistribution* of our metropolitan population. While the population of American Urbanized Areas increased by almost one-fourth between 1960 and 1970, the population of the central cities increased by only 10 percent, and that of the suburban fringe showed a gain of 44 percent. In 1960 approximately 40 percent of the metropolitan population was located in the fringe; by 1970 the figure had risen to 46 percent. By 1980 there will, in all probability, be more of the metropolitan population in the fringes than in the central cities. Thus the metropolitan communities are experiencing a net shift of the locus of the population. A large part of the net shift reflects migration of city residents to the fringe. But it also reflects the growth of the suburban population by higher rates of natural increase (births-minus-deaths) than the city population and the tendency for migrants to the metropolitan area to settle initially in the fringe rather than the central city. Consequently, we have annual rates of growth of the suburban population that exceed those of the cities. The long-run consequence of these growth differentials is the net redistribution of the metropolitan population from the city to the suburbs.

While the total population of the combined central cities of our Urbanized Areas has increased, there are many individual cities that have actually lost population while their fringes were growing. Table 2 provides data on city and suburban fringe growth of our largest Urbanized Areas. The figures show that cities that actually lost population between 1960 and 1970 were Chicago, Philadelphia, Detroit, Boston, Washington, Cleveland, St. Louis, Pittsburgh, Minneapolis-St. Paul, Baltimore, Milwaukee, Seattle, Cincinnati, and Buffalo. By 1970 many metropolitan areas had more of their population in the suburban fringe than in the central city. These included Los Angeles-Long Beach, Philadelphia, Detroit, San Francisco, Boston, Washington, Cleveland, St. Louis, Pittsburgh, Minneapolis-St. Paul, Seattle-Everett, Miami, Atlanta, Cincinnati, Kansas City, Buffalo, Denver, and San Jose.

TABLE 2. Population of Major U.S. Urbanized Areas and Their Components for 1960, 1970, and Change 1960-1970

COMMUNITY	1970 Population	Percentage	1960 Population	Percentage	Percentage of Change 1960–1970
New York	16,206,841	100.0	14,114,006	100.0	14.8
Central Cities	8,820,209	54.4	8,743,015	61.9	0.9
Clifton	82,437	0.5	82,084	0.6	0.4
Jersey City	260,545	1.6	276,101	2.0	−5.6
Newark	382,417	2.4	405,220	2.9	−5.6
New York	7,894,862	48.7	7,781,984	55.1	1.5
Passaic	55,124	0.3	53,963	0.4	2.2
Patterson	144,824	0.9	143,663	1.0	0.8
Fringe	7,386,632	45.6	5,370,991	38.1	37.5
Los Angeles-Long Beach	8,351,266	100.0	6,675,338	100.0	25.1
Central Cities	3,620,520	43.4	2,936,957	44.0	23.3
Anaheim	166,701	2.0	*		--
Garden Grove	122,524	1.5	*		--

TABLE 2 (continued)

COMMUNITY	1970 Population	Percentage	1960 Population	Percentage	Percentage of Change 1960–1970
Long Beach	358,633	4.3	344,168	5.2	4.2
Los Angeles	2,816,061	33.7	2,479,015	37.1	13.6
Ontario	*		46,617	0.7	--
Pomona	*		67,157	1.0	--
Santa Ana	156,601	1.9	*		--
Fringe	4,730,746	56.6	3,738,381	56.0	26.5
Chicago	6,714,578	100.0	5,961,634	100.0	12.6
Central Cities	3,697,144	55.1	3,898,091	65.4	-5.2
Fringe	3,017,434	44.9	2,663,543	34.6	46.2
Philadelphia	4,021,066	100.0	3,635,228	100.0	10.6
Central City	1,948,609	48.5	2,002,512	55.1	-2.7
Fringe	2,072,457	51.5	1,632,716	44.9	26.9
Detroit	3,970,584	100.0	3,538,495	100.0	12.2
Central City	1,511,482	38.1	1,670,144	47.2	-9.5
Fringe	2,459,102	61.9	1,868,351	52.8	31.6
San Francisco	2,987,850	100.0	2,395,098	100.0	24.7
Central Cities	1,143,968	38.3	1,107,864	46.3	3.3
Fringe	1,843,882	61.7	1,287,234	53.7	43.2
Boston	2,652,575	100.0	2,413,236	100.0	9.9
Central Cities	641,071	24.2	697,197	28.9	-8.1
Fringe	2,011,504	75.8	1,716,039	71.1	17.2
Washington	2,481,489	100.0	1,808,423	100.0	37.2
Central City	756,510	30.5	763,956	42.2	-1.0
Fringe	1,724,979	69.5	1,044,467	57.8	65.2
Cleveland	1,959,880	100.0	1,783,436	100.0	9.9
Central City	750,903	38.3	876,050	49.1	-14.3
Fringe	1,208,977	61.7	907,386	50.9	33.2
St. Louis	1,882,944	100.0	1,667,693	100.0	12.9
Central City	622,236	33.0	750,026	45.0	-17.0
Fringe	1,260,708	67.0	917,667	55.0	37.4
Pittsburgh	1,846,042	100.0	1,805,310	100.0	2.3
Central City	520,117	28.2	604,332	33.5	-13.9
Fringe	1,325,925	71.8	1,200,978	66.5	10.4
Minneapolis-St. Paul	1,704,423	100.0	1,377,143	100.0	23.8
Central City	744,380	43.7	796,283	57.8	-6.5
Fringe	960,043	56.3	580,860	42.2	65.3
Houston	1,677,863	100.0	1,138,819	100.0	47.3
Central City	1,231,394	73.4	938,214	82.4	31.2
Fringe	446,469	26.6	200,600	17.6	122.6
Baltimore	1,579,781	100.0	1,418,948	100.0	11.3
Central City	905,759	57.3	939,024	66.2	-3.6
Fringe	674,022	42.7	479,924	33.8	40.4
Dallas	1,338,684	100.0	932,349	100.0	43.6
Central City	844,401	63.1	679,684	72.9	24.2
Fringe	494,283	36.9	252,665	27.1	95.6

TABLE 2 (continued)

COMMUNITY	1970 Population	Percentage	1960 Population	Percent-age	Percentage of Change 1960–1970
Milwaukee	1,252,457	100.0	1,149,997	100.0	8.9
Central City	717,099	57.3	741,324	64.5	−3.3
Fringe	535,358	42.7	408,673	35.3	31.0
Seattle-Everett	1,238,107	100.0	864,109	100.0	43.3
Central Cities	584,453	47.2	557,087	78.8	−4.7**
Fringe	653,654	52.8	307,022	21.2	112.9
Miami	1,219,661	100.0	852,705	100.0	43.0
Central City	334,859	27.5	291,688	34.2	14.8
Fringe	884,802	72.5	561,017	65.8	57.7
San Diego	1,198,323	100.0	836,175	100.0	43.3
Central City	693,931	57.9	573,224	68.6	21.1
Fringe	504,392	42.1	262,951	31.4	91.8
Atlanta	1,172,778	100.0	768,125	100.0	52.7
Central City	496,973	42.4	487,455	63.5	2.0
Fringe	675,805	57.6	280,670	36.5	140.8
Cincinnati	1,110,514	100.0	993,568	100.0	11.8
Central City	452,524	40.7	502,550	50.6	−10.0
Fringe	657,990	59.3	491,018	49.4	34.0
Kansas City	1,101,787	100.0	921,121	100.0	19.6
Central City	501,859	45.5	475,539	51.6	5.5
Fringe	599,928	54.5	445,582	48.4	34.6
Buffalo	1,086,594	100.0	1,054,370	100.0	3.1
Central City	462,768	42.6	532,759	50.5	−13.1
Fringe	623,826	57.4	521,611	49.5	19.6
Denver	1,047,311	100.0	803,624	100.0	30.3
Central City	514,678	49.1	493,887	61.5	4.2
Fringe	532,633	50.9	309,737	38.5	72.0
San Jose	1,025,273	100.0	602,805	100.0	70.1
Central City	443,950	43.3	204,196	33.9	117.4
Fringe	581,323	56.7	398,609	66.1	45.8

*City not a central city that year   **Seattle only

Source: *1970 Census of Population, Number of Inhabitants, U.S. Summary PC(1) A-1,* (Washington, D.C.: U.S. Bureau of the Census, Dept. of Commerce). Table 20; "Population and Land Area of Urbanized Areas: 1970 and 1960."

As the populations of many metropolitan areas have decentralized so, too, have many industrial and commercial activities. Before the emergent supremacy of the motor truck, industries found it necessary to be located near centralized rail and dock terminal facilities in the urban core. Now the super highway and trucking technology have freed many manufacturing activities from the congestion, dirt, and outmoded facilities of the inner city allowing them to relocate in new fringe areas that are made highly accessible by the network of metropolitan highways. These fringe locations have proved a boon to management personnel whose commuter time is greatly reduced by the elimination of their daily run to the central city. The fringe location has proved to be much less beneficial to the urban blacks and low-income white employees who are unable to find adequate residential accommodations in the fringe. Thus, they must make the tedious trip out from the inner city to work in the fringe while hordes of fringe dwellers take to the freeways each morning for their nerve-jangling trip into the urban core. The net result is an enormous, twice-a-day cross-hauling each way. In such large metropolitan communities as Chicago the freeways are clogged both ways morning and night. Truly, like ships that pass in the night, the fringe dweller employed in the city and the city dweller employed in the fringe inhabit social worlds that regularly touch but never interpenetrate.

Retailing activities have been shifting from the core as well. The suburban shopping center has broken the suburban consumers' dependence on the Central Business District (CBD). While taking business away from the inner-city merchants, the shopping centers actually have extended the influence of the metropolis to farther segments of the hinterland than was possible when retailing was exclusively centralized downtown [Mark & Schwirian 1967]. Figures for many small towns and independent cities within easy driving distance of the suburban shopping centers on high-speed highways radiating from the metropolis have shown an erosion of their trading function as well. While the short-run trade picture for these metropolitan neighbors might be bleak, past experience has shown that they will quite likely experience a renaissance in the long run as the metropolis expands into the agricultural hinterland, converting previously rural communities into metropolitan suburbs or employing satellites.

The decentralization of manufacturing and retailing means that dynamic growth nodes are now emerging in the suburban fringe. These dynamic centers are affecting the economy and demography of their fringe sector. They are becoming vast organizing factors in their own right. They are harbingers of a new pattern of metropolitan organization, one in which the economic and organizational dominance of the CBD is broken and replaced with a series of growth nodes acting as dynamic influences in their own right. A prime example of such a center is the northwestern Chicago suburbs adjacent to and near O'Hare International Airport. In the early 1950s O'Hare was little more than a typical declining military air base, but its development as Chicago's principal jetport along with the confluence at O'Hare of major spokes of the freeway system have resulted in the location of approximately 30 percent of all suburban office space in the area. Nearby, old residential suburbs have greatly expanded and new residential developments have appeared in what formerly were open fields. Slick retail operations have spread throughout the area and gigantic shopping complexes are emerging. This subregion of the Chicago metropolis has a dynamism all its own and has significant secondary and tertiary effects on the economy and social organization not only of the CBD but of the whole metropolitan region.

City governments have not stood by idly while their populations and economic activities have spilled across the urban political boundaries. To attempt to recapture their human and economic wealth some cities have launched annexation programs. Annexation is, in effect, the extension of the city's corporate limits into the previously unincorporated fringe. On occasion formerly independent fringe communities will merge with the city in its amebic expansion. Between 1950 and 1970 the 290 largest U.S. cities expanded the territory within their borders by about 105 percent. The cities of the South and the West recorded the largest expansion rates while the northeastern and north-central cities displayed comparatively less expansion. Table 3 shows the land area for 1950 and 1970 and the degree of expansion in that period for selected U.S. cities. A number of cities recorded gigantic gains—Huntsville City was over twenty seven times larger in territory in 1970 as compared with 1950 while Nashville was twenty three and Phoenix was about fifteen times larger. Among the large cities that showed little or no expansion during the period were New York, Los Angeles, Chicago, Detroit, Philadelphia, and New Orleans. Many cities more than doubled; they are Houston, Indianapolis, Kansas City, San Diego, Fort Worth, San Antonio, Tulsa, San Jose, Columbus, Atlanta, El Paso, Mobile, Columbia, and Corpus Christi.

Who gains from annexation? It is not always easy to tell. Cities expand their tax base by including residential, commercial, or industrial land. But sometimes the cost of building streets, sewage systems, and street lights, and of extending security, educational, and sanitation services more than offsets the gain in property taxes. By being included within the city, residents experience some change in their taxes but many claim that the promised services are not always delivered. Delivered services often are not of the quality and quantity that was anticipated initially. The pros and cons of annexation are many and the hassles between the city and the fringe are likely to continue since we seem to have basic normative constraints that prohibit the evolution of sound metropolitan administrative integration.

TABLE 3. Area of Major U.S. Cities 1950, 1970, and Change 1950–1970

City	Area In Square Miles		Area 1970/Area 1950
	1950	1970	
New York	300	300	1.00
Los Angeles	451	464	1.02
Chicago	208	223	1.07
Detroit	138	138	1.00
Philadelphia	129	129	1.00
New Orleans	205	205	1.00
Oklahoma City	51	648	12.71
Nashville	22	508	23.09
Houston	160	426	2.66
Indianapolis	55	392	7.13
Kansas City	81	316	3.90
Dallas	112	266	2.38
Phoenix	17	248	14.59
San Diego	99	241	2.43
Fort Worth	91	205	2.25
San Antonio	70	184	2.63
Tulsa	27	166	6.15
San Jose	17	137	8.06
Columbus, Ohio	39	135	3.46
Atlanta	37	132	3.57
El Paso	26	118	4.53
Mobile	25	117	4.68
Huntsville	4	109	27.25
Columbia, S.C.	13	104	8.00
Corpus Christi	22	101	4.59

Source: Richard L. Forstall, "Changes in Land Area for Larger Cities, 1950–1970." *The Municipal Year Book*, 1972 (Washington, D.C.: International City Management Association, 1972. See Table 6/5 "Selected Cities with over 100 Square Miles of Land Area in 1970 with Areas for 1950, 1960, 1970).

The deconcentration of the metropolitan population has been accompanied by an increasing social differentiation between city and fringe dwellers. Table 4 presents a comparison of city and fringe populations in a number of social characteristics. The data are for all U.S. Urbanized Areas in 1970. The figures show that the rate of growth of the fringe population is roughly four times that of the cities. The percentage of nonwhite population is much greater in the cities—22.5 percent—than it is in the fringe—5.7 percent. The fringe's population is younger than that of the city as indicated by the larger percentage of those who are under 18 years of age and by the smaller percentage of those who are over 65 years of age. A larger percentage of fringe females 14 years and over are married than of the city women, and fringe females are more fertile than city females. For every 100 fringe women of child-bearing age there are 342 young children. For the city women there are 336 young children per 1000 women. Fringe households tend to be larger than city households and there is a slight tendency for city women to have higher labor-force participation rates than fringe females. The education level of suburban males and females is higher than that of their city counterparts. Family incomes are, on the average, greater for the suburbanites. The higher education and income levels of the total suburban population is also observed among black and Spanish fringe residents as compared with black and Spanish city dwellers. Finally, the percentage of suburban males in high-status occupations is larger than that of city males. The general picture that emerges is that the suburban population, as compared with that of the cities, is less ethnic, higher status,and more traditional in terms of females' roles and behavior. This is true for both the white and minority members of the suburban population as compared with their city counterparts.

General statements about the differences in social characteristics between city and suburban residents must be made cautiously because su-

T A B L E 4 .   Social Characteristics of City and Fringe Populations of U.S. Urbanized Areas, 1970

Characteristic	City	Fringe
Percentage of population growth, 1960–1970	11.7	44.0
Percentage of population Negro and other races Nonwhite	22.5	5.7
Percentage of population under 18 years of age	31.5	35.4
Percentage of population 65 years of age and older	10.7	7.8
Fertility ratio	336.0	342.0
Percentage of females 14 years and older married	56.1	63.8
Average number of persons per household	2.90	3.25
Median number of school years completed by males 25 years of age and older	12.0	12.4
Median number of school years completed by females 25 years of age and older	12.0	12.3
Percentage of all population 25 years of age and older with 4 years of high school or 1–3 years of college completed	66.3	70.0
Percentage of females 16 years of age and older who are in the labor force	44.5	42.5
Percentage of males 16 years of age and older with occupations classified as professional, technical and kindred, and managers	22.8	27.9
Median family income	$9,519.00	$11,771.00
Median school years completed for Negro males 25 years of age and older	10.2	10.5
Median school years completed for Negro females 25 years of age and older	10.6	11.0
Median school years completed for males of Spanish heritage 25 years and older	9.7	11.8
Median school years completed for females of Spanish heritage 25 years and older	8.9	11.2
Median family income for Negroes	$6,792.00	$7,795.00
Median family income for those of Spanish heritage	$7,195.00	$9,609.00

Source: 1970 Census, *Characteristics of the Population, Vol. 1 U.S. Summary. Part 1, Section 1.* (Washington, D.C.: U.S. Government Printing Office). Tables 99, 101, 102, 119.

burbia is not a homogeneous, undifferentiated lot. There are fundamental differences among suburban communities in their function, and there are status, ethnic, and family characteristics associated with such functional differentiation. For many years students of the suburbs have noted that there appear to be two major types of suburbs, which can be identified by the functions they perform. These two types of suburban communities are the *employing satellites,* or suburbs of production, and the *residential suburbs,* or the "dormitory" towns [Schnore 1959]. Basically, employing satellites have employment as their key function in the pattern of metropolitan organization. Usually they have large manufacturing or trade operations and daily attract to the community commuters who are employed there on a regular basis. Satellites usually have residents of their own but their principal function is that of providing goods and services for nonlocal consumption. One example of a dynamic employing satellite is the Chicago fringe community of Elk Grove Village. The large Centex Industrial Park located there has formed the hub for the relatively recent location of some 500 new companies in the community [Berry & Cohen 1973]. In 1970 the population of Elk Grove Village was 21,907, which represented an increase of some 232 percent over 1960. While the community has a large and rapidly growing population of white, middle-status residents, it still draws each day a very large labor force employed in the many and varied economic activities.

Residential suburbs are communities of homeowners and, in some cases, renters. Economic activities found in them are mainly retail trade and personal services for the residents. The total character is residential and attempts to introduce industry are usually met with resistance. These are the Park Forests, the Levittowns, the Upper Arlingtons, and the communities of the Palos Verdes peninsula. Each day these "dormitory" towns export their residents to work in jobs located in the city or in employing satellites.

To illustrate the differences in social characteristics between residential suburbs and employing satellites, table 5 summarizes several items from the 1970 census for the larger (10,000 and over) fringe communities of the Chicago Urbanized Area. To distinguish empirically between residential and employing communities we compare the patterns of aggregate employment in the suburb in the basic activities of trade and manufacturing to the number of local residents holding trade or manufacturing occupations. If the number of people employed in the suburb in trade and manufacturing greatly exceeds the number of residents with those types of jobs, then obviously workers must come in to the community daily to fill the jobs there. Thus, the community would be an employing satellite. On the other hand, if the number of residents holding jobs in manufacturing and trade greatly exceeds the number employed in trade and manufacturing, then it is obvious that the local residents must leave daily for work elsewhere. The suburb therefore is primarily residential in nature. The E/R ratio is a quantitative indicator of this pattern. The numerator, or E value, is the number of persons working in the community in trade and manufacturing. The denominator, or R value, is the number employed in trade and manufacturing activities living in the community. For example, in Arlington Heights, Illinois, the 1970 census shows that some 13,152 residents held jobs in trade and manufacturing. Also, there were only 3,454 persons employed in those two activities within Arlington Heights at about that time. The E/R ratio for Arlington Heights is

$$3{,}453/13{,}152 \ (100) = 26.3$$

Even if all 3,454 employed persons were residents of Arlington Heights, it would mean that 9,698 residents would have to be employed elsewhere! Thus the community clearly is highly residential in character.

Alternatively, there are 20,241 persons employed in trade and manufacturing in Joliet, Illinois. However, only 16,138 of Joliet's residents hold jobs in those employment categories. Therefore, even if all of these 16,138 Joliet residents worked within the city, 4,103 individuals still would have to come into Joliet to work in trade and manufacturing. Joliet's E/R ratior is 125.4, which indicates its stature as an employing satellite. In general terms of the E/R ratio a value of 85 or less is taken to represent a mainly residential suburb, while a value of 116 or greater is taken to represent a mainly employing satellite. Index values between 86 and 115 reflect a rather mixed pattern that cannot always be clearly interpreted. The E/R for the city of Chicago is 124.

The data in table 5 are for the 23 employing satellites with index values of 116 or greater and the 50 residential suburbs with E/Rs of less than 86. There were 14 Chicago fringe communities with values that indicated a mixture of residential and employment functions; these were excluded since adequate treatment of this mixed category would require almost a separate discussion of each community. Among the residential suburbs are such Chicago communities as Elmwood Park, Oak Park, Alsip, and Glen Ellyn. The employing satellites include Woodstock, Lincolnwood, Naperville, St. Charles, and Skokie.

The data in table 5 show that, on the average, the employing satellites are larger in population than the residential suburbs, but the residen-

TABLE 5. Social Characteristics of Employing Satellites and Residential Suburbs of the Chicago Urbanized Area, 1970

Characteristic	All Employing Satellites	All Residential Suburbs	Selected Residential Suburbs			
			Summit	Berwyn	Glen Ellyn	Winnetka
Average population	28,067	23,650	11,569	52,502	21,909	13,998
Average growth 1960–1970	41.6	91.8	11.5	-3.2	37.2	4.7
Percentage of adults with 4 years of high school or more	62.7	66.8	37.5	46.0	85.2	90.0
Percentage of families with incomes of $15,000 or more	39.3	42.8	20.2	29.7	61.5	79.3
Cumulative fertility women 35–44 years of age	2,842	2,924	2,882	2,214	2,910	2,882
Percentage of married women with young children and husband present who work	21.8	19.3	27.6	17.6	13.9	11.6
Percentage of the population foreign-born	28.5	26.7	26.7	45,2	17.4	20.8
Percentage of the population Nonwhite	3.0	2.9	19.5	0.4	0.7	1.3

Source: *County and City Data Book, 1972.*

tial suburbs are growing more rapidly. The average status level of the residents of suburbs is higher than that of satellite residents as indicated by the larger percentage of suburban residents that are high school graduates and the larger percentage of suburban families that have incomes of more than $15,000 per year. The fertility of the suburban women is higher than that of the satellite women. The cumulative fertility index is the number of children born per 1,000 women in the age cohort reaching the end of its fertile years—35 to 44 years of age. On the average, for every 1,000 women ages 35 to 44 in the residential suburbs 2,924 children were born while 2,842 were born to women in the same age group in the employing satellites. Thus, for every 1,000 women in the two communities the women in the residential suburbs gave birth to 82 more children.

The residential and employing communities also differ in the employment patterns of their women residents. A larger percentage of women with young children and their husbands present work in the employing satellites than in the residential suburbs. The employing satellites tend to have a greater representation of ethnics and blacks in their populations than do the residential suburbs. Thus, there is some tendency for the residential suburbs to be smaller, more rapidly growing, higher in status, more traditional in fertility and female employment matters, less ethnic, and less racially mixed than the employing satellites.

While there are apparent general differences between residential and employing satellites, there is still a great deal of variety among the residential suburbs themselves. I have selected four Chicago residential suburbs that well illustrate the point: Summit, Berwyn, Glen Ellyn, and Winnetka. The figures show these communities to be quite different from one another. While Berwyn and Summit are both of lower status than the other two, Berwyn is much larger than Summit. While Summit is experiencing modest population growth Berwyn is actually losing population. While the women in Summit are more fertile than those in Berwyn, there is a much greater tendency for the Summit married women with young families to work than for those in Berwyn. While Berwyn has a large concentration of ethnics, Summit has a comparatively large representation of black residents. Glen Ellyn and Winnetka are communities of substantial social status; however, Glen Ellyn is larger and is growing more rapidly than Winnetka. The Glen Ellyn women are both more fertile and more likely to work when their children are young than are those in Winnetka. Neither community has much black population and in both places about one-quarter of the population is first-or second-generation ethnic.

Indeed, there are many differences among suburban communities and these differences tend to persist through time. Reynolds Farley has shown that even though suburban communities experience rapid population growth their own relative position within the suburban social-status hierarchy tends to persist. In discussing the persistence, Farley has written:

> Evanston and Hammond are approximately equal in population size, at the same distance from Chicago's Loop, comparable in age, and both have Lake Michigan frontage. Yet the inhabitants of these suburbs have quite different characteristics. A meat packing plant was the first establishment to attract residents to Hammond, and excellent rail facilities fostered later industrial growth, while the history of Evanston was dependent upon Methodist institutions including Northwestern University.

> Parma and Shaker Heights, two of Cleveland's largest suburbs, were settled approximately at the same time and are the same distance from Cleveland. Census figures for 1960 show that college graduates and professional workers formed a sizably larger percentage of Shaker Heights' population than of Parma's. When these suburbs were laid out, real estate promoters planned numerous small homes in Parma and large, expensive homes in Shaker Heights.

> The specialization involved in the origin of a suburb may have implications for its distinctive socio-economic composition, so that once a suburb is established, the population that moves into that suburb tends to resemble the population already living there[1964, p. 47].

The deconcentration of the city into the fringe has been a somewhat selective process, as indicated by the gross differences between aggregate city and fringe populations. Yet, the movement to suburbia has not resulted in a homogeneous, undifferentiated residential plane. Our fringe areas have communities specialized in employment activities as well as places that are exclusively residential. Our fringe areas have communities that differ in social status, family characteristics, and ethnic and racial composition. Indeed, it seems that fringe communities are beginning to display the pattern of differentiation that have long been characteristic of city neighborhoods. In the past our suburbs have tended to maintain their relative position in the community status hierarchy. But what of the future? As suburban residential communities begin or continue to age, will they pass through a modified form of the neighborhood life cycle much like that of the inner city areas? Will slums appear in suburbia and will we see rebuilding programs much like those that now dot our cities?

Will deconcentration end? Will there be a return to the city? Whatever the answer to these questions, in all probability the CBD and the inner city will never again serve the centralizing and organizing role that they did earlier this century. Advances in transportation and communication have broken the necessity of and largely negated the need for a single-centered metropolitan complex. While the shift from a single-centered metropolis to a multinucleated region will not occur overnight, the economic and social forces are operating to produce a new pattern of social organization that will require new modes of institutional and personal adaptation. Neither annexation nor currently conceived metropolitan government has proved to be adequate adaptative mechanisms. The creativity of social and physical planners will undoubtedly be taxed as the necessity for innovative solutions to new as well as old metropolitan problems becomes imperative.

URBAN GEOMETRY

Urban sociologists have a long-standing interest in the extent and form of differentiation among urban neighborhoods. Differences in local histories, in population composition of neighborhood residents, in emergent forms of behavior, and in social pathologies have been of concern to an army of urban researchers. Their studies have sought to identify the particular geometry of neighborhood patterns and to explain such patterns in terms of broader processes of social organization and social change. Three basic perspectives have become the foci for much of the research and discussion: the concentric zone or distance gradient model [Burgess 1925], the sector model [Hoyt 1939], and the multiple nuclei model [Harris & Ullman 1945]. All three of these focus on the differential distribution of population and housing in urban space. These perspectives, or "models," argue that the gross distributional pattern of the city results from the interplay of socioeconomic forces of competition in the urban land market. In describing the process by which individuals become distributed in the city's neighborhood galaxy, Robert Park (who was a contributor, along with E. W. Burgess, to the development of the concentric zone model) argued that the city is a broad constellation of neighborhoods, each of which has its own unique niche in the city's ecological organization. Accordingly, the city is " . . . a great sifting and sorting mechanism" that selects the individuals best suited to live in each area [Park 1952, p. 79]. In such a system each urbanite finally lives in that area most closely attuned to his own characteristics and needs. In the aggregate, the impersonal "sorting" process results in a city whose neighborhoods are a collage of highly differentiated areas.

In addition to focusing on the operation of the urban land market, the concentric zone, sector, and multiple nuclei models share other assumptions. They are 1. the existence of social class gradations within the population; 2. a city that is large and growing in population and expanding in area and activities; 3. an economic base that is mainly an industrial-commercial mix; 4. private ownership of property and few strict regulations on land development; 5. specialization in land use; 6. a transportation system that is fairly rapid, fairly efficient, and generally available in terms of cost to the majority of the population; and 7. freedom of residential choice at least for the higher socioeconomic strata. Should any of these assumptions not apply in an individual city, we would not expect any of the three models to be adequate for analysis of the local urban geometry.

While these three models share a preoccupation with the operation of the broader socioeconomic forces within the city, the spatial configurations they propose differ quite markedly. The concentric-zone model argues that population and housing vary by distance gradient from the city's economic core or CBD. Chicago was viewed as the prototype of a concentric zonal city, although the eastern half of each of the set of concentric circles was preempted by Lake Michigan. Chicago's Loop was the CBD and it was around this node that the total pattern of land use and population distribution was organized. In the CBD are found the principal banking and financial institutions, hotels, restaurants, major retail stores, and the important office complexes that house the important national and regional offices of major corporations. Located around the CBD on all sides is the *zone in transition*. It is a concentric zone that is shifting from residential to industrial-commercial as the CBD expands and spills its various activities into this adjacent zone. The zone in transition is an area of intense land speculation and profit-taking by property owners. The blight and deterioration of the area, which drives out middle- and working-class residents, makes it an available place of residence for those individuals and groups that for one reason or another cannot obtain housing elsewhere. The zone in transition houses the segregated racial and ethnic minorities, the downwardly mobile, and those seeking imper- sonality, anonymity, and seclusion. It is a curious mix of social disor- ganization and social integration. The racial and ethnic ghettoes of the transition zone are tight islands of organized relationships within a broader sea of disorganization. The lack of social cohesion of the whole zone combined with the anonymity and seclusion make the area ripe for those activities publicly shunned by polite society. Gambling, prostitution, narcotics, and a wide variety of vices and perversions can be found in such areas and are given nearly free rein by indifferent or condoning law-enforcement agencies.

Just beyond the zone-in-transition is found the *zone of workingmen's homes*, which is followed successively by zones occupied by the middle status, the high status, and the commuters. With increasing distance the status of the residents rise. Consequently, anyone driving in any direction from the city's center to the periphery would pass through pro- gressively higher-status neighborhoods. Thus, the concentric zone scheme calls for a positive relationship between distance from the city center and social status. The concentric zone pattern for a typical city is shown in figure 4.

While the concentric zone model has a certain intuitive appeal to many and readily lends itself to post hoc explanations of certain aspects of the city familiar to all of us, significant questions have been raised as to the generality of the model to all cities. Indeed a number of critics have suggested that it does not even fit Chicago very well.

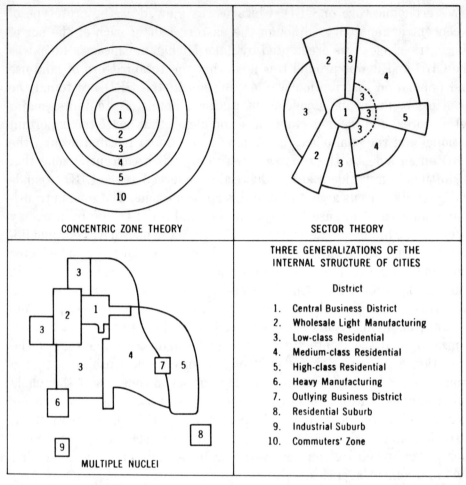

Fig. 4. Concentric Zone, Sector, and Multiple Nuclei Models (Source: Reprinted with permission from Chauncy D. Harris and Edward L. Ullman, "The Nature of Cities," the *Annals of the American Academy of Political and Social Science.* 1945, CCXLII November).

The most prominent alternative perspective is seen in Homer Hoyt's sector model. In a study of 142 American cities, Hoyt argued that the distribution of population is organized more in terms of homogeneous, pie-shaped sectors that run from the city's CBD to the periphery. Thus, the high-income areas of the city tended to be found in one or two major sectors rather than in a completely exclusive zone as predicted by the concentric zone scheme. There is an example of sectoral patterning in figure 4. It may be noted that the social-status level of an area is not related to its distance. Indeed, the types of neighborhoods that one would pass through in driving from the center to the periphery would basically depend on the sector in which one started.

A second alternative to the concentric zone model is the multiple nuclei perspective. The multiple nuclei model starts with a notion altogether different from the other two. Unlike the concentric zone and sector models the multiple nuclei does not view the city as being organized around a single, dominant focus as represented by the CBD. Rather, there are a number of different growth nuclei, each of which exerts influences on the distribution of certain activities and population. These nuclei specialize in markedly different activities, ranging from retailing through manufacturing to residential. Thus, the city is much like a patchwork quilt of differing nuclei that do not organize themselves around a single core area.

In addition to the different spatial geometries the three models differ somewhat in their treatment of the process of neighborhood change and development during urban expansion. According to the concentric zone model, change is described in terms of the processes of invasion, succession, extension, and concentration in which land use and population type in one zone initially invade and then succeed that of the adjacent zone. Thus, change is envisioned as being much like the dropping of a pebble in a lake: a series of ripples radiate from the point of impact pushing into each other in their outward flow. Much of the perspective and jargon for the analysis of neighborhoods undergoing racial transition from white to black stem directly from the concentric zone model, particularly such terms as *invasion* and *succession*.

From the standpoint of the sector model change involves the axial growth of the city along main transportation arteries and lines of least resistance. The key sector in change is that of high-status residence. Its location and expansion sets the parameters for the development of the other areas.

Some of the basic propositions describing sectoral change are [as summarized by Thomlinson 1969, pp. 146–147]:

1. High-rate residential growth tends to proceed from the given point of orgin, either along established lines of travel or toward another existing nucleus of buildings or trade areas.

2. The zone of high rent tends to occupy high ground that is free from risk of floods and to spread along lake, bay, river, and ocean ports where the waterfronts are not used by industry.

3. High-rent residential districts tend to grow toward the section of the city that has free open country beyond its edges and away from

"dead end" sections that are prevented from expanding by natural or artificial barriers.

4. The high-priced residential neighborhood tends to grow toward the homes of community leaders.

5. Sometimes trends in the construction of office buildings, banks, and stores pull the high-priced residential neighborhoods in the same general direction.

6. High-grade residential areas tend to develop along the fastest existing transportation lines.

7. Deluxe apartment areas tend to be established near the business centers in old established residential areas.

8. The growth of high-rent neighborhoods continues in the same direction for a long period of time.

9. High-rent neighborhoods do not skip about at random in the process of movement; they follow a definite path in one or more sectors of the city.

10. It is possible, under some conditions, for high-rent areas to "double back," or return toward the center of the city.

11. High-rent areas tend to be adjoined by medium-rent areas, sharp disjunctions in rental areas are not frequent.

Change is treated by the multiple nuclei model in terms of the factors that account for the emergence of separate nuclei within the city. The four factors that are involved in the development of the nucleated pattern are as follows: 1. Certain activities require specialized facilities located in only one or a few sections of the metropolis. 2. Certain like activities profit from adjacent congregation. 3. Certain unlike activities are antagonistic or detrimental to each other. 4. Certain activities are unable to afford the costs of the most desirable locational sites [Harris & Ullman 1945, pp. 7–17].

The obvious question at this point is: Which of the three different models is the correct one? Like so many other matters, none of them is completely right or completely wrong. Most cities display some features of each. In reviewing the recent research on these three models we need to focus on four topics: 1. the centralization of social status groups; 2. status gradients in cities of developing countries; 3. longitudinal analyses of neighborhood status levels; and 4. distributional patterns of urban social area analysis dimensions. Each of these four shall now be taken up in order.

1. The Centralization of Social Status Groups. The concept of *centralization* basically refers to how closely a group is located residentially to the city's center. By calculating indexes of centrality or centralization for the various social status groups and by comparing them we are able to draw some conclusions about the concentric zone model. It is consistent with the concentric zone model to expect that the highest status groups will be the least centralized and that the lower status groups will be the most centralized. Falling between the higher and lower status groups in degree of centralization are those of middle status. One measure of centralization is in terms of the average distance from the city's center of each member of a group. An example of this index is found in table 6. In the table is the average distance in miles from the center of San Juan of each educational status group [Schwirian & Rico-Velasco 1971]. On the average, those with no formal education live 2.3 miles from San Juan's center. Those with 1 to 4 years of education live 2.31 miles from the center; those with 5 to 7 years live 2.39 miles, and so on. The highest status category, those who have gone to college or beyond live 2.67 miles from the city's center. Thus, there is a consistent increase in average distance as educational level goes up. Thus, for San Juan at least, there is some support for the concentric zone or distance gradient model.

TABLE 6. Average Number of Miles Distance from the Center of the City of Each Educational Status Group, San Juan, Puerto Rico, 1960

Educational Status Group		Average Number of Miles from City Center
None		2.30
Grade:	1–4	2.31
	5–7	2.39
	8	2.41
High:	1–3	2.53
	4	2.58
College or More		2.67

Source: Schwirian and Rico-Velasco, 1971.

An alternative measure of centralization involves comparing the percentage of a given group living in the city rather than fringe to the percentage of the total population of the metropolitan area living in the city. Therefore, if 50 percent of the total population lives in the city but 80 percent of those with only a grade school education live in the city, we would say that this particular group is comparatively more centralized than the total population. This centralization index is

$$\text{Centralization of Group X} = \frac{\text{Percentage of Group X in City}}{\text{Percentage of Total Population in the City}}(100)$$

If the concentric zone model were correct we would expect to find that the lower status groups were the most centralized and the higher status groups the least centralized (and therefore the most decentralized). Table 7 gives the centralization values for various educational groups for four major U.S. Urbanized Areas. Detroit and New York represent patterns consistent with the concentric zone model. In both communities the most centralized groups (those with the highest indexes) are those of low educational attainment and the least centralized are the more highly educated categories. This pattern was found in 90 U.S. cities in 1960 by Leo Schnore and Hal Winsborough [1972]. However, many other places had other patterns. Twenty-four communities had an *inverse* status gradient. That is, those groups that were the most centralized were the higher status and the lower status groups least centralized. The figures for Tucson illustrate this pattern, which is the exact opposite of that predicted by the concentric zone scheme. A third pattern was found to describe seventy Urbanized Areas—it is one in which *both* the lowest and highest educational classes are centralized and the middle are decentralized. Los Angeles is representative of this pattern. Thus of one hundred eighty-four Urbanized Areas, ninety-four were found with pat-

T A B L E 7 . **Residential Centralization of Educational Status Groups in Four U. S. Communities, 1960–1970**

Educational Status Group	Detroit			New York			Tucson			Los Angeles		
	1960	1970	1970/1960	1960	1970	1970/1960	1960	1970	1970/1960	1960	1970	1970/1960
NONE	141	142	1.01	129	130	1.01	90	91	1.01	131	126	0.96
GRADE: 1–4	136	158	1.16	119	125	1.05	93	97	1.04	113	122	1.08
5–6	126	144	1.14	111	122	1.10	96	99	1.03	110	118	1.07
7–8	112	121	1.08	107	108	1.01	99	100	1.01	99	100	1.01
HIGH: 1–3	99	110	1.11	100	104	1.04	100	99	0.99	94	95	1.01
4	86	85	0.99	91	92	1.01	101	100	0.99	97	95	0.98
COLLEGE: 1–3	86	77	0.99	87	89	1.02	102	102	1.00	102	101	0.99
4 or more	77	65	0.84	84	86	1.02	103	101	0.98	106	105	0.99

Source: Schnore & Winsborough 1972; 1970 Census General Social and Economic Characteristics for Michigan, New York, Arizona, and Los Angeles.

terns contrary to that of the concentric zone model while ninety supported it. Does this mean that the concentric zone model is invalid?

While it seems clear that more U. S. cities deviate from the concentric zone model than support it, it must be kept in mind that the model was developed to describe the dynamics of the city; thus, to test the idea adequately data must pertain to the pattern of change through time. If the concentric zone pattern is correct, regardless of the centralization pattern at any one point in time, we still should find that through time there is a trend for the lower class to become centralized and the upper classes to become decentralized. A limited examination of this is presented in table 7. The ratio of 1970/1960 centralization scores tells us the direction of change in centralization for the educational groups. If the ratio exceeds 1.0 it means that the group was comparatively more centralized in 1970 than in 1960. If the index is less than 1.0 it means that the group was less centralized in 1970 than in 1960. Admittedly the ten-year time span is short to investigate such change in the distribution of so many people, but if the movement is there we should be able to detect it. For Detroit, where the low status residents are centralized and the upper-status residents are decentralized, the trend is for the low status groups to become more centralized and the high status groups to become less centralized. In New York it seems that all groups centralized slightly but the distance gradient was maintained. For Tucson it seems that although the inverse status gradient held for both 1960 and 1970 the ten-year change was in the direction of the low status groups becoming more centralized and the upper status groups becoming less centralized. We find Los Angeles also is moving in the direction predicted by the concentric zone scheme.

What accounts for the fact that some cities correspond to the concentric zone pattern whereas others do not? Research is currently probing for an answer. The general hypothesis to account for the relative decentralization of the higher status for which some support has been found is that " . . . dirt, noise, odors, physical hazards, residential crowding, and traffic congestion associated with a concentration of industry within a central city have drawn out the social elite and the broad middle class who have increasingly taken up suburban residences. More generally this notion suggests that the economic functions performed in the central city may be variously inimical to co-occupancy of the area for residential purposes, at least by economically favored status groups" [Schnore & Winsborough 1972, pp. 138–139]. As a result, we must look at the city's complex of productive activities and their residues to predict their impact on where various groups live—in town or at the metropolitan fringe.

So far we have ignored the *relative* descriptive power of the concentric zone model as opposed to the sector model. In other words, which seems to *best* fit the manner in which socioeconomic groups are located in a city. Many studies have concluded that in general, at a given point in time, status is described more by *sector* than by *distance*, although within individual sectors of the city there are status gradients. For example, in a study of Canada's eleven principal cities, Kent Schwirian and Marc Matre [1974] found that the status distribution in eight cities had more of a sector pattern than concentric zone pattern; two had primarily concentric zone patterns; and in one, status differences were associated with both sectors and zones. Interestingly, findings have shown that within given sectors of the city status and distance are differentially related. For example, Kent Schwirian and Ruth Smith [1974] report that within the northwestern sector of San Juan status has a strong negative relation to distance—the further the distance, the lower the status; but within the southwestern sector there is a positive relation between distance and social status, as would be predicted by the concentric zone model. In the southeastern and northeastern sectors no systematic relationship was found between distance and social status. It seems, therefore, that a main point to remember is that the distribution of social status groups within the city is not a topic about which we can make easy generalizations. There are sectoral, zonal, and even nucleal forces at work affecting where people live and where people work. These forces are themselves affected by the broader social and economic context including the age of the city and its industrial-commercial mix, its transportation system, property ownership pattern, level of racial and ethnic discrimination, and many other factors. These forces are covert and not easily detectable in our everyday observations. They operate through a set of social institutions generally called the urban land market. Unfortunately, we know little about the sociology of the land market, and we need to know much more. The topic of the land market is taken up later in this chapter.

2. Social Status Gradients in Developing Countries. Discussions of the location of various social status groups in developing countries have suggested that an *inverse* status gradient seems to characterize the emerging cities. Accordingly, the upper status groups cluster near the city's center, while the periphery contains those of lower socioeconomic status. The middle-status group, to the extent that there is one at all, supposedly falls between the other two. The difference between the direct status gradient and the inverse pattern of the developing cities is usually explained by some combination of the following factors: **1.** *Differences in Urban Functions.* Although U.S. cities are commercial-industrial based, many cities in developing countries are primarily (or were at the time during which their initial residential structures were evolving) administrative centers. The upper class located at the city's center near the complex of government and religious institutions that formed the hub of their life patterns. Lacking centralized industry, the inner city did not take on the negative characteristics of manufacturing slums. Thus, differences in primary functions resulted in different land use patterns and different residential structures. **2.** *Differences in Level of Transportation Technology and Transportation Ownership Patterns.* The spread of population in a city is a direct function of the major mode of transportation and the access to transportation of large segments of the population. In countries lacking good roads, high rates of auto ownership, and efficient and rapid mass transit, different forces work to sort the population. Proximity of residence to the city's center is much more desirable and sought after. In this process the upper classes have the distinct advantage and they preempt central and accessible location. **3.** *Level of Technology During the Period of the City's Initial Development.* Since initial urban patterns are influenced by transportation and industrial technology, they form the foundation on which all subsequent change is based. The initial distribution of people, businesses, and manufacturing cumulates to create an enormous resistance to change. A whole city's residential, commercial, and industrial pattern cannot be revamped overnight. When change does come in most cases it is slow, disjunctive, disruptive, and piecemeal. Barring major, constant, and pervasive forces for change, city patterns proceed much along the lines that emerged early in their development. To the extent that the cities of non-Western nations differ from those of the developed West, and to the extent that they have not experienced the pressures for change engendered by industrialization, they have maintained somewhat different ecological patterns including the residential patterning of their social status groups.

The vast number of studies of cities outside the United States leads to the conclusion that in terms of the gradient and sector models differences between our cities and those abroad are a result of differences in societal modernization—that is, differences in levels of industrialization and transportation technology, primary urban functions, and age of city. Furthermore, many of these studies assert or imply that the cities abroad are becoming more like cities in the United States as they take on greater commercial and industrial functions.

To date no formal attempt has been made to tie the urban geometric models into a developmental theory of society, even though such inferences abound in the literature. Perhaps the closest attempt at developing such a theory is that by Schnore in his review of the spatial structure of cities in North and South America. Schnore concluded, "What does emerge from this review is the possibility that (a) the Burgess concentric zone scheme, wrongly regarded as indigenous to the United States, and (b) the pres-industrial pattern, erroneously identified as unique to Latin America, are *both special cases more adequately subsumed under a more general theory of residential land use in urban areas,*" [1965, p. 374].

Schnore speculates that there might well be a sequential pattern of ecological change as societies modernize. In the early pattern of city development the "inverse gradient" characterizes the city in which the affluent population lives near the city's center and the lower income groups live toward the periphery. With growth, modernization, and aging the central portions of the city become less attractive residentially and the upper class migrates toward the periphery. The vacated areas in the inner portions of the city become targets for those urbanites who cannot survive the stiffer competition for fringe housing.

3. Longitudinal Analyses of Neighborhood Status Levels. As was pointed out in the discussion of residential centralization, cross-sectional analyses of residential patterns tell us nothing about the processes by which change occurs. Many studies have focused on the pattern of change in neighborhood composition with a view to assessing the correctness of the concentric zone model. The neighborhood life cycle concept emerged from such a study and has proved to be a useful aid in understanding residential change. In another study Lee Hagerty [1971] followed the changing social status positions of census tracts over a twenty-year period for Hartford, Rochester, Milwaukee, Minneapolis, Houston, Dallas, Denver, and Portland. For all of these cities, including those whose cross-sectional status distribution did not correspond to the positive gradient predicted by the concentric zone model, the longitudinal pattern of change tended toward the direct relationship between social status and distance. While these findings do not negate the sector perspective they do serve to reinforce the notion of change in terms of the processes described by Burgess and Park.

The fourth topic of importance for the consideration of urban spatial geometry is that of social area analysis. However, the ideas underlying social area analysis go beyond simple spatial structure. Therefore the topic is treated separately in the following section.

SOCIAL AREA ANALYSIS

Social area analysis is a perspective on urban structure closely tied to a theory of social organization and social change. Accordingly, the degree of social differentiation in life styles among individual urbanites and, at the aggregate level, among characteristics of city neighborhoods is a function of the *societal scale,* or degree of development of the society in which the city is located. Societal scale refers to the extent of the division of labor within society and the degree of elaboration of the integrative mechanisms and institutions centering on transportation and communication [Greer 1962]. High-scale societies, such as those of North America, are characterized by very complex occupational and industrial differentiation, by an intricate transportation web and by a pervasive system of rapid electronic communication. Low-scale societies, such as those of emerging Africa and Asia, have much more rudimentary occupational and industrial systems, embryonic transportation systems, and incomplete and chaotic communication patterns. As societies modernize or increase in scale the degree of social differentiation increases and this becomes reflected in the increasing specialization of urban land use and in the social characteristics of the population.

In terms of individuals and their life styles there are three basic dimensions around which life is organized and which are sensitive to broader changes in societal scale. There are social status, familism (sometimes called urbanism), and ethnicity. Indicators of social status include educational attainment and occupational standing. Income also is an indicator of status. Familism, or variations in life styles dealing with home and family, include indicators such as degree of fertility, female labor-force participation, and housing choice—single-family home or apartment. Ethnicity refers to racial and subcultural differences in such things as language, religious beliefs and practices, and physiognomy.

In small-scale societies, or societies that are low on modernization indicators, there is little social differentiation of these three dimensions; that is, social status is highly related to family patterns and both are related to ethnicity. In such a society, to know one's status is also to be able to successfully predict one's family patterns and ethnic standing. The extent to which these three dimensions are related means that differential population distribution in the city does not occur in terms of them. A neighborhood's ethnic standing as well as its family patterns are a function of the social status level of the population of the area in the city's ranking system. Thus, if one knows the neighborhood's population status level one can predict the ethnic and family patterns there.

In large-scale societies where social differentiation has occurred we now find people at each status level opting for different housing, fertility patterns, and family forms. Similarly, among all racial and ethnic groups there are great ranges in the social status of group members and a variety of family forms and housing options. At the neighborhood level there is specialization in status composition of residents. At each status level, neighborhoods have a variety of family forms present. And within ethnic areas there are status and family gradients. Knowledge of the social status of an area's population is in itself insufficient information to predict familism and ethnic composition because of the relative independence of the three dimensions.

Empirical studies utilizing the social area framework have been numerous. In general, their purpose has been to explore the extent to which social status, familism, and ethnicity are related to each other. The theory leads to the prediction that in low-scale societies the three are highly related whereas in developed societies they have a much lesser degree of interrelatedness. The studies have usually employed one of the techniques of the factor analysis family of statistics. Factor analysis provides the researcher with a mechanism for identifying a limited number of common underlying dimensions for a large number of specific indicators. The results of these studies for cities in low-scale societies such as Cairo and Alexandria, Egypt [Latif 1974], have consistently supported the social area notions. Indicators of social status, familism, and ethnicity have been shown to be quite highly related to each other. Thus, neighborhoods that differ in the status composition of their population also differ systematically in their family and ethnic composition.

Studies of cities in large scale societies are more numerous than those of cities in developing societies principally because of the greater availability of data for urban subareas in the cities of large-scale societies. The collection of comprehensive, valid, and reliable information on urban areas takes organizational mechanisms and professional skills and resources that are not readily available in the less developed countries. Most major cities of North America have been analyzed, as have many in Europe, Australia, and New Zealand. Collectively, the findings from the cities in large-scale societies show a much lower degree of relationship among status, familism, and ethnicity than do those from cities in the less-developed countries.

In societies in the midst of economic development, the rates of social change are not uniform across the whole society. Change proceeds at a much faster pace in the region of the primate city. The primate city is the portal for economic development. Change comes first to the primate city and then diffuses throughout the rest of society. Since there are differentials in the rate of change among cities there is also a bifurcation in the life styles and social organization between the primate's region and the other more isolated sections of the country. The primate city is the first to take on a changing ecological patterning. Therefore, in the midst of economic development, the primate city becomes very much like cities in large-scale societies while the smaller, more isolated cities maintain their traditional organizational pattern for a much longer time. In the primate city social status, familism, and ethnicity become less related to each other sooner than in the secondary urban centers [Schwirian & Smith 1974]. For example, in a study of Puerto Rico [Schwirian & Smith 1974] it was found that at the neighborhood level there was only a moderate relationship between social status and fertility ($r = -.59$) in San Juan, the primate city. In the secondary urban centers it was higher. For Ponce it was $r = -.72$ and for Mayaguez $r = -.90$. Puerto Rico is a society midway in economic development. San Juan historically has played the role of primate. It is Puerto Rico's gateway to the world. It is the filter through which the bulk of the development activities work. Ponce and Mayaguez are clearly secondary to San Juan. They are located in the more isolated sections of the island and their development has lagged markedly behind that of San Juan. Mayaguez is the smallest, most isolated, and least "modernized" of the three cities, and it shows the very traditional pattern of a strong negative relationship between social status and fertility.

The relationship between social status and familism all but disappears in high-scale societies. For example, for Ottawa, Canada, the r is only $-.06$. Even for smaller Canadian cities fairly comparable in size to Mayaguez we find a low relationship between fertility and status. For Kingston it is only $-.25$. Presumably as Puerto Rico continues to modernize and increase in societal scale the relationship between social status and fertility will decline in all three major cities.

The three social area dimensions—social status, familism, and ethnicity—are so fundamental for life's organization they become manifest properties along which urban neighborhoods may be distinguished. In figure 5, the census tracts of Ottawa have been plotted by their scores on social status and familism. The open dots are areas in the highest third of ethnicity and the black dots are in the lower two-thirds on ethnicity. Ethnicity is measured in terms of the percentage of the tract's population that is foreign born. Social status is a combined index mainly reflecting the educational and occupational level of the population [Schwirian & Matre 1974]. The familism index basically measures the extent to which local women are in the labor force and the propensity for residents to live in single-family dwellings as opposed to multiple-dwelling units. The distribution of points represents the galaxy of Ottawa's neighborhoods on the three dimensions. There are two tracts that are high on both social status and familism and low on ethnicity. They form a "social area" in this social space even though they may not be geo-

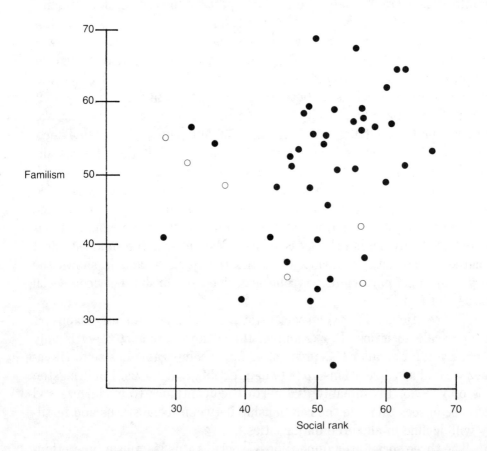

○ Indicates area of high ethnicity

Fig. 5. Ottawa's Census Tracts Plotted by Their Standard Scores on Social Status, Familism, and Ethnicity: The Social Area Galaxy of Ottawa

graphically adjacent. The important thing from the social area analysis standpoint is that these two areas are quite comparable in terms of the social characteristics of the people that live within them and they are quite different from people living in other segments of this social space, that is, other social areas.

The shape of Ottawa's neighborhood galaxy is not necessarily the same as that for other cities. Some cities have higher proportions of some social areas than do others. Such differences between cities reflect differences between them in industrial composition, employment opportunities, racial and ethnic mix, rate and recency of growth, and housing stock. It would be highly likely that the shape of the galaxy would change as cities grow, develop, and age. The change in location of individual neighborhoods in the social area galaxy seems to be fairly systematic. In a study of Chicago areas over a thirty-year period the following pattern was found by Hunter [1974]:   1. Neighborhoods at the sparsely settled fringe with low economic status but high familism are likely to experience an increase in their economic status as the city expands and includes the areas within the scope of its population decentralization.   2. Areas having achieved high familism and economic status are likely to experience a decline in familism as the areas age and as multiple family dwelling units invade. Younger families leave and ethnics begin to appear. It is only after the decline in familism that such areas also experience a downgrading of the population's social status. It seems that a decline in familism preceeds the decline in social status.   3. When central areas of low status and low familism change, they usually maintain their low social status but experience an increase in their familism as poor families move into the private housing of the area and as public housing units are developed primarily for families with young children. Thus, it seems that changes in familism and social status are related, and the process somewhat resembles that described in the neighborhood life-cycle model described earlier.

Studies have shown that among people living in different social areas different behaviors predominate. For example, in terms of social involvement with neighbors in four San Francisco neighborhoods, it has been shown that in areas low on both familism and economic status 58.2 percent of the adult males were socially isolated while in areas of high familism and high economic status only one-third of the males were isolated socially. Areas of low familism and high status had 51.3 percent of the males isolated but areas of high familism and low status had only 41.2 percent of the males isolated [Bell 1958]. The data also show that individuals whose occupations were atypical of those in the neighborhood, regardless of their occupations, were more isolated from their neighbors socially than those whose occupations were fairly typical of those of the area in terms of status. Thus it seems that social differentiation from one's neighbors in terms of the way one makes a living is associated with social isolation.

The three indicators of neighborhood social structure have been shown to be related to the voting of area residents. In a study of support for a welfare levy in a midwestern city it was found that over 60 percent of the variation in percentage of voters in favor of the levy was a function of social status, familism, and ethnicity of the areas. Ethnicity was the most important of the three—as the percentage of black and foreign born increased there was a large increase in the percentage of yes votes. Also, with status and ethnicity controlled, as the degree of familism decreased there was a moderate increase in support for the welfare levy. And, with the other two dimensions statistically controlled, there was a slight tendency for welfare support to rise with neighborhood social status [Ekstrom 1968]. Thus, the three social area dimensions tap individual and neighborhood characteristics that are relevant for understanding much of what is going on in our cities today.

While the social area analysis perspective developed fairly independently of the classic models there has been some interest in investigating the patterns of urban social areas in terms of concentric zones, sectors, and multiple nuclei. In studies of cities in the United States and Canada it was found that, overall, social status tended to be distributed *more* in terms of sectors than distance gradient. Familism was distributed more by distance gradient than by sector. The main reason for this is that the familism index's major component is the relative concentration of single-family dwellings as opposed to multiple-dwelling units. New housing at the fringe tends to be single family while other neighborhoods in the urban core are being converted from single family to multiple-dwelling units. Ethnicity was distributed neither by sector nor distance but tended to appear more in terms of highly clustered nuclei [Murdie 1969]. Thus it seems that the city is much like a multilayered club sandwich. Over the basic grid of streets we have a layer of social status sectors; then a layer of housing types distributed primarily by distance gradient; all topped off by a layer of nucleated racial and ethnic minorities. Social area analysis attempts to separate these layers and examine their individual contribution to the city and then recombine them to observe their total configuration.

NEIGHBORHOODS

Many people romantically view cities as gigantic collages of numerous, small, and highly variegated neighborhoods that offer the urbanite an antipasto of life styles and social types. Accordingly, each neighborhood is one of the building blocks that collectively constitute the city. Thus, neighborhoods are taken for granted and are seen as fairly fixed in terms of boundaries, population composition, dominant behavior patterns, and reputations. Residents of each neighborhood supposedly are held together by primordial sentiments that harken back to a more bucolic ambiance when the grass was mowed rather than smoked; the water was clean and pure; and the air clear and refreshing. Whatever change has taken place in city neighborhoods has meant that a basically wholesome environment has gone to the dogs.

A less romantic but more realistic view is to take as *variable* the extent to which any area of the city has an emergent social system closely linking the residents through reciprocal role relationships. To study neighborhoods a number of questions need to be raised: 1. Do the residents of the area have a regular set of relationships among themselves primarily based on propinquity?   2. What is the areal expansion of the relational network?   3. What is the nature of the social solidarity or social cohesion holding the relationships together?   4. What are the role relationships and role expectations for "neighbors"?

Many studies have shown that neighborhoods as social organizations are highly variable and quite volatile. They are not fixed entities that can be taken for granted. How then did we come to idealize the neighborhood as an ever-present and important social entity? The best place to start looking for an answer is in the work of the Chicago sociologists in the 1920's.

The concept of neighborhood as "natural area" came to prominence in the urban sociology of Park, Burgess, and their students at the University of Chicago. Urban neighborhoods were referred to as "natural areas" since they arose not from conscious planning efforts of outside organizations and agencies but as unplanned responses to the locational decisions of many individuals seeking suitable residential accommodations. The broad, impersonal processes of the urban land market, guided by natural economic laws operated so that according to Park " . . . every individual finds, eventually, either the place where he can, or the place where he must live" [1952, p. 79]. The city is then " . . . a constellation of natural areas, each with its own characteristic milieu, and each performing its specific function in the urban economy as a whole. . . . The metropolis is, it seems, a great sifting and sorting mechanism, which, in ways that are not yet wholly understood, infallibly selects out of the population as a whole the individuals best suited to live in a particular region and a particular milieu" [p. 79].

These "natural areas" grew out of, and were perpetuated by, the processes of residential selection. The residential coincidence of socially similar people generated differential natural areas. "Each separate part of the city is inevitably stained with the peculiar sentiments of its population. The effect of this is to convert what was at first a mere geographical expression into a neighborhood, that is to say, a locality with sentiments, traditions, and a history of its own" [Park 1952, p. 17].

Early students of the city began to view urban neighborhoods in highly romanticized ways. The neighborhood came to be seen as an expression of social solidarity based on common sentiments, beliefs, and values. It was like a village transplanted into the city's environment. It was with alarm and disdain that many students of the city noted that urban neighborhoods as social systems were disintegrating before their very own eyes as new migrants poured in. Impersonality, anonymity, transience, crime, violence, personal disorganization, and decay became the lot of the inner-city neighborhoods. Harkening back to a past that did not really exist the urbanists asked, "What's gone wrong with our cities?" "Why are neighborhood systems deteriorating?" Whatever the causes, many felt the only solution was to regenerate urban neighborhoods to make them vital, vibrant cores of city life. Commenting on recent planning attempts to rejuvenate urban areas along these lines, Jane Jacobs has written: "Neighborhood is a word that has come to sound like a Valentine. As a sentimental concept 'neighborhood' is harmful to city planning. It leads to attempts at warping city life into imitations of town or suburban life. Sentimentality plays with sweet intentions in place of good sense" [1961, p. 112].

The neighborhood as an appropriate unit of urban planning can be traced back to the work in 1929 of Clarence Arthur Perry. He suggested that an elementary school should form the core of the neighborhood, along with other necessary institutions. Shopping districts could be located along the neighborhood's periphery near traffic junctions and the shopping district of the adjacent area. The neighborhood's streets were to facilitate traffic movement within the area but to discourage through traffic. Major city traffic would not pass through the neighborhood but bypass it on some type of highway. The neighborhood unit as an object of urban planning became quite popular and was incorporated into the plans of many towns and cities during and following World War II. If the neighborhood is a reasonable unit for planning it is because it represents a basic expression of urban social life and not because it is an expression of primordial sentiments of social solidarity and territoriality that reached its zenith in the rural life of the nineteenth century.

When we talk of neighborhoods we can deal with varied expanses or levels of social organization. Gerald Suttles [1972] has suggested that in terms of patterns of social organization several types of neighborhoods can be found in the city: face-block, defended neighborhood, community of limited liability, expanded community of limited liability, and the contrived community. The *face-block* is the most basic form of city neighborhood. It consists of the immediate families and individuals whose dwellings share common egress and who use the same facilities on a regular basis. Most typically this neighborhood group consists of two sides of a block where dwellings face each other. Sometimes apartment complexes are characterized by the face-block pattern where courtyards, parking lots, back doors, and play areas are central to two or more buildings. Occasionally high rise apartment buildings may have the face-block pattern where hallways serve several apartments, and facilities such as laundry, storage, and swimming pools bring residents into regular contact. Face-blocks as neighborhoods are very loose networks of relationships. Much of the organizational patterns focus on the play pattern of children who are required by their parents to "stay on the block." Thus children's peer groups, limited largely by block bounds, emerge and become expressed as gangs or "corner-boys" as the children get older. Adult socialization patterns become influenced by propinquity as well as by the range and location of children's playmates. In describing the neighboring in Park Forest, William Whyte has written: "It is the children who set the basic design; their friendships are translated into the mother's friendships, and these, in turn, to the families" [1956, p. 375]. Whyte suggests that the local wives' kaffeeklatsch routes are the same as the range of the children's play.

For some adults the face-block may be a real source of social control and influence. Social pressure from neighbors may have its impact on some local residents in the style and maintenance of their dwelling and lawn, in consumption patterns, and in modes of child control.

But what makes a face-block area become a neighborhood? What leads to the development of relationships among the locals? Propinquity, where people live vis-à-vis each other, and the extent to which their paths cross in their comings and goings are only contributory conditions. Herbert Gans maintains that the necessary condition is social homogeneity, or similarity of the residents in basic characteristics. Gans has observed: "Although propinquity brings neighbors into social contact, a certain degree of homogeneity is required to maintain this contact on a positive basis. If neighbors are too diverse, differences of behavior or attitude may develop which can lead to coolness or even conflict" [1968, p. 155]. And, "Some propinquity results in visual contact whether voluntary or involuntary; it produces social contact among neighbors, although homogeneity will determine how intensive the relationships will be and whether they will be positive or not" [p. 158]. Conversely, relationships based on social homogeneity are reinforced by propinquity by making frequent contacts both more convenient and more likely. But what if the face-block dwellers are heterogeneous? Then it's not likely that a warm, cohesive face-block system will develop. Residents will look elsewhere for their friends and the significant contacts necessary for their well being. Work friends, clubs, and church groups are options for social interaction and they become likely arenas for those without meaningful neighborhood contacts.

The ingredient of homogeneity goes beyond the more general social characteristics of age, life-cycle position, education, income, and color. At the base of the relationship are the " . . . subjectively experienced definitions of homogeneity or heterogeneity which terminate in judgments of compatibility or incompatibility" [Gans 1968, p. 156]. Some have found that these subjective judgments focus on such things as child-rearing values and practices, temperament, political orientation, leisure-time interests, employment, and general world view. Face-blocks where people see themselves as being socially similar and compatible are characterized by fairly cohesive and complete interaction networks. People spend much of their leisure time together and sometimes form semiformal clubs to deal with their interests or concerns. Indeed, urban politicians will try to galvanize the block group into constituent actors by assigning block-captains or forming block clubs. By themselves such block organizations are simply too small and circumscribed to deal effectively with the neighborhood's major problems (such as garbage collection and street lighting) and must, when community issues arise, join with other like-intended blocks to develop some political muscle. On blocks where the residents are not socially or personally compatible a vibrant social interactional system does not develop. Interactions tend to be somewhat formal, stylized, and cool. Attempts to structure interaction about a common problem are difficult or nearly impossible. Residents spend their leisure time with others living elsewhere, in clubs or organizations, or in individual pursuits.

The second major category of neighborhood types is the *defended neighborhood*. It is a residential social system that shuts itself off from other areas and nonresidents through some social or physical mechanism. Examples of the means used to bound the defended neighborhood include delinquent gangs defending their turf; restrictive covenants excluding other status, racial, or ethnic groups; area reputation that says that you enter and remain here at your own risk; walls, gates, very dense shrubbery, moats, security guards, doormen, and other imposed barriers that keep residents in and out of view and strangers out; and sharp imposed boundaries such as freeways, rivers and canals, large park or green areas, railroad embankments or railyards, and industrial nuclei. But the defended neighborhood is more than just an area isolated from the rest of the city; it is an ongoing social system that has a corporate identity to both residents and outsiders. It is an area in which the residents have a relative degree of security as opposed to what they have in other adjacent areas. It is large enough in area to include most of the daily rounds of local movements. The people of the defended neighborhood share a common fate at the hands of the city and other key organizations, and their defensive posture serves as a source of social cohesion. Collective actions by the neighborhood's residents are reflected in protest groups, property-owners' associations, realty associations, and conservation committees. Such organizations usually emerge in response to given issues and may or may not remain viable for long periods of time.

A subculture develops among the defended neighborhood's residents. They come to share common values, beliefs, and local knowledge. The neighborhood becomes a source of personal identity for the residents. In discussing this identification process Ruth and John Useem and Duane Gibson have written: "The reputation of the larger neighborhood which the resident shares indicates to some extent the type of person he is. . . . Self-esteem is built upon a number of facets and the neighborhood reputation is one of these which a man uses to identify himself and to others. He becomes an instance of the reputation which the larger neighborhood has, i.e., he is the type of person who lives in that neighborhood" [1960, p. 75].

For many residents of the defended neighborhood, the area becomes an important framework for the individual's total entrance into various social systems, including the family and friendship clique. Conformity to local norms is necessary if the individual is to gain the social support of his neighbors. If the individual violates the trust of conformity bestowed upon him by his neighbors he becomes a threat to them, since he is no longer the type of person characteristic of the area—he becomes a threat to their very self-concept if they persist in their relationship with him. If the individual fails to conform to the defended neighborhood's norms and does lose the support of those around him, he suffers stress to the extent that he must look elsewhere for social support and regular positive social contacts.

The most classic examples of the defended neighborhood are the racial and ethnic ghettoes of large cities. The Jewish ghettoes found in medieval European cities were areas set aside by law for the Jewish population. Walled off from the remainder of the city they served not only to minimize the contact of the Jews with the gentiles but also to perpetuate the Jewish subculture. Contemporary cities in industrialized nations have seen the walls eliminated but still the ghetto remains. Louis Wirth's classic study of the ghetto has pointed out that "The Jews drifted into separate cultural areas not by external pressure but by deliberate design. To the Jews the geographically separated or socially isolated community seemed to offer the best opportunity for following their religious precepts, of preparing their food according to the established religious ritual, of following their dietary laws, of attending the synagogue for prayer three times a day, and of participating in the numerous functions of communal life which religious duty imposed upon every member of the community" [1958, p. 19].

The rich cultural life in the ghetto served to make the life of the urban Jew, in many ways, more warm and human than that of any other urban dweller. The high degree of identification of the Jew with his community is represented by the fact that even when the Jew moved from the ghetto he maintained many social relationships with the ghetto group. The culture that developed in the ghetto was so distinct from that of the other residential areas of the city that the migrant from the ghetto found obstacles and inner conflicts as he tried to adapt to a foreign cultural setting. Residential migration from the ghetto required the individual to make almost a complete readjustment of his life to the dominant patterns of the non-Jewish world. For those who do make the transition and move to other areas of the city, the ghetto, to some extent, is still a positive reference group for them in that it influences their behavior and colors their perception. For, as Wirth has written, "In their attempt to flee from the ghetto, the partially assimilated groups have found that the ghetto has followed them to their new quarters" [1958, p. 255].

Some migrant Jews and their families make the transition and become comfortably assimilated to the nonghetto forms of life. Others who find they cannot conform to the social expectations of the gentile world return to the ghetto where they generally may resume their place in the ethnic community. In some metropolitan communities today the suburban ghetto has appeared. With sizable numbers of "cultural" and/or "religious" Jews a series of organizations and institutions have emerged paralleling many of those of the inner city ghettoes of the 1920s. Different in content, to be sure, but still forming foci for community life, such institutions fill subcultural needs not obliterated by integration into the mainstream of American society.

Of course the ghetto form of organization is not unique to the urban Jew. The Italians, the Greeks, the Poles, the orientals—all have established ethnic, defended neighborhoods at one time or another in our large cities. These areas, by containing the social institutions required by the groups to work out their lives in the new world, have been major factors leading to the assimilation of the newcomers. Some of the areas have changed hands as invasion and succession have replaced one ethnic group with another, but many still retain visible signs of their ethnic heritages although occupied by newer urban ethnics—the blacks, the Puerto Ricans, the Cubans, and the Mexican-Americans.

The black ghetto has served to perpetrate the broad dichotomy between black and white in American culture. St. Clair Drake and Horace Cayton noted in an early, detailed study of Chicago's Black Belt: "While Bronzville's institutions differ little from those in other Midwestern Metropolitan communities, they differ considerably in content. This dissimilarity springs primarily from two facts: because the community is spatially isolated from the larger world, the development of its families, churches, schools, and voluntary associations has proceeded quite differently from the course taken by analogous white institutions; and second, Bronzville's 'culture' is but part of a larger national Negro culture" [1945, p. 396].

Defended neighborhoods also are found in white, nonethnic areas. Peter Binzen's description of the Kensington section of Philadelphia, and especially of its Fishtown area, reflects many of the organizational and interpersonal characteristics of the defended neighborhood. Kensington's existence as a viable residential community dates from 1730 when an English sea captain purchased ninety acres along the Delaware River about two miles northeast of Philadelphia's city center. This original settlement was called Fishtown and even though Kensington has grown much larger in response to the nearby location of many industrial employers, it has maintained its identity, homogeneity of population, and from time to time its residents have engaged in collective action for group goals. Binzen has written,

> . . . Fishtown survives today as a quaint urban hamlet of narrow, twisting streets, neighborhood groceries, corner bars, and row houses occupied by men and women who consider themselves the old, original Kensingtonians, and who yield to no one in their pride in their community or in their determination to keep it white. (In the summer of 1960 Fishtowners successfully routed from houses or apartments two Negro families, two Puerto Rican families, one dark-skinned Portuguese family, and a Cherokee Indian from North Carolina. In the fall of 1966 they joined in five days of rioting against a Negro family that moved into a near-by Kensington section.) [1970, pp. 85–86].

This collective action well illustrates the point that pressures and events from the outside world have much to do with the social constitution of the defended neighborhood. The threat to the local denizens served as a catalytic agent for collective organization and activities representing the values of the area's residents.

Today, the Fishtown neighborhood is sliding. The rate of deterioration of housing is rising as is the rate of poverty. However, in 1969 more than twenty Fishtown groups joined together and managed to obtain a promise from the Philadelphia City Council to build a much needed recreation center there. Surely the recreation center will not halt Fishtown's slide but the success of the neighborhood's groups bodes well for further local cooperation. The problem, of course, is for the neighborhood to sustain the enormous effort it requires to deal effectively and successfully with outside agencies. All too often groups from individual defended neighborhoods are simply unable to cope effectively with the large-scale bureaucracies whose decisions shape the areas' futures.

While the defended neighborhood has both formal and informal patterns of social organization, the index of the degree to which the neighborhood is viable is found in " . . . the extent to which certain groups, no matter how few in number, are able to keep intact neighborhood boundaries, to provide a general knowledge of its internal structure, and to keep alive the myth of unity and cohesion" [Suttles 1972, p. 41].

The third potential level for neighborhood social organization is the *community of limited liability*. The concept grows out of Morris Janowitz's study [1952] of the urban community press. Here the sense of community and the patterns of social organization are much more amorphous than those found in either the face-block or the defended neighborhoods. This is a local community whose definition, to a very large extent, is imposed and maintained by outside agencies. Cities spawn numerous administrative districts for education, fire protection, police protection, sanitation and sewage, welfare, and such special projects as model cities programs, restoration, and urban renewal. Each of these districts is established by a different agency. The agency dealing with the problem or program determines the scope of each district in the manner that best suits the goals and purposes of the agency, with little or no thought to coordination with other agencies or bodies. Thus, these districts have unique boundaries that throw together urbanites who in other services may be located in different districts. Residents of the same voting precinct may send their children to different schools and/or may be served by different police and fire districts. In addition, other nonpublic agencies get into the act and divide the areas other ways. Church parish boundaries, subdistricts of realty boards, circulation zones of the local "neighborhood" newspaper, and chapters of business and voluntary associations serve to cut the city up into a many-dimensional lattice of involvement and participation. Indeed each of these areas—the school district, the parish, the voting precinct—is an important focus of organizational involvement. However, in terms of the normal sweep of life, they demand highly segmentalized and limited social participation around very highly focused and specific problems. Each of such "neighborhoods" represents a tiny part of the totality of the resident's social involvement. The organization is limited to deal with only selected issues, problems, and matters.

The growth and expansion of large-scale urban administrative bureaus are giving rise to the development of a new neighborhood form— the *expanded community of limited liability.* This level of neighborhood refers to large sections of the city—the North Side or the Southeast, and so on. Such large areas have become the scale of administration and planning for many urban agencies. This new organizational operation is evident in the establishment of new levels of administration. For example, some urban school systems have developed a district level of organization that oversees numerous grade schools and many high schools in one large section of the city. The residents of one high school area no longer can deal directly with the principal on important matters. They must now deal at the subdistrict level that includes their school and many others as well. Thus, a large number of formerly separate areas are thrown together and must work out new patterns of relationships and organization in order to deal with the district office on pressing problems and issues. A new, expanded neighborhood of limited liability has emerged in response to expanded administrative areas.

The large-scale organizations are also reorganizing themselves in such ways so that decision-making responsibility is being both centralized and pushed upward in the organizational structure. This means that locals by themselves simply do not have the "muscle" to deal with the prestigious "downtown office." Local groups can only deal with these centralized bureaucracies by demonstrating that they do speak for vast segments of the population. Large-scale community organizations with professional credentials and experience in dealing with big bureaucracies are coming to the fore to represent these new expanded communities of limited liability. Indeed, Suttles [1972] has suggested that out of frustration many locals have engaged in demonstrations, protests, and other militant tactics. But such efforts are usually spotty and are easily written off as crank, lunatic fringe, or subversive behavior. And such activities often are actually counterproductive. One problem with the expanded community of limited liablility is that it can gain local consensus only on a few issues that face all (thousands or millions) in one large section of the city. Sacrificed are the issues specific to a few face-blocks, defended neighborhoods, or communities of limited liability. In many cases this level of neighborhood organization becomes so removed from the problems of blocks and individuals that at best it seems unreal and at worst just another large-scale bureaucracy meddling in the affairs of good, honest people.

Another form of neighborhood organization described by Suttles [1972] is the *artificial, or contrived neighborhood.* With the coming of the planners and developers prepackaged residential areas are erupting on the urbanscape. Many of these areas—some in the inner city and some at the fringe as well—seem to show three of the basic characteristics of the more traditional defended neighborhood. First, the boundaries are very clearly drawn. Streets, architectural design, and walls are used to mark off what is and what is not the contrived neighborhood.

Second, the area's identity is established and symbolized before the housing units are made available to renters or buyers. This manufactured image usually reflects some quaint, pseudohistorical, "Mad Avenue," or psychodramatic theme summarized in the development's name. Perusal of one metropolitan area's Sunday real estate pages revealed these names for such developments: Country Corners, Tall Oaks, Heritage, Peppertree, Valley Green, Shaker Square, Rolling Brook, and Coronado Woods. Public housing projects are usually called by the name of some former solid citizen whose descendants could only suffer pain in seeing their name affixed to some of the decaying developments. These images usually are accepted by the residents and become sources of identification.

A third characteristic of the contrived neighborhood, which is similar to that of a traditional defended neighborhood, is a degree of cultural homogeneity of the residents built into the structures through space and cost factors and enforced by the developer and owners or realtors. Through their distinctive and guarded boundaries, prepackaged but adopted identity, and their cultural homogeneity these new developments are becoming a form of neighborhood on the urban scene.

Collectively the types of neighborhoods discussed in this section are not mutually exclusive patterns of organizations. They are more properly seen as a series of decreasingly intense arenas of social organization that may or may not involve the residents of any locale. The face-block is the most basic and is based on primary relationships growing out of residential propinquity and social homogeneity. The defended neighborhood and its cousin the artificial, or contrived, neighborhood are the next level of organization. Covering a larger area but maintaining homogeneity, identity, and potential organizational structure, the defended neighborhood offers the residents a haven of security against the more hostile and impersonal outside world. The community of limited liability, primarily generated in response to the administrative patterns of the outside world both public and private, offers the individual an arena of participation, albeit a highly specialized and segmental one. The expanded community of limited liability carries the whole thing one step further as large-scale organizations centralize their decision making and create broader areal administrative components, which leaves our urban Don Quixote to tilt at bureaucratic windmills while the boys in the back room decide his fate.

SUMMARY AND A SIDE GLANCE AT THE URBAN LAND MARKET

In focusing on the internal structure of the metropolis the major topics explored were density gradients, neighborhood life-cycle patterns, city-fringe social and economic differentials, the geometry of urban space, social area analysis, and neighborhood social organization. Excluded from consideration has been the residential segregation of status, racial, and ethnic groups although such differentiation has been implicit in much of this discussion. The literature on residential segregation is one of the largest in all of urban sociology. We have, accordingly, separated segregation for treatment into its own chapter for this book.

The location of various groups and activities across the city, as well as patterns of change, are not the result of broad, amorphous forces operating beyond the human scene. Rather, the patterned internal structure of the metropolis is a direct result of the operation of the urban land market. Sociologists have left this topic largely to the economists who have tended to treat the land market in terms of the concepts of supply and demand. While a sociology of the land market remains to be developed certain basics need to be described.

William Form [1954] has suggested that to discover who are the basic groups interacting in those decisions involving land use we need to ask three basic questions: 1. Who are the really big consumers of land? 2. Which groups and individuals specialize in the buying and selling of land and in related transactions? 3. Which groups and organizations mediate conflicts and evolve control systems and mechanisms over land ownership, land use, and land transactions?

While there would be interesting, researchable differences among cities in American society there seem to be certain constant groups involved in land market activities. First, there are the real estate, building, and land development businesses. These groups are central in the buying, developing, and selling process. These are the big money-makers who profit from high rates on lucrative transactions. It is in their interest to keep the land pot boiling. Instead of being passive agents who act as intermediaries in land transactions, they are aggressive entrepreneurs for the development of new land uses, the redevelopment of the old, and the turnover of existing land. The second category of organizations operating in the urban land market consists of the large industries, businesses, and utilities. These groups purchase the largest and most strategic parcels of land. Their locational decisions often are major "priming actions" in land development and redevelopment. A priming action is an activity that sets the broad framework for a mass of secondary activities [Chapin & Weiss 1962, p. 431]. These priming actions trigger waves of activities by real estate and land developers, builders, bankers, and others. Priming actions affect the future location of other businesses, churches, schools, and various status and racial groups. For example, the location of a large, heavy industrial plant in a given tract of land will tend to exclude the development of residential areas nearby, especially those of middle and upper status, and will attract other heavy industry and related manufacturing and transportation activities. The location of Chicago's jetport at the O'Hare site has prompted many secondary locational activities throughout the metropolitan area's whole northwestern sector.

The third category of land market participants are the individual land owners and other small consumers. Unorganized, they tend to provide the volume of transactions needed by the realtors and developers to turn large profits. They represent a large component of the demand for land and housing but are essentially limited to responding to land market conditions produced by activities of developers, bankers, realtors, and public agencies. Some sociologists and geographers have explored individual decision making in terms of housing. They have viewed the processes by which people attempt to maximize status, space, and transportation concerns. Yet all of the decisions of individuals must operate within a framework largely determined by the big-money interests. To the extent that the context of the individual decision making has been ignored, the residential-choice models have been less than satisfactory in predicting urban form.

The fourth category operating in the land market consists of the government and public agencies that deal with land matters. School districts, fire and police agencies, zoning boards, and planning commissions are all involved to some extent at one time or another. Some of these groups are land consumers themselves, as in the case of municipal and school buildings. Others of these bodies serve as regulators of land use and land transactions. Within an individual community these groups sometimes actually work at cross-purposes, thus complicating the whole land market operation.

A number of factors need to be considered in attempting to identify the recurring regularities in the relationships among these categories: 1. What are the amounts and types of resources these groups bring to interactions over land matters? 2. What are the latent as well as manifest functions of each group in the land market and are these functions beneficial or deleterious for humane, efficient urban development? 3. How do the various organizational sectors align themselves on various kinds of land use issues and are the patterns of alignment stable over time? If the patterns change are the changes related to the specific content of the land issue? 4. What is the nature of the accountability patterns for the various groups and how does this affect their interactions? 5. What image of the city does each group have and how does the image become involved in the intergroup interactions? How much congruence in their image of the city do the groups have and to what extent do differences in image lead to conflict among the groups [Form 1954]?

Analysis of the various groups involved in land market machinations indicates that there are certain major value orientations that play determining roles in group actions. These value orientations are those stressing profit-making, the public interest, and culturally rooted matters [Chapin 1957, pp. 68–69]. Profit making is an obvious motivation for the realtors, land developers, and business users. Yet land use patterns do not reflect only the economic values of those involved in land transactions. Indeed, the public interest in health, safety, convenience, the public economy, and liveability becomes a major concern for groups acting in the public's behalf. Attempts at zoning, code development and enforcement, and long-range land-use planning reflect attempts to align economic and public concerns. Socially rooted values frequently lead groups to act to preserve or advance certain customs, beliefs, or traditions, as in the attempt to protect Beacon Hill, to redevelop Philadelphia's key historical sites, to maintain the San Francisco cable cars, and to preserve parks, cemeteries, and buildings in many cities.

While local groups may interact on the basis of differing value orientations, it must be kept in mind that the local community is no longer a system closed in from the outside world. As in the case of many aspects of local life, land-use decisions may be shaped by decisions made elsewhere. The decision in the New York home office of a large corporation to build a new plant in a given local community can have a major impact on the operation of the land market to the extent that such a decision becomes a "priming action." State and federal legislation on housing or transportation programs also affect local land-use decisions, as do federal and state regulations on land use, pollution, and money lending. If a national land-use policy is developed, as many hope, there will be an enormous redirection of the relationships among the various groups in local urban land markets that far surpasses that generated by recent federal urban renewal and housing legislation.

The social processes of competition, conflict, cooperation, collusion, and accommodation that characterize interactions among land market sectors underlie the density, factorial, geometric, and neighborhood patterns of the city. In the past, the land market was left to the economist and, occasionally, the political scientist. Ideally, the future will bring more sociological investigations, perspectives, and explanatory models to help us better understand the development process of the metropolis and to serve us as we move to ameliorate the obviously inhumane aspects of current urban structure.

BIBLIOGRAPHY

Peter W. Amato, "A Comparison: Population Densities, Land Values and Socio-Economic Class in Four Latin American Cities." *Land Economics,* 1970, 41:447–455.

Wendell Bell, "The Utility of the Shevky Typology for the Design of Urban Sub-Area Field Studies." *Journal of Social Psychology,* 1958, XLVII:71–83.

Brian J. L. Berry and Yehoshua S. Cohen, "Decentralization of Commerce and Industry: The Restructuring of Metropolitan America." In Louis H. Masotti and Jeffrey K. Hadden, eds., *The Urbanization of the Suburbs.* Sage, 1973.

Brian J. L. Berry, James W. Simmons, and Robert J. Tennant, "Urban Population Densities: Structure and Change." *Geographical Review,* 1963, 53:389–405.

Peter Binzen, *Whitetown, U.S.A.* Random House, 1970.

E. W. Burgess, "The Growth of the City." In Robert E. Park, E. W. Burgess, and R. D. McKenzie, eds., *The City.* University of Chicago Press, 1925.

F. Stuart Chapin, Jr., *Urban Land Use Planning.* Harper, 1957.

F. Stuart Chapin, Jr., and Shirley F. Weiss, eds., *Urban Growth Dynamics.* John Wiley and Sons, 1962.

St. Clair Drake and Horace R. Cayton, *Black Metropolis.* Harcourt Brace Jovanovich, 1945.

Beverly Duncan, Georges Sabagh, and Maurice D. Van Arsdol, Jr., "Patterns of City Growth." *American Journal of Sociology,* LXVIII:418–429.

Charles A. Ekstrom, "Community Social Structure and Issue Differentiation: A Study in the Political Sociology of Welfare." *Sociological Focus,* 1968, 1:1–16.

Reynolds Farley, "Suburban Persistence." *American Sociological Review,* 1964, 29:38–47.

Walter Firey, *Land Use in Central Boston.* Harvard University Press, 1947.

William H. Form, "The Place of Social Structure in the Determination of Land Use: Some Implications for a Theory of Urban Ecology." *Social Forces,* 1954, 32:317–323.

Herbert J. Gans, *People and Plans.* Basic Books, 1968.

Scott Greer, *The Emerging City.* The Free Press, 1962.

Avery M. Guest, "Urban Growth and Population Densities." *Demography,* 1973, 10:53–70.

Lee Hagerty, Jr., "Another Look at the Burgess Hypothesis: Time as an Important Variable." *American Journal of Sociology*, 1971, 76:1084–1093.

Chauncy D. Harris and Edward L. Ullman, "The Nature of Cities." *Annals of the American Academy of Political and Social Science*, 1945, CCXLII:7–17.

Edgar M. Hoover and Raymond Vernon, *Anatomy of a Metropolis*. Doubleday, 1962.

Homer Hoyt, *The Structure and Growth of Residential Neighborhoods in the United States*. Federal Housing Administration, 1939.

John T. Hough, Jr., *A Peck of Salt*. Little, Brown, 1970.

Albert Hunter, "Community Change: A Stochastic Analysis of Chicago's Local Communities 1930–1960." *American Journal of Sociology*, 1974, 79:924–947.

Jane Jacobs, *The Death and Life of Great American Cities*. Random House, 1961.

Morris Janowitz, *The Community Press in an Urban Setting*. University of Chicago Press, 1952.

Anthony J. La Greca and Kent P. Schwirian, "Social Class and Race as Factors of Residential Density." Paper presented at the annual meeting of the Southern Sociological Association, Atlanta, 1974.

A. M. Latif, "Factor Structure and Change of Alexandria, Egypt, 1947 and 1960." In Kent P. Schwirian, ed., *Comparative Urban Structure*. Heath, 1974.

Harold F. Mark and Kent P. Schwirian, "Ecological Position, Central Place Function, and Community Population Growth." *American Journal of Sociology*, 73:30–41.

Robert A. Murdie, *Factorial Ecology of Metropolitan Toronto, 1951–1961*. Department of Geography, University of Chicago Research Paper No. 116, 1969.

Richard F. Muth, *Cities and Housing; The Spatial Pattern of Urban Residential Land Use*. University of Chicago Press, 1969.

Robert E. Park, *Human Communities*. The Free Press, 1952.

Lee Rainwater, *Behind Ghetto Walls*. Aldine, 1970.

Leo F. Schnore, "The Timing of Metropolitan Decentralization: A Contribution to the Debate." *Journal of the American Institute of Planners*, 1959, 25:200–206.

Leo F. Schnore, "On the Spatial Structure of Cities in the Americas." In Philip M. Hauser and Leo F. Schnore, eds., *The Study of Urbanization*. John Wiley and Sons, 1965.

Leo F. Schnore and Hal. H. Winsborough, "Functional Classification and the Residential Location of Social Classes." In Brian J. L. Berry, ed., *City Classification Handbook*. Wiley-Interscience, 1972.

Kent P. Schwirian and Marc D. Matre, "The Ecological Structure of Canadian Cities." In Kent P. Schwirian, ed., *Comparative Urban Structure*. Heath, 1974.

Kent P. Schwirian and Jesus Rico-Velasco, "The Residential Distribution of Status Groups in Puerto Rico's Metropolitan Areas." *Demography,* 1971, 8:81–90.

Kent P. Schwirian and Ruth K. Smith, "Primacy, Modernization, and Urban Structure: The Ecology of Puerto Rican Cities." In Kent P. Schwirian, ed., *Comparative Urban Structure.* Heath, 1974.

Gerald D. Suttles, *The Social Construction of Communities.* University of Chicago Press, 1972.

Ralph Thomlinson, *Urban Structure: The Social and Spatial Character of Cities.* Random House, 1969.

Roy C. Treadway, "Social Components of Metropolitan Population Densities." *Demography,* 1969, 6:55–74.

Ruth Useem, John Useem, and Duane Gibson, "The Function of Neighboring for the Middle-Class Male." *Human Organization,* 1969, (Summer): 44–55.

William H. Whyte, Jr., *The Organization Man.* Doubleday, 1956.

Hal H. Winsborough, "An Ecological Approach to the Theory of Suburbanization." *American Journal of Sociology,* 1963, LXVII:565–570.

Louis Wirth, *The Ghetto.* University of Chicago Press, 1956.

4.

TYPES OF URBAN UNITS

Jack P. Gibbs

In highly urbanized countries such as the United States, virtually all sociological research now has an urban setting. Thus, in recent decades, sociological research on juvenile delinquency, collective behavior (e.g., riots), social stratification, voluntary associations, and race-ethnic relations has been largely restricted to urban populations. Consequently, urban sociology is now a field without a *distinctive* subject matter. As Ernest Manheim observed: "It appears sometimes as if urban sociology may become a mere label for cataloging American research" [1960, p. 228].

Sociologists are no longer particularly concerned with rural-urban differences because during this century those differences in highly urbanized countries have become very blurred. However, it remains the case (virtually by definition) that rural territory is characterized by a much lower population density and a much greater proportion of residents in agricultural occupations. Additionally, evidence indicates that at *some point* in the history of any country the rural population is characterized by a relatively greater fertility rate, a lower suicide rate, a lower divorce or separation rate, less anonymity, less creativity, and a more religious outlook, to mention only a few rural-urban differences [Sorokin & Zimmerman 1929; Abu-Lughod 1964]. Such contrast gave rise to the notion of "urbanism," meaning sociocultural patterns (or ways of life) that are supposedly peculiar to urban environments.

Since rural and urban populations may differ in all manner of ways, it may appear that urban sociology never had a distinctive subject matter. But the field was once united by a concern with two central questions: 1. Are there any *universal* sociocultural differences between rural and urban populations? 2. If there are such differences, can they be explained by reference to purely ecological and demographic contrasts such as population size, density, and nonagricultural employment? The second question extended research from strictly rural-urban contrasts to comparisons of territorial units that differed as to population size, density, and occupational composition. In other words, sociologists came to recognize that rural-urban differences are not truly qualitative; rather, they came to think in terms of a rural-urban continuum, meaning that all territorial units are "urban" to some degree and "rural" to some degree [Duncan & Reiss 1956]. Nonetheless, the central questions for urban sociology remained essentially the same.

The foregoing observations are not intended to suggest that urban sociology enjoyed great success. A truly systematic theory of rural-urban differences was never developed, and the reality or importance of a universal rural-urban continuum became suspect [Dewey 1960]. Even isolated generalizations about rural-urban differences came to be questioned, and today few sociologists would argue that there are truly *universal* differences between rural and urban populations [e.g., Abu-Lughod 1964; Fischer 1971; Greer 1956; Reiss 1959]. In the United States, for example, the difference between official suicide rates of the rural and urban population in the 1960s was much less than some 70 years ago [Gibbs 1971, p. 292]; and one could argue that the higher urban rate early in this century reflected the frustrations of rural migrants and immigrants in coping with the new environment they found in large American cities. To generalize the argument, a first-generation "urbanite" is one thing, but a second- or third-generation urbanite is quite another.

Whatever the reason for diminishing rural-urban differences, the trend itself does not account for the withering away of urban sociology as a distinctive field of study. Indeed, the trend only gives rise to some interesting questions, one being: do rural-urban differences follow a similar evolutionary course in all societies? The point is that urban sociology did not wither away because the practitioners answered all the important questions; far from it. The only conspicuous reason for the decline of the field is urbanization itself. Sociology flourishes only in highly urbanized countries (the United States especially); but once a high degree of urbanization[1] is reached, rural-urban differences blur and become less interesting. Above all, the locus of sociological research becomes urban because that is where one finds the "action."

One may or may not bemoan the fact that urban sociology is becoming little more than a label for sociological research in an urban setting. In any case, some of the older questions survive, whatever the focus of contemporary research may be. Specifically, what is an urban setting? The question recognizes that the rural-urban distinction remains relevant even in highly urbanized countries, but the distinction cannot be grasped without understanding the meaning of four terms—rural, city, urban area, and metropolitan area. Those terms are used in all manner

---

1. The degree of urbanization is the proportion of the total population (national or regional) that resides in some type of urban unit (a city, an urban area, or a metropolitan area). For elaboration on the meaning of degree of urbanization and observations on its importance see Davis and Golden [1954]. Here it will suffice to point out that urban sociology is not restricted to the study of particular urban units or comparisons of urban units. Research also extends to properties of urbanization (e.g., the degree of urbanization) at the international or global level [Davis 1973; Gibbs 1961].

of sociological studies, but what do they mean? One cannot comprehend or "do" urban sociology without an answer.

POINTS
OF POPULATION CONCENTRATION

At a very high altitude over any country, an observer would detect a significant feature of population distribution—places of residence are not located so as to maximize the distance between them. On the contrary, there are distinct points of population concentration in any country, and each point is not only a territorial unit in itself but perhaps also the center of a larger territorial unit. Thus, in flying up the coast of California an observer would identify one huge point of population concentration as Los Angeles, and the observer might also notice that somewhere past Los Angeles the predominant traffic flow changes from a southerly to a northerly direction. The change indicates that Los Angeles is more than a point of population concentration; it is also the center of a large region, the inhabitants of which look to Los Angeles as a place of employment, or for goods and services.

All social scientists are aware of population concentration, but they do not agree in their choice of terms to describe the phenomenon or on procedures for establishing the boundaries of points of population concentration. The social science literature offers a bewildering variety of terms—city, urban area, metropolitan area, community, and metropolitan region—all of which somehow relate to points of population concentration. Those terms are not used by scholars in the same way; worse still, writers commonly give vague definitions of the terms or leave them undefined. Moreover, there are no standard delimitation procedures. The meanings of each term can be clarified only by recognition that there is no *one* boundary for a point of population concentration. Rather, there may be several boundaries, each of which represents a distinct type of territorial unit.

URBAN UNITS

Scholars agree that most, if not all, points of population concentration are urban and that the remainder of the national area is rural. But the exact nature of the rural-urban distinction is debatable, and it is complicated by the variety of terms, such as cities, urban areas, and metropolitan areas, that are used to identify urban territory. Scholars commonly use one or another of these terms as though it were synonymous with "urban," but they disagree in their choice and one sociologist may speak of cities, while another speaks of urban areas.

The first step in resolving terminological anarchy is to recognize three types of territorial units—cities, urban areas, and metropolitan areas. None of these terms designate urban territory *in general.* If a generic term is needed, it should be "urban unit," meaning a city, an urban area, or a metropolitan area.

Cities

Few terms in sociology are used as uncritically as "city," and those who use the term rarely confront the question: what characteristics identify territorial units as cities? Consensus in answers to that question is not realized largely because social scientists commonly use the word city to denote *urban territory in general* [e.g., Mumford 1968; Sjoberg 1968; Walton & Carns 1973]. The usage leads to sterile arguments and divergent definitions, with one definition contradicting another because they refer to different types of urban units.

Proposed Definition

A city or municipality is a political entity with a definite administrative spatial boundary that was initially drawn to include all or part of an urban area. Like other types of civil divisions, a city is not politically autonomous, but it differs from other types of civil divisions in two respects. First, as already indicated, the boundary of a city was originally drawn in relation to an urban area. Second, if the boundaries of some type of civil division are contiguous (ignoring separations by water), then instances of that type are not cities, nor are they cities if all instances combined approximate the area of the country as a whole. The second contrast is essentially a negative definition of a city. Thus, in the United States, counties, wards, and precincts are not cities, as their boundaries are contiguous if separations by water are ignored. Specifically, any one county necessarily touches on or is adjacent to at least one other county, but the boundary of the typical city does not touch on the boundary of another city.

The boundary of a city may change over time, but it is changed only by administrative action. Further, the correspondence between the boundary of a city and that of the related urban area may not be close; and the divergence may increase to the point that the city boundary includes only a small part of the urban area, in which case the urban area *may* comprise more than one city.

The foregoing definition ignores certain features of cities, such as the form and functions of government. Although not politically autonomous, some city governments enact and enforce laws or ordinances. However, that conception of city government is ethnocentric since it does not apply to some countries, especially from a historical point of view. In other words, the "normative powers" of city governments are by no means the same, and no particular kind of "norm-making" power is true of city governments *by definition.*

The form and functions of city government vary so much internationally and historically that it would be questionable to refer to them in defining a city. Even in the United States, cities differ as to form of government. For example, the "commission" form of government did not appear until this century, and some American cities never adopted it [Gordon 1968]. City governments also differ as to functions, especially as regards ownership of public utilities. Finally, one cannot presume that cities share common demographic or ecological features, beyond the inclusion of all or part of an urban area. True, we tend to think of cities as large points of population concentration, but the number of residents varies enormously from city to city, even in the same country, and the stipulation of any minimum population size would be arbitrary.

Urban Areas

Urban sociology rests on the assumption that the population and area of a country are divided into two sectors—rural and urban. However, this would be a debatable distinction even if the rural territory and population were treated as residual categories (i.e., population and territory that are *not* urban are rural). Obviously, that simplification accomplishes very little. The literature clearly reveals such divergent conceptions of an urban area that there are distinct types of definitions.

One type of definition presumes that particular kinds of organizations, institutions, or styles of life distinguish rural and urban populations. For example, most Americans probably think of an urban area in terms of facilities—theaters, libraries, post offices, restaurants, parking lots, hospitals, and so forth. But a list of "urban" facilities usually reflects experience with a particular country, culture, or civilization, and it would be questionable to incorporate such a list in what purports to be a universal definition of urban areas. Indeed, it would be difficult to identify "essential" urban facilities in any country.

The second type of definition is labeled "ecological," for want of a better designation. Such a definition commonly considers population size, density, and/or nonagricultural occupations as "urban" characteristics. As we shall see, several difficulties are confronted when an urban area is so defined.

Toward an Ecological Definition

Contrary to common practice, the terms "city" and "urban area" should not be equated. For instance, Wirth [1938, p. 5] defined a city as "a relatively large, dense, and permanent settlement of socially heterogenous individuals," without any reference to political or administrative boundaries. No definition is right or wrong, but Wirth's nonpolitical definition is conducive to terminological confusion if one does not recognize that it actually pertains to urban areas, not to cities.

Most definitions of an urban area do not even suggest how such units are to be delimited; rather, the typical definition tacitly assumes a boundary and emphasizes the characteristics of the unit. Thus, Wirth speaks of a "permanent settlement," but without indicating how the boundary is to be determined.

All definitions of an urban area expressly or implicitly refer to a point of population concentration. Since even one place of residence may be taken as a point of concentration, an urban area is literally a "cluster of points of population concentration," the limits of which are not always obvious. Further, how one delimits a terrritorial unit determines the unit's characteristics. Population size is a function of the areal extent of the territorial unit, which means that the population can be "large" or "small," depending on the method of delimiting the boundary of the unit. The point is that a definition of an urban area should suggest how the boundary is to be delimited.

Consider Wirth's reference to "socially heterogenous individuals," an allusion to what is known as *urbanism*. It is a common practice to define an urban area in terms of such sociocultural features or "ways of life" as anonymity, cosmopolitanism, liberalism, and contractual relations. But such characteristics are vague, difficult to measure, and commonly defined in an arbitrary way. For example, even supposing that it is possible to measure "anonymity," at what point on the anonymity continuum does a population become "urban"? It is difficult to think of an answer that would not be arbitrary. Equally important, a definition of an urban area in terms of sociocultural features tends to be ethnocentric. Carried to its extreme, we have the idea that an urban area or "city" is a place where—to adopt an observation of Truman Capote's—one can get a shirt laundered at 3:00 A.M. The idea is only a special case of the "bright-lights" kind of definition, which takes London, New York, or some other large point of population concentration as the standard.

As for Wirth's reference to heterogeneity, social differences among individuals are multitudinous, and the definition unrealistically implies that the differences are all equally relevant. In any case, there is no indication as to the necessary degree of social heterogeneity, or how it is measured. Further, the amount of social heterogeneity depends on how one draws the boundary of the population. Social heterogeneity can be increased by simply extending the boundary, and the extent of the boundary also determines the level of population density. But note again that Wirth's definition does not suggest any procedure or criteria for delimiting a boundary. He simply assumes the existence of a boundary, which leaves only one question: taking the territorial unit as somehow given, is it rural or urban? That question appears to simplify matters, but it ignores a crucial consideration—the characteristics of a territorial unit depend on the way its boundary has been drawn.

The final problem with Wirth's definition is that population size and density are quantitative. Consequently, at what size and density level does a territorial unit become an urban area? Wirth recognized but did not answer the question, and any answer would be arbitrary. The same is true of any definition that refers to the proportion of the population engaged in or dependent on nonagricultural work. Thus, the typical "ecological" definition of an urban area is subject to some of the criticisms made of Wirth's definition.

The foregoing references to population size and density are especially important because those properties commonly enter into official or census definitions of urban territory. The United States Bureau of the Census recognizes "places" (with or without political boundaries) having 2,500 or more residents as "urban." That minimum number is clearly arbitrary and indefensible apart from convention or purely practical considerations (e.g., insufficient funds to tabulate data on smaller places). The point is emphasized because subsequent definitions of urban areas and other types of territorial units may strike the reader as unconventional. They are somewhat unconventional, but conventional definitions tend to be arbitrary and peculiar to particular countries.

Proposed Definition

An aerial view of an urban area does not reveal population size, density, or nonagricultural occupations. What one observes are manifestations of the use of space.

Some economic activities result in the extraction of objects or substances from the ground or bodies of water. In English-speaking countries those extractive activities are identified with the industries of agriculture, forestry, fishing, hunting, and mining. Some such activities are found in all countries, but the proportion of surface space under extractive use is by no means a constant, internationally or historically.

We now arrive at the *first component* of a definition of an urban area: there must be a continuous surface space that is used for some purpose other than extractive activities. Given the abstract terms in the definiens, the definition is not precise, and not a great deal can be done to achieve greater precision. Accordingly, in applying the definition, investigators may disagree somewhat in the identification and delimitation of urban areas, but clarification of certain terms will minimize disagreements.

Some land and water surfaces are not used and still others are used for multiple purposes (e.g., a body of water may be used for both commercial fishing and recreation). The major delimitation principle is that for surface space to be classed as urban it must be in use and the use must be exclusively nonextractive. The first requirement recognizes that some space may not be used for any particular purpose, although it may be "held" in anticipation of sale or future use. Such a case is not hypothetical since barren land surrounding residential areas in some parts of the United States is not used for any purpose, and its only value appears to be speculative.

The most difficult problem is temporal variation. Farm land may lie fallow for years, and space may be used for extractive purposes at one time and nonextractive purposes at another. Since land-use distinctions based on the amount of time are bound to be arbitrary, the only feasible criterion is to require that the use be clearly nonextractive when the urban area is delimited. Given doubts as to whether the space is being used or the nature of its use, *previous unquestioned use* is decisive.

Surface space used in agriculture, forestry, fishing, hunting, or mining is not urban territory. In the case of agriculture, the space includes both land under cultivation and pasture or grazing land. But the land must be used for "growing" animals, which means that land set aside for yards to hold or transfer animals is under nonextractive use. Although land used to raise animals as food for human beings is clearly extractive, the category also includes land that provides food for animals that are used in agricultural work, such as horses for herding cattle and oxen for plowing.

Even the notion that the cultivation of land constitutes an extractive use requires qualification. Some land on which plants are grown is not under extractive use, notably botanical gardens, parks, and golf courses. Whatever the plants, they must be extracted for human food, clothing, building materials, or for feed for domesticated animals.

Hunting and fishing are not clearly economic activities in *some* countries, such as the United States, where few individuals engage in those activities to obtain food. In one and the same space some individuals may hunt or fish for sport, while others engage in those activities for economic gain. Nonetheless, since both hunting or fishing are extractive activities, land or water used for either purpose is rural.

The term "mining" refers to the extraction of inanimate objects or substances from the earth. Given the concern with surface space, subterranean mining is of no concern in delimiting urban territory, but strip mining is a relevant extractive use of space.

Some of these qualifications may appear arbitrary, but they are less arbitrary than is defining an urban area in terms of population size, density, or nonagricultural employment. Moreover, the qualifications are of little practical importance. The use of space is commonly obvious, and the meaning of the terms in the definition is not so vague as to preclude agreement among observers in delimiting an urban area. One possible exception is "arterial urbanization," meaning the extension of urban territory along transportation routes, such as highways, waterways, or railroad lines. Objects or substances are not extracted from transportation routes, of course, but virtually all points of population concentration in a country are connected by transportation routes. The solution is to consider a transportation route as an extension of urban territory if, and only if, along one or both sides the space is under continuous nonextractive use, residential or otherwise. The only exceptions to the rule are bridges, which are treated by a special rule as though they were an extension of urban territory. Given that rule and the one exception, a transportation route is urban territory up to the point on each side where continuous nonextractive use of space ends. Both residential and commercial uses of land tend to expand along routes connecting two large urban areas (e.g., Dallas and Fort Worth) in the same vicinity, and eventually the two may become one urban area. According to the foregoing definition and qualifications, they become one urban area when the land along either side of a connecting transportation route is continuously under nonextractive use.

Observations on the extent of urban territory are suspect unless some definite criterion is specified. For example, the idea of a "megalopolis" stretching from north of Boston to south of Washington, D.C., has been popularized in recent years [Gottman 1961]. However interesting or horrifying that idea may be, the meaning of the term "megalopolis" is vague. If it refers to *continuous urban territory,* there are no urban units of that size in the United States.

Once the boundary of an urban area is delimited, it may be that enclaves of "extractive" space or unused space are surrounded by the area. Nonetheless, the urban area is continuous and surrounded by "extractive" space or space not in use. Yet an urban area is something more than space. All definitions recognize that an urban area contains permanent places of residence. Rather than stipulate some arbitrary minimum number of residents, the requirement is that the area contain at least two occupied places of residence or households. That criterion recognizes two major alternatives in the way of spatial organization—residences may be located so as to maximize or, alternatively, to minimize the distance between them. Since residential concentration reduces that distance, urban areas represent a distinct form in the spatial organization of human populations [Abler, Adams, & Gould 1971].

The notion of a residence itself needs to be clarified. It is not restricted to houses; rather, any structure where people sleep is a residence. Although residents of an urban area may move frequently, the places of residence are permanent in that there is some institutional arrangement by which individuals move into them once they are vacated. Finally, an urban area is not delimited in terms of places of residence alone. It also may contain nonresidential buildings (such as warehouses), stores, schools, factories, parks, lawns, airports, and cemeteries.

The term nonagricultural occupation or employment is used here in a narrow sense. Specifically, the category excludes occupations pertaining to farming, domestication of animals, forestry, fishing, hunting, and mining. As such, the term nonagricultural is equated with nonextractive. Surface space under nonextractive use indicates that some of the residents are engaged in nonagricultural occupations. However, rather than leave the criterion implicit, another element is added to the definition—at least one resident is engaged exclusively in a nonagricultural economic activity (i.e., a full-time nonagricultural occupation) *within the limits of the area*. The criterion recognizes that urban areas offer goods and services, but it does not stipulate that some particular *proportion* of the residents must be engaged in a nonagricultural occupation.

The first urban area represented a new form of social orginization, exemplifying Durkheim's notion of organic solidarity [1949], that is, integration through dependence. Socially speaking, residents of an urban area do not necessarily share anything in common other than proximity of residence, though all of them may depend on facilities in the urban area. In particular, all of the residents are not related by marriage or kinship, nor are they all members, employees, wards, or dependents of some association, organization, or agency. Hence, an *isolated* penitentiary, monastery, or military base is not by itself an urban area, though it may be a part of an urban area.

To summarize and repeat, an urban area is a continuous territorial unit in which: 1. the surface space is under nonextractive use; 2. there are at least two permanent and occupied places of residence or distinct households; 3. at least one resident is engaged exclusively in a nonagricultural economic activity within the unit; 4. not all of the residents are related by kinship or marriage; and 5. residence is not a matter of relation to a particular association, organization, or agency.

Two features of the definition are of significance. First, it is far less arbitrary than conventional definitions that stipulate some minimum as to population size, density, or nonagricultural employment. Second, the definition suggests how an urban area can be delimited. Of course, there will be objections to the definition, one being that a "village" is an urban area if only one resident pursues a nonagricultural occupation, and some of the inhabitants are not kindred. The objection erroneously presumes that conventional definitions provide nonarbitrary criteria for distinguishing villages from urban areas. Moreover, the definition proposed here does not preclude recognition of differences among urban areas as to population size, density, nonagricultural employment, or any other quantitative characteristic. The definition only identifies minimal criteria, which is to recognize that some urban areas are more "urban" than others. As for using the definition in international or historical comparisons of the degree of urbanization, all measures of degree consider only urban areas above some minimum population size (e.g., 5,000 or more inhabitants); and the present definition does not preclude such distinctions. However, since any minimum population size is bound to be arbitrary, the degree of urbanization is less defensible than a measure of the *scale* of population concentration [Gibbs 1966], which considers both the proportion of the national population who reside in urban areas (regardless of number of inhabitants) *and* the size of those urban areas. Since the present definition of an urban area avoids any reference to a minimum population size, it is particularly appropriate for a measure of the scale of population concentration.

Metropolitan Areas

In many Western countries for over 200 years there has been a conspicuous rise in the average distance between place of work and place of residence. The increase has become so obvious that movement between the two places is identified by a term—commuting.

Commuting is especially common around large urban areas, meaning that a large proportion of those individuals who work in the urban area reside in another urban area (usually a smaller one), or in rural territory. A less familiar commuter resides in a large urban area but works in a smaller urban area or in rural territory.

As commuting distance increases, economic activities transcend the boundaries of urban areas. Stated another way, the "effective" labor force of an urban area is no longer contained by the boundary of the urban area. Accordingly, when it comes to a study of an urban area's labor force, census data on the residents are not adequate, as they exclude individuals who work in the urban area but reside elsewhere.

The growing disjunction between place of work and place of residence led to the identification of the *metropolitan area,* a territorial unit that is larger than the urban area. Unlike an urban area, a metropolitan area is not a distinct physical or geographic entity. Its boundary cannot be detected from an aerial view. Rather, it is a "functional" entity in that its boundary reflects the spatial dimension of *dependence.* More specifically, individuals who work in an urban area but reside elsewhere depend on that urban area for employment, while those who reside in the urban area but work elsewhere depend on other territory for employment.

Dependence underlying a metropolitan area is *direct* and *territorial.* This means that individuals cannot work in one place and reside in another through an intermediary; obviously, they must travel between the two points. Indeed, if there were no separation of place of work and place of residence, there would be no metropolitan areas.

Definition and Delimitation

A metropolitan area can be defined in very simple terms: it is a territorial unit that contains at least one urban area and the surrounding territory in which   1. a substantial proportion of the *residents* work in the urban area and/or   2. a substantial proportion of *workers* reside in the urban area. The definition of a metropolitan area is scarcely a general guide for delimitation. As indicated previously, each urban area is a distinct geographical entity, the boundaries of which are fairly obvious from an aerial view, so much so that one can locate the approximate limits (roads, rivers, railroad lines) by simply walking around the urban area and noting where the nonextractive use of space ends. It is different for the metropolitan area, whose boundaries reflect commuting patterns that are not obvious from an aerial view. Accordingly, investigators are not likely to agree in identifying the boundary of a particular metropolitan area unless they follow the same procedures.

The most defensible approach to delimiting metropolitan boundaries is the "direct" procedure, which requires knowledge of where people work and reside. Delimitation begins with an inspection of all urban areas in the general vicinity to determine which is "primary" (i.e., the metropolitan center) and which are "secondary." The general notion is that some urban areas "dominate" others, but it is very difficult to define dominance. It might appear that the largest urban area dominates, but judgments based on size alone draw questionable inferences as to actual commuting patterns. To illustrate by reference to figure 1, it might appear that by virtue of size alone, urban area I is the center of a metro-

politan area, which includes other urban areas in the general vicinity.
But it could be that no one commutes between urban area I and say,
urban area VIII, in which case the two urban areas would not be in
the same metropolitan area.

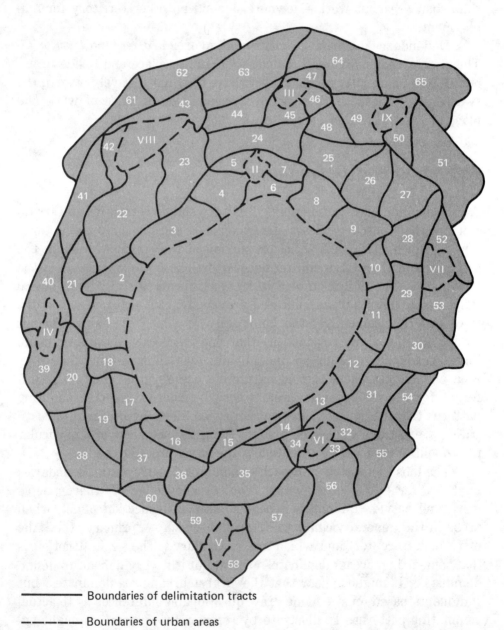

———————— Boundaries of delimitation tracts

– – – – – – – Boundaries of urban areas

Fig. 1. Urban Areas and Delimitation Tracts in a Hypothetical Region

Instead of inferring commuting patterns from the size of urban areas or proximity alone, one should consider three sets of figures for each urban area in the same vicinity: *A*, the number of individuals who work and reside in the urban area; *B*, the number of nonresidents who work in the urban area; and *C*, the number of residents who work outside the urban area. At first glance itmight appear that any urban area is "primary" if $B>C$ (i.e., *B* is greater than *C*). For example, suppose that 700 individuals work in urban area II, 500 of whom live in urban area I, and the remaining 200 live in urban area II. Since urban area II "imports" more workers than it "exports," that consideration may suggest that urban area II has its own metropolitan area. But urban area II clearly depends on urban area I for the bulk of its labor force, and the 500 who live in I but work in II may be only a very small proportion of the workers who reside in I.

As the foregoing suggests, the identification of primary and secondary urban areas may not be obvious in particular instances. It is clear that specific criteria are needed, but it is extremely difficult to stipulate criteria that are neither arbitrary nor limited to particular countries. An attempt is made here to formulate such criteria in the form of "rules," but it must be emphasized that these "rules" are debatable and will remain so until experience has been gained in applying them. The rationale for setting forth delimitation rules is that they further understanding of the term "metropolitan area."

For an urban area to be the center of a metropolitan area, *A* must exceed *B* plus *C* (i.e., $A>B+C$) and *B* must exceed *C* (i.e., $B>C$). That criterion is designated as *Identification Rule 1*. To illustrate the application of Rule 1, suppose that for urban area I $A=70,000$, $B=30,000$, and $C=10,000$. Since $A>B+C$ and $B>C$, urban area I is the primary center of a metropolitan area. Other urban areas would be "secondary" if $B+C\geq A$ and/or $C\geq B$, which is *Identification Rule 2*. Now suppose that for all other urban areas in figure 1 it is the case that $B+C>A$ and/or $C>B$. The conclusion would be that only urban area I is primary and the others (II–IX) are either secondary in the same metropolitan area *or* secondary in some other metropolitan area. Accordingly, the first step in the delimitation procedure would end with the identification of urban area I as primary (i.e., the center of a metropolitan area). The next major step is to draw the metropolitan boundary.

In addition to the primary urban area, a metropolitan area necessarily includes some rural territory and possibly other urban areas. There are eight urban areas (II–IX) in figure 1 that *could be* parts of the metropolitan area along with the center (urban area I). Consider urban area VI, which may or may not be a part of the metropolitan area in question. That distinction is determined by four numbers: W, the number of workers in a particular secondary urban area (VI in figure 1) who reside in a particular primary urban area (I in figure 1); X, the number of workers in the secondary urban area who do not reside there or in the primary urban area; Y, the number of workers who reside in the secondary urban area but work in the primary urban area; and Z, the number of workers who reside in the secondary urban area but who do not work in the secondary or primary urban area.

Suppose that we have the following numbers for urban area VI (secondary) in relation to urban area I (primary): $W=180$, $X=120$, $Y=80$ and $Z=40$. Those numbers would be assessed by *Inclusion Rule 1:* a secondary urban area is a part of the metropolitan area if $W>X$ or $Y>Z$. According to that rule, urban area VI is a part of the metropolitan area in which urban area I is the center, because $W>X$.

Rightly or wrongly, a metropolitan area is a conventionally thought of as a continuous territorial unit, that is, ignoring separations by water, each part touches on at least one other part. In the illustrative case, urban area VI is not adjacent to I, though both are parts of the same metropolitan area (by Inclusion Rule 1). Thus, two additional inclusion rules are needed. *Inclusion Rule 2:* given some territorial divison that is part of a metropolitan area, the space between that division and the primary urban area is also a part of the metropolitan area. *Inclusion Rule 3:* intervening space is limited to territorial divisions that are bounded in part by the closest public transportation route between the primary urban area and the division in question. Given Inclusion Rules 2 and 3, then the metropolitan area would also include (in addition to urban areas VI and I) tracts 13, 14, 32, and 34.

Inclusion Rules 2 and 3 refer to territorial divisions and, for delimitation purposes, two types are distinguished—urban areas and delimitation tracts. A brief explanation of delimitation tracts is in order. The delimitation of a metropolitan area requires that all territory surrounding urban areas be subdivided, with each division representing an area that is *not* traversed by a public transportation route (road, railroad, or waterway). Such divisions are designated here as delimitation tracts, and no tract contains all or part of any urban area.

The boundary delimited for any metropolitan area is, of course, only an approximation of the "true" boundary, and the correspondence between the two boundaries is largely a matter of the size of the delimitation tracts. Generally speaking, the smaller the delimitation tracts, the more realistic is the boundary.

As far as the delimitation procedure is concerned, *all* delimitation tracts are rural territory. However, workers in nonagricultural occupations may reside in delimitation tracts, and a substantial proportion of them may commute to work in an urban area. Alternatively, a substantial proportion of the individuals who work in a tract may reside in an urban area. As the first step toward specifying a criterion of "substantial proportion," we have *Inclusion Rule 4:* unless included by Inclusion Rules 2 and 3, a delimitation tract is a part of some metropolitan area only if $B+C>A$, where A is the number of workers (regardless of occupation) who reside and work in the tract, B is the number of individuals who work in the tract but reside elsewhere, and C is the number of individuals who reside in the tract but work elsewhere. To apply the rule, consider delimitation tract 37, and suppose that A is 70, B is 10, and C is 90. As such, the tract *could be* part of the metropolitan area of urban area I. To be so, it would have to qualify under *Inclusion Rule 5:* a delimitation tract is part of a metropolitan area if $W>X$ or $Y>Z$. Now suppose that tract 37 qualifies as part of metropolitan area I under Inclusion Rules 4 and 5. Then by Inclusion Rules 2 and 3, tracts 16 and 17 would also be part of the metropolitan area, even though they might not qualify under Inclusion Rules 4 and 5.

One major difficulty in delimiting metropolitan areas is that a secondary urban area or delimitation tract may qualify for inclusion in two or more metropolitan areas. Suppose, for example, that urban area IV qualifies for inclusion in metropolitan area I by Inclusion Rule 1 but delimitation tract 20 does not qualify under rules 4 and 5. In such a case tract 20 would nonetheless qualify for inclusion by rules 2 and 3. But suppose that tract 20 also qualifies for inclusion in metropolitan area XII (not shown in figure 1) by rules 4 and 5. The anomaly would be resolved by *Priority Rule 1:* Inclusion Rules 4 and 5 take precedence over Inclusion Rules 2 and 3, unless the principle of contiguity (no isolated parts of metropolitan areas) is violated, in which case inclusion rules 2 and 3 take precedence. Now consider the situation where tract 20 qualifies for inclusion in both metropolitan areas I and XII by rules 4 and 5, which could be the case if for tract 20 it is found that $W_1>X$ but $Y_{12}>Z$ or $W_{12}>X$ but $Y_1>Z$. The anomaly is resolved by *Priority Rule 2:* if a territorial division qualifies for inclusion in two or more metropolitan areas and the principle of contiguity is not relevant in either case, the direction of the greatest amount of commuting to and from that division is the criterion for inclusion. Now, suppose that for tract 20 it is found that $W_1 = 110$ (i.e., 110 residents of urban area I work in tract 20), $W_{12} = 40$, $Y_1 = 15$ (i.e., 15 residents of tract 20 work in urban area I), and $Y_{12} = 35$. As such, tract 20 could be a part of metropolitan area I or XII, since it might qualify for inclusion in either one by rules 4 and 5. However, given Priority Rule 2, tract 20 would be included in metropolitan area I, because $W_1 + Y_1 > W_{12} + Y_{12}$. Finally, observe that Priority Rules 1 and 2 apply to secondary urban areas as well as to delimitation tracts.

Inspection of the foregoing delimitation rules and general observations suggest certain characteristics of those territorial units that are not included in *any* metropolitan area. Delimitation tracts that do not qualify for inclusion are likely to be predominantly rural, with few residents in nonagricultural occupations. Urban areas that qualify neither as primary, nor as parts of a metropolitan area (i.e., $W \leq X$ and $Y \leq Z$ for commuting to and from any metropolitan center) are "interstitial" and especially common when commuting patterns are changing. Finally, an urban area may qualify as primary and yet not be part of a *larger* metropolitan area, that is, one that includes an urban area and at least one delimitation tract. In that case there is no metropolitan center or metropolitan area, and such an urban area is likely to be a small retail trading center in a predominantly agricultural region.

Some Alternatives

The foregoing delimitation rules are only illustrative and they are certainly disputable, but it is pointless to presume that there is or can be only one definition of a metropolitan area, let alone one delimitation procedure. In a sense, metropolitan areas are *created* by rules of delimitation; they are not distinct and obvious objects. So no definition of a metropolitan area or delimitation procedure is any more or less valid than others; they are merely different. Still another complexity is introduced by recognition that what is a defensible definition of a type of territorial unit (a metropolitan area or otherwise) or delimitation procedure depends on its use in theories. If a particular definition and delimitation procedure enhances positive tests of a theory, that is sufficient justification of the definition and the delimitation procedure. It may be that a particular definition can be used effectively in a variety of theories, but defensible judgments along that line cannot be made a priori.

Several national census agencies now draw the boundaries of metro-politan areas, and the rules employed by any particular census agency are alternatives to those proposed here. However, such rules are espe-cially subject to question because they are vague, relative to particular countries, or arbitrary.

The rules of delimitation used by a national census agency are com-monly vague. For example, officials of the General Register Office (Eng-land) made the following statement in describing *conurbations.* "A local area should be considered for inclusion in a conurbation to whose focal center it was strongly attached as a center for work. . . ." [1956, p. xv]. One must surely wonder what constitutes "strongly attached."

Even if the delimitation rules employed by a national census agency are very specific, they may be relative, that is, appropriate only for that country. For instance, in drawing the 1960 boundaries of Standard Met-ropolitan Statistical Areas, officials of the U.S. Bureau of the Census referred to the average number of telephone calls per month from one county to another as indicative of "integration" [1961, p. xxiv]. No stipu-lation was made as to the necessary or sufficient number of calls. In any case, the criterion would be questionable outside the United States, especially if applied to non-Western countries, and it would certainly not be applicable in any country prior to the nineteenth century.

The practices of the Bureau of the Census also illustrate how the rules of national agencies tend to be arbitrary. As a case in point, no city by itself can be the *central* city of a Standard Metropolitan Statisti-cal Area unless the resident population of the city equals or exceeds 50,000. Bureau officials may have some special reason for that rule (e.g., limited funds preclude considering central cities of less than 50,000 resi-dents), but the rule is arbitrary nonetheless.

Recognizing that the delimitation procedures of census agencies are extremely relative, urban sociologists have sought rules that are univer-sally applicable [Gibbs 1961; International Urban Research 1959]. Such rules emphasize the proportion of the labor force in nonagricultural em-ployment and/or population density as metropolitan characteristics. One rule might be that a territorial division is part of a metropolitan area if **1.** it touches on a part already included and **2.** at least 75 percent of the labor force are engaged in nonagricultural employment *or* the resi-dential density exceeds 999 residents per square mile. Those delimitation rules can be applied by investigators if they have access to published census data and maps, which means that they need not be physically present to draw the boundary or conduct a field study to gather the requisite data. Consequently, the rules of delimitation make no reference to commuting, about which few national census agencies publish any data, let alone the kind required for delimiting metropolitan areas. So some delimitation procedures emphasize density and nonagricultural employment as metropolitan criteria for the very simple reason that rules pertaining to commuting can be applied to census data for only a few countries. Nevertheless, rules that ignore commuting are questionable because **1.** the identification of metropolitan centers is arbitrary, **2.** the relation between commuting and density or nonagricultural employment is conjectural, and **3.** criteria pertaining to density and nonagricultural employment are inherently arbitrary.

Feasibility of the Present Rules

As already suggested, census data cannot be used in delimiting metropolitan areas by the procedure prescribed here. The procedure requires field studies in which investigators draw the boundaries of urban areas and gather requisite kinds of commuting statistics. Needless to say, the delimitation of even one metropolitan area would require substantial research resources.

Since application of the present delimitation rules is virtually precluded for practical reasons (the necessary resources are prohibitive), it may appear pointless to formulate those rules. Extending the objection, it could be argued that delimitation rules should be such that they apply to census data for most countries. However, rules that are applicable to census data have been formulated [Gibbs 1961; International Urban Research 1959], and they are not repeated here because they do not make reference to commuting, which is the basic consideration in examining the *notion* of a metropolitan area. Although application of the present rules is not now feasible, the rules do serve to clarify the meaning of "metropolitan area."

Metropolitan Areas as Urban Units

Since all metropolitan areas contain some rural territory, it may appear questionable to identify them as urban units. However, a metropolitan area is predominantly urban, especially as regards population. Nonetheless, in comparing countries or regions, two conceptions of urban population or territory should be distinguished. The *restrictive* conception encompasses only urban areas. The *inclusive* conception combines **1.** all urban areas *and* **2.** all rural territory within metropolitan areas. Accordingly, in comparing countries or regions as to amount of urbanization, the conception of "urban" should be either restrictive or inclusive for each country or region.

Once the urban boundaries are established, the rural population or rural territory of a country is a residual category. However, the *inclusive* conception of rural would extend to all territory *outside of urban areas* (that is, without regard to metropolitan area boundaries). By contrast, the *restrictive* conception limits the rural sector to territory outside of urban areas, as well as outside of metropolitan areas. A still more restricted conception of rural would exclude "associational" territory, where residence implies some relation to a particular organization or agency, such as an isolated monastery, penitentiary, or military base.

Metropolitan Areas and Ecological Problems

As recently as 1900, large urban areas were characterized by population densities that appear incredible today. It has been argued that high densities are conducive to high rates of mortality, so-called social pathologies (such as crime and racial strife), and all manner of psychiatric disorders. The argument is questionable, if only because very high urban densities also tend to be associated with inadequate sanitation facilities, poor medical care, and grinding poverty, which are scarcely conducive to physical or mental health. Accordingly, even if there is some relation between high residential density and social or psychological pathologies, the nature of that relation is debatable (that is, density may not be a *direct* cause of the pathologies). Nonetheless, a very high residential density in and of itself (regardless of other conditions) is not a congenial condition. When residential density reaches several thousand per square mile, a high noise level, restraints on physical movement, and invasions of privacy appear inevitable. Thus it is hardly surprising that, given the opportunity, individuals typically opt for residence in low-density areas. That opportunity comes with public transportation and/or the automobile, and it is manifested in the *horizontal* growth of metropolitan areas, with a decline in overall density. Viewed that way, metropolitan areas represent an escape from high densities, but the escapees are not the poor, who can afford neither the cost of housing nor the cost of commuting that is typical of suburban residence.

Without exception, the solution of any "ecological" problem creates others. As metropolitan areas grow horizontally, the problem of residential congestion is solved only at the expense of creating traffic congestion, for along with suburbanization there is an increase in average distance between places of work and places of residence. Although there has been a decentralization of places of work, as well as of residents, millions of suburbanites still commute "downtown." For that matter, the decentralization of places of work does not necessarily reduce commuting distance, since residents of one suburb commonly work in another.

Traffic congestion in metropolitan areas results in more than frustrated commuters. Emissions from combustion engines (primarily attributable to automobiles) are a major source of atmospheric pollution in American metropolitan areas. Of course, there are various technological solutions, such as anti-emission devices, automobiles that are not powered by hydrocarbon fuels, and more extensive public transportation systems; but they are not likely to reduce atmospheric pollution if metropolitan areas continue to grow at the current rate. The development of new power sources for automobiles, or even the perfection of anti-emission devices, will be costly undertakings. They will be resisted both by automobile manufacturers, who have a vested interest in the existing technology, and by consumers, who are likely to bear the cost. As for the development of public transportation systems in all metropolitan areas, no private corporation has the capital required for an undertaking of that magnitude, and the passenger fares necessary for a profitable enterprise would be so high as to preclude use by low-income citizens. In other words, a public transportation system of the scope contemplated could not yield a profit in strictly monetary terms. A public transportation system would be profitable if reduction of traffic congestion and atmospheric pollution is reckoned as a gain for all—an achievement that cannot be expressed readily in monetary terms.

It appears inevitable that a public transportation system of the requisite scope could be constructed and operated only by a governmental agency. However, governmental ownership is controversial, and local governments (city, county) appear unwilling or unable to finance public transportation systems of the scope required. Indeed, it is doubtful that the federal government could or would finance such systems for all large metropolitan areas, even presuming that there is no public resistance to federal intervention in local affairs. Above all, there is no assurance

that Americans would give up their extensive use of automobiles even
if an efficient public transportation system is developed. American
dependence on automobiles is not likely to be curtailed by anything less
than a major gasoline shortage, and the shortage itself would be a problem produced in part by the growth of metropolitan areas.

In contemplating solutions to such problems as traffic congestion,
atmospheric pollution, and fuel shortages, both the experts and the public are likely to presume that the problems can be solved without abandoning traditional values and privileges. Thus, the typical American
would not relish the legal proscription of commuting by automobile. Nor
does the American public fully recognize the extent to which the current
fuel crisis, traffic congestion, and the resulting atmospheric pollution reflect the separation of place of residence, place of work, and facilities
(for example, stores). Even if the consequences of those separations
were recognized, governmental action to substantially reduce commuting
is most unlikely. It would require controls over the location of places
of employment and facilities that are alien to the institution of private
property. It would be a mistake to assume, however, that solutions to
ecological problems are inimical only to the principles of capitalism.
Americans will not abandon numerous traditional freedoms that are
unrelated to capitalism, such as the largely unrestricted use of private
automobiles, selection of place of residence, and an unlimited choice of
facilities. Imagine, for example, a law that requires individuals to live
within 2 miles of their place of work. The result is an American myth:
ecological problems can be solved without major institutional changes.
The zero population growth movement is an extension of that myth. It
is entirely consistent with a hoary tradition (commenced by Malthus) of
attributing social problems to excessive population.

The proposed solution, reduction of the birth rate, ignores conflicting economic interests. One need only consider the distress expressed
by various interest groups in a typical American community when census
figures reveal a loss in population. The distress is not irrational, for a
population loss is likely to depress retail sales and employment opportunities. Indeed, the economic well-being of millions of Americans (e.g.,
elementary-school teachers, and workers who produce baby foods, toys,
and infant clothing) is jeopardized by a declining birth rate. One can
argue that the economic system should be able to withstand the adverse
impacts of a declining birth rate, but the argument is naive, because
it neither specifies the necessary changes in the economic system, nor
does it recognize that virtually any change will be resisted by powerful

interest groups. Advocates of zero population growth do not confront the issue, which suggests that an inordinate number of them are misanthropes who have never experienced prolonged unemployment.

Whatever the real or imagined benefits of zero population growth may be, it is most unlikely that they will include the solution of major ecological problems, particularly traffic congestion and atmospheric pollution. There is no compelling evidence that an end to population growth would check concentration in metropolitan areas or reduce the use of hydrocarbon fuels, both of which underlie many of the major environmental problems.

Automobiles are only one source of environmental pollution, and they are scarcely relevant in contemplating the pollution of surface and subterranean water. The primary considerations in that connection are agricultural practices and manufacturing industries, with the latter being also a major source of atmospheric pollution. Even if Americans are willing to control those sources of pollution through legal sanctions, municipal government in the United States cannot effectively exercise such control. With the growth of metropolitan areas, the atmosphere and waterways of cities are often polluted from external sources, that is, from factories located outside the jurisdiction of the city government. The same is true of the control of urban sprawl beyond the city limits, where land use is commonly unregulated by zoning ordinances.

Metropolitan regulatory agencies are needed to control "local" pollution and land use; but metropolitan areas are not administrative entities. Rather, a metropolitan area in the United States usually comprises several cities and parts of several counties. Arguments for "metropolitan" government have been made for generations, but very little has been accomplished in that direction [Wood 1968], partly because the boundaries of metropolitan areas are continually changing. It is doubtful, therefore, if "local" control of pollution is feasible. This means that only some combination of state and federal control would be effective, which is all the more desirable since it takes cognizance of the fact that local industries may have an environmental impact far beyond the metropolitan area in which they are situated. As has been noted, however, the sentiment in favor of local government is strong in the United States, and so the control of pollution involves still another kind of conflict of interests.

The horizontal growth of metropolitan areas creates more problems than traffic congestion, pollution, urban sprawl, and fuel shortages. Since much of the horizontal growth is due to residential movement of high-income families from cities to the suburbs, many large cities in the United States have lost population for decades, and the remaining city residents are increasingly members of racial or ethnic minorities (blacks, Chicanos) with very low incomes. Concomitantly, huge areas of the city become slums, the value of real estate declines, and business firms move to suburbs. One consequence is that the city government finds it increasingly difficult to obtain tax revenues, and it is forced to curtail services, such as public schools and public libraries. The decline in services makes the city an even less desirable place to live and population loss accelerates. Problems of city government are accentuated even more by the fact that suburban residents continue to use city facilities without a commensurate contribution to the city's tax revenues.

CENSUS DEFINITIONS

The foregoing definitions of cities, urban areas, and metropolitan areas are "universal" in that they are applicable regardless of the cultural or historical context (they could be applied to the United States or India today, or either country in 1800). However, investigators want to do more than delimit the boundaries of urban units. They also want to compile data (population size, occupations of the inhabitants, etc.) on those units. But it is a costly and time-consuming enterprise to delimit even one urban or metropolitan area, let alone to gather data on the population. Investigators, therefore, have little choice but to use data gathered by census agencies. Census data cannot be used, however, unless there is some *correspondence* between the "universal" definition of a type of urban unit and the definitions of territorial units that are used by census agencies.

Census terminology varies from country to country. Nonetheless, in some countries census officials delimit cities, urban areas, or metropolitan areas, although they may not use exactly those words. For example, in French census reports the word *ville* designates what is here called a city, while in England the census term "conurbation" designates metropolitan areas, or something akin to metropolitan areas.

Not all census reports use terms that correspond to city, urban area, and metropolitan area. On the contrary, census reports for a particular country may include a term that corresponds to "city," but there may be no terms in those reports that correspond to urban area or metropolitan area. Moreover, correspondence between census terms and the present universal terms cannot be established by reference to a multilingual dictionary. Correspondence can be determined only by inspecting the census reports of the country in question, specifically, the definitions of the various kinds of census territorial units, and of statements pertaining to delimitation procedure (i.e., how the boundaries of the units are established). For example, if a term is used in census reports to designate a type of territorial unit (such as "counties" in U.S. census reports), but the definition of the term makes no reference to land-use patterns or commuting, then that term cannot be construed as designating urban areas or metropolitan areas.

When the term city, urban area, or metropolitan area is used in a theory, a universal definition of it should be given as part of the theory. The theorist should stipulate whether or not census territorial units can be taken as instances of units designated by that term. If so, the theorist should stipulate criteria for determining if a given kind of census unit corresponds to the universal term—city, urban area, or metropolitan area. However, one need not presume a *perfect* correspondence between any kind of census unit and the universal unit. For example, U.S. census reports use the term "Urbanized Area" and specify a related delimitation procedure. That definition and procedure need not correspond exactly to those stipulated by a theorist in defining an "urban area"; the correspondence need only be *sufficient*. However, the theorist should state criteria by which investigators can judge the degree of correspondence between any type of census territorial unit and the type of urban unit in question—city, urban area, or metropolitan area. Subsequent investigators attempting to test the theory can then agree that a particular kind of census unit does or does not correspond sufficiently. As a case in point, some national census agencies use the term "agglomeration" to designate a particular kind of territorial unit. Accordingly, if the theorist's universal definition of a type of urban unit—city, urban area, or metropolitan area—and related instructions to investigators are adequate, then any two investigators working independently should agree that the census definition of "agglomeration" does or does not correspond sufficiently to the theorist's definition.

International Statistical Agencies

Census reports are not the only sources of data on urban units. The United Nations Statistical Office requests information from each national census agency as to the number and size of "localities" in the country. The information, which is published periodically by the UN Statistical Office, is strategic for urban research because **1.** national census agencies are asked to report the same kind of data on localities, thereby enhancing the international comparability of the statistics; and **2.** investigators need not search through the census reports of individual countries to obtain global urban data. However, the data are not perfect if only because some national census agencies fail to report, or they may not report data on localities in exactly the form requested.

The UN Statistical Office publishes international data on three types of localities, designated as *A, B,* and *C.* Type *A* is an *urban area; B* is a *city; C* is a *civil division.* Ignoring separations by water, the civil divisions of a country (e.g., counties or precincts) are contiguous, and all of them combined approximate the total area of the country. As such, the boundaries of civil divisions are largely unrelated to the rural-urban distinction and do not reflect land-use or commuting patterns. Accordingly, type *C* localities are not urban units.

Although some of the urban data published by international agencies can be used to test theories, no agency regularly gathers global data on metropolitan areas. Moreover, one should not presume that all urban data are internationally comparable. The urban data reported by the UN Statistical Office for one country may pertain to type *B* localities, while for another country the data pertain to type *A* localities; if so, it would be questionable to compare urban data for such countries. Thus a theorist's definition of a type of urban unit and the related instructions should be such that investigators will recognize that some of the urban data reported by the Statistical Office should *not* be used to test the theory in question.

UNITED STATES CENSUS DEFINITIONS AND DELIMITATION PROCEDURES

As already suggested, some national census agencies recognize and delimit territorial divisions that correspond to a universal type. The practices of the U.S. Bureau of the Census are especially instructive in that regard, for the Bureau recognizes a variety of territorial divisions, some of which correspond to universal types, as shown on page 244.

Universal Term	*U.S. Census Term*
1. Point of population concentration	1. Incorporated or unincorporated "place"
2. City	2. Incorporated "place" or city
3. Urban area	3. Urbanized Area or unincorporated "place"
4. Metropolitan area	4. Standard Metropolitan Statistical Area
5. Rural	5. Rural
6. Urban	6. Urban

Before commenting on the relation between each pair of terms, it is desirable to consider each census term.

Points of Population Concentration and Places[2]

Two major types of places are recognized in U.S. census reports, incorporated and unincorporated, as defined below.

Incorporated Places

These are political units incorporated as cities, boroughs, towns, and villages with the following exceptions: 1. boroughs in Alaska and 2. towns in New England, New York, and Wisconsin. Boroughs in Alaska are treated as county subdivisions and may include one or more incorporated places. Towns in New England, New York, and Wisconsin are minor civil divisions similar to townships in other states, and thus are not points of population concentration comparable to cities, boroughs, towns, and villages in other states. Similarly, in New Jersey and Penn-

---

2. All statements in this and subsequent sections pertaining to census practices in the United States were taken directly (with minor editing) from U.S. Bureau of the Census, *U.S. Census of Population: 1970*, PC(1)-A1, pp. ix–xiii, or from Bureau of the Budget, *Standard Metropolitan Statistical Areas: 1967* [Government Printing Office, n.d.], pp. 1-3.

sylvania some townships have governmental powers and functions similar to those of incorporated places, but they are not so classified. Thus, some minor civil divisions that are "incorporated" in one legal sense of the word are not regarded by the Census Bureau as "incorporated places." Otherwise, all of the towns or townships in New England, New York, Wisconsin, New Jersey, and Pennsylvania would be counted as incorporated places regardless of size, density, or concentration of population. However, the densely settled portions of some towns or townships are recognized as unincorporated places or as parts of Urbanized Areas.

In Hawaii there are no incorporated places in the sense of a functioning local governmental unit, but the state government has recognized places and established boundaries for them. Consequently, the Census Bureau has agreed to treat all such places as incorporated.

Unincorporated Places

In the 1950, 1960, and 1970 censuses, the Census Bureau delineated boundaries for closely settled population centers without corporate limits. Each place so delineated possesses a definite nucleus of residences and has its boundaries drawn to include, if feasible, all the surrounding closely settled area. Outside Urbanized Areas, those unincorporated places with a population of 1,000 or more are identified in the census reports in the same manner as incorporated places of equal size. Within Urbanized Areas, unincorporated places are shown only if they have 5,000 inhabitants or more, and there was an expression of local interest in their recognition. Since the boundary of an unincorporated place changes with changes in the settlement pattern, a place with the same name in 1970 as in previous decades does not necessarily have the same boundaries each census year.

The following modifications in the delineation of unincorporated places were introduced in the 1970 census:

1. Certain towns in New England and townships in Pennsylvania and New Jersey were no longer regarded as urban even though they were regarded as urban in 1960, but unincorporated places were recognized in the built-up area of those towns and townships (outside Urbanized Areas) in the same manner as for the rest of the country.

2. In Urbanized Areas outside of New England, unincorporated places with 5,000 inhabitants or more were recognized, whereas in 1960 only

places of 10,000 inhabitants or more were recognized. In New England, no unincorporated places were recognized within Urbanized Areas.

3. Built-up parts of military installations outside incorporated places were recognized as unincorporated places.

4. All places in Hawaii were treated as incorporated places, with boundaries defined by the state; but in 1960 all places other than Honolulu and Hilo were considered as unincorporated with boundaries defined by the Census Bureau.

5. Arlington County, Virginia, was treated as an unincorporated place, the only one that contains an entire county.

Extended Cities

During the 1960-1970 decade there was an increasing trend toward the extension of city boundaries to include essentially rural territory. Examples are city-county consolidations, such as the extension of Oklahoma City to include five counties. The classification of such cities as urban would include in the urban population individuals whose residential environment is primarily rural in character. To separate such individuals from those residing in the closely settled portions of cities, the Bureau of the Census examined patterns of population density and classified a portion or portions of "extended" cities as rural . An extended city contains one or more areas, each of at least 5 square miles with a population density of less than 100 persons per square mile, according to the 1970 census. The area or areas constitute 1. at least 25 percent of the land area of the city or 2. total at least 25 square miles.

An extended city thus comprises an urban part and a rural part. When an extended city is a central city of an Urbanized Area or a Standard Metropolitan Statistical Area, only the urban part is considered as the central city. If the extended city is shown separately under the area, the city name is followed by the term "urban part." Where the city name is not followed by this term, the population figure shown in tables of census reports is for the entire city.

Urbanized Areas

The major objective of the Census Bureau in delineating Urbanized Areas is to provide a better separation of urban and rural population in the vicinity of large cities. An Urbanized Area consists of a central city, or cities, and surrounding closely settled territory. The specific criteria for the delineation of an Urbanized Area follows:

1. (a) A central city of 50,000 inhabitants or more in 1960, in a census conducted by the Census Bureau since 1960, or in the 1970 census; or
   (b) Twin cities with contiguous boundaries and constituting, for general economic and social purposes, a single community with a combined population of at least 50,000, but no less than 15,000 residents in each city.

2. Surrounding closely settled territory, including the following:
   (a) Incorporated places of 2,500 inhabitants or more.
   (b) Incorporated places with fewer than 2,500 inhabitants, provided that each has a closely settled area of 100 housing units or more.
   (c) Small parcels of land normally less than 1 square mile in area having a population density of 1,000 inhabitants or more per square mile (large nonresidential tracts devoted to such urban land uses as railroad yards, airports, factories, parks, golf courses, and cemeteries are excluded in computing the population density).
   (d) Other similar small areas in unincorporated territory with lower population density provided that they serve:
   (1) To eliminate enclaves, or
   (2) To close boundary indentations 1 mile or less across the open end, or
   (3) To link outlying enumeration districts of qualifying density that are not more than 1.5 miles from the main body of the Urbanized Area.

The 1970 criteria are essentially the same as those used in 1960, with two exceptions. First, the extended city concept is new for 1970. Second, in 1960, towns in New England, townships in New Jersey and Pennsylvania, and counties elsewhere that qualified as urban in accordance with specific criteria were included in the contiguous Urbanized Areas. In 1970, only the portions of those towns and townships that met the rules followed in defining Urbanized Areas elsewhere in the United States were included as parts of Urbanized Areas.

All persons residing in an Urbanized Area are classified as urban. The Urbanized Area population is divided into those in the "central city or central cities" and those in the remainder of the area, the "urban fringe." The "central city" category consists of the population of the cities named in the title of the Urbanized Area. The title is limited to three names and normally lists the largest city first and the other qualifying cities in size order.

Standard Metropolitan Statistical Areas

The definition of a Standard Metropolitan Statistical Area involves two considerations: 1. the identification of a city as the central city and the county in which it is located as the central county; and 2. economic and social relations with contiguous counties. A Standard Metropolitan Statistical Area may include contiguous counties in different states. A "contiguous" county either adjoins the county or counties containing the largest city in the area, or adjoins an intermediate county integrated with the central county. There is no limit to the number of tiers of outlying metropolitan counties, as long as all the following criteria are met:

1. Each Standard Metropolitan Statistical Area includes at least:
   (a) One city with 50,000 or more inhabitants, or
   (b) Twin cities with contiguous boundaries and constituting, for general economic and social purposes, a single community with a combined population of at least 50,000, but no less than 15,000 residents in each city.

2. If two or more adjacent counties each have a city of 50,000 inhabitants or more (or twin cities under 1b), and the cities are within 20 miles of each other (city limits to city limits), they will be included in the same area unless there is definite evidence that the two cities are not economically and socially integrated.

The criteria of metropolitan character relate primarily to the attributes of the county as a place of work or as a place of residence for nonagricultural workers. Specifically, these criteria are:

3. At least 75 percent of the labor force of the county must be in the nonagricultural labor force, defined as those employed in nonagricultural occupations, members of the armed forces, and new workers.

4. In addition to criterion 3, the county must meet at least one of the following conditions:

   (a) It must have 50 percent or more of its population living in contiguous minor civil divisions with a density of at least 150 persons per square mile; and such minor civil divisions must radiate in an unbroken chain from a central city in the area. A contiguous minor civil division either adjoins a central city in a Standard Metropolitan Statistical Area or adjoins an intermediate minor civil division that meets the population density criterion. There is no limit to the number of tiers of contiguous minor civil divisions as long as the minimum density requirement is met in each tier. Central cities are those appearing in the Standard Metropolitan Statistical Area title.

   (b) The county must be the place of employment for a force of nonagricultural workers equal to at least 10 percent of the number of nonagricultural workers employed in the county containing the largest city in the area, or be the place of employment of at least 10,000 nonagricultural workers.

   (c) The county must be the place of residence for a nonagricultural labor force equal to at least 10 percent of the number of the nonagricultural labor force living in the county containing the largest city in the area, or be the place of residence of a nonagricultural labor force of at least 10,000.

5. In New England the city and town are administratively more important than the county, and data are compiled locally for such minor civil divisions. Accordingly, towns and cities are the units used in delimiting the Standard Metropolitan Statistical Areas of New England, and because smaller units are used and more restricted areas result, a population density criterion of at least 100 persons per square mile is the standard of metropolitan character.

   The criteria of integration relate primarily to the extent of economic and social communication between the outlying counties and the central county.

6. A county is regarded as integrated with the county or counties containing the central cities if either of the following criterion are met:

   (a) If 15 percent of the workers living in the county work in the county or counties containing the central city or cities of the area, *or*

(b) If 25 percent of those working in the county live in the county or counties containing the central city or cities of the area.

The Rural-Urban Distinction
As Recognized
by the U.S. Bureau of the Census

According to the definition adopted for use in the 1970 census, the urban population includes all persons living in Urbanized Areas or in places of at least 2,500 inhabitants outside Urbanized Areas. More specifically, the urban population includes all persons living in: 1. places of 2,500 inhabitants or more that are incorporated as cities, villages, boroughs (except Alaska), or towns (except in New England, New York, and Wisconsin), but excluding persons living in the rural portions of extended cities; 2. unincorporated places of 2,500 inhabitants or more; and 3. other territory, incorporated or unincorporated, included in Urbanized Areas.

The most important components of the urban territory are incorporated places with 2,500 inhabitants or more. However, a definition of urban territory restricted to such places would exclude a number of large and densely settled places merely because they are not incorporated. Prior to 1950, an effort was made to avoid some of the more obvious omissions by the inclusion of selected places that were classified as urban under special rules. Even with the acceptance of the rules, however, many large and closely built-up places were excluded from the urban territory.

In 1950, to improve its delimitation of the urban population, the Bureau of the Census adopted the concept of the Urbanized Area and delineated, in advance of enumeration, boundaries for *unincorporated* places. With the adoption of the Urbanized Area and unincorporated place concepts for the 1950 census, the urban population was defined as all persons residing in an incorporated or unincorporated place having 2,500 inhabitants or more. With two exceptions, the 1950 definition of urban was continued substantially unchanged in 1960 and 1970. First, in 1960 (but not in 1970) certain towns in New England, townships in New Jersey and Pennsylvania, and counties elsewhere were designated as urban (most of the population of these "special rule" areas would have been classified as urban in any event because they were residents of an

Urbanized Area or an unincorporated place of 2,500 or more). Second, the introduction of the concept of "extended cities" in 1970 had very little impact on the urban figures and the rural figures. In all census figures the population not classified as urban constitutes the rural population.

Commentary on U.S. Census Practices

Subsequent commentary on practices of the U.S. Bureau of the Census is critical, but it should be recognized that the Bureau's practices are largely dictated by practical considerations. The Bureau does not have unlimited funds or time to conduct a census and report the results; were it otherwise, the Bureau's practices would be less subject to criticism. Nonetheless, criticisms are desirable, if only to indicate some possible inadequacies of census data on the United States.

Incorporated and Unincorporated Places

Virtually all definitions of an urban unit presume a point of population concentration. Even though one place of residence could be construed as a point of population concentration, the term conventionally designates two or more places of residence in close proximity. Of course, any criterion of "sufficiently close" would be arbitrary, but that problem would be avoided by stipulating that a point of population concentration comprise two or more places of residence not separated by land under extractive use.

The recognition by the Census Bureau of places, incorporated and unincorporated, is important because a list of such "census places" in the United States would approximate a list of urban areas compiled in accordance with the universal definition. The two lists would not be identical, nor would the population and territory of all census places equal the population and territory of all urban areas. All such discrepancies would be due to questionable practices of the Bureau.

The legal boundary of an incorporated place may include only a part of a larger urban area, and the remainder may not be recognized by officials of the Bureau as part of the place. The remainder and the incorporated place itself would be recognized as components of one

Urbanized Area if more than 49,999 individuals reside in the incorporated place, but a multitude of incorporated places in the United States are smaller in size. As a result, urban territory outside of, but adjacent to, small incorporated places (less than 50,000 residents) may not be recognized as such by the Bureau. Consequently, the census figures probably underestimate the size of the urban population and the extent of urban territory. The underestimation would be eliminated by delimiting a nonadministrative boundary for all places, incorporated or unincorporated, regardless of their size; but that practice would make the census a much more costly undertaking.

Since there is no necessary correspondence between land-use patterns and the administrative boundary of an incorporated place, the boundary may include some rural territory. If the incorporated place is small (less than 50,000 residents), then the rural population and territory within its boundary are erroneously treated as urban, with the consequence being an overestimation of urban population and territory. That source of overestimation would be eliminated if the Bureau would commence drawing a nonadministrative boundary for all places regardless of their size.

Most important of all, the Bureau does not report a population figure for any place, incorporated or unincorporated, of less than 1,000 inhabitants. Therefore, many small urban areas in the United States do not appear on a list of census places (incorporated or unincorporated), nor are the residents reckoned as "urban" in the census figures.

Some of the census places are actually parts of an Urbanized Area, which is to say that they are not independent urban areas. Fortunately, at least some places in Urbanized Areas are identified in census reports, and hence they can be eliminated from a list of independent urban areas (such that the revised list would comprise Urbanized Areas and incorporated or unincorporated places outside of Urbanized Areas).

The foregoing commentary is relevant in reassessing the proposed universal definition of an urban area. Virtually all places, incorporated or unincorporated, recognized in U.S. census reports would qualify as urban areas, but a list of urban areas (universal definition) in the United States would include more than the places recognized in the census report. That discrepancy would be due to the Bureau's failure to recognize places with less than 1,000 residents. Thus, while the census figures do not reveal the total number of urban areas in the United States, they do reveal the approximate number of urban areas of a certain minimum size (1,000 or more residents).

Urbanized Areas

Since each Urbanized Area must contain at least one city (or incorporated place) of more than 15,000 inhabitants (50,000 if there are no "twin cities"), a list of Urbanized Areas would not remotely approximate a list of urban areas (the universal term) in the United States. The former list excludes urban areas that do not meet the population size criterion (15,000 or 50,000), but that criterion is clearly arbitrary. Note also that an Urbanized Area must contain at least one incorporated place (or city); but, apart from practical considerations, it is difficult to understand that requirement. The Bureau began delimiting Urbanized Areas in recognition that "city boundaries" commonly do not correspond to actual settlement patterns. There is every reason, therefore, to ignore city boundaries altogether in delimiting Urbanized Areas, especially since the population size of a city may reflect an "unrealistic" boundary. If the city is "underbounded," its boundary only includes part of a larger urban area, and it may not satisfy the Bureau's population size criterion (15,000 or 50,000) for delimiting an Urbanized Area. By contrast, if the city is "overbounded," then its boundary extends beyond the urban area, and it may satisfy the population size criterion for delimiting an Urbanized Area only because it includes rural territory. The possiblity of an overbounded city is taken into account by the Bureau's notion of an "extended" city, but it would be much better to delimit Urbanized Areas without any regard to administrative boundaries.

In addition to at least one city, an Urbanized Area includes surrounding territory that meets certain criteria stipulated by the Census Bureau. All of those criteria are subject to question. As for the inclusion of additional cities (incorporated places), the administrative boundaries of those cities may not correspond closely to land-use patterns. No less important, the census criteria pertaining to population size, density, areal extent, and distance are all arbitrary.

The foregoing criticisms do not mean that there would be very little correspondence between an "Urbanized Area" and an "urban area" if the boundary of the latter were drawn in accordance with the universal definition and delimitation procedure. On the contrary, even though the procedure for delimiting an Urbanized Area does not focus exclusively on land use (nonextractive use in particular), there is every reason to believe that the boundary of any Urbanized Area would correspond fairly closely to a boundary drawn in accordance with the proposed universal definition of an urban area.

Standard Metropolitan Statistical Areas (SMSAs)

According to the Census Bureau's criteria, cities in the United States with less than 50,000 inhabitants may not have a metropolitan area. However, the volume of commuting to and from a city cannot be judged accurately from the size of the city, and the figure of 50,000 residents is arbitrary. In all probability, numerous less populous cities have a metropolitan area. Consequently, the number of SMSAs is probably far less than the number of territorial units that would qualify as metropolitan areas by the universal definition.

Even if the Bureau should consider all points of population concentration, the delimitation of a metropolitan area in terms of counties would be questionable. Counties are simply too large (especially in the West) for any but the grossest kind of delimitation. Suppose, for example, that a particular county is adjacent to and west of a central county (a county that contains the central city of an SMSA). Now it may well be that a very large proportion of the residents in the eastern part of the adjacent county work in the central county, but the adjacent county may be so large that very few of the residents in the western part work in the central county. Consequently, the *proportion* of the total employed residents of that adjacent county who work in the central county may be so small that the adjacent county does not qualify for inclusion in the SMSA. Of course, in such a case only the eastern part of the county should be included; but the census rules are such that *all* of a county must be either included or excluded. Even when the SMSA includes only one county, it is conceivable that commuting between the central city and certain parts of the county is negligible, especially if the county is large and the central city small (slightly over 50,000).

Even if the Bureau used smaller delimitation units than counties, the procedure would not be free of criticism. The criteria of a sufficient amount of commuting are arbitrary, and the rationale for the other criteria (those not pertaining to commuting) is obscure.

The Rural-Urban Distinction

Reduced to essentials, there are three major components of urban territory as defined by the Bureau of the Census: 1. all Urbanized Areas, 2. all *incorporated* places with 2,500 or more inhabitants located outside of an Urbanized Area, and   3. all *unincorporated* places of 2,500 or more inhabitants located outside of an Urbanized Area. Other census territorial units are rural.

The Bureau's rural-urban distinction is subject to all of the criticisms made of Urbanized Areas. Observe again that the Bureau does not draw an Urbanized Area boundary for all incorporated places; consequently, urban territory outside of, but adjacent to, small incorporated places may be treated as rural. More important, no incorporated or unincorporated place of less than 2,500 inhabitants is treated as urban if it is outside an Urbanized Area. Those exclusions are difficult to defend because the minimum size limit is arbitrary, and many of the places excluded are clearly urban by virtually any universal definition.

All of the foregoing criticisms reduce to one major point—the Census Bureau's rural-urban distinction probably results in substantial underestimation of urban territory and urban population in the United States. Unfortunately, the amount of underestimation cannot be ascertained with any degree of accuracy.

THE COMMUNITY AS ANOTHER TYPE OF TERRITORIAL UNIT

As previously noted, a metropolitan area boundary extends beyond the limits of urban areas and hence includes some rural territory. Metropolitan areas are thus urban units only in that the vast majority of the residents live in urban territory. However, two other types of territorial units also may have an "urban center" but extend so far beyond the center that the majority of residents are rural. One of these two types is here designated as a community.

The term "community" is difficult to define for several reasons, one being that the term is used by social scientists, scholars, and laymen alike in an indiscriminate manner. Thus, when someone speaks of the "business community" or the "academic community," the terms only loosely designate the members of some association, organization, or interest group. As such, the usage is clearly contrary to the notion that a community is a territorial unit. Certainly that notion is more conventional [Bell & Newby 1971, p. 29], and for that reason alone it is questionable to refer to a population that is not spatially distinct as a "community." For example, the term "academic community" does not denote a spatially distinct population; thus one should speak of, for example, "Oregon academicians," "American academicians," or some particular association of academicians. Obviously, the term "academic community" is not needed unless one yearns for ambiguity.

Even if a "territorial" conception of community is adopted, an explicit definition is needed, but such definitions of community are notoriously divergent. Of the ninety-four definitions analyzed by Hillery [1955], even those that clearly reflect a territorial conception differ in several important respects. Nonetheless, most of them are subject to the same criticism—they are so vague as to preclude application. Consider MacIver and Page's well-known definition: "The mark of a community is that one's life *may* be lived wholly within it. One cannot live wholly within a business organization or a church; one can live wholly within a tribe or a city. The basic criterion of a community, then, is that all of one's social relationships may be found within it" [1949, p. 9]. The reference to what individuals "may" do makes the definition extremely difficult to apply when it comes to identifying and delimiting actual communities.

The criticism of MacIver and Page's definition does not extend to all other definitions of a community; but those other definitions differ in several respects, and one is hard pressed to make a defensible choice among them. The divergence is not surprising, however, as definitions of a community tend to reflect particular research and theoretical interests. It is not surprising that a geographer would define a community one way, a sociologist another way, and a political scientist still another way. Such differences cannot be resolved, and it is idle to presume that there is or can be only one definition of a community. With that consideration in mind, the proposed definition is explicitly limited to an ecological conception of a community.

A community is a territorial unit that contains two or more facilities and a resident population that is directly dependent on these facilities. So defined, a community is not a geographic entity with boundaries that can be observed from an aerial view. Like a metropolitan area, a community is a functionally integrated territorial unit, with integration manifested in the use of facilities. Individuals who make use of a facility may be said to depend on them, and the dependence is direct, not through some human intermediary (as when a postman delivers mail to a residence) or through technology (e.g., utility lines). Therefore, the notion of "facility use" is restricted to instances where a resident travels to and from the facility.

Communities and metropolitan areas are alike in that direct dependence is the basis of territorial integration. However, the notion of a facility includes *more* than places of employment; it also includes any place, agency, or organization that offers some product or service, such as churches, hospitals, parks, stores, theaters, cafes, schools, bus stops, airports, railroad stations, and even houses of prostitution. Since facilities offer more than employment opportunities, the boundary of a community may include much more territory than a metropolitan area. Thus, someone who resides 60 miles from an urban area is not likely to work there, but he or she may make extensive use of the facilities in that urban area.

A better understanding of the definition is realized on recognition that a community is a form of spatial organization, one that solves a universal human problem. The problem is that movement through space requires an expenditure of energy and time, both of which are limited for any individual. Consequently, we would be dumbfounded to discover a San Francisco resident who uses only Los Angeles facilities. This would require such a staggering amount of energy and time, so much that we expect San Francisco residents to use San Francisco facilities. That very expectation is tacit recognition of community as defined here. However, the argument is not that individuals always locate so as to reduce to a minimum the time and energy entailed in facility use, or that they choose among alternative facilities only with that end in mind. Nonetheless, for the vast majority of individuals there is some association within fairly broad limits between the location of residence and the location of facilities used.

Whatever else it may be, a community is both a territorial unit and a population. That point can best be illustrated by considering the extreme case—a locality where there is no community. Suppose that *no two* residents of the locality make use of *any* facility in common; if so, that locality is not a community or a part of any one community. Now consider an even more extreme case—a country in which there are no communities. That would be the case if there were no association whatever between place of residence and facility use, such that no two residents use the same facilities. Described in this way, it is difficult to imagine any country without communities. It is difficult because we recognize that residential proximity commonly gives rise to a "commensalistic" relation, meaning one in which the parties depend on something in common, in this case on the same facilities. But the very notion of a community suggests that facilities in the same locality are likely to have a commensalistic relation in that they depend on the same population for clients, customers, or members. So a country without communities can be described another way—no two facilities in the country provide a product or service for the same individual.

Each facility or class of facilities (e.g., all retail stores in a vicinity) has a service area [Galpin 1915], meaning territory where most of the residents use the facility. Viewed that way, a community is a general or composite service area, one in which most of the residents use two or more facilities in common. While the proposed definition of a community is not difficult to understand, at present it cannot be extended to a specific procedure for delimitation. Because patterns of facility use are exceedingly complicated, there is no obvious defensible procedure for delimiting communities. Indeed, in the United States and probably in all highly urbanized countries, community boundaries are becoming less and less obvious; consequently, the delimitation techniques employed by early investigators are no longer applicable. For example, early in this century such rural sociologists as C. J. Galpin [1915] developed some ingenious procedures for delimiting the community boundaries of small urban areas. One of the procedures was the ultimate in simplicity. By inspecting wheel ruts at road intersections, one could detect the general flow of traffic. The point where the traffic turned away from the urban area in question marked *one* point on the outer limit of the community.

What with the advent of the automobile and the paving of roads, the procedure is no longer applicable. Even early in this century the procedure or a variation of it (e.g., direct counts of traffic flow at intersections) would have been questionable if applied to large urban areas, because one cannot justifiably assume that all of the facilities in a large urban area provide goods and services for the same population.[3] Taking any Los Angeles resident at random, there are thousands of facilities in the urban area that the resident never uses. It is thus difficult to see how the Los Angeles urban area is the center of *one* community. Instead, it is a mosaic comprising scores of communities. Such considerations make the delimitation of communities a very complicated matter. One may object that the subdivisions of a large urban area are "neighborhoods," not communities. But the meaning of a "neighborhood" is no more clear than the meaning of community, and hence it is difficult to distinguish between them [Greer 1968]. A neighborhood can be defined

---

3. Galpin and others did not rely exclusively on traffic flow as a criterion for delimiting communities. However, their other procedures are subject to the same objection if applied to large urban areas.

and delimited without explicit reference to facility use (e.g., a certain kind of pattern in social relations, such as visiting, among residents of the same locality), in which case community boundaries and neighborhood boundaries may not correspond. But if the definition of a neighborhood or related delimitation procedure is couched in terms of facility use, then there is no basis for distinguishing between neighborhoods and communities.

Although there is a pressing need to develop procedures for community delimitation, it is most unlikely that any procedure can be applied without enormous research resources. The problem is all the more difficult since few if any national census agencies delimit territorial units that qualify as communities. As a result, social scientists who rely on census data have little choice but to conduct their research on cities, urban areas, and metropolitan areas rather than on communities. The point deserves emphasis because investigators have gone so far as to use census data on counties, yet refer to the research as a study of communities. Counties are communities only in a nominal sense, and the same is true of cities, urban areas, and metropolitan areas.

The paucity of research on genuine communities is most unfortunate. Of course, one may regard all that has been said about facility use as obvious but, like most obvious things, its significance is likely to be overlooked. After all, it is the use of facilities that accounts for most traffic congestion; it is the use of facilities scattered hither and yon that precludes a sense of membership in a distinct community; it is the use of different facilities (especially schools and churches) that diminishes meaningful interaction between social classes and races; it is the reliance on facilities that makes us anything but masters of our own fate; and it is the use of highly specialized facilities that contributes to the growth of "inhumanly" large urban areas.

OTHER TYPES OF TERRITORIAL UNITS: METROPOLITAN REGIONS

Consider a farmer who resides near a small urban area some 200 miles southwest of Denver. Because of the distance, the farmer is not likely to make regular use of the facilities located in Denver; rather, he and his family are likely to use the stores, hospitals, schools, and churches of the nearby urban area. However, suppose that virtually all of those facilities look to warehouses, wholesale outlets, and marketing facilities in Denver. If so, the farmer, the residents of the small urban area, and the residents of the community around the small urban area depend on the Denver metropolitan area. To be sure, the dependence is not direct because residents of the community (including the small urban area) may not travel to Denver; but the dependence is territorial and scarcely less important even if indirect.

Therefore, a survey of types of territorial units would be incomplete without recognition of still another type of territorial unit, the *metropolitan region*. Defined explicitly, a metropolitan region comprises at least one metropolitan area and the surrounding territory in which the residents are directly or indirectly dependent on the metropolitan area. Like a community, a metropolitan region is not an urban unit, for it typically contains a very large rural territory and rural population, along with one huge urban area (the regional center) and numerous smaller urban areas.

There is as yet no defensible procedure for the delimitation of a metropolitan region in any country, let alone a procedure that can be applied universally. Indeed, there is not even a defensible criterion for identifying regional centers. In one of the most systematic investigations of a metropolitan region ever undertaken, Bogue [1949] considered 100,000 or more inhabitants as a necessary condition for identifying a U.S. city as a regional center, but that size criterion is clearly arbitrary.[4] Moreover, even if regional centers could be identified in some defensible way, there would still be the problem of locating the regional boundary, and very little can be said in favor of procedures that have been employed to date. For example, some investigators have taken the spatial extent of newspaper circulation from the regional center as indicative of a regional boundary; but as Green has argued, "metropolitan newspaper circulation tells us about metropolitan newspaper circulation" [1955, p. 285]. Green's criticism can be illustrated by the hypothetical case at hand. Even if all of the households in the small urban area subscribe to a Denver newspaper, it does not follow that all or most retail stores in that urban area look to wholesale outlets in Denver. Some of the retail stores may depend on Denver, others on Albuquerque, and still others on Salt Lake City. If so, where is the small urban area located relative to those three

---

4. Bogue speaks of "metropolitan communities" rather than metropolitan regions, but the instances that he delimited in the United States are so large that they involve more than the *direct* dependence of residents on metropolitan centers.

regional centers? Such a question arises if it is assumed that regional boundaries do not overlap; and it is complicated by recognition that agencies, organizations, and all types of business firms (not just retail stores) must be considered in delimiting regional boundaries.

The foregoing observations should be sufficient to indicate why it is extremely difficult to formulate specific rules for the delimitation of metropolitan regions, especially with a view to avoiding arbitrary distinctions and procedures that are applicable in only a few cases. [For a more extensive commentary on these problems and procedures, see Duncan et al. 1960, pp. 36–45, 90–104]. The difficulties are magnified by a purely practical consideration. One is hard pressed to imagine any defensible delimitation procedure that could be applied without enormous resources, which may be the primary reason why national census agencies do not delimit metropolitan regions. In any case, census data are not available for metropolitan regions, and it is not surprising that so little research has been done on that type of territorial unit.

Whatever the reason for the paucity of research on metropolitan regions, it is most unfortunate. Many of the major environmental problems confronting industrialized countries will be solved, if at all, only by taking the metropolitan region as the appropriate unit for "ecological" planning and programs, governmental or otherwise. In particular, it is the concentration of population in metropolitan areas that gives rise to traffic congestion, urban sprawl, and pollution of such magnitude that it cannot be dissipated by air or water currents. The conventional explanation of such concentration is that residents of small urban areas and rural territory are attracted to metropolitan centers by greater employment opportunities. Much can be said for that explanation, but it ignores another feature of metropolitan centers—they offer a much greater variety of goods and services than do small urban areas. The contrast as regards variety of goods available would be even greater were it not for the institutional and technological arrangements that enable residents of small urban areas and rural residents to depend *indirectly* on metropolitan centers, so that they need not travel to those centers for goods. However, when it comes to services, the situation is quite different. Obviously, in the ordinary sense one does not "indirectly" use a ballroom, a psychiatric clinic, a museum, a literary club, or a massage parlor, and such facilities tend to be concentrated in metropolitan centers. However, it is not difficult to imagine a mass transportation system so efficient and inexpensive that one could reside in a small urban area but make frequent use of metropolitan facilities. For that matter, one can think of innovations that would *bring services to* the residents of small urban areas—indeed, radio and television now provide such an entertainment service.

Putting the argument all too briefly, it is difficult to imagine population concentration being checked, let alone reversed, without **1.** technological changes that markedly reduce the time-cost distance of travel and communication *within* metropolitan regions and **2.** organizational innovations that promote the delivery of "metropolitan" services to small urban areas. The delivery of such services would not reduce employment opportunities in metropolitan centers relative to those in small urban areas, but a sharp decline in the time-cost distance of transporting goods and people within a metropolitan region could lead indirectly to an increase in employment opportunities in small urban areas. Firms, organizations, and agencies that provide goods or services for a national or international market need not locate in large metropolitan centers, but a trend toward their location in small urban areas is unlikely without a sharp reduction in the time-cost distance of travel and communication within metropolitan regions. Such a sharp reduction is not an immediate prospect, largely because of a preoccupation with transportation *in* and *between* metropolitan areas.

Plans and programs for mass transportation rarely extend beyond isolated metropolitan areas, and the interstate freeways only traverse metropolitan regions (they connect metropolitan centers and only rarely form a transportation network *within* a metropolitan region). No less important, the most dramatic change in the technology of transportation, large and swift aircraft, has facilitated travel between metropolitan centers, but it has done little to reduce the time-cost distance of transportation within metropolitan regions.

OVERVIEW

As previous observations have suggested, there may be as many as five boundaries associated in some way with a point of population concentration. Those boundaries are ordered in terms of approximate areal extent as follows: the city (smallest), urban area, metropolitan area, community, and metropolitan region (largest). However, some points of population concentration are only *secondary* centers in metropolitan areas, communities, and metropolitan regions.

Since so little work has been done on metropolitan regions and especially on communities, it is difficult to say what relation their boundaries have to cities, urban areas, and metropolitan areas. When a large number of defensible delimitations have been made, it may be discovered that the relation between the community boundary and that of the city, the urban area, and the metropolitan area is not the same in all localities. In particular, the community boundary may extend beyond the city, urban area, and metropolitan area only in the case of small points of population concentration.

Figure 2 illustrates relations among the five boundaries. In contemplating that illustration recognize that it is unrealistic in three respects. First, whereas only one city, urban area, metropolitan area, and community are shown, there may be numerous instances of each type within the boundary of a larger unit (e.g., two or more metropolitan areas in one metropolitan region). Second, in the case of very large urban areas, there may be several communities, some of which are entirely within the urban area. And, third, it is extremely unlikely that the boundary of any type of territorial unit conforms closely to any geometric figure, a circle or otherwise.

Several features of macroscopic spatial organization are not revealed by figure 2. Communities and metropolitan regions are inclusive territorial units in that instances of either type taken together encompass all of the country. Thus, one may or may not reside in a city, in an urban area, or in a metropolitan area; but all places of residence are located in some community, and all places of residence are located in some metropolitan region. Finally, although it has not been documented by systematic research, there seems to be an evolutionary trend in the areal extent of certain types of territorial units; an ever-increasing size ratio of urban areas to cities, metropolitan areas to urban areas, and metropolitan regions to metropolitan areas.

Along with the evolutionary trend in relative areal extent, numerous points of population concentration become secondary centers, that is, only parts of larger territorial units. That trend has importance for all manner of programs and planning, with an increasing need to broaden the *territorial scope* of programs and plans. Whatever the sociological and psychological significance of "identification with the local area," it may well decline to the point that individuals think of residence largely in terms of metropolitan regions. Surely it is difficult to conceive of such identification as other than the most impersonal kind. Identification with the local area has already declined to the point that many individuals

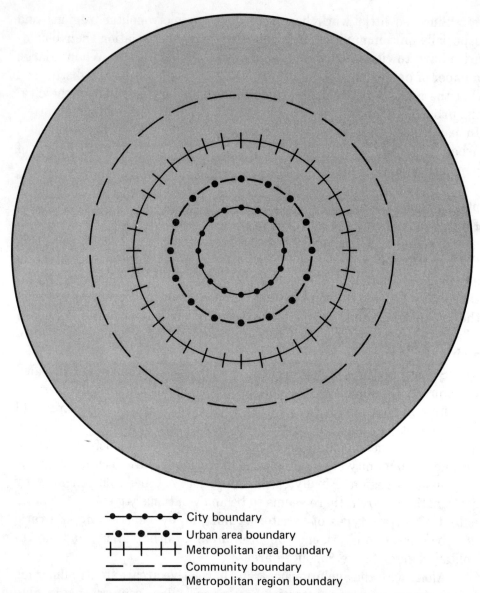

●–●–●–●	City boundary
–●–●–●–	Urban area boundary
+++++	Metropolitan area boundary
– – –	Community boundary
———	Metropolitan region boundary

Fig. 2. Boundaries of Five Types of Territorial Units: Hypothetical Instances

evidently do not value that identification or attach significance to it. In any case, the trend clearly exemplifies a maxim of ecological organization—populations never gain anything without giving up something. Wittingly or unwittingly, Americans and residents of other highly urbanized countries are increasingly abandoning identification with the local area and a "sense of community" for access to a greater variety of goods and services.

Bibliography

Ronald Abler, John S. Adams, and Peter Gould, *Spatial Organization*. Prentice-Hall, 1971.

Janet Abu-Lughod, "Urban-Rural Differences as a Function of the Demographic Transition: Egyptian Data and an Analytical Model." *American Journal of Sociology*, 1964, 69:476–490.

Colin Bell and Howard Newby, *Community Studies*. Praeger, 1971.

Donald J. Bogue, *The Structure of the Metropolitan Community*. University of Michigan, 1949.

Kingsley Davis, "Introduction." In *Cities: Their Origin, Growth and Human Impact*. Readings from the Scientific American, W. H. Freeman, 1973.

Kingsley Davis and Hilda Hertz Golden, "Urbanization and the Development of Pre-Industrial Areas." *Economic Development and Cultural Change*, 1954, 3:6–26.

Richard Dewey, "The Rural-Urban Continuum: Real but Relatively Unimportant." *American Journal of Sociology*, 1960, 66:60–66.

Otis Dudley Duncan et al., *Metropolis and Region*. Johns Hopkins Press, 1960.

Otis Dudley Duncan and Albert J. Reiss, Jr., *Social Characteristics of Urban and Rural Communities: 1950*. Wiley, 1956.

Emile Durkheim, *The Division of Labor in Society*. Free Press, 1949.

Claude S. Fischer, "A Research Note on Urbanism and Tolerance." *American Journal of Sociology*, 1971, 76:847–856.

C. J. Galpin, *The Social Anatomy of an Agricultural Community*. University of Wisconsin Agricultural Experiment Station, Research Bulletin No. 34, May 1915.

General Register Office, "Report on Greater London and Five Other Conurbations," *Census, 1951, England and Wales*. London: Her Majesty's Stationery Office, 1956.

Jack P. Gibbs, ed., *Urban Research Methods*. Van Nostrand, 1961.

Jack P. Gibbs, "Measures of Urbanization." *Social Forces*, 1966, 45:170–177.

Jack P. Gibbs, "Suicide." In Robert K. Merton and Robert Nisbet eds., *Contemporary Social Problems*, 3rd ed. Harcourt Brace Jovanovich, 1971, Chapter 6.

Daniel N. Gordon, "Immigrants and Urban Governmental Form in American Cities." *American Journal of Sociology*, 1968, 74:158–171.

Jean Gottman, *Megalopolis*. Twentieth Century Fund, 1961.

Howard L. Green, "Hinterland Boundaries of New York City and Boston in Southern New England." *Economic Geography*, 1955, 31:283–300.

Scott Greer, "Urbanism Reconsidered: A Comparative Study of Local Areas in a Metropolis." *American Sociological Review*, 1956, 21:19–25.

Scott Greer, "Neighborhood." In David L. Sills, ed., *International Encyclopedia of the Social Sciences,* Vol. 11. Macmillan, 1968, pp. 121–125.

George A. Hillery, Jr., "Definitions of Community: Areas of Agreement." *Rural Sociology,* 1955, 20:111–123.

International Urban Research, *The World's Metropolitan Areas.* University of California Press, 1959.

R. M. MacIver and Charles H. Page, *Society: An Introductory Analysis.* Rinehart, 1949.

Ernest Manheim, "Theoretical Prospects of Urban Sociology in an Urbanized Society." *American Journal of Sociology,* 1960, 66:226–229.

Lewis Mumford, "Forms and Functions of Cities." In David L. Sills, ed., *International Encyclopedia of the Social Sciences,* Vol. 2. Macmillan, 1968, pp. 447–455.

Albert J. Reiss, Jr., "Rural-Urban and Status Differences in Interpersonal Contacts." *American Journal of Sociology,* 1959, 65:182–195.

Gideon Sjoberg, "The Modern City." In David L. Sills, ed., *International Encyclopedia of the Social Sciences,* Vol. 2. Macmillan, 1968, pp. 455–459.

Pitirim Sorokin and Carl C. Zimmerman, *Principles of Rural-Urban Sociology.* Holt, 1929.

U.S. Bureau of the Census, *U.S. Census of Population: 1960,* Vol. I, Part A. Government Printing Office, 1961.

John Walton and Donald E. Carns, eds., *Cities in Change.* Allyn and Bacon, 1973.

Louis Wirth, "Urbanism as a Way of Life." *American Journal of Sociology,* 1938, 44:1–24.

Robert C. Wood, "Metropolitan Government." In David L. Sills, ed., *International Encyclopedia of the Social Sciences,* Vol. 2. Macmillan, 1968, pp. 459–466.

5.

RESIDENTIAL SEGREGATION IN URBAN AREAS

Avery M. Guest

Residential segregation in cities is a recent phenomenon. For most of their history, humans have been migratory, living in what are known as hunting and gathering bands. These bands depended primarily on the good will of nature for their survival, moving their residence as the weather changed, as the plants bore food, and as the environment provided warmth and shelter. Given the primitive technology, the earth could support economically only a small population. And most of these bands probably had little contact with each other, since movement by foot was slow [Lenski 1970].

Between 10,000 B.C. and A.D. 1800, man developed rudimentary agricultural tools—the plow and the domesticated animal—and techniques leading to a more sedentary residential pattern. The earth could now support more individuals at specific geographical points, but technology and social organization were still unable to support large settlements or cities. For instance, Davis [1955, p. 433] estimates that by 1800 only about 1.7 percent of the world lived in cities of more than 100,000. Most settlements consisted of a few hundred persons and were often nothing more than agricultural villages, where workers ventured forth each day to till nearby fields.

Since 1800, the world has been engaged in a great social-demographic revolution in which large cities are becoming the dominant settlement pattern. Humans have used their advanced technology, as represented by such inventions as the automobile, tractor, and truck, to increase agricultural productivity severalfold, and in turn, to free millions of persons to become urban dwellers. In the United States the urban population has increased from 5 percent of the total population in 1790 [Bogue 1955, p. 473] to over 70 percent today. And many of the remaining "rural" dwellers live in small villages or settlements, close to cities. Only about 5 percent of adult American men still farm.

By its very nature, urbanization has led to the residential segregation of persons and groups within cities. Given large concentrations of population, given the heterogeneity of industrial society, and given differences in life style and culture, it is almost inevitable that persons will sort themselves from other persons on the basis of subjectively important criteria. It would indeed be amazing to find urban concentrations where all neighborhoods or blocks of cities had exactly the same types of persons.

The recent development of large numbers of cities, therefore, takes us to our principal concern, the analysis of residential segregation in North American (United States and Canadian) cities. We shall focus on three population dimensions by which sociologists generally distinguish one neighborhood from another: family composition, social rank, and race/ethnicity. These distinctions should not be surprising because they are major variables distinguishing groups in most institutions of American society.

Family or life-cycle segregation results from the fact that most of us pass through a series of life-cycle changes after our childhood, involving early adulthood without marriage, early adulthood with marriage but without children, early and middle adulthood with children, late adulthood with adult children, and widowhood. Each expansion or contraction of the family creates needs for certain types of housing, particularly in terms of space or room, and for certain types of neighbors, particularly those in the same stage of the life cycle.

Social rank segregation involves the tendency of individuals to segregate themselves on the basis of their occupational positions, educational achievements, or incomes. We may also refer to this as segregation by social class or social status. The existence of segregation by social rank in an industrial society should be expected, for highly urbanized societies often have great social inequalities. In fact, the United States has maintained roughly the same degree of inequality in income since about 1920 [Kolko 1962].

Ethnicity or racial segregation must be partially defined by cultural criteria since most Americans come from the Caucasian racial stock, and the physical differences among persons from some European countries are minimal. Origin from different geographic areas presumably creates special interests and heritages that are reflected in the spatial location of individuals. Ethnicity or racial segregation may also be based on physical characteristics, such as Asian or black Americans versus white Americans. While many sociologists have perceived American urban society as a melting pot for ethnic groups, current evidence suggests this may not be so; there seems to be persistence of ethnic traits, even 50 years after the great waves of European migration have ended.

These three dimensions of segregation may be studied independently, and in fact, our analysis would be simplified by treating them separately. But the hard realities of the sociological world indicate that they are related, and we will want to discuss the extent to which one dimension is really a part of another dimension of segregation. For instance, is racial segregation between blacks and whites a result of social rank differences between blacks and whites? Is the persistence of ethnic communities in American cities the result of older "ethnics" continuing to live in the same neighborhood, while younger members of the ethnic group have moved away?

WHO CARES?

Why should we be interested in residential segregation in a society? Four reasons might be suggested. First, because the degree of residential segregation between groups may be considered an indicator of their degree of social inequality or social distance; second, the segregation or integration of neighborhoods and parts of the city will have consequences for the resulting types of community institutions and characteristics; third, segregation of neighborhoods may affect the collective behavior of groups; fourth, residential segregation may affect the life chances of individuals, their ability to achieve, or not achieve, what are conventionally considered indicators of social success. We shall examine each of these issues.

The first reason for studying residential segregation, as an indicator of social distance, was eloquently stated by Robert E. Park, a sociologist in the early twentieth century at the University of Chicago. He wrote,

> It is because social relations are so frequently and so inevitably correlated with spatial relations, because physical distances so frequently are, or seem to be, the indexes of social distances that statistics have any significance whatever for sociology. And this is true, finally, because it is only as social and physical facts can be reduced to, or correlated with, spatial facts that they can be measured at all [Park 1967, p. 68].

Park's arguments have far-reaching implications for the study of society. It is implied, for instance, that we could learn much about the changing nature of social relationships in a society by studying the changing spatial relationships. Thus, changes in the social relationships between blacks and whites should also be reflected in changes in spatial relationships. It is also implied that the relative importance of two types of social relationships may be studied by analyzing the degree of residential segregation by these characteristics. Thus, one may infer the importance of racial versus social rank relationships in our society by comparing the degree of residential segregation by race with the residential segregation by social rank. Finally, Park implies that the sum of individual psychological feelings of one group about another are summarized in the spatial location of one group in relationship to another. To put it another way, hate and love get worked out in the city by the physical distances between groups.

These reasons alone would be enough to justify the study of residential segregation. But segregation also has consequences for the types of institutions and characteristics that develop in the urban community. Some sociologists [Greer 1962, pp. 105–110] allege, for instance, that many central city communities are having difficulties in solving problems because whites and the middle and upper status groups, often sources of civic leadership, have left for the suburbs. As another example, many communities in the 1960s faced serious financial difficulties in their educational systems as a swelling population of children produced shortages of schools and teachers. The swelling number of children stemmed at least partially from the family composition of the area. Finally, the development of racial residential segregation is certainly a major cause of racial segregation in our schools. Controversies over busing to achieve integrated schools would be unlikely if blacks and whites lived in approximately the same proportions in each neighborhood.

Statements about the importance of residential segregation in determining group collective behavior have a venerable history in sociology. In the nineteenth century, the sociologist Karl Marx contended [Bendix & Lipset 1966, p. 11] that residential proximity among blue-collar workers would encourage a sense of class consciousness and anger against the employer class. Workers would be able to communicate their grievances with each other and develop a shared sense of hostility toward other agencies of the society. The Marxist analysis probably has its modern relevance in explaining the urban racial uprisings of the 1960s. The black population, almost completely segregated from whites, developed a shared racial consciousness and grievances against the white community, and this hostility was undoubtedly an underlying factor in the massive destruction directed against the established agencies of the dominant white society, such as police and businessmen.

A recent debate has raged among sociologists about the effects of residential segregation on individual life chances.[1] Some sociologists contend that individual school achievement of lower-class youth is enhanced by contact with upper middle-class children, and others contend that aspirations for further education are also enhanced by this process.

While much needs to be known about the basic causes and dimensions of residential segregation, even more needs to be known about the

1. For a summary of some of the literature and discussion concerning the effects of race and class on achievement, see Armor [1972] and Coleman [1966]. For a full discussion of the effects of neighborhood status on college attendance, see Sewell & Armor [1966], Sewell [1966], Turner [1966], Michael [1966], and Boyle [1966].

consequences of segregation. Without qualification, I would argue that almost all allegations concerning consequences of residential segregation should be currently considered assertions rather than empirically verified propositions. In this chapter, I do not attempt to evaluate most of these alleged consequences, although in the last section I describe my own views on the positive and negative benefits of residential segregation by race and social rank.

MEASURING SEGREGATION

Sociologists are also citizens, and as a result they have focused most of their research in the area of residential segregation on racial patterns, to a moderate extent on ethnic and social rank patterns, and to a small extent on family composition patterns. The amount of research is in rough relationship to the degree to which these dimensions are perceived as social problems. Few American citizens or sociologists would be outraged at the thought that old people tend to live in different neighborhoods from young people, but more would become excited about the existence of segregation by social rank and ethnicity, and many would become outraged at the thought of continued racial segregation. The reasons for these feelings are relatively simple. Many Americans probably share an aversion to the treatment of persons based on racial criteria, seeing such treatment as an affront to American values of egalitarianism and universalism, and some of us feel that social rank distinctions are too great in our supposedly egalitarian society.

In studying residential segregation, sociologists have developed a vocabulary of conceptual terms and a methodology for measuring these terms. In talking about spatial location, sociologists often distinguish among three terms: *segregation, concentration,* and *centralization.*

Segregation means dissimilarity in residential distribution—that is, the tendency of one type of person to live separately from another type of person in one small area of the city. Thus, racial segregation would be indicated by whites having a dissimilar residential distribution from blacks over city blocks or neighborhoods. The opposite of segregation would be integration, and a process in which segregation is being abolished would be called desegregation.

Segregation may, but does not necessarily, also take the form of concentration. If members of a group are segregated so that all live in one region or large area of the city, they are concentrated. In the case of black-white segregation, the existence of large racial ghettoes would be considered an example of concentration. But a group may be segregated without being concentrated, as would be indicated by a pattern of city blocks being completely white or completely black, but these blocks being randomly distributed around the city.

Concentration may also take the form of centralization, although centralization is only one form of concentration. If groups are concentrated close to the Central Business District (CBD), or downtown, of the city, they are considered centralized, while if they are concentrated toward the outskirts, they are considered decentralized. The most classic example of concentration but no centralization would be *sectoral location,* in which a group locates primarily on one side of the city but is found in all areas of this sector, both close to and distant from the CBD.

Most studies of residential segregation are based on census tract or block data collected by the U.S. Bureau of the Census.[2] The census tract is an area of the city with a presumably homogeneous population, in terms of various social characteristics, such as familiy composition, social class, and ethnicity. Census tract populations may vary widely, but they often contain 3,000 to 5,000 people, and large metropolitan areas in the United States will have several hundred census tracts. The block is a smaller unit than the census tract and consists only of the small area bounded by a series of streets. City blocks rarely contain more than 20 to 30 dwellings, or 50 to 100 residents. The data on population characteristics by census tracts and blocks are published in special reports every 10 years for most large metropolitan areas in the United States. In the 1970 census, each Standard Metropolitan Statistical Area (SMSA) had its own census tract report. SMSAs are defined as central cities of 50,000 or more plus surrounding counties that are socially and economically integrated with the central city.

Using census tract data, one may easily determine the degree of residential segregation among various groups, as all the raw data are given in the tract reports. It is also possible to trace the concentration or centralization of groups by using the maps of cities found in census tract reports. The census tract data are less valuable for determining why patterns of segregation occur, as the reports do not clearly tell why persons live in certain neighborhoods. Intention may be inferred by investigating the distribution of housing types found in tract reports in

---

2. Census tract data are found in most university libraries, and it is therefore possible for students to study many of the issues raised in this chapter.

relationship to the types of persons. For instance, one may find that deteriorated housing is highly correlated with the residential location of lower status persons. Yet, we cannot test for other possible explanations, such as lower status persons having a particular desire to live near other lower status persons. In summary, the nature of the data leads more to description of residential patterns than to analysis of why they occur.

To measure segregation, we shall use the index of dissimilarity.[3] It is computed over census tracts or blocks and may vary from 0, no segregation, to 100, which is complete segregation. That is, an index of 0 would be found when every neighborhood actually had the same proportion of two social groups, such as the rich and poor, and the index would be 100 when every neighborhood had either all rich or all poor. Fortunately, the index values have a substantive interpretation, indicating the percentage of one group that would have to change neighborhoods in order to be equally distributed with another group. An index of 0 would indicate 0 percent would have to switch neighborhoods, while an index of 50 would indicate that either 50 percent of the rich or 50 percent of the poor would have to shift blocks to be equally distributed. In the Appendix, we show how to compute the index.

The measurements of concentration and centralization are more elusive. More often than not, the concentration of groups is determined by mapping locations by census tracts. Contiguous neighborhoods with large numbers of specific groups are considered concentrations. Centralization is often measured in two ways: **1.** by some measure of association between distance and status, such as the Pearsonian correlation coefficient or Goodman's gamma;[4] or **2.** by change in status as one moves out each mile or distance zone from the CBD. Thus, one might be interested in the change in the proportion of white-collar workers for each mile moved from the CBD.

WHY SEGREGATION?

Sociologists have spent nearly half a century disputing whether residential segregation results from the action of unconscious, largely nonper-

---

3. For an excellent discussion of various approaches to measuring residential segregation, see Taeuber and Taeuber [1969, pp. 155–245].

4. For a good discussion of the Pearsonian correlation coefficient, you may consult most statistics textbooks. For a good discussion of gamma, see James A. Davis, *Elementary Survey Analysis*, [Prentice-Hall 1971].

sonal forces or from conscious acts by individuals and groups, which we shall call "personal" causes. Nonpersonal acts lead indirectly to residential segregation. That is, groups become segregated from each other not because they particularly dislike or fear each other at a conscious level, but because they wish to locate in proximity to some special features or attractions found in neighborhoods. Personal acts are largely premeditated, based upon a desire of individuals or groups to live close to or far away from other groups. Our argument in the following section is also shown in figure 1.

We might think of nonpersonal segregation as resulting from such features of the city as the distribution of deteriorating housing. Obviously, higher status persons would not want to locate in areas of deteriorated housing, and thus we could expect some social class segregation in the city as a result of the distribution of housing, unaccompanied by any particular attitudes of higher status persons toward lower status persons. Personal segregation would occur when groups located in a

Fig. 1. Causes of Segregation

- Non-Personalistic Factors
  - Morphological Features
    - a. character of housing
    - b. crowding - congestion
    - c. land uses (business, industrial)
  - Sentimental Features
    - a. historical traditions
    - b. "arty" or cultural reputation
    - c. family history

- Personalistic Factors
  - Individual Desire
    (similar life styles-values)
  - Institutional Action
    - a. realtors and contractors
    - b. industrial, business, utility firms
    - c. individual home owners
    - d. governmental agencies

neighborhood because of the types of people there. It is often alleged, for instance, that whites flee neighborhoods when blacks move in, perpetuating a system of segregation in which most neighborhoods are all white or all black.

Nonpersonal segregation may be considered a product of two possible causes: 1. sentiments and symbolism attaching to certain areas of the city, and   2. morphological or structural features of neighborhoods. Thus, referring to sentiment and symbolism, higher status persons may seek location in some neighborhoods because they have an "arty" character or they have a long historical tradition of being a center of literary thought and ideas. Or, referring to morphological features, we could argue that higher status persons may seek location in a neighborhood because it has large and spacious homes, regardless of its literary charm or historical character.

At the same time, personal segregation may be due to: 1. the actions of individuals, or   2. the actions of institutions or specialized agencies within the community. Thus, there is some debate about whether racial segregation results directly from whites individually refusing to let blacks buy in their neighborhoods, and whites individually fleeing blacks when they move into neighborhoods, or whether segregation results from the actions of institutions such as realtors and government agencies. For instance, it is frequently alleged that racial segregation, while sought individually by at least some whites, is actively created by the actions of realtors who may refuse to show neighborhoods to blacks, raise the price of white housing when showing it to blacks, and so on, and then may attempt to "panic" whites into selling when blacks move in.

In a provocative analysis, Form [1954] suggested four types of institutions that might have important effects on urban land use: the real estate and building business; large industrial, business, and utility firms; individual home owners and other small-scale users of land; and zoning boards, planning commissions, school boards, and other agencies of local government. The interactions among these sets of units, according to Form, are affected by the resources each can command, the manner in which the set normally functions, the kind of internal organization each possesses, the pressure to which each is exposed, and the image of the city held by each set of groups. Unfortunately, Form's ideas for research have rarely been pursued.

While little is known definitively about the causes of residential segregation, it shall be argued in the following pages that segregation by family composition and social rank primarily results from nonpersonal factors. And within the nonpersonal causes, morphological factors are more important than sentiments or symbols. Family composition of neighborhoods is particularly affected by the size and age of housing. Social rank segregation is affected by both the quality of the housing, in terms of size and structural condition, and by the quality of the neighborhood, in terms of population congestion and the presence of business and industry. Ethnic-racial segregation, on the other hand, arises primarily from personal causes, from the desire to live close to or away from other groups. But I would argue that this type of segregation, particularly between blacks and whites, is probably created more by institutions than individuals.

THE BURGESS HYPOTHESIS

A starting point for an analysis of residential segregation—its degree, spatial patterns, and its causes—is the Burgess theory of urban growth [Park & Burgess 1967, pp. 47–62], sometimes known as the Burgess hypothesis.[5] The theory, developed in the 1920s by Ernest W. Burgess, a University of Chicago sociologist, has stimulated several generations of research and theorizing on urban spatial patterns. And, in fact, it may be considered the only theory of residential segregation that is relatively complete. That is, it explains in a fairly clear-cut manner why segregation of different types of residential groups will occur, and it shows how the residential segregation pattern develops spatially as the city grows. All other so-called theories of residential segregation are primarily negative and positive comments on aspects of the Burgess framework.

The essential goal of Burgess' theory was the portrayal of the spatial organization of the urban community in the same framework as the spatial organization of the plant and animal community. Out of this framework arose what is known as the human ecology perspective in sociology, or the Chicago school of ecology.

Burgess became fascinated with the relationship of the human and plant communities after observing that plant communities near Chicago along Lake Michigan were organized in rough concentric rings emanating from the water. A central ring contained only sand, followed by a ring

---

5. The Burgess theory is also outlined in various other places. For a description of the zonal scheme with an emphasis on families, see Burgess, Locke, & Thomas [1963, p. 64].

of light shrubs, and then rings of progressively thicker vegetation as one moved outward, until the forest was reached. These rings grew or contracted by nonpersonal forces, as the environment changed by alteration of temperature and climate.

Burgess suggested that the spatial pattern of the typical American city, as represented by Chicago, could also be portrayed in a series of concentric rings, or zones, emanating from the CBD. These zones changed as the population of the metropolis grew. The first zone, the "Loop" or CBD, generally contained disproportionate amounts of retailing and wholesaling establishments and was the commercial hub of the metropolis. The second zone, sometimes called "The Zone in Transition," was continually being invaded by commercial interests expanding from the CBD. Housing was often deteriorated, and many rooming houses were also found. The population was disproportionately composed of homeless or unattached men and women, first generation ethnic and racial groups, and lower status persons. The third zone, the "Zone of Workingmen's Homes," had little commercial activity and was primarily an area of small single-family dwellings for the stable working class, and second-generation immigrants. The fourth and fifth zones, High-Class Apartments/Single-Family Dwellings, and the Suburban or Commuters' Zones, generally contained the high-status population, families in the childbearing stage, and spacious single-family dwellings—sometimes intermingled with apartment houses.

While Burgess used Chicago to illustrate the zone concept, he obviously intended his theory to be applicable to most cities. Due to its location on a lake, Chicago grew in a half circle. But Burgess saw this as only an artifact of nature; the typical city would be circular and would have zones emanating in a 360 degree arc.

Burgess' ring concept seemed to be primarily a heuristic device to show how activities and groups become segregated, concentrated, and centralized in the city. The zones were meant to indicate general tendencies of location, rather than hard and fast zones. It follows from his theory that higher status persons, single and unattached persons (including homeless men and women), and ethnic and racial minorities should generally be located near the center of the city (centralized), while higher status persons, third-generation Americans and families with children should generally be located on the urban outskirts (decentralized).

Within Burgess' model, the primary force producing the segregation of groups was economic competition for centrality around the Central Business District. The process worked something like this: First, the CBD was desired as a site for many urban activities. Retailers and wholesalers desired location in the CBD to be near their suppliers and the harbor and rail terminals; retailers also desired the CBD because it was the most accessible point for customers. The CBD also assumed particular value to specialized luxury types of businesses because they could be located close to other similar businesses, and customers could shop comparatively. For the individual resident, location near the CBD was desired because workplaces were often located there, and travel time to work could be reduced by close residential proximity.

Second, the bidding for central location led to increases in central land prices, and the activities with the most money and most desire for the CBD disproportionately occupied it. In most cases, businesses disproportionately occupied the CBD, while residences were driven out. The remaining residential population had to live at very high densities or great congestion in order to afford the central rents. These densities were generally accommodated by apartment houses.

Third, as the population of the metropolis grew, there was an increased demand for central land, and it could be accommodated only by the outmovement of the CBD. As this movement occurred, owners of residences allowed them to deteriorate because they could sell the property at a high price to the expanding businesses. The commercial establishments were presumably not interested in the buildings themselves.

Out of this economic competition came a sifting and sorting of persons by social rank, ethnicity, and family composition. The city in its early history had a relatively random distribution of persons by population characteristics, but segregation, concentration, and centralization began to appear as the population grew. Higher status persons fled the center of the city as the congestion increased, the housing deteriorated, and unpleasant business and commercial interests inhabited neighborhoods. The center of the city was generally left to lower status persons. Since Burgess generally assumed that generation in the United States was closely associated with status, it followed that first-generation ethnic groups should be found near the center of the city while later generations would be found progressively outward. Families with children also deserted the center of the city, for the housing space there was small, and the outskirts contained ample yard space and ample internal house space. The apartment and rooming houses of the center were left to single and homeless persons.

In summary, groups became segregated in the city, not because they had a particular like or dislike for other groups, but because changes in the city's structural or morphological features led them to live in certain areas of the city. Within the context of possible causes of segregation, the theory emphasized the nonpersonalistic framework.

While the causal mechanism of the theory may seem complex, the actual argument is relatively simple. As cities grow in population size, segregation among groups becomes pronounced, and the segregation takes the form of a centralization-decentralization pattern.

Burgess' theory also had implications for understanding changes in the population characteristics of neighborhoods. Early in its history, a neighborhood contained a variety of population groups, although higher status persons, native urban dwellers, and families with children would predominate. As the CBD expanded, the previously peripheral neighborhood would become desired for other uses, setting off a process of invasion and driving out higher status persons, native Americans, and families with children. Eventually, a complete process of succession would occur so that the neighborhood population disproportionately consisted of lower status residents, the foreign born and ethnic population, and homeless men and women, or at best, the single and childless population. A similar conception has been used by the economists Edgar Hoover and Raymond Vernon [1962, pp. 183–198] in explaining the development of neighborhoods in the New York Metropolitan Area.

Several critiques of the Burgess hypothesis clearly miss the mark. For instance, it has been argued [Alihan 1938, pp. 224–225] that clear concentric zones cannot be distinguished in the city, but Burgess obviously intended for the zonal concept to be used primarily as an analytical scheme for explaining general tendencies. Burgess has also been criticized because individual American cities do not fit his scheme [Davie 1937, pp. 133–161]. Yet, Burgess was clear that the zonal concept should apply only to particular types of cities—those that were large and had relatively flat planes so the economic competition could reign unchecked. Spatial patterns could be altered by differences in topography. Burgess has also been criticized because his theory does not seem to explain residential patterns in non-American cities, particularly in less developed countries. But Burgess obviously assumed that cities had to have some advanced technologies, such as transportation systems, so that the upper status groups could desert the center. Since most less developed countries have very primitive forms of transportation, Burgess' scheme was not intended to apply to them. For a complete discussion of differences in urban structure between developed and less developed countries see Schnore [1965, pp. 347–398].

Rather than make a full commentary on the Burgess hypothesis at this point, I would prefer to deal with the more cogent criticisms in the sections analyzing the nature of segregation by family composition, social rank, ethnicity, and race. Some of these criticisms are persuasive, and the Burgess hypothesis should by no means be accepted uncritically.

To this point, we have raised more questions than we have answered. In the following sections, we deal with various questions related to the residential segregation of persons by family composition, social status, and ethnicity. We will devote separate attention to research findings related to the general phenomena of ethnic segregation among whites and selected nonwhite groups as opposed to racial segregation between blacks and whites. Among the questions we shall answer are the following: How much segregation is found by the various social characteristics, and how does the degree of segregation affect the concentration and centralization of groups? What are trends in segregation over time? Why does the segregation occur? Is it due to personal or nonpersonal causes? Can we specify the exact nonpersonal mechanisms? Can we specify the role that institutions play in furthering personal segregation? We shall also be interested in whether the various types of segregation are likely to decrease or increase in the coming years.

In a final section of this analysis, we shall deal with some of the consequences of residential segregation, whether social class and racial segregation are good or bad. Is it a serious social problem, or is it a nonserious hindrance to some desired goals?

Our mode of analysis involves moving from the type of segregation that we know the least about, family composition, to the type about which we know the most, racial segregation. As we have pointed out, our knowledge is not independent of our social concerns as Americans, for few of us would see the existence of family segregation as a "social problem," while many would feel otherwise about racial segregation.

FAMILY-LIFE CYCLE SEGREGATION

Americans have undergone a change in family arrangements, moving from a system where generations of the same family often lived together in the same house to a system in which every generation expects to set up living arrangements separate from every other generation. Some indication of this trend is suggested by data on married couples. In 1940, 93.3 percent of all married males, wife present, had their own households, while in 1970 the figure had grown to 98.7 percent [see U.S. Bureau of the Census 1943a, table 9, 1943b, table 11; U.S. Bureau of the Census 1973a, table 2].[6] In the older system, each household often contained a married couple with children still in school, adult age children, whether single or recently married, and other relatives, such as unmarried brothers and sisters, married or widowed mothers and fathers.

This situation has apparently changed in recent generations, as increasing family incomes have permitted segments of the family system to set up separate households. Now it is likely that the child, upon reaching adulthood, will move away to a small apartment, and will continue there in the first years of marriage, and perhaps even the first years of parenthood. But gradually, as the family expands in size, and perhaps as the family income increases with job promotion, the family decides that it needs more housing space, both internal space, or rooms for eating and sleeping of all the family members, and external space, or yard room for recreation and leisure activities. In all likelihood, the typical young married family with one or two children will seek a home in which to live for their period of child-raising, which often lasts up to 20 years.

For mom and dad, now in their late 40s or early 50s, the growing up of children means that the need for a large home has now ended, although they may hang on to the home for a number of years for reasons of nostalgia, because friends live in the area, because their children and grandchildren will occasionally visit. But eventually, the home becomes more bother than it is worth. Taxes may be high, and as retirement nears, income to pay those taxes may be low. As old age slows down energy and drive, the costs of maintaining a residence increase. And, eventually, one spouse will probably die so that little is left to share in the old household. As a consequence, we may predict, the older married couple or the widowed individual tends to seek again a small apartment as living quarters for the last years of life.

For purposes of analysis, the life-cycle pattern may be summarized in terms of three major groups: 1. households of married couples in the age period 22–45, with children under 18 present; 2. households of

---

6. Households are separate living units according to the U.S. census. They may contain several families, or related groups of people. In most cases, although not all, each household contains one family. In the following discussion, we use the terms household and family interchangeably, although, in fact, they are not exactly the same.

Fig. 2. Patterns of Family Location

Family	Types of Housing	Spatial Location
● Childbearing Couples	a. recently built b. single family, spacious	décentralized
● Older Couples	a. older housing b. single family, spacious	neither centralized nor decentralized
● Non-married Families	a. sometimes older housing b. multiple unit, non-spacious	centralized

married couples in the age period over 45, generally without children present; 3. households in which no or very few married couples or children are present, generally containing the young, single population, the older, widowed population, and the divorced-separated population. Our argument about the relationship of these family types to housing characteristics and spatial location is shown in figure 2.

Each of these groups should have clear housing needs related to the size and age of housing. The families in the middle of the child-bearing stage should be located in spacious housing, in terms of both internal room and external yard space, while the households without children present or married couples should be located in less spacious housing, given their small household size. The households of married couples in the age period over 45 might also be located in spacious housing, if only as a relic of their past housing needs. Families in the middle of the child-bearing period might also be found in new housing, since it seems reasonable that many families move into new housing when they start the child-bearing period and remain in the housing for a long period of time. For the same reason, households of married couples in the age period after 45 should be disproportionately found in neighborhoods of older housing since they have presumably aged with the neighborhood. The age of housing should be less related to the location of households without children or married couples present, due to the age diversity of this group. However, the presence of older widows within this group may produce some tendency to be found in older neighborhoods. In summary, married couples in the childbearing stage should primarily be found in areas of spacious, new housing, while married couples past the childbearing stage should be found in areas of spacious, older housing. Other types of families should primarily locate in smaller older housing.

Given these housing needs, families in the city are likely to be segregated from each other, as long as the housing is also segregated by its age and space. This also follows from the Burgess hypothesis because it is a fact of life that new areas of the city are almost always on the outskirts. And we also know, from the Burgess hypothesis, the competition for land around the Central Business District means that most central residential housing will be multi-unit apartment houses, and most spacious single family homes will be found on the urban outskirts.

One would also predict, therefore, the concentration and centralization of certain family types based on this distribution of housing. That is, families in the childbearing stage should be decentralized or concentrated on the outskirts, while older families and families not in the childbearing stage should be relatively concentrated or centralized in the city. Households of married couples beyond the childbearing years would not be particularly centralized or decentralized. Their location in single-family housing would pull them toward the outskirts, while their location in older housing should pull them toward the center.

This analysis also has its implications for understanding changes in neighborhood character. One would predict that apartment house areas of the city would be primarily transient and perpetually diverse in population character—that is, these areas would have persons in a wide range of family relationships and ages. Individuals—single, widowed, divorced, separated—would be moving in and out of the neighborhood as they sought housing for what are generally short-term stages in the life cycle. Areas of single-family homes would disproportionately contain married couples and would pass through age-life cycles, having young, married couples early in their history, and older married couples, those over the age of 45, later. As these older households break up, the neighborhood might again pass through another life cycle.

My interpretation of segregation by family composition, therefore, is primarily nonpersonal, seeing it result from the search of persons for certain attributes of neighborhoods rather than for certain types of persons. I also see the segregation as resulting primarily from structural or morphological features of neighborhoods rather than from sentimental features. It is, of course, likely that some families do seek residential neighborhoods for personal reasons. Thus, a family with children may locate in a neighborhood because other families with children (potential playmates) are also there. But since most neighborhoods of single-family dwellings already have a large number of families with children, this should not be a principal direct concern in neighborhood location. Certain types of families probably locate in relationship to other morphological features of the neighborhood besides housing. One would speculate, for instance, that families with children would also be interested in the quality of schools, the number and quality of the recreational areas, and the safety of the streets. Older persons might be particularly interested in the proximity of stores and service institutions for their needs.

In recent years, there have been several studies of why people move and these seem to be consistent with the view that most families pick a residence on the basis of housing needs. For instance, Peter Rossi [1955], in a study of residential mobility in Philadelphia, found that his respondents were almost unbelievably narrow-minded in their likes and dislikes of neighborhoods. The space, quality, and structural character of housing was the overwhelming concern, and most of the families moving or planning to move were doing so to adjust housing needs with life-cycle changes. Other features of neighborhoods such as the noise levels, neighborhood appearance, and quality of schools drew some attention but were relatively unimportant. In a comprehensive review of the literature on urban mobility, James Simmons [1968] also agreed that the dominant cause of mobility in the metropolis was the life-cycle search for types of housing.

Some feeling for the degree of residential segregation by life-cycle stage may be gained by investigating measures of the differences in residential distribution of six types of households in the Cleveland, Ohio SMSA in 1960. These were defined by the availabilty of census data. Indicators of segregation in table 1 for four types of married couples are presented: Young Couples, in which the head of the household is under 45 and has no children present; Young Families, in which the head of the household is under 45 but has children present; Old Families, in which the head of the household is over 45 and has children under 18 present; and Old Couples, in which the head of the household is over 45 but no children under 18 are present. These four types of married couples roughly follow the typical sequence of married life, from having no children (Young Couples), having young children (Young Families), having teenage children and a declining family size (Old Families), and having grown children (Old Couples). Data are also presented for two other types of families: nonrelated households, persons living alone or with one or two other nonblood related persons; and related heads, households in which a married couple is not present but related persons do live together. These last two types of families disproportionately consist of young single persons, widowed, and divorced and separated persons. They are, therefore, typically persons who are very early in their adult life cycle or at the end of the adult life cycle.

T A B L E 1. Indices of Dissimilarity for Family Types Cleveland, Ohio, SMSA, 1960

	YC	YF	OF	OC	RH	NRH
Young Couple	–	20	21	25	22	28
Young Family	20	–	20	16	30	37
Old Family	21	20	–	14	24	30
Old Couple	25	16	14	–	31	38
Related Household	22	30	24	31	–	22
Nonrelated Household	28	37	30	38	22	–

Source: Guest 1970, p. 193.

According to the segregation measure (the index of dissimilarity), most families in the Cleveland SMSA are not very segregated from each other, and this result is consistent with my study of segregation by these family types for 16 other metropolitan areas in 1960 [Guest 1970]. For instance, the segregation index of 20 between Young Families and Young Couples indicates that only 20 percent of Young Couples or Young Families would have to move from current neighborhoods to other neighborhoods to be equally distributed. Remember that if the two groups were perfectly segregated the index would be 100, while no segregation would mean an index of 0. The least segregation seems to occur between families in similar stages of the life cycle, such as Young Couples and Young Families, or Old Families and Old Couples; yet, even the difference between dissimilar types of families is not very great. For instance, Young Families have a segregation index of only 37.1 from Nonrelated Households, presumably composed disproportionately of single persons and widows. In summary, the results suggest that residential segregation by family type is low in degree, at best.

Even though segregation by family type is not very great, it is worthwhile to know if it can be explained by housing types. In an analysis of the Cleveland data, not reported here, I found this to be the case [Guest 1972a]. For instance, Old Families tended to be found in different neighborhoods from Young Families because the single-family housing in the neighborhoods differed in periods of construction. Young and Old Families differed in residential location from Related and Nonrelated Households primarily because housing is distributed differently across neighborhoods in terms of its internal and external space.

Finally, I showed [Guest 1972a] that most of the decentralization or centralization patterns of families could be explained by the types of housing that were decentralized or centralized. In particular, Young Families were decentralized, both because of the age of the household head and the need for single-unit housing. Related and Nonrelated heads were particularly centralized, both because of the age of the housing and the use of apartment housing. Old Families and Old Couples showed some decentralization, although less marked than Young Families. Once housing character had been controlled (or the effects resulting from difference in housing across census tracts had been eliminated), there was almost no tendency for types of families to be particularly centralized or decentralized. This further suggests that nonhousing factors could only be a small component in explaining the location of types of families.

I have also plotted the spatial location of these various types of families in sixteen other American metropolitan areas [Guest 1970], selected to represent a variety of population sizes, regional location, and period of early development. Similar centralization-decentralization patterns were found for the various types of families, indicating a rather regular and universal pattern over metropolitan areas. In fact, the decentralization-centralization pattern was much more characteristic of families than of social status groups, white ethnic groups or racial groups —suggesting that family composition is the most clear-cut characteristic distinguishing the center from the outskirts of the American metropolis. On the whole, the study of the seventeen metropolitan areas showed little tendency for family segregation to vary in clearcut concentration patterns other than centralization-decentralization.

In summary, while segregation by family-life cycle stage exists in cities, it appears to be minimal at best. Most neighborhoods contain a diverse array of families. Furthermore, most of the segregation that does exist seems to result from the different spatial distribution of types of housing. And finally, segregation by family-life cycle pattern is heavily represented by the centralization-decentralization spatial pattern. These conclusions are thus generally compatible with the Burgess hypothesis.

In the future, will residential segregation among families increase or decrease? No longitudinal studies of the question exist, and it is therefore impossible to extrapolate past trends. Two factors would seem relevant. First, the recent trend toward the construction of complete communities for persons at various stages in the life cycle, such as "swinging" singles developments and old age condominiums, should lead to increasing segregation. These developments are increasingly being located in suburbs, and may therefore affect some of the patterns of concentration on a central-decentralization basis which I found. Second, family-life cycle segregation may also increase if segregation by social class and ethnic-racial status decreases. Due to their low incomes and subordinate ethnic-racial status, many minority families—regardless of their life cycle stage, may find themselves limited to small parts of the metropolis. In the case of the black population, for instance, most families with children have only a limited number of single family dwellings available within the established racial ghetto. If and when social rank and ethnic-racial segregation decrease, urban communities may organize themselves spatially to a greater extent on the basis of family needs and related housing needs.

SOCIAL CLASS SEGREGATION

American society has great social inequalities. For instance, while 10.6 percent of persons over 25 were college graduates in 1970, some 15.5 percent had finished less than 8 years of education. [U.S. Bureau of the Census 1973b, table 1]. While 5.3 percent had family incomes over $25,000 per year in 1971, some 8.2 percent had incomes less than $3,000 per year [U.S. Bureau of the Census 1972a, pp. 1261–1262]. According to most studies of changing income inequality in the United States, the distribution of income in the United States has not changed drastically since about 1920 [Kolko 1962]. Within the context of these great differences in social rank among the American population, it would not be surprising to find at least moderate degrees of segregation by occupation, income, and education.

Among sociologists, the cause of segregation by social rank has provoked a wide-ranging debate on whether it results from personal or nonpersonal causes, and within each perspective there is disagreement about whether nonpersonal segregation results from structural or symbolic factors, and whether personal segregation results from the behavior of individuals or institutions. More has been written on the cause of segregation by social rank, than by other dimensions, but less is probably known definitively.

There has also been a long-standing debate on whether social class groups are segregated on the basis of centralization-decentralization, or whether segregation occurs more on the basis of sectors or wedge-shaped areas emanating from the Central Business District. We turn to each of these issues.

Exponents of the role of nonpersonal, structural factors in determining social class segregation generally agree with Burgess' hypothesis of urban growth. The fundamental view is that persons of higher social status have certain desires or tastes for types of neighborhoods, and that they use their income to purchase location in accordance with their tastes. For instance, Amos Hawley argues [1950, p. 282] that "rent, operating through income, is a most important factor in the distribution and segregation of familial units."

As Burgess suggested, there may be several features of the neighborhood in which higher status persons prefer to buy—little congestion, little business and industry, and generous amounts of internal and external housing space.

The most famous defense of this position has been made by Otis Duncan and Beverly Duncan [1955] in a study of occupational segregation in the Chicago Metropolitan District in 1950. Their study has been replicated in various metropolitan areas with the results generally supporting the Duncan and Duncan study. I discuss their results, using the Cleveland SMSA as an example.

Using census tracts as the unit of observation, I determine the residential segregation (as indicated by the index of dissimilarity) among eight major occupational groupings used by the U.S. Bureau of the Census. These occupations and the indices of dissimilarity are shown in table 2. The occupations can be ranked roughly in terms of their prestige in American society, from high to low. Duncan and Duncan found that occupations with similar degrees of prestige also had low segregation from each other, while dissimilar occupations had much higher degrees of segregation. And this is true also for Cleveland. For instance, professionals had a segregation index of only nineteen from managers but an index of fifty-four from laborers. Note that the indices of segregation by occupation tend to be moderate; they are greater than those found for family groups, and either about the same or less than those found for ethnic and racial groups.

Importantly, the Duncans showed that the degree of segregation among groups was heavily related to differences in income. Occupations with similar average income levels were relatively unsegregated from

T A B L E 2. Indices of Dissimilarity for Occupational Types, Males Only, Cleveland, Ohio, SMSA, 1960

	PR	*MA*	*SA*	*CL*	*CR*	*OP*	*SE*	*LB*
PR	–	19	17	30	31	44	40	54
MA	19	–	17	34	36	48	44	56
SA	17	17	–	31	35	46	40	53
A	30	34	31	–	17	21	21	35
CR	31	36	35	17	–	19	26	36
OP	44	48	46	21	19	–	21	23
SE	40	44	40	21	26	21	–	24
LB	54	56	53	35	36	23	24	–

C O D E :

PR Professional, technical and kindred

MA Managers, officials and proprietors

SA Sales

A Clerical and kindred

CR Craftsmen, foremen and kindred

OP Operatives and kindred

SE Service workers

LB Laborers, except miners

Source: Guest, 1970, p. 195.

each other, while occupations with dissimilar incomes were relatively segregated. The most noticeable exception to this case involved craftsmen and clerical workers. While craftsmen had higher incomes than clerical workers, they were also more segregated from the other white-collar workers than were clerical workers. This represented an anomaly in the finding, although Duncan and Duncan pointed out that craftsmen spent a lower proportion of their income for housing than did clerical workers. Once again, in the case of Cleveland, it can be seen that clerical workers are less segregated from other white-collar workers than are craftsmen.

Service workers also seemed to be less segregated than would be expected on the basis of their general standing in the community, but Duncan and Duncan pointed out that many of them were live-in servants, and thus they had an artificially low index of segregation.

In general, then, Duncan and Duncan's finding seemed to support the traditional ecological view that segregation was primarily a result of differences in income and occupational status.

Consistent with this view, I have shown [Guest 1971] that the proportion of white-collar workers (as opposed to blue-collar workers) in census tracts of 17 SMSAs in 1960 was highly dependent on the types of housing, particularly the number of rooms in the dwelling and the structural condition of the housing (whether deteriorated or in sound condition). These results would thus suggest that higher status persons use their money primarily to purchase certain types of housing, and to the extent that this housing is also segregated, it tends to produce segregation among occupational groups. Housing patterns also accounted for most of the tendency of higher status persons to be centralized or decentralized in the same metropolitan areas.

Of the various criticisms of the traditional ecological view, Walter Firey's [1945] emphasis on the importance of sentiment and symbolism in the location of higher status persons has probably attracted the most attention. Firey shared the ecologists' view that nonpersonalistic factors were important in determining residential segregation by social rank, but disagreed on the importance of morphological or structural features of neighborhoods and the importance of income purchasing power.

Firey's attack was based on an intensive study of Beacon Hill, an old higher status neighborhood near the Boston downtown area. Firey wondered why this central neighborhood had maintained its high status for several decades, when other Boston central neighborhoods had declined in status over time. He felt that the existence of a high-status neighborhood in the central part of an old, large city was inconsistent with the Burgess hypothesis.

Beacon Hill continued to be attractive to higher status persons, Firey suggested, for several reasons. First, it had a quaintness and charm stemming from the days of Boston's founding. The streets were built with cobblestones, and the housing was traditional colonial. Second, Beacon Hill had an important literary and cultural tradition. Many of Boston's early great literary figures, such as Harriet Beecher Stowe and William E. Channing, had lived on the Hill. Third, many of Boston's foremost and earliest families had lived on the Hill, and many of their descendants felt a continuing desire to live there.

While Firey makes some interesting points, we find his arguments less persuasive than those of the human ecologists. First symbolism cannot have an overwhelming role, even in Boston, because most of the city's central neighborhoods followed the classical patterns suggested by Burgess. Beacon Hill seems to be an exception to the general rule. Symbolism would therefore seem to be, at best, a residual explanation beyond the ideas of the ecologists. Second, Beacon Hill has paid an economic price in order to maintain its high-status character. At the present time, much of the previous single-family housing has been subdivided into apartments, thus splitting the high costs of rent for the land. For instance, in 1970, of all dwelling units in the Boston census tract (201) roughly encompassing the Beacon Hill area, only 9 percent were single family dwelling units [U.S. Bureau of the Census 1972b, table H–2]. Third, one may also argue that Beacon Hill maintains its high-status character not particularly because of "symbolism," but due to the desire of some higher status persons to live in close proximity to the Central Business District. While Burgess suggested that most higher status persons would be willing to trade off longer travel time to work for the attractions of the urban outskirts, it seems believable that a segment of the high-status population would prefer not to do so, and Beacon Hill thus was an attractive site. Many large cities have maintained downtown luxury neighborhoods for a select group of the elite who prefer to live near downtown and are willing to accept apartment living.

Other criticisms of the ecological view have argued that location patterns arise from personal action by social class groups to locate and defend their common territory. This position is not rejected by many ecologists, but is considered relatively unimportant. As Hawley notes

> A number of similar units can create by their congregation various amenities that are not inherent in the location. If together in sufficient number, they can attract special services to their area, can engage in their own peculiar forms of collective behavior, and can when necessary offer relatively effective opposition to undesirable encroachments from without. [1950, p. 282]

Whether higher status neighborhoods protect their character through individualistic or institutional means is also vigorously debated. In one research effort from the individualist perspective, Arnold Feldman and Charles Tilly [1960] showed that the residential locations of different occupational groups for Hartford, Connecticut fit the pattern shown by Duncan and Duncan. In other words, they replicated the Duncans' study of differences in residential location among occupational groups for Chicago. They then controlled for the average education and income levels of census tracts and determined the degree of occupational segregation. Consistent with their thesis that social class segregation resulted more from the search for others with the same life style (as measured by education) than from income, they found that controls for education produced less occupational segregation than similar controls for income. In other words, segregation among occupational groups seemed to be more responsive to differences in educational than income levels.

Feldman and Tilly's analysis was valuable for suggesting that the concept of social rank or social class segregation is multidimensional, that it cannot be completely reduced to a single factor of purchasing power. Their conclusion is thus consistent with other research on social stratification which suggests that occupational levels, educational achievement, and annual income are only moderately related and that each often has a separate effect in explaining human behavior. Yet, given some methodological problems of Feldman and Tilly's study, I have some trouble accepting their conclusion that persons seek to locate near persons of a similar life style more than they seek to buy certain types of housing according to their incomes.

As one example of methodological problems, Feldman and Tilly controlled for the average educational and average income level of the tract, rather than for the educational and income levels of various occupational groups. The issue at hand would seem better tested by the second procedure. It is also an open question whether the same results would occur if the analysis were replicated for other cities, and it would be particularly valuable to replicate the study for Chicago, the city emphasized in the work of both the Duncans and Burgess. If one wants to challenge another ideological position, what better place to start than home?

Feldman and Tilly's article places primary emphasis on individual desire as the cause of segregation; other researchers have emphasized the role of institutions in encouraging and maintaining segregation by social rank.

The most common argument views zoning as a principal means by which higher status persons keep lower status persons out of their neighborhoods. For instance, analyzing the effects of zoning, Paul Davidoff, Linda Davidoff, and Neil Newton Gold argue:

> Restrictive zoning and land use controls in suburban areas constitute the principal barrier preventing the development of job-linked moderate-cost housing in the suburbs. Among the specific devices that suburban governments have used to prevent construction of such housing are: minimum lot size requirements, minimum house size requirements, restrictive subdivision regulations, and unduly expensive building standards. In addition to these devices, many suburban communities have adopted zoning ordinances that prohibit all forms of multifamily housing within their jurisdiction. Taken together, these restrictive zoning and land use controls have been remarkably effective in preventing low- and moderate-income families from penetrating suburban housing and land markets [1970, p. 14].

Zoning undoubtedly serves the interests of higher status persons, and does have some effect in maintaining the status character of neighborhoods. But the real issue is whether zoning has any impact independent of what would happen anyway. Does zoning merely legitimate residential segregation or does zoning actively encourage it? For instance, higher status persons have various indirect means of keeping lower status persons out of their neighborhoods. Social and political pressure may be exerted against any builder or individual who wants to construct lower status housing. Lower status persons can be socially ostracized once they have moved into a higher status neighborhood, and lower status persons might have second thoughts anyway since they would probably not have a great deal in common socially with higher status persons, even if they were neighbors.

T A B L E 3. Indices of Dissimilarity for Occupational Types, Males Only, Houston SMSA, 1960

	PR	MA	SA	CL	CR	OP	SE	LB
PR	–	16	15	31	45	54	59	67
MA		–	16	26	37	47	52	59
SA			–	24	39	49	53	62
CL				–	23	32	39	50
CR					–	19	40	47
OP						–	29	32
SE							–	24
LB								–

C O D E : See Table 2

Source: Guest 1970, p. 155.

A crucial test of the effects of zoning would involve a comparison of social rank segregation in metropolitan areas without zoning and social rank segregation in metropolitan areas with zoning. Unfortunately for research purposes, only one large metropolitan area, Houston, does not have zoning. Nevertheless, we have presented in table 3 the indices of occupational segregation for the Houston SMSA in 1960, and these may be compared with the indices for the Cleveland SMSA in 1960, shown in table 2. Cleveland, like most large metropolitan areas, has well-developed zoning.

If anything, occupational segregation is greater in Houston. Other factors, of course, may make Houston's social class segregation particularly high, independent of zoning (for instance, Houston's large black and Spanish-American population). Yet, I have compared four other metropolitan areas with Houston and none of them has greater occupational segregation than Houston [Guest 1970]. The burden of proof would seem to be on those who believe that zoning does have significant *independent* effect on social class segregation.

As in the case of life cycle segregation, we know little about longitudinal trends in social rank segregation, as no comprehensive study has been made. One would be surprised at any clear cut trend in residential segregation by social rank since social inequality, at least as crudely measured by such factors as income, seems to be relatively constant in the United States. John Fine, Norval Glenn, and J. Kenneth Monts [1971] have shown that occupational segregation is about the same within suburban and central city rings of eight metropolitan areas, and one would expect changing patterns of occupational segregation to be reflected in different trends for the new part of most metropolitan areas, the suburbs. They also compared residential segregation among occupational groups in 1950 and 1960 within the central city and suburban rings, and they found similar patterns in both years, or little change in the degree of segregation within the central city and suburban territories.

We also know little about comparative patterns of occupational segregation across metropolitan areas. As we shall point out in the next sections, racial segregation is very high in American cities, and to the extent that blacks hold lower social class position (in terms of income, occupation, and education), one might expect racial segregation to be confounded with occupational segregation. As a result, cities with large black populations may have somewhat higher overall levels of social class segregation than cities with small black populations. Furthermore, one might speculate that the nature of industrial relationships would also effect occupational relationships. In cities that depend primarily on manufacturing or large plants, there may be great social distance between employees and employers; whereas in a city where retailing was dominant, employers and employees might work more closely together. But there are no studies bearing on this question.

Another important determinant of social class segregation might be the location of workplaces. In cities where workplaces are concentrated together, particularly "dirty" industrial plants, upper status workers might be especially inclined to seek distant, relatively private residences, while the area around the plants would be left for manufacturing workers. For instance, Beverly Duncan [1964] has shown that manufacturing workers in Chicago tend to concentrate disproportionately around plants that happen to be located in the central city. Leo Schnore and Hal Winsborough [1972] have shown that metropolitan areas with large amounts of industrial activity, presumably concentrated in the central city, also have a disproportionate tendency for higher status persons to live in the suburbs. Schnore [1965, pp. 169–183] has also shown that industrial suburbs generally tend to contain lower status residents than suburbs that are primarily residential areas.

In summary, my own view probably coincides most closely with the Chicago ecologists in their emphasis on social class segregation as resulting from nonpersonal processes, and particularly from structural features of neighborhoods such as the congestion, deterioration, amount of business and industry, and the housing space. As is true of most issues in sociology, there is probably something to be said also for the other viewpoints, although the supporting evidence seems rather fragmentary and not particularly persuasive. It may be said with some certainty that we know more about the pattern of spatial location of socioeconomic groups than we know about the cause of that pattern.

CLASSES AND SPACE

According to the Chicago ecologists, social classes should be concentrated primarily in a centralized-decentralized pattern, with the highest status population found on the outskirts of the metropolis. This pattern should be particularly clearcut in the largest metropolitan areas.

In a series of studies, Schnore [1972] has imaginatively investigated the average status of American central cities compared with the average status of their suburban rings. Central cities are generally close to the CBD, and suburbs are generally far away, and it is thus possible to make some statements about the centralization-decentralization of status groups in American metropolitan areas. Schnore found in 1960 that most suburban rings were higher in status than their central cities, regardless of whether occupational status, educational level, or family income was compared. However, many metropolitan areas had higher central city than suburban status, and, in fact, only about half the metropolitan areas had suburbs with higher suburban occupational status (as measured by the proportion of white-collar versus blue-collar workers). In two studies [Guest 1971, 1972b] I have also shown that the tendency of occupational and educational status to increase with each mile from the CBD is generally slight, and thus it would appear that status groups are not clearly centralized or decentralized.

In attempting to explain the differences in centralization, Schnore [1965, pp. 201–241; 1972] has found on the whole that population size of metropolitan areas is not related to the location of higher status groups in central cities or suburbs. This would seem to be incompatible with the original Burgess hypothesis suggesting that the city developed a pattern of higher status decentralization in population as it grew.

The strongest variable in predicting central city-suburban status differences has been metropolitan area age. Older metropolitan areas, that is, places that attained 50,000 population in their central cities early in American history, were most likely to have higher suburban than central city status. Most of the older metropolitan areas are found on the eastern seaboard and in the Middle West, while most of the "new" areas are located in the South and on the West Coast.

Schnore [1972] interprets the cross-sectional results to be largely consistent with the Burgess hypothesis—that metropolitan areas show a pattern of higher status decentralization as they age. The patterns currently found in the older areas will presumably be found eventually in the "new" places. Schnore does not explain why the evolution is related to age, rather than population size, which was the driving mechanism of the Burgess hypothesis.

My view is that the Burgess hypothesis was quite important for understanding the spatial development of the American metropolis until at least the 1880s and possibly until the 1920s. But in the 1880s, the development of the electric streetcar reduced some of the pressure on the Central Business District, and the mass diffusion of the automobile to the American population in the 1920s reduced this pressure even more. Both developments in transportation reduced pressure in several ways. First, travel time to work could be faster, and workers no longer needed to worry so much about locating close to jobs, often around the CBD. Businessmen no longer needed to work in close geographic proximity to all customers, since travel time was relatively rapid. Furthermore, many businesses wanted to follow their customers outward as the streetcar and automobile opened up new areas for settlement. A derivative of the automobile, the truck, permitted the development of transportation facilities on the urban outskirts, and even further reduced the need for location around the CBD by business and industry.

Another technological change should also be mentioned. Recent advances in building construction have permitted the CBD to build up, rather than outward. Previously, buildings were quite limited in height by the quality of building materials, and the lack of knowledge about how to erect high structures.

One can hypothesize that the reduced pressure on the CBD left many older metropolitan areas with a core area of great congestion, housing deterioration, and large amounts of retailing, wholesaling, and manufacturing. But the changes in technology never led to the same consequences for newer cities and so, as a result, they never developed the classical Burgess pattern. As a result, higher status persons were not driven to the outskirts. This view suggests that the new metropolitan areas are not just young precursors of older areas. Rather, I would argue, the tendency toward "evolution" of metropolitan areas by social status is probably not very great. And in fact, most neighborhoods have probably persisted in their basic status character for some time.

This view is buttressed by three pieces of evidence found in the work by Reynolds Farley [1964], and a paper of mine [Guest 1974]. First, in a study of the Cleveland metropolitan area from 1940 to 1970, I found that older neighborhoods had not been undergoing clear declines in absolute levels of status but were instead persisting in their status levels. Second, in a study of twelve other metropolitan areas between 1960 and 1970, I found a very high persistence of status over the decade. There was only a very slight tendency for older neighborhoods to lose in status while newer neighborhoods gained in status. Third, Farley showed for seventeen large metropolitan areas that the absolute status of the central city changed very little between 1950 and 1960, although the absolute status of the suburbs did increase slightly. He also showed that older suburbs in several large metropolitan areas had remained practically constant in relative status during two periods, from 1920 to 1960 and 1940 to 1960. Why the suburban rings generally could increase in status while individual suburbs persisted in status is not clear, although the increase in total ring status could be due to the development of new suburbs that were not included in the Farley study of suburbs over time.

In any case, the debate on why higher status persons are centralized or decentralized in certain places may be as important as a molehill on a mountain. As I have shown recently [Guest 1971, 1972b], the actual tendency of social status to vary with each mile of distance from the CBD in American cities is not great, and thus we are really trying to explain only slight tendencies, if present at all, of status to increase with distance from the CBD.

The major spatial alternative to the Burgess centralization view, the sector theory, portrays another form of concentration. Its major exponent, the economist Homer Hoyt [1939], sees the sector theory as somewhat complementary to the concentric zone thesis, although he clearly believes the former to have greater explanatory power. Sectors may be considered wedge shaped slices of a pie that emanate from the CBD and overlap several concentric zones. Hoyt's perspective on the existence of sectors was supported in an analysis of the location of high rent districts in some sixty-four American cities in 1934. The importance of sector versus concentric zonation for the location of status groups has been demonstrated in a study by Theodore Anderson and Janice Egeland [1961] of four Midwestern cities in 1960.

Hoyt's explanation of residential segregation is similar to the Chicago school's in that he sees higher status groups primarily motivated by nonpersonal and structural criteria, but he sees these criteria as varying more by sectors than by concentric zones. Thus, Hoyt argues that higher status neighborhoods are not found in areas with large amounts of industrial activity but are found in areas with such scenic environments as hills and waterways. Hoyt also argues that the sectors often form around major transportation lines emanating from the CBD, such as rapid transit lines or major highways. Accessibility makes the land valuable, and higher status persons are willing to pay for such location. Hoyt also sees sectors as developing in the same direction as the already existing distribution of higher status homes. This seems reasonable, since urban residents generally possess the most information about areas near them, and it would only seem natural, therefore, for higher status persons to seek new homes nearby.

In a study of four American cities (Atlanta, Indianapolis, Syracuse, and Wichita), Phillip Peters [1964] generally found support for Hoyt's views about why sectors appear, although he did not find strong evidence that higher status areas located in high ground, open country, or shoreline areas—especially if these areas were common.

A general problem with Hoyt's view is that sectors are primarily determined on an ad hoc basis, by plotting the actual location of higher status neighborhoods on a map, rather than by any clear deductive logic. Thus, it is easy to test the Burgess hypothesis across cities by comparing central city versus suburban social status, or determining the relationship between distance from the CBD and social status of tracts. But, it is not intuitively obvious how one would determine the presence or absence of sectors across cities, except by mapping locations of groups.

If the location of higher status persons is based on a centralization-decentralization pattern most frequently in older, eastern cities, it seems most likely that the sectoral pattern is also found least often there. Sectors would presumably be more important in new, western cities, while the centralization-decentralization pattern would be less evident. But again, there are no relevant data available.

In summary, segregation by social rank seems to be moderate in degree. While there is some confusion about its causes, we believe that nonpersonal, morphological features of cities are most important in determining the location of higher status versus lower status persons. It is likely, however, that other factors also have some importance. While segregation by social rank varies slightly with distance from the CBD, the relationship is generally not strong, and is most present in older eastern cities. A major alternative explanation of spatial location is Hoyt's sectoral theory, and current evidence indicates that it may be a more accurate explanation of concentration than the Burgess hypothesis.

ETHNIC SEGREGATION

To repeat a cliché, America is a nation of immigrants [See Irwin & Warren 1972; Keeley 1971, 1972; Taeuber & Taeuber 1967]. The history of American society is also a chronology of massive migrations from Europe, Africa, and Asia. For migrants or their children, the American city has been the eventual destination. Often migrants have settled initially in rural areas but eventually have begun the process of urbanization. For some of America's first immigrants, the African population, large-scale urbanization waited until World War I, nearly 300 years after their arrival. For Jews, from northern and eastern Europe, urbanization occurred almost immediately after their arrival in the late nineteenth and early twentieth centuries.

Migration to the United States reached a peak in the early twentieth century, but then declined rapidly as the chaos of World War I cut off the European migrants. And the flow was legally controlled by restrictive federal legislation in the early 1920s. It is only recently that foreign migration to the United States has begun to increase again, as the result of liberalization during the 1960s of previously restrictive migration laws. In fact, about 25 percent of the U.S. annual population growth is due to foreign migration, and the annual number of migrants now ranges between 250,000 and 300,000. In contrast with older migrant streams, the new migrants tend to come more frequently from non-European parts of the globe, so that today new communities of Chinese and Asiatic Indians are found in many of our large cities, and some cities, such as Miami, have very large colonies of Cuban exiles.

Undoubtedly, the most interesting current migrations to the city involve citizens of the United States for several generations—the African-Americans, Mexican-Americans, and Puerto Ricans. Black urban migration began in earnest in the World War I period; Puerto Rican migration to mainland U.S. cities has primarily been a phenomenon of the post-World War II period; Mexican-Americans have been entering the United States and its cities for some decades now.

For most cultural groups in the United States, ethnicity is officially determined by membership in the foreign stock population. According to the U.S. Census, one is foreign stock either by being born outside the United States or being the child of at least one parent who was born outside the United States. Relying on the reports of individual citizens, the census can then categorize Americans by their foreign stock country. About 4.7 percent of the U.S. population were foreign born in 1970, and another 11.8 percent were of foreign-born parentage [U.S. Bureau of the Census 1973c, table 1].

Unfortunately, the United States census does not collect data on the ethnicity of most of the remaining U.S. population. A general ethnicity question has been asked in some sample surveys, but the results have been too disappointing to pursue the issue further. Apparently, many third-generation Americans either cannot clearly describe their ethnicity or insist that they have no particular ethnicity but are "Americans."

Among white Americans, only the Spanish surname population, heavily Mexican and Puerto Rican in descent, is identifiable for the third and later generations. The Spanish surname population is generally determined by matching the last name of household respondents with a list of usual Spanish surnames.

Nonwhite Americans may be identified by racial questions on the census forms. By these questions, it is possible to investigate at least some population and housing characteristics of the black, Asian-American, and native American population.

Until recently, most sociologists treated ethnicity as an aspect of social rank. Ethnic identification was seen as a temporary manifestation of the migrant's low economic status in American society. And it was presumed that distinctive ethnic traits would disappear as the migrant was assimilated economically into the society. The "teaming masses" presumably arrived uneducated, unskilled and uncultured in the United States, and then fought their way upward in the social structure over generations.

In the forceful statement of this perspective, Robert Park, a close associate of Burgess, noted:

> Assimilation, as the word is here used, brings with it a certain borrowed significance which it carried over from physiology where it is employed to describe the process of nutrition. By a process of assimilation, somewhat similar to the physiological one, we may conceive alien peoples to be

incorporated with, and made part of, the community or state. Ordinarily assimilation goes on silently and unconsciously, and only forces itself into population conscience when there is some interruption or disturbance of the process [1967, p. 120].

Using this perspective, one might divide the process of assimilation into roughly four stages: 1. arrival in the United States with low socio-economic status and low degree of acculturation;   2. the formation of separate residential communities, because low status relegates the group to certain areas of the city and discrimination forces the group to band together;   3. a gradual upward movement in social status and the break-down of the ethnic community;   4. the complete integration of the group into American society.

Within the context of this perspective, ethnic residential segregation may be seen as either a cause or a consequence of other ethnic group characteristics. For instance, just as inability to speak English may cause an ethnic group to live together, the fact of living together may be a cause of the group's inability to learn English.

This perspective, in seeing status and ethnicity as very similar, seems to follow the view that residential segregation arises primarily from nonpersonal causes. That is, ethnic groups become segregated primarily because their income and status relegate them to certain types of housing and neighborhoods in the city. However, there may be certain personalistic components of the segregation because the ethnic group, due to its low status, seeks out others of the same ethnicity in order to protect and defend its interests.

On the whole, Stanley Lieberson's most comprehensive study [1963] of ethnic residential segregation among European stock groups in American society seems to share this perspective, arguing that the following are all closely related for ethnic groups: time in the United States, social status, degree of residential segregation from the native population, and various indicators of assimilation such as the ability to speak English and the percentage of naturalized citizens. His study focused on cross-sectional correlates of residential segregation and changes in the degree of segregation for political wards, 1910–1920, and census tracts, 1930–1950. He selected for analysis ten large northern cities, with significant foreign-born populations.

Lieberson found that the average segregation of foreign-born groups from the native population decreased over time, although the declines were not great. For instance, over the ten cities, the average index of dissimilarity of the foreign-born white ethnic groups from the native white population was 43.9 in 1930 and 38.6 in 1950 [1963, pp. 66–67]. This level of segregation at both time points would be similar to the degree of occupational segregation and it would be somewhat higher than the degree of family segregation, which were noted previously in this paper.

Furthermore, according to Lieberson's results, the old immigrant groups, those primarily from Northern Europe and Scandinavia, were weakly segregated from each other and the native whites, while the new immigrant groups, primarily from Eastern and Southern Europe, were more strongly segregated from the old immigrant and native white groups. The older immigrant groups were also higher in status and other alleged characteristics of assimilation.

Consistent with Lieberson's results, Taeuber and Taeuber [1964] showed a general decrease in the segregation of foreign-born ethnic groups in Chicago from the native white population during the 1930 to 1960 period. This decrease was particularly characteristic of the "new" immigrant groups, or Southern and Eastern Europeans.

In a provocative critique of Lieberson and the Taeubers, Nathan Kantrowitz [1973] has argued that the declines in residential segregation, which were far from strong in the first place, may be artifacts of the definition of the native white or nonforeign stock population. In the early part of the twentieth century, the native white population was primarily composed of persons from Northern European stock, although they were not immigrants or the children of immigrants themselves. However, over time, as the Southern Europeans had children and grandchildren, the composition of the native white population became more diversified. Kantrowitz' intriguing idea is that declining segregation between immigrant groups and the surrounding native population may be largely an artifact of the changing composition of the native population, so that it was becoming more similar in national origin to the various foreign stock groups.

If Kantrowitz is correct, then the traditional process of ethnic segregation has not been occurring in American cities. Unfortunately, the current census statistical data do not permit researchers to determine whether the alleged declining residential segregation is a statistical artifact or not, since the nonforeign stock (native) population is not divided in reports by ethnicity.

What Kantrowitz [pp. 18–19] does show, using the New York Metropolitan Area in 1960 as an example, is that a high degree of residential segregation remains among the foreign stock population of New York. For instance, among ten foreign stock groups of European heritage, Kantrowitz found an average index of dissimilarity of 46.4 for first- and second-generation Americans. More specifically, as examples of patterns, foreign-stock Swedes and Norwegians, both presumably similar in culture, had a segregation index of 45.8. Italians and Irish, both heavily Catholic, had a segregation index of 48.0. In general, the lowest indices were found within the Eastern European and within the Northern European populations, respectively, but the indices clearly suggested that segregation by ethnicity had far from ended, at least in New York City.

Kantrowitz' general view about the remaining importance of ethnic segregation is supported in two studies of residential segregation in the Toronto metropolitan area. The Canadian census provides extensive data on ethnicity and immigration for all its citizens, and the data may assume more meaning than in the United States, since Canada has had large waves of immigration since World War II. In one study, A. Gordon Darroch and W. G. Marston [1971] found that segregation among ethnic groups in Toronto in 1961 could be explained only slightly by the social class differences of the groups. The article also showed that social class segregation in Toronto was roughly equal to segregation by ethnicity. In another article, Darroch and Marston [1969] argued for a multidimensional concept of ethnic residential segregation, showing that ethnic segregation seemed to be explained by a variety of factors: period of immigration to Canada, religion, mother tongue, and country of birth. The researchers also showed that ethnic segregation could not be explained by period of immigration to Canada alone, indicating that it was not simply an artifact of having new, low status immigrants.

Kantrowitz and Darroch and Marston do not explain why ethnic segregation should persist in American society, but it is likely that ethnic groups find residential proximity to members of their own group valuable for several personal reasons. First, as Nathan Glazer and Daniel Moynihan [1970] argue, ethnic identification may be a basis for conflict over issues not obviously identified as such. The recent struggles of the Jewish-dominated teachers' union in New York City with black and Puerto Rican political groups over changes in the organizational and administrative structure of the public school system was generally not fought openly on the basis of racial and ethnic interests. However, in actuality, the Jewish community in New York tended to side with the teachers' union, while the black and Puerto Rican communities became mobilized in opposition. Second, and probably more important, is the nature of social relations in a large metropolis. Most city dwellers do not have close, off-the-job associations with coworkers and undoubtedly seek out other personal ties in the metropolis. Ethnic identification is certainly one viable means of building ties, and this may be indicated by the separate residential location of people.

While Kantrowitz' study is valuable, it is limited to the New York City area, and there are reasons to believe that ethnic segregation might be stronger there than in other cities of the country. Canada is also a society with very high rates of recent in-migration. New York, for instance, grew to great size during the periods of great migration from Europe, and segregated ethnic communities originally developed at that time. These communities may have simply persisted over time for reasons of inertia, if nothing else. Ethnic segregation may be less clearcut in newer American metropolitan areas, such as West Coast cities, which developed after the period of the great migration. Anthony Henzell [1973], in a replication of Kantrowitz' study for selected ethnic groups in the new West Coast city of Seattle, found similar overall patterns but lower overall degrees of segregation. Furthermore, New York City, because of its sheer size, has extremely large ethnic groups, and it is therefore more possible to maintain a network of ethnic community institutions and ties. In cities with smaller total populations, ethnic groups may have difficulty in maintaining strong ties over time.

Since most European migration came to an end around World War I, most foreign stock persons in the United States are relatively old. It is interesting to speculate whether the continued existence of ethnic segregation in the United States is largely a product of age segregation in metropolitan areas. That is, older members of ethnic groups continue to live in the neighborhoods where they first settled upon arrival, but their children may have dispersed in the metropolis. For instance, in the New York SMSA, 29.9 percent of the foreign born males are over 65 years of age. The foreign born make up 41.1 percent of the foreign stock population in New York [U.S. Bureau of the Census 1972b, table 15].

Unfortunately, the degree of concentration or centralization of white ethnic groups in American society is not well understood. According to the traditional Burgess hypothesis, assimilation in culture and social mobility should be accompanied by decentralization of population groups, and, in fact, Paul Cressey [1938] and more recently Richard Ford [1950] have shown that ethnic groups did move outward from the center of Chicago during the early part of the twentieth century as they increased in socioeconomic status. Ford's study, the more empirical of the two, stopped with the year 1940, and Ford noted little outward movement of the ethnic population from 1930 to 1940. In another study [Guest 1971], I have shown some general tendency for the white ethnic population in American cities to be centrally located, but this centralization was apparently not determined primarily by social rank.

Since social rank does not vary clearly with distance in American metropolitan areas, it seems unlikely that the central or peripheral location of ethnic groups in most American cities could be considered indicative of ethnic assimilation.

Clearly, more needs to be known about the spatial location of ethnic groups and the reason for their location. Others have suggested that ethnic groups spatially concentrate themselves on nonpersonal symbolic bases. This perspective differs from the Kantrowitz view and the Burgess ecological perspective. Consistent with this view, Christen Jonassen [1945] argues that Norwegians in New York City have located close to the sea and semirural areas, because they remind Norwegians of their native land. For instance, Staten Island—until recently a lightly populated part of New York City—has been a favorite location for Norwegians. In Seattle, the Scandinavian population is particularly located around the Puget Sound shoreline, with clear views of the water and the imposing Olympic Mountains.

Non-European minorities, such as Spanish-Americans, Puerto Ricans, and Asian-Americans, are also segregated in American cities; yet, their segregation from the dominant white population does not approach the segregation of blacks from whites, and current evidence suggests that the above minorities are also highly segregated from blacks. This last finding is particularly interesting since in some cities the black population does not differ clearly in socio-economic status from the Spanish-American and Puerto Rican populations. In the Southwestern states (Texas, Colorado, New Mexico, Arizona, and California), most cities have both large black and large Mexican-American populations in addition to the usually large white or "Anglo" population. Most of these places also have small nonwhite populations other than blacks, such as Native Americans, and Japanese- and Chinese-Americans. In a study of residential segregation in 35 Southwestern cities, Leo Grebler, Joan Moore, and Ralph Guzman [1970, pp. 271–285] compared the degree of residential segregation of these four groups over census tracts and found residential separation, in at least moderate degrees, among all four groups. The highest average degree of segregation, 80.1, was between "Anglos" and blacks, but "Anglo" vs. Spanish surname was also a relatively high average of 54.5 In addition, the Spanish surnamed were also relatively segregated, on the average, from blacks, with an average index of 57.3.

In studies of Chicago and New York, Taeuber and Taeuber [1964] and Kantrowitz [1973] showed that Puerto Ricans are less segregated from the native white and Northern European foreign stock groups than blacks are, and Kantrowitz also showed that Puerto Ricans are also highly segregated from blacks. Compared with other ethnic groups, Puerto Ricans were also among the most residentially segregated from the native white or Northern European populations.

As far as I know, the degree of segregation between Asian populations and the native white population is not well understood. In the Grebler, Moore, and Guzman [1970, p. 277] study of Southwestern cities, including California with a large Asian population, nonwhite nonblacks (predominantly Asian-Americans) had an average segregation index from "Anglos" of 62.5—relatively high. In a study of the large Japanese-American population in San Francisco, however, Harry Kitano [1960, p. 184] concluded on the basis of his observation that "ethnic colonies of Japanese are gone or rapidly going" and documented the rapid socio-economic advance of the Japanese. This conclusion was generally documented by Taeuber and Taeuber [1969, p. 67] in a study of changes in white-Asian residential segregation for San Francisco between 1940 and 1960. Hashimoto [1973] found residential segregation between Asians and whites in Honolulu was decreasing between 1960 and 1970, and there was clear evidence of individual neighborhoods becoming more mixed in their racial composition.

RESIDENCE AND RACE

During the past 60 years, American urban society has witnessed one of the great population movements in history, as the black population has left the rural South for cities in both North and South. In 1910, 73 percent of the black population lived in rural areas [Taeuber & Taeuber 1969, p. 1] and 89 percent in the census-defined South, largely the old Confederacy [U.S. Bureau of the Census 1913]. By 1970, only 20 percent of the black population lived in rural areas and about 53 percent was left in the South [U.S. Bureau of the Census 1973d].

Why did the movement begin, almost half a century after the emancipation of the slave population? [Farley 1968]. The primary pull attracting blacks to cities was undoubtedly World War I. As the economy generated many new jobs due to the war effort, a serious labor shortage occurred. The shortage was increased by two other events—large numbers of able-bodied whites marched off to war, and migration ended from war-ravaged Europe.

Few blacks had previously left the South, but it was hardly because of strong attachment to the life of the region. After briefly flirting with racial equality after the Civil War, the South had restored a strict system of racial segregation symbolized by the "Jim Crow" laws. During this same period, the mechanization of southern labor had led to a declining need for unskilled black labor on the farms, and the spread of the infectious boll weevil (which killed cotton crops) further increased the black labor surplus.

Once the flow started, it swelled into hundreds and thousands of persons. The out-migration of blacks from the South is still occurring, although a few still work as farmers. Most now live in southern cities or small towns.

The decade-by-decade inflow of blacks into some cities has been massive. For instance, the black percentage of the central city population of Chicago grew steadily decade by decade: 1900, 1.6 percent; 1910, 2.0 percent; 1920, 4.1 percent; 1930, 6.9 percent; 1940, 8.2 percent; 1950, 13.6 percent; 1960, 23.0 percent; 1970, 32.8 percent. During the same period, the total population of Chicago grew from 1.7 to 3.4 million. [The data on Chicago are drawn from Duncan & Duncan 1957, p. 25, and Hermalin & Farley 1973, p. 599.]

The pre-World War I black population of many northern cities was relatively low in social status and relatively segregated residentially; yet differences between the races should not be overemphasized. For instance, a residential segregation index of 69.2 was found in 1910 for census tracts in Cleveland—high, but far from complete, segregation, and in 1890, there were some blacks in the city working in various professional, managerial, and skilled trades. Of the 1,237 black males in Cleveland in 1890, 6 were physicians, 2 each were lawyers and engineers, 28 were carpenters, 24 were masons, and 80 were barbers (a trade later closed to most blacks) [U.S. Census Office 1897, table 118].

The post-World War I flow of blacks into cities had to be accommodated in some way. Northern whites could have accepted some types of residential and social integration of these new urban immigrants, permitting them to reside in many white neighborhoods and encouraging their educational and economic advancement in the urban job structure. Rather than attempt an accommodation, however, the white community generally resisted contact and association with blacks. The result was the rapid development of separate black and white communities. For instance, in Cleveland, the index of segregation increased from 69.2 in 1910 to 71.6 in 1920, to 82.8 in 1930, and to 85.8 by 1940 [Taeuber & Taeuber 1969, p. 53]. In order to find new housing, blacks had to either push whites out of already established neighborhoods or they had to accept the housing left behind by whites when they moved to the suburban neighborhoods.

The black communities in American cities at the turn of the century appeared at specific spatial points of concentration for a multitude of reasons. Once established, the black communities generally continued to develop from their initial points. Gilbert Osofsky [1968], for instance, reports in his study of race in New York City that the black population was located on the southern part of Manhattan Island until the late 1800s, when the growth of the CBD led to the destruction of centrally located black residential districts. Since whites resisted residential integration of all neighborhoods, it was inevitable that a new black section of New York would appear in some part of the white community. The new black community, in Harlem, appeared indirectly as a result of the construction of a subway line about 1890. Land speculators saw the subway stop as a central site for residences and hurriedly constructed more new houses than demand from whites warranted, leaving many of the homes permanently or periodically unfilled. Within this context of a loose housing market, some of the speculators began renting their apartments and homes to the New York black population, recently displaced from its former area near the CBD. At first slowly and then quickly, the Harlem area changed from pure white to an almost completely black area. By 1914, some 50,000 blacks lived in the Harlem area [Osofsky, p. 105]. The pace of change was stimulated by the development of black-owned real estate companies such as the Afro-American Realty Company, which dealt actively in the Harlem market.

The change was fraught with tension, as was often the case in northern cities. Neighborhood "improvement" organizations formed to fight the in-movement of blacks in Harlem legally, through social pressure, and sometimes through violence. As John G. Taylor, the founder of the Harlem Property Owners Improvement Corporation, noted in 1913, "We are approaching a crisis. It is a question of whether the white man will rule Harlem or the black" [Osofsky, p. 107]. At another time, Taylor exclaimed in an angry tirade, "Drive them out and send them to the slums where they belong" [Osofsky, p. 107]. Yet black individuals were willing to suffer the great abuse if the alternative was no housing at all.

The Harlem experience has since been matched in dozens of other cities. In the search for housing in a "tight" market, blacks find some property owner—often white—who is willing to sell. And then, given the pent up demand for black housing, pressure from other black families follows. This process of change is often encouraged by such tactics as "block busting," in which realtors warn white homeowners that their neighborhood is about to change racially, and that they should get out early. The white housing is then presumably bought at an extremely low price and resold at a high price to a black family.

In a pioneering study of racial change in Chicago, Otis Dudley and Beverly Duncan [1957] argued that neighborhoods underwent a sequence of changes: invasion, early consolidation, consolidation, late consolidation, and piling up, in which the neighborhood became overwhelmingly black—often with crowded living quarters. Their view was generally consistent with the picture of neighborhood change presented by Burgess [Park & Burgess 1967, pp. 47–62] in the "Growth of the City." While the Duncans' terminology may seem to have racist overtones, it was actually drawn from some ecological literature on change in plant and animal communities. For instance, an area supporting one type of tree, such as birch or alder, might be invaded by another type, such as the pine, so that over time the nature of the area would change.

The reaction of the white community to the growth of the black community may be seen as somewhat irrational, from the black viewpoint. Given a situation in which a black population in a city is growing and no newly constructed housing is being made available to the minority group, blacks will almost inevitably try to locate in white housing, generally near the already established black area. Since the black population rarely consists of more than 15 to 20 percent of the total population of any metropolitan area, most of the black population could be accommodated by the whites without ending white supremacy in any neighborhood. Instead of attempting to plan together—with each other and with blacks—white neighborhoods have competed with each other to see who could keep out the black population. In this competition, some neighborhoods were certain to be "losers."

TRENDS IN SEGREGATION

A recent pattern of high and pervasive segregation has been carefully documented by Taeuber & Taeuber [1969] in a study of segregation between whites and nonwhites (primarily blacks) in 109 American cities between 1940 and 1960. They used blocks rather than census tracts as the unit of analysis, and the indices are slightly inflated by the use of the smaller areal unit.

The researchers found [1966, p. 44] the following average indices of racial segregation: 1940, 85.2; 1950, 87.3; 1960, 86.1; indicating no clear downward trend. The levels of segregation are much higher than found for families, occupational groups, and European ethnic groups vis-à-vis the native white population.

The greatest regional gains in racial segregation, Taeuber and Taeuber found, have been made in the South, primarily the Old Confederacy, where the average index climbed from 84.9 in 1940 to 90.7 in 1960, that is, racial segregation is even more prevalent today in the South than it had been previously. Leo Schnore and Philip Evenson [1966] argue that the particular increase in segregation is due to the transition in social relationships within the South. In the pre- and early post-Civil War period, many blacks continued to live near their white masters or employers in southern cities. The black population often lived in servant quarters on alleys or side streets, or lived in white homes as servants. Over time, as the South has begun to industrialize, the old traditional southern pattern of race relations disintegrated, presumably being replaced by the northern pattern where blacks and whites live in clearly demarcated neighborhoods. In recent years, the court-ordered desegregation of southern schools presumably has further stimulated this process, as white parents have sought neighborhoods where their children would not have to attend schools with large numbers of blacks.

In analyzing the changes in segregation between the 1950 and 1960 decade, Taeuber and Taeuber suggested [1969, pp. 76–77] that decreases in segregation or slow increases in segregation for some cities may have been a transitory phenomena. They suggest that during the 1950s many whites deserted older, central neighborhoods, for the suburbs, leaving them open for black occupancy. In cities where the black population expanded rapidly in numbers and also increased its socio-economic position, blacks moved into these vacated housing units in large numbers, creating a semblance of temporary integration. Taeuber and Taeuber suggest that this integration may be purely temporary, however, as the remaining whites in these neighborhoods leave and blacks continue to move in.

The data from the 1970 census on racial segregation between blacks and whites have yet to be fully analyzed; still, there is fragmentary evidence, based on limited studies in the 1960s of some cities [Farley &

Taeuber 1968], that residential segregation by race is not decreasing and is probably increasing.

Why does racial segregation occur? I have already argued *how* it occurs—by the expansion of blacks into previously white neighborhoods. There are essentially four major hypotheses about why it occurs. One hypothesis, which is primarily nonpersonal, suggests that racial segregation is largely a consequence of class differences between blacks and whites. The other hypotheses essentially emphasize personal causes of segregation. Two of them argue that segregation results from the desires of individuals—either the preference of whites not to live with blacks or the preference of blacks to live with other blacks. A fourth hypothesis argues that racial segregation is created primarily by institutions, particularly realtors and possibly the government.

In particular, Edward Banfield [1970, pp. 67–87] has suggested that racial segregation between blacks and whites is primarily a consequence of economic or social class differences between the two groups. By implication, racial segregation will disappear when differences in social rank also end. But Taeuber and Taeuber [1969, pp. 78–95], after a careful analysis of the effects of class differences on racial residential segregation, concluded that class or economic factors could explain only about one-third of the racial segregation in a sample of fifteen large northern and southern cities. The effects of class factors decreased between 1940 and 1960, and class factors explained the smallest proportion of segregation in northern cities, where blacks have generally made the greatest economic gains relative to whites. The implication of such an analysis is, of course, that economic equivalence between whites and blacks will not lead quickly to residential equivalence. The Taeuber and Taeuber analysis is so persuasive that a research tour de force would be required to prove segregation by race would not occur if social rank were the same.

The argument that racial segregation results from the overwhelming personal preference of whites to maintain segregation is not well supported by recent public opinion polls. For instance, national samples of the white population have been asked: "Which of these statements would you agree with: White people have a right to keep Negroes out of their neighborhoods if they want to, or Negroes have a right to live wherever they can afford to, just like anybody else?" [Campbell 1971, pp. 133]. From 1964 to 1970, the percentage of whites who agreed that white people had a right to keep blacks out declined from 29 percent to 21 percent, while the percentage who argued that blacks have a right to live wherever they can afford to increased from 53 percent to 67 percent. The rest said that "it depends" or they "didn't know." In response to the question: "If a Negro family with about the same income and education as you moved next door to you, would you mind it a lot, a little, or not at all?" [Campbell 1971, p. 8] the 1970 sample of whites had 19 percent minding a lot, and 25 percent minding a little, while 53 percent either did not mind at all or already had a black family next door.

These patterns seem to be recent; public opinion polls of previous decades show greater resistance to racial integration. I interpret the more recent polls to indicate that some whites are still strongly opposed to integration, and it is likely that most whites are not strongly in favor of integration—willing to move into neighborhoods that are clearly changing racially. Yet, it is clear that racial segregation at the present time cannot result from the simple addition of individual white attitudes.

Another hypothesis—that racial segregation results from the personal desires of black people to segregate themselves from white people—is not supported when public opinion polls of the black population are analyzed. For instance, black samples were asked [Campbell 1971, p. 136] in 1964, 1968, and 1970 whether they were in favor of desegregation, strict segregation, or something in between. The question did not refer just to residential patterns but to general social patterns. The percentage of blacks supporting desegregation was 72 percent in both 1964 and 1968 and 78 percent in 1970. In 1964, 6 percent favored strict segregation, and this had decreased to 5 and 3 percent in 1968 and 1970, respectively. Blacks also overwhelmingly endorse the necessity for open housing laws [Campbell 1971, p. 133]. I do not interpret the results to indicate that blacks have a particular liking for whites over blacks, but rather that blacks would prefer a wide choice of neighborhoods and housing. I, therefore, tend to reject the hypothesis that blacks have a particularly strong desire to live next to other blacks.[7]

7. Banfield [1970, p. 75], in support of the idea that blacks prefer racial segregation, cites a 1964 poll of blacks responding to the question of what type of neighborhood would be preferred if all were equally well kept up. The sample of metropolitan blacks showed 55 percent, preferring "mostly Negro," 38 percent "mixed or "no difference"; 4 percent, "mostly white"; 3 percent, "don't know." Even if one assumes that a slight 55 percent majority clearly indicated black desires, several questions may be raised. First, the question assumes that blacks make a clear distinction between black and white neighborhoods in selecting a desired nieghborhood. The black-white preference is not compared with other possible desirable features of neighborhoods, such as housing quality and size in making location decisions. Second, the data suggest that blacks most desired living with blacks in southern cities, where racial barriers and hostilities are generally greater than in the North. Blacks may have been answering in terms of how they perceived their chances of being treated with respect by white neighbors, rather than their particular liking of blacks versus whites.

Unfortunately, we know little about the behavior of institutions such as realty companies, but there are certain documented cases of realtors refusing to show homes to blacks. Take for example, a recent Chicago study [Molotch 1972, pp. 20–34] of real estate dealers in apartment management. Of the 177 Chicago realtors interviewed, only 29 percent gave the only legal (in light of the Chicago Fair Housing Ordinance) response: that they would rent to blacks anywhere at any time regardless of local market conditions or existing racial composition of building or neighborhood. Of the other respondents, 7 percent would rent after one black was already on the block; 11 percent when the block is less than one-fourth black but at least two black families were already in residence; another 10 percent would rent to a black if the block population was between 25 and 50 percent black; 6 percent indicated they would rent to blacks only if half the block was already black; 3 percent indicated they would not rent to blacks under any circumstances. Ten percent of respondents refused to specify a policy, indicating that the decision was made by the owner, not the agent; 22 percent of respondents either evaded answering or offered another kind of response.

Why would realtors discriminate in housing if most whites do not particularly favor racial segregation? The attitude of realtors may stem primarily from the realization that a few whites strongly oppose integration and few are strongly in favor. Given the profit margins of most small businesses, it hardly pays to risk the wrath of any customer, no matter how unusual his attitudes may be.

Recent activities of the federal executive and legislative branches in favor of civil rights legislation and equal racial opportunities would suggest a strong positive role in ending racial segregation in housing. The federal government certainly has the power to affect the housing market, as it is estimated that about one-fourth of all housing starts are subsidized in some way by federal money [Lawson 1971, p. 18]. The federal government can require nondiscrimination in much housing by contractors, home owners, and apartment managers. And officially, housing-oriented agencies such as the Department of Housing and Urban Development do have policies requiring and encouraging nondiscrimination in housing.

There seem, however, to be two practical problems with the federal government as an agency for racial integration. [The following summary is drawn from Lawson 1971.] First, President Nixon interpreted the federal government's position as being against racial segregation but pro-social class segregation. That is, the federal government opposes neighborhood segregation on the basis of race alone but will not object to higher status persons keeping lower status persons out of their neighborhoods. While it is clear that all lower income persons are not black and all blacks are not lower income, persons of lower socioeconomic position are found more often in the black population. And it is possible that racial discrimination in housing sometimes occurs and is justified on the basis of what are proclaimed as social class factors. Second, the federal government apparently does not actively enforce its official position. A recent report by the U.S. Civil Rights Commission studied major agencies in local housing markets such as bankers and realtors. The study found a flagrant and open disregard for federal antidiscrimination policy at the local level; local institutions paid lip service to antidiscrimination measures, but in practice ignored them.

In summary, my view is that racial segregation is probably created primarily by institutions, particularly realtors and other organizations in the local housing market. Their actions are at least partially stimulated by some popular desire for racial segregation, in the absence of strong sentiment for racial integration. It should be emphasized, however, that most whites do not favor residential segregation by race.

Lest the above statements about realtors and the government seem irresponsible, it should be pointed out that some social agencies must be facilitating racial segregation because it does not decrease, and there is little strong support for it among most whites.

COMMUNITY WITHIN COMMUNITY

The net result of the creation of black ghettoes is the development of a community within a community. Separate shopping or business districts in the city develop, and the black community sometimes organizes itself around these business districts, much as the white community organizes itself around the major business district for the metropolis. For instance, Frazier [1937] plotted the spatial location of families around the major shopping center in the Harlem area of Manhattan and found regular change in the incidence of families with children and indicators of social status, as Burgess suggested for the larger total community.

When the black community does not organize itself around its own shopping centers, there is often a process of sorting on the basis of the Central Business District for the total metropolis. Schnore [1965, pp. 254–308], for instance, found that social status, as measured by education, income and occupation, generally tended to increase with distance from the CBD in the nonwhite communities of twenty-four large cities. The pattern was most clear for northern industrial cities and less common for southern and western cities. I found [1970, pp. 133–154] that the patterns of spatial location of black families in five large metropolitan areas tended to mirror the location patterns of families in the total population—that is, families with children tended to be located on the outskirts, and unattached and single individuals tended to be located near the center of the city.

In their study of racial segregation, Taeuber and Taeuber [1969, pp. 246–254] determined the degree of segregation among occupation groups in ten large nonwhite communities. They found some increases in occupational segregation between 1940 and 1960, although the levels of segregation seemed below those found in white and total communities of large cities. Kantrowitz [1973, pp. 39–41] computed indices of residential segregation by income groups for both black and white (non-Puerto Rican) communities. He found that segregation within both communities was high and relatively equal.

NEIGHBORHOOD CHANGE

Much of the literature on racial segregation has focused on the process of racial change in neighborhoods, partially because such research indicates the demographic and ecological process by which the black community expands, and also because such research indicates the nature of white feelings about the in-movement of blacks.

There are several folk arguments about the nature of racial change, which may eventually be proved correct; yet, present research finds little support for them.

One argument holds that the black population invades the worst, deteriorated sections of the white community. As Abrams notes, "Obsolete and run-down areas inhabited by whites are the most susceptible candidates for the sequence of desertion, infiltration, and influx by nonwhites" [1955, p. 276]. But, according to Taeuber and Taeuber, this image is not correct, particularly in Northern cities.

> The data for the six Northern and border cities indicate that, in the initial year of each decade, the average educational and occupational level of the white population in Invasion tracts was usually higher than that of the . . . (white population) . . . in the all-white Rest of the City. Negro invasion, then, was not limited to deteriorated areas, but occurred in some of the better areas. However, levels of owner-occupancy were lower, and

levels of room-crowding were higher among whites in Invasion tracts than in the Rest of the City. Improvement in the four socioeconomic characteristics during each decade was usually less for whites residing in Invasion tracts than for whites residing in the Rest of the City [1969, pp. 155–157].

Another argument is that blacks moving into changing areas are often low in social and economic status, and thus threaten the status character of the previously white neighborhood. But Taeuber and Taeuber [1969, pp. 156–163] found that blacks in Invasion tracts "are often of higher educational status and more likely to be home-owners than whites in these tracts, both before and after invasion." However, blacks were clearly at a lower occupational status (fewer in white collar jobs), presumably resulting from discrimination in the economic sector.

In fact, the evidence of Edwards [1972], and Guest[1970, pp. 133–154], and Taeuber and Taeuber [1969], suggests that racially changing areas attract the same types of individuals as suburban white areas: relatively high in status, relatively young, and often in the process of forming a family. The process of invasion and succession for the black population may be seen as roughly analogous to the general growth of the city suggested by Burgess.

It has also frequently been argued that the movement of blacks into an area has clearly negative effects on property values, the presence of blacks presumably being a negative environmental factor. This argument would have to deal with two competitive processes. On the one hand, whites may, in fact, interpret the presence of blacks as being a negative factor in determining property values. On the other hand, the pent-up demand for housing among the black community may drive house prices up rather than down in changing neighborhoods, as blacks realize that they may purchase them.

There is clearly a desperate need for more research in this area. But the most comprehensive study of the question, done during the 1950s, concluded that racial change had no measurable negative impact on housing prices. Laurenti [1960], in a study of primarily single-family neighborhoods in San Francisco, Oakland, and Philadelphia, compared housing prices for neighborhoods similar in most characteristics except for the fact that some were changing racially. During this 1-year observation period, about 41 percent of the matched neighborhoods had no noticeably different trends in housing prices; in another 44 percent of the comparisons, the housing price in the changing neighborhood ended relatively higher than the control price, by margins of 5 to 26 percent.

Another common argument suggests that whites "flee" when blacks move into a previously all-white neighborhood. The flight may be stimulated by fright over declining property values, the rise of crime, and the like. Yet, while there is clear evidence that neighborhoods frequently become all-black once they contain a substantial proportion of blacks, say 25 to 50 percent, no clear evidence exists that there is a process of white "flight" in early stages of racial change. In talking about the possibility of flight, it must be realized that most urban neighborhoods have a high turnover of residents each year, roughly 20 percent, and 50 percent or more within 5 years. Within the context of the high mobility, it is possible for white neighborhoods to become almost completely black within a decade or so as whites move out gradually, and almost all the new residents are black. That is, neighborhoods may change by whites refusing to buy-in to the neighborhood, rather than by already present whites fleeing.

In a comparison of two similar Chicago central city communities, South Shore (racially changing) and Rogers Park (stable white), Molotch [1969] could find little evidence that property sales within a 6-month period were unusually high in South Shore. The neighborhoods were matched on various nonracial characteristics, such as the presence of apartment housing, the age of the housing, and the housing values. Guest and Zuiches [1971] in an analysis of changing neighborhoods in Cleveland, looked at the mobility rates for various types of neighborhoods after the effects of all other mobility-inducing factors had been eliminated, such as the presence of apartment housing, and the age of the residents. They found that, typically, racially changing tracts had only slightly higher rates of out-mobility than would be predicted by knowing the other characteristics of the area. Yet, a few of the changing neighborhoods had much higher mobility than would be predicted by knowing the housing and population characteristics of the neighborhoods. It may be that some neighborhoods change gradually, while other neighborhoods change rapidly, perhaps stimulated by the block-busting tactics of realtors or explosive racial incidents.

Other research also suggests that little relationship exists between racial attitudes and willingness to live near blacks. For instance, Wolf and Lebeaux [1969], in a study of a changing neighborhood (the Bagley area) in Detroit found little correlation between the attitudes of the residents and their later disposition to move out once the neighborhood clearly began to change. Rapkin and Grigsby [1960] found that a proposed interracial housing project in Philadelphia primarily attracted whites who were concerned about obtaining a good housing value, and most of the prospective white residents were little motivated by racial concerns pro or con.

In future attempts to reduce racial segregation in American society, the transition neighborhood theoretically may be a good starting point. After all, the existence of blacks and whites together in a neighborhood is what we generally mean by racial integration. At the present time, however, it does not appear likely that many changing neighborhoods are or can be stable in racial composition. As Molotch [1972] points out in a study of changing neighborhoods in Chicago, only unusual features of changing neighborhoods will encourage whites to continue moving in after the change process begins. For instance, Molotch [pp. 169–171] notes that the Hyde Park area has been integrated for a long period of time, primarily because the nearby University of Chicago needs a neighborhood for its employees, and tremendous pressure has been exerted to maintain a white presence in the area. In this way, Hyde Park differs greatly from South Shore, which also made strenuous efforts to maintain an integrated character, through various community organizations, but eventually failed. South Shore was an attractive community, but not attractive enough to ensure a large in-flow of white families to replace those leaving.

The transition neighborhood may become a fulcrum of integration, however, if two things occur. First, housing opportunities must be opened for the black population in new, single-family developments. While black income is still far below white income, there is a developing black middle class that can afford suburban, tract-type housing. The development of black alternative housing opportunities would reduce the tremendous pressure within the black community to buy the housing in a changing neighborhood once it has been entered. Second, alternative employment opportunities must be created for the black population in a large number of American cities. The black population is increasingly concentrating in a few large cities, and the resulting pressure on transition neighborhoods must be particularly great. In 1970, 4 out of 10 blacks in the United States were living in the 30 cities with the largest black population. This percentage of the total black population of the United States residing in the 30 selected cities has shown a steady increase from the computed 30 percent in 1960 [U.S. Bureau of the Census 1971, p. 17].

Some observers of black residential patterns suggest a general dispersal of the black population into the suburbs. This is generally seen as consistent with the upward social and economic advancement of the black population. As Birch noted:

> While all the recent evidence on black migration is spotty and subject to confirmation by the 1970 census, it all points in the same direction. Blacks finally appear to be moving throughout the metropolitan region in something like the way that other immigrants did before them. As educational opportunities have opened up, and as incomes have risen, blacks seem to be forming stable family units, and those units are moving into better neighborhoods as fast as they can [1970, p. 74].

The evidence, however, is not consistent with this thesis. In a study of 29 large urban areas, Hermalin and Farley [1973] found that the average percentage of blacks in suburban rings had increased from 4.1 percent in 1950 to 4.6 percent in 1970. This compared with the growth of the central city black population from an average of 12.7 percent to 25.9 percent.

In an earlier study of black suburbs in 1960, Farley [1970] claimed that most could be divided into three types: 1. "new" segregated tract developments of single-family homes, particularly those found in the South; 2. population replacement of whites in older, densely settled suburbs, containing or near employment centers; 3. slum suburbs with inadequate sewer and water facilities, containing dilapidated homes of low value, and having exclusively black populations. None of these types suggest that the small suburbanization of blacks is followed by their racial integration, especially in middle class white residential communities.

Clearly, then, very few blacks are decentralized in the suburbs. We know little about black location patterns within central cities, although maps of 10 American cities show [Taeuber & Taeuber 1969, pp. 256–275] the black population to be heavily concentrated in sectors with some concentric function. The sectoral pattern would be compatible with Hoyt's view and incompatible with the Burgess perspective.

SEGREGATION— ITS CONSEQUENCES AND ITS FUTURE

In this unit, I have summarized some of the literature on residential segregation in urban areas—its degree, its causes, its spatial location. As the reader hopefully has discovered, much is unknown about the subject, and the unanswered questions would provide enough research work for several lifetimes.

Should we be for or against residential integration? The issue is not easy to resolve, and positions seem to be based as much on philosophy as on fact.

Some social critics have strong views on the general positive value of having demographically diverse neighborhoods in cities, regardless of whether the issue is family composition, social rank, or ethnicity. For instance, one sociologist, Richard Sennett [1970], has argued that Americans are driven by a spirit of "purification," an effort to shut themselves out from different ideas and groups. Presumably, this drive toward purification has led to more homogeneous neighbors, and as a result, the city is less livable and exciting. Sennett argues that neighborhood homogeneity is leading to a decrease in tolerance of other ideas and a general inability of diverse groups to communicate with each other and solve problems.

Another social critic, Jane Jacobs [1961], shares many of Sennett's fears about the trend toward neighborhood homogeneity. She argues that heterogeneity increases contact with new ideas and, in turn, stimulates cultural creativity and economic innovations.

Both Sennett and Jacobs attack urban planners for what they see as an effort to make all urban neighborhoods homogeneous. Many planners would undoubtedly disagree with this analysis, and it does seem difficult to find many planners who seriously suggest that all neighborhoods should have just one type of population group.

Debate has been sharper on the value of specific types of segregation. In particular, the negative functions of racial integration or segregation have attracted a great deal of attention in the past decade, and increasingly, social activists have attacked social class segregation in our society.

A few persons naively see residential segregation as a direct cause of general segregation within our society. That is, if we could eliminate residential segregation by race and by social class, we would take a long step toward eliminating all distinctions on the basis of race or social class in our society.

This position seems flawed to me, as I see racial and social class segregation as resulting primarily from the existence of inequalities in income and social power within our society. As long as some people have more money than others, ways will be found to maintain social class segregation. As long as the white population, including realtors, has the desire and power to control the spatial location of the black population, high levels of racial segregation in residence will continue.

More common positions on residential segregation call for an alteration in its pattern because it will open up opportunities in the society for social and economic progress. It is a means to an end rather than an end in itself. A great deal has been written about the advantages of ending racial segregation in particular, and many of the arguments may also be used to jusify ending social class segregation.

Traditionally, those who support racial segregation have seen it as a means of maintaining the black population in a position of subordination. But more recently, advocates of racial equality in the United States have sometimes taken the position that equality will be achieved only by intensifying the current pattern of black residential segregation.

Each of these positions deserves attention, for the light it sheds, or does not shed, on the value of integration within our industrial society. We call the pro-integrationist stance the White Liberal position, since it is more often held by reform-minded whites than by reform-minded blacks. The "new" pro-segregation position is called the Black Power position.

The White Liberal position points to several deleterious effects of racial segregation:

First, it is alleged, the existence of all-black neighborhoods creates all-black schools, and this is detrimental to the education of black children. More recent versions of this argument suggest that the costs of going to an all-black school are primarily socio-economic, rather than simply racial. According to this argument, children learn heavily from other children, and in particular, lower status children benefit from their contact with higher status children. Since black children are disproportionately of lower status, other black children have trouble learning from them. This argument has increasingly been questioned [Armor 1972] and it seems unclear whether there are, in fact, positive or negative learning benefits for black children who attend white schools.

Second, it is argued, racial segregation prevents the necessary interracial contacts among groups that will lead to an understanding of each other's positions and some effort at a common resolution of mutual problems. Sophisticated exponents of this thesis admit that contact between blacks and whites in itself will not necessarily lead to understanding, for there is evidence that contact may, in some cases, actually lead to greater hostility. Pettigrew [1971, pp. 255–334] argues that contact will reduce tensions between groups if the two groups: 1. possess equal status, 2. seek common goals, 3. are cooperatively dependent upon each other, that is, are not in a situation where economic or social interests are strictly based on racial lines, and   4. interact with the positive support of authorities, laws, or customs.

Unfortunately, these four conditions are rarely found together in our society when blacks meet whites, although they probably exist more frequently today than a few years ago. In any case, given these principles, it hardly seems likely that having blacks and whites live in the same neighborhood will immediately lead to contact, liking, and mutual aid. In fact, recent research on neighborhoods in racial transition suggests that their spatial integration is not matched by social integration [Molotch 1972]. As the transition occurs, separate areas and institutions of the community become set aside for separate groups. On the whole, it seems likely that greater contact among whites and blacks may lead to an improvement in the position of blacks; yet, it is unclear how much positive effect such contact would have.

Third, some social scientists argue that racial segregation prevents blacks from attaining decent jobs [Kain & Persky 1969]. The essential argument is this: blacks live in the central city but jobs are increasingly in the suburbs. As a result, jobs are limited for the black population, particularly since many blacks do not have automobiles, and mass transit lines often do not connect well between ghettos and suburban job sites. While this argument may have some validity, it is rarely pointed out that many, if not most, jobs are still found in the central city, including the CBD [Hawley 1971, p. 173]. The proximity of the black population may make them particularly good candidates for these jobs. For instance, the most rapid job gains of black women during the past decade have been in clerical occupations [U.S. Bureau of the Census 1971, p. 61]. One possible explanation is the close location of many black communities to the CBD, which disproportionately contains businesses employing large numbers of clerical workers.

Fourth, racial segregation may be an important deterrent to housing opportunities for blacks. While the evidence is not entirely clear, some [Duncan & Hauser 1960, pp. 168–233] suggest that blacks clearly pay more than whites for the same quality housing, given constant income levels. In comparison with white families of similar status, black families are also more apt to occupy substandard housing. Richard Muth [1969, p. 12], on the basis of a study of Chicago, has argued, however, that previous studies have seriously overestimated the inferiority of black housing compared to white housing. More needs to be known, but it does seem clear that blacks suffer to some extent from racial segregation; the question is how much.

Fifth, one may argue, racial segregation must be destroyed because it symbolizes the existence of continued inequities and discrimination in American society. Racial segregation is incompatible with American ideals of egalitarianism and universalism. This is essentially an ethical, or philosophical, not an empirical argument, and its power depends on the extent to which one shares the sentiment. I share the sentiment and find this argument, along with the consequences of segregation on the housing supply, to be the most forceful argument for racial integration of housing.

Opponents of racial integration in society ("Black Power" advocates) both attack some of the arguments that are made for residential integration, primarily on empirical grounds, and also argue that continued residential segregation may have powerful positive effects in creating a unified black community and political movement.

Advocates of this position generally *do not* believe that the present system of racial segregation has positive effects for the black community but believe it has *potentially positive* benefits. Thus proponents of black power, such as Stokely Carmichael and Charles Hamilton [1967], recognize that most of black business is controlled by whites and that blacks currently have little control over the political destiny of the black community, but they argue that these conditions could change.

According to this perspective, a concentrated black community has the potential for developing its own independent institutions and services that can provide jobs for other blacks, can facilitate the development and transmission of black culture, which will lead to racial pride and solidarity, and it can facilitate the development of black political movements, since political representatives are generally elected on the basis of geographic areas.

What this perspective does not deal with is the possibility that this program of action may actually benefit those committed to the racial status quo in the United States. Blacks comprise only about 10 percent of the American population, and thus do not generally have the political power to organize and seize control of all the political institutions of the population. Within the demographic dilemma faced by blacks, it seems unlikely that the development of black pride alone will be able to effect political change in the condition of black people, nor is it likely that having 10 percent of the political representatives in the society would necessarily lead to political and social equality.

The continued segregation of blacks in ghettos may create some business and professional jobs; yet it is questionable whether the black population alone in many cities is large enough to support certain types of viable businesses. For instance, there has been a trend toward large chain stores, and these chain stores can offer low prices only as long as there is a large customer population to purchase a large volume of goods. Furthermore, chain stores are often linked with other chain stores so that costs of administration may be cut. The individual black store will often not be able to afford the low retail prices of the chain competition, and may therefore be in a weak economic position.

On the whole, it seems to me, forces for reform of the society will have to come out of the organization of the black population, but this organization need not be based on a geographic basis. Blacks can form coalitions in integrated neighborhoods with other out-groups in the society, and therefore form a more massive group for change. Such coalitions with other groups would involve compromise and moderation; still it seems difficult to believe that 10 percent of the society can liberate itself by shutting itself off.

Many similar arguments to those of the White Liberal position are made concerning reasons for residential integration of neighborhoods by social and economic status. Specifically, it is alleged that school achievement and job opportunities will increase. The arguments have many of the same problems as the arguments for racial integration: it is unclear whether contact among school children of different classes has the alleged positive effects; it is unclear whether contact between members of different socio-economic groups will necessarily lead to understanding, it is unclear whether lower status persons are really hindered much in job possibilities by geographical location.

On the other hand, for those interested in distributive justice in the society, there seems to be little reason to support residential segregation by social class. One would presume that the worst urban services from government are provided in lower status neighborhoods. For instance, it is likely that streets are maintained below the city average, and that parks and recreational services are not well-developed.

I personally favor efforts to reduce racial and social class segregation in our society since I see few positive benefits to be gained from their continuation. However, I am not convinced that an end to racial and social class segregation would have profound impact on other areas of urban life.

In every society, only some goals can be pursued, given the limitations of personal time and societal resources. I would opt for indirect attacks on residential segregation by attacking the basic existence of social and economic inequality. Thus, I would favor all programs that would potentially increase the job and economic status of the black population. I would favor all programs that would increase the economic rewards of holding less skilled jobs in our society relative to the more skilled jobs. And I would favor efforts to make certain that all Americans have a decent income, since many of the low-income population cannot work, due to their age, physical disabilities, or their family responsibilities (such as caring for children below school age).

Such programs would provide social class groups with the economic power to purchase housing in desired neighborhoods. Such programs would not end racial segregation, since it is not now explained by social class differences between blacks and whites. Yet, it seems difficult for me to believe that high residential segregation in the United States could survive indefinitely in a condition where blacks and whites were equal in economic and occupational position. The economic power of many blacks would inevitably lead to a relatively free choice of housing.

In the end, then, residential segregation is another indicator of the social and ethnic inequalities that exist within our industrial society. In the long run, it will increase or decrease as these inequalities increase or decrease.

Appendix: Computing the Index of Dissimilarity

As pointed out in the body of the chapter, the index of dissimilarity indicates the percentage of one group that would have to change neighborhoods in order to be equally distributed with another group. It may vary from 0 (no segregation) to 100 (complete segregation).

The essential idea of the index is the comparison of the percentage of groups across census tracts or blocks. We may determine the percentage of group A in each areal unit, and we may also determine the percentage of group B in each areal unit. The index is a summary measure of how equally or unequally the groups are distributed across the real units. The formula of the index is

$$1/2 \sum_{1}^{k} [x_i - y_i]$$

where x_i is the percentage of a group found in areal unity i, y_i is the percentage of another group found in area unit i, and k equals the last areal unit.

Let us demonstrate the computation of an index. Assume Podunk, U.S.A. has two city blocks. On Block A, we have two Martians and one Slobovian. On Block B, we find two Martians and four Slobovians. Following the formula for the computation of the index of dissimilarity, we first determine the percentage of each group in each block.

	Martians	*Slobovians*
Block A	50% (2)	20% (1)
Block B	50% (2)	80% (4)
Total	100%	100% (5)

We then determine for each block the percentage of Martians minus the percentage of Slobovians. For block A it is +30 (50−20), and for block

B it is −30 (50%−80%). We then add up the absolute values of 30+30, and divide by 2, giving us an index of 30.

Bibliography

Charles Abrams, *Forbidden Neighbors: A Study of Prejudice in Housing.* Harper, 1955.

Milla Aissa Alihan, *Social Ecology: A Critical Analysis.* Columbia University Press, 1938.

Theodore R. Anderson and Janice A. Egeland, "Spatial Aspects of Social Area Analysis." *American Sociological Review,* 1961, 26:392–398.

David J. Armor, "The Evidence on Bussing." *The Public Interest,* 1972, 28:90–126.

Edward C. Banfield, *The Unheavenly City.* Little, Brown, 1970.

Reinhard Bendix and Seymour Martin Lipset, "Marx's Theory of Social Classes." In Bendix and Lipset, eds., *Class, Status, and Power.* The Free Press, 1966.

David L. Birch, *The Economic Future of City and Suburb.* Committee for Economic Development, 1970.

Donald J. Bogue, "Urbanism in the United States, 1950." *American Journal of Sociology,* 1955, 60:471–486.

Richard P. Boyle, "On Neighborhood Context and College Plans (III)." *American Sociological Review,* 1966, 31:706–707.

Ernest Burgess, Harvey J. Locke, and Mary Margaret Thomas, *The Family.* American Book, 1963.

Angus Campbell, *White Attitudes Toward Black People.* Institute for Social Research, University of Michigan, 1971.

Stokeley Carmichael and Charles V. Hamilton, *Black Power: The Politics of Liberation in America.* Vintage Books, 1967.

James Coleman. *Equality of Educational Opportunity.* Government Printing Office, 1966.

Paul Frederick Cressey, "Population Succession in Chicago: 1858-1930." *American Journal of Sociology,* 1938, 44:59–69.

A. Gordon Darroch and W. G. Marston, "Ethnic Differentiation: Ecological Aspects of a Multidimensional Concept." *The International Migration Review,* 1969, 4:71–95.

A. Gordon Darroch and W. G. Marston, "The Social Class Basis of Ethnic Residential Segregation: The Canadian Case." *American Journal of Sociology,* 1971, 77:491–510.

Paul Davidoff, Linda Davidoff, and Neil Newton Gold, "Suburban Action: Advocate Planning for an Open Society." *Journal of the American Institute of Planners,* 1970, 36:12–21.

Maurice R. Davie, "The Pattern of Urban Growth." In George P. Murdock, ed., *Studies in the Science of Sociology.* Yale University Press, 1937.

Kingsley Davis, "The Origin and Growth of Urbanization in the World." *American Journal of Sociology,* 1955, 60:429–437.

Beverly Duncan, "Variables in Urban Morphology." In E. W. Burgess and D. J. Bogue, eds., *Contributions to Urban Sociology.* University of Chicago Press, 1964.

Beverly Duncan and Philip M. Hauser, *Housing a Metropolis—Chicago.* The Free Press, 1960.

Otis Dudley Duncan and Beverly Duncan, "Residential Distribution and Occupational Stratification." *American Journal of Sociology,* 1955, 60:493–503.

Otis Dudley Duncan and Beverly Duncan, *The Negro Population of Chicago.* University of Chicago Press, 1957.

Ozzie Edwards, "Family Composition as a Variable in Residential Succession." *American Journal of Sociology,* 1972, 77:731–741.

Reynolds Farley, "Suburban Persistence." *American Sociological Review,* 1964, 29:38–47.

Reynolds Farley "The Urbanization of Negroes in the United States." *Journal of Social History,* 1968, 2:241–258.

Reynolds Farley, "The Changing Distribution of Negroes within Metropolitan Areas: The Emergence of Black Suburbs." *American Journal of Sociology,* 1968, 75:512–529.

Reynolds Farley and Karl E. Taeuber. "Population Trends and Residential Segregation Since 1960." *Science,* 1968, 156:953–956.

Arnold S. Feldman and Charles Tilly, "The Interaction of Social and Physical Spaces." *American Sociological Review,* 1960, 25:877–884.

John Fine, Norval Glenn, and J. Kenneth Monts, "The Residential Segregation of Occupational Groups in Central Cities and Suburbs." *Demography,* 1971, 8:91–101.

Walter Firey, "Sentiment and Symbolism as Ecological Variables." *American Sociological Review,* 1945, 10:140–148.

Richard G. Ford, "Population Succession in Chicago." *American Journal of Sociology,* 1950, 56:156–160.

William Form, "The Place of Social Structure in the Determination of Land Use: Some Implications for a Theory of Urban Ecology." *Social Forces,* 1954, 32:317–323.

E. Franklin Frazier, "Negro Harlem: An Ecological Study." *American Journal of Sociology,* 1937, 43:72–88.

Nathan Glazer and Daniel P. Moynihan, *Beyond the Melting Pot,* 2nd ed. M. I. T. Press, 1970.

Leo Grebler, Joan W. Moore, and Ralph C. Guzman, *The Mexican American People.* The Free Press, 1970.

Scott Greer, *Governing the Metropolis.* Wiley, 1962.

Avery M. Guest, "Families and Housing in Cities." Ph. D. dissertation, University of Wisconsin, 1970.

Avery M. Guest, "Retesting the Burgess Hypothesis: The Location of White Collar Workers." *American Journal of Sociology,* 1971, 76:1094–1108.

Avery M. Guest, "Patterns of Family Location." *Demography,* 1972a, 9:159–171.

Avery M. Guest, "Urban History, Population Densities, and Higher Status Residential Location." *Economic Geography,* 1972b, 48:375–387.

Avery M. Guest, "Neighborhood Life Cycles and Social Status." *Economic Geography,* 1974, 50:228–243.

Avery M. Guest and James J. Zuiches, "Another Look at Residential Turnover in Urban Neighborhoods." *American Journal of Sociology,* 1971, 77:457–467.

Cheryl K. Hashimoto, "Residential Segregation in Honolulu, Hawaii." Unpublished paper, Department of Sociology, University of Washington, 1973.

Amos H. Hawley, *Human Ecology: A Theory of Community Structure.* Ronald Press, 1950.

Amos H. Hawley, *Urban Society: An Ecological Analysis.* Ronald Press, 1971.

Anthony Henzell, "Ethnic and Racial Segregation in Seattle, Washington." Unpublished paper, Department of Sociology, University of Washington, 1973.

Albert I. Hermalin and Reynolds Farley, "The Potential for Residential Integration in Cities and Suburbs: Implications for the Bussing Controversy." *American Sociological Review,* 1973, 38:595–610.

Edgar M. Hoover and Raymond Vernon, *Anatomy of a Metropolis.* Doubleday, 1962.

Homer Hoyt, *The Structure and Growth of Residential Neighborhoods in American Cities.* Federal Housing Administration, 1939.

Richard Irwin and Robert Warren, "Demographic Aspects of American Immigration," in The Commission on Population Growth and the American Future, Research Reports, Vol. I. *Demographic and Social Aspects of Population Growth.* Ed. by Charles F. Westoff and Robert Parke, Jr. Government Printing Office, 1972.

Jane Jacobs, *The Death and Life of Great American Cities.* Vintage Books, 1961.

Christen Jonassen, "Cultural Variables in the Ecology of an Ethnic Group." *American Sociological Review,* 1945, 14:32–41.

John F. Kain and Joseph J. Persky, "Alternatives to the Gilded Ghetto." In *Race and Poverty: The Economics of Discrimination.* Prentice-Hall, 1969.

Nathan Kantrowitz, *Ethnic and Racial Segregation in the New York Metropolis.* Praeger, 1973.

Charles B. Keely, "Effects of the Immigration Act of 1965 on Selected Population Characteristics of Immigrants to the United States." *Demography,* 1971, 8:157–169.

Charles B. Keely, "Immigration Considerations on Trends, Prospects, and Policy." In Commission on Population Growth and the American Future. Research Reports. Vol. I. *Demographic and Social Aspects of Population Growth.* Ed. by Charles F. Westoff and Robert Parke, Jr. Government Printing Office, 1972.

Harry L. Kitano, "Housing of Japanese-Americans in the San Francisco Bay Area." In Nathan Glazer and Davis McEntire, eds., *Studies in Housing and Minority Groups.* University of California Press, 1960.

Gabriel Kolko, *Wealth and Power in America.* Praeger, 1962.

Luigi Laurenti, *Property Values and Race.* University of California, 1960.

Simpson Lawson, "Seven Days in June: The Great Housing Debate." *City,* 1971, 5:17–25.

Gerhard Lenski, *Human Societies.* McGraw-Hill, 1970.

Stanley Lieberson, *Ethnic Patterns in American Cities.* Free Press of Glencoe, 1963.

John A. Michael, "On Neighborhood Context and College Plans, (II)." *American Sociological Review,* 1966, 31:702–706.

Harvey Molotch, "Racial Change in a Stable Community." *American Journal of Sociology,* 1969, 75:226–238.

Harvey Molotch, *Managed Integration: Dilemmas of Doing Good in the City.* University of California Press, 1972.

Richard Muth, *Cities and Housing: The Spatial Pattern of Urban Residential Land Use.* University of Chicago Press, 1969.

Gilbert Osofsky, *Harlem: The Making of a Ghetto.* Harper Torch Books, 1968.

Robert E. Park, *On Social Control and Collective Behavior.* University of Chicago Press, 1967.

Robert E. Park and Ernest W. Burgess, *The City.* University of Chicago Press, 1967.

Phillip D. Peters, "Residential Sectors and Urban Expansion." Master's thesis in regional planning, Cornell University, 1964.

Thomas F. Pettigrew, *Racially Separate or Together?* McGraw-Hill, 1971.

Chester Rapkin and William Grigsby, *The Demand for Housing in Racially Mixed Areas.* University of California Press, 1960.

Peter Rossi, *Why Families Move.* The Free Press, 1955.

Leo F. Schnore, *The Urban Scene.* The Free Press, 1965.

Leo F. Schnore, "On the Spatial Structure of Cities in the Two Americas." In Philip M. Hauser and Leo F. Schnore, eds., *The Study of Urbanization.* Wiley, 1967.

Leo F. Schnore, *Class and Race in Cities and Suburbs.* Markham, 1972.

Leo F. Schnore and Philip C. Evenson, "Segregation in Southern Cities." *American Journal of Sociology,* 1966, 72:58–67.

Leo F. Schnore and Hal H. Winsborough, "Functional Classification and the Residential Location of Social Classes." In Brian J. L. Berry, ed., *City Classification Handbook: Methods and Applications.* Wiley, 1972.

Richard Sennett, *The Uses of Disorder.* Knopf, 1970.

William H. Sewell and J. Michael Armor, "Neighborhood Context and College Plans." *American Sociological Review,* 1966a, 31:159–168.

William H. Sewell, "Reply to Turner, Michael and Boyle." *American Sociological Review,* 1966b, 31:707–712.

James W. Simmons, "Changing Residence in the City: A Review of Intra-Urban Mobility." *The Geographical Review,* 1968, 58:662–651.

Karl E. Taeuber and Alma F. Taeuber, "The Negro as an Immigrant Group: Recent Trends in Racial and Ethnic Segregation in Chicago." *American Journal of Sociology,* 1964, 69:374–382.

Karl E. Taeuber and Alma F. Taeuber, "Recent Immigration and Studies of Ethnic Assimilation." *Demography,* 1967, 4(2):798–808.

Karl E. Taeuber and Alma F. Taeuber, *Negroes in Cities.* Atheneum, 1969.

Ralph H. Turner, "On Neighborhood Context and College Plans (I)." *American Sociological Review,* 1966, 31:658–702.

U.S. Bureau of the Census, 13th Census of the United States. *Abstract of the Census.* Government Printing Office, 1913.

U.S. Bureau of the Census, Population and Housing. *Families.* Government Printing Office, 1943.

U.S. Bureau of the Census, *The Social and Economic Status of Negroes in the United States, 1970.* Government Printing Office, 1971.

U.S. Bureau of the Census, Current Population Reports, Series P-60, No. 85. *Money Income in 1971 of Families and Persons in the United States.* Government Printing Office, 1972a.

U.S. Bureau of the Census, Census of Population and Housing:1970. *Census Tracts.* Final Report PHC(I)-29. Boston, Mass., SMSA. Government Printing Office, 1972b.

U.S. Bureau of the Census, Census of Population: 1970. Subject Reports.Final Report PC(2)-4B. *Persons by Family Characteristics.* Government Printing Office, 1973a.

U.S. Bureau of the Census, Census of Population: 1970. Subject Reports. Final Report PC(2)-5B. *Educational Attainment.* Government Printing Office, 1973b.

U.S. Bureau of the Census, Census of Population: 1970. Subject Reports. Final Report PC(2)-A. *National Origin and Language.* Government Printing Office, 1973c.

U.S. Bureau of the Census, U.S. Census of Population, 1970. Subject Reports.

Final Report PC(2)-1B. *Negro Population.* Government Printing Office, 1973d.

U.S. Census Office. *Report of the Population of the United States at the Eleventh Census—1890.* Part II. Government Printing Office, 1897.

Eleanor P. Wolf and Charles N. Lebeaux, *Change and Renewal in an Urban Community.* Praeger, 1969.

Part Three

Problems, Politics, and Planning

6.

CRITICAL URBAN PROBLEMS

Anthony J. La Greca

Historically, many of man's greatest accomplishments and many of his most cherished institutions have been centered in the city. As a nation's intellectual and administrative heart, the city has been idealized throughout the centuries as the showplace of a people's finest accomplishments. In contemporary America, however, the city is often more of a disgrace than a showplace. Problem after problem confronts modern American urbanites. Headlines and newscasts are filled with reports of urban decay and disorganization. Cries of "crisis in the city" are heard from the lips of revolutionaries in the ghettoes, professors in the universities, members of the United States Congress, and Americans in all walks of life. Most of us wish that the crisis in American cities could have been avoided by proper planning years ago, but there can be no doubt that American cities are faced today with problems that threaten their physical and social environments. The "Columbus Challenge" is a rallying cry for those who predict that in the last forty years of the twentieth century America must build ". . . as many new homes, roads, schools, shopping centers, and the like . . . as we did from the time of Columbus up to 1960" [Downs 1970, p. 3].

At a time when over 70 percent of all Americans live in cities, the United States is confronted by a sad situation: not only is there confusion concerning the cause and extent of its urban problems but, stemming from this confusion, there appear to be no readily available solutions for solving these problems—problems that are rooted in a lack of planning and preparation on the part of those most readily accountable for shaping the cities of the 1970s. Federal leaders, city mayors, and private citizens share the responsibility for the turmoil and inadequacies encountered by modern urbanites. One thing is certain: the problems of America's cities are not isolated happenings; rather, they stem from an overall breakdown in man's ability to cope effectively with his physical and social milieu.

Realistically, the problems of the city cannot be swept under the carpet with sanguine expectations that they will somehow solve themselves. A fast-paced country dictates solutions that emerge quickly and take effect quickly; unfortunately, such solutions are often shallow and treat only the most visible symptoms. Underlying any possible effective, long-term solutions to the problems of the city is the nagging realization that often we neither understand the complexity of the whole problem nor are able to cope with the various blocks—legal, economic, and social—to true reform.

The situation is further complicated by the fact that many present-day city dwellers are relatively new migrants. The long-term movement of rural people into cities has been coupled in recent decades with the massive influx of blacks and other minorities into cities. Migrants present cities with diverse problems and concerns and, along with the natural increase in population, have helped to account for a massive increase in America's urban population—a population whose needs have not been adequately anticipated.

One must also realize that there are at least three cities in each urban area. One is the inner-city ghetto populated by blacks and other minorities, such as Puerto Ricans. Ghetto residents have made great strides in advancement, yet still occupy a socioeconomic status below that of Americans as a whole. Another group is the typically stereotyped suburbanite who has left the central city to avoid its problems while retaining access to its benefits. Caught in between are a great number of urban residents who either do not have the ability to leave the central city or do not desire to do so. For these people, the expansion of the ghetto represents a detrimental encroachment on their lives, while the suburbs represent an unattainable or undesirable area of residence. Each of these three populations is itself highly differentiated internally and each has its own vested interests and struggle to gain and maintain power. Each adds its own elements, therefore, to an already overly complicated situation: "A fundamental problem in studying and understanding modern urban communities is that internally they are highly differentiated: they consist of many different social worlds which are complexly interrelated" [Popenoe 1973, p. 35].

Not only are there different social worlds within a city, but the urban setting itself serves to accentuate inequalities between them. As one travels through the city one may readily distinguish areas of sheer poverty from those of great wealth. Although the city lends some anonymity to the individual in terms of his legal or social identity, there are distinct contrasts between the wealthy and the poor, middle-class homes and ghetto dwellings, suburban schools and street schools of the inner city, and so forth. These contrasts provide all too excellent a medium for cultivating the intense alienation and distrust that is so frequently found in modern, urban America.

In the 1950s C. Wright Mills, a strong spokesman for the social activist element of sociology, asked some somber questions of urban scholars in particular and the public in general:

. . . consider the metropolis—the horrible, beautiful, ugly, magnificent sprawl of the great city. . . . What should be done with this wonderful monstrosity? Break it all up into scattered units, combining residence and work? Refurbish it as it stands? Or, after evacuation, dynamite it and build new cities according to new plans in new places? What should those places be? And who is to decide and to accomplish whatever choice is made? [Mills 1959, p. 10].

Some people feel that the problems of American cities have reached so great a crisis that they have actually resorted to the tactics of destruction in the hope that replacement would be better than present reality. The urban riots of the 1960s have awakened America's concern for the city. The shock waves that came from Watts, Newark, and Detroit placed America's urban and social ills on the front page of world awareness. The countless commissions, boards of inquiry, special committees, and the like bear witness to Americans' preoccupation with trying to solve the problems of their cities.

Chief among these problems are   1. to provide housing that is both physically and socially adequate;   2. to eliminate urban poverty;   3. to give all people an equal opportunity to benefit from the city's educational system;   4. to make available the necessary and essential health services to ensure community-wide medical care;   5. to develop a transportation system that would give all citizens equal access to all areas of the city; and   6. to establish some means of ensuring that the cities and their respective governmental bodies and agencies have the fiscal support to carry out programs to alleviate the plight of America's cities. In this chapter each of these six problem areas is discussed. The extent and depth of each of these six concerns is described and some of the various approaches, either proposed or implemented, toward solving these problems are reviewed.

FINDING A HOME FOR EVERYONE

For modern Americans, housing is something much more than shelter. Instead, a home is both a private protection from the world that people want to lock out and a most convenient insulator for the world that people want to lock in. The monetary and intrinsic value of a house depends not only on the degree of privacy it affords but also on the extent to which it is a *home*. As a home, any housing unit projects its own status in the following terms: 1. structure, which refers to all the physical attributes of the dwelling itself and the land it is on;   2. accessibility and utilities, which refer to the tangible services rendered to the dwelling unit by the general community;   3. rights, which refer, mainly, to the community's legal norms that apply to the home owner; and   4. neighborhood, which refers to the surrounding houses and area [Smith 1970]. Ultimately, housing status is, of course, defined by the dominant sector of society. America's white middle to upper classes believe that the closer one goes to the city center, the lower the status of the available housing. In this sense there is a built-in negative perspective on inner-city housing that, in turn, has detrimental effects on the inner-city population itself.

This negative perspective stems from the differentiation among social classes regarding attitudes toward housing. Basically, slum dwellers are thought to view housing mainly in terms of shelter; the traditional working-class population sees it in terms of an expression against outside threats to privacy and protection and as a means of maintaining "cozy" living surroundings; the modern middle class sees housing in a more complete perspective of shelter, pleasant surroundings, and living up to the mainstream of modern American community life [Rainwater 1966]. The media have provided an increased awareness of how others live, but this is balanced by the anticipation of a gradual erosion of such different class-related perspectives. More and more Americans, regardless of their social class, are expected to seek housing that goes beyond the category of "adequate" (in terms of plumbing, heating, cleanliness, and security from floods and so forth) and to search for a life in pleasant surroundings as well.

For the present, however, the notion of housing status per se is still, by default, most applicable to the lower middle class and those higher up the social class hierarchy, both of whom can afford the luxury of "keeping up with the Joneses." For these people, the physical amenities of the home and lot, the prestige of the neighborhood, and the accessibility to key community activities all take on a great importance. And with the high inflation rate of the 1970s, housing status becomes even more of a concern, since many Americans must be content with their present housing-status level.

Housing the Poor

Although being able to afford housing is a concern for everyone in the market for a home, "the housing problem, in its most basic and traditional form, can be defined as one of an adequate living environment for people too poor to pay for decent housing at market prices" [Frieden 1971, p. 322]. And what about these poor people who cannot even see beyond the survival of another day, let alone the status of the home they live in? What about the people who live in the urban slums of America's cities and must struggle merely to sustain an "adequate" level of existence? Most Americans have little realization of the deplorable conditions existing in the homes of many inner-city people. The filth alone would be enough to sicken most people, yet there is a pathology that goes hand in hand with the slum—a pathology that physically kills, psychologically alienates, and socially disorganizes slum dwellers.

Although there are, for some, a few sources of satisfaction in slum life—chiefly close family ties and social cohesion with peers [Fried & Gleicher 1961]—for most the chief effort is directed simply at staying alive: "We're still where we were, so far as knowing where your next meal is coming from. When I go to bed at night I tell myself I've done good, to stay alive and keep the kids alive, and if they'll just wake up in the morning and me too, well then, we can worry about that, all the rest, come tomorrow" [Quoted in Coles 1971, p. 104].

The slum is a defeating environment, an isolated city within the city, surrounded by social and economic barriers that guide and control the lives of its inhabitants. A great deal of life centers around the home [Suttles 1969], which serves as the focal point of much of the social activity and street life. In the urban slums, housing conditions are seen at their worst, and the worst is deadly. The pathological effects of poor housing can be grouped into three main categories: 1. those affecting one's health: 2. those affecting one's psychological well-being: and 3. those affecting one's social life both in terms of local surroundings and in terms of society as a whole. As Gunnar Myrdal wrote: " . . . Any common sense evaluation will tell us that the causation, in part, goes *from* poor housing to bad moral, mental and physical health" [Myrdal 1944, p. 1920].

In terms of all housing variables, the adverse effects of crowding—a critical problem of inadequate housing—is probably the most extensively investigated phenomenon [Schorr 1970, p. 715].[1] More and more research

---

1. Probably few areas of housing environment are receiving more attention than density. As with many topics related to physical health and mental well-being, much of the earlier work on human density relied on research done with animals [Calhoun 1966, 1962; Christian, Flyger, & Davis 1960; Marsden 1970]. A recent trend in relating density to human pathology centers on the task of seeing if high density pathologically affects humans when income, education and other social factors are taken into account [Mitchell 1971; Schmitt 1965; Winsborough 1965]. A further concern of research on density stems from considering how density varies by social class, race, and physical considerations (such as distance from the city center) [La Greca & Schwirian 1974]. For a review of much of the research on density see Carnahan and Galle [1973], Carstairs [1969 chap. 21] and Stokols [1972].

points to the deleterious effect of crowding on physical well-being [Galle, Gove, & McPherson 1972; Schmitt 1966; Schwirian & La Greca 1971]. Thus, not only are the actual structural deficiencies of slum housing a cause for alarm (infested homes *do* breed disease), but high density also contributes to poor health conditions.

The high density of slum dwellings has also been linked to severe psychological disorders. This link between density and psychological disorders runs the gamut from great stress and mental anxiety [Davis 1946; Marsella, Escudero, & Gordon 1970; Plant 1960], to admissions to mental hospitals [Galle, Gove, & McPherson, 1972]. In discussing "Density and Sanity," Carl George and Daniel McKinley [1974] go so far as to say that the high density of people crowded into small areas has resulted not only in mental illness but also in a failure for many to adequately interact within society.

This failure in interaction has produced the social effects of poor housing that contributed to the turmoil of the urban uprisings and riots of the 1960s. Be they black or white, Indian or Mexican-American, inhabitants of America's slum housing face an almost totally uphill struggle in overcoming their surroundings.

Over thirty-five years ago, R.E.L. Farris and H.W. Dunham [1939] pointed out that slum conditions are highly correlated with high density and social pathology. Since that time, it has been found repeatedly that " . . . extremely overcrowded conditions do, in fact, influence social behaviors in a negative fashion" [Griffitt & Veitch 1974, p. 137]. The extreme lack of privacy in such crowded situations negates one's ability to escape others and be alone with oneself or to withdraw from an unsettling situation. A typical child-parent disagreement becomes a seething source of frustration and anxiety, as neither party has the physical room to completely withdraw from the situation. The child can not go to his room upstairs since he is sharing his room with several brothers and sisters or even with his parents. In such an instance, the avenue of withdrawal is the street, an arena of crime and idle people, who themselves feel crowded by a world they did not make. In the streets there is only an intensification of the anger born in the home. A simple family argument mushrooms, then, into the awareness that there is no real escape. Fear of one's surroundings instigates a fear of what one might become in life. This perception of a negative future gives birth to an alienation that keeps slum dwellers locked into the slum [Bullough 1967].

Fear, fatalism, and alienation all combine to form a severe hatred and distrust of the general society that tolerates slum conditions. It does not take long for a slum child to realize that he does not have the environment for a pleasant life nor will he necessarily ever possess the means to move out of his present locale. No one needs to be told that they are at the bottom. The causal cycle is completed: poor housing helps lead to alienation and distrust of the larger society; these, in turn, lead the individual to reject participation in the few societal means available for leaving the slum. If the slum dweller is black, the distrust and alienation are even more pronounced: "Peter already seems a grim and unhappy child. He trusts no one white, not his teacher, not the white policeman he sees, not the white welfare worker, not the white storekeeper. . . . At nine he has learned to be careful, wary, guarded, doubtful, and calculating" [Coles, 1971, p. 110]. Peter's plight is not unique to him or to modern America. Ever since its rapid urbanization process began, America has had a housing problem. Today, it is a problem that goes even beyond the slums and into lower-middle and middle-class areas of the city as well. Anthony Downs estimates that 26 million housing units must be built by 1980 to solve the housing problem [1970, p. 118]. Although 6 million of these units would be earmarked for low- and moderate-income families, there is doubt now as to whether Down's estimate might be too conservative. Accustomed to a relatively high standard of living, middle-class America is constantly raising its standards and expectations; consequently, the price of new housing is constantly increasing. How this nation will deal with a disgruntled middle class that cannot buy the housing it wants remains to be seen. But no matter what answer is given to the housing crisis, any proposed housing policy must be securely grounded in the broad context of solving contemporary urban problems [Frieden 1971].

In 1934, the U.S. government went on record as having a total commitment to provide housing for America by passing the National Housing Act. Through subsequent legislation (see urban renewal discussion below), the government has presented a public posture of taking an active role in the housing sector. Although this is true to a limited extent, the fact remains that there is no systematic, national policy regulating housing and housing development in the United States. Left to the business sector of society, housing needs have not been met, and there has been greater and greater citizen discontent with the free enterprise system's inability to meet housing needs [Reilly 1973].

An increasing distrust of business is voiced not only by people espousing radical ideologies but also by the average citizen. Efforts by large private corporations to do something about housing are often viewed with skepticism and met with criticisms of profiteering [Cohen & Weiss 1971]. Those economists who have argued that housing needs could be met in the "traditional economic market" [Muth 1973; Olsen 1969], have been criticized for ignoring basic human needs and social values [Cohen & Weiss 1971; Downs 1973]. Those who have gone so far so as to make predictions based solely upon economic considerations have seen them fail because of the influence of societal variables not found in the conventional "supply-demand" curve. Frank Kristof [1965], for example, predicted that by 1980 New York City could meet all its housing needs within the "normal" housing market; but it is already apparent that such a goal cannot be met within the traditional housing market.

Solving the Housing Crisis: Rent Strikes

Other solutions aimed at meeting the demands of the housing crisis center chiefly around the immediate and most pressing problem of slum clearance. Such solutions can generally be grouped under the following main headings: 1. measures taken by individual housing occupants, such as rent strikes   2. local attempts by a particular community toward solving its own housing problems; and   3. federally financed and directed large-scale relocation and urban renewal.

Rent strikes are based on two main considerations: 1. the poor lack both economic and political power; and   2. many of those subjected to exorbitant rent demands are blacks who have suffered mammoth economic, political, and social discrimination. Table 1 shows that, for selected urbanized areas, the majority of blacks live in rented housing. This holds true especially for cities with populations over 500,000, regardless of region. According to a federal housing survey [Mandelker & Montgomery 1969], blacks have a renter rate that is much higher than that of the white population. Further, lower income blacks (like lower income groups in general) spend from 20 to 40 percent of their income on housing-rent—a percentage that far exceeds the American average. Since they are also faced with severe discrimination in the housing market, low-income blacks have, at times, joined low-income whites in staging rent strikes both to decrease actual rental rates and to improve housing conditions.

One of the most famous contemporary rent strikes occurred in 1963 and 1964 when Jesse Gray led the residents of over 100 Harlem slum tenements on a crusade to show New York City and America what "renter-power" could do. Through the tactic of withholding rent, Gray

TABLE 1. Percent of Blacks Owning and Renting Homes for Selected Standard Metropolitan Statistical Areas *

City	Population	Percentage blacks owning home	Percentage blacks renting home
New York, New York	11,571,883	18.5	81.5
Los Angeles-Long Beach, California	7,036,463	37.7	62.3
Chicago, Illinois	6,974,906	26.3	73.7
Cleveland, Ohio	2,064,194	39.8	60.2
Houston, Texas	1,984,985	48.4	51.6
Newark, New Jersey	1,856,556	25.1	74.9
Minneapolis-St. Paul, Minnesota	1,813,647	42.5	57.5
Dallas, Texas	1,556,048	45.4	54.6
Seattle-Everett, Washington	1,421,859	49.9	50.1
Milwaukee, Wisconsin	1,403,688	33.2	66.8
Atlanta, Georgia	1,390,164	39.9	60.1
Denver, Colorado	1,227,531	46.2	53.8
Indianapolis, Indiana	1,109,882	49.1	50.9
New Orleans, Louisiana	1,045,809	31.2	68.8
Columbus, Ohio	916,228	44.3	55.7
Omaha, Nebr.-Iowa	540,142	49.1	50.9
Tulsa, Oklahoma	476,945	58.0	42.0
Fresno, California	413,053	42.8	57.2
Mobile, Alabama	376,690	54.2	45.8
Tucson, Arizona	351,667	53.9	46.1
Albuquerque, New Mexico	315,774	46.4	53.6
Des Moines, Iowa	286,101	55.4	44.6
Fort Wayne, Indiana	280,455	53.0	47.0
Eugene, Oregon	213,358	12.1	87.9
Lincoln, Nebraska	167,972	41.4	58.6
Odessa, Texas	91,805	65.9	34.1
Pine Bluff, Arkansas	85,329	55.9	44.1
Owensboro, Kentucky	79,486	42.9	57.1
San Angelo, Texas	71,047	54.9	45.1
Meriden, Connecticut	55,959	22.4	77.6

*Source: Data for the table is taken or computed from the U.S. Bureau of the Census, *County and City Data Book, 1972* (A Statistical Abstract Supplement) [U.S. Government Printing Office 1972].

was able to help lay the basis for tenant-reform laws in New York City, but he had little success in improving the actual slum conditions as such.

Intrinsically, rent strikes face an almost totally uphill fight because 1. they are illegal, thereby subjecting participants to be branded as criminal (slum landlords need not worry about their decrepit holdings, since few laws exist against the landlord);   2. those who carry on a rent strike are usually the poor, who do not have the economic or legal resources to gain desired goals;   3. the leaders of a rent strike run into great difficulty in trying to maintain the involvement of a people who have lived so long in an environment of fatalism; and 4. as Michael Lipsky [1969] points out, a rent strike is an unconventional tactic that directly impinges on a traditional political process of power; by its nature, such a tactic often alienates even the third parties (e.g., liberal groups) or the public at large who might help the renters in their plight.

One way to overcome some of the above difficulties of a rent strike is for tenants to form a tenants union, thereby establishing a legitimate basis for future actions. However, nothing guarantees that such a union will be recognized by landlords or by city officials, because most laws affecting the tenant are written from the landlord's perspective. Nevertheless, a tenant union is an approach that still might be effective in the future. The Berkeley (California) Tenants Union, among others, is still waging its battle for better housing. The main points of its bargaining agreement include these provisions: 1. to prohibit unfair and exploitative rents; 2. to include a statement of the landlord's responsibility to keep the premises in good, safe, sanitary condition; and 3. to prohibit the owner from evicting tenants for withholding rent [see Jones 1971, pp. 90–91]. A further attribute of the Berkeley Tenants Union is that it encompasses whites as well as blacks and is aimed at all levels of housing, not just slum housing. It is too early to assess properly the overall impact of individuals collectively organizing to form a tenants union. To be successful, however, any tenants union must ultimately gain acceptance by the local community, and that in itself is an almost impossible task.

Solving the Housing Crisis: Community Action

Individual community actions to improve housing are best exemplified by the Boston Rehabilitation Plan (BURP) [Urban Planning Aid, Inc. 1969]. This plan incorporates some key voluntary associations in the community (e.g., the Black United Front), as well as some of the legally chartered groups of the community (e.g., the New Urban League and Fair Housing, Inc.). BURP tried to correct slum housing in the Roxbury–North Dorchester area of Boston. As a group recognized by government officials, BURP was able to overcome some of the legitimization deficiencies of rent strike groups or tenant unions. Even with this seeming advantage, BURP leaders soon found themselves at odds with the Federal Housing Administration (FHA). BURP's chief aim—to improve slum housing—was thus compromised, in part, by the FHA and participating developers who limited the decision-making power of BURP officials and other local tenant groups. Although not a total failure (some improvements were made), BURP does point to the failure local communities are likely to experience without the establishment of a nationwide federal housing plan. Given the great involvement of the federal government in mass housing, local and state governments have little leverage and few resources for adequately dealing with the housing crisis.

Taxation is one area in which state and local governments do have influence concerning housing costs. Although property taxes provide municipalities with lucrative incomes, they are, nevertheless, usually discriminatory in that they favor large corporate concerns and, through increased taxation, punish home improvement. The rationale for proposing property-tax reform as a cure for the housing problem is an involved, legally technical one that can not be explored in depth here [Wittman 1972]. Suffice it to say, however, that through such tactics as tax rebates, rewarding slum renovation with a decreased tax, and the like, tax reformers hope to make it economically advantageous to make housing improvements, as well as to own housing in the central city. As will be seen, however, in this chapter's section on urban financing, cities are already in a state of financial disarray. The likelihood of property-tax reform to improve slum housing is, therefore, probably one of the most unattainable of all the possible cures for America's housing ills. In fact, despite political rhetoric to the contrary, local communities are relying more and more on the federal government to be their savior in the area of housing needs.

Solving the Housing Crisis: Federal Action

As noted earlier, the main thrust of the federal government's involvement in urban housing had its genesis in 1934 with the passing of the National Housing Act, one of the many pieces of New Deal legislation aimed at combatting the Depression. The act—passed at a time when many conservatives adamantly opposed governmental "intervention" into housing— provided the groundwork for and the orientation toward accepting the legislation called the Housing Act of 1937. It was at this time that further sanction was given to the federal government's role of helping people to obtain mortgages to buy homes, and it was also the beginning of the federal government's role of helping to provide housing for those who could not afford it. The 1937 Housing Act also began the tradition of building high-rise, high-density public housing in the area known today as the inner city. As more and more Americans overcame the effects of the Depression, the mortgage-loan assistance aspects of the Housing Act of 1937 were seen as justifiable means of helping the working class buy a home, while the slum-clearance aspects of the act were criticized as "handouts." The public housing program became more and more unpopular and the government began to drift away from it.[2] Criticism of federal public housing reached its pinnacle with the debate over the Taft-Ellender-Wagner Bill, better known as the Housing Act of 1949. Conservatives, led by Senator Robert A. Taft of Ohio, argued that while slum demolition could be tolerated, excessive federal intervention into urban housing could not. Although the 1949 legislation provided for public housing, it placed such severe restrictions on it that conservatives saw the law as a chance to keep the federal role in housing at the same level established in 1937. Title 1 of the 1949 Housing Act helped private entrepreneurs sell more land and homes but it did little to alleviate America's housing problems, although the act itself was dressed in the terminology of "urban renewal."

The greatest assistance to urban housing up to that time came with the Housing Act of 1954. It was in this act that urban renewal got its real impetus. As emotions ran high (and still do) over the role of the federal government in housing, even the meaning of the term "urban renewal" was debated. Basically, the federal government perceives urban renewal as having three main purposes:

1. To speed up the clearance of slums and badly blighted areas

2. To facilitate the provision of decent, low-income housing by helping to finance the acquisition and preparation of appropriate sites, including in-site preparation of public facilities that would contribute to a "suitable living environment"

---

2. It should be noted that today even the mortgage aspects of this and other housing acts have come under severe criticism. Michael E. Stone [1973] has said that federal housing laws have done nothing more than safeguard the lender (who gets his money from the borrower) from ever losing money through mortgage default. However, according to Stone, the borrower is made to take the risk, as well as to provide the lender with exorbitant interest payments, thereby further strengthening the economic power of the lender. All of this leads, in Stone's words to " . . . creating the illusion of homeownership for millions of people, while the actual owners are the mortgage lenders" [1973, p. 79]. Although many, if not most, traditional economists would disagree with Stone, he does, nevertheless, provide an insightful objection to a housing market system that is taken for granted by many. It should also be noted that space does not permit a detailed account of all federal housing legislation; for a detailed history of the evolution of the urban renewal program see Foard and Fefferman [1960, pp. 635–684].

3. To give private enterprise "maximum opportunity" to take part in redeveloping these areas [The National Commission on Urban Problems, 1968, p. 152.]

Although the actual interpretation and implementation of these three purposes is still subject to debate, it is generally held that urban renewal is a significant attempt by the federal government to bring federal funds to the city for the purpose of preserving neighborhoods and rebuilding slum housing. Technically, a city cannot qualify for urban renewal funds until it has a workable program that: 1. establishes a code of minimum standards of housing,   2. provides a plan to relocate those displaced by demolition, and   3. provides a means of some sort of involvement by local citizens. The degree to which individual cities have adhered to these points has varied and this variance is itself one of the reasons for the misunderstanding of urban renewal. As an added note, the 1954 Housing Act allowed federal money to be used for nonresidential redevelopment, which decreased some of the funds available for slum clearance and public housing construction. Furthermore, before cities can even count on getting federal funds, they must establish a local urban renewal authority. Depending on the city's charter, this can come about either by an administrative decision of the city council or by a vote of the people. Where required by law, the latter approach often faces stiff opposition from an electorate that is afraid, mostly through ignorance, that urban renewal means more local taxation and more blacks or other "undesirables" moving into its neighborhoods. Once established, local urban renewal authorities usually become manipulated by the vested interests of the powerful actors of the community, making urban renewal a source of windfall profits for private developers and land owners and of a pitifully inadequate relocation process for those in slum housing. Consider coming home one day and finding the following urban renewal notice on your door:

> The building in which you now live is located in an area which has been taken by the Boston Redevelopment Authority according to law as part of the Government Center Project. The building will be demolished after the families have been relocated and the land will be sold to developers for public and commercial uses, according to the Land Assembly and Redevelopment Plan presently being prepared [Quoted in Anderson 1971, p. 93].

This Boston urban renewal notice is typical of the thousands seen by the countless numbers of people affected by an urban renewal program.

The trouble with relocation is that it is too often planned by middle- and upper-class professionals who have little knowledge of the social life of the individuals to be relocated. Little attention is given to preparing residents for the possible loss of nearby friends, the task of getting used to new shops, grocery stores, and so forth [see Fried 1963; Gans 1959]. As one person who was caught up in an urban renewal program said, "I don't know where to go. If I leave this area I am lost. I have lived here for thirty-seven years. The streets know me" [Quoted in Bellush & Hausknecht 1969, p. 370]. Thus, although the "large-scale relocation of families and individuals, such as that occasioned by . . . urban renewal, necessarily raises basic questions of social welfare and public policy" [Hartman 1967, p. 315], these questions are either ignored or the people who are to deal with them are actually incompetent to do so. Few city administrators and few developers, if any, have the psychological and sociological expertise necessary to deal with the multifaceted complexity of relocation.

Moreover, even the federal government admits that relocating to an urban renewal project usually means that the relocated person will 1. pay a higher rent for his new housing than he was previously paying, and 2. pay a higher proportion of his income on rent than he previously did [U.S. Bureau of the Census 1965]. Admittedly, the new housing is structurally better than the slum housing, but, for the relocated individual, that does not mitigate the often impossible task of paying the increased rent. Such a demand on a person only further intensifies the frustration experienced by people living in slum-housing areas.

Urban renewal programs also have been criticized, and rightly so, for not giving proper attention to housing design. The darkened halls of high-rise apartments provide excellent locations for crime but difficult ones for family life. With no real backyard or other private outside area, the family must limit much of its informal activity to indoors. Even more important, how can a mother cook dinner and at the same time watch her children at play when they are eleven floors below in a common playground that may be half a block away?

One of the most obvious monuments to improperly designed housing for the poor is the massive Pruitt-Igoe project in St. Louis, Missouri. Started in 1954, Pruitt-Igoe was a large planned-housing development for the poor. Its eleven-story buildings attracted national attention as a possible model for future housing projects. However, the high-rise design of the buildings, the crowded conditions, and the inability to maintain a racially integrated population all helped to convert the "model" buildings into vertical ghettoes by the 1960s.

The design of mass housing must, therefore, take into account the future inhabitants' stages in the family-life cycle (e.g., the presence or absence of children), general life-styles, local customs and values, and attitudes toward what they want in a home [Brolin & Zeisel 1968; Michelson 1967].

Finally, urban renewal can be criticized for the manner in which redevelopment sites are chosen. As Herbert Gans points out:

> . . . many clearance areas . . . were chosen . . . not because they had the worst slums, but because they offered the best sites for luxury housing. . . . Since public funds were used to clear the slums and to make the land available to private builders at reduced costs, the low-income population was in effect subsidizing its own removal for the benefit of the wealthy [Gans 1973a; p. 163].

Although such an account is appalling, it should not be shocking, given the power that private business now holds in America. In fact, there are those who argue that " . . . the very nature of our society and culture leads to a lack of attention to the housing problems of the poor" [Bellush & Hausknecht 1967, p. 414]. Consequently, public housing projects are doomed to automatic failure. Bellush and Hausknecht go on to say that proponents of public housing are themselves handicapped by the lack of a well-funded professional congressional lobby and by the lack of a strong political base to give them support. What then should be done with public housing?

Gans [1973a] argues that urban renewal should not be discarded but should, rather, be redirected toward urban housing as such. This means that urban renewal would also entail the finding of housing for the poor outside of the slum area of a city. Such a suggestion, however, is not feasible, given the present level of Americans' housing discrimination toward blacks and other minorities. In fact the Model Cities Program, launched in 1966, sought to overcome many of the social and economic problems in the task of housing the poor. At best, the program could lay claim only to modest success. Given the lack of enthusiasm of the Nixon and Ford administrations for Model Cities, it does not look as though broad, encompassing housing programs have a very bright future.

This is not a blanket condemnation of all federal housing proposals. They are a beginning, but they are not enough, particularly for those who must spend another day in an urban slum. This nation has yet to even adopt stringent, uniform housing codes [Greer 1965, pp. 22–24] or national zoning requirements, let alone a workable, systematic means

---

3. For a more extensive treatment of housing codes, see The National Commission on Urban Problems, *Building the American City* [1968, pp. 273–284] and Teitz and Rosenthal [1971]. Most housing codes are quite ineffectual; even where strongly enforced, housing codes alone cannot have a totally ameliorative effect on the housing problem.

of finding a home for everyone.[3] What is needed is not another housing program but a dedicated thrust toward solving the real underlying dimension of slum housing: poverty.

SLUM HOUSING AND POVERTY: A VICIOUS CIRCLE

The housing programs that have been described were aimed at trying to treat the problem of housing as such but have had only a minimal effect on eradicating poverty, the main urban crisis facing America today. Although not confined to the city, poverty affects the quality of urban life more than any other factor. Perhaps no other topic affecting American society is more complex or more politically volatile than that of trying to erase poverty.

Who are the poor of America's cities? They are the over 10 percent of all urbanites who cannot afford the essential food, shelter, and services for maintaining a minimum standard of living. They are the twenty-five out of every one hundred urban blacks who live from day to day. They are the "other America" [Harrington 1962] who are either invisible to or ignored by the majority of Americans. Not only are their incomes below minimum standards designated by the federal government, but their purchasing power is also below that of the rest of society [Rasmussen 1973]. They expend, for example, a far greater proportion of their income on food and rent than any other element of society.

When poverty is masked by the color on one's skin, it becomes even more damaging. Table 2 shows the consistently higher median income enjoyed by urban whites over urban blacks. It also shows that in most American cities a minimum of 20 percent of the black population is living below the poverty level. Race then, because of discrimination, becomes an important variable in accounting for the high degree of American urban poverty.

Some have argued that poverty will never disappear until it becomes dysfunctional for society [Gans 1973b, p. 181]. Among its other functions, Gans holds the position that poverty provides the following positive functions for the nonpoor of America: 1. poverty ensures that there will be a population destitute enough to have to do the "dirty work" of certain industries and services; 2. the poor help create jobs for professions that serve the poor or protect the rest of society from them; included here are such occupations as police, prison workers, and pawn-shop owners; 3. poverty helps to provide status differentiation so that the nonpoor

TABLE 2. Income and Poverty Levels for Selected Standard Metropolitan Statistical Areas over 250,000*

City	Median White Family Income	Median Black Family Income	Percentage of Black Family Members Below Poverty Level
Over 2 Million			
New York, New York	11,538	7,309	22.2
Los Angeles-Long Beach, California	11,352	7,571	23.0
Chicago, Illinois	12,644	8,032	23.0
Detroit, Michigan	12,814	8,639	19.7
St. Louis, Missouri	11,038	6,659	29.6
Baltimore, Maryland	11,305	7,412	24.5
Cleveland, Ohio	11,899	8,005	23.4
1,000,000–1,999,999			
Houston, Texas	11,054	6,210	29.6
Newark, New Jersey	12,763	7,642	21.3
Minneapolis-St. Paul, Minnesota	11,748	7,665	23.1
Dallas, Texas	11,113	6,137	29.9
San Diego, California	10,304	7,366	22.5
Buffalo, New York	10,647	6,936	26.2
Miami, Florida	9,818	5,980	30.9
500,000–999,999			
Columbus, Ohio	10,760	7,663	23.0
Louisville, Kentucky-Indiana	10,196	6,338	29.7
Sacramento, California	10,497	7,068	25.9
Birmingham, Alabama	9,338	5,212	37.1
Jersey City, New Jersey	9,920	7,365	22.8
Omaha, Nebraska-Iowa	10,451	6,450	28.5
250,000–499,999			
Orlando, Florida	9,549	4,511	43.2
Harrisburg, Pennsylvania	10,133	6,535	27.4
Wichita, Kansas	9,609	6,137	31.4
Columbia, South Carolina	9,738	5,329	38.2
Jackson, Mississippi	10,253	4,291	49.2

*Cities are listed in order of descending size. Median income for both whites and blacks is in terms of dollars and is based on 1970 figures. Poverty level is based upon the poverty index adopted by a Federal Interagency Committee in 1969 and is computed from 1969 figures. The poverty index provides a range of income cut-offs or "poverty thresholds" adjusted to take into account such factors as family size, sex and age of the family head, the number of children, and farm-nonfarm residence. For a nonfarm family of four with a male as the head of the household, the poverty threshold is $3745. Data is taken from the U.S. Bureau of the Census, *County and City Data Book, 1972* (A Statistical Abstract Supplement) [U.S. Government Printing Office 1973] and the U.S. Bureau of the Census, *Census of Population: 1970* [U.S. Government Printing Office 1972].

can always know that someone is below them on the social ladder; 4. as the most powerless group in America, the poor are often made to suffer the high cost of progress: highways can be pushed through poorer neighborhoods easier than through middle-class ones; and   5. given the American value system of hard work, individuality, and delayed gratification, the poor can easily be identified as "deviants" toward this value system, thereby legitimizing the dominant—and chiefly middle-to-upper class—values of our society.

It seems highly unlikely that, for several generations to come, poverty will become dysfunctional for America as a whole. Although its mere presence eats at the moral fiber and life-quality of America, poverty is not being fought by enough members of our society to be defeated soon. As a matter of historical account, it has been the federal government that has been the main influence in helping the poor. However, there are still many within our society who oppose any governmental "intervention" in trying to break the chains that keep the poor poor. Given such reasoning as that of William F. Buckley [1974] that unemployment can be a sign of a healthy economy, it is clear that not all segments of our society are alarmed by poverty, nor do they even feel that something should be done concerning it. "After all," it is argued by some more affluent people, "who helped me or my parents during the Depression years? No one! We had to pull ourselves up by our own bootstraps." This argument is spurious. During the Depression the majority of Americans suffered its consequences and there were few people who could carry the economic burden of financing poverty programs. What is more, the government *did* play a major role in the 1930s in helping those adversely affected by the Depression.

Welfare Programs: Promises and Pitfalls

Given the assumptions   1. that society as a whole benefits when all its members live well and   2. that society as a whole has the obligation to see that this is the case, America has its work cutout in trying to overcome poverty.

One of the chief weapons used by the federal government, the corporate representative of the people, to combat urban poverty is the welfare program. Unfortunately, these programs, initiated to help the poor, are often characterized by corruption and a bureaucratic ineptness that gives more money to the administrators of the programs than to the poor themselves. Furthermore, welfare recipients, no matter how legitimate their plight, are stigmatized by the larger society as shiftless parasites who, going against the value of individuality, are willing to take charity. Thus their status degradation is further intensified [Coser 1965].

Besides being stigmatized in such ways, welfare recipients also are used as political issues by those politicians who play on the notion that the poor would not be poor if only they would do something about it. Such a stance, although true in some cases, of course, ignores the contemporary complexities of an America in which unemployment is on the rise, inflation is in a runaway pattern, and racial and ethnic prejudice persists. Because of their nature, welfare programs actually make recipients directly subservient to the status–preserving "establishment" that supervises and finances the "war on poverty."

Beyond Welfare: Business, Community Action, and Cultural Change

Charles A. Valentine [1968] proposes that the impoverished of America's cities be given not only economic aid but also special rights and positive discrimination to provide them with the *power* to overcome their plight. By giving the highest employment priority to the poor, he hopes to eradicate the bulk of welfare programs, and thus to rid the poor of the welfare stigma. However, a large part of his plan depends on the private sector's provision of jobs for all Americans—an obligation that is still ignored or denied by many in the business community.

The Economic Opportunity Act of 1964 was another attempt to overcome the poverty problem. This legislation required the "maximum feasible participation" of the poor as active planners and administrators in developing policies to eliminate poverty in their local communities. Conservative critics, both in and out of Congress, have branded community-action programs as nothing less than a "blueprint for revolution" [Rubin, 1972, p. 98]. And, with recent budget cuts by the executive branch, attempts at impounding some poverty-directed funds, and maneuvers to abolish the Office of Economic Opportunity altogether, most reformers see little immediate hope in the long struggle to escape the poverty dilemma.

Herbert Gans [1968] takes a more inclusive view of poverty by attempting to incorporate the cure for poverty into the general area of cultural change. He seeks to establish an understanding of the normative basis for the poor's reaction to new opportunities and of how this normative basis can best be suited or even altered to fit antipoverty proposals. In such an approach, opportunities for the poor are not given by governmental or bureaucratic fiat. Instead, they are based on discovering which aspects of the working-class culture are shared by the poor and how these aspects can best be put to use. Of course, such a proposal to restructure opportunities for the poor has society-wide ramifications that can only be dealt with when, and if, Gans's idea becomes a reality.

Other Proposals: Guaranteed Income and Negative Income Taxes

One of the most controversial solutions for poverty is that involving the notion of a guaranteed income. This notion postulates that "Income . . . should be guaranteed and paid by the government, regardless of work done in exchange" [Walinsky 1973, p. 241]. Senator George McGovern alienated many Americans with just such a stance in the 1972 campaign. Although proposed with good intentions, guaranteed income still has the deficiency of keeping the poor dependent on the larger society. As nothing more than a dole, it carries with it the stigma of welfare and maintains the relative powerlessness of the poor. Although a guaranteed income plan might be a temporary solution to help the poor secure life-sustaining benefits, its potential as an overall cure is minimal, especially in light of public opposition to it.

The negative income tax, although similar to the guaranteed income, goes beyond the idea of an actual dole as such. David Rasmussen [1973] suggests that one of the ugliest aspects of poverty is seen when a person who maintains a full-time job cannot, because of low wages, sustain a family above the poverty level. As Elliot Liebow puts it:

> The objective fact is that menial jobs in retailing or in the service trades simply do not pay enough to support a man and his family . . . the plain fact is that, in such a job, he cannot make a living. Nor can he take much comfort in the fact that these jobs tend to offer more regular, steadier work. If he cannot live on the $45 or $50 he makes in one week, the longer he works the longer he cannot live on what he makes [1972, p. 69].

To combat this and similar situations, Rasmussen proposes a negative tax that would guarantee a minimum level of income while, at the same time, encouraging people to work. A family earning no income would receive the "negative income tax" (similar to a tax overpayment worth $3000) equal to the legal minimum income established by the government (for example, $3000 for a family of four). A family's directly taxable income begins only at some predetermined moderate income level (such as $6000 for a family of four). Therefore, a worker could earn $3000 from his job, yet his family would receive $6000 in nontaxable income.

According to Rasmussen, such a plan involves transfer payments from the national income tax itself and not direct welfare payments. The validity of this contention is still subject to economic debate, as is the whole notion of worker incentive. In actuality, proponents of a negative income tax must grapple with the problem of getting people to work to earn more money even though this would place them in a higher tax bracket.

Even the negative income tax idea still speaks of "giving" money to the poor. To overcome this, Ben Seligman [1965] suggests, as Valentine's positive discrimination does not, that society actually has a directed goal of creating and financing, as much as necessary, new jobs for the poor. Although the Job Corps and similar federal programs sought, in part, to do just this, the financing of these programs was high and private businesses could not (or would not) easily absorb the semiskilled workers coming out of these programs. And, with persistent congressional opposition by conservatives to a high minimum wage many employers can easily get away with offering low wages. What is more, even if all the present unemployed in search of a job became employed, poverty would still not be eliminated because   1. many wages have not kept up with inflation   2. many poor people, chiefly because of family responsibilities, cannot leave their homes to go to work. For these people, some type of welfare system is the only solution.

Welfare: Toward New Concepts

Richard Cloward and Frances Fox Piven [1967] give a succinct summary of some of the legal rights of welfare recipients. They cite, for example, a Georgia case where a group of ADC (Aid to Dependent Children) mothers contested the assumption that a mother must try to find suitable employment before she can go on welfare. In actuality, a mother with, for example, four children to care for would serve society better by staying home than by finding a low-paying job and not being able to care for her children. Although some more affluent people become indignant at the notion of "welfare rights," it appears that more and more federal courts are saying that society cannot make excessive demands of welfare recipients.

Furthermore, there is also every indication that the poor in general and welfare recipients in particular are organizing more and more to make their voices heard. Not all poor people are willing to be told how they must live or under what conditions they can receive aid [Wright

1968]. With effective leadership and planning, there is a trend for the poor themselves to play an ever-increasing significant role in directing society's attempts to overcome poverty [Gove & Costner 1969; Zurcher & Key 1968].

What is more, the notion of welfare could, of course, be altered so that it is more readily acceptable to the general American public. Bernard Beck argues that when seen as a moral category " . . . welfare activities on the part of agencies and institutions of the society, welfare careers, and so on are in no structural way differentiable from agencies, institutions, careers, and uses in the non-welfare areas of the society" [1972, p. 246]. Viewed in its technical and moral aspects, welfare could, Beck implies, soon gain prominence as a legitimate societal function.

Whether one of those above or some other proposal will be the ultimate solution to the poverty problem cannot be determined here. With an all-encompassing belief in "free enterprise," an aversion to federal welfare programs, and a lack of general public concern for the poor, it does not appear, however, that any solution will be in sight for a very long time. It has been more than a decade since President Lyndon Johnson declared war on poverty and poverty is still "winning" the confrontation.

A vicious circle exists that goes from poverty to poor housing and back to poverty again. Everywhere one looks for a remedy, another liability seems to appear. Even the traditional institution of education, long seen as a cure-all for many societal ills, no longer provides a ready solution for overcoming poverty. Especially for the poor, who *must* have an education to break the poverty cycle [Rasmussen 1973], urban schools are faltering in their job and suffering from their own malaise.

URBAN EDUCATION: CHALLENGES FROM ALL SIDES

Besides being one of the chief socializing agents of society, the institution of education has usually been regarded as a type of equalizer in America. That is, it is thought to have the capacity of providing all people with an equal opportunity to gain the knowledge and background necessary for an individual to pursue a particular (usually career-oriented) goal in life. With such a large mandate, American education has borne the brunt of much of the criticism concerning the problems facing this country today.

The poor and others who are culturally deprived present education with one of its gravest problems: how to make a relevant education available to all [Trow 1966]. In urban America such a concern is especially important in light of the poverty and other ills of the nation's cities. But the urban poor are not the only ones presenting education with a great challenge. In light of the 1954 Supreme Court desegregation ruling and the present turmoil over "busing," urban education is also challenged by the urban white population. Both the task of educating the poor and the task of dealing with severe racial problems contribute a very real crisis in urban education [Levine 1972].[4] Of course, the crisis facing contemporary urban schools, like all social problems, did not arise overnight [Hummel & Nagle 1973; HEW Urban Task Force 1970]. Yet knowing this does not in any way mitigate the gravity of the situation.

Schooling: Programs for Failure

One of the most comprehensive, most discussed, and most criticized surveys of education in America was done in 1966 by the Department of Health, Education, and Welfare and entitled *Equality of Educational Opportunity*, although it is commonly called the Coleman Report [Coleman et al. 1966]. The report has been criticized for some possible methodological and procedural deficiencies [Bowles & Levin 1968], but it has been widely recognized as an authoritative citation of   1. inequities between predominantly black and white schools;   2. regional differences throughout America regarding the quality of education;   3. the effect of student peer-group structure on achievement; and other pertinent aspects of America's educational system. James Coleman and his co-authors clarified the almost impossible dilemma faced by education, which is how to carry out an educational process when that process is itself so highly influenced by external factors. " . . . Schools bring little influence to bear on a child's achievement that is independent of his background and general social context" [1966, p. 325].

Increasingly, one's social class, family background, and race have a serious impact on the type of education one will receive in today's cities. Patricia Sexton [1961] argues that many of the students from the lower

---

4. This crisis is further underscored by the more general category of complaints against overall educational curriculum, teacher-training, and other topics that go beyond the scope of this chapter. For a review of these and other topics see Bode [1965], Corwin [1974], Cronbach and Snow [1969], Dreeben [1968], Gideonse [1970], Miller [1967], Scriven [1967], and Travers [1973].

class are looked upon as inferiors by their teachers and as not worth the time needed to educate them. What is more, their parents are often judged to be indifferent to their children's education. In a national study of urban schools it was found that

> The lower the School SES [socioeconomic status], the smaller the percentage of parents reported to attend school events, to initiate talks with teachers, or to give their children adequate supervision. Principals and teachers believe that the attitudes of parents match their behavior, for the lower the School SES, the smaller the percentage of parents said to be interested in the school work of their children [Herriott & St. John 1966, p. 204].

Obviously, there are intraclass differences among the poor and lower-class populations, but this does not negate the fact that the majority of high school dropouts and "problem" students come from this segment of society. Who, however, is to blame for this—the poor or the school itself?

Paul Lauter and Florence Howe [1970] maintain that through the use of outmoded procedures, an orientation toward white, middle-class values, and the like, urban schools are "rigged for failure" in trying to educate the poor. The authors go on to categorize urban schools as servants of the private business sector by providing it with "a disciplined and acquiescent work force." Lauter and Howe indict the common use of "tracking" within urban schools. By grouping students according to their ability—an ability determined by questionable IQ tests—tracking is bitterly chastised as a system for controlling the manpower specialties of society; that is, it groups students together to help ensure that they do not get too much education so that, by necessity, they will have to work in the lower and more menial job categories.

Others argue that not only is education not serving the poor, but it is especially failing with urban blacks. Nowhere is this failure more pronounced than in the American urban ghetto. With an emphasis on routine and an adherence to outdated teaching techniques, school administrators in the ghetto emphasize control more than they emphasize education [Levy 1970]. Although illegal in some of the areas where it is practiced, overt physical force is sometimes used to maintain order [Levy 1970].

Jonathan Kozol notes that a booklet for Boston teachers, places major emphasis on maintaining the child's obedience. Kozol's personal reaction is that "there is too much respect for authority in the Boston schools, and too little respect for the truth" [1973, p. 277]. This practice of teaching ghetto students submission, Kozol contends, is not only highly detrimental to learning but also has a detrimental effect on how the black student views the American educational process.

Schooling: Isolation and Inadequacy in the Ghetto

The teacher, caught between the student and the administrator, is victimized by a training that did not include preparation for ghetto education [Ornstein 1972].

> The room in which I taught my Fourth Grade was not a room at all, but the corner of an auditorium. . . . They had desks and a teacher but they did not really have a class. . . . In case a reader imagines that my school may have been unusual . . . I think it's worthwhile to point out that the exact opposite seems to have been the case [Kozol 1972, pp. 322–325].

Faced with such deplorable conditions, the urban teacher finds himself in a situation for which he was improperly trained. All of this leads to the absence of an "atmosphere of learning" [Sizer 1967] and to the development of a breeding ground for " . . . a growing atmosphere of hostility and conflict in many cities [Urban American and the Urban Coalition, Inc. 1969].

Intrinsic to the problems faced by ghetto schools is the racial segregation of the ghetto school itself. Opposing this segregation is the widespread, although not unanimous, belief that children of different races must learn, in the school, to live and work together [Sizer 1967].

> But we are forced . . . to ask the harder question, whether in our present society, where Negroes are a minority which has been discriminated against, Negro children can prepare themselves to participate effectively in society if they grow up and go to school in isolation from the majority group. We must also ask whether we can cure the disease of prejudice and prepare all children for life in a multiracial world if white children grow up and go to school in isolation from Negroes [Frankie Freeman, quoted in Schwartz, Pettigrew, & Smith 1972, p. 91].

Despite one's belief in the benefits of integrated urban schools, one must, however, grapple with the reality of segregation. The U.S. Commission on Civil Rights [1967], in a special study, reported that in America's seventy-five largest cities, an overall average of three-fourths of all black students attended urban schools that were 90 percent or more black. Such a finding, though disturbing, is not surprising, considering the high level of residential segregation found in American cities [Taeuber & Taeuber 1965].

Segregated schools, when not brought about by intentional public policy, are thought to be consequences of de facto segregation. Historically, such segregation has been described as being more pronounced in northern than in southern cities. This contention is, of course, grounded in the theory that the South, because of slavery and Reconstruction, has traditionally followed a pattern of segregation of the races. However, present analysis increasingly leads to the conclusion that the North is itself plagued by rampant segregation that cannot be totally explained as de facto. In the North, as elsewhere, politics has played a major role in the segregation of urban schools [Sizer 1967]. Although segregation in Northern cities was not brought about by policies aimed toward establishing segregation as such, the lack of effective state and local policies to prohibit segregation is itself a strong policy influence on the mammoth level of segregation of northern cities.[5]

Schooling: Is Integration the Solution?

Segregation within urban school systems has the dire consequence of fragmenting a child's complete socialization into a society comprised of both black and white people. For white and black students, segregation only serves to feed prejudicial attitudes and behavior. For black students, it has the added effect of isolating the process of education within the confines of the ghetto. Such an isolation distorts and impairs the black students' perception of the relevancy of modern education.

> What strikes one is the feeling of irrelevance. The distance between much of what the children are asked and what they perceive as their needs is great. The formality of the school doesn't mesh with the informality out of school. School language isn't their language [Sizer 1967, p. 347].

Although the major part of segregation is due to economic, social, and racial barriers against blacks, some segregation, as a result of Black Power ideas and the like, is voluntary. Preston Wilcox [1971], however, argues that no matter what the black student does, it is a losing battle. Given the present structure of education in the United States, Wilcox feels that both integrated and segregated schools are manipulated and controlled by white America. For Wilcox, even black separatist–type schools are mere colonies of the white colonizer. "The skin color, life style, and mores of Black people have required that they think and behave white, and reject themselves and the Black masses . . ." [Wilcox 1971, p. 234]. Regardless of Wilcox's contention, the banner of integration is

---

5. Some states do have statutes against de facto segregation. Massachusetts has one of the nation's more rigorous ones. New York, New Jersey, Illinois, and California also give some evidence that individual states are trying to limit segregation. However, most states have either ignored the subject or have enacted relatively ineffective antisegregation laws. For a more detailed discussion of this, see Dye [1968], U.S. Commission on Civil Rights [1967].

still carried by those who see it as the only way out of the racial crisis of America's cities.

Any plan for integrating urban schools must, by necessity, have some legitimate basis. Although the civil rights movement of the 1960s led by the NAACP, CORE, and similar groups had integrated schools as one of its chief goals, many whites did not recognize this movement as a legitimate forum for either promoting or implementing integration. When confronted by the racial problem more-recognized legitimate bodies, such as school boards, are often besieged by angry (and scared) whites who, for whatever reason, see integrated schools as a liability for the education of their children. Few scenes are as ugly as the confrontation between pro- and anti-integration factions that converge on and batter their local board of education. Although such cities as Chicago and Cleveland, have implemented desegregation policies, most local urban school boards have not met the problem head-on except when required to do so by the federal government.

Regardless of the professional character attributed to educators, most urban school boards (which are usually controlled by noneducators) respond directly to the wishes of the white electorate and to the powerful actors within the city.

> When members of the mayor's staff or members of the civil elite choose school board members (and in most cities they do choose them), they have in mind an operational image when they say they want a "good man" for the job. It is hardly a surprise that they get the kind of man they want most of the time. These men then control the schools' "image" on racial matters and to a limited extent this style can filter down to the classroom [Crain & Street 1969, p. 120].

This practice has served as a moderating, if not stifling, influence on desegregation.

Whether desegregation of the nation's schools will come about in this or the next generation is problematic. Given the high degree of urban residential segregation and the deeply rooted opposition to integration in both the white and black communities, one cannot be very optimistic that integration will be a reality of the near future. Nor can one properly perceive school integration as a panacea for the crisis in urban education: integrated education is not necessarily *good* education.

Although all three branches of the federal government have openly espoused a commitment to integrated schools, neither Johnson's "Great Society," the 1954 Brown decision by the Supreme Court, nor the threat by Congress to withhold funds from segregated schools has had a powerful impact on lessening the inequities between predominantly black and predominantly white urban schools. In its desire to integrate, the federal government—especially the judiciary—has sought to overcome segregation by moving students rather than by integrating neighborhoods. This attempt at a cure has resulted in one of the most bitterly divisive practices found in urban America: busing.

On the surface, busing students to achieve integration appears to be a viable temporary alternative to segregated schools. But the recent turmoil in Pontiac, Michigan; Richmond, Virginia; Boston, Massachusetts; and other cities is visible proof that busing is the greatest Pandora's box of modern federal policy. In impassioned pleas, whites (and some blacks) have opposed the forced movement of their children from local schools to schools miles away. Some argue that busing prohibits one's children from participating in extracurricular activities that require additional after-school hours of attendance. Others fear for the safety of their children both in the bus journey itself, as well as in the actual integrated context of the school. It should be noted, however, that blacks have long been bused by local school boards to maintain segregation, and little outcry from whites was ever heard concerning this practice. Moreover, it must be stressed that at this point in history, busing is sometimes opposed on the grounds of prejudice, although different reasons are verbalized.

Boston and Louisville are two recent arenas for the busing controversy. In a 104 page court order issued in May, 1975, Federal District Court Judge W. Arthur Garrity ordered the busing of over 21,000 Boston students, 12,000 of whom were in grades 1 through 5. His plan not only called for busing, but it also called for the actual closing of 20 schools and the creation of nine new local school districts. All this, according to Garrity, is necessary for Boston public schools to approximate the Boston ratio of a student population that is 37% black. Boston City Council member Louise Day Hicks, an avowed anti-busing advocate, said the court order would be ". . . the death knell of the city" [*Time* 1975]. Some of the white residents of South Boston seemed to agree with Hicks' dire prediction as they prepared to battle integration with the defiant call of "Southie's on the warpath, ooh-ah!" [*Newsweek* 1975]. The subsequent rioting and violence in Boston in both 1975 and 1976 has been on a scale beyond most experts' fears. The situation in Boston remains so unstable that the city has prepared a general protection plan for the safety of the children in Boston's public schools.

1975 also saw racial turmoil over court ordered busing in Louisville. What started as a peaceful and orderly, although sometimes boycotted, busing program soon turned into a riot necessitating the calling out of the national guard by Kentucky's Governor Julian Carroll. However, the officials of Louisville presented a strong backboned policy of determinism to make sure that the busing order would be carried out. Stating that rioters had ". . . insulted the dignity of the community," Judge James Gordon banned demonstrations near public schools. He also forbade the gathering of three or more people along bus lines while the buses were carrying out the court order [*Time* 1975]. As the school year proceeded, the tension in Louisville subsided, but as anticipated, many parents began to seek private schools for their children.

Besides racial tension and turmoil for some cities, what consequences has busing had? For one thing, it has, in effect, helped integrate schools in many American cities that have peacefully adjusted to limited busing programs. The impact of busing in helping to achieve this integration is underscored by the research of Reynolds Farley who studied 143 Northern and Southern school districts and concluded that:

> . . . the greatest decreases in segregation occurred in those districts where many students were bussed to achieve racial balance. If a law banned such busing, the courts and administrators would lose an effective tool, and within urban areas, schools would be segregated because of neighborhood patterns [Farley 1975, pp. 22-23].

In actuality, therefore, busing is America's main, present thrust toward racial integration. But does this busing have other effects on the future overall residential integration of urban populations? In terms of the long range impact of bringing blacks and whites together at a young age, this question cannot be answered as yet. But what about the anticipated short range result of busing's intensifying the "white flight" to the suburbs? At a 1975 symposium at the Brookings Institution, a group of scholars, whose participation was funded by the National Institute of Education, disagreed with the notion that busing causes any further increase in "white flight" [*National Institute of Education Information* 1975]. The panel felt, in general, that the movement of whites to the suburbs already had its momentum before busing became an issue. Yet, this white flight, regardless of its impetus is a major obstacle to further integration of urban schools. "The panelists generally agreed that, with continuing white flight to the suburbs, only a metropolitan, inter-district desegregation plan would turn the tide of black and white segregation in the schools" [*NIE Information* 1975, p. 1]. Whether or not the courts will be able to support this type of interdistrict school desegregation is doubtful.

Although busing had been consistently supported by the federal courts, the Supreme Court ruling of July 25, 1974, placed a new restriction on the practice of busing. In a five-to-four decision, the Court, led by conservative Justice Warren Burger ruled that ". . . busing pupils across district lines from a black inner city to white suburbs was improper and contrary to the tradition of local school control" [*Miami Herald,* July 26, 1974]. This decision is particularly detrimental to predominantly black central cities that are surrounded by white school districts. Although praised by then–Vice-President Gerald Ford as a "victory for reason," the decision represents, in the opinion of some people, a major retreat by the federal court from implementation of a school desegregation policy. In his strong dissenting opinion, Justice Thurgood Marshall called the ruling "a giant step backwards" that supported segregated and unequal schools. For the moment, the ruling does alleviate the growing and intense white backlash against forced integration; however, America must someday face the problems stemming from segregated schools.

Schooling: Experiments and Proposals

Of course, the involvement of the federal government is not limited to busing. In fact, all recent federal legislation dealing with education has, somewhere within it, some type of plan to alleviate the problems facing urban education. As part of President Johnson's war on poverty, the Head Start program was implemented to give culturally deprived pre-schoolers exposure to American education. Based on a social pathology model of poor blacks, Head Start sought to overcome the "deficiencies" experienced by disadvantaged children in their home lives. With such a rationale for implementation, it is little wonder that the program has been soundly opposed by those who dislike the value-laden "deficiency" notion [Baratz & Baratz 1970]. Furthermore, the small size of Head Start classes did not, in actuality, prepare preschoolers for the large classes they would eventually attend in regular schools. Also, the rather innovative teaching techniques followed in Head Start classes did little to prepare students for more traditional teaching methods. All in all, evidence seems to show that the Head Start child's school performance is not distinguishable from his culturally deprived counterpart who was not enrolled in the Head Start program [Grosser 1973].

Although there are many other federal programs dealing with urban education, one of the major thrusts of federal involvement with urban schools comes in the form of financing. Before local school districts can get federal funds, they must meet the prerequisites established by

Congress when it passed a particular piece of legislation. In this way, the federal government has a certain "veto power" over many local programs. This veto power is justified not only on the grounds that the source of funds (in this case the federal government) has the privilege of determining how these funds are to be spent but it is also justified by the fact that local governments simply cannot provide enough funds for local education [Rasmussen 1973, p. 136]. Although this veto power does exist, it must be emphasized that local school districts still have great control over the extent to which the federal government can tell them what to do.

Most urban schools are financed by a mixture of federal and state money and local property taxes. The latter have been a source of discontent for urbanites who already feel overtaxed. When increased funds are needed by a school district, the board of education must not only justify increased expenditures but they must also justify an increase in property taxes to support these expenditures [Alford 1971]. It is difficult to persuade the electorate to vote for such increases and in poor school districts it is not even possible to meet them.

Financial burdens are especially pronounced in inner-city schools where the population itself cannot adequately support schools, although nearby suburban districts enjoy less trouble in raising funds. Without a consolidation of funds, inner-city school systems remain plagued by money problems; with a consolidation of funds, suburban populations become angered at having to pay for educational services that do not directly affect their children.

With a broadly based tax, such as the sales or income tax, some of the financial troubles of urban schools—especially inner-city schools—could be lessened. However, given the present power structure of most cities, a strong shift from the property-tax base is not likely. Other suggestions to alleviate the financial problems of education include various proposals subsumed under the category of "voucher schemes."[6] With a voucher system, much of the direct public financing of education would be eliminated, and parents would receive an equal share of funds to use as they wish for the education of their children. Under voucher schemes

---

6. There are various, complicated voucher schemes proposed by both economists and educators. Many such schemes are proposed by those who view total public financing of education as an "intrusion by the government," as well as unfair competition to free-market educational facilities. For a greater discussion of voucher schemes see Benson [1968], Coleman [1967], Friedman [1963], Levin [1968], Sizer & Whitten [1968]. Also, both sales and income tax systems are potentially regressive (see the Urban Finance section of this chapter).

parents could supplement their share of public funds with their own money in order to send their children to private schools. On the surface, voucher schemes appear to be one way of introducing flexibility into education, since different schools would provide different educational emphases and programs. However, Rey Carr and Gerald Hayward [1970] correctly argue that most voucher schemes place too much emphasis on education as a market system. Also, by steadily eliminating direct governmental control of education, the voucher system could only increase the number of segregated schools, since many black families could afford only minimally adequate schools—schools that would be avoided by a more affluent white population.

One cannot argue against the fact that marked disparities exist between wealthy school districts and poorer ones. Nor can one deny that these differences influence the quality of education offered. However, there is still no agreement as to how—or even whether—these differences should be eliminated [Cohen 1969].

One proposal that actually claims to lessen city educational expenditures is the educational park. The educational park is usually a multigrade (for example, kindergarten through high school) campus that has extensive facilities and services in a single area. Not only do educational parks have a wide variety of vocational and academic curriculums but they also seek to become the center of local community life. During school hours, the auditorium and gymnasium, for example, are used by students. In the evenings they are used for community musicals, plays, and family recreation.

Specifically, the greatest benefit of educational parks is that they offer a variety of educational programs in one area. For racially heterogeneous communities educational parks can provide for a mingling between races, as well as for an education geared toward different racial groups. Some educational parks with high school campuses even have a unique curriculum that allows students to have a great voice in their studies. Some of the better known educational parks are Parkway in Philadelphia, Brandywine in Wilmington, Delaware, and Educational Park in Camden, New Jersey [Allen 1970]. If properly planned, educational parks could also serve as an opportunity for racially segregated communities to integrate blacks and whites by combining several neighborhood schools into one single campus. Such a plan would have to overcome opposition to the loss of neighborhood schools and to transportation costs for bringing students to and from the campus. Admittedly, these are major problems, but educational parks are one of the few bright prospects in contemporary urban education.

Major attention toward alleviating urban educational problems goes beyond such specific programs as educational parks and is directed toward the advancement of local community control of education. For the sake of clarity, we will point out at the outset that local community control is not the same as decentralization; the two concepts cannot be used interchangeably. Decentralization specifically means " . . . the transfer of the power to make certain decisions from a central office or staff to a number of subordinate offices or staffs which serve smaller parts of a large district or area or population" [Havighurst 1971, p. 296]. Although decentralization *might* entail the active participation of the local citizenry, the local school is still governed by the larger school system. What is more, most decentralization plans call for subdivisions governing 20,000 or more students and most plans delegate relatively few items (such as the selection of textbooks) to the decentralized bodies.[7]

Local community control, which by definition involves some degree of decentralization, refers to " . . . a pattern of organization in which the local community has power over decisions" [Glazer 1971, p. 234]. Although local community control does not mean that professional competency is ignored in making decisions, it does mean that the average citizen will have a greater, if not the main, voice in deciding how the school his child attends is run. An urban school district is literally divided into smaller communities of no more than about 50,000 people and 10,000 to 12,000 students [Havinghurst 1971]. This division is based not only on numerical considerations but also on racial and socioeconomic considerations. Local community control, if fully implemented, would, for example, give a ghetto population greater control over finances, personnel, curriculum, and other administrative decisions.

Proponents of local community control argue that such control would
1. increase the relevancy of education, since it would be geared directly to a specific subset of the city population and not to the city as a whole;
2. mark a return to the "participatory democracy" of early America;
3. instill in the public a sense of responsibility toward maintaining urban education; 4. give parents a greater understanding of the complexities involved in education; and 5. help parents to more willingly finance education [Fantini 1968; Gittell 1968; Havinghurst 1971]. In part, the proposing of these positive effects is based on the Coleman Report [Kleinfeld

---

7. Decentralization is severely limited by the areas of decision making allotted by the larger school district. Although decentralization has been implemented in some cities (New York, Chicago, Los Angeles, Detroit), its relative effectiveness is weakened by this lack of decision making power for decentralized officials. For a further discussion of the disadvantages and advantages of decentralization see Epstein [1968], Etzioni [1969], Featherstone [1969], Ornstein [1972, ch. VI].

1971], emerging new directions in community processes [Altshuler 1970; Grosser 1973], and the demand by some segments of the public—especially blacks—for a greater voice in deciding the dynamics of the organizations that influence them.

Even on a minor scale, any local community control plan involves an organizational restructuring of the entire city. In a real sense, it is giving power to people who are presently quite powerless. Local community control of education also opens the door to local community control of other city institutions such as the police [Ostrom & Whitaker 1973] and any other presently centralized urban organization or service. Whether this is a positive or negative trend cannot be determined here. However, there are some basic objections that pertain to the local community control of education as such. First, the average layman is often felt to be improperly trained to deal with the problems facing urban education. Second, education would run the risk of parochialism in that each local community would be providing its own form of education. Third, as a result of this parochialism, the general role of education to prepare one for interaction in American society as a whole would be mitigated. Fourth, the entire national educational system would have to be revamped, since some local communities, by making nontraditional demands of a traditional institution, would require personnel and curriculums not presently anticipated. Finally, local community control could easily lead to the death of integrated schools, since white and black local communities would both have their own miniature school systems.

Whether the positive or negative aspects of local community control prevail will only be decided by future history. It is certain, however, that this plan will be tried again and again, and that educators and the public at large have only begun to see what profound ramifications local community control will have on the city as a whole.

Regardless of how urban schools are changed to meet modern demands, we are learning more and more that society itself must undergo major changes before the urban educational crisis is solved [Jencks et al. 1972]. H. G. Wells stated insightfully that history is a race between education and catastrophe. As seen throughout this discussion, the basis of catastrophe is already present in our nation's urban schools. Poor housing, poverty, inadequate schools, and racial clashes all have additive, adverse effects on the cities. As will be shown in the next section, even the basic services of the city are faltering in meeting the demands of the people.

URBAN SERVICES: OUTMODED DELIVERY SYSTEMS

One of the often overlooked facets of the city is its service sector. More and more of America's urban labor force is being devoted to the provision of intangible services to the public. Both of these services are distributed or delivered to urbanites, and how these services meet the needs of urban people has a powerful effect on the quality of life that urban people experience.

Nelson Foote and Paul K. Hatt [1953] developed the generally accepted typology for classifying the main services of American society. In essence, this typology is divided into three distinct groupings based on the extent that a given service helps the recipient and on the extent that a service maintains or expands America's complex division of labor.

> a) *tertiary services* provide direct and rather immediate benefits to the recipient: for example, barbershops, laundries, repair services, and other domestic or semi-domestic services;
> b) *quarternary services* help to maintain a division of labor by providing the essential services of transportation, administration, communication, and commerce;
> c) *quinary services* are the most basic services since they are the ones that improve or change the essential character of the recipient: for example, health care [Foote & Hatt 1953, p. 365].

Time and space prevent us from discussing all of the services listed, but two of them are of special relevance to contemporary cities: health care and transportation. Urban health-care delivery systems are receiving greater attention today than ever before. This is due not only to the fact that health care is an all-encompassing, essential, cradle-to-grave service but also because it is being challenged as a service that mainly serves the more affluent urban population and not the city as a whole. Transportation is discussed more and more not only because of the energy crisis but also because of the role it plays in the distribution and movement of people, goods, and other services throughout urban space.

Health Care: For Whom and at What Cost?

One of the paradoxes of modernization is that the more a society advances, the less an individual can actually do regarding certain functions.

For example, now that many Americans have modern home furnaces, few people are equipped with the facilities or the know-how to provide their own heat; with modern grocery stores and refrigeration, even fewer could provide or preserve food for their families if forced to do so. There are countless such examples, but one of the most glaring is in the area of health maintenance. Having become accustomed to modern health care and a long life expectancy, modern Americans are nearly totally dependent on the American health institution to provide them with medical care. Yet, in spite of its basic importance, American health care is viewed as being in a state of crisis. American medical services have been accused of failing to provide proper medical care to all and of converting " . . . inner cities into medical wastelands" [Medical Committee for Human Rights 1970].

As the health industry becomes increasingly technical and monopolistic in character, a type of "American Health Empire" is seen as emerging [Ehrenreich 1970]. Also, as mental health, psychological well-being, dental care, and the like become more important, the health crisis is only worsened by the increasing demands made of it. Such demands only further exacerbate what is already a severe shortage of medical personnel. In 1970, Assistant Secretary of Health, Education, and Welfare Roger Egeberg, estimated that the nation had an immediate need for 50,000 more doctors and for almost 200,000 more nurses [Jones 1971, p. 55]. And Selig Greenberg reports that by 1975 America's supply of doctors will fall short of its needs by at least 80,000 [1971, pp. 125–126].

Although this shortage is more stringently felt in small communities, even the nation's cities are suffering from this lack of personnel. Also, the shortcomings of health-care delivery systems in the cities are especially pronounced in poverty areas, where such services are gravely lacking.

Not even an insured middle-class family is free from the possibility of crippling health bills. For the poor, who cannot even afford health insurance, this possibility increases geometrically. Also, as we have seen in the discussion on housing, the poor are made to suffer the physically pathological effects of poor housing. When combined with a lack of funds to secure good medical care, the health of the poor is further worsened. The Urban Coalition claims that the urban poor lose twice as many days from work as the nonpoor, and that "they suffer four to eight times the incidence of heart disease, arthritis, and other chronic conditions" as the nonpoor [George & McKinley 1974, p. 69]. In the ghetto, the health-care delivery system is at its worst.

There's the city hospital, but it's no good for us . . . [it's] far away, and I didn't have money to get a cab . . . My kids, they get sick. The welfare worker . . . took my daughter and told her she had to have her teeth looked at. . . . So, I went. . . . And I had to pay the woman next door to mind the little ones, and there was the carfare. . . . So, I figured it would take more than we've got to see the dentist [A black ghetto mother, quoted in Coles 1971, p. 106].

Even the poor who are able to gain access to health care are confronted by the seemingly endless amount of bureaucratic red tape that accompanies health services for the poor. Lester Breslow outlines the experiences of a young mother whose family is receiving aid under the ADC program. Even though she has had the foresight to receive prenatal care from her local health agency, when she is ready to have her baby, she is referred to a public hospital. Her records are often lost in the process with the result that at the height of her labor she is confronted with a battery of procedural questions; additionally, she is surrounded by unfamiliar personnel. After delivery, her baby is examined by another doctor who will never see the baby again. Once home, she takes the baby to another local health agency that can provide only routine check-ups for a healthy baby; of course, more questions are asked for their records. If the child becomes seriously ill, the mother is referred to a local physician who is paid through a welfare agency; the physician requires yet another round of questions and forms to ensure that he will get paid for his services. If the child requires hospitalization, the mother is sent again to the public hospital, since the physician's hospital does not accept welfare patients. If the child is afflicted with a certain ailment that comes under a different welfare program, the mother is referred to yet another source to receive that aid [Breslow 1966]. In this entire process, both mother and child have seen many different doctors, and the mother has had to repeat her private life history and background over and over again —all in the pursuit of essential health care.

Such procedures are rationalized on the premise that health agencies must answer to whomever is funding them. Each funding program has its own narrow set of bureaucratic requirements and procedures that agencies must strictly adhere to in order to receive funding. This adherence is repeatedly carried to extremes, as evidenced by a recent Jacksonville, Florida, incident. Having gone into labor, a young mother went to the emergency room of a local hospital. When hospital personnel discovered that she had been on welfare and could not pay her hospital bills herself, they refused her admittance. In spite of the fact that she was bleeding, she was literally forced to leave the hospital. An hour later, she delivered her child in the home of a midwife. The hospital administration, when pressed by reporters, was forced to acknowledge that admittance is never refused to those who can pay.

Walter Vandermeer desperately sought help from over seven "welfare" agencies, but was either turned down by some who felt he did not fit their requirements or discouraged by others who asked countless questions. At the age of twelve, he became the youngest person ever to die in New York City from an overdose of heroin: "The agencies had exhausted their routine procedures before he died; only his file continued to move" [Lelyveld 1970]. For Walter, at the age of twelve, even a bureaucratic health agency was too late.

Middle-class Americans, with their private physicians, would never tolerate such runarounds. Nor would they tolerate being asked, "Do you know who the father of the child is? Is the man living with your mother married to her? Where will the money come from to pay for your visit?" (Even middle-class America, long too tolerant of demeaning health care for the poor, is now also being asked more questions about its ability to pay than about its ailments!)

Most health care agencies are administered by people who have little contact with poverty except through forms and records. Even hospitals, the centers of care for the very ill, are governed by boards of trustees who are usually drawn from the business community and who have made, or may make, monetary donations to the hospital. The physicians come from predominantly middle- and upper-class backgrounds. Almost all of the hospital personnel have had little training in taking care of the poor, who are often erroneously viewed as being too ignorant to know whether they are sick or not. The clerks and office personnel are usually socialized into a highly patronizing and negative view of the poor who come to the hospital [Roth 1969]. As a result of all this, the poverty-stricken patient is subjected to a depersonalization process that goes far beyond the usual trauma accompanying a hospital stay.

Health Care: Some Solutions

The situation is rather clear: it takes money to receive good health care. American medical care is big business. Each year over $65 billion is spent in this nation on health care. With doctors' fees, drugs, hospital fees, and all medical expenses on the rise, proper medical care is definitively out of the reach of the poor and is fast becoming a strain on America's middle-class. Each passing day makes it clearer that private health insurance companies are not the answer. While the private sector has been losing its capacity to meet the financial demands of medicine, the government has been taking a greater role in financing medical programs. The main involvement of the federal government began in the mid-1930s under President Franklin D. Roosevelt. The Wagner Act of 1939 was this nation's first attempt at a national health program. Subsequent federal legislation has mostly dealt with assistance programs aimed at helping the blind, the aged, and disabled people in general. Historically, the federal government has been averse to direct involvement in health insurance programs. However, with support from Presidents Kennedy and Johnson, Congress in 1965 passed Medicare, health insurance for the aged, and Medicaid, which was to help the indigent [Falk 1973]. Unfortunately, Medicaid was severely hampered by the fact that only a few wealthy states could meet the expenditures required on the state level. Both Medicare and Medicaid have increased administrative red tape at the local level and have, in actuality, intensified health-care delivery problems at the local level [Falk 1973]. Realizing the need for a national, comprehensive health insurance program, both the executive and congressional branches are coming up with legislation to reach this goal. With the support of such powerful lobbyists as the American Federation of Labor, the United Auto Workers, and other labor and activist groups, it is only a matter of time until some form of national health insurance is enacted. Yet, none of this legislation is expected to go beyond the "market mentality" that rules the economics of medical care. With such a mentality, there is little hope that any national health insurance will actually guarantee that medical care is successfully conveyed to all who need it. As long as medicine is dominated by profit and market concerns, the provision of decent health care may be completely thwarted by financial problems.[8]

In trying to offset the burden of medical-care financing on the poor, increased attention has been given to community health centers. In 1962, under President Kennedy, the federal government and various private foundations established the National Commission on Community Health

---

8. In addition to the problem of financing medical care, there are many specific aspects of health care (e.g., training of personnel, expansion of medical schools) that can not be elaborated on here. For these and related topics, the reader is referred to Bazell [1971], Cartwright [1967], Coe [1970], Creel [1966], Friedson [1970], Mechanic [1968], Mumford and Skipper [1967], Richmond [1969], and Strauss [1967].

Services. As a partial result of the commission's findings, Congress in 1966 passed legislation providing some funds for health-planning agencies at the regional, state, and community levels. Unfortunately, only a fraction of these funds reach local poverty communities, and many of the appropriations have since been vetoed by President Ford. However, the demand for local community health care increases daily.

To be truly effective, any urban health-care delivery system must entail involvement of the local citizenry, and it must be client-centered. Too often, health agencies are set up for the comfort of those who run them and not for the sick who come to them.

One of the most exhaustive attempts to have such client-centered health care is found in Redwood City, California, in a racially mixed poverty area of 15,000 people. Working from the premise that American medical care is set up to make money and not actually to serve the sick, the People's Medical Center (PMC) [1970] sought to change the relationship between the doctor and the patient. Volunteers helped the PMC to convert a warehouse into a clinic. Other noteworthy features of the PMC are that it publishes a bilingual (English and Spanish) monthly newsletter, provides free transportation to and from the clinic, and has a board of directors composed of members of the clinic *and* active representatives from the local poverty community. No one is refused care for a lack of funds; so far, the PMC has sustained itself through the payments of those who can afford to give some money for care received.

Community health centers, similar to the People's Medical Center, have a future that is dependent not only on the local community but also on American society as a whole. And until something is done about medical costs, even Americans above the poverty level might soon be getting medical care from local community health centers rather than from private physicians. Although health is a community affair, there is little reason to think that this fact will actually be widely recognized and acted on in America for years to come. Although a strong health care delivery system is essential for all Americans, it appears that the poor of the cities will not see the full benefits of this essential, quinary service for a longer time than is tolerable.

So far, we have concentrated only on the health-care service sector. However, any delivery system, to be effective, must be able to meet the demand of bringing the service to the people or the people to the service. With this in mind, we now turn to a look at transporation, one of the most important aspects of America's cities.

Transportation: Providing Access for All

The contemporary concern with urban transportation goes beyond the single dimension of energy supply and conservation. For the modern urbanite, transportation is the means of access to the resources and services of the city. Any impingement on this needed transportation differentially affects the various social strata of the city.

For too many Americans highways are little more than concrete conveyances for auto travel. In a more comprehensive perspective, highways are actually the lifelines of the cities, and today's cities reflect the historical development of these lines of transportation. Unfortunately, modern highways exist only at a cost that goes beyond monetary considerations. With the construction of any highway in a city, there is certain to be destruction of some homes and the removal of a population that must yield to eminent domain.[9] Since facilities and people tend to move with advances in transportation, access to highways has allowed people who could afford it to move farther out into the urban fringe.

Many employers have followed this movement of people to the suburbs. Increasingly, the trend is for factories and business to move away from the central city, leaving behind those who simply cannot afford the transportation costs of working in the suburbs and the urban fringe.

> For some segments of the lower-income populations, locational inaccessibility to employment . . . erects an additional handicap which acts to further depress earning capacities. Especially for Negroes seeking work in the suburbanizing manufacturing and wholesale industries, exclusion from the suburban housing market couples with deficient outbound commuter service to make these growing job opportunities relatively inaccessible, while opportunities near their central-city homes are contracting [Webber 1968, p. 12].

In a very real sense, therefore, urban highways are powerful determinants of urban life—determinants that cover the whole spectrum from necessary travel to work down to accessibility to the community swimming pool.

---

9. Eminent domain is the legal term applied to the sovereign power of the state over all property. Under eminent domain, private property can be taken for highway construction as long as compensation is given to the owner. Such compensation is influenced by the power an individual has at his disposal to fight for a given price for his land and the building(s) on it. Often, lower-class people who own their homes are not able to afford the legal fees necessary to help them get fair compensation for their homes. Furthermore, people sometimes oppose highway construction not only because of an unjust use of eminent domain but because of its effect on both the physical and social environment of a neighborhood [Brown 1972].

Few American scenes are more common than rush-hour traffic jams on the nation's urban freeways. In spite of new highway construction, most freeways are inadequate by the time they are completed. Since 1950, the number of families owning two or more cars has increased by over 250 percent, and no highway construction can keep up with that type of an increase. Although they are latent consequences of many individual decisions, traffic jams are a visible proof that the auto is America's chief vehicle for travel and that something must be done to cure urban traffic congestion.

Some have argued that the problem of traffic jams can be handled within an economic framework. Rasmussen [1973] suggests that electronic detectors could be installed in cars to bill people monthly for their driving into a congested area. Others argue that raising gasoline prices and parking fees is one means not only of conserving energy but also of forcing people to form car pools. The District of Columbia has implemented a plan that it hopes will force 25 percent of its 380,000 commuters to leave their cars at home by 1975. An essential aspect of the plan is to raise parking fees substantially and limit the number of new parking lots (*U.S. News and World Report,* 1972). However, this and all other economic plans to curb traffic congestion are not actually aimed at providing transportation for all urban citizens. What is more, until all people have equal access to all major parts of a city, low-income groups will still be victimized by poor transportation. Any major proposal to ease urban transportation must entail a comprehensive public mass-transit system that is priced within the reach of all segments of the population.

This history of America's attempts at developing urban mass-transit systems is dismal. Between 1950 and 1967, for example, the number of passengers carried by buses decreased by 39 percent; for electric railway cars, the decrease was 64 percent; and for mass transit as a whole, the decrease was 52 percent. Table 3 shows that for 1970, few major cities had more than 10 percent of their work force using mass transit to get to work. No city of over 1 million people had more than 25 percent mass-transit usage except New York City. And Norwalk, Connecticut, is the only city of the 48 listed with under a million people that even has 10 percent of its work force using mass transit.

With such a small percentage of usage, how can it be said that mass transit is a cure for our cities' transportation ills? There are three basic justifications for this contention:

1. The automobile wastes energy and space. (For example, 50 percent of downtown Los Angeles is devoted to freeways, parking spaces, and garages) [Temko, 1969].

TABLE 3. Persons Using Public Transportation to Work for Selected Standard Metropolitan Statistical Areas*

City & Population	Percentage of Workers Using Public Transportation to Work	City & Population	Percentage of Workers Using Public Transportation to Work
Over 2 million		*250,000–499,999*	
New York, New York	48.0	Tulsa, Oklahoma	2.3
Los Angeles-Long Beach,		Orlando, Florida	3.5
California	5.6	Fresno, California	1.5
Chicago, Illinois	23.2	Harrisburg, Pennsylvania	4.7
Philadelphia, Pennsylvania-		Charlotte, North Carolina	6.9
New Jersey	20.6	Knoxville, Tennessee	3.9
Detroit, Michigan	8.2	Wichita, Kansas	2.4
San Francisco-Oakland,		Lansing, Michigan	1.7
California	15.4	New Haven, Connecticut	9.5
Boston, Massachusetts	20.0	Peoria, Illinois	2.7
Baltimore, Maryland	13.8	Albuquerque, New Mexico	2.5
		Trenton, New Jersey	8.0
1,500,000–1,999,999		Des Moines, Iowa	4.7
		South Bend, Indiana	3.6
Houston, Texas	5.4	Jackson, Mississippi	2.9
Newark, New Jersey	18.5		
Minneapolis-St. Paul, Minnesota	9.1		
Dallas, Texas	6.3	*100,000–249,999*	
		Colorado Springs, Colorado	1.4
1,000,000–1,499,999		Raleigh, North Carolina	3.8
		Eugene, Oregon	1.0
Seattle, Everett, Washington	7.1	Lowell, Massachusetts	4.7
Milwaukee, Wisconsin	12.0	Macon, Georgia	5.5
Atlanta, Georgia	9.4	Modesta, California	.3
San Diego, California	4.3	Savannah, Georgia	9.3
Buffalo, New York	10.4	Cedar Rapids, Iowa	2.5
Miami, Florida	9.1	Green Bay, Wisconsin	3.0
Denver, Colorado	4.4	Portland, Maine	6.5
Indianapolis, Indiana	5.8	Altoona, Pennsylvania	4.2
San Jose, California	2.3	Decatur, Illinois	2.5
New Orleans, Louisiana	20.4	Norwalk, Connecticut	10.3
		Abilene, Texas	1.2
500,000–999,999		Gainesville, Florida	1.9
Phoenix, Arizona	1.3	*Under 100,000*	
Columbus, Ohio	8.1		
Rochester, New York	8.0	Sioux Falls, South Dakota	2.6
Louisville, Kentucky-Indiana	6.7	Dubuque, Iowa	4.6
Sacramento, California	2.3	Albany, Georgia	2.6
Birmingham, Alabama	6.2	Billings, Montana	1.0
Oklahoma City, Oklahoma	1.6	Rochester, Minnesota	2.5
Salt Lake City, Utah	2.3	Columbia, Missouri	2.0
Omaha, Nebraska-Iowa	7.2	San Angelo, Texas	1.3
Jacksonville, Florida	6.7	Bristol, Connecticut	.9

*Cities are listed in order of descending size. Public transportation refers to the chief means of public travel or type of conveyance used in traveling to and from work on the last day the person reporting worked at the address given as his or her place of work. Data is taken from the U.S. Bureau of the Census, *County and City Data Book, 1972* (A Statistical Abstract Supplement) [U.S. Government Printing Office 1973].

2. Autos provide America with at least half of all urban air contaminants [Hawkins 1973].

3. As pointed out, highways alone simply cannot handle transportation needs; nor can they provide for equitable access to all parts of the city for all urbanites.

The task, then, is to provide a mass-transit system that will be used by a nation accustomed to hopping into the car to go wherever it wishes. Such a system must meet the following minimum criteria:

1. It must have broad, citywide support.

2. It must provide access to all major areas of the city for all people.

3. It must be convenient for people to use.

4. It must charge low fares (or no fare at all).

5. It must provide travel that is comfortable and safe from accidents and crime.

6. It must be fast.

7. It must have a firm financial basis supporting it.

8. It must be relatively free of noise and air pollution.

9. It must be aesthetically pleasing (e.g., electric trains must fit into the urban environment).

10. It must be built with as little disruption to settled populations and facilities as possible.

A system that meets these ten requirements would be more than just a mover of people; it would also serve the social-welfare function of providing transportation for lower-income populations who are presently deprived of such services.

Transportation: Some Experiments

For the present, proposed mass-transit systems would utilize buses (powered by gasoline), trains (powered by diesel fuels), or train-type vehicles such as monorails (powered by electricity). Unfortunately, the success of any mass-transit project is often short-lived. In spite of a massive amount of both local and national publicity, San Francisco's Bay Area

Rapid Transit (BART) service is seeing a marked decrease in passengers. The history of BART is a nightmarish picture for those who seek to convince Americans to make the transition from the auto to the bus or train.

Construction of BART, "the miracle transit system," began in 1962. However, many cautioned overly optimistic city fathers that there were several structural and design problems inherent in the system. Unfortunately, these harbingers of caution were not fully heeded and BART has been plagued by mechanical and electronic problems ever since its maiden voyage in 1973 [*The New York Times* 1974]. The problems became most pronounced when a BART train was involved in an accident that, although it claimed no lives, was the poorest of publicity for getting people to use the service. The computerized control system has failed often, doors have opened while the train is in full motion (80 miles per hour), and passengers have had the train doors open with no platform for detraining in sight [*The New York Times* 1974].

Although one can claim that the mechanical troubles of BART are due to poor planning, one still must grapple with the fact that the financing of this type of modern system cannot be handled by fares alone. The managers of BART already claim a need for several million dollars to continue service, and federal and state monies must come to the rescue to keep the system in operation [*The New York Times* 1974].

Urban transportation experts are still rather optimistic about BART's potential despite all its apparent woes. When it works efficiently, few deny that it provides a fast, comfortable, clean ride. However, San Francisco Bay area officials must still continue the "hardsell" to get people to use the trains.

An equally challenging solution to urban transit problems is being undertaken in Atlanta, Georgia. The Metropolitan Atlanta Rapid Transit Authority (MARTA) set out in 1971 to build a rail transit system that would provide rapid transit to Atlanta's citizens by 1979. Because of funding delays, the completion date has been pushed back to 1980 at the earliest, and Atlanta officials are in a quandry similar to that of BART officials—where to get financing.

There are indications that MARTA's proposed $1.7 billion price tag will go higher, and Atlanta faces the further obstacle of competing with cities all across America for a share in the small amount of federal mass-transit funds. With the advent of the fuel crisis, cities have tried harder than ever to gain a share of federal transit funds. More and more of these funds are going to smaller communities (100,000 to 500,000), since even these cities face transportation problems brought about by pollution, congestion, and fuel shortages.

Atlanta is seeking over $291 million annually from the federal Urban Mass Transportation Administration (UMTA). But because UMTA has a total pool of funds of less than $900 million for the whole nation, Atlanta cannot have too much faith in gaining full funding from UMTA. Atlanta hopes to avoid the funding problem by borrowing money against MARTA's own sales-tax income and by issuing revenue bonds. Yet, since there are limits to the extent that these two sources can be tapped for money, MARTA's future is still not secure [*The Atlanta Journal* 1974].

MARTA brings another complicating factor into the transportation picture in the form of pollution control. Ironically, MARTA, whose use by commuters would cut down on auto pollution, was delayed by an Environmental Impact Study (EIS) required by Washington. Atlanta was used as a model for future EIS studies, and federal officials took their time in assessing the antipollution potential of MARTA, thereby further delaying its construction.

In addition to such highly technical systems as BART and MARTA, some cities have tried to make a better use of buses for mass transit. Seattle's program of free bus rides in the downtown area has been only moderately successful and, with the passage of time, enthusiasm for the program is waning. Commerce, California, is one of the few cities in America that has totally free bus service. Yet, only about 7 to 8 percent of its 10,500 residents are using the buses [*U.S. News and World Report* 1972].[10]

Proposals of reduced fares, subsidized fares, or, in the case of Commerce, no fares at all, are heard across the country in cities of all sizes. And, although a highly used mass-transit system can gain a sizable revenue from fares, fares alone cannot meet transit costs, since too high a fare would severely limit the use of mass transit.

Another problem is that transportation, whatever the type, is now governed by highly irrational pricing practices [Vickrey 1973]. What must be done is to carry out a public information program to let citizens know that in the long run, mass transit is the cheapest possible form of urban travel. William Vickrey [1973] points out that on the basis of a 1963 study done in Washington, D.C., a person who spent $3,000 on a car

---

10. There have been many local attempts to improve mass-transit systems other than those discussed here. Some are quite innovative—for example, the monorail system being developed in West Virginia. But most merely rely on an increased use of buses and are sadly nonsystematic in their development and execution.

to get to work downtown would require the city to spend $23,000 on highways and supportive services in order for that car to be used [Vickrey 1973, p. 183]. With the present prices of automobiles, gasoline, and highway construction and maintenance increasing rapidly, a family could actually save a sizable sum each year by supporting mass transit and not buying one or more cars. By spending less on highway construction, the average city could provide quick, citywide bus service with no increase in local taxes.

Once the federal Department of Transportation gains some power in Congress, it can also serve as an effective coordinator for those lobbying for more mass-transit funds. Presently, both the executive and congressional branches of government are giving only token financing to mass transit. This tokenism is a result of the power of those groups opposing mass transit. Not surprisingly, the American Automobile Association (AAA), the auto industry, highway construction companies, and the oil and gasoline industry are among the chief lobbyists against mass transit. There is great concern over the effect mass transit will have on these groups (although the "needs" of the AAA are hardly crucial to America). Ideally, any comprehensive, national mass-transit program will *effectively* utilize such industries as automobile manufacturing to develop and build mass-transit systems.

Even if such systems are developed and well financed, America must also rid itself of the idea that mass transit is essentially a service to the downtown area. Although such a service is of immense help to a city like New York, which has over 800,000 people leaving the central business district (CBD) during peak rush-hour traffic [Rasmussen 1973, p. 124], it would do little for most smaller cities, which usually have, at most, only 10 to 15 percent of their population working in the CBD. Rather, mass transit must be comprehensive enough to serve the city as a whole. Although it is difficult for us to imagine taking a Sunday ride on a monorail or a bus, this is exactly what must come about, given our present large urban population and our need to conserve energy.

Any good mass-transit system would not only have to be convenient and comfortable, but it would also have to serve as an impetus for curbing urban crime. People can hardly be expected to use a bus or train if there is a high probability that they will be mugged or assaulted in the process. Of all the problems discussed in this chapter, urban transportation could be the one most readily solved once a national commitment was made to mass transit. And a good mass-transit system would also increase the visibility of all aspects of the city to all people. In the long run it is hoped that this visibility would, in itself, help urbanites to understand that their community is made up of a wide variety of people with diverse needs and interests. Should this understanding ever come about, mass transit would be helping not only to transport people but also to foster a sense of community spirit.[11]

As a final note to this discussion of urban delivery systems, it should be apparent that all urban services, and not just health and transportation, are faced with nearly overpowering financial problems. In fact, all problems discussed in this chapter require some type of financial strength as a major factor for the solution of the problem. In the next section, we see that although a great deal is asked from urban financing, it has only been able to deliver economic resources that are far below what is needed.

URBAN FINANCES: SOME WOULD CALL IT BANKRUPTCY

In addition to the economic complexities associated with the problems already discussed, each American city has its own financial crisis in trying to provide funds for all the services, facilities, and personnel supported by the city. The National Commission on Urban Problems has concluded that there is " . . . extensive evidence of a present and growing crisis for urban government financing" [1968, p. 355]. According to this commission, this crisis is brought about by   1. an increased demand for urban services,   2. a rapid rise in overall urban expenditures,   3. mounting opposition to urban taxation, and 4. the inability of most cities to tap the economic capacity of the entire metropolitan area surrounding them [1968, p. 355].[12]

---

11. The actual influence that transportation will have on the communication between subpopulations of the city is not yet known, but its impact will be great. What is more, as modern systems of communication increase (especially those aided by computers and visual images), the urbanite of the future will be able to do at home many tasks that once required a journey to the CBD, a local bank, and so forth. For some interesting speculation on the future role of communications and transportation, see Johnson [1971].

12. All financial decisions of the city are governed by political processes discussed elsewhere in this book. Also, there are specific economic considerations (such as the manufacturing and consumption of goods) that affect the city but are not germane to the discussion here. The reader is referred to the following for an understanding of these topics: Baumol [1967], Buchanan [1970], Perloff and Wingo [1968], Weisbrod [1964], and Whitelaw [1970].

The increasing deficit of urban finances is nearing bankruptcy. The National Committee for Economic Development made the projection that between 1965 and 1975 urban revenues will have increased by 82.4 percent while urban expenditures will have increased by 102.9 percent [Rasmussen 1973, p. 141]. Although this financial dilemma has long been predicted [Still 1974], like all other urban problems, little or nothing has been done to prevent it from reaching crisis proportions.

Finding Money: Taxes

Most local urban revenue has been gained through taxation. However, taxes alone cannot even begin to meet expenditures, nor are they equitable in their application. Property taxes usually are erroneously assessed below real property values [Goodall 1968] and are often assessed so as to place a greater burden on the private home owner, thereby favoring business and industry. A local sales tax not only increases the price of any retail good but is also regressive in that the poor are forced to pay the same rate of tax as the rich [Netzer 1970]. Any local income tax also favors the wealthy if it is based on one's federal income tax. Finally, some cities tax utilities or charge a service fee for sewage, water, and other related urban utilities and services. Again, such practices are regressive in that large users of such services (such as, local industry) are not charged the same percentage as the average private citizen.

In addition to the inequities of these taxes and their inability to meet urban expenses, the urban financial crisis is being compounded by a growing hostility to any additional increase in taxes. More and more bond and revenue issues are being defeated in the cities despite urgent appeals for their passage. Although most citizens are dissatisfied with the services and government of their city, few want to pay higher taxes in order to improve them.

However, probably no financial problem facing the city is as great as the fiscal fragmentation that exists in most metropolitan areas. Increasingly, cities are becoming surrounded by suburban and satellite communities that are themselves incorporated. Although the residents of these areas utilize the central city for shopping, business transactions, and recreation, they provide little or no overall input into local government revenues. Rasmussen summarizes the intensity of this fragmentation by pointing out, "Only six of the 117 large SMSA's have fewer than 20 political subdivisions, while 29 have more than 200" [Rasmussen 1973, p. 145].

The fiscal imbalance that exists between the central city and municipal areas surrounding it is especially serious when one considers the intensity and scope of the problems of the central city. As seen previously, the effects of poor housing and of inadequate educational, health, and transportation facilities affect the poor of the central city more adversely than any other segment of urban population. Yet, it is this same population that is forced to live with a local government that cannot meet the expenses for possible solutions to these problems.

Some cities have tried to overcome this problem through a high sales tax. Anything the suburbanite buys in the city contributes to the tax revenues of the city. But, as previously pointed out, the poor of the central city suffer from such a tax. Other cities have tried to put a "work-tax" into effect so that those who work in the central city must pay a type of income tax even though they do not live in the city. This tax is difficult to implement, since it is strongly opposed by businesses whose employees would suffer from such a tax. Also, the legality of this type of tax has not yet been fully adjudicated.

A final solution to fiscal fragmentation comes in the form of consolidation, that is, the entire metropolitan area, or county it is found in, is consolidated under one government. Most consolidation, however, is not so all-encompassing. Present attempts at consolidation usually retain the legal integrity of all participating communities while providing for the sharing of certain services in common. More often than not, consolidation extends to only some services (e.g., fire protection, weed control) while leaving basic institutions (such as, education) in the hands of the individual communities. Such limited consolidation is a reflection of the compromises necessary to get noncentral-city dwellers to agree to even partial involvement with the central city.

Jacksonville, Florida, represents one of the few examples of total consolidation. Through voter approval, Jacksonville established a consolidated government that covers all but four small communities of Duval County, in which Jacksonville is located. As a result of this consolidation, Jacksonville, with an area of 827 square miles, is now the largest city of developed land in the Western Hemisphere. Although such a consolidation eliminates duplication of personnel and services throughout Duval County, its effectiveness has still not been established.

Jacksonville can hardly serve as a model for all of America because most states have stringent laws governing consolidation. It also is difficult, if not impossible, to get suburban voters to approve consolidation. Most communities surrounding a central city either have been there for generations or were developed by people who "fled" the problems of the central city. These people see little or no advantage in coming under the auspices of one central government. A more recent obstacle to consolidation stems from a latent consequence of the Supreme Court ruling on busing of July 25, 1974. As noted earlier, this ruling prohibits busing across school district boundaries. Opponents to consolidation can now appeal to prejudice by pointing out that suburbanites can retain their segregated schools only if they retain control of their community. Central cities will have to look elsewhere for a solution to fiscal fragmentation, since consolidation is simply not a viable alternative for most cities.

Finding Money: The Federal Government

Having realized that consolidation is often impossible and that local taxes cannot meet financial needs, leaders of cities are forced to seek out federal funds allotted to various federal programs. But, as discussed earlier in this chapter, these funds, when tied to a particular program, greatly inhibit local control and are often too narrow in scope to help the city fully. More and more cities, therefore, are turning to the federal government not for bureaucractic programs but for *direct* financial help. The famed economist John Kenneth Galbraith states the rationale for such a trend in the most emphatic of terms: "The great economic anachronism of our time is that economic growth gives the federal government the revenues while, along with the population increase, it gives the states and especially the cities the problems. The one unit of government gets the money, the other gets the work" [Quoted in Weidenbaum 1971, p. 134]. Galbraith's words take on a greater significance when one considers the fact that although more than seven out of ten Americans live in cities, the term "city" is not even mentioned in the United States Constitution. Such an omission is based on the historical dual partnership of federal and state governments. As Article X of the original Bill of Rights states, "The powers not delegated to the United States by the Constitution, nor prohibited by it to the states, are reserved to the States respectively, or to the people." Although the Founding Fathers could not foresee the dominant role that cities would eventually play in America, through practice the city has been added as the third partner of the federal and state governments [Martin 1965, p. 108]. This active interplay between cities and the federal government began in the 1930s as a result of the Depression. However, even as late as the early 1960s, direct federal grant-in-aid payments to cities still comprised less than 15 percent of all federal payments to state and local governments [Martin 1965].

To increase the direct flow of funds to the cities, Professor Walter W. Heller, an economist from the University of Minnesota, proposed a significant new plan while serving under Presidents Kennedy and Johnson. Under the Heller Plan, some portion of the national income tax would be shared with the states for them to spend as they saw fit [Heller & Peckman 1967]. The eventual adoption of a modified version of the Heller Plan has placed American cities on a new course of financial action known as revenue sharing.

The primary aim of revenue sharing is the congressional sharing of funds with states, major cities, and urban counties [The National Commission on Urban Problems 1968, pp. 378–379]. The actual revenue shared comes from a trust fund established by Congress; local shares of this fund are allotted according to population.

Major revenue sharing legislation was passed by Congress in the State and Local Fiscal Assistance Act of 1972. The trust fund established by this act runs for five years and totals $30.2 billion for allocation to 38,000 state and local governments [Teska 1972].

The rationale for revenue sharing is based both on the financial crisis confronting local governments and on the premise known as "the new federalism," which affirms that local governments, and not the federal government, must play the major role in America's internal policies [Heller 1973]. On the surface, the notion of revenue sharing and the rationale of "the new federalism" sound as though they were made to order for America's cities. However, both revenue sharing and "the new federalism" may be only temporary pain-killers. First, in spite of all the political rhetoric to the contrary, there is nothing inherent in revenue sharing that would cause cities to act quickly and wisely in solving urban problems. In fact, throughout this chapter we have made reference to a *national* housing policy, a *national* commitment to eradicating poverty, and so forth. This call for a *national* perspective goes against the notion of the new federalism, since the latter is really a step backward to the days in which the groundwork for many of America's contemporary urban problems was laid. Second, revenue sharing, as such, mainly provides cities with a limited amount of money. Governor Bruce King of New Mexico, criticized Congress for not giving the states and cities enough money in its first try at revenue sharing. Although Governor King and others who hold this position may be correct about the need for more money, their demands only point to the fact that local governments will be asking for larger and larger revenue sharing funds to spend as they wish. The crisis of the nation's cities dictates that any revenue sharing program must be tied in with national policies that can be effectively carried out at the local level. To allow cities, for example, to use revenue sharing funds to build more segregated schools or more highways will only worsen the educational and transportation problems of the city. Revenue sharing per se, therefore, cannot solve the problems of the cities if cities are allowed to pursue their present course of avoiding the underlying dimensions of urban problems: poverty, prejudice, poor planning, and public apathy. A redefinition of priorities must be established to break the chains holding civic leaders to past spending behavior. Urban officials must no longer be allowed to make budget decisions on the basis of the wishes of powerful business and special-interest groups.[13] More often than not, such groups do not represent the needs of the people as a whole. Only a watchful public concerned about its plight can ensure that urban funds are spent on problems affecting them.

A FEW FINAL WORDS

Today's critical urban problems must be solved before "the urban crisis" becomes "the urban catastrophe." Although our discussion has at times been very critical of some of the attempts to cure America's cities of their ills, such criticism is not totally negative. At least these attempts are a beginning from which we can learn. At the same time, however, we owe it to both present and future generations to move on to new solutions. Too often, when people think of needed resources for the solving of urban problems, they think only in terms of money; most assuredly, little can be done in modern America without a great deal of funds. Yet, in the truest sense of the word, resources also include the imagination, involvement, and dedication of people. At the beginning of this chapter we quoted C. Wright Mills's provocative words concerning the challenge of the cities. However, in light of what has been presented here, a redirecting and rewording of Mills's quotation is in order.

> Or consider America—the most prosperous nation in the world. What should be done concerning its urban problems? Leave them to politicians and

---

13. Urban officials also are often ill-trained in the management and spending of money. In fact, many budget proposals and decisions are left in the hands of individual bureaucrats and agencies. The P.P.B.S. (planning-programming-budgeting system) is one technique to overcome this practice. Under P.P.B.S., overall urban goals are established and local urban funds are allotted from a central government to accomplish these goals [Weidenbaum 1971]. Of course, even such a plan as P.P.B.S. does not guarantee that money will be directed toward problem-solving goals.

short-sighted administrators? Let them continue on as they have in the past? Or ignore them and let our cities be destroyed? If not, how do we make people aware of the problems facing them? And how do we get these people to do something about them?

The answer to these questions comes in the form of urbanites finding a sense of community in the city they live in. It also comes in the form of all Americans realizing that urban problems are societal problems and must be dealt with on a national level. National programs must be taken away from the vested interests of a few powerful business and political groups and must be reoriented to a face-to-face confrontation with the task of actually *solving* urban problems. The federal government must work closely with the people of the city (and not just with the city's officials) to discover the needs of the city as well as the talent available for solving these needs. "We need, quite literally, to 'go to the people' with a question that is almost never asked of them: 'What kind of a world do you want ten, twenty, or thirty years from now?' We need to initiate, in short, a continuing plebiscite on the future" [Toffler 1970]. In essence, federal programs must not only be carried out *for* people but also *with* people. Furthermore, federal standards must be developed and enforced to ensure that cities carry out programs directed at curing urban problems. Such standards would also ensure a national uniformity of procedure as well as a national commitment to enforce the effective planning and implementation of policies aimed at helping urban populations directly [Martin 1965]. To do this, Americans must acknowledge the fact that national standards and programs facilitate the centralization needed for a coordinated effort at problem solving.

Finally, it must be emphasized that although this chapter and the extensive references accompanying it provide the student with an overview of some of the nation's most critical urban problems, it is up to the student to pursue an even deeper understanding of the problems presented here.

BIBLIOGRAPHY

Albert L. Alford, "Nonproperty Taxes for Schools." In Patricia C. Sexton, ed., *School Policy and Issues in a Changing Society.* Allyn and Bacon, 1971.

LeRoy B. Allen, "Replications of the Educational Park Concept for the Disadvantaged." *Journal of Negro Education,* Summer, 1970: 225–233.

Alan A. Altshuler, *Community Control: The Black Demand for Participation in Large American Cities.* Pegasus Press, 1970.

Martin Anderson, "The Myth of Urban Renewal." In Robert L. Branyan and Lawrence H. Larsen, eds., *Urban Crisis in Modern America.* D. C. Health, 1971.

The Atlanta Journal. "MARTA Marriage." 17 April 1974, p. 20A.

Stephen S. Baratz and Joan C. Baratz, "Early Childhood Intervention: The Social Science Basis of Institutional Racism." *Harvard Educational Review,* 1970, 40: 29–47.

W. J. Baumol, "Macroeconomics of Unbalanced Growth: The Anatomy of Urban Crisis." *American Economic Review,* 1967, 57: 415–426.

Robert J. Bazell, "Health Radicals: Crusade to Shift Medical Power to the People." *Science,* 1971, 173: 506–509.

Bernard Beck, "Welfare as a Moral Category." In Max Birnbaum and John Mogey, eds., *Social Change in Urban America.* Harper & Row, 1972.

Jewel Bellush and Murray Hausknecht, eds., *Urban Renewal: People, Politics, and Planning.* Anchor Press/Doubleday, 1967.

C. S. Benson, *The Economics of Education.* Houghton Mifflin, 1968.

B. H. Bode, *Modern Educational Theories.* Vintage Books, 1965.

Samuel Bowles and Henry M. Levin, "The Determinants of Scholastic Achievement—An Appraisal of Some Recent Evidence." *Journal of Human Resources.* Winter, 1968.

Lester Breslow, "Changing Patterns of Medical Care and Support." *Journal of Medical Education,* 1966, 41:318–324.

Brent C. Brolin and John Zeisel, "Mass Housing: Social Research and Design." *Architectural Forum,* July–August 1968.

Barry A. Brown, "Citizen Opposition to a Suburban Freeway, A Semi-Hypothetical Scenario: The Seattle Experience." *1972 Urban Law Annual.* Washington Universtiy Press, 1972.

James M. Buchanan, "Public Goods and Public Bads." In John P. Crecine, ed., *Financing the Metropolis.* Vol. 4. Urban Affairs Annual Reviews. Sage Publications, 1970.

William F. Buckley, Jr. "Unemployment: A Key to Affluence." *Cincinnati Enquirer,* 14 April 1974.

Bonnie Bullough, "Alienation in the Ghetto." *American Journal of Sociology,* 1967, 72:469–478.

J. B. Calhoun, "Population Density and Social Pathology." *Scientific American,* 1962, 206:139–148.

J. B. Calhoun, "The Role of Space in Animal Sociology." *Journal of Social Issues,* 1966, 22:46–59.

Douglas L. Carnahan and Omer R. Galle, "Needed Research in the Study of Population Density." Report Submitted to the Southern Regional Demographic Group, June 1973.

Rey A. Carr and Gerald C. Hayward, "Education by Chit: An Examination of Voucher Proposals." *Education and Urban Society,* 1970, 2:179–191.

George M. Carstairs, "Overcrowding and Human Aggression." *The History of Violence in America.* Bantam Books, 1969.

Ann Cartwright, *Patients and Their Doctors.* Atherton Press, 1967.

J. Christian, V. Flyger, and D. Davis, "Factors in the Mass Mortality of a Herd of Sika Deer *Cerus Nippon.*" *Chesapeake Science,* 1960, 1:79–95.

Richard A. Cloward and Frances Fox Piven, "We've Got Rights! The No-Longer Silent Welfare Poor." *New Republic,* 5 August 1967, pp. 23–37.

Richard M. Coe, *Sociology of Medicine.* McGraw-Hill, 1970.

David K. Cohen, "The Economics of Inequality." *Saturday Review,* 19 April, 1969, pp. 64–65, 76–79.

Fred Cohen and Marc Weiss, "Big Business and Urban Stagnation." In W. Ron Jones, ed., *Finding Community.* James E. Freel and Associates, 1971.

J. S. Coleman, "Toward Open Schools." *Public Interest,* Fall 1967, pp. 20–27.

J. S. Coleman et al. *Equality of Educational Opportunity.* U.S. Government Printing Office, 1966.

Robert Coles, "Like It Is in the Alley." In Ted Venetoulis and Ward Eisenhauer, eds., *Up Against the Urban Wall.* Prentice-Hall, 1971.

Ronald G. Corwin, *Education in Crisis: A Sociological Analysis of Schools and Universities in Transition.* John Wiley and Sons, 1974.

Lewis A. Coser, "The Sociology of Poverty." *Social Problems,* 1965, 13:140–148.

Robert L. Crain and David Street, "School Desegregation and School Decision-Making." In Marilyn Gittell and Alan G. Hevesi, eds., *The Politics of Urban Education.* Praeger, 1969.

Stephen M. Creel, "Our Backward Medical Schools." *Atlantic,* 1966, 217:46–50.

L. J. Cronbach and R. E. Snow, *Individual Differences in Learning Ability as a Function of Instructional Variables.* U.S. Office of Education. U.S. Government Printing Office, 1969.

Allison Davis, "Motivation of the Underprivileged Worker." In William F. White, ed., *Industry and Society.* McGraw-Hill, 1946.

Anthony Downs, *Urban Problems and Prospects.* Markham, 1970.

Anthony Downs, "Comments." In Daniel R. Mandelker and Roger Montgomery, eds., *Housing in America: Problems and Prospects.* Bobbs-Merrill, 1973.

R. Dreeben, *On What Is Learned in School.* Addison-Wesley, 1968.

Thomas R. Dye, "Urban School Segregation: A Comparative Analysis." *Urban Affairs Quarterly,* 1968, 4:141–165.

Barbara Ehrenreich, *The American Health Empire: Power, Profits and Politics.* Random House, 1970.

Jason Epstein, "The Politics of School Decentralization." *New York Review of Books,* 6 June, 1968, pp. 26–31.

Amitai Etzioni, "The Fallacy of Decentralization." *Nation,* 25 August 1969, pp. 145–147.

I. S. Falk, "Medical Care in the U.S.A.—1932–1972." *Milbank Memorial Fund Quarterly,* 1973, 51:1–32.

Mario Fantini, "Community Participation." *Harvard Educational Review,* 1968, 38:160–175.

Reynolds Farley, "Racial Integration in the Public Schools, 1967 to 1972: Assessing the Effect of Governmental Policies." *Sociological Focus,* 1975, 8(1):1–26.

R. E. L. Farris and H. W. Dunham, *Mental Disorders in Urban Areas.* University of Chicago Press, 1939.

Joseph Featherstone, "The Problem Is More Than Schools." *New Republic,* 30 August 1969, pp. 20–23.

Ashley A. Foard and Hilbert Fefferman, "Federal Urban Renewal Legislation." *Law and Contemporary Politics,* 1960, 25:635–684.

Nelson N. Foote and Paul K. Hatt, "Social Mobility and Economic Advancement." *American Economic Review,* 1953, 43:364–378.

Marc Fried, "Grieving for a Lost Home." In Marc Fried, ed., *The Urban Condition.* Basic Books, 1963.

Marc Fried and Peggy Gleicher, "Some Sources of Residential Satisfaction in an Urban Slum." *Journal of the American Institute of Planners,* 1961, 27:305–315.

Bernard J. Frieden, "Housing and National Urban Goals: Old Policies and New Realities." In Louis K. Loewenstein, ed., *Urban Studies.* The Free Press, 1971.

M. Friedman, "The Role of Government in Education." In C. S. Benson, ed., *Perspectives in the Economics of Education.* Houghton Mifflin, 1963.

Eliot Friedson, *Profession of Medicine: A Study of the Sociology of Applied Knowledge.* Dodd, Mead, 1970.

Omer R. Galle, Walter R. Gove, and J. Miller McPherson, "Population Density and Pathology: What Are the Relations for Man?" *Science,* 1972, 176:23–30.

Herbert J. Gans, "The Human Implications of Current Redevelopment and Relocation Planning." *Journal of the American Institute of Planners,* 1959, 25:15–25.

Herbert J. Gans, *On Understanding Poverty.* Edited by Daniel P. Moynihan. American Academy of Arts and Sciences. Basic Books, 1968.

Herbert J. Gans, "The Failure of Urban Renewal: A Critique and Some Proposals." In David W. Rasmussen and Charles T. Haworth, eds., *The Modern City: Readings in Urban Economics.* Harper & Row, 1973a.

Herbert J. Gans, "The Uses of Poverty: The Poor Pay All." *Readings in Social Problems 1973–74*. Dushkin, 1973b.

Carl J. George and Daniel McKinley, *Urban Ecology: In Search of an Asphalt Rose*. McGraw-Hill, 1974.

Hendrick Gideonse, *Educational Research and Development in the United States*. U.S. Office of Education. U.S. Government Printing Office, 1970.

Marilyn Gittell, "Community Control of Education." *Urban Riots: Violence and Social Change*. Proceedings of the Academy of Political Science, 1968, 29:60–71.

Nathan Glazer, "For White and Black, Community Control Is the Issue." In Ted Venetoulis and Ward Eisenhauer, eds., *Up Against the Urban Wall*. Prentice-Hall, 1971.

Leonard Goodall, *The American Metropolis*. Charles E. Merrill, 1968.

Walter Gove and Herbert Costner, "Organizing the Poor: An Evaluation of a Strategy." *Social Science Quarterly*, 1969, 50:643–656.

Selig Greenberg, *The Quality of Mercy*. Atheneum, 1971.

Scott Greer, *Urban Renewal and American Cities*. Bobbs-Merrill, 1965.

William Griffitt and Russell Veitch, "Hot and Crowded: Influences of Population Density and Temperature on Interpersonal Affective Behavior." In Rudolf H. Moos and Paul M. Insel, eds., *Issues in Social Ecology*. National Press Books, 1974.

Charles F. Grosser, *New Directions in Community Organization: From Enabling to Advocacy*. Praeger, 1973.

Michael Harrington, *The Other America: Poverty in the United States*. Macmillan, 1962.

Chester W. Hartman, "The Housing of Relocated Families." In Jewel Bellush and Murray Hausknecht, eds., *Urban Renewal: People, Politics, and Planning*. Anchor Press/Doubleday, 1967.

Robert J. Havighurst, "Decentralization Versus Local Community Control in Large City School Systems." In Robert Havighurst, Bernice L. Neugarten, and Jacqueline M. Falk, eds., *Society and Education: A Book of Readings*. Allyn and Bacon, 1971.

Betty D. Hawkins, "Cities and the Environmental Crisis." In Melvin I. Urofsky, ed., *Perspectives on Urban America*. Anchor Press/Doubleday, 1973.

Walter W. Heller, "Should the Government Share Its Tax Take?" In David W. Rasmussen and Charles T. Haworth, eds., *The Modern City: Readings in Urban Economics*. Harper & Row, 1973.

Walter W. Heller and Joseph A. Peckman, *Revenue Sharing and Its Alternatives: What Future for Fiscal Federalism?* Hearings before the Subcommittee on Fiscal Policy of the Joint Economic Committee of the United States, 1967.

Robert E. Herriott and Nancy Hoyt St. John, *Social Class and the Urban School: The Impact of Pupil Background on Teachers and Principals*. John Wiley and Sons, 1966.

Raymond C. Hummel and John M. Nagle, *Urban Education in America: Problems and Prospects.* Oxford University Press, 1973.

Christopher Jencks et al. *A Reassessment of the Effect of Family and Schooling in America.* Basic Books, 1972.

Nicholas Johnson, "Urban Man and the Communications Revolution." In Ted Venetoulis and Ward Eisenhauer, eds., *Up Against the Urban Wall.* Prentice-Hall, 1971.

W. Ron Jones, ed., *Finding Community: A Guide to Community Research and Action.* James E. Freel and Associates, 1971.

Judith Kleinfeld, " 'Sense of Fate Control' and Community Control of the Schools." *Education and Urban Society,* 1971, 3:277–300.

Jonathan Kozol, "Death at an Early Age." In J. John Palen and Karl Fleming, eds., *Urban America: Conflict and Change.* Holt, Rinehart & Winston, 1972.

Jonathan Kozol, "Death at an Early Age." In A. David Hill et al., eds., *The Quality of Life in America.* Holt, Rinehart & Winston, 1973.

Frank S. Kristof, "Housing Policy Goals and the Turnover of Housing." *Journal of the American Institute of Planners,* 1965, 31:232–245.

Anthony J. La Greca and Kent P. Schwirian. "Social Class and Race as Factors of Residential Density." Paper presented at the Human Ecology session, Southern Sociological Society, Atlanta, Georgia, 1974.

Paul Lauter and Florence Howe, "How the School System is Rigged for Failure." *The Conspiracy of the Young.* World, 1970.

Joseph Lelyveld, "Obituary of Heroin Addict Who Died at 12." *The New York Times,* 12 January 1970, pp. 1 and 18.

H. Levin, "The Failure of the Public Schools and the Free Market Remedy." *Urban Review,* 1968, 2:32–37.

Daniel V. Levine, "The Crisis in Urban Education." In Melvin I. Urofsky, ed., *Perspectives on Urban America,* Anchor Press/Doubleday, 1972.

Gerald Levy, *Ghetto School.* Bobbs-Merrill, 1970.

Elliot Liebow, "Men and Jobs." In Susan S. Fainstein and Norman I. Fainstein, eds., *The View From Below: Urban Politics and Social Policy.* Little, Brown, 1972.

Michael Lipsky, "Rent Strikes: Poor Man's Weapons." *Trans-Action,* February 1969, pp. 10–15.

Daniel R. Mandelker and Roger Montgomery, eds., *Housing in Urban America: Problems and Prospects.* Bobbs-Merrill, 1973.

H. Marsden, "Crowding and Animal Behavior." Paper presented at the American Psychological Association Annual Convention, 1970.

Anthony J. Marsella, Manuel Escudero, and Paul Gordon, "The Effects of Dwelling Density on Mental Disorders in Filipino Men." *Journal of Health and Social Behavior,* 1970, 11:288–293.

Roscoe C. Martin, *The Cities and the Federal System.* Atherton Press, 1965.

David Mechanic, *Medical Sociology.* Free Press of Glencoe, 1968.

Medical Committee for Human Rights. "Statement to the American Medical Association." Presented at the American Medical Association National Convention, 1970.

William Michelson, "Social Insights to Guide the Design of the Housing for Low Income Families." *Critical Urban Housing Issues,* 1967, pp. 60–68.

Richard I. Miller, *Perspectives on Educational Change.* Appleton-Century-Crofts, 1967.

C. Wright Mills, *The Sociological Imagination.* Oxford University Press, 1959.

R. Mitchell, "Some Social Implications of High Density Housing." *American Sociological Review,* 1971, 36:18–29.

Emily Mumford and J. K. Skipper, Jr., *Sociology in Hospital Care.* Harper & Row, 1967.

R. F. Muth, "Urban Residential Land and Housing Markets." In Daniel R. Mandelker and Roger Montgomery, eds., *Housing in America: Problems and Prospects.* Bobbs-Merrill, 1973.

Gunnar Myrdal, *An American Dilemma.* Vol. 1. Harper, 1944.

The National Commission on Urban Problems, *Building the American City.* Report to the Congress and to the President of the United States. U.S. Government Printing Office, 1968.

National Institute of Education Information, "White Flight to Suburbs not Caused by Busing." Fall 1975, p. 1.

Dick Netzer, "Tax Structures and Their Impact on the Poor." In John P. Crecine, ed., *Financing the Metropolis.* Vol. 4. Urban Affairs Annual Reviews. Sage Publications, 1970.

Newsweek, "Battle of the Buses." 26 May 1975, 85(21):74.

The New York Times, "News Supplement." Reprinted in Gainesville, Florida *Sun,* 8 April 1974.

Edgar O. Olsen, "A Competitive Theory of the Housing Market." *American Economic Review,* September 1969, pp. 612–622.

Allan C. Ornstein, *Urban Education: Student Unrest, Teacher Behaviors, and Black Power.* Charles E. Merrill, 1972.

Elinor Ostrom and Gordon Whitaker, "Does Local Community Control of Police Make a Difference? Some Preliminary Findings." *American Journal of Political Science,* 1973, 17:48–76.

People's Medical Center, "The People's Medical Center." Redwood City, California, 1970.

Harvey S. Perloff and Loudon Wingo, Jr., *Issues in Urban Economics.* Johns Hopkins Press, 1968.

James S. Plant, "Family Living Space and Personality Development." In Norman W. Bell and Ezra F. Vogel, eds., *A Modern Introduction to the Family.* Free Press of Glencoe, 1960.

David Popenoe, "Urban Residential Differentiation: An Overview of Patterns, Trends, and Problems." *Sociological Inquiry,* 1973, 43:35–56.

Lee Rainwater, "Fear and the House-as-Haven in the Lower Class." *Journal of the American Institute of Planners*, 1966, 32:23–37.

David W. Rasmussen, *Urban Economics*. Harper & Row, 1973.

William K. Reilly, ed., *The Use of Land: A Citizen's Policy Guide to Urban Growth*. Crowell, 1973.

Julius B. Richmond, *Currents in American Medicine*. Harvard University Press, 1969.

Julius A. Roth, "The Treatment of the Sick." In John Kosa, Aaron Antonovsky, and Irving Zola, eds., *Poverty and Health: A Sociological Analysis*. Harvard University Press, 1969.

Lillian B. Rubin, "Maximum Feasible Participation: The Origins and Implications." In Susan S. Fainstein and Norman I. Fainstein, eds., *The View From Below: Urban Politics and Social Policy*. Little, Brown, 1972.

Robert C. Schmitt, "Implications of Density in Hong Kong." *Journal of the American Institute of Planners*, 1965, 29:210–217.

Robert C. Schmitt, "Density, Health and Social Organization." *Journal of the American Institute of Planners*, 1966, 32:38–40.

Alvin L. Schorr, "Housing and Its Effect." In Robert Gutman and David Popenoe, eds., *Neighborhood, City, and Metropolis*. Random House, 1970.

Robert Schwartz, Thomas Pettigrew, and Marshall Smith, "Fake Panaceas for Ghetto Education." In Max Birnbaum and John Mogey, eds., *Social Change in Urban America*. Harper & Row, 1972.

Kent P. Schwirian and Anthony J. La Greca, "An Ecological Analysis of Urban Mortality Rates." *Social Science Quarterly*, December 1971, pp. 574–587.

M. Scriven, "The Methodology of Evaluation." In R. E. Stake, ed., *Perspectives of Curriculum Evaluation*. Rand McNally, 1967.

Ben B. Seligman, *Poverty as a Public Issue*. Macmillan, 1965.

Patricia Cayo Sexton, *Education and Income: Inequalities of Opportunity in Our Public Schools*. Viking, 1961.

Theodore R. Sizer, "The Schools in the City." In James Q. Wilson, ed., *The Metropolitan Enigma*. Doubleday, 1967.

T. Sizer and P. Whitten, "A Proposal for a Poor Children's Bill of Rights." *Psychology Today*, 1968, 2:58–63.

W. F. Smith, *Housing: The Social and Economic Elements*. University of California Press, 1970.

Bayrd Still, *Urban America*. Little, Brown, 1974.

Daniel Stokols, "A Social-Psychological Model of Human Crowding Phenomena." *Journal of the American Institute of Planners*, 1972, 38:72–83.

Michael E. Stone, "Housing, Mortgages, and the State." In Daniel R. Mandelker and Roger Montgomery, eds., *Housing in America: Problems and Prospects*. Bobbs-Merrill, 1973.

Anselm L. Strauss, "Medical Ghettos." *Trans-Action*, 1967, 4:7–15.

Gerald D. Suttles, "Anatomy of a Chicago Slum." *Trans-Action*, 1969, 4:16–25.

Karl E. Taeuber and Alma F. Taeuber, *Negroes In Cities*. Aldine, 1965.

C. Teitz and Rosenthal. *Housing Code Enforcement in New York City.* Rand Institute, April, 1971. Also found in Daniel R. Mandelker and Roger Montgomery, eds., *Housing in Urban America: Problems and Prospects.* Bobbs-Merrill, 1973.

Allan Temko, "Good Buildings and the Good Life; An Interview with Allan Temko." *The Center Magazine,* 1969, 11:56–63.

Anona Teska, "The Federal Impact on the Cities." In Melvin I. Urofsky, ed., *Perspectives on Urban America.* Anchor Press/Doubleday, 1972.

Time, "Phase Two For Boston." 26 May 1975, 105(22):64.

Time, "Busing and Strikes: Schools in Turmoil." 15 September 1975, 106(11):35–36.

Alvin Toffler, *Future Shock.* Random House, 1970.

Robert M. Travers, "Educational Technology and Related Research Viewed as a Political Force." In Robert M. W. Travers, ed., *Second Handbook of Research on Teaching.* Rand McNally, 1973.

Martin Trow, "Two Problems in American Public Education." In Howard S. Becker, *Social Problems: A Modern Approach.* John Wiley and Sons, 1966.

Urban American and the Urban Coalition, Inc., *One Year Later.* Praeger, 1969.

Urban Planning Aid, Inc., "Evaluation of the Boston Rehabilitation Program." Urban Planning Aid, Inc., 1969.

U.S. Bureau of the Census, *Survey of Families Recently Displaced from Urban Renewal Sites.* U.S. Government Printing Office, 1965.

U.S. Commission of Civil Rights, *Racial Isolation in the Public Schools.* U.S. Government Printing Office, 1967.

U.S. Department of Health, Education, and Welfare. Urban Task Force. *Congressional Record.* U.S. Government Printing Office, 1970.

U.S. Department of Housing and Urban Development. *Housing Surveys, Part I.* "Occupants of New Housing Units, 1969." In Daniel R. Mandelker and Roger Montgomery, eds., *Housing in America: Problems and Prospects.* Bobbs-Merrill, 1973.

U.S. News and World Report, "Mounting Pressure to Curb Downtown Driving," 13 March 1972, pp. 74–77.

Charles A. Valentine, *Culture and Poverty.* University of Chicago Press, 1968.

William S. Vickrey, "Pricing in Urban and Suburban Transport." In David W. Rasmussen and Charles T. Haworth, eds., *The Modern City: Readings in Urban Economics.* Harper & Row, 1973.

Adam Walinsky, "Keeping the Poor in Their Place: Notes on the Importance of Being One-Up." In A. David Hill et al., eds., *The Quality of Life in America.* Holt, Rinehart and Winston, 1973.

Melvin M. Webber, "Comprehensive Planning and Social Responsibility." In Bernard J. Frieden and Robert Morris, eds., *Urban Planning and Social Policy.* Basic Books, 1968.

Murray L. Weidenbaum, "The Sagging Finances of States and Cities—How Washington Can Help." In Ted Venetoulis and Ward Eisenhauer, eds., *Up Against the Urban Wall*. Prentice-Hall, 1971.

Burton A. Weisbrod, "Collective Consumption Aspects of Individual Consumption Goods." *Quarterly Journal of Economics*, 1964, 78:471–477.

W. Whitelaw, "The City, City Hall, and the Municipal Budget." In John P. Crecine, ed., *Financing the Metropolis*. Vol. 4. Urban Affairs Annual Reviews. Sage Publications, 1970.

Preston Wilcox, "Integration or Separatism in Education." In Robert Havighurst, Bernice L. Neugarten, and Jacqueline Falk, eds., *Society and Education: A Book of Readings*. Allyn and Bacon, 1971.

H. Winsborough, "The Social Consequences of High Population Density." *Law and Contemporary Problems*, 1965, 30:120–126.

Dennis L. Wittman, "Property Tax Relief: A Viable Adjunct to Housing Policy?" In *1972 Urban Law Annual*, Washington University Press, 1972.

Nathan Wright, *Let's Work Together*. Hawthorne, 1968.

Louis Zurcher and William Key, "The Overlap Model: A Comparison of Strategies for Social Change." *Sociological Quarterly*, 1968, 10:85–96.

7.

VIOLENCE IN URBAN SOCIETY

Robert M. Jiobu

Violence in the city has become a major social problem. Scarcely a day passes without some news reports of homicides, muggings, rapes, and collective turmoil. In the back of their minds, many, perhaps most, residents of large cities constantly fear violent assault, theft, and burglary. Indeed, the problem of "law and order" emerged as a major campaign issue during the 1968 presidential election and remains a current topic.

In this unit we will be considering the problem of urban violence: what is it and what causes it? Because so many acts of violence are illegal, we will also consider selected aspects of crime. But, as with any objective discourse, it is first necessary to arrive at a clear understanding of what is meant by the central subject matter, in this case, violence.

WHAT IS VIOLENCE?

Everyone has some notions about the meaning of violence, but it is extremely difficult to specify a precise working definition that is suitable for social science analysis. *Webster's New World Dictionary* includes the following in the definition of violence: physical force used so as to injure or damage; use of force so as to injure or damage; severity; as, the violence of the storm; unjust use of force or power, as in deprivation of rights; great force or strength of feeling; distortion of meaning, phrasing; as, to do violence to a text; desecration; profanation.

The term violence obviously possesses many different meanings For our purposes, however, employing such a diversity of meanings would lead to a great deal of confusion. Consequently, for now, let us restrict our nominal usage of the term to the second meaning, that is, the use of force so as to injure or damage. Even this restriction leaves us with large areas of ambiguity. What, for example, constitutes force and injury or damage? The answers to such questions can be quite philosophical, but in this unit, the meanings shall be restricted to *physical* force and *physical* damage or injury. At the same time, we should recognize that we are leaving out vast areas of behavior. A great deal of damage and injury is caused by verbal and social abuse; yet if we were to include this category of behavior in our inquiry we would be drawn into an almost endless discourse that touched upon such topics as arguments, child-parent relations, marital discord, and the like. Lastly, let us specify that the physical abuse or damage must be done by humans. Although we will be examining, in passing, some studies performed with animal subjects, we shall do so in order to illuminate human behavior.

By restricting our inquiry to humans, we remove from consideration behaviors such as dogs biting men. It is not that these behaviors are unimportant, but simply that to consider them would lead us rather far afield from our main concern.

Thus far we have been discussing a nominal definition of violence, that is, a definition framed solely in terms of conceptual categories without actually looking at specific behaviors to ascertain whether or not people would consider them acts of violence. The question of the operational definition of violence, that is, which acts are considered violent, makes the inquiry even murkier. For example, a recent national survey of American males conducted by the Michigan Survey Research Center, presented respondents with a list of specific behaviors and asked if they were considered violent. Their findings are presented in table 1.

T A B L E 1. Percentage of Respondents' Definitions of Certain Acts as Violence (N = 1,374)

Do you think of _____ as violence?

	Yes (%)	No (%)	Both (%)	Total (%)
Looting	85	3	12	100
Burglary	65	5	30	100
Draft card burning	58	4	38	100
Police beating students	56	14	30	100
Not letting people have their civil rights	49	8	43	100
Student protest	38	15	47	100
Police shooting looters	35	8	57	100
Sit-ins	22	9	69	100
Police stopping to frisk people	16	10	74	100

Source: Adapted from Blumenthal et al. 1972.

The table shows that the majority (over 50 percent) of respondents considered many acts of force that were directed against inanimate targets to be violent. For example, looting, burglary, and draft-card burning were considered violent acts, but these do not involve human targets, although they are obviously carried out by humans. Conversely, several acts involving humans were not considered violent by the majority of respondents: police shooting looters, police stopping to frisk people, and depriving people of their civil rights. Of these behaviors, one involves physical damage by a human to another human (police shooting looters). Also note that only a scant majority (56 percent) felt that police beating students was an act of violence.

What does all this mean? If nothing else, it demonstrates the disparity that is often seen when comparing nominal definitions with operational ones. Police shooting looters is not perceived to be violent, but the act of looting itself is considered violent. It has been suggested [Blumenthal et al. 1972] that whenever the legitimate arm of society engages in physical force to damage or injure someone, ipso facto this is not an act of violence. In other words, the legitimacy of the actors at least partly defines violence. No matter what our political orientation towards the police, the fact remains that they are the sole body that has the legal and legitimate right to commit violence in order to insure compliance. Obviously, this is not an unrestricted right, but the average citizen has virtually no right personally to commit violent acts.

Legitimacy has been defined as the collective judgment that attributes goodness, morality, or righteousness to behavior [Ball-Rokeach 1972]. As such, it plays a powerful role in guiding behavior. Legitimacy may be thought of as a continuum, ranging from legitimate at one pole to illegitimate at the other. Between these two extremes lies an area of nonlegitimacy (neutral). Consequently, the question is *how* legitimate is an act of violence. In addition, we must ask, "legitimate for *whom?*" Are the standards of the broader society involved or are they the standards of some special subgroup? [Gerson 1968] From this perspective, certain factors that might influence the degree of legitimacy of a specific violent act are specific subgroup criteria. For example, if "supermasculinity" is highly valued among many delinquent gangs, individual members can validate their status through engaging in violence. A number of other factors that influence legitimacy have been identified [Ball-Rokeach 1972]:

1. *The social closeness of the person(s) to each other.* For example, when a person commits an act of violence, he may feel compelled to legitimize the act to those who are close to him—friend, family, neighbors, and the like. Similarly, those close to the person may be especially prone to accepting claims to legitimacy as a means of justifying the action.

2. *Criminal status of the act.* Regardless of whether close friends and family accept the legitimacy of a violent act, certain acts are generally regarded as violent by the society at large. For example, terrorist activity such as random bombings may appear to be quite illegitimate to the population at large, and constitute a crime.

3. *Novelty of the violent act.* For certain acts, it may be that they are so new that no consensus exists as to whether the act is legitimate or not. Some recent investigations into the killings of participants in protest, such as occurred at Kent State University where National Guardsmen fired into a crowd of students, basically seek to resolve the question of whether the acts were legitimate.

4. *Value conflicts.* There are certain areas for which no consensus really exists, or for which the existing consensus is brought into question. Much of the furor over abortion results from the conflicting opinions as to whether or not the killing of the foetus is legitimate. (No one argues that the foetus is not alive, although much debate centers about whether or not it is really human.)

5. *Justification.* Societal consensus provides several legitimate reasons for committing violence. First, in many instances the end justifies the means. National security, law and order, and self-defense are common justifications for the use of violence. When the justification is accepted, the violence becomes legitimate. Second, obedience to higher authority may be invoked. "I was simply following orders" is often used, particularly in a military or police situation. This justification has been invoked from the Nuremberg war trials to Mai Lai to the shootings at Kent State. Indeed, one of the central concerns in investigation of the Kent State shooting was whether or not National Guardsmen were in fact following orders from higher authority. Finally, extenuating circumstances may be used to justify violence. Common defenses for homicide are temporary insanity, the influence of drugs or alcohol, and extraordinary circumstances such as combat. The important point is that we normally accept certain justifications for violence and once they are accepted, the issue is "resolved." While these justifications may not legitimate the acts, they at least prevent both legal and social sanctions.

Closely related to questions of legitimacy, is the role that intent plays in defining violence. Presumably, when the policemen shoots a looter, he intends to enforce the law; he is not simply striking out at anyone without reason. By the same token, when a parent spanks his child or when a doctor performs surgery, the intent is to benefit someone else. Normally, such behaviors are not classified as illegitimate violence, but if a mugger cuts a victim or a parent beats his child with a club, these are considered illegitimate violent acts. Is it an act of violence when a motorist accidently runs over a pedestrian? The answer is not quite so clear, presumably because of the absence of intent on the part of the motorist, although he had no legitimate right to hit the pedestrian.

Finally, the whole issue of legitimacy can be put aside by simply defining certain categories of persons as "nonhumans," or by increasing their remoteness. Slaves, members of certain minority groups, "the enemy," and others may at some time fall into this category. When they do, the necessity to legitimate acts of violence against them ceases to exist since they are outside the framework to which legitimacy applies. Roy Bean, the famed judge of the Old West, is reputed to have dismissed charges against a cowboy who killed a Chinese person on the basis that homicide laws only applied to whites. In other words, the act was nonlegitimate as opposed to illegitimate.

Making the object of violence remote also tends to remove the necessity to legitimate violence. It may be easier for a bomber pilot to kill one hundred people than for a foot soldier to kill one person. For the bomber pilot, the consequences of violence are remote: he neither sees nor hears the results of his bombs. The foot soldier must confront his victim face to face.

These points illustrate some of the mechanisms by which violent acts are redefined as legitimate. Thus, violence is divided into two types: "good" violence and "bad" violence. Every society accepts certain violent acts as necessary and commonplace (although not every member of society must agree). The issue is not whether we should tolerate violence, the controversy centers instead on the goodness of specific acts of violence. As was shown in table 1, a certain amount of disagreement on this question exists; and, as one might guess, the legitimacy of a violent act varies in different subgroups within society. For example, the data shown in table 1 may be rearranged as follows in table 2 (see page 6).

Note that the overwhelming number of both blacks and college students view police beating students as violence whereas less than 50 percent of white union members do so. Moreover the denial of civil rights is viewed as violence by the majority of college students and blacks, since both groups may feel particularly oppressed in this regard. Finally, note that less than 50 percent of college students and only 23 percent of white union members consider police shooting looters as violence but 59 percent of blacks do consider it violence. That the black percentage is so low attests to the powerful role that legitimacy plays in defining violence since blacks are the most probable target. In addition to specific acts then, the answer to the question of "what is violence?" depends

T A B L E 2. Percentage of Respondents' (in Selected Subgroups) Definition of Certain Acts as Violent

Do you think of _____ as violence?

	College Students (%)	College and Post Graduate Degree Holders (%)	White Union Members (%)	Blacks (%)
Police Beating Students	79	66	45	82
Police Shooting Looters	43	50	23	59
Police Frisking	16	16	10	34
Looting	76	79	91	74
Burglary	47	54	67	70
Student Protest	18	22	43	23
Sit-ins	4	13	24	15
Draft Card Burning	26	35	63	51
Denial of Civil Rights	54	45	40	70

Source: Adapted from Blumenthal et al. 1972.

on the legitimacy of the act, and this is determined by several factors outlined above. Moreover, table 2 indicates that there is widespread consensus as to legitimacy on only a few acts (for example, looting, frisking, and sit-ins) among different groups in American society. Consequently, the controversy surrounding the problem of violence is not surprising. Violence is dramatic and, in many cases, horrifying, but it is a commonplace occurrence about which a great deal of dissensus exists.

In sum, when discussing violence, it is vitally important that we recognize precisely what we mean by the term. Several elements must be taken into account including damage or injury, human versus nonhuman aggressors, legitimacy, intent, and nominal versus operational definitions. All of these factors play a role, and the importance of any one factor will vary in accordance with the purpose of the discussion. For example, in studies of criminal violence, intent and legitimacy may be quite important because they, in part, are what determines whether or not a crime has been committed. If a policeman intended specifically to kill a looter who could have been easily subdued by verbal commands, the policeman may be charged with a crime. Thus, we might define *violence* as *the physical injury of a human or property by another human with the intent to injure and without the legitimate right to do so in that situation.*

The necessity for understanding precise terminology is also emphasized by the existence of other frequently encountered terms. *Aggression* is a broader psychological term that refers to attacking behavior, usually coupled with the emotional state of the attacker. *Conflict* is a form of social interaction in which rivals attempt to neutralize, injure, or eliminate each other [Coser 1956, p. 7]. As such, not all conflict is violent (as here defined) since neutralization or elimination can be accomplished nonviolently, as when one co-opts another party, or banishes a political foe. *Turmoil* is generalized disorder and may or may not include violent acts, while *civil strife* may be thought of as "collective nongovernmental attacks on persons or property that occur within a political system, but not individual crimes" [Gurr 1969, p. 573]. *Social violence* is an "assault upon an individual or his property solely or primarily because of his membership in a social category" [Grimshaw 1969b, p. 817]. The commonly heard term, *race riot* is frequently defined or subsumed under social violence since members of racial groups (or their property) are assaulted simply because they happen to be members of the particular race. Lastly, the term *agnostic behavior* is sometimes encountered and refers to fighting behavior itself, apart from moral or motivational concerns. As commonly used, the term is most often applied to animals because it is so difficult to ascertain their moral or motivational status.

The last background point we wish to consider concerns variations in types of violence. For our purposes, violence may be classified as individual versus collective, and rational versus expressive. First, *collective violence* is that which is influenced by immediate, ongoing social processes. More specifically, members of a collectivity share common norms and values that emerge or become salient as a function of immediate group experiences. Mob behavior and race riots are examples. *Individual violence,* in contrast, is performed primarily without reference to immediate group processes. Fist-fights between two people are a case in point. Here the face-to-face interaction and the predisposing personality factors may be sufficient to account for the outbreak and course of the fight.

The distinction between rational and expressive violence is also important. *Rational violence* may be either collective or individual as long as it is committed for an instrumental purpose, that is, to gain some exterior goal. An example of individual rational violence is a successful political assassination. Presumably such acts (at least when committed by mentally competent people) are done in order to bring about some explicit political change, hence the goal is exterior to the individual committing the act. In contrast, an example of *collective and expressive violence* is a mob attack upon referees, as sometimes occurs in European and Latin American soccer matches. Such acts may function primarily as a catharsis to release pent-up hostilities and are not committed with the explicit goal of changing the game's outcome (unless it causes a disqualification of one team or another).

As with attempts to define violence, attempts to classify the different types of violence are important because the same causes may not apply equally to all types. Indeed, it would be surprising if the cause of political assassinations turned out to be the same as the cause of race riots.

APPROACHES TO VIOLENCE

Macrosociological approaches tend to emphasize or look for the causes of urban violence in reference to broadly defined conditions of American society, such as racism and poverty. From this perspective, urban violence has basically the same root causes as violence in any other locale, but the urban environment is thought to aggravate the nature of certain conditions. The underpinnings of this approach tend to be based on two views of society. These are sometimes referred to as the "Integrative Model," and the "Conflict Model." These distinctions are perhaps most closely associated with the sociologist Ralf Dahrendorf.

Briefly, Dahrendorf [1958] argues that any society has certain problems that are satisfactorily explained by the integrative model, others that may be explained only by the conflict model, and some to which both models may apply. It is important to realize that these "models" are really sets of assumptions guiding one's observation and explanations, and are not meant to describe literally every feature of society.

The integrative model is based upon the assumptions that:

1A. Every society is relatively stable.

2A. Every society is a well-integrated structure.

3A. Every feature of society works to maintain the integration of society.

4A. Every societal feature is based upon a consensus of values.

Conversely, the conflict model is based upon vastly different assumptions that almost directly contradict the assumptions of the integrative model:

1B. Societies are constantly changing.

2B. Every society displays dissensus and conflict.

3B. Every feature of society works to disintegrate and change society.

4B. Every society is based on the coercion of some members by others.

The conflict approach naturally leads one to examine how the conflict is resolved. The answer is coercion (assumption 4B); some members of society must continually exert authority, force, or, ultimately, coercion, in order to maintain the society as a relatively efficient and effective unit. From the perspective of the integrative model, violence, particularly mass violence, represents a force that ruptures and rends the structure of society; it is perhaps the ultimate outcome of dissensus because the model maintains that society is held together by consensus (assumption 4A). Consequently, violence is viewed as "abnormal," "pathological," "disruptive," and as something to be suppressed and/or eliminated.

On the other hand, the conflict model views violence as part of the glue that binds a society together because coercion is ultimately based on force. Eliminate this glue, and the society tends to disintegrate and become uncoordinated. Moreover, violence may be a positive force in the limited sense that it promotes several desirable ends. Karl Marx viewed violence (that is, the revolution of the worker) as the solution to an oppressive political and economic system, while Georges Sorel [1960] saw the violence of revolution as having a cleansing function—the elimination of undesirable elements. At its extreme, this viewpoint is summed up in a saying attributed to Chairman Mao, "Anything can grow out of the barrel of a gun."

Admittedly, the above models are abstract, as they were intended to be; nonetheless they do tend to permeate the sociological analysis of urban violence. Several sociologists have applied either the integrative or particularly, the conflict model, as a means of explanation.

Superordinate and Subordinate Relationships

American society may be viewed as a structure composed of layers in which upper layers dominate lower layers. Social stratification is a case in point. Clearly upper-class persons have a great deal more political power than lower-class persons. The answer to the question, "Who has the power?" is, "The upper strata, by and large." The division of society into superordinate and subordinate relations appears to be a fundamental fact, particularly in regard to racial divisions. Blacks have always been a subordinate group dominated by whites (except briefly after the Civil War). Assuming that these types of relations are inherently unstable over a long period of time—subordinate groups will attempt to shift the power relations—violence is likely to occur when the superordinate/ subordinate relations lose their vitality and viability. This may occur when the upper strata loses its power and/or when the subordinate group gains more power [Grimshaw 1969a, pp. 488–501].

Urban racial violence has often been interpreted along such lines. For example, the race riots of the 1960s have been viewed as an attempt on the part of blacks to fundamentally change their subordinate position within American society. The ghetto has always been rather powerless in the face of the dominant community; powerless in the sense that its residents tend to be impoverished, discriminated against, and hence to lack control over most ghetto economic institutions, such as retail outlets, the city budget, police force, and the like. The black ghetto has been described as a colonial territory occupied by whites [Blauner 1969]. Consequently, the "guiding impulse in most major outbreaks has not been integration with American society, but an attempt to stake out a sphere of control by moving against the society and destroying the symbols of its oppression" [Blauner 1971, p. 238].

Other observers have voiced related interpretations. Characteristically, the looting that took place during the riots of the 1960s was highly selective along racial lines; rioters frequently attacked white-owned or white-controlled stores while ignoring similar stores that were owned by or run by blacks. A common sight during the Watts riot of 1965 was a store window sign reading "Blood Brother." (Incidentally, the protective value of such signs was quickly recognized by many Oriental merchants in the Watts area who quickly proclaimed themselves to be "Blood Brothers" as well.) This selectivity suggests   1. that riots are not irrational, senseless acts; they are not total chaos; participants do behave in a rational manner as individuals;   2. that riots have a symbolic political meaning; they represent a form of violent communication protesting and expressing discontent with white domination.

A more precise analysis of these looting patterns has been provided in terms of the redefinition of property rights [Quarantelli & Dynes 1970]. Looting commonly refers to the taking of goods and possessions; that is, physical things. However, the concept of property refers to the rights one has over certain physical things. For example, the owner of a television set has the right to sell it, to give it away, to paint it, and so on. While this bundle of rights to a particular good is recognized in law, it is also part of the common culture of most people and takes the form of a group of norms concerning "who has the right to do what" to certain possessions.

However, during a period of great and rapid stress, the normative consensus regarding property rights breaks down, and people must operate in a state of flux with few norms to guide their behavior. Many everyday guides to behavior temporarily cease to exist and the question of property rights can undergo a rapid redefinition. Looting becomes normatively defined as the proper behavior and in this sense, represents conformity with commonly shared expectations (norms) rather than deviance. Thus, looting during racial disturbances symbolically represents a redefinition of property rights. In particular, whites lose their rights to certain physical goods that become the property of the black community, available to any black daring enough to take them.

It is important to emphasize that looting remains illegal and a violation of the collective norms of the broader community. Moreover, the redefinition is temporary, associated with the ongoing racial turmoil and quickly disappears when calm returns. Nonetheless, looting appears to be an almost institutionalized part of riot behavior. Police are unable or unwilling to prevent it, and participants show little fear of being apprehended or even recognized. Even though looters may participate for purely selfish motives, the important point is that this behavior is made possible by the alteration of the normative structure concerning property rights. Consequently, looting may represent a form of black protest centering about economic exploitation of ghetto residents.

As previously discussed, the riots of the 1960s may represent a form of black protest against their subordinate and unequal position in American society. Obviously, not all collective violence represents protest (for example, a barroom brawl or gang fight) from the viewpoint of the public at large. Protest has been defined as being an expression of a grievance reflecting the inability of the protesters to directly correct the situation by their own efforts. The protest action is intended to draw attention to the grievances and to lead to corrective steps on the part of the target group; and finally, protesters depend on a combination of fear and sympathy to move the target group on their behalf [Turner 1969].

Whether or not the public at large considers riots to be a form of protest is vitally important; if the public does, then the likelihood of action designed to correct the causes of the violence is enhanced. Public support and pressure for corrective action are brought to bear, either directly or indirectly, on public officials who are in a position to take action. On the other hand, if riots are considered as aberrations or senseless acts perpetuated by outside agitators and deviants, then the emphasis shifts to controlling such people (for example, by jailing them). It is important to bear in mind that this is the public definition, not the definition of actual participants; but in terms of policy the public definition may be the more relevant one since the public can exert pressures for change. Consequently, it is important to ascertain the factors that determine whether an act of violence is defined as protest.

In order to explore this topic empirically, whites residing in the Los Angeles area were surveyed as to their reactions to the 1965 Watts riot [Jeffries, Turner, & Morris 1971]. A scale composed of three questionnaire items[1] was constructed to measure the extent to which whites defined the Watts riot as black protest. One of the most significant findings concerned the relation between perceived discrimination and protest definition of the riot, as the following table shows.

T A B L E 3 .   Protest Definition by Beliefs in Discrimination and Attitudes Toward Blacks

| | Attitudes Toward Blacks | | | |
| | Favorable | | Antagonistic | |
Scale: Belief That Riot Was Protest	Racial Discrimination High* (%)	Racial Discrimination Low (%)	Racial Discrimination High (%)	Racial Discrimination Low (%)
Riot Was Protest	67	36	48	23
Riot Was Not Protest	33	64	52	77
Total	100	100	100	100

Source:Adapted from Jeffries et al. 1971.

*Believe that large amounts of black discrimination exists.

It is particularly interesting to note that being favorable or antagonistic toward blacks makes no difference in the relation between defining the Watts riot as protest and beliefs in the existence of racial discrimination. Regardless of this attitude, whites who believed that high levels of racial discrimination existed tended to define the riot as black protest (67 percent versus 36 percent, and 48 percent versus 23 percent). Apparently, one can be antagonistic toward blacks and still believe that discrimination is operative, and it is this belief that leads to the protest definition of the riot. This suggests that recognition of preexisting injustice, particularly discrimination, is of more importance than favorable attitudes towards blacks, at least insofar as protest definitions are concerned. Thus, increasing the level of public awareness about discrimi-

1. Items: Agreement that the riot was protest; feeling the riot was caused by such things as police brutality, discrimination,etc.; and agreeing that steps to prevent future riots should involve factors such as better black housing, jobs, education, etc.

nation would seem to be a promising strategy in order to muster support for changing the levels of black deprivation. Unfortunately, this does not appear to be an easy task; at least at the time of this survey, more than one half the white respondents felt that blacks were only subject to little or no discrimination. This type of thinking exists even at high levels of government. A survey of congressmen [Hahn & Feagin 1970] showed widespread beliefs that the 1967 riots were caused by "joblessness and idleness, especially among young Negroes" (68 percent surveyed), lack of responsibility among Negroes (47 percent), and "outside Negro agitators" (46 percent). Apparently congressmen felt that the riots were caused by moral characteristics of blacks (idleness, lack of responsibility) or agitators. In contrast, "white indifferences to Negro needs" and "insufficient Federal Aid in education, job training, etc.," were mentioned by only 26 percent of congressmen. On this basis it would seem that those persons in a position to actually do something about the black situation are not particularly likely to view riots as protest. If one accepts that recent riots were in fact protest, then the policy implications of such research are not too promising.

The preceding explanations of riots provide one avenue toward understanding. They are not, however, the total explanations; other factors can also be considered. As noted, not all violence is alike, nor do seemingly similar acts of violence necessarily have the same political meaning. Although perhaps superficially the same as outbreaks of the 1960s, earlier incidents may represent white attempts to maintain the status quo. For example, the infamous Detroit riot of 1943, was characterized by whites attacking blacks. Large numbers of whites, usually in the form of small groups or larger mobs, ran rampant throughout the black areas of Detroit attacking both property and persons. The largest riot in American history occurred in New York City during the Civil War and involved an estimated several thousand whites. The riot began as a protest against Union draft policies, and escalated and spilled over into the city at large. During the course of the violence, resentment against blacks living in New York, some of them freed or escaped slaves, was acted out. This resentment had long smouldered as whites saw blacks as competitors for their jobs. This is how one observer described the situation:

> Two boarding houses were surrounded by a mob [of whites]. The desperados, finding only the owner left behind [a black], wreaked their vengeance on him, and after beating him unmercifully, broke up the furniture and then fired the building . . . . A negro lodging-house

in the same street next received visit of these furies, and soon was a mass of ruins. Old men, seventy years of age, and young children too young to comprehend what it all meant, were cruelly beaten and killed. It was a strange spectacle to see a hundred Irishmen pour along the streets after a poor negro . . . . All this was in the nineteenth century, and in the metropolis of the freest and most enlightened nation on earth [Headley 1970, pp. 207–208].

What, then, do such incidents as these signify? A common interpretation is that the violence perpetrated by whites on blacks (and there was very little, if any black violence perpetrated on whites) served to maintain the prevailing social structure. That is, it helped insure that the whites remained in superordinate positions and the blacks in subordinate ones. It did this directly by attacking certain blacks or "uppities" but more pervasively, it symbolically served notice as to the consequences of black mobility.

It should be emphasized that the foregoing interpretation does not mean that individuals necessarily participate in racial violence in order to personally express protest. Although some may be so motivated, the question of individual motivation is really not germane to the argument. What is of primary importance is the nature of the societal conditions, notably the existence of what has been termed "structural strain," coupled with inequality between blacks and whites. When strain is present it means that the society is undergoing some adjustment (or maladjustment); that is, according to the integrative model, the consensus is breaking down. Times of national turmoil, such as depressions, wars, or even unexpected and great prosperity, serve to weaken the prevailing consensus. What has been commonplace and ordinary becomes an issue for debate. The legitimacy of black subordination was a long accepted fact of American race relations, and it is only recently that it has been challenged on a large and forceful scale. The civil rights movement may be thought of as both a consequence of and a stimulus to this challenge. Other nonrace related movements concerning women, homosexuals, and the rights of the foetus to life, demonstrate the weakening of societal consensus about certain of the society's features; which, in turn, subject the society to strains.

The conjunction of these strains, along with racial inequality, opens the way for violent protest. In fact, the legitimacy of violence itself may come under challenge. As discussed, legitimacy defines violence as "good" or "bad"; hence, when the consensus that violence is "bad" disintegrates, restraints on its use are greatly diminished. In terms of individuals' participation in racial violence, none of them may actually realize or be able to articulate the political implications of the violence, but it suffices that those former constraints on the use of violence are weakened, making violence a reasonable alternative or mode of behavior.

The Role of Culture

The notions of subordinate-superordinate relations and strain are sometimes reinforced by the addition of the component of culture to the explanation. Culture refers to the totality of learned experiences passed on from one generation to the next; consequently, it is possible that certain cultures, or subcultures, within a society emphasize the use of violence to resolve disputes. This so-called "subculture of violence" has been defined as the "prevalence of customs and expectations which legitimate and honor the violent settlement of interpersonal disputes" [Glaser 1970] and most frequently has been applied to the analysis of interpersonal violence, notably homicide. The following table shows homicide rates for selected countries (note that the rates are per 100,000 persons and are not percentages).

T A B L E 4. Homicide Rates (per 100,000) for Selected Countries, 1966

Colombia	21.2	Canada	1.3
Mexico	18.7	Scotland	1.1
Thailand	14.9	W. Germany	1.1
Philippines	10.10	Italy	0.9
Venezuela	8.7	Sweden	0.8
Chile	6.4	France	0.7
United States	5.9	England	0.7
Argentina	5.8	N. Ireland	0.5
Australia	1.3	Ireland	0.4

Source: *World Health Statistics Annual*, 1966; and *World Health Organization*, Geneva, 1969.

Contrary to some popular beliefs, the United States homicide rate is high only in comparison to developed countries. Several nations, notably Colombia, have rates far exceeding that of the United States, but the United States rate far exceeds those of other highly developed Western countries such as Canada, Sweden, and England. Moreover, within a country the homicide rate is likely to vary from region to region. In 1969 Georgia, Alabama, and South Carolina had rates exceeding 11.0 while Iowa, New Hampshire, and Vermont had rates of less than 3.0 [Bureau of the Census 1971, p. 141].

Variations in rates have been explained by the concept of the "subculture of violence"; several aspects of this subculture have been identified [Glaser 1970]. First, the high rates in Latin American countries suggest that some cultures contain the normative expectation that honor shall be satisfied by violence. Sometimes referred to as "machismo," this code specifies the violent settlement of interpersonal disputes. It has been thought to be particularly pronounced among lower-class juvenile gangs of all ethnic backgrounds and, of course, among those of Latin American descent.

Second, the Southwest and South-Central states have about twice the homicide rates of the rest of the country. A variation of the machismo theme has been applied to explain this and may be called a "regional subculture of violence." In particular, the South as a region has long emphasized the values of manliness, individual self-protection, and the right of an individual to enforce the law himself. It is not surprising that within such a regional subculture, resorts to violence will be relatively high. The similarity between the concepts of regional subculture and machismo may be noted; they are not too distinct.

A final factor involved with the subculture of violence is quite different from those just mentioned—it is the relative inability of the criminal justice system to handle the volume of cases brought before it. When the courts and correctional institutions cannot act on arrests, the police are reluctant to become highly involved. In other words, if convictions are not forthcoming, the police have little motivation to make formal arrests; instead they tend to harass or to simply "keep things cool." Thus, such forms of interpersonal violence, as muggings and rapes are not likely to be given a great deal of attention by the police (by and large), and this in turn reinforces the effectiveness of the violent subculture. In short, if violence is not punished, the cultural prescriptions favoring violence are left relatively intact.

As with racial violence, no one maintains that the concept of violent subculture predetermines what any particular individual is likely to do; rather, it is argued that the outcome of conflict between persons is more likely to be violent if people are socialized into a violent subculture. It may be noted, moreover, that the subculture also plays a role in determining how the violence will be enacted. In Texas, the majority of homicides involve guns, while in New York the majority involve knives, clubs, and the like. In Texas guns are widely available, as they are throughout several southern and western states, whereas in New York, state law greatly reduces the availability of firearms.

Frustration, Aggression, and Deprivation

Explanations in terms of subordinate-superordinate race relations attempt to resolve some of the political symbolic meaning of race riots, as well as take into account culture and societal strains. This section deals with a related line of argument. According to several sociologists and psychologists deprivation leads to frustration which, in turn, leads to aggression. (This is abbreviated DFA). In the DFA argument *deprivation* refers to goals that objectively would be desirable or attractive, if obtainable. *Frustration* emerges when people anticipate the pleasure to be derived from these goals, but they are thwarted in their efforts to reach them. In short, frustration is a blockage of goal-directed activity [Berkowitz 1969]. Note that in this formulation, deprivation leads to frustration only to the extent that goal-directed activity is blocked; deprivation is a necessary but not a sufficient cause of frustration. Moreover, frustration is usually considered an unpleasant or even painful emotional state. The assumption is that the greater the unpleasantness or pain is, providing it does not debilitate, the more aggressive the resulting response will be. However, unpleasant and painful experiences may result from sources other than frustration (for example, insults and physical attacks). In a broad sense, frustration may thus be considered one type of noxious stimulus. Diagramatically, the DFA argument may be represented as follows.

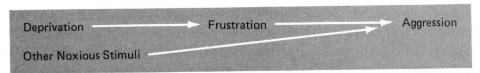

Fig. 1. The DFA Argument

Since deprivation along racial lines obviously exists (on the average blacks are less well off than whites) as a fundamental fact of United States society, it follows that, on the average, blacks will suffer from higher levels of frustration than whites and (again, on the average) consequently will engage in more aggression. It is important to realize that this argument begins with certain societal features, notably the institutionalized deprivation of blacks. As a result, DFA is a macrosociological explanation and should not be confused with theories, using the identical terms and much the same logic, that are anchored in the psychology of individual, idiosyncratic experiences. For example, it is quite possible for a child deprived of his toys to become frustrated and strike his mother; but this is far different from the race riot induced by the institutionalized deprivation of an entire subpopulation.

There are several variants of the deprivation-frustration-aggression model. Unfortunately, the same terms are used frequently but in different ways. This is an area in which experimental laboratory studies with both humans and animals have contributed to the development of sociological theory.

Frustration
and Aggression—
Evidence from Laboratory Studies

The relation between frustration and aggression has probably been evident throughout history; however, its scientific analysis was first given prominence about thirty years ago. Since that time, a great deal of research has been conducted and it seems fairly clear that frustration leads to aggression *under certain* conditions but not others. The specification of these circumstances or conditions still remains an important area of research.

For example, we could train our family dog to run to the kitchen in order to obtain food everytime he heard us call. Having thoroughly trained him, if we then suddenly slammed the kitchen door in his face when he was running to his feeding dish, this would be defined as "frustration" in operational terms. Similarly, if we were eating dinner and a salesman interrupted us, this would also lead to frustration. In both cases a goal-directed, ongoing activity has been blocked.

It is this state of frustration that leads to aggression; the aggression may be overt and violent, or it may simply take the form of symbolic attacks ("damn him!"), or aggression may not result at all. In particular, three areas of laboratory research have been undertaken: cues, justification, and arousal [Geen 1971].

There is some evidence that certain stimuli elicit aggressive responses when presented to frustrated subjects. Frustrated pigeons become quite aggressive towards other pigeons placed in their cages, while frustrated rats apparently attack other moving rats, but not those that are dead [cited in Berkowitz 1969]. In another study human subjects were frustrated by giving them unsolvable puzzles and it was found that they became more aggressive *only* if permitted to view a movie depicting a bloody prize fight. Apparently, the fighting in the movie acted as a cue that triggered the aggressive response. Another experiment [Berkowitz & LePage 1967], in which college students were used as subjects, induced frustration with minor electric shocks. Some students were frustrated in the presence of a gun that had been left on a shelf, while others did not see the weapon. Subsequently, both groups were allowed to deliver shocks to the person supposedly responsible for their initial shocks. The frustrated subjects who had been exposed to the weapon were significantly more aggressive, as measured by the number of shocks they delivered to their supposed tormentor.

These results make good sense; one would suppose that in our culture weapons are closely associated with the idea of aggression. Hence, when persons are frustrated, the weapon serves as a cue suggesting the aggressive response. Obviously, such evidence strongly supports the notion that widespread ownership of weapons should be minimized in order to reduce the number of aggressive cues in the environment. In this sense, one sometimes hears the statement, "the trigger pulls the finger." However, a more recent experiment fails to support such an assertion. This experiment used the same basic procedures as before, but found that frustrated students actually emitted *fewer* aggressive responses (shocks) in the presence of a weapon than did those for whom a weapon was not present [Ellis, Weinir, & Miller 1971]. Moreover, weapons reduced aggression even when subjects were not frustrated.

While such inconsistencies between experimental results have not been fully resolved, the results do emphasize the complexity introduced by past learning of culturally acceptable forms of aggression. Weapons apparently serve as cues to aggression depending on certain conditions, particularly the "meaning" of the weapon, including the circumstances in which it is found. Would a weapon elicit an aggressive response if associated with a baby? Probably not, but if it was associated with a mugger, it might. In other words, the broader circumstance may function to determine aggression-eliciting behavior. In this sense, weapons do not cause violence. This does not mean that gun legislation is without merit; the absence of weapons may make it more difficult to carry out lethal aggression while doing very little to reduce the aggression levels per se.

In addition to the role of environmental cues, research has also examined the effects of justification or legitimacy on the frustrations-aggressions hypotheses. In a study similar to the one just mentioned, subjects were assigned certain tasks and then insulted by the experimenter. They were subsequently shown part of a movie depicting a bloody prize fight in which the protagonist was badly beaten. Half of the subjects were led to believe that the protagonist was a "bad guy" who deserved what he got; the other half of the subjects were told that he was a "good guy." Those in the "bad guy" situation displayed significantly less aggression (as measured by electric shocks they were permitted to give to the researcher who had initially insulted them) than those in the "good guy" group. Seemingly, legitimacy plays a role in controlling aggressive responses; legitimizing aggression in one situation and of one particular kind (the movie) predisposed subjects to be less aggressive towards something totally unrelated (the experimenter's insult). While persons may have certain inhibitions against acting out violence, observing legitimate violence may have the effect of reducing those inhibitions.

It is, of course, possible that aggression results from simple arousal in combination with certain cues. Subjects were permitted to view the boxing film and then express their aggression level by shocking another person. Those persons subjected to loud (nonpainful) noise in addition to viewing the film proved the most aggressive. Presumably, the effect of noise was the strong arousal of subjects to perform at high rates of any activity. When combined with the aggressive cue, the activity is directed toward aggressive behavior. Without the arousal, the aggression simply remains dormant.

If this is true, then any environmental feature that arouses but does not debilitate may be conducive to aggression. Newspaper accounts suggest that mob violence typically occurs during or after highly important sports events. Riots typically occur during "long, hot summers." Homicides frequently occur during or after quarrels. All of these behaviors (excitement, discomfort, anger) might serve to increase arousal levels, and when the cue is manifested (a thrown bottle at a game; a police arrest, the presence of a gun) violence becomes probable. This may be particularly likely if the violence towards the object of attack can be legitimated.

Relative Deprivation

Closely related to the DFA argument, is the theory of relative deprivation. Indeed, this theory builds upon DFA; in effect, deprivation is defined as the gap between what people hope for (aspirations) and what they can attain. Deprivation per se is thought to have few consequences for violence; however, when people begin to aspire to a better standard of living and equality, and to view these goals as legitimate and reasonably attainable—but not forthcoming—the amount of relative deprivation increases. To put it another way, relative deprivation is the gap between what people want and what they get. In turn, relative deprivation leads to frustration, which leads to some form of aggression. It is necessary to add the qualification, "realistic" because people obviously have aspirations that they recognize as outside the realm of possible attainment. In this formulation, self-definition and self-perception determine relative deprivation regardless of how outsiders may view the situation. If persons consider themselves relatively deprived, then they are so deprived, no matter what their "objective" levels of comfort and possessions may be. It follows that relative deprivation can exist as long as some persons are better off than others and persons aspire (realistically) to emulate them.

Note that when we speak of deprivation in relative rather than absolute terms, it becomes necessary to state what the deprivation is relative to. In order to perceive the gap between aspiration and present reality, individuals or groups must be comparing themselves to someone else or to some future state. Although sometimes left vague, most applications of the theory to blacks have implicitly assumed that they are relatively deprived compared to whites and further assumed that blacks *define themselves* as so deprived. It is also possible for blacks not to compare themselves to whites, but to other blacks. In other words, blacks may take either whites or other better off blacks as the reference group. This is an important distinction, as we shall see when we examine some of the empirical work done on riot participants.

It is also important to note that two factors account for the amount of relative deprivation: 1. the amount of aspiration or hope that persons have, and 2. the extent to which those hopes are already fulfilled. Diagrammatically, these situations are depicted as follows in figure 2 (see p. 424) [after Gurr 1968].

Actually, there are an almost limitless number of forms for each line (curve) and combinations thereof; however these four (A through D) are commonly discussed because they are thought to depict actual situations. Considering these possibilities, diagram A shows that relative deprivation can increase as expectations increase even if the possibility and rate of fulfillment of those expectations remain constant. This might be called a situation of "false promises," that is, if people are led to

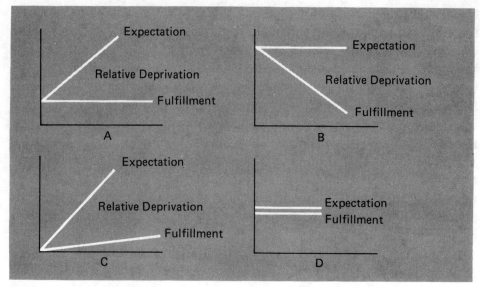

Fig. 2. Relative Deprivation

believe expectations will be fulfilled but no real changes occur, then relative deprivation will be high and aggression likely. Conversely, even if expectations remain the same but fulfillment decreases, relative deprivation is again high (figure B). It is possible for societal conditions to deteriorate as the result, for example, of depressions, famines, and so on. Unless expectations are commensurately decreased, aggression is a likely outcome. The difference between this situation and one of absolute deprivation is that the absolute DFA postulates that violence erupts as a consequence of misery and suffering associated with poverty, and not because of the gap between deprivation and expectation. Figure C illustrates the situation most frequently used to analyze recent race riots. It is presumed that the expectations level of blacks has increased over the past years; the emphasis on civil rights, public accommodation, integration, suffrage, and so on, coupled with the mass influence of television in conveying and dramatizing these issues, have all increased expectations. Unfortunately, while some of these hopes have been fulfilled, they have not been fulfilled as quickly as the expectation levels have increased; consequently, relative deprivation has been high in the black community. Lastly, figure D shows the situation of no relative deprivation; expectation and fulfillment are precisely equated (actually the expectation curve would lie on the fulfillment curve).

Relative deprivation is perhaps the theory most widely used to explain both collective and individual violence. Numerous studies have reported data that suggest the validity of the theory with regard to racial violence. The Kerner Commission [1968], which studied the urban violence of the 1960s, concluded that the typical black rioter had a better job than the average ghetto black. Furthermore, riot participants and militants are slightly better educated [Caplan 1970]. Thus riot participants are those who, compared to other blacks, could be in a state of relative deprivation. They have somewhat more education and see large differences between poor and affluent blacks. It is also presumed that persons with higher education have been socialized into believing that richer rewards will follow their education (that is, they have realistic hope for improvement) but to the rioters these rewards appeared not to be forthcoming.

An analysis of blacks living in the Watts ghetto provides an example of how relative deprivation theory has been applied. The researchers [Sears & McConahay 1970] discussed relative deprivation in terms of Comparison Levels (abbreviated CLs), which are defined as "some model or average value of all outcomes known to the person (by virtue of personal or vicarious experience), each outcome weighted by its salience" [Thibaut & Kelley 1959]. The modal or average CL is considered a neutral point with outcomes above the CL being satisfying and outcomes below the CL being unsatisfying. This is a compact and meaningful way of discussing relative deprivation since all of the concepts are embodied in the CL notion.

Several months after the 1965 Watts riot, interviews were conducted with blacks living in areas that had been subject to curfew. The CL level was measured by responses to the following questions: "What kind of work are you doing?" and "If you could have any job, what would you most like to do?" By comparing the answer to the first question with the answer to the second, it was possible to compare respondents' job aspirations with their actual level of job attainment. Numerical scores (1-8) were assigned to each job category according to the job's prestige and a CL score was then calculated. For example, if a respondent was a menial laborer that job received a score of 1; if he aspired to be a physician, that job received a score of 8. Subtracting the two scores gave a single number, 7, representing his CL. It was found that 30 percent of the sample was satisfied since there was no difference between the job they held and the one they aspired to; 35 percent were moderately deprived (scores of 1-3) and 35 percent were highly deprived (scores of 4-8). Finally, respondents were asked if they had participated in the riot.

Is relative deprivation as measured in this fashion related to prior riot participation? Table 5 documents the response to this question in Watts.

T A B L E 5. Relative Deprivation and Riot Activity

Level of Relative Deprivation (All Respondents)	Participated in the Watts Riot
None	16%
Moderate	25%
High	31%
Level of Relative Deprivation (Young Respondents: Ages 15-29)	
None	20%
Moderate	40%
High	44%

Source: Adapted from Sears & McConahay 1970.

According to table 5, the percentage of persons involved in the riot increased as the level of relative deprivation increased. This suggests that the level of relative deprivation was indeed related to participation in the Watts riot. Moreover, the table shows that the amount of participation was greater among younger blacks than the Watt's black population at every level of relative deprivation. This is not surprising since younger blacks have been reared in a more promising society; that is, the young are more likely to be affected by and accept racial changes than their parents, who were socialized when the structure of race relations was comparatively rigid. Note that consideration of age brings another variable into the analysis: socialization. We mentioned previously that learning culturally acceptable forms of aggression plays an important role in determining the outcomes of frustration. The same is true for relative deprivation.

This formulation, incorporating socialization, cultural values, and relative deprivation, has been used to explain other forms of violence in addition to race riots. It is a known fact that the vast majority of homicides occur among the deprived. For example, in Philadelphia during the period 1948–1952, 90 percent of all persons charged with murder had occupational categories ranging from semiskilled to unemployed [Wolfgang 1958].

Lower-class persons, it is thought [Coser 1967, pp. 53-71], tend to socialize their children by means of external controls such as punishment in an attempt to obtain conformity. In contrast, middle-class parents tend to emphasize the development of internalized controls within the child rather than compliance to external controls. Consequently, lower-class persons have fewer built-in, internal controls to prevent them from acting out aggression.

At the same time, the cultural values of social mobility and equality tend to reinforce the notion that the "good life" is the legitimate right of all people. Members of the lower class are thus likely to compare themselves to the middle and upper classes and to view the attainment of that life style as a realistic goal. Consequently, relative deprivation may be high among that group of persons who live in a violent subculture, which has only external controls preventing violence.

Moreover, women, even within the lower strata, appear to have a significantly lower homicide rate than men. Recalling that alternatives or aspirations must be realistic and legitimate, it may be that some women do not see sex equality as a realistic and/or legitimate alternative and, consequently, their level of relative deprivation is low. However, assuming that women will increasingly challenge their status, we would predict that the female homicide rate will begin to approximate the male rate as sexual equality is attained.

Second Thoughts About Relative Deprivation

The political scientist T. R. Gurr is probably the leading proponent of relative deprivation theory. He says that

> 'Frustration' or 'discontent' is the root cause of rebellion . . . and the basic relationship is as fundamental to understanding civil strife as the law of gravity is to atmospheric physics: relative deprivation, the phrase I have used, is a necessary precondition for civil strife of any kind, and the more severe is relative deprivation, the more likely and severe is strife [Gurr 1968, p. 52].

> Underlying this relative deprivation approach to civil strife is the frustration-aggression mechanism, apparently a fundamental part of our psychological make up [Gurr 1968, p. 53].

These are rather grandiose claims. Not surprisingly, numerous criticisms have been leveled against the theory of relative deprivation. At a fundamental level, since relative deprivation is thought to lead to frustration which, in turn, leads to aggression, the relationship between the latter two variables is a vital link in the theory. What relative deprivation specifies is how the frustration arises, *not* how frustration leads to aggression. Thus anything that tends to vitiate the relation between frustration and aggression also vitiates the relative deprivation argument, since, without that link, it is difficult to specify how deprivation (relative or absolute) leads to aggression.

Empirically DFA has not fared too well as an explanation for recent race riots. Several of the previously cited studies, as well as others, were compared and reanalyzed in order to ascertain if there was widespread evidence for the proposition that deprivation-frustration is related to riot participation [McPhail 1971]. Since different studies asked slightly different questions, the various measures were summarized into three categories: deprivation, frustration, and deprivation and frustration combined. The following summaries were obtained.

T A B L E 6. Deprivation-Frustration-Aggression Relationships by Strength of Association with Riot Participation

	Strength of Association with Riot Participation			
	Due to Chance (%)	Low (%)	Moderate (%)	Total (%)
Deprivation*	38	58	4	100
Frustration**	23	65	12	100
Deprivation and Frustration***	43	54	3	100

Source: Condensed from McPhail 1971, table 2.

*Deprivation: 50 different measures, e.g., education, income, and occupation.

**Frustration: 84 different measures, e.g., political attitudes, police malpractices, and housing.

*** 39 different measures referring to a mixture of * and ** above.

Table 6 reveals scant support for DFA theory. A large percentage of the relationships could be due to chance (38, 23, and 43 percent for deprivation, frustration, and deprivation and frustration, respectively). This means, for example, that of the 84 different relationships between frustration and riot participation, 19 (23 percent) could have arisen from chance factors alone. When a study fails to reject chance as a plausible explanation, it is generally assumed that the initial hypothesis (frustration leads to aggression in this case) cannot be supported.

It should also be noted that the majority of relationships were of low strength and only a few of moderate strength. In other words, although the chance explanation can be rejected, relationships of low and moderate strength are tenuous at best. Clearly, we could not measure educational deprivation, for example, and then predict participation in a riot to any meaningful degree. To perform such a task, the relationships would have to be of very high strength, but none achieved that level. Moreover, although table 6 suggests that slight correlations might exist, they could come about as a simple function of age.

In this regard, a survey was conducted of blacks arrested for riot participation during the 1967 Detroit riot [Geschwender & Singer 1970]. As a control group, a similar number (approximately 450) blacks were surveyed from the black community at large. It was found that black arrestees tended to be better educated at the level of "some high school" than the community sample (50 percent versus 31 percent) and, in general, had a slightly higher median level of education. On the surface, this would support the notion of relative deprivation; those blacks achieving more (education) would expect more in return; when this result is not forthcoming frustration and then aggression follow. However, the preponderance of youth in riot activity has long been noted and the black arrestees in this study were no exception. On the average, they were younger than the community black, hence their higher level of riot participation may have had little to do with relative deprivation but may have been simply a function of their youth. In fact, when age is taken into account, the community blacks had achieved higher levels of education than the arrestees (44 percent completed high school as opposed to 31 percent for arrestees). The same general finding was also true for income, occupational status, and employment.

If anything, then, it is the deprived portion of the black population that becomes involved in riot behavior, and the evidence to date suggests little, if any, support for the notion of relative deprivation. But if absolute deprivation is the causal factor, then this is contradictory to a general conclusion we previously mentioned, namely, that the most deprived segment of the black population is passive and apathetic. Consequently, we are currently left in a state of limbo insofar as DFA theory is concerned. Upon reanalysis none of the empirical evidence turns out to support the theory. It should be emphasized that in this regard we are speaking of race riots and not other violent behaviors.

Given that the empirical evidence for the DFA argument is tenuous at best, what might be wrong with the theory? Several logical criticisms have been made, particularly as the notion has been applied in survey research [McPhail 1971]. First, when conducting surveys (unlike laboratory studies) it is virtually impossible to work with the correct chronological sequence since feelings of deprivation and/or frustration are measured after the subject has already participated in the violence. One does not really know if the attitudes expressed lead to participation, or if they have arisen as a result of participation. A reasonable suspicion is that persons participate and subsequently express attitudes that they have learned, or have been made salient by the experience. The expressed attitude thus serves to legitimate participation in an activity that runs counter to most cultural norms.

Second, and most important, the basic idea that attitudes determine behavior is not well established. Even if one feels politically oppressed, does this mean one will participate in some overt action to lift the oppression? In actuality, so many things can intervene between the attitude and the behavior that the predicted behavior may never occur. Other factors that may actually determine riot participation include one's state of health, responsibilities to family, job, and feelings of daring. In short, asking an individual how he feels about something, even if the time sequence is correct, does not necessarily suffice to predict a given behavior, particularly when that behavior is disapproved of by the larger society.

Third, what we loosely call a "riot" actually involves a whole series of behaviors. A single person may participate in numerous activities such as the following: throw bricks, loot a store, aid a friend, secure his family, and so forth. If this is so, then the question may be raised as to when the DFA sequence comes into play? Is it operative when the person is throwing bricks, and does it then suddenly switch off when he helps a friend? On a more general scale, does the DFA mechanism determine whether the individual participates in the first place, and is subsequent behavior during the violence controlled by other factors? If so, what are these factors? While such a switching process is conceivable, it hardly seems likely that it is the operative mechanism because there are simply too many switches that have to be activated in the proper sequence.

The frustration-aggression link also has been subject to much criticism. Many theorists no longer view the relation as invariant, maintaining that frustration does not always lead to aggression. Recall that laboratory studies suggested the importance of generalized arousal, aggressive cues, and legitimacy of the aggressive response. These factors may well modify or even override the aggressive response. For example, without a legitimate target, high levels of frustration may never result in a violent outburst. In fact, since frustration is assumed to be a noxious stimuli, one might just as well postulate that the response will be directed towards reducing the frustration rather than exploding into violence. Additionally, frustration may result in exhaustion and apathy, or it may be channeled into highly productive and creative endeavors. In the Newark and Detroit riots of 1967, survey data showed that blacks of the lowest socioeconomic status were the least likely to riot [Caplan 1970]. Blacks in this position may: 1. not aspire to improvement goals because they are not realistic, hence they are not frustrated, or 2. if frustrated, become apathetic rather than aggressive. In short, laboratory and some survey research indicates that there is little basis for believing frustration *always* leads to aggression. At best, frustration is a generalized noxious stimulus that tends to arouse. Whether or not violence is the outcome of this arousal is determined by the other factors that we previously discussed.

Moreover, it has also been claimed that "the most satisfying inherent response is to strike out at the source of frustration" [Gurr 1968, p. 53]. This claim is probably invalid and it is surely misleading. 'Striking out' may not occur and if it does there is no guarantee that it will be the most satisfying response that could be made in a given situation. In fact, pacifists may find violence the most unsatisfying alternative. Although one could debate the proposition that the aggressive response is inherent, it suffices to note that there is little basis for believing that it is genetically transmitted. This proposition—the innate character of aggression in humans—has never been proven; indeed, it is difficult to know how one could, as a practical matter, go about demonstrating its validity.

Finally, it should be noted that frustration-aggression may be best applied to spontaneous, expressive violence rather than to rational violence. For example, a cold-blooded killing or an instrumental riot necessitates that someone carefully choose, calculate, and commit the violence. This process requires a certain amount of time. Hence, if frustration-aggression theory is used to explain these types of violence, one must assume that the relationship is extremely strong and durable because the more time that elapses between frustration and the act, the more likely other factors are to intervene. The frustration itself may dissipate; the arousal level may decline; reassessment of cues and legitimacy may occur; alternate responses may be envisioned; and the consequences of aggression may be taken into account. The laboratory evidence clearly suggests that a much more tenuous relationship exists between frustration and aggression than is capable of sustaining this type of instrumental violence. Consequently, to claim that frustration is a "necessary precursor of civil strife of any kind, excluding crime" [Gurr 1968, p. 52] is to apply the theory to the wrong type of violence. It is more likely, if the theory applies at all, that it applies to "crimes of passion" such as the majority of homicides. In these cases, the time lapse between the frustration and violent act is quite short.

In sum, it would appear that the DFA explanation for violence has serious shortcomings, despite the fact that it is probably the most widely accepted contemporary explanation. In one form or another it constantly reappears in both technical and popular media. In order to rectify some of these shortcomings, it has been suggested that more emphasis be placed on sampling riot behavior during the course of the violence; obviously a highly difficult strategy. However, closer attention to the riot process—that is, the behaviors and activities of persons during a riot—might lead to a more satisfying explanation. Moreover, emphasis on ecological factors would add potentially important dimension to understanding riots. It could be that the reason youths tend to participate is relatively straightforward: they are simply more available. The explosion of racial violence during summer months certainly suggests that this might be operative since school-age children are on vacation and often have little to do.

Alienation

Another attitudinal factor that is possibly related to violence is alienation. Modern, urban society is mass society; that is, processes such as bureaucratization and industrialization may have led to the detachment of individuals from the society in which they live. A so-called lack of "integration" with society is thought to result in: 1. feelings of powerlessness (lack of control over events that affect one),   2. isolation from meaningful contacts with others, and   3. a generalized dissatisfaction with one's life situation [Ransford 1968]. Isolation may be considered a structural characteristic since it is partially determined by one's life situation (how many friends one has, where one works, and so forth) whereas powerlessness and dissatisfaction refer to subjective states—how one feels about something.

A survey of blacks conducted almost immediately following the 1965 Watts riot applied this sociological perspective. Questions were asked about racial isolation, and about feelings of powerlessness and dissatisfaction. In addition, the respondent's "willingness to use violence to obtain Negro rights" was ascertained. The most highly alienated persons were defined as those with low social contacts and high feelings of powerlessness and dissatisfaction. Blacks scoring high on only one of the three measures were considered intermediate, and those scoring low on all three were considered nonalienated. The results of the survey are summarized in table 7.

T A B L E 7. Percentage willing to Use Violence by Alienation

Level of Alienation	Willing to Use Violence(%)	Not Willing to Use Violence(%)	Total (%)
High	65	35	100
Intermediate	24	76	100
Nonalienated	12	88	100

Source: Adapted from Ransford 1968.

The table shows that the majority of highly alienated blacks were favorably disposed toward violence (65 percent) but only a small minority (12 percent) of the nonalienated were so disposed. As postulated, there is obviously a clear relation between alienation and proviolence attitudes. However, an important qualification to this general finding concerned the role of education, as table 8 shows.

T A B L E 8. Percentage Willing to Use Violence by Alienation and Educational Attainment

Dimension of Alienation	Level of Education	
	High School or Less (%)	Some College or More (%)
High Isolation	52	24
High Powerlessness	51	18
High Dissatisfaction	59	17

Source: Adapted from Ransford 1968.

Among blacks with low levels of education (high school or less), the majority of those high in isolation, powerlessness, or dissatisfaction favored violence. However, for the college-educated group, favorableness was far reduced; in fact, only a small minority of college-educated blacks advocated the use of violence to obtain Negro rights. This suggests that alienation, insofar as it leads to proviolent attitudes, is operative only for those less willing to risk their social position despite feelings of alienation. To put it simply, they have more to lose; hence they presumably opt for more institutionalized methods of obtaining Negro rights. Additionally, more educated persons may have been socialized into believing that violence is not a legitimate means for redressing grievances, even if the grievances themselves are legitimate ones. For example, many of the nonviolent civil rights organizations in the black community are predominantly controlled and oriented towards middle-class blacks and traditionally were not in favor of militant tactics. In contrast, lower-strata blacks may not have been so socialized (or may have been socialized to lesser degrees) and, at the same time, have little to lose from violence.

A more complex theory suggests that rioters should be characterized predominantly as dissidents (that is, they have low trust in the government but are intellectually informed about how government operates), rather than alienated (low trust in government and little intellectual knowledge of government). The dissidents are likely to feel that the political system can and should be changed, hence they may be more likely to engage in radical or violent political activity. In contrast, the alienated tend to be apathetic and are unlikely to engage in political activities. In a sense the alienated simply drop out of the political system.

A survey that was conducted after the 1967 Newark riot provided information on this theory. Respondents in the riot zones were asked if they participated in the riot, how much trust they had in the Newark city government, and were given a test concerning knowledge of their city government [Paige 1971]. Over 60 percent of those persons classified as dissidents (low trust, high knowledge) participated in the riot, whereas less than 30 percent of the alienated participated.

Comparing this with the preceding study, note that alienation is operationally defined in different ways. In the Ransford study alienation was considered in terms of isolation, powerlessness, and dissatisfaction while Paige used knowledge and trust. Which of the two authors is "correct" is a moot question; they may be using the same term—alienation—for different things. Nonetheless, both studies suggest that some area of trust and a feeling of being a meaningful part of the political and social system are related to violence.

As with DFA theory, it should be borne in mind that the relation between a subjective state, in this case "alienation," and a behavior is problematic. Moreover, in Ransford's study, as in so many studies of racial violence, retrospective, imaginary behaviors are being used as the dependent variable rather than actual participation itself. In this case, the willingness to use violence was a hypothetical question. People who say they are willing to participate may decline to do so in an actual situation. On the other hand, the existence of attitudinal support for violence may contribute to a normative structure (climate of opinion) that is conducive to the occurrence of violence. Finally, note that the violence in question had a strong aura of legitimacy (gaining Negro rights) and should not be interpreted to mean that alienation leads to all types of violence.

Other Explanations of Riot Behavior

Although the protest interpretation of riots is being stressed, alternate explanations do exist. These go under various names and can be categorized as conspiracy, riffraff, and youth [Lupsha 1969]. Edward Banfield's widely read book *The Unheavenly City* [1968], interprets riots in terms of the "youth theory." He argues that four types of riot exist: rampage, outburst of righteous indignation, foray for pillage, and demonstration. Probably most riots are some combination of these four. Banfield, however, argues that rampages, consisting of "an outbreak of animal—usually young animal—spirits" and pillages (motivated by the desire to steal) are the dominant types. Hence, they represent "fun and profit." In terms of causes, the most fundamental are the background causes: large numbers of boys and young men, and the exclusion of lower-class people from political institutions. It is the young, lower class male who must release "animal spirits," and in former times this release was accomplished by institutional participation. For example, the system of political bossism permitted young people to actively participate in political institutions at the local ward level by providing jobs in exchange for party loyalty and services. However, nowadays this and other types of participation are no longer available, having been replaced by professional and bureaucratic machinery. Consequently, these pent-up animal spirits are released in rioting. Moreover, the presence of middle- and upper-class blacks residing in the ghetto (either because they like it or because they are excluded from the suburbs) provides some riot leadership and legitimation. Even if social improvements are accomplished (which Banfield claims is not too likely) "boys and young men of the lower classes will not cease to 'raise hell' once they have adequate job opportunities, housing, schools, and so on" [Banfield 1968, p. 205].

This thesis has drawn heavy fire from numerous social scientists, and is not generally accepted by most sociologists. Banfield's analysis of riots relies heavily on motivation; it describes four reasons why persons riot. Unfortunately, no data is presented that would substantiate his claim. He provided ancedotes, selected, and perhaps biased observations. Additionally, his thesis of "lower class, animal spirits" is simply stated without evidence and, from a logical point of view, borders on the mystical and tautological. It can hardly be identified (what it is, how does it work, where it comes from), but even if it could, the idea provides little in the way of explanation. We could just as well say that lower-class boys and young men instinctively riot. Finally, Banfield appears to be highly selective in the issues and research he cites to bolster his contentions. Most of the research that contradicts his thesis is simply ignored; the same may be said concerning his arguments on social class. [A series of criticisms and Banfield's reply can be found in *Social Science Quarterly* 1971, 816-859.]

Conspiracy theories are another widely publicized explanation. Conspirators (sometimes secret) are blamed for either planning or deliberately provoking the violence. This explanation is a comforting one as it places the blame on "outside" sources. Neither residents nor officials are at fault if conspirators or outside agitators caused the riot. As might be expected, the conspiracy theories are widely held. After the 1967 riots, a survey of congressmen showed that 46 percent thought outside agitators were of great importance in causing the violence [Hahn & Feagin 1970]. At the same time, 45 percent of the white public concurred in this belief [Lupsha 1969].

Actually, this view is an old one. The previously described New York Draft Riot of 1863 was once blamed on political conspirators. In addition to the comfort the theory brings, the tenacity with which it is held may result from the difficulty involved in disproving it. Although investigative committees can find no evidence that conspiracies existed, proponents can counter that the investigators simply were duped and did not search hard enough. After all, conspirators are not dumb, and they do not leave evidence of their participation.

Granting, for the sake of argument, that conspirators exist, (and there is no evidence that they do, although some groups may claim credit *after* the riot), it is difficult to understand how they can instigate collective violence. Riots are rather poorly understood and cannot be produced at will; to do so would require a great deal more knowledge on the conspirator's part than probably exists. Moreover, even if the conspirators could produce a riot, it is difficult to explain the mass support they gain without recognizing the existing social conditions. If people were content, they would not participate in the first place.

Another theory suggests that riffraff are the cause of riots. This, too, conjures up potentially comforting visions of deviants, petty criminals, drunks, and other similar types that elicit little sympathy from many people, or even represent immoral elements who are said to have no one to blame but themselves. Moreover, if the riffraff theory is true, then one can maintain that the lot of the average black is not so bad (the average black did not riot) and one's conscience can be assuaged. As we have seen, however, there is little empirical support for this notion. Typically rioters are fairly well off compared to nonrioters and even if they are not, there is no evidence to suggest they are riffraff.

The Mass Media

Several of the laboratory studies mentioned are relevant to another issue; namely, the impact of the mass media on violence. This topic has been investigated by several commissions. It has been estimated that one-half the characters shown on television commit some act of violence, while 6 percent commit homicide and 3 percent are victims [*U.S. News and World Report,* 24 October 1973, pp. 33–36]. This amount suggests that the media teach people to be violent. On the other hand, the mass media may simply reflect the level of violence in society and/or provide the amount and type of violence desired by the viewing audience. Certainly voluminous incidences and examples can be cited to show that American culture contains and glorifies violent acts. From this viewpoint media violence does not lead viewers to engage in more violence than they otherwise would. In short, the argument is that viewers get what they want. Unfortunately, this issue is an emotional one, particularly when it comes to the effects on children.

In a widely quoted experiment [Bandura 1968], preschool children were exposed to three different stimuli: 1. an adult striking a Bobo doll while the attacker exclaimed "punch him," "hit him";   2. the same scene but shown on film;   3. a similar scene with the adult attacker dressed as a cartoon cat; and   4. a control group not exposed to the violent model. After exposure, the amount of violence displayed by the children was assessed by observing their play behavior, particularly in regard to types of toys. Both aggressive (a Bobo doll, darts,) and nonaggressive toys (crayons, coloring paper) were provided. Children exposed to the violent models, whether on film or the actual adult, displayed considerably more aggression than the control group. Notably, they tended literally to imitate the adult's behavior in striking the Bobo doll, often using the same expressions ("hit him"). Thus the effect of viewing aggression seems to bring a reduction in inhibitions toward acting it out, as well as suggesting the form or method in which the aggression is actually conducted. These conclusions are consistent with those already discussed, and would seem to suggest that the media can induce people to commit violent acts.

Before drawing conclusions about this or related issues, however, we should note the difficulties in generalizing laboratory studies beyond the confines of the laboratory. In assessing scientific evidence, validity is sometimes divided into two types: internal and external [Campbell 1957]. The former refers to the ability to attribute the cause to the effect. It seems reasonably clear that in the studies cited, the causes (frustration, cues, and so on) were linked to the effects (shocks, striking the Bobo doll), hence internal validity is high. In contrast, external validity is the ability to generalize the relationships to the real world and it is in this regard that laboratory studies are comparatively weak. Along these lines, it has been suggested that the following criteria should be met before generalizing laboratory research to the real world [Hartley 1964, pp. 131-139].

1. The subjects must be representative of the population to which the results are to be generalized. This is clearly not the case in most laboratory studies, particularly in the social sciences. Subjects are often college students selected for their convenience. Unfortunately, college students do not represent the population at large; they tend to be middle class, better educated, more intelligent, holding to unique value systems and living within a college subculture. We can ask how likely are the laboratory results to generalize to, for example, lower-class persons, the elderly, different occupational groups and different ethnic groups. These questions, in most cases, must remain unanswered.

2. The laboratory conditions must be reasonably similar to those that occur in real life. Although laboratory studies attempt to emulate real life situations, at least to the extent that experimental manipulations are made believable to the subjects, there are obvious and severe shortcomings in this regard. For example, few persons actually are frustrated in the manner commonly used in laboratories, and fewer still have the opportunity to express aggression in terms of electric shocks. Normal everyday life does not take place in a laboratory ac-

companied by detailed instructions, researchers, apparatus, and the general knowledge that one is a guinea pig.

3. The "stimulus" must be similar to the material encountered in real life. In terms of cues (for example, the prize fight film, the exposed gun on the shelf) since they are drawn from everyday material, this criterion appears to be satisfied. However, only short clips from the film were typically shown. Consequently, the viewers did not see the film in its entire context; the fight scenes, being isolated, were made much more salient. The same may be said of the gun; a gun lying on a shelf in a laboratory is quite stark. In short, persons respond to cues embedded in a sequence of events within a particular social context and this context tends to be lacking in laboratory research.

4. The dependent variable (aggression) must be similar to the real life behavior whose likelihood of occurrence is being predicted. In most laboratory studies this is not the case. As we have seen, electric shock is often used to measure aggression; yet few people have access to this method of expression in real life. It would be more appropriate, for example, to allow the subjects to use knives, guns, or fists. However, if this were done, moral and practical considerations aside, would we then predict aggression? This is still an open question.

5. The social context of the behavior must be similar to the social context of real life in which the dependent variable would occur. Again, the laboratory is not real life; consequently the total social context in which behavior occurs is not taken into account.

In sum, laboratory studies tend to be artificial and thus to ignore the social context in which real life behavior occurs. What, then, are the values of the laboratory research? Why is it done? At least three answers to these questions may be suggested for consideration:

1. Internal validity is high. In laboratory studies researchers are relatively certain, at least when compared to field studies, that the cause is linked to the effect. Without this assurance, it is difficult to say much about anything. Since it is difficult to maximize both internal and external validity at the same time, the laboratory provides valuable information on that point.

2. In the absence of the ability to maximize both internal and external validity simultaneously, it makes sense to study a given problem from both the viewpoints of the laboratory and the field. Relationships

found to be true within the laboratory can be verified in the field and suggestions from the field can be reexamined in the laboratory. When the two give consistent results, we are then on much firmer ground in drawing conclusions.

3. Finally, depending on one's philosophical bent, it can be argued that the laboratory is not so different from real life as one might think. Replicating every nuance of real life is not necessary as long as we can isolate and manipulate a few crucial dimensions. Assuming this is done, then one can generalize the fundamental relationships to more realistic settings, as long as the differences between the real world and the laboratory are borne in mind.

APPROACHES TO URBAN VIOLENCE

Thus far, our discussion of violence, particularly racial violence, has been from a general rather than a uniquely urban perspective. The various explanations offered, DFA, alienation, and so on, are not anchored in urban phenomena per se. Presumably they refer to societal conditions and/or to social and psychological characteristics, and attitudes of individuals. Unless one assumes that these characteristics and attitudes vary by city, they have very little to do with the nature of urban life. That is, are blacks more subordinate in one city than another? Are they more relatively deprived? More alienated? If the answer to such questions is "no," then some other factors are required to account for the fact that race riots, at least in the 1960s, predominantly took place in urban ghettos, and that large cities have disproportionately higher rates of criminal violence. On the other hand, there may be urban characteristics—that is, features of urban life that are not found in other areas—that vary from city to city and are the causes of violence. The predominant approach to this type of reasoning has consisted of assessing different city characteristics (for example, population size, percent of Negro population) as to their relationship with violence. Usually, heavy reliance is placed on the use of data accumulated by the United States Bureau of the Census to measure city characteristics, and to the extent possible, the use of newspapers, mass media, and other sources to accumulate data on violence.

This body of research is characterized by an emphasis on the effects of urban structural conditions. By this is meant relatively enduring urban social patterns, such as the segregation of blacks into urban cores; the unequal distribution of persons into various socioeconomic strata; and the relative number of blacks versus whites. Consequently, less attention is given to characteristics and attributes of individuals. The occurrence and/or severity of race riots is examined quite apart from individual motivation, while, in the case of criminal violence, the crime *rate* is emphasized rather than the reasons why a particular person engages in crime. This does not mean, however, that the various aforementioned theories are simply ignored; in fact they quite often serve as the starting point of constructing hypotheses relevant to urban structure.

The events of the 1960s apparently spurred research applying this approach to the problems of racial violence. A widely known study examined incidents of racial violence (riots) that occurred between 1913 and 1963 in the United States [Lieberson & Silverman 1965]. The first question addressed was whether or not riots occurred randomly over time and between different American cities. A statistical procedure was employed in which were determined the number of riots expected on the basis of chance for both time and city. The findings are summarized in table 9.

T A B L E 9. Number of Race Riots Actually Occurring Compared to Number Expected by Chance

By Years, 1913–1963			By Cities		
Riots per Year	*Riots Occurred*	*Expected by Chance*	*Riots per Year*	*Riots Occurred*	*Expected by Chance*
0	26	11	0	300	281
1	10	17	1	25	47
2	7	13	2	3	4
3	2	6	3	3	0
4	1	2	4	1	0
5	0	1	5-14	1	0
6	0	0			
7	2	0			
8	1	0			
9	1	0			
10	0	0			
11	1	0			

Source: Adapted from Lieberson & Silverman 1965.

Table 9 reveals that in the 50-year-period between 1913 and 1963, there was no riot in 26 of those years. Yet, on the basis of chance, only 11 no-riot years would be expected. In a like manner, there would be no years in which 8 riots occurred by chance. Yet one such year was observed. In considering the distribution of riots over 333 cities with 1960 populations of at least 50,000, 300 experienced zero riots per year. However, on the basis of chance, only 281 should have done so. Similar conclusions, based on alternate statistical techniques, have been reported for riots occuring between 1961–1968 [Spilerman 1970]. Thus it seems clear that the location and timing of riots are not random events.

Given the difficulty in predicting where and when riots will occur, this is not an idle issue. Since they are not random events, it follows that something, potentially discoverable and meaningful, leads to their distribution over time and place. Moreover, the foregoing emphasizes a difference in approach. We previously explored theories explaining why individuals are favorably disposed toward or actually participate in riots. In contrast, the emphasis in this section is on the occurrence and/ or severity (however measured) of riots. Obviously, if everyone absolutely refused to participate, a riot could not occur. However, this has not been the case, and we can inquire if certain characteristics of a city facilitate or predispose that city towards having riots, and if they occur, lead to different degrees of severity.

Several of these characteristics were assessed in this study [Lieberson & Silverman 1965]. The authors found that low Negro unemployment, a low proportion of Negro police, high population per councilmen, and a low proportion of Negroes in occupations usually considered black and menial, all distinguished cities that had riots from those that did not. Unemployment, lack of store ownership, and occupational restrictions imply that, in some cities, economic institutions have not adequately served the black population. A large number of persons per councilmen suggests that less attention can be paid to individuals, that the councilmen's constituency is massive and anonymous, and, consequently that it is difficult to obtain action on grievances. Similarly, the presence of black policemen may represent the willingness of citizenry and municipal government to take the black community into account. Collectively, these characteristics suggest that riots tended to occur in those cities characterized by inadequate social institutions, particularly the economic ones, and by unresponsive government.

While this and several other studies consider the occurrence (that is, frequency) of riots, a related issue is their severity. Some riots obviously cause more damage, involve more persons, more deaths more casualties, and extend over wider areas. Are there some urban characteristics that predispose a city towards having severe riots independent of their frequency? In other words, a city might have one severe riot while another city might have several less severe riots. Consequently, some urban characteristics may lead to severity while others may lead to frequency, and there is no particular reason why the two must be related. Having one riot does not necessarily guarantee that a city will not have another of unknown severity. In fact, the frequency with which riots occurred in 1967 bore no relation to the severity of riot. This result holds whether or not severity is measured by a scale composed of such factors as the number of riot-produced fires, amount of looting and size of crowds, a descriptive account provided by newspaper reporting, an index based on the number of riot-related injuries, or a rather sophisticated scale based on descriptive accounts provided by mayors of riot-torn cities [Jiobu 1969].

A related issue deals with the question of where severity measures should be anchored. That is, should a city with zero frequency of riots be considered to have riots with zero severity, or should the severity measures only apply to those cities having riots. Both strategies have been used at one time or another, although there seems to be some consensus that severity is applicable only to cities experiencing a riot.

In one study [Wanderer 1969], mayors were requested to provide information on the riots occurring in their cities during 1967. On the basis of their responses it was possible to construct a Guttman scale of riot severity. According to the Guttman scale, if highly severe behaviors (e.g., riot related death) occurred, then less severe behaviors also occurred (e.g., vandalism). Conversely, if only the less severe behaviors occurred, then the highly severe ones did not take place. This is made clearer by considering the following:

T A B L E 10. Guttman Scale of Riot Severity

Riot Behaviors	Severity Score	Percent of Cities
None	8 (least severe)	4
Vandalism	7	19
All Above + Interference with Firemen	6	13
All Above + Looting	5	16
All Above + Sniping	4	13
All Above + Called State Police	3	7
All Above + Called National Guard	2	17
All Above + Law Officer or Civilian Killed	1 (most severe)	11

Source: Adapted from Wanderer 1969.

For example, 11 percent of the 75 cities considered in this study experienced riots of the most severe type (severity score = 1), which meant the riot included killings, calling of the National Guard, state police, sniping, looting, interfering with firemen and vandalism. In contrast, 19 percent of the cities had rather mild riots (severity score 6) that involved only interference with firemen and vandalism. The fact that these riot behaviors form a Guttman scale suggests that severity represents a single dimension. This is an important point because it means that riots do not become severe by some helter-skelter, random process. If there is order then presumably we are potentially capable of understanding it. To put it another way, all of the events in the scale share a common attribute: severity. Moreover, it is possible to interpret the events sequentially: first vandalism occurs, then there is interference with firemen, then looting, then sniping, then the state police are called, then the National Guard, and finally a killing occurs. If this interpretation is correct, then presumably one can intervene in this process to prevent more severe events from occurring. For example, the way to prevent sniping is to prevent looting and interference with firemen. Obviously, such an interpretation may not fit literally every riot; however, it provides a preliminary model or conceptual start for analyzing the problem of severity. (It should be noted that for technical reasons beyond this unit's scope, this type of interpretation of Guttman scales is not advocated by everyone.)

This scale of riot severity proves to be related to a number of urban characteristics such as the percentage of increase in nonwhites between 1950 and 1960, the percentage of nonwhites living in housing constructed between 1950 and 1960, (no data for 1970 was then available), and two police-preparedness indexes: the use of police dogs and the existence of a riot plan. The relation between severity and increases in the nonwhite population is interesting because it is sometimes thought that rapid population gains burden and strain the city's ability to cope with new problems and the demands for services such as trash collections, sewers, police, and schools are inadequately met.

At the same time, the nonwhite percentage can increase because whites move to other areas of the metropolis, leaving nonwhites behind. This movement has been going on for the past two decades. Consequently, those nonwhites "left behind" in the central areas of the city may become more isolated, have fewer contacts with whites and because the remaining citizens tend to be poorer, the city has a smaller revenue base and consequently cannot provide adequate services. In terms of riots, such processes among nonwhites, virtually all of whom are Negro, may lead to disorganization and grievances which, in turn, aggravate and increase the severity of a riot once it does occur. Another measure, the percentage of nonwhites residing in newer housing could indicate the existence of segregation and discrimination inasmuch as blacks traditionally have been forced into central areas where housing is older and of poorer quality. Finally, the two police variables could suggest that cities that are better prepared to meet riots and to use more extreme methods accurately assessed how severe the riots might be. On the other hand, a self-fulfilling prophecy might be at work—being prepared leads to the use of extreme methods that, in turn, lead to more severe riots.

The general influence of city population size on riot severity has been documented using a measure of riot severity based on economic and property losses. It was found that the proportion of the metropolitan population within the central city was related to riot severity. For low-severity cities the proportion was 65, while for high-severity cities it was 60 [McElroy & Singell 1973]. Another study, based on cities of at least 25,000 population, found that sheer size was also strongly related to riot severity as measured by an index based on amounts of looting, arson, sniping, and window breaking. Size of city has also been found to be related to *occurrence* of riots [Jiobu 1971], as well as to rates of violent crime [Kerner Commission 1968].

What is it about size that predisposes a city towards more severe violence? The answer to this question is difficult to document directly, but it is sometimes believed that large city size creates certain problems. Because of the sheer number of people, larger cities may be more impersonal and bureaucratic, and the access of citizens to government may be much more limited. While in a small town, citizens can know their councilmen on a personal basis; in large urban areas few people even know who their representatives are, much less how to express a grievance. The same point may be made about such other government officials as policemen and firemen.

Moreover, in the large city environment, people are believed to interact less and have less personal involvement with other people. A case in point involves a woman stabbed repeatedly on the streets of a respectable residential neighborhood late at night. Although almost forty people admitted they heard her screams for help, no one even called the police until she was dead. Given the nature of urban life, this is a tragic but understandable result. First, urban life lacks the compactness of small-town living; friends and kin may be quite distant while those physically close (in the next apartment house) may be strangers. Thus the murder victim was a stranger to the neighborhood residents, and no one had a vested interest in coming to her aid. Second, public murders are relatively rare, particularly in middle-class suburbs, and persons were more likely to interpret the screams as a quarrel or prank; and, in an anonymous urban environment there is little reason for one to investigate the behaviors of strangers. Finally, involvement is dangerous. The average middle-class person is inept in the act of violence, and even telephoning the police could lead to subsequent revenge by the assailant or his friends. In sum, the urban environment may be conducive to violence because individuals do not perceive their self-interests as being involved with the "strangers" who are their neighbors [Milgram & Hollander 1964].

Impersonal as they are, large cities also tend to be older cities with higher levels of deterioration and congestion. Moreover, they tend to have higher numbers of less well-off people, as measured by welfare expenditures. This generally depressed population, an impersonal, bureaucratic government structure limiting access to government, and a general "lack of community" may provide an environment highly conducive to violence of all types.

A related consideration concerns the size of the black population. The vast majority of riots during the 1960s did not involve interracial violence; seldom did blacks and whites directly confront each other. Instead, black aggression was often directed at symbols of the white population, such as white-owned stores and white policemen. Since this is the case, the number of blacks in a city may heavily influence the probability of riot outbreaks, and once the riot is under way, the seriousness of the violence. Obviously, some minimum black population must be necessary; if there were no blacks, there would be no riot participants. In fact, it has been found that the number of blacks residing in a city is one of the most powerful predictors of riot occurrence [Spilerman 1970]. Data for 413 communities was gathered and the effects of 16 different urban characteristics was assessed. In some cases these characteristics proved strongly or moderately related to riot occurrence. For example, consistent with the studies discussed previously, persons per councilmen was a factor that was strongly related to riot frequency. However, after all 16 characteristics are taken into account, the most powerful predicter of riot frequency was the size of the black population. It is important to realize that we are discussing the sheer size (that is, number) of blacks and not the percentage of blacks in the population.

In some instances a rather small number of black residents might constitute a large percentage of the total population (for example, 500 blacks in a city of 1,500, represent 33.3 percent of the total population).

This study implies that urban characteristics are of little importance insofar as riot frequency is concerned. Certain urban features, such as persons per councilmen, appear to be related to riots because this characteristic tends to be present wherever there are large black populations. The same may be said of many other urban characteristics. In short, different cities are more or less likely to have riots because they vary in the number of blacks residing within them. What then does the number of blacks represent? On the basis of this research Seymour Spilerman concluded:

> I would argue that although different communities are not equally prone to racial disturbance, the susceptibility of an individual Negro to participating in a disorder does not depend upon the structural characteristics of the community in which he resides. As for the community propensity, it is an aggregate of the individual values—the larger the Negro population, the greater the likelihood of a disorder. Little else appears to matter [Spilerman 1970, p. 645].

This conclusion is consistent with the argument that the race riots of the 1960s reflected black protest that was not centered on any particular feature of urban structure or life. Instead, the situation of blacks is perceived as uniformly bad, a consequence of societal pressures such as racism and discrimination. If each individual black feels and protests against this situation, then the larger the number of blacks in a city, the greater the collective feelings of resentment will be. Consequently, the size of the black population determines the occurrence of the riot. Note that nothing is said about the severity of the riot, although presumably the greater the discontent, the more severe the violence.

The relation between discontent and riot severity has been assessed in a study of the 1967 violence based on forty-two cities [Morgan & Clark, 1973]. Housing inequality, measured by the percentage of blacks in substandard housing minus the same percentage for whites, was strongly related to the severity of the riot. Presumably, blacks living in cities of high housing inequality were more likely to be dissatisfied and to express this dissatisfaction in high levels of violence. Strangely, job inequality, measured by the percentage of blacks in low-status jobs minus the white percentage, tended to decrease the severity of violence. Possibly, where there is more racial inequality in jobs, blacks have come to accept their subordinate status and are less motivated to engage in violence, or any form of social action. Nonetheless, this finding is contradictory to most theoretical arguments and it is difficult to explain. Finally, city size proved to be related to severity. For reasons already discussed, this is not surprising.

THE POLICE

Whatever the causes, when collective violence occurs, the police must confront the situation, and their behavior is subject to both criticism and acclaim. The police are sometimes thought of as the thin blue line between hordes of criminals, chaos, and disorder on the one side, and the decent, law-abiding, God-fearing people on the other. Yet, the Kerner Commission [1968], which investigated the racial violence of 1967, concluded that these riots were almost invariably precipitated by an act committed by a white policeman. For example, the Watts riot reportedly was triggered when a white policeman attempted to give a ticket to a Negro youth. In the ensuing confrontation, a crowd gathered and grew threatening, more police were called and, from that seemingly innocuous incident, one of the largest riots in history exploded. Similar incidents can be recounted for numerous other riots. Even incidents of earlier years show the same pattern. Police were engaged in 20 percent of the incidents that precipitated the riots occurring between 1913 and 1963 [Lieberson & Silverman 1965]. This does not mean that police "cause" riots, but rather that they act as sparks to ignite an already smouldering situation. The simple performance of routine duties by white policemen in the ghetto provided a highly visible symbol against which widespread resentment could be focused.

Not only are police believed to be involved in a disproportionately large number of precipitating incidents, but their activities during the riot are often thought to increase the severity of the riot rather than to contain it. There is an adage stating that "riots don't begin until the police arrive."

This view is particularly congruent with the fact that many blacks and police share a mutual dislike for each other. From the perspective of blacks, white police represent about the only direct contact they have with the white power structure. The police are charged with enforcing the law in the black ghetto, yet they are virtually aliens, representatives of a system that has systematically discriminated against blacks. Applying the colonial analogy, the police are sometimes treated as an army of occupation. Not surprisingly, they are disliked. One author concluded that, "Anger, hatred, and fear of the police are a major common denominator among black Americans at the present time" [Skolnick 1969, p. 242].

Blacks are harassed more by the police than whites, a pattern which has been found over the last several decades. For example, in 1935 a commission report stated that ". . . the insecurity of the individual in Harlem against police aggression is one of the most potent causes for the existing hostility to authority" [Skolnick 1969, p. 243]. In a different vein, a survey of blacks in fifteen different cities was undertaken for the Kerner Commission. One section dealt with police abuse of citizens and asked: "Some people say police rough up people unnecessarily when they are arresting them or afterwards. Do you think this happens to people in this neighborhood?" "Has it ever happened to you?" The results of this survey question are given in table 11.

T A B L E 11. Perceptions of Police Abuse

	Black	*White*
Think it happens in this neighborhood	35%	10%
Don't think it happens in this neighborhood	41	78
Don't know	24	12
Total:	100	100
Yes, it has happened to me personally	4%	1%
No, it has not happened to me personally	53	20
Don't know	2	1
No, don't think it happens in this neighborhood	41	78
Total:	100	100

Source: Adapted from Campbell & Schuman 1968, p. 43.

Apparently, blacks believe that police mistreat persons to a considerably higher degree than whites (35 percent versus 10 percent). Whether or not this belief is based on fact, it nonetheless affects black attitudes towards police. Roughing people up is not something that leads to harmonious relations between police and citizens and, as long as people believe this is the way police behave, they will base their attitudes on that belief. Moreover, if we assume that a person's experiences are valid, then the table shows that blacks personally have been roughed up four times more than whites. The numbers of personal incidents are not trivially small. If we assume that each person answering "yes" has been roughed up twice sometime during his lifetime, apply these figures to the national population, and take into account the number of police, then on the average, there are 7.5 roughing incidents per policeman [Stark 1972].

Another indirect way of estimating the amount of police violence is suggested by injury figures from Detroit. In 1964, 1,048 citizens were reported as injured by policemen (either justifiably or not). Of that number, 59 percent were black. Clearly, the relative number of injuries to blacks is disproportionately high since Detroit as a whole was only 29 percent black. Moreover, of all those injured, 66 percent suffered facial damage; and of the 580 injuries to the police, 52 percent were on the hand, knuckles, and fingers [Brooks 1968]. It seems more than coincidental that the majority of citizens are injured in the face while the majority of police are injured in the hand.

It is equally apparent that the many police dislike blacks. Several observers have noted the high levels of police prejudice. In studies of the Boston, Chicago, and Washington police, 72 percent of the policemen were considered prejudiced as indicated by spontaneous remarks, slurs, and epithets against blacks [Black & Reiss, cited in Stark 1972]. If anything, this would tend to underestimate the amount of prejudice since the expressions were spontaneous and, presumably, some prejudiced policemen would not display their attitudes in the presence of researchers.

Moreover, this hostility is not reserved solely for blacks; it applies to many other ethnic minorities, as well as to atypical social groups such as hippies and long-haired college students. To put it another way, police tend to emphasize and respect the status quo and view anything that changes it as potentially dangerous. One of the most widespread incidences of illegal uses of force and violence by police was directed at college students at the University of California, Berkeley. A force of Berkeley regular and reserve police, augmented by county sheriffs "forcefully dispersed—with tear gas, riot batons, kicks, stones and curses—a peaceful crowd of several hundred persons gathered on Telegraph Avenue" [Stark 1972, pp. 32–33]. An observer described the incident as follows: "The first stones were thrown at the police. Gas cannisters were caught and hurled back. More beating and gassing by the police occurred and [it] eventually turned into what can only be described as a police rampage against unarmed and mainly nonprovocative citizens. For several nights many policemen were lawless, dangerous rioters against a terrorized community" [Stark 1972, p. 33].

Not only are blacks and students often the target of police violence, but on at least one occasion a crowd with many middle-class and professional persons were the subject of indiscriminate violence. This crowd had gathered in front of a plush Los Angeles hotel to protest the Vietnam war on the occasion of the late President Johnson's visit to Los Angeles. Apparently, someone gave the order to disperse the crowd and a wild, club swinging melee ensued.

Why do police become rioters? They are the ones charged with maintaining law and order, yet, under certain circumstances, only their uniforms and weapons enable observers to distinguish between them and the "other rioters." However, as with any other collective violence, not all persons become lawlessly and violently engaged. During riots large, but undetermined proportions of the crowd are not active participants; many are simply spectators, hangers-on; passersby, and the like. Similarly, we should not expect all policemen to become lawless and violent. Yet, when even a minority do so, it constitutes a major social issue for a fundamentally simple reason: if the police violate the law, then to whom can we turn to enforce it?

Several factors about modern police forces have been suggested to account for police behavior in general and police riots in particular. Let us examine some of these.

Basically, the police are charged with making arrests, not adjudicating behavior. The question of guilt or innocence is a matter for the courts, yet police have great latitude in carrying out their responsibility. Not all police encounters lead to arrests; persons may be warned, frisked, or taken in but released without charge. Not only is there latitude in making arrests, police also have a great deal of latitude in how they respond to given situations. Essentially, since police training emphasizes individual decision making during encounters when the officer is isolated from his superiors (as on a patrol), the individual policeman decides the amount of force or restraint necessary to carry out his duty. At the same time, police are trained and given the authority to use violence; hence, when violence is used, it tends to be viewed as legitimate unless proven otherwise. Even when use of violence is questioned by others, investigations are usually conducted by the police department itself rather than by an outside group. Only rarely do criminal proceedings ensue. For example, a study [Robin 1963] of Philadelphia revealed that during 1950–1960, thirty-two persons were killed by the police. At the inquest, the policemen in thirty of these cases were exonerated on the basis of justifiable homicide and two cases resulted in jury trials at which the officers were found innocent. By and large, the police were found to have acted with due restraint; twenty-five victims resisted physically and seven attempted to flee. While one can debate whether or not killing represented the "last resort," these figures do show that police officers are rarely brought to trial. Moreover, police have vigorously opposed any attempts to impose external controls over their activities. Numerous efforts to establish civilian review boards have failed, in part due to the campaigns waged by the police [Stark 1972].

Given this set of circumstances, there are few external constraints on police violence, particularly when the target is a powerless group without political influence or the resources necessary to bring charges. As with many other professions (for example, physicians), the primary constraints are internal; that is, reliance is placed on adherence to standards, regulations, norms, and values generated within the profession itself. Unfortunately, police organization tends to lead in the opposite direction—away from nonviolence towards an emphasis on violence as a means of social control. Stark [1972] suggests a line of argument for this. One reason is the physical danger involved in police work. In comparison to some other types of work, the police actually have less dangerous occupations than is sometimes realized. For example, the rate of work-related deaths is almost three times greater for mining than for police work, while contract construction is almost two-and-one-half times as dangerous [Robin 1963]. In a way, such figures tend to understate the amount of danger involved. Compared to clerical work, police work is extremely dangerous. Further, the rate undoubtedly varies according to the specific type of work the policemen is engaged in; those filling out forms in the police station are obviously safer than those patrolling in high-crime-rate areas of the city. Nonetheless, police work is not as dangerous as the police assert. Many policemen spend an entire career without having to fire their guns in the line of duty. However, policemen *believe* their work is extremely hazardous, even though the amount of perceived danger is far greater than the objective amount.

There are several factors responsible for these beliefs. First, police are in close contact with potentially violent episodes. Although the vast majority of police calls do not result in actual violence, the situations may be ripe for it. Even something as mundane as responding to a call involving a family quarrel is laden with violent overtones; persons are emotionally and angrily aroused, and it is probable that some physical aggression between the parties has already taken place. Not only do individual policemen encounter many similar episodes, they have the opportunity to informally exchange information with other policemen in the course of their work and during their off-duty hours. Hence, since they are often immersed in violent or potentially violent activity, either personally or vicariously, the perceived threat may be magnified out of proportion to the actual threat. Second, police are trained in the use of violent tools: guns, clubs, blackjacks, and chemicals such as mace. These tools are constantly present and carried on their person. Both in fact, and symbolically, these tools represent violence. It seems reasonable to expect that under potentially danger-ous situations these violent tools will be used. Indeed, policemen may be foolish not to use them in the face of danger. However, the point is that violence is part and parcel of the policemen's job.

Finally, unlike many dangerous occupations, police experience per-sonal violence; that is, they are subject to dangers directed at them from other persons. This may lead police to view their safety as manageable. If the proper precautions are taken, which includes being armed, and being prepared to use those arms when threatened, then their own safety can be maintained. Hence, a large amount of police violence is psycholo-gically and morally justified on the grounds of preemptive violence—it is better to strike before the other person strikes you.

No one denies the police the right to be concerned with their own safety, and society certainly does not expect them to be so much cannon fodder. On the other hand, police also accept the responsibility for public safety and the common good. Which of these two should be given the first priority? From a societal view, the common good is obviously more important, and police are paid to accept a certain amount of risk and danger [Stark 1972]. Conversely, the personal safety of the police can be given priority and the latter view tends to predominate; investigative bodies have consistently pointed out the dangers faced by police during riots and have accepted that as a legitimate reason for violence.

Another consistent finding is that police form an extremely cohesive subculture, far stronger than is typically found in other occupational groups. They are highly secretive and clannish, characteristics that permeate both their working and private lives. Police and their wives tend to associate primarily with other police families through a variety of clubs, lodges, and fraternities. The code of secrecy is particularly strong when it comes to testifying against another police officer concern-ing charges of abuse; it is simply not done [Stark 1972].

Several reasons undoubtedly exist for this subcultural development. Obviously, police share common interests and occupational experiences. One consequence of shared dangers is to increase the solidarity of the threatened group [Coser 1956]. People come together in order to face the common danger, and there is no reason to believe that the police are any different in this respect.

They also tend to have similar personality profiles (highly authoritarian) [McNamara 1967], and to justify the use of force to obtain "respect" from persons they encounter [Westley 1953]. Finally, the police are a paramilitary organization and tend to view the civilian life as the "outside" in much the same way the military does.

Moreover, for most people, police represent an authority they are uncomfortable confronting. People routinely commit "minor" crimes such as speeding, littering, and swearing in public. This puts the policeman into a state of conflict between his duty to intervene and his obligation to be friendly. At the same time, even the police engage in such behaviors during their off-duty hours although they realize that the public expects them to be extremely law abiding; thus, police may feel much more comfortable in the presence of other police. In sum, there are strong pressures that lead the police to become very cohesive as an occupational group.

As a result of such cohesiveness, group decisions are especially binding on group members. The norm of secrecy is easy to maintain; the toleration of violence is socially reinforced, as is the prejudice against minority groups. Any attack on one member of the group is perceived as an attack on all members, whether the attack is physical, verbal, or in the form of civilian complaints.

Police administrators are also bound up in this system. Most have long police experience, having worked their way up from the ranks. Even if administrators were not part of the system, they would face extreme difficulty in attempting to impose external changes in the face of such cohesiveness. Moreover, there is very little public support for changes. Public opinion polls suggest that few people approve of illegal police violence. But the polls also suggest that the majority of people do not believe it takes place [Stark 1972]. Police violence is simply not an issue, except in an academic sense.

Given the above factors, a major decrease in the amount of police violence appears unlikely. The police essentially represent the dominant middle and upper classes [Galliher 1971]. The lower classes are powerless and make easy targets. More important, the interests of the middle and upper classes may be in direct conflict with the lower classes or racial minorities. The former may want order and harmony since changes might disrupt their life styles. At the same time, these are often the very changes for which the lower classes may strive. Obviously, the upper strata have more political and financial influence, and police departments tend to behave in a manner consistent with their desires. As one author said, ". . . police tend to function to control the poor and Black Americans in any way necessary while other citizens can continue to believe this is a free democratic society and yet have their property protected at the same time" [Galliher 1971, p. 315].

However, note that the preceding analysis, while critical of the police, is based upon institutional arrangements and not directed at any particular department or individual. For example, it is not surprising that police departments reflect the middle and upper classes, nor that policemen develop an occupational subculture; most institutions develop along such lines. Hence, in a fundamental sense, police violence is "natural" and simply a reflection of the society that supports the police.

At the same time, police work is "dirty" work. In their daily routines, policemen must confront and deal with persons and activities that the average member of the middle class shuns. Moreover, police are obviously the targets of much abuse, and the individual policeman is placed in a role that it is virtually impossible to fulfill. Remember that we expect police officers to deal with potentially dangerous or disagreeable situations; to impartially uphold the law; to prevent (not just respond to) crime; and to render aid when we need it. At the same time, all of these tasks must be done perfectly: the police officer must show the judgment of a judge, apply the law like a lawyer, be as empathetic as a social worker, and be prepared to use violence if necessary.

An instructive insight into these problems is provided by the experiences of an academic criminologist who became a police officer [Kirkham 1974]. When confronted by an angry crowd that had gathered when he attempted to give a traffic ticket, he says that he suddenly recalled his professorial arguments that policemen should not carry shotguns and realized that his role as policeman had changed his perspective radically.

> As a criminology professor I had always enjoyed the luxury of having great amounts of time in which to make difficult decisions.
> As a police officer, however, I found myself forced to make the most critical choices in a time frame of seconds, rather than days.
> To shoot or not to shoot, to arrest or not to arrest, to give chase or let go . . . .

As these experiences serve to emphasize, the job of a policeman is one of the most difficult jobs there is; perhaps few people have the psychological make-up to cope with it to the degree of perfection we demand. Perhaps in a broader sense, we simply expect too much from our police forces; perhaps policemen should not be expected to perform social work roles (e.g., collecting drunks or resolving family arguments). In short, society places demands on police forces that may, given their current social organization, be impossible to fulfill.

CONCLUSION

As we have seen, violence is a very complex topic. Not only is it difficult to arrive at a universally agreed upon definition of violence, but once having found a working definition, we find it may be divided into various types. Each type, in turn, may be analyzed in numerous ways. At first blush, this seeming hodgepodge of findings, opinions, and theories may seem more confusing than enlightening. However, in addition to the detailed information provided by the literature, more general conclusions can be briefly suggested. These are meant more as a frame of reference rather than as master conclusions.

First, violence is socially defined behavior; what is violent by the standards of one group may not be so defined by another. Consequently, the attribution of morality to agnostic behavior is relative to one's socially defined perspective.

Second, all human behavior takes place in a social context and violence is no exception. Thus, it is not surprising that much violence occurs within societies (or subgroups of societies) that are organized in certain ways and supported by certain cultural prescriptions.

Third, we can see that the question, "what causes violence?" is far too simple minded and hardly worth asking except in a pedagogical or rhetorical sense. The answer will naturally vary depending on the *type* of violence, the *situation* in which it occurs, and the *conceptual viewpoint* used to analyze it.

Finally, since new research is constantly being done, we should not be surprised to find that some of what we have read will, in the future, become "outdated." Consequently, we should not be misled into seeking immutable answers, at least at this stage of sociological knowledge. Perhaps the greater wisdom would come from recognizing what is known and what is doubtful, and accepting the limits of knowledge as they constantly change before us.

Bibliography

Sandra J. Ball-Rokeach, "The Legitimation of Violence." In James F. Short, Jr., and Marvin E. Wolfgang, eds., *Collective Violence.* Aldine-Atherton, 1972, pp. 101-111.

Albert Bandura, "What TV Violence Can Do to Your Child." In Otto N. Larson, ed., *Violence and the Mass Media.* Harper & Row, 1968, pp. 123–130.

Edward C. Banfield, *The Unheavenly City.* Little, Brown, 1968.

Leonard Berkowitz, "The Frustration-Aggression Hypothesis Revisited." In Leonard Berkowitz, ed., *Roots of Aggression.* Atherton 1969, pp. 1–28.

Leonard Berkowitz and A. LePage, "Weapons as Aggression Eliciting Stimuli." *Journal of Personality and Social Psychology,* 1967, 7:202–207.

Robert Blauner, "Internal Colonialism and Ghetto Revolt." In James A. Geschwender, ed., *The Black Revolt.* Prentice-Hall, 1971.

Donald Block, and Albert J. Reiss, Jr., *Patterns of Behavior in Police and Citizens Transactions.* U.S. Government Printing Office, 1967.

Monica Blumenthal, Robert L. Kahn, Frank M. Andrews, and Kendra B. Head, *Justifying Violence.* Ann Arbor: Institute for Social Research, 1972.

Thomas R. Brooks, "Necessary Force—Or Police Brutality?" In Shalom Endleman, ed., *Violence in the Streets.* Quadrangle, 1968, pp. 403–413.

Angus Campbell and Harold Schuman, "Racial Attitudes in Fifteen American Cities." *Supplemental Studies for the National Advisory Commission on Civil Disorders.* Praeger, 1968.

Donald T. Campbell, "Factors Relevant to the Validity of Experiments in Social Settings." *Psychological Bulletin,* 1957, 54:297–312.

Nathan Caplan, "The New Ghetto Man." *Journal of Social Issues,* 1970, 26:59–73.

Nathan Caplan and J. M. Paige, "A Study of Ghetto Rioters." *Scientific American,* 1968, 219:15–21.

Lewis A. Coser, *The Function of Social Conflict.* The Free Press, 1956.

Ralf Dahrendorf, "Out of Utopia." *American Journal of Sociology,* 1958, 64:116–127.

Desmond Ellis, Paul Weinir, and Louis Miller, III, "Does the Trigger Pull the Finger?" *Sociometry,* 1971, 4:453–465.

John F. Galliher, "Explanation of Police Behavior." *Sociological Quarterly,* 1971, 12:308–318.

Raymond Gastil, "Homicide and the Regional Culture of Violence." *American Sociological Review,* 1971, 36:412–427.

Russel Geen, "Some Implications of Experimental Social Psychology for the

Study of Urban Disorders." *Sociological Quarterly,* 1971, 12:340–350.

Walter M. Gerson, "Violence as an American Value Theme." In Otto N. Larson, ed., *Violence and the Mass Media.* Harper & Row, 1968, pp. 151–162.

James A. Geschwender and Benjamin D. Singer, "Deprivation and the Detroit Riot." *Social Problems,* 1970, 17:457–463.

Daniel Glaser, "Violence and the City." In Daniel Glaser, ed., *Crime and the City.* Harper & Row, 1970.

Allen D. Grimshaw, "The Changing Pattern of Racial Violence in the United States." In A. D. Grimshaw, ed., *Racial Violence in the United States.* Aldine, 1969a.

Allen D. Grimshaw, "Violence." *George Washington Law Review,* 1969b, 37:816–834.

Ted Robert Gurr, "Urban Disorder." In Louis H. Masotti and Don R. Bowen, eds., *Riots and Rebellion.* Sage, 1968, pp. 51–67.

Ted Robert Gurr, *Why Men Rebel.* Princeton University Press, 1970.

Ted Robert Gurr, "A Comparative Study of Civil Strife." In Hugh Davis Graham and Ted Robert Gurr, eds., *Violence in America.* Bantam, 1971, pp. 572–632.

Harlan Hahn and Joe R. Feagin, "Rank and File versus Congressional Perceptions of Ghetto Riots." *Social Science Quarterly,* 1970, 51:361–373.

Ruth E. Hartley, "The Impact of Viewing 'Aggression'" (summarized by Joseph T. Klapper). In Otto N. Larson ed., *Violence and the Mass Media,* Harper & Row, 1964, p. 131–139.

Joel Tyler Headley, *The Great Riots of New York.* Bobbs-Merrill, first publication 1873.

Vincent Jeffries, Ralph H. Turner, and Richard T. Morris, "Public Perception of the Watts Riot as Social Protest." *American Sociological Review,* 1971, 36:443–451.

Robert M. Jiobu, "City Characteristics, Differential Stratification, and the Occurrence of Interracial Violence." *Social Science Quarterly,* 1971, 50:508–520.

Robert M. Jiobu, *Conflict and Integration.* Ph.D. dissertation, University of Southern California, 1969.

Kerner Commission, *Report of the National Advisory Commission on Civil Disorders.* Otto Kerner, chairman. U.S. Government Printing Office, 1968.

George L. Kirkham, "Professor Turned Cop." Reprinted in the *Columbus Citizens Journal,* March 6–8, 1974.

Stanley Lieberson and Arnold R. Silverman, "The Precipitant and Underlying Causes of Race Riots." *American Sociological Review,* 1965, 30:887–898.

Peter A. Lupsha, "On Theories of Urban Violence." *Urban Affairs Quarterly,* 1969, 4:273–296.

Jerome L. McElroy and Larry D. Singell, "Riot and Nonriot Cities." *Urban Affairs Quarterly,* 1973, 8:281–302.

John H. McNamara, "Uncertainties in Police Work." In David J. Bordua, ed., *The Police*. Wiley, 1967, pp. 152–163.

Clark McPhail, "Civil Disorder Participation." *American Sociological Review,* 1971, 36:1058–1073.

Stanley Milgram and Paul Hollander, "The Murder They Heard." *The Nation,* 15 June, 1964.

William R. Morgan and Terry Nichols Clark, "The Causes of Racial Disturbances." *American Sociological Review,* 1973, 38:611–624.

Jefferey M. Paige, "Political Orientation and Riot Participation." *American Sociological Review,* 1971, 36:810–820.

E. L. Quarantelli and Russel R. Dynes, "Property Norms and Looting." *Phylon,* 1970, 31:168–172.

Edward H. Ransford, "Isolation, Powerlessness, and Violence." *American Journal of Sociology,* 1968, 73:581–591.

Gerald D. Robin, "Justifiable Homicide by Police Officers." *Journal of Criminal Law, Criminology and Police Science,* 1963, 54:225–231.

David Q. Sears and John B. McConahay, "Racial Socialization, Comparison Levels, and the Watts Riot." *Journal of Social Issues,* 1970, 26:121–140.

Jerome H. Skolnick, *The Politics of Protest*. Ballantine, 1969.

Social Science Quarterly, "The Unheavenly City: Acrimony and Accolades." *Social Science Quarterly,* 51:816–859.

Georges Sorel, *Reflections on Violence*. T. E. Huline and J. Roth, trans. London: Collier-MacMillan, 1960.

Seymour Spilerman, "The Causes of Racial Disturbances." *American Sociological Review,* 1970, 35:627–649

Rodney Stark, *Police Riots*. Wadsworth, 1972.

J. W. Thibaut and H. H. Kelley, *The Social Psychology of Groups*. Wiley, 1959.

Ralph Turner, "The Public Perception of Protest." *American Sociological Review,* 1969, 34:815–831.

U.S. Bureau of the Census, *Statistical Abstracts of the United States*. 92nd ed. Government Printing Office, 1971.

U. S. News and World Report, "Violence on TV." 24 October, 1973, pp. 33–36.

Jules J. Wanderer, "Index of Riot Severity." *American Journal of Sociology,* 1969, 74:500–505.

William A. Westley, "Violence and the Police." *American Journal of Sociology,* 1953, 59:34–41.

Marvin Wolfgang, *Patterns in Criminal Homicide*. University of Pennsylvania Press, 1958.

8.

POWER,
POLITICS,
AND
DECISION
MAKING

David G. Bromley

The field of urban politics involves the study of the connection between two sets of social structures and processes—one labeled "urban" and the other "political." This area of inquiry is labeled a "field" since urban studies and research on politics fall into the domain of several disciplines including sociology, history, political science, economics, and psychology. What is unique in a sociological approach to urban politics, then, is the perspective taken on the subject matter rather than the subject matter itself. For urban sociologists, understanding the politics of urban communities involves an examination of the relationship between the emergence, change, structure, and functioning of urban society and one of its constituent elements, the local community political institution. Such a task necessarily includes an analysis of the relationships among component units of the political institutions, with other communities, and with supra-community organizations.

URBAN SOCIOLOGY AND URBAN POLITICS

The study of urban politics in the context of urban sociology is based on several important premises: 1. the emergence of urban society constituted a basic transformation of human societies;   2. in highly specialized, interdependent urban societies local communities remain viable social units; and   3. the study of community political relationships yields insight into the structure and process of urban society. A brief commentary on these premises and important dimensions of urban society may provide some perspective on the context within which the study of urban politics has developed.

The Emergence of Urban Society

Both urban and political sociology reflect the absorption of sociology as a discipline with the breakdown of traditional society and the emergence of modern urban society. Perhaps no better evidence of this can be cited than that most of the founding fathers and many subsequent theorists have attempted to describe the nature of this transformation through a comparison of traditional, transitional, and modern urban social orders. This orientation is reflected in dichotomous typologies such as Durkheim's mechanical and organic, Tonnies' *Gemeinschaft* and *Gesellschaft,* Redfield's folk and urban, Weber's traditional and rational, and Maine's status and contract. Their concern with this transformation is not surprising for throughout most of human history societies have been small, relatively static, culturally homogeneous, and structurally undifferentiated. They were held together by commonality of social activities, kinship, tradition, and values. The Reformation and the French and Industrial Revolutions saw the emergence of large, heterogeneous societies, growing and changing at an unprecedented rate. An extensive division of labor created complex, functionally differentiated institutions and a concomitant decline in common cultural beliefs and values. Social thinkers were profoundly disturbed, raising apprehensions about what would hold such societies together.

Within this framework urban sociologists have sought to determine the nature of urbanism, those qualities possessed by urban communities and the way of life, characterized "urban," that occurs within those communities [Gutman & Popenoe 1970; Meadows 1969; Popenoe 1969; Sjoberg 1965]. For political sociologists the analogous question has been how complex urban societies could withstand continuous conflict among their members and still retain social cohesiveness and the legitimacy of state authority [Coser 1966; Lipset 1959; Nordlinger 1970]. What would be the relationship between the state and other social institutions? Much of the current research in sociology is the continuation of a century-long dialogue with theorists who began trying to answer such questions.

The Significance of Community

The viability of communities is an important issue. Although there has been considerable fluctuation in the popularity of community as an object of inquiry, historically the concept has been central in sociological analysis. Recently there has been a resurgence of interest in community studies, but the utility of the concept as a unit of sociological analysis still is widely debated [Bonjean 1971; Kaufman 1966; Warren 1969].

It has been argued that local communities are outmoded since they are no longer autonomous and no longer shape the behavior of their members through a shared local culture, life style, and set of institutions. However, the assertion that communities once were autonomous units is dubious since their existence implies some supra-community level of organization. Communities represent a specific form of social organization within a society, one that involves the relationship between a population and its territorial location. The emergence of urban-industrial society has not caused the demise of communities as effective locality units, but it has resulted in the same kind of structural and functional specialization that has occurred in other organizations and institutions.

The Significance of the Political Process

The significance for sociology of research on urban politics lies in the general knowledge of urban society, which is acquired through an understanding of community political institutions and the relationship between those institutions and their community and extra-community environment.

The political process is of particular sociological importance since it is a major determinant of the degree to which various groups within communities will experience relative privilege or deprivation. Community resources are generated and allocated; disputes over the criteria, process, and substance of resource allocation are resolved, and the rights and obligations of subgroups are defined through the political process.

In urban-industrial societies the political institution becomes increasingly important. First, as political institutions assume responsibility for a wide array of functions that were previously performed by other institutions, the scope of their activity and the size of the political economy grow correspondingly. Second, the potential sources of conflict that must be resolved politically multiply [Bredemeir & Stephenson 1962, pp. 367–391]: 1. Cultural heterogeneity results in very different conceptions of "morality" and "truth." 2. The combination of diverse interests and interdependence creates controversy over the rights and obligations of subgroups. What kinds of demands, restrictions, and freedoms are obligatory? For whom? Under what conditions? 3. Change is endemic to urban society. Yet some groups inevitably absorb more of the costs and consequences of social change than others. 4. Resources are limited and so, at least on a relative basis, there must be "haves" and "have-nots." How should scarce and valued resources be distributed? 5. Specialization and differentiation create real and perceptual differences in definitions of subgroup and societal interests.

As the importance of the political process and the sources of potential conflict grow, both the necessity and the difficulty of coordinating and regulating diverse, but interdependent, social units increase. Viewing urban society through the political process, therefore, is uniquely revealing of the nature and extent of value consensus and dissensus, the ranking of social priorities, the distribution of power resources, relationships among institutions, and the degree and type of societal integration. Each of these phenomena can be observed in the structure and process of urban communities.

Some Key Dimensions of Urban Society

The urban-industrial revolution transformed the nature of local communities and their institutions. In order to explore the political concomitants of this revolution, it is important to identify some of its key elements. These elements have been conceptualized and categorized in a variety of ways [Reissman 1965, pp. 150–194; Warren 1972, pp. 53–94]. We shall now consider some of those that are particularly relevant to the structure and functioning of the political institutions.

Urban Growth

The term "urban growth" refers here to both urbanization and industrialization. Urbanization denotes an increase in the number of urban centers, their size, and the proportion of the population located within them. Industrialization refers to the shift from an agriculture-based to a manufacturing-based economy. They will be considered jointly, however, since they coincided spatially and temporally in the United States.

By the middle of the nineteenth century the urban population was growing rapidly. As table 1 shows, only 10 percent of the population was urban in 1840, but it was 25 percent urban by 1870 and reached 50 percent by 1920. In 1840 there were only 5 cities with populations over 50,000, but there were 144 in 1920 and 385 in 1970. The overwhelming majority of urban population growth has occurred through migration; very little has been the result of natural increase. Many of the early British, German, Dutch, and French immigrants were induced to leave the coastal cities by the availability of rich farm land in the interior. The first group of immigrants to remain in the cities were the Irish, several million of whom arrived in the United States between 1850 and 1860 in the wake of a severe potato famine in Ireland. Successive waves of German, Dutch, Swiss, and Scandinavian immigrants arrived between 1860 and 1890. They were followed in the next few decades by large numbers of southern and eastern Europeans. When foreign immigration was virtually halted in 1920 by restrictive immigration laws, rural areas within the United States became the chief source of urban population growth.

After the Civil War industrial growth accelerated very rapidly and the number of workers in agriculture and related occupations began to decline. Productivity and the amount of land in farms, however, has continued to increase. In 1870, 54 percent of the labor force was employed in agricultural, forestry, and fishing industries, but by 1920 that proportion had dropped to 28 percent [Hawley 1950, p. 376]. As a result of declining agricultural employment, the rural population has grown very slowly in comparison with the urban population, and the absolute size of the rural farm population has declined.

The combination of population and industrial growth transformed cities. Urban populations reached unprecedented size, density, and social and cultural diversity. Cities were restructured as commercial and industrial activities assumed central locations, homes and workplaces separated, and population and industry began to disperse over ever wider areas. The cities became the dominant centers of expanding hinterlands, transportation and communication hubs to which raw materials were shipped for processing, storage, and redistribution to distant markets. As the urban-industrial economy developed, the economic and political center of gravity shifted to the cities.

The transformation of urban communities created a myriad of new problems for which there were no institutional solutions. Explosive growth

TABLE 1. Characteristics of the Urban Population

Year	Percentage of total U.S. population Urban	Rural	Number of places over 50,000	SMSA Population as a percent of Total U.S. population	Distribution of SMSA Population Central City	Outside
1970	73.5	26.5	385	67.0	45.8	54.2
1960	69.9	30.1	320	63.0	51.4	48.6
1950	64.0	36.0	232	59.1	58.7	41.3
1940	56.5	43.5	199	55.1	62.7	37.3
1930	56.1	43.9	191	54.3	64.6	35.4
1920	51.2	48.8	144	49.7	66.0	34.0
1910	45.6	54.4	109	45.7	64.6	35.4
1900	39.6	60.4	78	41.9	62.2	37.8
1890	35.1	64.9	58	-	-	-
1880	28.2	71.8	35	-	-	-
1870	25.7	74.3	25	-	-	-
1860	19.8	80.2	16	-	-	-
1850	15.3	84.7	10	-	-	-

Source: Data obtained from U.S. census publications.

and high densities compelled cities to institute water, sanitation, and waste-disposal systems. More efficient forms of transportation were needed to link residences and workplaces and to facilitate the flow of raw materials and finished products. In addition to innovations in the physical plant, new mechanisms for social control and coordination were required. Social and cultural diversity led to growing conflict, crime, and disorder. Large numbers of unskilled and uneducated immigrants arrived without even the ability to speak English. The combination of lack of skills, economic dislocations, and unfettered capitalism resulted in high rates of unemployment and desperate poverty. Since most of these problems could be attacked only through collective action, local governments soon began expanding their field of activity, assuming a central role in facilitating and dealing with the consequences of urban growth.

Suburbanization

During recent decades the growth rates of most large cities have slowed and many have experienced absolute declines in population [Hawley 1956; Schnore 1957; 1962]. Urban growth now occurs principally in the incorporated and unincorporated areas surrounding these cities. As table 1 shows, the proportion of the U.S. population within metropolitan areas has steadily increased, from just over 40 percent in 1900 to almost 70 percent in 1970. At the same time, the distribution of that population within metropolitan areas has shifted. In 1900 over 60 percent of the metropolitan area population resided within central cities, but by 1970 the balance had shifted, with 54 percent in the suburban areas.

Decentralization began relatively early in the nineteenth century, but travel distances were severely limited by the relatively primitive means of transportation. As technological innovations in transportation were made, these distances steadily increased. However, the dramatic growth of suburban areas did not begin until 1900, with the advent of the automobile. In every decade since 1920 suburban areas have grown faster than central cities [Hawley 1956; Schnore 1959].

In many ways suburbanization represents a continuation of the process of urban growth. Since early cities usually encompassed only a few, densely settled square miles, new growth tended to occur on the periphery of the built-up area. Therefore, some initial suburbanization simply was the result of such new growth spilling over existing municipal boundaries. When more distant locations became accessible, however, they offered large tracts of land for development, relief from city taxes, and freedom from the multitude of problems that beset cities.

The first suburbanites were drawn largely from upper status groups since they were able to absorb the longer time and higher monetary costs of commuting. As a result, particularly in larger, older metropolitan areas, there is a clear socioeconomic division between central cities and suburban rings [Schnore 1963; 1964; 1965, pp. 169–183]. As a larger proportion of the population suburbanized, the heterogeneity of suburban rings has grown. The caricature of suburbs as middle-class, white havens is losing its validity, although it is true that only a small percentage of suburbanites are black [Grodzins 1972, pp. 91–99]. Despite such overall diversity, the characteristics of individual communities have tended to persist [Farley 1972, pp. 82–96].

The outgrowth of these processes has been the division of the suburban population into a number of small, independent political jurisdictions. Thus, while metropolitan areas constitute a single system socially and economically, they are politically fragmented. For this reason it is important to distinguish between urban and suburban growth. Metropolitan area communities vary markedly in population size and composition, economic base, fiscal resources, municipal service mix, type of government, policy outputs, and power structure. The result is a tremendous variety of types of political relationships within communities, among these independent communities, and with supra-community-level institutions.

Organizational Complexity

Another major aspect of urban-industrial development has been the increasing bureaucratization and professionalization [Alford 1973] of organizations. Bureaucratization refers to a structure and a process whereby the differentiated roles within an organization are rationally and hierarchically organized. Professionalization signifies that organizational positions are filled on the basis of technical expertise, and the trained experts perform their assigned functions according to professionally designated standards. Despite its pejorative connotation, bureaucratization is an effective social mechanism for coordinating highly differentiated systems by institutionalizing regularity, precision, impersonality, integration, and centralization of authority.

Rising expectations for efficiently administered services and the problems attending urban growth have led local governments to become increasingly professionalized and bureaucratized. There are significant implications for the political process. Bureaucracies constitute organizational vehicles for administering policy; in this sense their existence denotes that major value commitments and social policies have already been formulated. The bureaucratic organization of government tends to result in decision making by specialists rather than through a more public process. It also tends to formalize relationships with other organizations and individuals, and centralizes control in the hands of professionals to whom access is limited. As a result, the movement toward bureaucratization and professionalism restructures access, the decision-making process, and the perspective of decision makers.

Vertical Integration

Vertical integration refers to the structural and functional relationships of community social units to the larger social systems of which they are a part [Warren 1972, pp. 237–266]. The specialization of communities has increased their dependence on and involvement in vertically organized systems. The multiplicity of specific functions that communities perform as manufacturing, wholesaling, retailing, transportation, residential, recreational, governmental, or military centers suggests their specialized roles in metropolitan, regional, state, and national systems.

Communities are territorially based units, but increasingly the interests of their residents and the larger system organizations that operate within them do not coincide with their geographic boundaries. In this sense, many organizations and individuals are "in" but not "of" the community. The policies of supra-community organizations reflect their own goals and priorities. While their decisions have a profound impact on the community, they frequently are made outside of and with limited consideration of their consequences for the locality. The careers and aspirations of individual members of the community are tied to these organizations rather than to the place itself. Vertical integration tends to reduce communities' social cohesiveness and control over their own fate.

Politics within urban communities strongly reflects the impact of this vertical integration. Local governmental structure, at least to some extent, is adapted to the specialized role the community plays within the larger system. The local political economy that provides resources for public services is dependent on funding from higher levels of government and taxes on business. The flow of these resources hinges on the extent to which community policies conform to the needs and priorities of supra-community organizations. Effective local political leadership, therefore, often mandates the maintenance of extra-community ties as well as a community political base. Finally, policy outputs are shaped by the interaction of many diverse community and extra-community interest groups. Thus, important elements or determinants of community power structure, such as governmental structure, economic resources, and policy outputs, have been reshaped by the rapidly growing involvement of communities in vertical systems.

Cultural Context

The growth and development of American cities is best understood within the context of dominant cultural goals and values. The emergence and character of urban society were shaped by the American cultural tradition of which the cities were part. As Sam Warner, among others [Merton 1973; R. Williams 1970], has noted, American culture has been dominated by a tradition of privatism.

> Its essence lay in the concentration upon the individual and the individual search for wealth. . . . [It meant that cities] depended for their wages, employment, and general prosperity upon the aggregate successes and failures of thousands of individual enterprises, not upon community action. It also meant that the physical forms of American cities, their lots, houses, factories, and streets, have been the outcome of a real estate market of profit-seeking builders, land speculators, and large investors. Finally, the tradition of privatism has meant that the local politics of American cities have depended for their actors, and for a good deal of their subject matter, on the changing focus of men's private economic activities [Warner 1968, pp. 3–4].

Among the triumvirate of values to which the leaders of the French Revolution appealed—liberty, equality, and fraternity—the first two received priority in the United States [Advisory Commission on Intergovernmental Relations 1962c, pp. 8–20]. Both liberty and equality tend to be universalistic. Liberty values relate to individual freedom, protection of minority group members, and the defense of property rights. Equality values imply broadly based citizen participation in government. The abolition of slavery, granting of women's suffrage, and elimination of property ownership as a voting qualification are instances of the extension of equality values. Both liberty and equality values, at least as they have been expressed in the United States, imply limited governmental power. Equality traditionally has been defined as equal opportunity rather than equal condition; liberty as "freedom from" constraint. Liberty values translate into governmental functions such as maintaining vital records on individuals and property and the administration of justice. Equality values translate principally into regulation of electoral rules and procedures.

Fraternity values, by contrast, imply a collectivistic rather than individualistic orientation. Although individuals benefit from their implementation, fraternity values are group oriented. Indeed, individual interests sometimes must be sacrificed for the collective interest. Governments seek to promote the welfare of the community as a whole rather than operating as agencies that merely provide a set of services paid for by tax revenues. As fraternity values are implemented, the scope of governmental activity widens and resources channeled through the political economy grow. Public education, protective police and health services, and land use planning tend to reflect welfare values; yet the dominance of the privativistic tradition is evident from the fact that development of welfare functions was later, more limited, and aroused greater controversy than either liberty or equality functions.

Although there are a host of other important values that characterize American culture, the tradition of privatism has been central in the formation of urban communities and in the governance of those communities. Although the types and levels of municipal service outputs and the order of their enactment document the commitment to government as the defender of liberty and equality values, the exploitation of capital outlays for municipal services for personal gain, as well as the use of political office as a mechanism of social mobility, reflect the preeminence of economic success as a cultural goal. The early dominance of political office by the economic elite, their later withdrawal, and the restructuring of local governments to coincide with economic interests documents the central role that economic institutions played in shaping the role of other institutions. These and other prominent features of urban political histories underscore the significance of the tradition of privatism in shaping the character of and the American response to urban growth.

THE EMERGENCE OF URBAN GOVERNMENTS

The Expansion of Urban Service Functions

The expanded scope of activities of municipal governments is attributable both to the problems attending urban growth and to Americans' conception of the kinds of functions that local government ought to perform. The initial impetus for expansion was rooted in the physical and social realities of the urban industrial revolution. The way that expansion occurred and the nature of the governmental structure that emerged also were influenced by cultural definitions of the proper role of government. The explosiveness of urban growth literally overwhelmed the institutional structure of urbanizing communities. For example, Chicago, which had a population of only 30,000 in 1850, had grown tenfold to 300,000 by 1870. By 1890 it had reached the million mark, and it absorbed an average of half a million new inhabitants during each of the next four decades. As the population size of cities increased, so did density. By 1850, for instance, the density of New York City had climbed to 136 persons per acre. It rapidly became imperative to institute formalized means of social control; to improve transportation and communication technology; to assimilate and acculturate vast numbers of immigrants; to provide basic literacy and skills for members of the labor force; and to protect the health, safety, and welfare of community members. The way that these functions were organized and performed was determined in large measure by the American tradition of privatism and a commitment to ever-increasing levels of efficiency and production.

The expanded scope of local government had important implications for the political process within urban communities. Many activities that formerly had been carried out by private initiative, other institutions (e.g., the family), or voluntary associations were transferred to the political institution. In this sense, decision making and policy outputs became the product of "political" rather than "market" forces. As the scope of governmental activity increased, so did the size of the political economy and the importance of political decisions for groups and individuals within urban communities.

The expansion of local government constituted the creation of new centers of power, which, in the aggregate, had the effect of restructuring community power. It has been commonplace to think of municipal services in "administrative" rather than "political" terms because in many communities they have become relatively standardized and routinized. The political implications of these services often become apparent only when issues such as neighborhood control of schools, zoning for racial segregation, or police brutality surface. However, it is important to emphasize that the objectives and style of implementation of new municipal agencies did not serve the needs and interests of all groups within urban communities equally. The relative distribution of their benefits and costs are revealing indices of community power structure. From this perspective the structure of government represented an answer to the question, "What functions should governments perform and for what purposes and clientele?"

As local governments began to perform a wider array of functions, the exigencies of urban growth and the tenets of privatism interacted to shape the type, level, and extent of services. Water, fire prevention, and sewage disposal were services necessitated by the increasing size, density, and complexity of urban communities. Such services helped ensure the orderly growth of the industrial city, which otherwise might have been undermined by the uncontrolled ravages of disease and fire. The tradition of privatism stipulated that these services be designed to foster economic growth rather than to promote the general welfare by ensuring the health and safety of all individuals. Similarly, public education arose to combat problems such as poverty, illiteracy, and unemployment among the urban migrants. Not long after their inception, however, public schools began to see their task in terms of a limited set of objectives congruent with the emerging industrial order, forgoing many broader social objectives in the process [Lazerson 1971].

The organization of welfare services documents the impact of privatism even more clearly. Despite the existence of deprivation, poverty, and substantial unemployment, local governments assumed little responsibility for the poor. Public assistance was minuscule, and communities relied heavily on private charity. Higher levels of government intervened only when severe economic dislocation made action unavoidable. The development of local police forces also illustrates the response to the disorder accompanying urban growth. In addition, police agencies were a dramatic instance of the consequences of creating power centers. Once created, centrally organized police forces could be used for a variety of purposes, in the service of various interests. The question of the responsiveness of police agencies to governmental leaders and community members is a continuing dilemma.

Water, Fire, and Health Services

Early in the nineteenth century many growing communities found the quality and quantity of their water supplies to be grossly inadequate for the control of fires and the provision of drinking water [Blake 1970; Still 1970]. Each household provided for its own water supply and waste disposal through family wells and privies. Households banded together in common defense against fires. However, the devastating fires that swept through a number of cities during the eighteenth and nineteenth centuries provided compelling evidence that a more reliable and abundant water supply was indispensable.

During the same period, as population densities increased, the quality of family water supplies deteriorated. Wells, which often were dug near and below the level of privies and cemeteries, soon became contaminated through seepage. Demands for a potable community water supply followed the uncontrollable epidemics of smallpox, yellow fever, and cholera that often were attributed to contaminated water supplies. Thousands were afflicted by these diseases, principally the poor and immigrant groups, and a large proportion of the population fled to the countryside until the epidemics had abated. For example, in New York and Philadelphia nearly 10,000 people died in epidemics during the last decade of the eighteenth century alone [Blake 1970]. In fact, the technical knowledge needed to establish municipal water works had long been available and awaited only public recognition of its import. By the mid-nineteenth century water was being brought into some cities from outside rivers and lakes through aqueducts, and there was a movement to construct sewer lines.

The costs and disruptions of these recurrent crises necessitated a collective response in the form of an expanded municipal administration, which provided other new services and regulated individual and organizational conduct. Semiprofessional fire departments arose to operate the increasingly sophisticated equipment. City ordinances were passed regulating the construction of wooden buildings and the uses of fire, chimneys, and boilers. Boards of health were established to gather and disseminate information on the sources and outbreak of epidemics, inspect immigrants for disease, order the removal of public nuisances, and require vaccination [Still 1970]. However, the tradition of privatism dictated that the goals of public health services be limited to insulating individuals from one another to free them to conduct their personal affairs, not to raise the living standard of the more deprived classes [Warner 1968, pp. 99–124].

Police Departments

Traditional American opposition to a large, powerful government and fear of despotism were most evident on the local level in the controversy over the organization, composition, and operation of police forces. Americans were acutely conscious of the potential for abuse of power by centralized authority. It is not surprising, then, that through the first half of the nineteenth century the police function was filled by the night watch—a small, inefficient force of untrained, often politically appointed men who patrolled the street arresting those disturbing the public order, reporting fires, and attempting to recover stolen goods. They did little in the way of investigation or prevention of crime, and lacked central organization [Richardson 1972].

Only sharp increases in violence and disorder in fast growing cities impelled the establishment of large, centrally organized police forces. In the early years of the nineteenth century many cities were hit by major social disorders and upheavals. For example, between 1830 and 1860, there were thirty-five riots in Baltimore, Philadelphia, New York, and Boston alone, including labor, election, anti-abolitionist, anti-Negro, and anti-Catholic riots. During the 1860s draft riots erupted, and the 1870s saw a violent nationwide railroad strike [Brown 1969]. The disturbances stemmed from the vulnerability of the industrial labor force to the economic dislocations that accompanied industrialization; the competition for jobs and housing among immigrant groups; the clash of immigrant values and life styles with those of already established, dominant groups; and the poverty, unemployment, long work hours, and low salaries among industrial laborers. Events such as these precipitated fears among the citizenry that order and stability were being undermined and brought demands for more effective means of social control.

The creation of police forces has had important political ramifications. First, whenever collective protest or violence among antagonistic groups has erupted police have stood between those groups and their targets, usually in the position of defending status quo interests [Richardson 1972]. Second, dominant status groups within communities have, at various times, attempted to dictate their value preferences through the use of criminal laws and sanctions. Laws regulating gambling, sexual conduct, the sale and consumption of alcohol and drugs, and the operation of businesses on Sunday dealt with activities that required the tacit or overt support of a sizable portion of the community for their continued existence [Schur 1965]. The open flourishing of vice was regarded by some elements of the community as an affront to decency and morality [Haller 1972]. They point to the sale of liquor to minors, desecration of the Sabbath, the frequenting of saloons by members of the underworld, and corruption of governmental officials as inevitable concomitants of vice. To others the issues were personal freedom and maintenance of cultural and social traditions and life styles. Government, they contended, had no place in such matters. The police who were empowered to enforce these statutes earned the enmity of the groups that such laws were designed to constrain. As a result, the questions of how responsive the police ought to be and to whom have created persistent dilemmas in many communities [Wilson 1973b].

The expanded power resources of police departments and their exploitation for partisan purposes stimulated reform efforts that met with only partial success. Reformers sought to remedy political abuses through the creation of a civil service bureaucracy that would remove the police from politics [Lane 1970; Richardson 1972]. However, bureaucratization had a number of other unanticipated consequences. Advancement depended on loyalty and length of tenure; departmental leadership was recruited from within and hence reflected the values and predispositions of rank-and-file officers; and the insularity of the bureaucracy made it highly resistant to change [Richardson 1972; Wilson 1973b]. The combination of an insular bureaucracy, the relatively low esteem accorded the police, the inevitably conservative role police agencies played in defending the status quo, the hostility directed against the police by minority groups, which often saw them as oppressor rather than public servant, and the tendency of communities to regulate conduct on which there is substantial dissensus through criminal law has left police community relations inherently unstable. Many cases of police brutality [Burnham 1973], extreme secrecy [Goldstein 1973; Westley 1973] and corruption [Richardson 1972; Wilson 1973b] can be traced to the structural situation in which police agencies have been placed. While these issues remain unresolved, they do illustrate the impact of governmental expansion on community power relationships.

Public School Systems

Education traditionally has been valued in American society although often as a means rather than as an end. The development of public education can be better understood, however, as a product of tensions created by the urban-industrial revolution than as the implementation of the tenets of a democratic order [Schultz 1972]. As early as the 1820s crimes against the public order, unemployment, illiteracy, and poverty had become major problems in urban areas. Institutional responses to the mounting crises included public education and welfare systems as well as police forces.

Early in the nineteenth century the public schools were attended by only a small percentage of the young. Charity schools for the poor were not well attended and public schools were attended principally by children of the middle classes. Families that could afford to do so sent their children to private schools. The public school movement began in the 1820s and by mid-century free public education systems were becoming commonplace in urban areas. Soon thereafter school attendance became compulsory—in Boston by 1852 [Schultz 1972] and in Philadelphia by 1895 [Warner 1968, pp. 99–124].

Although the formation of public school systems in the 1820s and 1830s represented an attempt to broaden the base of public education, the actual commitment usually was to little more than basic literacy [Power 1962].

Education was seen both as a panacea for such problems attending urban growth as poverty, unemployment, petty crime, drunkenness, vagrancy, dependence on public assistance, disease, filth, and ignorance, which increasingly disturbed public leaders [Drake 1955, pp. 165–195; Rosenberg 1972; Schultz 1972], and as a means of maintaining moral, social, and political order. In fact, through the latter half of the nineteenth century the policy of using the public schools to perpetuate traditional agrarian ideals persisted. There was strong suspicion of and antipathy toward developing urban values and life styles [Lazerson 1971; Sizer 1968]. The school was to preserve traditional rural values, provide manual training to inculcate work values, prepare youth for participation in the labor force, and compensate for the demise of the apprenticeship system. In addition, kindergartens were instituted to reshape urban family life by educating the young and, through them, acculturating their parents. Evening classes were established to offer adults the opportunity to achieve basic literacy and exposure to the tenets of the American creed.

Expansion of the public school system was supported by a number of groups with various motivations [Drake 1955, pp. 165–195]. Business leaders saw education as a means of supplying a more productive labor force, teaching sound economic doctrine, and forestalling radical labor movements. Organized labor enthusiastically supported public education in order to provide the quality of education working-class families desired for their children but could not otherwise afford. Those concerned with the issues of sectionalism and nationalism saw education as a means of promoting national unity. Finally, the democrats and humanitarians, whose faith in the fundamental goodness of human nature led them to trust the people's judgment over that of governmental leaders, saw education as the only hope of a free, democratic society [Ulich 1967, pp. 225–254].

Once it had become apparent that schools were unable to meet these lofty expectations, faith in the schools as vehicles of broad social change declined. As school systems sought to reach an increasingly larger proportion of the eligible population, their clientele became ever larger and more diverse. Mass production techniques, overcrowding, staff mediocrity, rigidity, and narrowly conceived objectives became increasingly serious problems and produced increasing disaffection among students as schools sought to reach the entire community and hold pupils for extended periods [Schultz 1972; Warner 1968, pp. 99–124]. Further, educational systems were in competition for limited resources with other municipal agencies addressing themselves to the problems of urban growth.

The goals of the public education system gradually shifted in emphasis. Toward the end of the nineteenth century and during the first decades of the twentieth century, public schools began to accommodate themselves to the industrial society rather than trying to perpetuate agrarian ideals. Although the latter theme persisted, schools accepted the value priorities of an industrial order that emphasized increasing productivity and preparation of individuals for specific productive roles within that order. Schools, like other municipal agencies, became professionalized and bureaucratized stressing efficiency, regulation, and standardization. Manual training was replaced by vocational training for specific occupations. Public education directed itself toward combating the disorganization of the city, providing an opportunity structure for the disadvantaged, and assimilating newcomers.

Many of the early objectives of local public schools still underpin American public education. The cry for relevance of education continues. The preschool movement has reappeared, and school systems mold children to prevailing cultural and institutional systems [Baratz & Baratz 1972; I. Sloan 1972]. However, the narrowness of purpose, irrelevance of the system to many of its clients, inadequacy of staff and facilities, and lack of vitality and imaginativeness meant that, for many, the schools had little to offer and the minimizing of class difficulties in opportunity remained an unfilled promise [Coleman 1972; Kozol 1972].

Welfare Institutions

The most direct antecedent of American welfare practice was European policy, although the notion of charity itself is deeply rooted in Judeo-Christian tradition [Fink, 1974a]. The policy of a locally financed and administered welfare system based on aid to the unemployable and work for the able-bodied dates back to the sixteenth century when restrictions were placed on those who could legally beg for alms, local officials were mandated to eliminate begging by providing public assistance, and small taxes were levied on the community for support of the impoverished. The conviction that poverty was attributable principally to character deficiency led to welfare programs designed to ameliorate the physical condition of the poor, uplift their moral character, and make relief as uninviting as possible.

Throughout the first half century of the industrial revolution, communities typically supported almshouses with a small tax, furnished medical care for the sick poor, but relied on personal benevolence for most of the assistance to the needy [Still 1970]. Charitable assistance flowed from a variety of sources. Religious groups often expressed their commitment to the welfare of others through voluntary associations dedicated to assisting the needy. Nationality groups formed organizations to assist their compatriots who migrated to America [Fink 1974b]. It was the third quarter of the nineteenth century before the charity organization movement arose to coordinate the efforts of these autonomous private agencies. Settlement houses, supported by the middle classes, were founded on the conviction that the more fortunate could help uplift the poor.

The tradition of localism characterized American welfare practice until the 1900s. Communities maintained almshouses in which alcoholics, mentally ill, disabled, and the sick were housed. Jails, which were the only institutional alternative, also contained a mélange of individuals. The "overseer" of the poor dispensed whatever cash or food was available and administered the almshouse. [The first statewide organization of welfare did not occur until 1863 in Massachusetts; however, the initial state board lacked administrative and control powers.] After 1900, statewide organization and control began to emerge as it became apparent that there were individuals in each community with specialized needs and problems, but for whom local communities lacked the resources and numbers of cases to support specialized facilities. States gradually began to assume responsibility for providing institutions to which communities could refer appropriate individuals. There were some early examples of such institutions, but these were exceptions to the general pattern of local responsibility.

The pressure for welfare services mounted as the urban-industrial revolution progressed [Jacobs 1968]. The economy of the South was devastated by the Civil War, and a depression had occurred between 1857 and 1859. As a result, unemployed workers in a number of cities rose up in protest. Public funds were appropriated for relief in many cities, and the federal government assumed some responsibility for assisting veterans and the families of soldiers killed in the conflict. Another depression occurred in 1873 in which police crushed the demonstrations; in 1894 Coxey's Army marched on Washington. A panic in 1907 and depressions between 1914 and 1915 and 1920 and 1922 were followed by the major depression of the 1930s. Although the federal government had previously provided states with land and cash grants for various purposes, the 1930s marked a turning point in the delivery of welfare services. The need caused by the Great Depression was inescapable. Local and state governments were unable to cope with the rising tide of unemployment. In 1929 there were 3,000,000 unemployed; by 1931 the figure had doubled; and by 1933 it had doubled again [Fink 1974c]. The federal government responded with legislation and financial assistance of unprecedented magnitude. Since the 1930s the federal government has assumed major responsibility for welfare services, although many federally funded programs are locally administered.

Structural Changes in Urban Governments

Early Developments

The few, small antebellum cities in the United States were modeled, naturally enough, after English communities. By contemporary standards they were not very democratic. Borough powers were vested in a single body, the borough council, composed of councilmen and aldermen (council members with magistrate duties) with lifetime tenure. Vacancies were filled by a vote of the council. The mayor, the council's presiding officer, also was selected by vote of the council. Administrative powers rested with council committees, not the mayor.

After the American Revolution the charters of new communities reflected the same mistrust of unchecked power that led the framers of the Constitution to construct an elaborate system of checks and balances and to a commitment to greater popular participation in the political process. Many municipal councils became bicameral, and the direct election of mayors began to supplant council appointments. Administrative tasks relinquished by the council were allocated to the administrative heads of departments to avoid centralization of power in the executive.

The trend toward direct election of public officials also received support from the proponents of Jacksonian democracy [Hugins 1973]. This movement represented an attempt by skilled workers and small businessmen to shed their political, social, and economic disabilities. Based both on their own interests and on humanitarian impulses, they advocated the direct election of mayors, abolition of the general ticket system of nominations, smaller electoral districts, and payment of aldermen so that more working-class people could participate in government. As a result the number of elective offices was expanded to include clerks, judges, and administrative heads of departments. The Jacksonians felt that any man had the ability and should have the opportunity to hold public office, that public office was an honor to be sought, and that maximum participation could best be attained by keeping tenure in office short and discouraging reelection. The combination of these forces led to the gradual abandonment of property ownership and tax payment as qualifications for voting. By the early twentieth century, universal white male suffrage was generally established.

The Rise of Political Machines

Urban growth and its attendant problems led to an expansion in the scope of local governments. The joint effect of Jacksonian democracy and the system of checks and balances was to diffuse authority. Responsibility for specific functions was carefully divided to prevent centralized control. The large number of elective offices meant that officials were not accountable to any central source of authority within the government. As a result, power within urban governments was hopelessly fragmented. Positive, decisive action was all but impossible but rapid growth and

change combined with the increasing involvement of municipal government in these processes to make political decisions ever more necessary
and important. Since the formal structure of government was so cumbersome and fragmented, an informal structure arose to provide coordination
and integration. These political organizations have been popularly termed
"machines" and their leaders "bosses."

The history of political machines and bossism is considerably longer
than their heyday during the last half of the nineteenth and first few
decades of the twentieth century would suggest [Jackson & Schultz 1972].
However, the conditions in cities at that time were particularly conducive
to machine politics, consequently, their number and their hegemony
within urban governments were unmatched before or since. (The term
"machine" is heavily laden with negative connotations, but it is more
important to examine the social forces that supported their existence
than to merely document their obvious excesses.)

Machines are political organizations that are involved in politics as
a business. Their success and survival depended on their ability to act
as brokerage units for a diverse set of interest groups [Hays 1973; Merton
1973]. They were responsive to interest groups that found it necessary
or expedient to obtain governmental assistance or favors but lacked adequate access. Political bosses simply exploited the opportunities with
which rapid, disorganized change and lack of adequate social mechanisms
to accommodate that change presented them. Machines arose not because
evil men were able to take over city governments but because bosses
were able to represent the people's interests more effectively and had
sufficient political strength to keep their candidates in office.

Bosses gained and maintained their control over the governmental
structure through domination of a political party. A candidate had little
chance of being elected to public office without the machine's support.
As head of the party the boss controlled a substantial vote in the primary
[Kent 1969; Meyerson & Banfield 1969]. Since few voters typically participated in the primary election, party workers could muster the loyal vote
for the machine candidate. Usually the boss himself and many of his
subordinates held no formal position in the government.

A party nominee's success in the general election hinged on the vigor
with which party regulars campaigned and on access to funds from the
party's war chest. Both sets of resources were securely in the hands
of the party boss. Party workers frequently held appointed positions in
the city government. This patronage was contingent on their contribution
of time and money to the election campaign. Substantial financial re-

sources flowed to the party from businessmen for whom the boss had arranged political favors or governmental contracts. Even once elected, an official remained dependent on the party for renomination, patronage appointments for his supporters, and support on council committees to furnish municipal services and improvements in his ward. Machines were thus able effectively, if informally, to coordinate the legislative and executive branches and the myriad of directly elected officials [Ford 1969] and, at the same time, to provide a direct avenue of access to government for powerful interest groups.

Sources of Machines' Strength

Political machines derived much of their strength from the support of lower status ethnic groups. Although members of these subcommunities usually lacked financial resources, it was their ability to deliver large blocs of votes that helped ensure the election of party candidates. The machine offered help to immigrant groups living in squalor and poverty, working long hours for meager wages, and subject to unpredictable economic dislocation. Members of these subcommunities were treated as individuals with real personal and neighborhood problems. There was food for families of the unemployed, assistance for citizens who ran afoul of public agencies, informal mediation of landlord-tenant disputes, improvements in municipal services—important concerns to local residents but apparently inconsequential to bureaucratic agencies. For the beleaguered lower classes, local problems far outweighed national issues and defense of abstract political principles. Machine leaders could get things done, and the things they got done mattered [Handlin 1969].

Ethnic group support was further enhanced by ethnically balanced tickets. Each group received some patronage jobs and some formal representation. The name of an ethnic group member on the ticket fostered identification with the party that persisted for relatively long periods of time [Wolfinger & Field 1970]. Ward leaders asked only for loyalty on election day in return for their patronage and favors. To those groups for whom life was a constant struggle, this was small enough repayment for such direct and visible assistance [Whyte 1969]. Although it would be easy to overestimate and overplay the legendary tales of beneficence to families, ethnic representation, and patronage appointments, numbers were not all-important. A few visible, strategically placed favors had an impact out of proportion to their apparent value. As symbols of acceptance and caring, they forged a link between ethnic group and party that lingered long after ethnic identities began to pale.

The machine offered favors, preferential treatment, and circumvention of the bureaucratic decision-making process to business interests. To businessmen such access was simply good business. Cities were making large capital outlays for the development of some new municipal services and awarding franchises to private enterprise for the provision of others. The acquisition of land, construction, and service provision all offered lucrative profits. Money, power, and prestige went to those willing to seize these opportunities by the most expendient means. Business interests had another reason to seek preferential treatment. As the trend toward popular democracy shifted control of municipal governments to the urban masses, their ability to influence the decision-making process declined. Businessmen who felt that the business of the city should be business, whose economic power was vastly greater than their formal representation, and who were frustrated by the fragmented, cumbersome governmental structure saw informal influence as a means of getting "important" things accomplished [Ford 1969].

The Decline of Political Machines

If the machine was so successful as a broker for these various types of interest groups, why have they largely disappeared from the American political scene? To put it simply, times changed. The machine was a response to one set of needs and problems, but its very existence constituted part of a new social structure that resolved some of those problems and thereby altered the conditions that led to its inception. Further, the continued development of urban society changed communities and institutions, and the relationship between the two, in such a way as to undermine its viability.

Political machines always involved some type of coalition among diverse and, to some extent, opposed interest groups. To maintain these uneasy alliances, concessions had to be made to each of the groups. While patronage appointments, preferential treatment in obtaining government contracts, sanctioning illicit activities, and defending subcultural life styles were the standard fare, other issues also were involved. Some policies designed to accommodate the interests of constituents in the long run diminished the indispensability of the organization to these very constituents.

For instance, Cincinnati Boss Cox's Republican machine formed a coalition involving upper status groups residing on the periphery of the city and middle status groups living just outside the city's core. These two groups offset Democratic strength in the lower status core area [Miller 1968]. Both sets of groups had to be offered political concessions that included reduction of the rapid turnover in public office, elimination of petty graft, and corporation raiding, and support for the secret ballot, voter registration, enfranchisement of blacks, and state laws designed to stabilize and centralize governmental structure. In addition, a number of basic services such as police and fire protection, streets, sewers, parks, and waterworks were expanded or professionalized. Sunday saloon operation, public gambling, and brothels were suppressed. However, the political reforms that the machine conceded crippled many of its more lucrative, as well as flagrant and abusive, practices. The expansion of a municipal services bureaucracy created a core of officials whose commitment to universalistic standards, formal rules, proper administrative procedures, and efficient and economical service delivery based on professional standards undercut the informal arrangements on which the machine thrived.

During the progressive era a number of national reforms—the adoption of the Seventeenth Amendment providing for the direct election of senators, revival of the Interstate Commerce Commission, establishment of the Federal Trade Commission, and passage of Workingmen's Compensation and Child Labor laws [Huthmacher 1970]—constituted an effort to redress some of the abuses accompanying industrialization. They signified the increasing political influence of urban areas, and were indicative of the emergence of a national system of interdependent institutions and communities. Reforms during this era accorded greater political access to the urban populace and thereby reduced their vulnerability to economic exploitation. Protection of the type that machines granted informally to some extent became a right rather than a privilege. Of course, an even more dramatic expansion of social welfare legislation occurred during the 1930s.

These and other reforms—such as factory safety legislation, tenement laws, widow pension provisions, and hours and wages legislation—were supported by elements of both the upper and lower classes. Reform was rooted in a mixture of selfishness and altruism [Huthmacher 1970]. The upper classes were concerned with bettering the lot of the impoverished urban masses through paternalistic labor and social welfare legislation. For some groups, however, the major objective was to wrest political control from immigrant and lower class groups. For their part the working classes showed considerable enthusiasm for liberal legislation. They were less attracted by appeals to maintain free enterprise and individualism than by a pragmatic concern for their own safety and security.

At the height of their hegemony, many machines appeared to be monolithic and invincible since their life spans frequently could be measured in decades, the organization survived incompetent leadership, and sporadic reform efforts were much more successful in prosecuting individuals than in dismantling the organization itself. In New York, for example, although the Tweed Ring was openly corrupt for years, reformers found it almost impossible to obtain the kind of evidence that could be used for legal prosecution or to dispel public apathy [Callow 1973]. However, in reality, the size, composition, and stability of the coalitions supporting machines varied considerably among cities and within individual cities over time. In Cincinnati, for example, Boss Cox's Republican machine functioned for a decade without the support of the lowest status groups, but in the following decade came to rely principally on their support.

As the groups supporting machines found less need for the kinds of services they offered, their real vulnerability became apparent. Naturally, some were more ingenious than others in adapting to change. However, the fact that machines generally arose, flourished, and declined during the same time period suggests that the real explanation for their decline lies in the changing structure of urban society. When successful attacks were launched against machines, they gave the somewhat misleading appearance of being the result of idiosyncratic events or the efforts of individuals. Disgruntled members of the Tweed Ring furnished *The New York Times* with hard evidence of massive, pervasive corruption that launched a reform crusade [Callow 1973]. In Cincinnati a persistent county prosecutor finally obtained an indictment for perjury against Boss Cox, which forced his resignation [Z. Miller 1972]. These, however, were the precipitating incidents and not the real causes for the decline of political machines.

The Restructuring of Urban Governments

Perhaps the single most important factor in undermining political machines was the determination of upper status business and professional groups to restructure local governments to wrest control from lower status groups. Although their proposals for redressing the balance of power diverged widely, they shared a skepticism that the urban masses were capable of assuming responsibility for their own governance. Structural reformers regarded the organization of government as the source of the problem. Among the most frequently decreed structural "deficiencies" were the separation of powers [Ford 1969], partisanship [Whitlock 1969], and the division of the city into small wards [Hays 1973]. They contended that the business of cities should be provision of municipal services, a function that bore no relation to politics. Hence the cliché: "There is no Republican or Democratic way to pave a street." As one observer [White 1969] put it, cities are corporations whose function is the creation and control of city property. In these activities politics have no part; rather those in the city who have title to or substantial part in it (the equivalent of corporate shareholders) should be the controlling influence.

The reformers frequently depicted themselves as fighting for the "people" and against "corruption." It became clear, however, that in the government that they envisioned, some would be more equal than others. They shared a basic mistrust of popular democracy that in their eyes had allowed the urban masses undue influence and had spawned the chaos afflicting urban communities. Moreover, businessmen were not aroused over corruption as such for business interests had profited handsomely from their dealings with machines. The real problem was that even if businessmen could obtain the preferential treatment they needed under this system, each new favor had to be negotiated. It was a costly and whimsical system that was inconsistent with orderly administrative practice.

Since the machinery of government had been found to be defective, the obvious solution was to restructure it so that men of substance, men who could clearly see the interests of the larger community, would be at its helm. The problem was to devise a strategy that would generate sufficient popular support for this process. Machines and bosses offered the visible symbols of evil and corruption that reformers needed to ignite public sentiment. However, the themes that they stressed in their campaigns—efficiency, economy, orderliness, and professionalism—were more indicative of their true goals. They sought to introduce the same rationality and order into government that they had achieved in economic affairs.

A series of reform mayors attacked different elements of the governmental structure but always from the same perspective [Holli 1972]. In New York, for example, between 1872 and 1874, William Havemeyer, a retired businessman, cut taxes, work relief, and some important public services. Three decades later Seth Low fought to reduce the municipal debt, tighten the tax system, and introduce nonpartisanship and a centralized administration. In 1914 John Purroy Mitchell, seeking to cut governmental costs, reduced educational funding and support for "feebleminded" children. Under James Phelam in San Francisco a reform administration advocated a merit system, short ballot, strong mayor, at-large elections, and rigid fiscal controls. Phelam also lowered taxes, which curtailed the delivery of some municipal services.

The lower classes, of course, were most affected by these fiscal austerity programs but their support generally was necessary in order to assure the adoption of reform proposals. Members of the working classes usually were selective in the progressive reforms they supported. They were indifferent to structural reforms but opposed Prohibition, blue laws, immigration restrictions, and the closing of parochial schools [Hays 1973; Huthmacher 1970]. Nevertheless, the reformers' strategy of attacking machines, bossism, and corruption was soundly conceived. In case after case reform administrations were elected, not because there was a groundswell of support for structural reorganization, but in order to "throw the rascals out of office" [Hays 1973; Holli 1972; Mann 1972; Z. Miller 1972]. The downfall of machines did not require massive desertions but merely the erosion of solid support for a straight party ticket. The reformers succeeded in creating enough mistrust to bring about ticket splitting. These reform movements spanned several decades however, as machines survived periodic onslaughts. Their persistence may be attributed in part to reformers' short-lived forays into politics, their penchant for abstract ideals, a mechanistic conception of government, and a fundamental mistrust of popular democracy that inspired little confidence or trust in them among the urban masses.

The Structure of Reform Governments

While structural reformers advanced a variety of innovations such as public ownership or regulation of utilities, better accounting procedures, tighter tax systems, initiative, referendum, and recall, the centralization of administrative authority was at the heart of their reform efforts. The two major types of reform governments were the commission and council-manager plans.

The commission plan was born in Galveston, Texas, in 1900, not as a part of the reform movement but in response to a savage storm that totally destroyed half of the city and left the rest a shambles. Faced with a breakdown in municipal services, food and housing shortages, lootings, and absence of real emergency powers the citizenry mobilized and formed a relief committee that operated as the de facto government. Each member of the committee was assigned and had total responsibility for some municipal service function. The citizens were so impressed with their newfound political organization that they solicited and received from the Texas legislature a new city charter that included the basic elements of the relief committee. The government that emerged had five elected officials, a mayor, and four commissioners, each of whom was administrative head of a municipal department.

The commission plan achieved immediate, if short-lived, acceptance. By 1918, there were 500 cities with commission governments. Thereafter its obvious deficiencies reduced its popularity, and 40 years later only 320 cities still retained the plan [Schnore & Alford 1963]. The system had two important features of the reform model—the short ballot and concentration of power in an elected council; elections usually were at-large and nonpartisan. The concentration of power in the council was designed to eradicate the disjointedness caused by the separation of powers but to retain direct control of governing officials. At-large, nonpartisan elections would assure that the commissioners would be the "right" types of individuals. The short ballot protected the electorate from having to select officials for a myriad of minor posts. Rather, minor officials would be appointed on the basis of merit and would be part of a rationally conceived and organized administration.

It quickly became apparent, however, that there was no strong executive who could assert policy and administrative leadership. In theory each commissioner was to carry out the council's mandates, but in fact council members were reluctant to intervene in department operations for fear that some day the tables would be turned. Further, commissioners typically were not experienced administrators. As a result, they were forced either to abdicate all but very general control over their departments or risk intervening in specialized tasks about which they had limited knowledge.

If the commission plan's shortcomings left reformers disenchanted, the council-manager plan came much closer to fulfilling their aspirations. The manager plan originated in Staunton, Virginia, in 1908. In 1914, Dayton, Ohio, became the first major city to adopt this plan. By 1958, 885 cities had adopted the plan [Schnore & Alford 1963], and adoptions have continued at a high rate since that time. Like the commission form, council-manager government was designed to limit the number of elected offices and place a small city council in full control of the government [Price 1969]. Nonpartisan, at-large elections also were usually part of the reform package. Ideally, the council, headed by the mayor, would hire the chief administrative office, the manager, who served at their pleasure. Other administrative officials would be appointed by the manager on the basis of merit.

Like the commission plan, council-manager government does not operate precisely as its founders and proponents envisioned. The organizational blueprints called for the separation of policy-making and administrative functions, but this distinction has proven to be artificial and untenable [Adrian 1967]. Managers often do try to maintain a low political profile by soliciting policy innovations from civic groups and governmental agencies. Yet policy and administrative function includes making recommendations to council, preparing the budget, and assessing the adequacy of existing practices and programs. The strong policy leadership that was expected to emanate from a popularly elected council also has not always been forthcoming. Council members are elected officials for whom strong positions on controversial issues can spell political disaster. They also lack the staff, resources, and expertise to formulate policy alternatives [Kovner 1969]. As a result, administrative agencies, advisory committees, and civic organizations are the principal sources of policy innovation. The relative lack of leadership has not created insurmountable problems, however, since most cities infrequently encounter issues over which there is intractable conflict.

The Diffusion of Reform Governments

Although a large number of communities have adopted reform governments, the diffusion process has been strongly patterned along a number of demographic and socioeconomic dimensions. Council-manager governments tend to be found in medium-sized cities. Very small communities usually have mayor-council governments since municipal affairs are not sufficiently complex to demand full-time professional management and the cost of retaining a manager may be prohibitively high. Mayor-council governments also are likely to be found in large cities that contain a diverse array of interests that periodically are in conflict. In these communities the government constitutes an arena in which opposed interests are reconciled; the political process is the business of government.

Other characteristics of mayor- and manager-headed cities also differ in a fairly consistent pattern. Mayor-council governments occur more frequently in communities that are growing at a modest rate and have populations with a high proportion of blue collar workers, ethnic group members, and low-income families [Alford & Schoble 1970; Gordon 1968; Kessel 1967; Schnore & Alford 1963]. Communities organized under the council-manager plan tend to be growing more rapidly and have higher status populations. Rapid growth creates a need for the extension of municipal services, the kind of task that lends itself to professional management. Upper status communities, which are likely to be homogeneous, have fewer political conflicts and contain residents supportive of the concept of managerial government.

Although structure of government is related to community socio-economic characteristics, a variety of other factors also are operant: 1. States do not make statutory provision for all types of governmental organization.   2. Political party names are not permitted to appear on the ballot in some states [Cutright 1967]. This occurs most frequently in states dominated by a single political party.   3. Political organizations do adapt to changing social conditions. Even if the size and composition of a community changes, the form of government may not unless a major political crisis arises.

Further, reform governments are not always adopted as a package; consequently, many governments are of mixed types [Wolfinger & Field 1970]. For example, a city may retain a mayor-council government but institute nonpartisan elections and a strong (popularly elected) mayor. Indeed, although partisan, ward elections usually accompany a mayor-council government, these relationships are not as strong as those between council-manager government and nonpartisan, at-large elections. The weakness of the former set of relationships is attributable to the fact that older communities that operated under the mayor-council system for some period of time may modify but usually will not completely alter the governmental structure. By contrast, newly incorporating communities adopting the council-manager plan do not face established structures that would have to be altered with either unknown or disadvantageous consequences for certain interest groups. As a result, they are much more likely to adopt the entire reform package.

The Effects of Reform

The formal structure of local government has been fundamentally altered, and, in general, services are delivered more efficiently and with less graft and corruption than they were under the older weak mayor-council system [Lowi 1973]. The trade-off costs have been in the opportunities for popular participation, which have declined correspondingly. Bureaucratization and professionalization of local governments have removed many decisions from the public arena and formalized channels of access to government [Alford 1973]. Yet, despite attempts to centralize authority in the executive, power is more decentralized than the reform model would suggest. Bureaucratically organized departments remain islands of power over which the executive has limited control. Since agencies are relatively autonomous, departmental jurisdictions overlap, and all interest groups do not have equal institutional representation. Cities often are efficiently administered but ungoverned [Lowi 1973].

The kinds of interests to which these governmental agencies are responsive has changed. Instead of small, homogeneous wards electing representatives to defend ward interests, pressure groups, whose interests are not territorially based, attempt to influence those governmental agencies regulating matters of importance to them [Morlan 1969]. The way that government responds to interests also has changed. Instead of responding to particularistic interests, agencies provide services based on universalistic standards and professional criteria. Administrative experts are not neutral specialists, however, for they have a vested interest in defining and resolving problems in a manner consistent with professional and agency interests.

The evolving structure of local governments has been a response to the new problems and centers of power that emerged in the process of urban and industrial development. The structure of reform government has been consistent with the organization of urban society and the interests of dominant segments of that society to the extent that the primary function of local governments has been to efficiently provide municipal services, and there have been few significant sources of conflict within the community. Reform governments have not been as responsive to minority groups whose needs and values were not adequately represented by existing institutions and those segments of the population that were locally oriented or lacked the capacity to participate meaningfully in extra-local institutions.

THE POWER STRUCTURES OF URBAN COMMUNITIES

Methodologies in the Study of Power Structure

In order to discuss studies of community power structure and change in that structure it is important to review the research methodologies that have been employed. Each methodology contains implicit or explicit assumptions about what constitutes the most significant questions to be explored, the way power is structured, and how that elusive entity "power" may best be measured. Theory and methodology, therefore, are not independent. The different perspectives of each approach have produced diverse and sometimes conflicting conclusions.

The Positional Method

Prior to the publication of Floyd Hunter's classic monograph, *Community Power Structure,* in 1953, the positional method was the principal approach used to describe or analyze community power relationships. It was assumed that individuals gained power by occupying offices in major institutional complexes and that key decisions were made by those in authority. The greater the number and importance of offices held, the greater one's power. Those individuals who held no formal positions were largely disregarded.

It was a convenient and concrete method of analysis since individuals and positions were readily observable, and data could be obtained from organizational blueprints. While there were some technical problems with this type of analysis (such as variations in the titles of comparable positions in different organizations), the major deficiency was that the positional method assumed precisely what had to be demonstrated. The possibility of examining the relationship between the ideology and reality of political decision making, between authority and control was effectively precluded. The obvious drawbacks to the positional approach have reduced its implementation as a primary method of analysis, although positional surveys sometimes have been conducted in conjunction with reputational and/or decisional analysis.

The Reputational Method

Hunter's work triggered a major controversy as both his methodology and substantive findings were challenged. In sharp contrast to previous research, Hunter concluded that Regional City (Atlanta) was run by a group of forty leaders, most of whom held no formal positions in government. In fact, only four held governmental office; the majority of the others had careers in commerce, finance, or industry. This leadership group, he reported, was highly integrated through common ecological patterns, interlocking organizational memberships, business contacts, and consciousness of their status within the community.

His findings that most of the key decisions in the central city of a major metropolitan area were made by a small, cohesive elite, composed predominantly of businessmen, had major implications both for American ideology and previous research findings (if they were accurate and characterized other cities as well). Hunter's monograph was followed by a number of other studies that, by and large, confirmed his observations on Atlanta [Agger & Ostrum 1969; Klapp & Padget 1969; D. Miller 1969]. It was not long, however, before critiques began to appear that at first prompted rejection and later acceptance of a modified, narrower role for the reputational method in community power studies.

Hunter [1953] began his research by compiling lists of leaders in civic, business, and governmental organizations as well as of socially prominent and wealthy individuals. He assumed that persons holding such positions were involved in or knowledgeable about community power relations and therefore could identify the actual community leadership and any sub rosa leaders. These four lists were given to fourteen judges, who were long-time residents and knowledgeable about community affairs. The judges were instructed to rank the ten most influential (defined as ability to lead others) persons from each list containing the names of fifty nominees. The results showed a very high degree of consensus among the judges. Having identified community leadership, Hunter proceeded to explore their relationships with each other and with the rest of the community.

The reputational approach has been widely criticized as its implicit assumptions and implications have been recognized. Among the objections that have been raised are the following:

1. It is implicitly assumed that power is exercised by an elite that operates behind the scenes. Indeed, reputational research does not

ask "Who governs?" but rather "Who are the rulers?" This assumption is supported by the use of arbitrarily designated cut-off points on compiling lists of nominees. Hunter simply selected the ten top-ranked individuals from each of the four lists and treated them as categorically different from all other nominees.

As a result, the discovery of an elite is in the nature of a self-fulfilling prophecy. If the research does not uncover a monolithic elite, it can always be argued that the leaders who have been identified in actuality are only the subordinates of the real power holders or that an elite does exist but is so well concealed that it has not been discovered. This is the problem of infinite regress. The assumption that a power elite exists that is not publicly visible may preclude the possibly valid findings of a coincidence of power with authority or of a pluralistic system.

2. Even if it can be assumed that a covert elite sometimes exists, the unique ability of a panel of lay judges to identify them is open to question. Public opinion surveys have consistently shown that even the best-informed citizens have surprisingly little knowledge about most public affairs, particularly of municipal governments [Ehrlich 1968]. If, as Hunter finds, there is a high degree of consensus on the composition of top leadership, this consensus both belies the assumption that elites are not publicly visible and suggests that other more direct, valid, and reliable procedures, such as using social scientists as participant-observers, could be employed.

3. It is hazardous to assume that the researcher and informants all share the same definition of "power." Judges are likely to assess power on the basis of the nominee's formal position or social rank. In this event findings may mirror general status hierarchies [Ehrlich 1968], but any relationship between status and participation in decision making or possession of other power resources should be empirically demonstrated. Further, there must be bias among the judges in their evaluation of nominees. Politicians and labor leaders, for example, may be held in low esteem, and segregated subgroups such as the black community may receive few nominations because they are socially and ecologically isolated. In fact, Hunter was forced to conduct a separate study of the black community for precisely this reason [Hunter 1970a; 1970b]. The combination of predetermined or ad hoc limits on the number of nominees and bias in the judges selections is likely to lead to some who are influential not being so labeled and some individuals who are not influential being included in the designated elite.

4. Even if the attributional reputations of judges are accurate, critics have contended that this technique actually measures the reputations for power rather than power itself. It is perhaps more productive to view reputation as constituting one type of power (if power is defined as capacity or ability to influence). Reputation, then, is not irrelevant to the study of power but it is only one power resource. To the extent that individuals or organizations modify their actions in response to perceptions of the distribution of power the study of reputations has significance. The impact of reputations is, of course, an empirical question that must be investigated. Where reputation has been utilized as an index of actual behavior, it would be preferable to gather data on the behavior itself.

5. The assumption that a small group of top leadership necessarily constitutes an elite also has been a major point of dispute. A small, tightly knit group of individuals totally dominating a community's political life is the limiting case and probably rarely occurs. There virtually always are cases in which powerful individuals or groups do not attain or are compelled to modify their objectives. Indeed, Hunter notes that Atlanta's elite sometimes found it necessary to bargain in order to get programs they wanted [Kaufman & Jones 1970]. This suggests, first of all, that power is not asymmetrical; that is, power is not an all-or-none resource. If power resources are distributed, to whatever degree, among groups within a community and the dominant group does not always achieve its objective, the question arises, "When can a powerful group be labeled an elite?"

Robert Dahl has listed four conditions that must be met in order to demonstrate the existence of an elite [Anton 1970]: **1.** The controlling group must be less than a majority of the population. **2.** Its preferences must regularly prevail when there are differences of preference. **3.** The composition of the elite must be specific in order to avoid the problem of infinite regress. **4.** A series of concrete decisions must be examined in order to confirm the dominance of the controlling group.

Dahl contends that elite theorists have confused elites with groups having a high potential for control. An elite is likely to emerge when there is both a high potential for control and a high potential for unity —that is, when members are willing to act together for control. The mere unequal distribution of power does not constitute grounds for concluding that a ruling elite exists nor can elite membership be imputed from class membership. In addition, he contended that since elitists had generalized from a single type of community decision, the possibility that different groups or individuals controlled different sets of decisions had been ignored. Based on these and similar considerations, Nelson Polsby defined an elite as a group of persons, but less than a majority vote, standing at the apex of community power, and exercising influence over a wide range of issues [Rose 1967, pp. 255–297].

6. Since power is not asymmetrical and leadership groups are not always unified, then a methodology that implicitly assumes that there is a ruling elite may obscure the divisions within or among top leadership groups. The exertion of influence or dominance may vary over time and among issues. Critics have contended, therefore, that it is important to examine specific decisional outcomes. Preferably a wide range of decisions would be studied in order to assess the degree of coincidence that exists among decision makers across issues.

The Decision-Making Method

The volley of criticism aimed at the positional and reputational methods discredited them as the sole methods of investigating community power. The distinctions among the approaches should not be drawn too sharply, however, since each approach incorporates elements of the other. For example, researchers working on reputational studies often first compile lists of nominees by interviewing positional leaders. Positional analysis assumes that the officials of certain organizations make key decisions, but if no analysis of decisions involved, then the selection is based at least partly on reputational factors. Decision-making research has relied on something akin to a reputational process in selecting issues for study. Dahl prefaced his classic study *Who Governs?* [1961], an analysis of decision making, with historical and positional-reputational survey of New Haven.

Adherents of the decision-making approach contend that no a priori assumption can be made about a community's power structure. Only an empirical investigation of decisional outcomes can reveal who actually exercises power rather than who merely has the positional resources or reputation for doing so. Of course, not all community decisions can be examined; therefore, a sample from the universe of all community decisions must be selected. Dahl [Rose 1967, pp. 225–297] has stated that it is impossible to delimit the universe of decisions precisely, and, further, that this is unimportant to do. The principal concern is that those issues that are chosen represent "sectors of issues" whose importance would be generally accepted. Several sectors are necessary so that generalizations about the exercise of influence are not formulated on the basis of a narrow range of issues. Once a series of decisions has been analyzed, the relative power of the participants can be ascertained by weighing their impact on decisional outcomes.

Like other methodologies the decision-making approach was subjected to considerable criticism after an initial period of acceptance and popularity. Most of the critiques concern the process by which issues are selected and the validity of studying decisions.

1. Since only a few decisions can be studied, this approach involves a commitment to an intensive study of a single community. Considerable time and effort are necessary in order to gather extensive data on complex decision-making processes. Historical records and secondary sources must be consulted if the issue has been recurrent or emerged over a long time period. For more current or sensitive issues, gaining the confidence of key informants may require considerable time and patience. The smaller the number of issues and communities and the shorter the time span studied, the more hazardous it is to generalize findings to other communities.

2. Several problems surround the selection of issues. One of the most important is the criteria on which a choice is based. Dahl, for example, is more concerned with sectors of issues than issues within sectors. Yet in order to claim validity for findings both must be representative. The question of what constitutes a representative set of decisions goes to the heart of the problem. Dahl suggests that they should be of obvious importance. However, this amounts to the use of the reputational approach if opinions rather than objective consequences determine the choices. There are, moreover, a number of criteria that might be preferred for both importance and representativeness.

   Decisional research has tended to focus on issues that arouse conflict or controversy, but if findings are to have theoretical importance, other aspects of the decisions may be important [Barth & Johnson 1970]. First, some issues tend to recur while others do not. Unique issues produce an emergent, ad hoc leadership that must generate resources and create an organizational base in order to exert influence. Since ad hoc organizations have less of a vested interest in status quo arrangements, many normal sanctioning procedures are ineffective. When issues recur, an organizational structure for their resolution typically evolves over time. Unique and recurrent issues therefore are likely to vary in their visibility, tactics, leadership, organizational contests, and outcome. Unique events may be significant in understanding social change or precedents that affect later policy formulation, whereas recurrent events that involve major social organizations may be more indicative of basic divisions, interest group organizations, and power structure within a community.

Second, issues that arouse public controversy but are of little consequence to most leaders, such as fluoridation, may produce considerable publicity but only limited involvement by leaders. On the other hand, actions that affect leadership but apparently are of minor consequence to the public, such as administrative reorganizations, may receive little publicity despite having greater implications for future policy formulation.

Third, the extent to which objective conditions can really be altered may determine whether substantive or symbolic activity occurs. It has been noted, for instance, that outbreaks of racial violence have been followed by the formation of commissions to study the causes and consequences of racism whenever the situation must be defused but meaningful political, social, or economic changes cannot be implemented [Lipsky & Olson 1968; Marx 1968]. Finally, decisions that affect local communities increasingly involve higher levels of government; hence the alternative lines of action are limited by forces beyond the local control. These considerations suggest that the depiction of a community power structure may be determined by the type as well as the representativeness of issues selected.

3. While issues relating to the sampling process are important, a more fundamental problem is trying to determine the meaning of whatever findings emerge from decisional analysis. Can data on any set of decisions be used to determine the nature of the community power structure? Peter Bachrach and Morton Baratz [1970] contend that it is not instructive to study community power structure by asking either "Who governs?" or "Who are the elite?". They maintain instead that it is imperative to investigate the "mobilization of bias," that set of values, beliefs, and "rules of the game" that systematically benefit some groups at the expense of others. The mobilization of bias is integral to all social organizations, and those groups whose interests have institutional and cultural preference usually are in a strong position to maintain the status quo. Often no direct action is required to ensure

the formulation of favorable policies as they will flow naturally from the system through the process of nondecision making.

Nondecisions are those that block any challenge to the interests of the decision maker before they are articulated, gain access to a decision-making forum, or can be implemented (so that reallocation of benefits and privileges does not occur). There are a variety of nondecision-making tactics such as exerting force; threatening the use of sanctions, working rules, or precedents; or strengthening the mobilization of bias as a hedge against future challenges. If these strategies are successful, there may be few, if any, major controversies involving the interests of the "status quo" groups. Therefore, any analysis based solely on overt decisions would encounter only "safe" issues. Further, since many decisions do not involve power relationships, many would not be very revealing of community power structure.

4. The critics of the decision-making approach point out that few generalizations about community power structure have emerged from this line of research. They attribute this to the fact that power is not activated in many decision-making situations, that all operant factors in decision making tend to be treated as equally important, and that situations in which conformity is gained by threatening severe deprivation are confused with those in which it is not.

Another way of conceptualizing certain of these problems is to create a typology of levels of outcomes [Alford 1967]. For example, particular acts may be labeled "decisions," a series of decisions of a particular type, "policies," and a commitment to certain types of policies, "the role of government." Decisions are likely to be influenced by a variety of situational, and perhaps idiosyncratic, factors, such as strategy, motivation, and leadership. The prediction of decisional outcomes is, therefore, inordinately difficult. Since so many nonrecurrent factors are operating and different groups participate in or dominate individual decisions, the analysis of a series of specific decisions may lead to the conclusion that there is no concentration of power and may frustrate efforts to isolate those factors that are of primary importance in predicting outcomes.

Policies are more stable than decisions. The role of government is even more enduring. There are many conflicts over specific decisions but fewer at the higher levels that involve increasingly more basic, unchallenged assumptions. Once policies have been formulated and the role of government established many decisions become routine. Frequently there will be no threats of sanctions since consensus or nondecisionmaking will shape the context of the decision-making process. Consequently, an examination of only decisional outcomes that reflect situational factors may obscure fundamental, recurrent patterns in policy making and the role of government. At the same time, knowledge about patterning at the higher levels may not lead to accurate predictions about decisional outcomes. Generalizations will emerge only when the three levels of outcomes are studied concurrently.

Comparisons and Developments

There is a developing consensus that the three major methodologies have tapped different aspects of community power. A number of comparative studies have been undertaken in order to compare results obtained by the three methods. A comparison of the reputational and positional methods showed substantial agreement in the designation of leaders [Freeman et al. 1968], although there is some conflicting evidence [Schulze & Blumberg 1970]. However, little agreement was registered between these two and decision-making activities. Vaughn Blankenship [1970] reported similar findings. Reputational leaders' involvement in decision-making activities varied widely among communities, and their participation produced a reputation for power only when it extended over a number of issues. On some occasions the two types of leaders joined in decision making, but this occurrence varies. He concluded that the two methodologies turned up different types of leaders, although the distinctions were not sharp. Several secondary analyses have confirmed that positional-reputational research is more likely to report a pyramidal power structure and decisional analysis a pluralistic power structure [Aiken 1970; Gilbert 1968].

The developments that have occurred in community power methodology have more than procedural implications since built-in assumption have been revealed that partly predetermine the findings. Each approach provides a narrow, incomplete, yet valuable perspective on community power structures. Reputations constitute only one type of power resource; participation of reputational leaders in decision making varied by issue and community and over time within communities [Ehrlich 1968]. Positional leaders tended to be active in certain types of decision making, and some of those most active on a range of issues developed a reputation for leadership. While comparative research has furnished evidence that decisions constitute an accurate index of some kinds of political outputs, it also is clear that there are a number of types and levels of outputs that must be distinguished conceptually and empirically. Critiques of the prevailing methodologies have fostered a greater awareness of the complexity of analyzing power structures, more sophistication in conceptualizing "power," explicit articulation of assumptions involved in research techniques, and conceptual separation of distinct but related concepts.

These developments have produced a new focus in community power research [Bonjean & Olson 1970, pp. 203–215]. Both theoretical [Alford 1967; Clark 1968] and empirical [Aiken 1970; Gilbert 1968; Walton 1971] attempts have been made to piece together previous research as a basis for further exploration. Research methodologies now are more likely to be combined in an integrative rather than an additive fashion. Intensive studies of single communities have given way to comparative studies, including examination of larger numbers of communities and cross-cultural research. Scholars studying urban politics have become aware of the range of possible types of communiy power structures and the diverse set of factors that shape them. The outcome has been research that is more narrowly focused on selected aspects of power structure and process. Finally, an interdisciplinary expertise has been brought to the study of urban politics in recognition of the complex interdependencies characterizing urban-industrial societies. The field of urban politics now receives contributions from sociologists with interests in community studies, urban sociology, and political sociology and political scientists concerned with local government and intergovernmental relations.

Historical Trends

Toward a Definition of "Community Power Structure"

The urban-industrial revolution had the effect of expanding and, ultimately, bureaucratizing and professionalizing local governments. The distribution of community power resources also was transformed in the process. The most widely studied and extensively documented trend in community power structures has been the increasing dispersion of power resources. Power structure typologies [Aiken 1970; Mott 1970a; Rossi

1968; Walton 1971] usually have distinguished several types of community power structures that vary along a dispersion-concentration continuum. John Walton [1971], for example, defines four types:

1. *Pyramidal:* monolithic; monopolistic; single, cohesive leadership group

2. *Factional:* at least two durable competing factions

3. *Coalitional:* leadership varies with issues and is made up of fluid coalitions of interested persons and groups

4. *Amorphous:* absence of any pattern of leadership or exercise of power

Walton defines power as "the capacity to mobilize resources for the accomplishment of intended effects with recourse to some type of sanctions to encourage compliance" [1971, p. 192]. Power thus refers to the possession of resources (such as money, access to media, prestige, physical strength, personal persuasiveness) and the ability to utilize those resources (which depends on the extent of value sharedness, the proximity and accessibility of organization members, perception of a threat to the organization, and countervailing sources of power). Power structure is defined as "the characteristic pattern within a social organization whereby resources are mobilized and sanctions employed in ways that affect the organization as a whole" [Walton 1971, p. 192]. Communities with competitive power structures experience more frequent overt conflict since opposed interest groups attempt to utilize power resources in order to achieve their objectives. In more monopolistic structures opposition to a powerful, united elite is of limited utility and has predictable consequences.

Preindustrial Communities

The relative autonomy, horizontal integration, and cohesiveness of American communities before the urban-industrial revolution is reflected in the convergence of social, economic, and political power [Schulze 1970]. The dominant source of influence was a relatively small group of notables. For example, in New Haven, Dahl [1970] observed three stages in the transition "from oligarchy to pluralism." During the oligarchic period, from the end of the eighteenth century to the middle of the nineteenth, public affairs were dominated by lawyers and educators affiliated with Yale University.

In the oligarchic period local political activity by elites was consistent with both the structure of the community and their status within the community. Commercial and agricultural activities were locally oriented and were owned by the community elite. Since their own well being and that of the community depended on the prosperity of these enterprises, the elite naturally had a direct interest in local politics. Participation in community affairs was regarded as an obligation and election to high office an honor. The elite often held state and/or national offices as well [Rossi & Rossi, 1973]. Because social, economic, and political resources resided with the same individuals it was not always necessary for the elite to hold public office in order to exert influence [French 1969]. As a result of their prestige and leadership within the community, however, they were consulted when major decisions were being made and appointment to formal positions often followed.

Industrializing Communities

Urban growth led to a change in the composition of political leadership. The coincidence of wealth, power, and prestige decreased as a new class of industrialists amassed huge fortunes and commanded vast organizational resources. By the middle of the nineteenth century in New Haven [Dahl 1970], as in many other cities, businessmen and entrepreneurs began to supplant the social notables as the dominant force in local politics. At the outset of the industrial revolution, economic growth had the effect of increasing the involvement of businessmen in local government. Industrialization had a direct economic interest in the expansion of public services to ensure the development of their own business, because municipal services themselves were economic pursuits on which fortunes could be built and were a means of attracting new population and industrial growth. Local industrialists soon realized that some cities would rise to regional or national preeminence, and others would be relegated to more specialized, ancillary roles within the economic system. Businessmen, therefore, had dual motivation for active participation in local politics.

Not all cities proceeded through precisely the same stages. A historical comparison of mayoral recruitment in New Haven and Chicago has shown that the former had a long history prior to industrialization during which mayors were selected from the city's leading families [Bradley & Zaid 1970]. Chicago, by contrast, was a community of only 100 in 1830 but grew to 120,000 by 1860. Hence, Chicago, which lacked a long preindustrial history dominated by social notables, was governed almost from the outset by an industrial and commercial elite.

The Withdrawal of Economic Dominants from Local Politics

As a national, corporate economy developed, a complex of institutions shaped the niche of each community within the larger system and consequently, the role of economic dominants in local communities. Important industrial concerns no longer were local in organization or orientation. They became vast enterprises with branch plants scattered throughout the country serving regional or national markets. In many communities, the local industry became, in reality, the branch of a national corporation or absentee-owned by a corporate conglomerate. Local community affairs were of marginal importance to these organizations. Most of the services that economic enterprises needed already existed although they might have had to be tailored to company needs. With many communities competing for new industry, corporations negotiated favorable tax and service arrangements as part of their site selection process. The balance of power clearly had shifted as the fate of local communities hinged more on corporate decisions than did corporate profits on community policies.

The people who managed absentee-owned companies were corporate representatives, whose principal commitment was to that organization and not to the communities in which they were located. Their careers made them transients, moving from locality to locality as company needs dictated. They did not necessarily reside in the same community in which the branch plant was located. As a result, from both the executive's and the corporation's point of view civic activity became less vital.

Studies of election to governmental office in Chicago, New Haven, Bay City, Cibola (Ypsilanti), Wheelsburg (Dearborn), and Cornucopia all recorded a decline in office-holding and, to some extent, in voluntary association membership by economic dominants. Of course, the rate and pattern of decline varied since a variety of other factors were operant in individual communities [Gordon 1973]. The pace of withdrawal was slower in Wheelsburg, a major automobile production center, than in Cibola, one of its satellites, apparently because central city political affairs were of greater consequence to the corporation. In Bigtown [Pellegrin & Coates 1973] there was greater political participation by absentee-owned corporation executives than might have been expected. Because the dominant economic concerns (oil companies) were less mobile than some other industries and the local market for oil products was substantial, they were concerned with good community public and political relations [Clark 1968]. In addition, since Bigtown was the state capital and oil companies had an interest in state regulation of depletion allowances, oil leases, and severance taxes, local politics and state politics were integrally related [Pellegrin & Coates 1973]. There also was evidence that region was a factor. Industrial leaders in the South adopted a more traditional, paternalistic stance toward the communities in which they were situated [Clark 1968, Gilbert 1968; Gordon 1973; Pellegrin & Coates 1973]. Although there was a clear trend toward the withdrawal of economic dominants from local politics, it was not uniform in extent or timing.

The formal participaton of absentee-owned corporations and their executives in local government declined, but many remained involved in civic affairs. Companies varied in the extent to which they encouraged their officials to participate in civic activities. In his study of Cibola, Schulze [1970] concluded that corporations opposed managerial involvement in politics since any political activity might antagonize some segment of the community, company-community disputes could create role conflicts for executives, and political activities might negatively affect the company's image in other communities.

In a reexamination of these conclusions, Mott [1970b] found that, in fact, automobile manufacturers in Cibola varied considerably in their support for employee civic activities. Ford had an active, somewhat decentralized community relations program. Management within each locality rewarded employee civic activity, assisted charities, and provided speakers and films. General Motors, by contrast, operated a more centralized community relations program closely oriented to corporate interests. While companies varied substantially in their orientation to local communities, public relations programs hardly matched the involvement of early industrialists.

Despite corporate officials' participation in local government and public relations programs to smooth company-community relations, corporate policies still had a major impact on the political economy of local communities. The larger the proportion of the resident labor force directly employed by or indirectly supported by large economic units, the more vulnerable the community was to decisions beyond its control. The effects of corporate policies were complex, having mixed benefits and costs to various segments of the community. At the worst, an industry could curtail or terminate its local operations, seriously threatening the community's economic stability or viability. Imposition of a national wage scale also might adversely affect the competitive position of local firms. On the other hand, the corporation might contribute substantially to the community's tax base, commercial prosperity, and support of municipal services. Corporate expansion had mixed consequences—increasing land values but also housing costs, capital outlays, and taxes. Some of these effects, which resulted from the changing position of an industry within the economy or a corporation within an industry, transcended corporate policy as well.

The effects of corporate policies were not always visible. Decisions not to intervene or not to support local initiatives had as great an impact as positive actions. For many community programs active corporate support was a prerequisite for successful implementation. Further, corporate policies often aroused little controversy because community leaders recognized the central role the company played in the community's well being; and they shared with corporate leaders a commitment to the economically oriented value system. The appearance of noninvolvement, therefore, could have been simply that. As long as the community policies were compatible with business interests, corporations had little interest in local affairs. Community relations programs and civic participation forewarned or forestalled conflicts and helped to maintain a favorable public image.

Other Sources of Dispersion

After 1900, control of local government shifted to working- and middle-class members of ethnic groups for whom politics was a career [Dahl 1970]. This trend was the product of a number of factors: 1. The extension of the voting franchise and direct election of most important public officials provided growing numbers of ethnic group members who would represent their interests. 2. The appeal of businessmen as candidates declined as ethnically balanced tickets became more imperative for electoral success. 3. The era in which industrialists could simultaneously build both a business and a government career passed as each activity became a full-time career and the relationship between business success and governmental service declined.

The vertical integration of local communities further contributed to the dispersion of power structures. The development of reform governments was one index of the increasing importance of the vertical system.

The principal impetus to reform was the demand for efficiency, predictability, and compatibility with the larger institutional system by dominant interest groups. Yet professionalized bureaucracies centralized control only in theory as semiautonomous governmental agencies became centers of control over specific functions. The number of interest groups that attempted to influence these power centers also expanded as communities became specialized components of a larger system. Not only competing business interests but civic groups, labor unions [McKee 1970], governmental regulatory agencies, and other municipal bureaucracies all became potential participants in the political process. Many of these organizations, such as state and federal agencies, were supra- or extra-local.

Summary

Communities were characterized during their early histories by coincidence between political power, wealth, and social prestige. Industrialization had the effect of separating wealth and creating a new set of organizations that had the need and capacity to influence the political process. Leadership of municipal governments, therefore, was captured by those for whom the political institution was instrumental in fostering urban growth.

As the locus of the industrial economy gradually shifted to corporate organization, the importance of the local political scene declined. Important decisions were made elsewhere. Industrialization also produced an expanded labor force composed primarily of foreign immigrants and rural migrants. Their numbers, cultural diversity, and deprivation created a new source of political power that ultimately transferred control of city governments anew and further dispersed power resources. Yet the continued development of an urban-industrial economy generated mounted pressure for community organizations consistent with that development. The outgrowth of these pressures, the installation of reform governments, rendered community governmental structure more consistent with the organization of the larger society and community power structures more decentralized. Thus the unmistakable trend, fed by a force arising out of the urban industrial revolution, had been away from pyramidal power structures and toward more centralized organization of local governments. In the process the politics of local communities has been transformed.

Political Structure and Policy Formation

Although there has been a general trend toward the dispersion of power resources within urban communities, the power structures of contemporary American cities still vary enormously. One important aspect of the greater functional specialization of urban communities has been social, economic, and political relationships that are increasingly complex and interdependent. Social scientists slowly have begun to recognize the importance of delineating the conditions under which various types of power structures emerge, the consequences of their occurrence, and the complex relationships among the component elements of community power structures. This recognition has led investigators to broaden the scope of their research beyond the question, "Who governs?" to explore the salient social dimensions along which power is structured and the consequences of various power arrangements. Among the issues that have received attention are the extent to which power structures are centralized and the consequences of concentration or dispersion of power resources for policy innovation, the consistency and coordination of policy outputs, and the types and levels of political outputs. While centralization of power is acknowledged as one important dimension of community power, a number of others also have been studied, such as governmental structure, individual municipal agency organization, community resource capacity, and political values. Since much of this research has been done quite recently theoretical integration is lacking. Nevertheless, the relationships discussed here suggest some important dimensions along which communities vary politically and some of the implications of those differences.

Power Structure and Policy Consistency

Socially differentiated communities are likely to be characterized by decentralized power structures. Since power resources within governments also tend to be fragmented, coordination among the various power centers can be difficult to effect. In their study of New York City politics, Wallace Sayre and Herbert Kaufman [1968] essentially came to this conclusion. New York was described as an extremely heterogeneous city in which political dominance has not been achieved by any single group. Instead, there were a number of powerful participants in the political process—political party leaders, governmental officials, nongovernmental organizations and associations, and the electorate.

Each group in New York City constituted a decisive force with respect to certain sets of decisions. Political parties controlled nominations for elective office, effectively limiting the alternatives presented to the electorate, which selected governing officials from among the party nominees. Heads of the various departments and agencies were the principal decision makers within functional areas. Each decision-making center was the object of pressure from interest groups such as professional associations, private enterprise, labor unions, civic organizations, and mass media, with some stake in policy outputs. Decisions were influenced most by those well-organized, nongovernmental interest groups that had a substantial, enduring interest in agency policy. Such groups typically included those subject to governmental regulation, which competed for government contracts, or whose operations were affected by tax and wage legislation. While civic groups, ad hoc groups, and the media exerted influence intermittently, it was the sporadic nature of their efforts that assured that their effects would be minor and transitory.

The mayor and city council provided limited coordination for New York's government. There were some constraints on each power center that inhibited pursuit of agency goals to the exclusion of all other concerns. Legislative and executive leaderships, central budgeting, and pressure from other agencies, civic groups, the press, and the electorate all exerted a general, diffuse influence on agency practices. These restraints had a limited effect and tended to produce compromise, mutual accommodation of interests, bargains, and alliances rather than a consistent, coordinated policy. In many cases it was difficult even for one department to implement a coordinated policy. Although bureaucracies were sufficiently independent to control certain sets of decisions, jurisdictions overlapped enough so that they could not insulate themselves from the effects of other agencies' policies. For example, while one department attempted to rejuvenate and expand public transportation facilities, others supported the development of an elaborate highway network.

New York, of course, is a unique case and is instructive principally as a polar type. However, other studies also have reported that more consistent, coordinated policy outputs occur in communities in which the decision-making process is centralized. A comparative study of two communities hosting military bases [Present 1971] showed that the leadership of Elmwood, the smaller community highly dependent economically on military contracts, was more cohesive and in agreement on matters relating to military contracting. The elite in Elmwood were faced with the necessity of maintaining unity if effective pressure was to be brought to bear on the federal government and an appealing community image was to be effectively communicated to new industries that could help diversify the community's economic base. Centerville, a neighboring community that served as a regional trading center, as well as hosting a military base, had a more diffused power structure. The community was less vulnerable to changes in the flow of military contracts and was more flexible and permissive in initiating change.

Power Structure, Innovation, and Output Levels

The evidence on the relationship between power structure centralization and policy innovation and output levels is less conclusive [Aiken 1970]. It has been argued that centralized power structures are more conducive to policy innovation and high output levels since the elite share a common set of values and coordination among subsystems can be achieved more easily. The reverse has been argued on the basis that decentralized power structures have separate, specialized decision making units, each of which is concerned with policy formation in a limited functional area and is supported and influenced by a constellation of interest and clientele groups. Since these decision-making centers have a focused concern on a limited set of problems, they are more likely to identify existing or emergency needs and formulate policy responses. In addition, interest groups are able to channel their resources into influencing specific decision-making centers, thereby magnifying their influence and the probability that action will be initiated.

Although the evidence is not consistent, in part because the sample of communities and decisions studied, indices and techniques of analysis employed, and control variables introduced vary [Aiken & Alford 1973; Clark 1971; Hawley 1968], several studies have reported a positive association between decentralization and innovation and high output levels. In his secondary analysis of 57 cities, Aiken [1973] found that communities with decentralized power structures were more likely to become involved in public housing, urban renewal, and model cities programs, to enter the first two of these and the War on Poverty sooner, and to achieve greater outputs on the latter three programs. He concluded, therefore, that more rapid innovations and higher levels of output were attributable to large specialized staffs administering each functional area, providing the requisite knowledge for initiating new policies. Further, it was necessary to mobilize only that limited part of the local population and organizational network concerned with each specific policy area in order to produce a coalition of forces sufficient to stimulate action.

Other research that had postulated a positive association between centralization and output levels [Clark 1968; 1971] found an inverse relationship between total community budget size and urban renewal expenditures. The research suggested that some types of decisions were easier to implement in decentralized than centralized power structures. Decisions that were innovative, involved change, and generated opposition could be more easily implemented when power was more centralized. On the other hand, for less fragile decisions, compromise was likely to increase outputs, and so the level of outputs could be expected to be higher. In fact, communities with decentralized power structures appropriated more funds for construction of housing and had higher levels of expenditure under traditional urban renewal programs. While inconclusive findings and speculations about intervening variables currently remain unresolved, they do underline the need for broader comparative research and the development of a more sophisticated model of the structure of community decision making.

Governmental Structure, Innovation, and Output Levels

In theory council-manager governments centralize decision making to a greater degree than either the mayor-council or commission forms. The manager ideally is a nonpartisan, professional administrator who appoints departmental heads and coordinates their activities. As we noted earlier, the elements of reform government, professional administration and at-large, nonpartisan elections had the effect of decreasing the political representation of lower status and ethnic groups. Party politics was replaced by interest group politics, and preponderant influence shifted to the middle classes, business, civic, and other interest groups. Therefore, structural reform did not reduce potential sources or conflict or socioeconomic and ethnic cleavages; it merely reduced the political representation of lower status groups.

Since unreformed governments were more responsive to cleavages within the community, they were more likely to innovate and maintain higher output levels. Here again, however, the type of policy was an intervening factor. Studies of participation in urban renewal and poverty programs suggested that unreformed governments applied for the financial resources available under these programs sooner, disbursed them more quickly, and had higher output levels than reformed governments [Aiken 1970; Aiken & Alford 1973; Greenstone & Peterson 1968]. With respect to innovation and outputs involving monetary resources, then, partisan administrations appeared to be much more successful in obtaining and dispensing them. On the other hand, when the outputs were political in nature, involving the reallocation of political power, reformed governments appeared better able to initiate change and facilitate the extension of political resources to additional interest groups.

One study [Greenstone & Peterson 1968] hypothesized that these differences were attributable to the organizational characteristics of the two types of government. The study of four cities' participation in the War on Poverty revealed that reform governments were better able to implement the "maximum feasible participation" clause whereas unreformed governments dealt more effectively with the economic aspects of poverty. Unreformed governments tended to disburse rewards based on partisan interests. To the extent that party organizations functioned by representing the particularistic needs of a variety of ethnic and class groups, dispensing monetary resources through the antipoverty program was consistent with old-style patronage. Distributing these resources enhanced and solidified the position of politcal leaders. A partisan organization was more likely therefore to suppress any dissention over innovation and quickly institute programs that were directly related to the maintenance of its political hegemony and the satisfaction of its constituents' needs. By contrast, the development of autonomous bases of political power within neighborhoods, as envisioned in the now-famous "maximum feasible participation" clause, constituted a major threat; if the party faithful were able to forge connections with power and revenue sources outside the control of the local party and government, the political support-patronage underpinnings of partisan government were endangered. In fact, mayors in these cities used their state and national party connections to resist such encroachments on their power bases.

Reform governments did not have the strong partisan leadership with extra-local party affiliations with which to blunt the impact of federal programs. The importance of political parties and geographically based constituencies was attenuated and power dispersed among a variety of interest groups in these cities. As a result, the formation of additional interest groups was less threatening. In the event that quiescent groups mobilized by such programs could be co-opted to form a broadened base of support for governmental officials there were some tangible gains from encouraging the political organization of lower status groups. Almost inevitably, however, interest groups clashed over the desirability of and procedures for administering any new program. Although the government as a whole might not be threatened by increased pluralism, some governmental agencies, their clientele, and ancillary interest groups were likely to be affected by any change in the provision of services. Conflicts among these interest groups made the implementation of the poverty program slower and more difficult. The result was that monetary output levels tended to be lower since the government had a less vital stake in dispensing material rewards, but political outputs were greater since there was less organized resistance to political participation by the poor.

Under certain conditions reform governments might be able to innovate more readily since professionalization and centralization of authority make them less vulnerable to minority opposition. In a study of several hundred communities that considered proposals to fluoridate municipal water systems, Rosenthal and Crain [1968] concluded that council-manager governments were more likely to adopt such proposals than mayor-council governments. Most public officials and civic and business groups did not perceive fluoridation to be a crucial issue. Any opposition that arose, therefore, tended to come from small, vocal minorities organized on an ad hoc basis. In the absence of interest group mobilization a single official could sometimes block adoption, but officials usually had little to gain by taking a strong position on the issue. As a result, the manager's commitment to efficient, enlightened administration combined with an uninformed electorate and interest group apathy could override such limited protest. If opposition groups succeeded in mobilizing powerful interest groups or a sizable proportion on the electorate, however, the odds of success or failure were dramatically altered. The vulnerability of reform governments to interest group pressures was further documented by the finding that even after fluoridation proposals had been adopted, reform governments were more likely to reconsider these decisions.

Political Culture and Policy Outputs

Community policy outputs reflect a commitment to a set of goals and values as well as social structural characteristics. Value preferences shape expectations about the kinds of actions that governments ought to undertake, the style in which politics should be conducted, the legitimacy with which various groups within the community can press for governmental response to their needs or interests, and the obligation of government to respond to such petitions and pressures. Adequate conceptualization and measurement of community value systems has proven to be a difficult, complex task. Value systems often have been inferred from policy outputs or structural attributes; in fact, value systems are cognitive and, therefore, are not identical with their behavioral manifestations.

One classic study [Wilson & Banfield 1970] postulated that communities tended toward either "public" or "private regarding" value systems. The former was characteristic of communities populated by the middle classes and Yankee-Protestants for whom the community good and disinterested civic participation were valued above individual needs. These communities, they reasoned, should endorse and institutionalize efficient, rational, nonpolitical governments that eschew partisanship and favoritism. They anticipated finding partisanship and favoritism in communities populated predominantly by ethnic groups. Immigrants and their descendants were thought to be more familiar and comfortable with hierarchically organized power structures, to maintain the same feelings of personal obligation in political life that typified their kinship relationships, and to prefer governments that were responsive to their economic, political, and social problems. Therefore, governments that distributed material benefits to neighborhoods or wards were expected to be congruent with their needs and preferences.

An empirical investigation of public and private regardingness by Raymond Wolfinger and John Field [1970] examined the relationship between the size of ethnic populations and the adoption of reform government, civil service coverage, and urban renewal programs. They concluded that the two ethics that James Wilson and Edward Banfield described did not exist, that they were not differentiated along ethnic lines as predicted, and that other factors were important in understanding political structures and policies. Indeed, Wolfinger and Field suggested that regional differences in the timing and rate of community growth and the structure of communities in which immigrants settled were more important factors than the size of the ethnic population.

Other studies have attempted to distinguish value preference regarding the role local government ought to play in community life. Oliver Williams and Charles Adrian [1968] described four such roles: 1. Promoting economic growth. Wealth and/or population was sought on the premise that a growing community was a thriving community, one presenting opportunities to furnish products and services to its new residents and businesses. 2. Providing and securing amenities. These communities found rapid growth objectionable. Their preference was for a safe, quiet, beautiful, convenient community. The range and level of services was adapted to attaining these objectives rather than to fostering community expansion, provision of welfare services, and so on. 3. Maintaining traditional services. The laissez-faire orientation of these communities legitimated expenditures or budget increases only for maintenance of the traditional functions at established levels. The community's orientation was individualistic rather than collectivistic, and so community tax revenues were kept at the minimum level necessary to maintain core services. Any problems created or confronted by caretaker communities typically were passed on to higher levels of government. 4. Arbitrating among conflicting interests. In this type of community the objective of the political process was the reconciliation of competing interests. A motley collection of interest groups coexisted with varying degrees of access to and representation in the formal political process, but each had to be considered when decisions were formulated.

Williams and Adrian reported that very different sets of policies followed from these diverse types of values and goals. For example, cities seeking growth attempted to attract industry and population through favorable tax and zoning arrangements, expanded services, annexation, and financial and political stability. Those governments that were dedicated to providing amenities implemented a narrow range of policies (e.g., traffic, zoning) in which high output levels were expected. In communities maintaining traditional services the narrowest possible range of such services was provided at minimum output levels. Governments that arbitrated among competing interests were forced to resolve the same kinds of issues confronting the other types of cities, but theirs was a procedural, as much as a substantive, orientation. No single, overriding goal shaped individual decisions; instead, compromises were made to particularistic interests on each substantive decision.

Williams and Adrian [1968] also noted that community values and goals are not sufficient to explain decision and policy outcomes. Communities can simultaneously pursue contradictory policies, albeit unconsciously. The demographic composition of the community, its governmental structure, and situational factors also determine policy choices. Indeed, in another study Williams and others [1965] observed that policy choices were influenced by a combination of factors including needs (e.g., population composition, available space), resources, and value preferences. While they conceded that decisions did not necessarily reflect value preferences, they also concluded that community assessments of service needs were influenced more by conceptions of the proper role of government than by resources and needs.

Agency Structure and Policy Outputs

Several studies have documented the impact of governmental and nongovernmental boards and agencies on outputs. An exploration of public school desegregation decisions in eight cities [Crain & Vanecho 1968] revealed that integration plans were not fashioned either in response to direct influence on school board members by political or economic leaders or by the level of civil rights activity. The economic elite had limited knowledge of or interest in the impending decision; it was the composition of the school board itself that was the determinative factor.

School boards composed of civic elites were more liberal than those dominated by political elites, predispositions that were acquired prior to assuming board membership. The more liberal boards made up of civic elites were much more likely to acquiesce to the federal desegregation orders. Liberalism and implementation of desegregation plans were most highly related where board members were appointed or their elections were uncontested. The ability of these school boards to function freely was attributable in large measure to a broad consensus on community values and goals. When there was value dissensus, elections were hotly contested and acquiescence much lower.

To a certain extent the composition of the school boards was a product of community values. In cities where governmental reform had been carried out, school board activities were relatively autonomous; intervention from outside occurred principally in recruitment of new board members and financing of elections. Through their individual participation in community affairs and their common commitment to governmental reform, economic development, and community harmony, the civic elite made a continuous imput into community decision making. However, they acted as individuals, sharing a common ideology, rather than as a cohesive group seeking to control local politics. To the extent that they were successful in bringing the "right" kind of men into government, school-board decisions were likely to be generally consistent with their value orientation. This did not imply that specific policies, such as integration, failed to arouse controversy or individual economic or political leaders did not disagree with specific decisions. Despite such disagreements, since the board was not acutely sensitive to political pressures, its own composition and internal operations were important determinants of decisional outcomes.

A study [Derthick 1968] of the administration of public assistance programs in Massachusetts towns further confirms the importance of agency structure for policy outputs. The organization of public welfare has shifted from a locally appointed and controlled welfare board to a state and federally funded civil service bureaucracy. Local public assistance constitutes a small proportion of welfare payments compared with the federally funded, state-regulated Aid to Families with Dependent Children (AFDC) program. It might be expected that under AFDC the number of recipients relative to the eligible population and the size of payments to families would not vary significantly among cities. However, case studies of two demographically similar Massachusetts cities [Derthick 1968] uncovered substantial disparities both in the proportion of the eligible families receiving assistance and the size of payments to recipients. One city simply dispensed state-prescribed minimums; the other exercised discretion to expand the number of recipients and the size of payments.

The more liberal board financed moving expenses, paid overdue utility bills to prevent termination of service, authorized advance payments for transportation to obtain emergency medical care, and increased rental allowances. These added benefits were attributable to a client-oriented, permissive welfare administration in which executives allowed caseworkers considerable individual discretion. Since workers tended to be liberal and lenient with their constituents, output levels were higher. The more restrictive agency, by contrast, demanded strict conformity by caseworkers to executive-approved rules and procedures. Flexibility in serving client needs was discouraged. The fact that such differences were observed in similar communities despite state guidelines indicated that municipal agencies retained considerable autonomy and that policy outputs were not solely a function of the community resource base or need levels. Agencies clearly differed in their definitions of agency goals and responsibilities.

The importance of political leaders' perceptions of problems, the mutuality of these perceptions, and their implications for policy outputs were highlighted in a longitudinal study of city council policy formation in seventy-seven local governments in the San Francisco metropolitan area [Eulau & Eyestone 1970]. Results indicated that population size, density, and growth, but not resource capacity, were related to policy development. Nevertheless, they concluded that policy outputs could not be explained simply in terms of environmental challenges or availability of resources since the variance in the perception by council members of conditions as "problems," the mutuality of these definitions, and consensus on the community's future intervened between environmental conditions and policy outputs. Advanced cities, those with the highest output levels, were characterized by definition of more conditions as problems, greater agreement regarding which conditions were problems, consensus on which problems were most pressing, and a common conception of future development leading to an industrial or balanced economic base.

Community Resources and Policy Outputs

A number of separate investigations have reported that ecological and demographic characteristics of communities, such as size, density, growth, socioeconomic status, distribution of the population, community economic base, and land available for development affect the type and level of policies and outputs [Eulau & Eyestone 1970; Derthick 1968; O. Williams et al. 1965; Wood 1961]. These kinds of factors, of course, were related to income distribution and land and property value structure, which, in turn, were the sources of governmental revenue. To some extent these studies have assumed that communities with similar demographic-ecological characteristics could be expected to generate about the same types and levels of outputs. Most research has confirmed that community resources were related to outputs, but most also have concluded that community policies and output levels were not solely a function of needs and resources.

Robert Wood, in his classic monograph on the New York metropolitan area, *1400 Governments* [1961], reported that population size was the best predictor of community expenditures although other factors such as industrialization, housing density, age distribution of the population, socioeconomic factors, and available reserve land also were significant. Size was a particularly critical factor for smaller places. Expenditures to communities under 10,000 were governed by the size of available revenues. In larger communities the range and level of services provided also was contingent on the needs, preferences, and power of various segments of the community. For example, small communities typically expended more funds for police protection and street maintenance; large communities allocated resources more evenly and were able to direct more funds into fire protection, sanitation, and social services.

Given any level of resources, however, communities have adopted a variety of strategies for coping with the pressures generated by community growth and composition. Resources have been increased by manipulating the assessed valuation and tax rates. New industry has been solicited to increase revenues. Special district governments have offered a means of coping with problems that transcended administrative boundaries and an opportunity to create new units of governments with independent tax powers. The impact of urban growth in some cases has been blunted by planning for future growth, zoning to assure orderly land use development, and attracting "desirable" types of industry. Appeals have been made to higher levels of government for additional revenues and easing of tax and debt ceilings. Such strategies have been variably successful and, of course, past decisions have cumulated to narrow future alternatives. Those communities, for example, that from the outset were overwhelmed by urban growth and attempted to develop additional sources of revenue through expansion found that population and industrial growth created ever-increasing demands on the political economy. Some of these communities that reached very high densities discovered that higher business property valuations did not offset the reduced residential tax base. For them the point has long since passed when an alternative strategy based on control of urban growth through planning, zoning, and selective recruitment of industry could be implemented. Thus current policies reflected communities' developmental histories, and variance in outputs was attributable not only to environmental conditions but also to the strategies adopted to deal with them and the cumulative impact of similar choices made in the past. These strategies developed out of value preferences regarding community goals and the proper role of government, perceptions of conditions as problems, and the structuring of political organization and access.

Summary

Research on the political process within urban communities has documented a number of important components of power structures and relationships among them. Centralized power structures are likely to achieve greater coordination and consistency, but innovation and output levels tend to be lower. Governmental structure, likewise, has an impact on policy innovation and output levels; innovation and some types of outputs tend to be lower in reform governments, for example. Resources available to the political economy appear to influence the type and level of political outputs, although the values and goals to which a community is committed are of equal or greater import. There are, of course, a number of intervening factors in these relationships such as the type of decision and limitations improved by previously formulated policies. While these and other findings require further substantiation and integration with previous research, greater methodological sophistication and sensitivity to various aspects of community power structure have been achieved. Considerable evidence on certain political processes and relationships has already been gathered. One such area of specialized research is evident in the recent spate of studies dealing with majority-minority political relationships.

The Position of the Black Subcommunity

From the time that America was "discovered" it has been truly a land populated principally by immigrants and their descendants. The new arrivals have confronted the established residents with and were themselves confronted by enormous problems. The immigrants who flooded into American cities to provide the labor force for the Industrial Revolution entered cities just as urban institutions were beginning to take shape. They were socially and culturally diverse, largely unskilled, pushed from their homelands by lack of opportunity and/or political despotism, and pulled to the United States by the promise of freedom and opportunity. For many early immigrants it was several generations before the promises on which their hopes were based bore fruit; for others, the promise remains long deferred.

The established residents of the communities to which the new Americans came reacted tc them and their problems with an ambivalence that has persisted despite changes in the composition of immigrant groups. On the one hand, Americans demonstrated a resilient faith in America as a melting pot, in an open democratic society in which no man was better than any other, and in the United States as a sanctuary for the poor and oppressed of other lands. On the other hand, fear and prejudice have been directed toward ethnic group members with distinctive values and life styles and have led to discrimination, segregation, and outright violence. The new arrivals did not meld as quickly and easily as their hosts had expected. Many clung tenaciously to their native social and cultural traditions, reinforced partly by their ecological and social separation into ethnic subcommunities.

Blacks in the United States are unique to the extent in which they have suffered social, economic, and political disabilities. The destructive effects of long-term subjugation and racial visibility are an onus that other groups have been spared [Bromley & Longino 1972]. Resistance to subjugation is as old as the slave rebellions and has changed only in character as blacks' status within the society has been altered. Nevertheless, blacks remain physically and socially isolated, and, as a result, some observers have contended that black politics can be better understood in terms of a colonial than a cohesive ethnic group model.

Robert Blauner [1972] described the internal colonialization model in terms of four components: 1. involuntary entry, 2. destruction or transformation of indigenous values and ways of life, 3. administration of the colonized group by representatives of the dominant power, 4. definition of the colonized group as inferior. Members of other ethnic groups migrated to the United States partly by choice, were not politically subjugated and administratively controlled for extended periods, and were able to adapt their values and life styles to those of the indigenous culture as this transformation worked to their advantage. Although the degree of ethnic group assimilation and acculturation should not be overemphasized, many groups inhabited lower class slums for only a few generations. Blacks, by contrast, remain to a significant degree, trapped within ghettoes. The economic and political organization of their subcommunities is controlled by the white community, and they lack meaningful access to the governmental structure and political process.

Reputational and Positional Leadership

Numerous studies of black subcommunities reveal the extent to which blacks have been politically isolated. Reputational research, for example, has produced few nominations of blacks as community leaders [Barth & Abu-Laban 1970; Hunter 1970b]. Because no blacks were nominated as community leaders in Atlanta, Hunter [1970b] conducted a separate investigation of the subcommunity power structure. The economic disabilities of the black subcommunity were underlined by the fact that reputational leaders included a publisher, banker, minister, educator, politician, social worker, insurance executive, civic worker, and lawyer; whereas white community leaders were found predominantly in commerce and industry. More women and ministers were found among the second level of leadership in the subcommunity; and religious, along with fraternal and welfare, were among the most influential subcommunity organizations.

Positions research also indicated that blacks traditionally have held positions of only minor importance within municipal governments. Consequently, the decisions in which they participated had limited consequences for the community as a whole. Although other minority groups have encountered prejudice and discrimination, the hostility directed toward blacks has extended beyond the usual time lag between an ethnic group's arrival in the community and significant ethnic representation in the political institution [Wilson 1973a]. The length of that time lag varied among cities depending on size, density, rate of growth of the black population, and the size of the wards.

A recent survey of policy-making positions in Chicago [Baron et al. 1972] revealed that while blacks constitute 20 percent of the population, they held fewer than 3 percent of the policy-making positions in all major institutions and only about 5 percent of such positions in the local government. The study concluded that the actual power vested in black policy makers was only one-third as great as the percentage of positions they held. Black representation in policy-making positions frequently constituted "tokenism" or occurred in organizations that were all black. For example, two large black insurance companies accounted for the vast majority of blacks in policy-making positions, and black councilmen represented predominantly black wards.

Black representation in important local offices reached a turning point toward the end of the 1960s. In a number of cities the black population became the largest single minority group or even a majority as black populations within cities continued to grow while the white middle classes moved to the suburbs. Under these circumstances the probability of a major party endorsing black candidates for major elective offices increased. Indeed, in 1967 Carl Stokes and Richard Hatcher were elected as mayors in Cleveland, Ohio, and Gary, Indiana, respectively [Hadden, Masoth, and Thiessen 1970]. These elections were hotly contested, and race was the central issue. Voting was split along racial lines with the black candidates' victory resting on solid support among black voters and some support from white liberals. The importance of race as a factor in these elections are underscored by the narrow margins of victory Hatcher and Stokes recorded [Stokes, for example, a former state legislator and mayoralty candidate with Democratic party, labor, and media support won by only 1500 votes].

As a result of the narrow margins of victory and the fragility of their coalitions, the newly elected black mayors were forced to proceed cautiously. Policies that would have initiated major changes designed to uplift the condition of black populations also would have generated massive resistance among the whites, undermining already tenuous coalitions. In order to preserve their power bases, the new mayors were forced to share power with whites and seek incremental change. Since 1967 blacks have captured the mayoralty in other cities. Race was a factor, sometimes a decisive one, in such elections. However, as whites began to perceive that black mayors would not propose radical policies or change, the importance of race as an issue, although not as a source of voting support, has diminished. Yet the individuals who have been elected had to be moderate, constrained by the very victories they had achieved. As a result, the tangible gains that have occurred for the masses of the black poor were modest, although the election of major officials constituted a symbolic victory.

Barriers to Political Equality

While some blacks have achieved important offices in a variety of institutions, for the mass of black urban poor there have been few avenues for effective actions to better their lot. Perspective on their continuing plight can be gained by reviewing the historical context of the urbanization of the black population. Blacks did not begin to migrate in large numbers to urban areas until World War I [Palmer 1972]. Political disenfranchisement and racial violence in the South coupled with the expanding opportunities of a wartime economy in northern cities provided the impetus for the first major migration of blacks northward. This movement was dwarfed in size by World War II and postwar migrations. Black migrants who availed themselves of these economic opportunities often found themselves unemployed after peace was concluded. The later migrants moved into an economy in which there was a shrinking demand for unskilled labor, which had offered employment opportunities to so many earlier migrants.

In addition, they confronted discrimination in hiring practices and union membership, inferior and segregated schools, and residential segregation, all of which served to constrict economic opportunities.

There were political obstacles as well. Unlike many previous immigrant groups, blacks were unable to utilize local governmental institutions as a vehicle for social mobility or to increase their political strength. The reform of local governments brought with it larger wards or at-large elections, which diminished the ability of ecologically segregated minority groups to elect locally responsive representatives; civil service bureaucracies, which reduced patronage appointments; and managerial executives, who were relatively impervious to influence from geographically organized constituencies. Unreformed governments with political "machines" simply absorbed blacks into the existing structure [Wilson 1973a].

Examples of the political discrimination directed against blacks abound. In many communities reapportionment plans, annexation programs, and electoral procedures were designed to dilute black voting strength. In Philadelphia, for instance, legislative reapportionment had the effect of reducing the black population within city districts [Strange 1969]. Baltimore also attempted to institute a reapportionment plan highly unfavorable to blacks during the 1960s, although it was ultimately defeated. Lakeland, Michigan, altered its electoral system so that each district nominated two candidates for the general election, reducing the chances of black nominees in all but overwhelmingly black districts [Sloan 1969]. Ironically, by the time blacks constituted a substantial enough segment of the population to secure some major elected offices, many cities were overwhelmed by deteriorating physical plants, the flight of industry and white middle-class residents to the suburbs, eroded tax bases and expanding municipal debt, and high assessed valuations and tax rates.

During recent decades most of the major initiatives in establishing racial equality and improving opportunities for blacks have come through federal intervention. However, federal programs usually have been channeled through local communities, and the impact of these programs on existing political arrangements has been carefully contained. The antipoverty program provides one illuminating illustration of the frustration blacks have faced in attempting to increase their political participation and influence. The Economic Opportunity Act of 1964, which launched the "War on Poverty," contained a number of provisions for combating poverty. Among them was Title II, the "Urban and Rural Community Action Program," which provided 90 percent federal financing for local community programs that provided services or assisted in eliminating poverty. The most controversial aspect of Title II was the stipulation that programs were to be developed, conducted, and administered with the "maximum feasible participation" of area residents.

Community action programs were predicated on the assumption that institutions were unresponsive to the needs of the poor and that poverty stemmed from these structural barriers rather than personal pathology. The poor were those who, for a variety of reasons, were prevented from achieving culturally defined goals through existing institutional arrangements. The community action concept represented a sharp break with tradition since the new programs were designed to mobilize the poor for the purpose of removing these structural barriers. Existing welfare institutions had been designed to deliver services to the poor on a casework basis, not to increase access to decision-making arenas. These agencies essentially were social answers to the questions, "Why is there poverty?" and "What ought our society to do about the existence of poverty?" Their organization and goals reflected the traditional American view of poverty as a personal rather than as a social problem.

From the point of view of local officials, the notion of providing the quiescent poor with a source of organization and funding independent of governmental control had very little to recommend it and a number of obvious, serious disadvantages. 1. Organization of the poor ultimately would lead to demands for political change or better services, demands that would be aimed at local officials. Governmental leaders already faced with deficit spending and political pressures from all sides for additional resources could hardly have been expected to respond enthusiastically. 2. Many of the demands that the poor might have made would have been certain to alienate other crucial constituencies and bureaucracies. Calls for civilian review boards to monitor police activities, better physical services for ghetto areas, expanded welfare programs, community control over public housing, or rent controls would have been certain to antagonize members of important agencies within the government (e.g., police department), private interest groups (e.g., real estate interests), or middle-class taxpayers [David 1971]. 3. Expanded services could have resulted in higher taxes, redistribution of scarce resources, or reallocation of power. 4. Even the potential gains in political support within the black subcommunity were unpredictable since some conservative black leaders also opposed changes that might weaken their own control over poor blacks.

It is not surprising, therefore, that local officials attempted to retain control over community action programs through such techniques as limiting the number of poor on community action boards, hand-picking representatives of the poor, retaining centralized control over the grant application process and administration of funded programs, encouraging proposals that expanded social services rather than community organization, prohibiting community action workers from engaging in political activities, and lobbying for changes in the federal enabling legislation. Ultimately, through some combination of such practices, many mayors were able to retain substantial control over local community action programs.

There was, however, considerable variation in the extent to which governmental leaders accepted or encouraged oranization of the poor [David 1971]. For example, in New York Mayor Robert Wagner's administration had less to gain politically from such programs than John Lindsay's administration. Wagner was elected by a coalition of middle-income white ethnic group members, low-income nonwhite groups, and reform Democrats. While some concessions on participation of the poor were made to placate them, Wagner was careful to maintain a tight reign lest the former groups be alienated by insatiable demands from the poor. Lindsay, on the other hand, who was a fusion candidate, had a much more unstable constituency. Community action offered him an opportunity to erode some of the bloc support the Democratic party held in poorer areas. There was a real possibility of making inroads into traditionally Democratic constituencies. The risks involved in allowing the poor to establish their own political organizations were reduced by retaining considerable control in proposal formulation and the administration of funded proposals. Thus, even in those administrations where community action fared best, the groups that controlled the decision-making forums were willing to advance the well-being of the poor, but balked at redistributing political resources or restructuring institutional arrangements.

So while urban communities have become increasingly pluralistic and governmental decision making, particularly in larger cities, has been decentralized, it cannot be concluded that the political process has been equally accessible to all groups. As a group, the black poor in urban areas have been left out of the legitimate access structure. They lack financial resources, technical and professional expertise, cohesiveness, and political experience. Consequently, they have not been politically active despite real needs and grievances that could have been accommodated within the political system. In general, they have not formed interest groups to levy pressure on public officials or coalitions with other groups sharing similar interests. The many autonomous decision-making agencies, have, therefore, both reflected the prevailing mobilization of bias and been most accessible to permanent, well-organized and well-financed interest groups. Public agencies were set up to deal with needs and problems as they had already been defined and not to redistribute political power. Consequently, decision-making arenas have generated outputs that both appeased deprived groups and perpetuated the existing distribution of power.

In these already-established systems the defenders of the status quo had a major advantage. The forces for change usually were not as well organized as those which they confronted. Status quo organizations represented the prevailing mobilization of bias that in itself made dissent from prevailing practices difficult. Service-oriented programs were launched in order to undercut the appeal of militant groups that might provoke a direct confrontation; militant leaders were co-opted; procedural requirements sapped the energies of emergent organizations; overlapping responsibilities interminably delayed decisions and prevented agencies from becoming visible targets for demands or hostility; and divisions among black leadership were exploited. For their part, change-oriented groups had to be successful in all decision-making arenas in order to implement change but status quo forces had only to succeed in controlling one such arena in order to block change. Constituents were divided, difficult to mobilize, and anxious to avoid conflict. Further, it proved difficult to convince them of the relationship between their individual problems and institutional arrangements. However, the continuing frustration and anger that those without access to the political system experienced has periodically erupted into protest activities that were political in nature but took place outside the normal, established political channels and institutions.

The Rise of Militancy

There have been some general trends in the black protest against their ascribed status [Downes & Burks 1968] that reflect changing majority-minority political relationships. Traditionally, black leaders tried to accommodate themselves to white society on the assumption that moderate demands for equal rights, responsible leadership, and efforts to assimilate blacks into white society were the most effective means of gaining social acceptance. Therefore, most black political organizations were extra-governmental (e.g., NAACP, Urban League, CORE, SCLC) and were dedicated to advancing greater equality, integration, and representation in white-dominated institutions. Virtually all the issues with which they were concerned were race-related civil rights, segregation, housing, and welfare. It is indeed a significant commentary on racism in American society that most important black political activity has had a single focus—dealing with the disabilities created by their ascribed racial status. In many communities black leaders had some access to white leaders for redress of grievances, were sometimes consulted by white leaders when decisions affecting the black subcommunity were formulated, and could bargain for (but not demand) political concessions. However, initiative, resources, and final authority were securely in the hands of white leaders. Historically, then, the relationship of the black to the white community has been predominantly one of accommodation and compromise [Killian 1969; Killian & Smith 1970; Pfautz 1969].

The 1954 Supreme Court school desegregation order signified the beginning of a major change in the relationship between the black subcommunity and the larger community. The NAACP had used the courts and due process to achieve this landmark decision. Yet the decision did not produce immediate school integration, much less dramatic changes in the lives of most urban blacks. The South reacted initially with defiance and then with delaying tactics to desegregation orders. For urban blacks in the North, who were confronted by de facto segregation that, if less visible, was equally insidious, the Court decision was an even more hollow victory. The school desegregation order was followed the next year by a ruling against segregated public transportation and two years later by the dispatch of federal troops to Little Rock, Arkansas. While the fruits of the desegregation order were not realized immediately in or outside the South [Coleman et al. 1972] and the inferior quality of education [Kozol 1972] and other more subtle aspects of racism [Baratz & Baratz 1972; Sloan 1972] persisted, the judicial decisions did lead to a more militant type of protest. The 1960s were characterized by mass protests, confrontations, and direct action as it became apparent that court decisions would not be followed by remedial change but by defiance, evasions, and tokenism. Black leaders began to perceive how deeply racism was embedded in American cultural and institutional systems and recognized that the removal of legal barriers was necessary but not sufficient for equal membership in American society.

Beginning in 1963 with the rioting in Birmingham, Alabama, and culminating in the hundreds of separate disorders in 1967, blacks directly confronted white society [Downes 1971]. These hostile outbursts differed from earlier racial confrontations. Prior to the seven major race riots in 1919, most mob violence was initiated by whites against blacks. Over 3000 lynchings occurred between 1880 and 1915 as a means of "keeping niggers in their place" [Brown 1969; Downes & Burks 1968]. In the 1919 riot in Chicago, the 1935 Harlem violence, and the 1943 Harlem and Detroit disorders, blacks and white alike initiated violence against members of the opposite race. Both of these types of collective behavior must be distinguished from the 1960s disorders, which have been deemed "hostile outbursts" rather than "riots" (a legal-adminstrative term) since hostility was directed against those agents that blacks perceived as responsible for the deprivations that they had suffered.

Considerable controversy has been aroused over the meaning of the disorders. Explanations [Banfield 1968; Fogelson & Hill 1968; Lupsha 1968] have run the gamut from conspiracy theories that attributed them to the work of "outside agitators" to the "riffraff" theory, which fixes responsibility on criminals, juveniles, agitators, the unskilled, uprooted, and unemployed, to the theory that rioting was conducted mainly for "fun and profit" rather than as social protest. An impressive amount of evidence has been gathered, however, that suggests that such theories are misinformed and that the disorders may be best understood as a continuation, although modified in form, of the protest movement. Among the research findings that support the collective protest view are the following:

1. More than a tiny percentage of blacks were involved in the protests [Downes 1971; Fogelson & Hill 1968; Hahn 1973]. Fifteen percent of the black population often was actively involved, and, of course, some of the participation rates would increase if age, sex, proximity to the riot area, and other related factors were controlled. In addition, bystanders tacitly indicated approval of the disorders by their own inaction to terminate them or to prevent illegal activities and by their encouragement of the active participants [Hahn 1973; Quarentelli & Dynes 1971].

2. A substantial percentage of blacks defined the riots as necessary or inevitable, having a purpose, giving the victims their just deserts, increasing white awareness and sympathy, and assisting the ends that civil rights groups had sought [Fogelson & Hill 1968; Hahn 1973]. While blacks clearly preferred negotiation or nonviolent protest, and there was ambivalence about the effectiveness of violence as a tactic, there also was a fatalistic feeling that such violence was unavoidable and would recur.

3. The personal characteristics of participants in the disturbances were similar to those of nonparticipant ghetto dwellers [Fogelson & Hill 1968; Lupsha 1968]. Since most black ghetto dwellers were lower class, a number of the traits delineated in the "riffraff" theory were characteristic of a large segment of the subcommunity; however, they were not disproportionately represented among self-reported participants or among those arrested in the disorders. Participants tended to be young, male, and residents of the community; they were somewhat more likely than nonparticipants to have unskilled occupations or to be unemployed. Like a sizable proportion of ghetto males, they had had previous encounters with the police. Participants had higher median education levels than nonparticipants, although their incomes and occupational status were likely to be lower [Geschwender 1971]. This pattern suggests that participants were more likely to have experienced status inconsistently than nonparticipants.

4. Riot supporters tended to perceive the disturbances in political or change terms more often than nonsupporters [Geschwender 1971; Hahn 1973]. Politically disaffected individuals were more likely to define the riots as helpful, seeking political objectives through nonsanctioned methods. Supporters typically saw the disturbances as calling attention to needs, were opposed to the incumbent mayor, were not disposed to work through conventional political channels, and were disenchanted with federal poverty programs.

   Those who perceived the disturbances as calling attention to their needs also felt that riots were inevitable, that leaders could not meaningfully respond to their problems, and that outsiders would not understand the disorders. Thus, while participants felt that the disorders were politically purposeful, they were not aimed at publicizing their needs or forcing expansion of existing programs. Rather their rejection of law and authority was a more basic repudiation of their subjugation. From their perspective the political system had failed to deal with their problems. Although they clearly were not fomenting revolution, participants were attempting to confront the larger society with its failures through direct, dramatic action, which they hoped might lead to a modification of the means by which solutions to problems were sought.

5. The popular belief that the disorders were meaningless, destructive outbursts was founded in part on the facts that many of them coincided more closely with oppressive summer weather than with salient political

events and that they were not preceded by, or sometimes even accompanied by, formal political demands [Lang & Lang 1971]. Yet there was discernible patterns of behavior that indicated the general objectives of and limitations observed by the participants.

First, although many whites were in the riot areas, there were few interracial assaults unless the individuals were perceived as members of the "white power structure" against which the protests were directed (e.g., police, firemen, media representatives) [Obershall 1971]. Even when violence was employed it was clearly limited. Some individuals were beaten and snipers occasionally harrassed police and firemen, but whites at the mercy of rioters were not beaten or shot to death.

Second, the rioters were selective in picking targets for arson and looting [Geschwender 1971; Quarentelli & Dynes 1971]. In general, stores owned by blacks, churches, schools, and post offices were not burned or looted whereas grocery, furniture, apparel, and liquor stores were ransacked. It is also significant that looting was not an individual, covert activity but rather a group, public activity in which numerous members of the community participated and that was openly or tacitly supported by many others. Looting may be interpreted as involving a temporary redefinition of property rights. The repudiation of norms regulating individuals' access to culturally valued items represented a form of collective protest against existing institutional arrangements.

Third, there were no attempts at armed resistance or efforts to hold territory that might be expected in revolutionary activity. The disorders were intended to dramatically and directly confront the white society with the failure of its institutions to meet the needs of black Americans and not to totally repudiate that system. Fourth, only certain norms were violated. Participants were observed obeying traffic ordinances, for example, while actively involved in the disorders.

6. The general objectives of the civil rights movement and the disorders were similar despite the greater legitimacy accorded the former. While the participants in the hostile outburst were largely unorganized and their strategy and tactics for attaining full acceptance in American society were not logically developed, their activities were related to those of more conventional civil rights organizations. Black protest has taken a variety of forms, all the way from slave uprisings and escape, black separatism, accommodation, legalistic confrontation, and race riots to direct action in hostile outbursts.

It has been the failure of attempts to appeal to the political system for redress of legitimate grievances that led to the adoption of more violent tactics to produce change. Over the last 300 years virtually every major gain by blacks has occurred only after a crisis situation has forced white leaders to respond [Downes & Burks 1968]. The use of violence to achieve what more orderly tactics had failed to accomplish constituted a protest even if the individuals were not consciously attempting to communicate this message. If the level of organization was primitive and the demands inarticulate, this was due primarily to the participants' lack of any clear conception of how to institute meaningful change. When all else failed, massive refusal to honor the normative order had the effect of forcing political leaders to respond to the dissidents' demands or to assume the enormous burden of attempting to continuously enforce compliance.

7. The occurrence and intensity of the hostile outbursts varied among cities [Geschwender 1971; Lieberson & Silverman 1971; Wanderer 1971]. Several studies have shown that the occurrence and intensity of hostile outbursts was associated with a number of social and political characteristics of cities such as population size, density, and stability; a large, growing black population; low education and income levels; high unemployment; deteriorating housing; higher governmental debt and expenditure levels; partisan elections; larger city councils and longer tenure in public office. While some of these findings were not startling in themselves, they indicated that the disorders did not occur randomly but were related to community structure.

Summary

The evidence on black subcommunity participation in urban politics strongly indicates that blacks have had little access to the community political system. Most of their limited resources have been directed toward removing social, economic, and political disabilities. Such protests have taken a variety of forms as the structure of the black subcommunity, the local community of which it is part, and the larger society have changed. The changing character of black political activity in urban areas has been partly a function of the urbanization of the black population, the formation of ghettoes, governmental reform, economic dislocations, and other related factors that can be linked to the urban-industrial revolution. However, despite a variety of other social changes, much of the political activity of the black subcommunity has taken place outside the framework of the local government; unlike political activity in the conventional sense, it has been directed at the political system from outside.

Political Relationships Among Urban Communities in Metropolitan Areas

Urbanization and industrialization in the United States transformed community structure and the relationship between community and society. Like other components of urban society, communities became specialized units, performing specific roles within the larger systems of which they were part. Their increasing complexity, specialization, and interdependence were reflected politically in general trends toward greater dispersion of power resources within communities, more diversity among community power structures, and greater salience of extra-community institutions in the local political process. Preceding sections have traced a number of the factors that have shaped community power structures, governmental policies, and political decision making. In this section attention will focus on the political relationships among urban communities themselves, and on the politics of metropolitan areas in particular. Intercommunity political relationships at once reinforce and are an outgrowth of the functional specialization and complex interdependencies that characterize urban society.

A clear majority of the U.S. population currently resides within metropolitan areas, and a substantial proportion of the metropolitan area population lives in the urban fringe surrounding central cities. Usually the urban fringe contains a large number of local governments, including incorporated municipalities, townships, counties, and special districts, with overlapping jurisdictions and responsibilities. Although a metropolitan area, taken as an aggregate, is extremely heterogeneous, individual communities tend to be much more homogeneous, fulfilling a specific role within the larger metropolitan systems. Since many political units occupy the same field, their actions, whether coordinated or uncoordinated, have a decided impact on surrounding communities. Suburbia and the multiplicity of local governments frequently are assumed to be a normal feature of urban life. However, metropolitan politics would now be quite different if the incorporation of suburban communities had been prevented, central cities had enlarged their boundaries to recapture new fringe growth, or metropolitan area-wide governments had been established. It is the plethora of local governments that has transformed local politics by adding intergovernmental to citizen-government relationships within metropolitan areas. The reasons for the evolution of metropolitan areas as we now know them are rooted in a set of historical conditions that reflect the dynamics of urban growth and the culture of privatism.

In several respects the phenomenon labeled "suburbanization" is simply an extension of the process of urban growth. 1. Although urban populations are divided among a number of governmental jurisdictions, both the proportion of the U.S. population residing within metropolitan areas and the scale of individual metropolitan areas are increasing. 2. Urban growth has engendered greater heterogeneity of metropolitan areas as aggregates but greater homogeneity of subareas (e.g., neighborhoods, municipalities). The process of suburbanization has continued the trend toward ecological segregation of various types of land uses and population groups. 3. The evolution of metropolitan areas exemplifies the individualistic orientation of the culture of privatism. As one observer has pointed out: The development of cities has occurred through unplanned, historically developed cooperation of thousands of actors largely unconscious of their collaboration to this individually sought end. "Much of what occurs seems to just happen with accidental trends becoming cumulative and providing results intended by nobody" [Long 1970, p. 11]. Suburban growth has continued that pattern with individual communities and metropolitan areas as a whole manifesting a lack of coordination and integration.

The Advent of Suburbanization

Prior to the Industrial Revolution cities were rather small by modern standards, serving principally commercial and residential functions. The upper classes lived close to the city center and lower status groups were located on the periphery. Neighborhoods within preindustrial cities tended to be fairly heterogeneous [Taylor 1970]. There were autonomous communities located in the areas surrounding preindustrial cities that served a limited residential function for and maintained economic and social interaction with the larger city [Singleton 1973]. The relationship of these fringe communities to the larger centers can be better characterized as interdependence than dominance-subservience, a pattern that emerged later.

Industrialization dramatically altered both the scale and ecological organization of urban areas. The influx of industry into cities increased their population and physical size. Heavy industry spawned subsidiary economic enterprises; the industrial labor force mushroomed the size of urban populations; and retail and service industries proliferated to meet the needs of the expanding population. Congestion became a serious problem since the level of technology limited the height and density of buildings as well as the distances over which people and goods could be transported economically. As time went on, technological innovations such as steel-frame buildings, elevators, and steam and electrically powered vehicles permitted urban expansion both upward and outward.

Rapid increases in city size and density forced much of the new growth to the periphery of the built-up area where large tracts of land were available for new building sites. Since the administrative boundaries of cities usually had been established at the time of their initial incorporation and were drawn closely around the built-up areas, much of the new urban growth spilled over municipal boundaries. Many cities initially were able to expand their boundaries to recapture these outlying populations; however, keeping pace with urban growth proved problematic for a variety of reasons [ACIR 1961]. **1.** Many cities were literally overwhelmed by the magnitude and rapidity of urban growth. The increasing number and levels of municipal services demanded by city residents placed a heavy burden on the political economy; funds to support services for outlying populations were not readily available. **2.** Many states passed liberal incorporation statutes that permitted outlying populations to form autonomous communities rather than merge with central cities. As a result, a substantial part of the tax-generating population became immune to annexation, and suburban communities were obstacles to further central city boundary expansion. **3.** Once established, suburban communities themselves attracted population and industry that found suburban locations desirable.

The pace of suburban growth initially was limited by primitive transportation technology [Taylor 1970]. Major development in public transportation began by 1830 as the horse-drawn omnibus was put on rails; later electrically powered streetcars and subways replaced horse-drawn coaches, and railroads began offering commuter service. Although the number of suburbanites steadily increased, the automobile was the single greatest impetus to suburban growth [Schnore 1959]. The earliest suburbanites were drawn largely from upper status groups, which first took advantage of new forms of transportation [Singleton 1973]. As industrialization proceeded, residences in and around the core areas of cities were displaced by industrial and commercial units. The latter required contiguity to other economic units, proximity to transportation lines that radiated outward from the center of the city, and maximum accessibility to consumers. Business and industry were better able to compete for valuable land at the center of the city than residential units. In addition, the conditions accompanying urban growth such as congestion, pollution, disease, crime, and the influx of lower status groups made centralized residential locations less attractive to the upper classes. Upper status groups were best able to absorb the greater temporal and monetary costs of suburban locations, which necessitated commuting. The resultant pattern, which characterized the first decades of suburbanization and still characterizes many larger, older metropolitan areas, was a pronounced socioeconomic gradient outward from city centers. Lower status groups tended to cluster more closely around the core area, and middle and upper status groups increasingly located in suburban communities [Schnore 1963].

Suburbanization began as a middle-class residential movement, but, over time, suburban areas have become as diverse as central cities themselves. There are still numerous upper status communities that are principally residential, allowing only shopping centers and the "right kind" of business and industry within their borders, but these no longer typify suburbia. Suburbs now vary widely in class structure, size and density, economic base, governmental organization, and degree of dependence on central cities. Decentralization of industry, followed by retail and service activities, gradually transformed suburbia from "its traditional role as dependent 'urban fringe' to independent 'neo-city'" [Masotti 1973, p. 15]. Suburbs now are less dependent on central cities; they have become functionally specialized communities within metropolitan areas. The decreased dominance of central cities is reflected in the distribution of population and industry and movement patterns. Larger proportions of formerly centralized economic units have relocated along radial highway networks. The once-predominant pattern of suburb to central city commutation also has been supplanted by greater travel among suburban areas and from central cities to suburbs. While suburban communities have become less dependent on central cities, they have also become increasingly interdependent. The distinguishing feature of suburban areas is not the establishment and maintenance of homogeneous, distinct subcommunities; it is that ecological segregation has been reinforced by political autonomy.

The Political Organization of Metropolitan Areas

The political organization of metropolitan areas has become as diverse and complex as their social and economic organization. Early urbanites were reluctant to move beyond the administrative boundaries of central cities partly because of the unavailability of municipal services in outlying areas. County and township governments usually serviced areas adjoining cities, but these governments were designed to meet the needs of rural populations. As urban populations outside central cities began to swell in size, the availability of urban services also increased.

Both the number and type of political units grew to meet the needs of growing suburban populations [Wood 1961]. Dozens, and in some larger metropolitan areas even hundreds, of incorporated communities of various types sprang up (e.g., villages, boroughs, cities). These incorporated municipalities fell within (and sometimes overlapped) township and county boundaries. In addition, a multitude of special districts arose from school districts to pollution- or mosquito-abatement districts, from bridge and tunnel authorities to port and airport authorities. Each of these jurisdictions had a separate corporate existence and taxing power; each provided a limited range of services to a population whose boundaries overlapped existing township, county, and municipal boundaries. The proliferation of local governmental units meant that suburban populations and industry could locate within any of a variety of types of incorporated municipalities offering different site advantages and service mixes. Alternatively, they might choose locations within unincorporated areas serviced by some combination of special districts, county governments, and private service suppliers.

In some important respects metropolitan areas may be conceived of as social systems. Within metropolitan areas ecological subareas are highly specialized; each performs a specific function within the larger area. Further, performance of a function within one subarea presumes the performance of reciprocal functions elsewhere. For example, in order for some subareas to serve principally as employment centers, others must be given over to residential use. The existence of homogeneous, white, middle-class suburbs presumes other residential areas that are principally black. Ecologically, then, metropolitan areas are composed of subareas that are both specialized and interdependent. As a result, changes or conditions in one part of the system have implications for all other parts of the system. The degree of specialization, of course, varies and is influenced by a number of factors [Williams 1968]. For instance, larger, older metropolitan areas and those located in states with permissive incorporation statutes may tend to have more specialized municipal units.

One significant aspect of this functional and ecological division of labor is that subareas generate different types of resources and needs that correspond to their functions. If a metropolitan area were subsumed by a single political economy, resources generated in some areas could be allocated for the specific needs of subareas and the system as a whole. The political fragmentation of metropolitan areas in effect has created a large number of political economies. Social and economic specialization and interdependencies have been juxtaposed with local political autonomy. The needs of each jurisdiction, therefore, must be met with the resources available within its boundaries. For some governmental units resources match or outdistance expenditure needs; for others some needs cannot be met with existing resources. The unequal distribution of needs and resources has both internal and intercommunity political consequences.

Internal Consequences of Political Fragmentation

A number of studies have delineated different types of metropolitan area communities. Oliver Williams and his associates [1965] distinguished four types of communities based on demographic composition, density, and functional specialization: 1. industrial and commercial centers, 2. residential high-density suburbs, 3. residential low-density suburbs, and 4. enclaves. Robert Wood [1961], although his analysis was not typological, identified density, degree of industrialization, size, and age as key dimensions on which communities vary. Schnore [1957] constructed four types of suburbs based on economic base-land use patterns: 1. residential suburbs, 2. industrial suburbs, 3. employing suburbs, and 4. satellite suburbs. Schnore and Alford [1963] classified suburban communities according to their form of governmental organization. Bryan Downes [1968] created four community types based on land use patterns and expenditure, receipt, and tax levels. These typologies suggest the kinds of specialized functions communities serve within metropolitan areas, and each is constructed on the basis of a single (or series of) demographic, ecological, or organizational factor(s).

Some studies have attempted to demonstrate that a large number of other community characteristics tend to accompany the typological criteria. Leo Schnore and Robert Alford [1963], for example, found that different forms of government tended to be associated with other community characteristics such as age and class structure, ethnic group mix, population size and growth, and the age and quality of housing stock. Other studies have shown that policy outputs vary by type of community. Wood [1961], for example, found that population size accounted for a large proportion of the variance in community operating expenditures. These and other studies have confirmed that there is a strong relationship between community policy outputs and their social, economic, and political characteristics.

There is considerable evidence that goals and value preferences, as well as needs and resources, are important in determining policy choices. Nevertheless, preferences are established to some extent in the context of existing needs and available resources, the cost of realizing some alternatives is related to resource availability, and some types of services cannot be provided within the limits of existing resources. As Wood [1961] pointed out and the criteria for typing communities implied, the decisions to zone out industry or to aggressively solicit new industry and to maximize or stabilize population growth committed communities to certain types and levels of expenditures. Large industrialized central cities, for instance, generally had higher operating expenditures and tax rates than suburbs, with the exception of school taxes, which tended to be a higher proportion of suburban expenditures [Dye 1970]. Increasing density, industrialization, and size created spending pressure, but total wealth per capita declined as higher business property valuations did not balance the contracted residential tax base relative to the populations to be serviced. As a result, these communities had higher expenditure levels irrespective of their wealth and continuously attempted to extend service in order to meet problems generated by density and industrialization.

Affluent communities, by contrast, were able to be more selective in their service mix and levels since problems associated with industry and congestion were avoided. By attracting only "desirable" types of business, planning for future growth, and zoning to control industry and multifamily dwellings, expenditures for many problems such as crime, fire, pollution, and public welfare were limited. Thus, some communities were able to maintain low assessed valuations and tax rates by using such tactics and yet support needed or desired services. From the point of view of the internal operation of local community units, then, the consequences of political fragmentation in large part revolves around the imbalance of community needs and resources. For some communities there is abundance; for others there are needs that cannot be satisfied.

External Consequences of Political Fragmentation

Political fragmentation has consequences for inter-governmental relation-ships as well as intra-governmental policy. Many problems that occur within metropolitan areas are area-wide in character and hence cannot be meaningfully resolved by any single locality. The inability of localities to resolve such problems is not merely a matter of the relationship between needs and limited resources. Rather, it is attributable to the facts that coordination is all but impossible to achieve among separate jurisdictions and that the administrative boundaries of individual municipalities do not correspond with the boundaries of the problem. It is because subareas within metropolitan systems are politically autonomous and have different needs, resources, and value priorities that policies with respect to these problems are varied and uncoordinated. It is because they are socially, economically, and ecologically interdependent and unable to "internalize" these problems that their individual policies have important consequences for subareas and the system as a whole.

Local policies with respect to area-wide problems have consequences for other localities that usually are unintended and indirect. In this sense they are not related to the objectives for which the policies were formu-lated. These indirect effects have been termed "externalities" or "spill-over effects." Of course, externalities created by one community can have either desired or undesired consequences for surrounding communities. One community may benefit from another's superior education system and suffer from others' inattentiveness to pollution control.

The more area-wide a problem is, the less effective any community will be in coping with it, irrespective of its resources. Governmental func-tions can be placed on a continuum [ACIR 1963] from most local to most area-wide as follows: fire, public education, refuse collection and disposal, libraries, police, health, urban renewal, housing, parks and recreation, welfare, hospitals, transportation, planning, water supply, sewage dis-posal, and air pollution. However, it should be emphasized that various components or phases of the delivery of each service are differentially located along the local–area-wide continuum.

For the more locally oriented services many costs and benefits can be adequately internalized within existing municipal boundaries; there are fewer and/or less serious repercussions of local policy for surrounding areas. Further, while some benefits theoretically might accrue from greater efficiency and economies of scale, there are significant limitations on the extent to which such gains would actually materialize [Hirsch 1968]. 1. Of the many diverse governmental purchases, few items are ordered in sufficient bulk to secure major price reductions. 2. The nature of the services and public expectations keep facilities small and localized. 3. Economies of scale are difficult to achieve since the services are labor intensive. Centralized facilities could improve economy only by reducing duplication. Since major capital outlays have already been made for existing plants and equipment, economies of scale would await replacement or expansion of present facilities.

Services such as refuse collection usually can be operated by localities with few spillover effects, although refuse disposal can produce negative externalities such as air pollution, water pollution, or disease. Under certain conditions (e.g., disposal through incineration, a shortage of appropriate land-fill sites) central organization may offer some advantages. Fire protection services also tend to be localized, in part due to the need to locate stations and equipment strategically. The need for localized protection reduces the desirability of achieving economies of scale, although some area-wide economies can be achieved in recruitment, training, and prevention activities. While fires may spread from one community to another, the spillover of costs and benefits is relatively low.

Police services traditionally have been highly decentralized in the United States. Local control reflects a strong preference for law enforcement agencies that are accessible to the citizenry and reflective of community values as well as a profound mistrust of centralized power. However, jurisdictionally fragmented police responsibilities create a variety of externalities. The prevention and repression of some types of crime, the apprehension of offenders, and the recovery of stolen property often are unrelated to political boundaries. Paradoxically, perhaps, the spillover of benefits from rigorous law enforcement is not as great as the costs of inadequate enforcement. Persistent, effective enforcement practice in one community has the effect of driving some kinds of deviant activities into surrounding jurisdictions. There are other problems as well. Interjurisdictional rivalries and jealousies reduce responsiveness and efficiency. Many communities lack sufficient resources for special investigative units (e.g., detective squads) and specialized equipment (e.g., communication systems, police laboratories) and facilities (e.g., jails). Limited man-power renders police incapable of dealing with emergency situations. Despite some limited attempts at cooperation such as sharing of radio bands and "hot pursuit" agreements, community policies are largely uncoordinated and many mutual problems go unresolved.

Those problems that are most area-wide in character are well beyond the capacity of localities and, in some cases, of the metropolitan area as a whole to resolve. In the absence of metropolitan area government, area-wide problems create large-scale spillovers that affect individual jurisdictions and the area as a whole. One result of uncontrollable spillovers has been the increasing involvment of state and federal agencies. In this sense insoluble local problems have been passed along to higher levels of government. However, state and federal intervention have not necessarily remedied these problems. Most federal funding to localities has been in the form of project grants, many of which do not require the chief executive's approval at either the state or local level. As a result, federal aid has fostered fragmentation of local government structures [Fox 1972].

An urban transportation system constitutes a single type of service function, although a number of different forms of transportation, including automobiles, trucks, trains, buses, and subways, are involved. The elements of an urban transportation system, which include vehicles, tracks, roads, terminals, loading and unloading facilities, and control facilities, are located throughout the metropolitan area, and various components of the system serve major parts of the area. Therefore, area-wide planning, construction, and maintenance are indispensable for orderly, efficient, economical vehicle movement. Area-wide organization permits coordination and integration of the elements of the transportation system, such as meshing highway and mass transit or parking and highway facilities, and development and implementation of priorities concerning the most effective means of transporting people and goods.

The political fragmentation of metropolitan areas creates major spillovers and decreases the efficiency of urban transportation systems. First, transportation system planning and coordination are lacking, and, consequently, all localities pay the costs of inefficiency. The local level lacks sufficient interest and resources to develop a metropolitan transportation system. As in most other policy areas, community decisions tend to be made in the context of local resources and priorities. Further, the large capital outlays requisite for obtaining land and equipment cannot be financed unless the fiscal base coincides with service boundaries. As a result, the elements of the total transportation system lack balance. For example, the rapid growth of highway networks and the preeminence of automobile commuting have created severe pollution and congestion as well as large budget expenditures for street maintenance and traffic control. As rapidly as highways have been built, usage has reached capacity levels. It has become apparent that continuous new highway construction is not an adequate solution to urban transportation problems. Yet public transportation (subway, railroad, bus) traffic has declined. Mass transit facilities in suburban areas often are impractical because of urban sprawl, encouraged in part by reliance on automotive travel. For the most part, central cities are hard-pressed to maintain existing road systems without attempting to extend them or undertake a revitalization of mass transit systems. With declining public transportation ridership, revenues drop, fares increase, service schedules are curtailed, deficits grow, and aging equipment is not replaced. Higher level governmental involvement by and large has not resolved the lack of coordination because there is little integration among the numerous separate state and federal agencies that support the development and operation of various types of transportation.

Second, there are a variety of spillover effects. The costs of providing municipal services associated with automobile use exceed user charges. In essence, this means that in heavily traveled areas such as central cities commuting is subsidized by city residents. If suburban commuters impose some costs on central cities, they in turn must bear the cost of inadequate street and parking facilities in cities. Central city voters are unlikely to show enthusiasm for expanding street networks to accommodate commuters. In short, the service users (suburban commuters) lack political representation in the service-dispensing jurisdictions (central cities), and service suppliers (central city residents and officials) lack access to the fiscal resources (suburban tax base) to finance adequate service levels.

The development of suburban–central city and radial highway networks also have consequences besides facilitating movement through the metropolitan area. Highways create or imperil site advantages of local communities by changing patterns of access. Some communities by choice or over their opposition are linked more closely with other parts of the metropolitan area; some communities prosper as locations for regional shopping centers or industrial parks; and some communities find traffic, but also potential clientele, are diverted from downtown shopping areas. Finally, the emphasis on automobile commuting and highway development creates unequal burdens. While many suburbanites have access to suburban and central city labor markets, lower status central city populations face unemployment or lengthy commuter trips as industrial and business enterprises continue to decentralize.

The task of providing safe, decent, sanitary housing is another function that demands area-wide coordination. Although private industry undertakes the vast majority of new housing construction, governmental policy impinges on the housing industry in at least two important respects: 1. Public funding supports construction and maintenance of housing for low-income groups when private enterprise is unwilling or unable to accommodate their needs. 2. Governmental land use planning, subdivision regulation, zoning, and building codes have the effect of controlling the quality and location of housing.

The political fragmentation of metropolitan areas imposes a variety of social and economic costs with respect to the supply and distribution of housing: 1. Zoning, subdivision, and building regulations vary substantially among communities. This very lack of uniformity results in diseconomies since builders are unable to accumulate large tracts of land suitable for development or to build to a single set of standards and specifications. To the extent that conflicting construction regulations and standards raise building costs, all communities pay a price for political autonomy. 2. Municipal ordinances that regulate the location and quality of housing have an impact on the housing stock in surrounding jurisdictions. For example, inadequate codes make it difficult to maintain health standards and property values. Such problems often exist in unincorporated fringe areas where the absence of municipal ordinances permit mixed land use patterns and substandard housing impose costs on surrounding areas. By contrast, when codes contain very high standards, the result is to bar lower status groups. Indeed, zoning and buildings sometimes are employed precisely for such purposes. The effect of these policies is to concentrate lower status populations in certain communities, particularly central cities, where older housing, often substandard in quality, is available in large quantities. In essence suburban communities force central cities to allocate substantial resources for public housing, slum clearance, health, welfare, and police-related services. Naturally, the problems must be met with meager resources since the city's tax base declines or upper status populations and industry, which seek to avoid city problems and high tax rates, move to more "desirable" suburban locations.

Political Integration Within Metropolitan Areas

The reason why political fragmentation persists within metropolitan areas must be sought in the goals that suburban communities pursue, in the functions that they serve, and in the balance of interests (real or perceived) within individual communities once they have become established. Metropolitan area communities are more than just political or economic entities [O. Williams 1968]. If community goals were simply political, integration might reasonably be expected to ensue. There are a number of factors operant within metropolitan areas, such as geographical proximity, social homogeneity, mutual knowledge of each other, shared functional interests, and previous cooperative experiences, which might exert an integrative influence [Jacob & Teune 1964]. However, political integration has not been forthcoming despite the facts that 1. communities within metropolitan areas are socially and economically interdependent; 2. many problems of concern to all communities go unresolved; and 3. communities experience higher service costs, inefficiencies, and spillovers. In fact, the proportion of urban population residing outside of central cities and the number of governmental units within metropolitan areas has continued to grow.

Similarly, metropolitan areas cannot be viewed as a free market in which individual communities offer different bundles of services [Ostrom, Tiebout, & Warren 1967]. Many of the conditions associated with a free market economy are not operant in metropolitan areas. Political fragmentation limits mobility, impedes the free exercises of consumer preference, and magnifies externalities such that they may exceed the magnitude of internalized costs and benefits [Netzer 1968]. Community boundaries have not been drawn so as to maximize the efficiency economy, or diversity of service provision. As a result, there are disparities between needs and resources, uncontrollable externalities, an underallocation of resources to the public economy, and a dysjunction between the locus of political representation and the locus of service consumption.

It is precisely because suburban communities do not seek merely political or economic goals, narrowly construed, that political fragmentation persists. These communities also seek to facilitate and defend various life styles and locational advantages. Thus, despite inefficiencies and spillovers, cooperation and integration occur within the context of preserving locational advantages. The conditions under which integration occurs and the degree to which it occurs are indicative of the priorities of suburban communities.

There are three basic means by which greater political coordination and integration can be achieved in metropolitan areas [Bollens & Schmandt 1970; Jones 1942; Ostrom, Tiebout, & Warren 1967]. 1. Municipalities can voluntarily cooperate to resolve problems. Intergovernmental agreements facilitate cooperation on issues of mutual interest without disturbing existing governmental arrangements. 2. Political units can be reconstituted so that political service boundaries coincide more closely.

There are different kinds and degrees of governmental reorganization. Extraterritorial powers grant cities control over certain functions, such as zoning or land use planning, within a prescribed radius around its borders. Formation of special districts entails creation of new governmental units that deliver a specific set of services and whose boundaries are delimited with reference to the boundaries of that service problem. Annexation involves the expansion of municipal boundaries to include adjacent unincorporated population and territory. Consolidation entails the merger of two or more existing units of government, such as municipalities, special districts, or counties. Federation involves the creation of a metropolitan area-wide government. Local governments cede certain powers to a central body while retaining their corporate existence and autonomy in performing other functions. 3. Higher levels of government can assume responsibility for some types of services and problems. State and federal government agencies frequently provide financial support to local jurisdictions for various purposes. Federal control or discretion is maintained, for example, by proffering grants for specific purposes, requiring local support for a given program in order to attain eligibility for federal assistance, or requiring agency approval of each local project [Fox 1972].

Once communities have been established there are a variety of barriers to reducing their powers or autonomy. Even unincorporated populations maintain service arrangements with special district, counties, or private suppliers. Merger with an incorporated community can raise tax rates, change zoning ordinances, alter service provisions, and decrease the significance of other governmental units that lose population (e.g., counties or townships). Once communities have incorporated, additional impediments to change arise, such as corporate status, debt incurred, local organizations and officials whose existence or livelihood are linked to that of the municipality. In addition, few organizations seek change for its own sake. Unless problems create an impetus for change, the combination of satisfaction with existing arrangements, apathy, and uncertainty about the implications of change limit the appeal of governmental reorganization [ACIR 1962b].

The available evidence suggests that integration is less likely to occur when important life-style values are involved and when integration might disrupt vested interests. In short, the more far-reaching the political reorganization proposal, the lower its probability of acceptance; and the more life-style values are altered (or potentially altered), the lower the probability of political integration occurring. The importance of life-style values can be illustrated by examining the patterning of intergovernmental agreements. Such arrangements occur frequently because they lower unit costs by facilitating economies of scale, create greater coincidence between service and administrative boundaries, and eliminate the necessity of creating additional units or layers of government—all without modifying the structure of existing governments.

One study of intermunicipal cooperation among communities in the Philadelphia metropolitan area [Dye et al. 1963] reported that cooperation occurred principally with respect to school systems, police radio systems, sewer systems, water and solid waste disposal, although there were scattered cases of cooperation in other functional areas as well. The functions for which voluntary agreements are negotiated probably vary among metropolitan areas depending on the number and size of suburban communities, critical service problems within the area, and state regulations.

Three important conclusions emerge from this research. 1. Voluntary agreements tend to occur when the interests of local governments coincide and occur with frequency because existing units of government are undisturbed. 2. Most instances of cooperation involved system maintenance facilities [O. Williams 1968]—libraries, sewers, water, waste disposal, and police radio. The major exception was education, an important life-style value. However, many joint educational arrangements were an outgrowth of difficulties faced by small districts attempting to finance independent building programs and state regulations establishing a minimum population size for school districts. 3. A comparison of cooperating and noncooperating urban communities for educational, police communication, and sewer systems revealed that cooperating pairs were more similar with respect to predominant party affiliation, community wealth, and social rank than noncooperating municipalities.

Differences among cooperating and noncooperating communities were smallest with respect to the sharing of a common police radio network. Since the financial commitments were small, public involvement minimal, and the issue was regarded as a technical one, there was little hesitancy over establishing cooperative arrangements. Both school and sewer systems, by contrast, involved expensive plant facilities, although the social and cultural connotations of the two types of systems were enormously different. It appeared that when communities became involved in cooperative ventures that committed substantial financial resources, they tended to select similar communities as partners.

For those types of integration that involve the transfer of territory and/or the restructuring of local governments, such as annexation, special district formation, consolidation, and federation, similar patterns emerge. The more minor forms of restructuring that least disturb existing governmental arrangements predominate, and there are few successful cases of metropolitan area-wide political integration. For any particular type of restructuring, small or limited instances far outnumber larger or more general cases. With respect to the approximately 20,000 special district governments in the United States, most provide a single service function over a limited area, and hence multiply the number of small local governments and constitute a minor threat to existing governmental arrangements. There are only about 100 metropolitan area-wide (and, in some instances, multipurpose) districts, which represent a more significant movement toward political integregation.

Further, the vast majority of special districts, local and metropolitan alike, deal with system maintenance functions, such as utilities and central facilities, not life-style functions [O. Williams 1968]. As John Bollens and Henry Schmandt report: "Providing port facilities and sewage disposal are easily the most frequent functions, followed by airports, mass transit, parks, public housing, and water supply" [1970, p. 314]. Thus parks and public housing are among the least frequently occurring, and district library services are even more rare. Bollens and Schmandt note the virtual absence of some types of districts (which deal with life-style functions). "Strangely enough . . . certain functions considered by some people to be definitely area-wide in character—law enforcement in particular—are not provided by any metropolitan districts" [1970, p. 314].

Annexation and consolidation, which involve the transfer of territory and authority, currently have a limited impact on metropolitan area organization. However, both processes have played a major role in the growth of central cities and prevented even more extensive fragmentation of metropolitan areas. Between 1840 and 1960, over 5500 square miles of surrounding territory were annexed by central cities [Bromley & Smith 1973]. Similarly, 196 metropolitan area communities consolidated, principally suburbs with central cities, between 1900 and 1950 [Hawley 1959]. Nevertheless, neither annexation nor consolidation have kept pace with the territorial and population growth of fringe areas or the proliferation of new units of government. Since 1900 the number of consolidations has continuously decreased, and annexations have declined, particularly in the most fragmented metropolitan areas. For example, there were 71 consolidations between 1910 and 1920 but only 15 between 1940 and 1950 [Hawley 1959]. Although more land was annexed by central cities between 1950 and 1960 than during any previous decade, 42 central cities in northeastern metropolitan areas annexed a total of only 11 square miles of land while 60 central cities in southern metropolitan areas annexed 1,700 square miles of adjoining territory [Bromley & Smith 1973].

The historical and current role of annexation and consolidation within metropolitan areas can be readily summarized. First, the vast majority of annexations and consolidations have been small, changing the face of metropolitan areas only slightly. Second, most large annexations and consolidations were prodded or facilitated by state government rather than local initiative. During the nineteenth and early twentieth centuries, for instance, a number of large cities consolidated with their counties or were separated (usually accompanied by large annexations) from their counties [ACIR 1962a; Bollens & Schmandt 1970, pp. 297–311]. Boston (1821), Philadelphia (1854), New Orleans (1813), and New York (1898) were consolidated with the counties in which they were located. Baltimore (1851), San Francisco (1856), St. Louis (1876), and Denver (1902) were separated from their counties. There were few subsequent consolidations of note until this step was taken by Baton Rouge (1947), Nashville (1962), and Jacksonville (1967). Although the special state enabling legislation that stimulated early metropolitan reorganizations now occurs infrequently, large annexations currently occur principally in states that grant virtually unilateral annexation powers to municipalities [Wheeler 1965].

Third, political integration is sought or accepted by suburban areas most often when service provision is inadequate [ACIR 1962b; Manis 1959]. Only when suburban areas find it difficult or impossible to function independently is merger perceived as desirable. For example, Los Angeles was successful in using its water supply system as a weapon to impose annexation on fringe areas that lacked the resources to develop their own systems [Bollens & Schmandt 1970, p. 176]. Fourth, the chances of political integration are greatly enhanced when the units involved are socioeconomically similar. Central city growth through annexation has been greatest where the city-suburban socioeconomic gradient was smallest [Dye 1967]. In general, the socioeconomic gradient is smallest in younger, smaller, southern and western metropolitan areas. Both annexation and proposals for more extensive reorganization efforts have been most successful in these areas [ACIR 1962b].

Finally, considerable opposition to metropolitan reorganization emanates from local groups that perceive that their interests will be adversely affected [ACIR 1962b]. Minority group leaders who fear dilution of their constituencies voting strength; suburban newspapers, commercial interests, and governmental officials whose prosperity or careers hinge on local autonomy; and agricultural interests that anticipate higher tax rates are all sources of opposition. In the face of suburban residents' general satisfaction with existing governmental arrangements; apathy with regard to area-wide problems; organized, vocal opposition groups; few interest groups that will profit from reorganization; and uncertainty about the implications of reorganization, it is small wonder that major reorganization efforts are so seldom successful.

Summary

Suburbanization in several important respects constitutes an extension of the urbanization process. The genesis of suburbia is rooted in the urban-industrial revolution that led to the industrialization of cities, the separation of residence and workplace, advances in intra-urban transportation systems, and the gradual decentralization of business, industry, and residences. Over time suburban areas have become as specialized and diverse as subareas within cities. However, it was the development of politically polycentric metropolitan areas that sharply distinguished city and suburb and transformed the character of urban politics.

The existence of specialized, interdependent communities that are politically autonomous has created a variety of problems for individual communities and the metropolitan area as a whole. There is an imbalance between needs and resources; problems of an area-wide nature go unresolved; service provision is costly and inefficient; and individual community policies have a variety of external consequences for surrounding jurisdictions. However, despite these obvious problems, polycentric metropolitan areas persist because communities are more than political or economic entities. They also defend life-style values and established local interests. As a result, some cooperation and integration occurs, but it is limited by and takes place within the context of the goals and value priorities of the existing polycentric metropolitan area structure.

BIBLIOGRAPHY

Charles Adrian, "Leadership and Decision-Making in Manager Cities." In T. Dye and B. Hawkins, eds., *Politics in the Metropolis.* Charles E. Merrill, 1967, pp. 315–325.

Advisory Commission on Intergovernmental Relations, *Governmental Structure, Organization, and Planning in Metropolitan Areas.* U.S. Government Printing Office, 1961.

Advisory Commission on Intergovernmental Relations, *Alternative Approaches to Governmental Reorganization in Metropolitan Areas.* U.S. Government Printing Office, 1962a.

Advisory Commission on Intergovernmental Relations, *Factors Affecting Voter Reactions to Governmental Reorganization in Metropolitan Areas.* U.S. Government Printing Office, 1962b.

Advisory Commission on Intergovernmental Relations, *State Constitutional and Statutory Restrictions upon the Structural, Functional, and Personnel Powers of Local Government.* U.S. Government Printing Office, 1962c.

Advisory Commission on Intergovernmental Relations, *Performance of Urban Functions: Local and Areawide.* U.S. Government Printing Office, 1963.

Robert Agger and Vincent Ostrom, "The Political Structure of a Small Community." In R. French, ed., *The Community: A Comparative Perspective.* Peacock, 1969, pp. 235–243.

Michael Aiken, "The Distribution of Community Power: Structural Bases and Social Consequences." In M. Aiken and P. Mott, eds., *The Structure of Community Power.* Random House, 1970, pp. 487–525.

Michael Aiken and Robert Alford, "Community Structure and Innovation: The Case of Urban Renewal." In D. Gordon, ed., *Social Change and Urban Politics.* Prentice-Hall, 1973, pp. 278–297.

Robert Alford, "The Comparative Study of Urban Politics." In L. Schnore and H. Fagin, eds., *Urban Research and Policy Planning.* Sage Publications, 1967, pp. 263–304.

Robert Alford, "The Bureaucratization of Urban Government." In D. Gordon, ed., *Social Change and Urban Politics.* Prentice-Hall, 1973, pp. 263–277.

Robert Alford and Harry Scoble, "Political and Socioeconomic Characteristics of American Cities." In J. Goodman, ed., *Perspectives on Urban Politics.* Allyn & Bacon, 1970, pp. 393–413.

Thomas Anton, "Power, Pluralism, and Local Politics." In M. Aiken and P. Mott, eds., *The Structure of Community Power.* Random House, 1970, pp. 321–339.

Peter Bachrach and Morton Baratz, "Decisions and Nondecisions: An Analytical Framework." In M. Aiken and P. Mott, eds., *The Structure of Community Power.* Random House, 1970, pp. 308–320.

Edward Banfield, "Rioting Mainly for Fun and Profit." In J. Wilson, ed., *The Metropolitan Enigma.* Harvard University Press, 1968, pp. 283–310.

Steven Baratz and Joan Baratz, "Early Childhood Intervention: The Social Science Base of Institutional Racism." In D. Bromley and C. Longino, eds., *White Racism and Black Americans.* Schenkman, 1972, pp. 303–325.

Harold Baron, Harriet Stulman, Richard Rothstein, and Rennard Davis, "Black Powerlessness in Chicago," In D. Bromley and C. Longino, eds., *White Racism and Black Americans.* Schenkman, 1972, pp. 442–451.

Ernest Barth and Stuart Johnson, "Community Power and a Typology of Social Issues." In M. Aiken and P. Mott, eds., *The Structure of Community Power.* Random House, 1970, pp. 304–307.

Nelson Blake, "The Need for an Urban Water Supply." In A. Wakstein, ed., *The Urbanization of America: An Historical Anthology.* Houghton Mifflin, 1970, pp. 117–127.

Vaughn L. Blankenship, "Community Power and Decision-Making: A Comparative Evaluation of Measurement." In M. Aiken and P. Mott, eds., *The Structure of Community Power.* Random House, 1970, pp. 348–358.

Robert Blauner, "Internal Colonialism and Ghetto Revolt." In D. Bromley and C. Longino, eds., *White Racism and Black Americans.* Schenkman, 1972, pp. 427–441.

John Bollens and Henry Schmandt, *The Metropolis: Its People, Politics, and Economic Life.* Harper & Row, 1970.

Charles Bonjean, "The Community as Research Site and Object of Inquiry." In C. Bonjean, T. Clark, and R. Lineberry, eds., *Community Politics: A Behavioral Approach.* The Free Press, 1971, pp. 5–16.

Charles Bonjean and David Olson, "Community Leadership: Directions of Research." In M. Aiken and P. Mott, eds., *The Structure of Community Power.* Random House, 1970, pp. 203–215.

Donald Bradley and Mayer Zald, "From Commercial Elite to Political Administrator: The Recruitment of Mayors of Chicago." In M. Aiken and P. Mott, eds., *The Structure of Community Power.* Random House, 1970, pp. 46–59.

Harry Bredemeir and Richard Stephenson, *The Analysis of Social Systems.* Holt, Rinehart and Winston, 1962.

David Bromley and Charles Longino, "On White Racism." In D. Bromley and C. Longino, eds., *White Racism and Black Americans.* Schenkman, 1972, pp. 1–16.

David Bromley and Joel Smith, "The Historical Significance of Annexation as a Social Process." *Land Economics,* 1973, 49:294–309.

Richard Brown, "Historical Patterns of Violence in America." In H. Graham and T. Gurr, eds., *Violence in America: Historical and Comparative Perspectives,* Vol. II. U. S. Government Printing Office, 1969, pp. 35–64.

David Burnham, "Police Violence: Changing Pattern." In A. Niederhoffer and A. Blumberg, eds., *The Ambivalent Force: Perspectives.* Rinehart Press, 1973, pp. 174–178.

Alexander Callow, "The City in Politics: Introduction." In A. Callow, ed., *American Urban History.* Oxford University Press, 1973, pp. 213–219.

Terry Clark, "Community Structure and Decision-Making." In T. Clark, ed., *Community Structure and Decision-Making.* Chandler, 1968, pp. 91–126.

Terry Clark, "Community Structure, Decision-Making, Budget Expenditures, and Urban Renewal in Fifty-One American Communities." In C. Bonjean, T. Clark, and R. Lineberry, eds., *Community Politics: A Behavioral Approach.* The Free Press, 1971, pp. 293–313.

James Coleman et al., "Equality of Educational Opportunity." In D. Bromley and C. Longino, eds., *White Racism and Black Americans.* Schenkman, 1972, pp. 291–302.

Lewis Coser, "Introduction." In L. Coser, ed., *Political Sociology.* Harper & Row, 1966, pp. 1–9.

Robert Crain and James Vanecho, "Elite Influence in School Desegregation." In J. Wilson, ed., *City Politics and Public Policy.* John Wiley & Sons, 1968, pp. 127–148.

Phillips Cutright, "Nonpartisan Electoral Systems in American Cities." In T. Dye and B. Hawkins, eds., *Politics in the Metropolis.* Charles E. Merrill, 1967, pp. 298–314.

Robert Dahl, *Who Governs: Democracy and Power in an American City.* Yale University Press, 1961.

Robert Dahl, "From Oligarchy to Pluralism: The Patricians and the Entrepreneurs." In M. Aiken and P. Mott, eds., *The Structure of Community Power.* Random House, 1970, pp. 31–45.

Stephen David, "Welfare: The Community-Action Program Controversy." In J. Bellush and S. David, eds., *Race and Politics in New York City: Five Studies in Policy-Making.* Praeger, 1971, pp. 25–58.

Martha Derthick, "Intercity Differences in Administration of the Public Assistance Program: The Case of Massachusetts." In J. Wilson, ed., *City, Politics, and Public Policy.* John Wiley & Sons, 1968, pp. 243–266.

Bryan Downes, "Suburban Differentiation and Municipal Policy Choices: A Comparative Analysis of Suburban Political Systems." In T. Clark, ed., *Community Structure and Decision-Making: Comparative Analyses.* Chandler, 1968, pp. 243–258.

Bryan Downes, "Social and Political Characteristics of Riot Cities: A Comparative Study." In J. Geschwender, ed., *The Black Revolt.* Prentice-Hall, 1971, pp. 332–349.

Bryan Downes and Stephen Burks, "The Black Protest Movement and Urban Violence." Paper presented at the 1968 annual meeting of the American Political Science Association, Washington, D.C., 1968.

William Drake, *The American School in Transition.* Prentice-Hall, 1955.

Thomas Dye, "Urban Political Integration: Conditions Associated with Annexation in American Cities." In T. Dye and B. Hawkins, eds., *Politics in the Metropolis.* Charles E. Merrill, 1967, pp. 424–438.

Thomas Dye, "City-Suburban Social Distance and Public Policy." In J. Goodman, ed., *Perspectives on Urban Politics.* Allyn & Bacon, 1970, pp. 363–373.

Thomas Dye, Charles Liebeman, Oliver Williams, and Harold Herman, "Differentiation and Cooperation in a Metropolitan Area." *Midwest Journal of Political Science,* 1963, 7:145–155.

Howard Ehrlich, "The Social Psychology of Reputations for Community Leadership." In W. Hawley and F. Wert, eds., *The Search for Community Power.* Prentice-Hall, 1968, pp. 171–179.

Heinz Eulau and Robert Eyestone, "Policy Maps of City Councils and Policy Outcomes: A Developmental Analysis." In J. Goodman, ed., *Perspectives on Urban Politics.* Allyn & Bacon, 1970, pp. 525–558.

Reynolds Farley, "Suburban Persistence." In J. Kramer, ed., *North American Suburbs.* Glendessary Press, 1972, pp. 82–96.

Arthur Fink, "The Development of Social Services: European Background." In A. Fink, ed., *The Field of Social Work.* Holt, Rinehart and Winston, 1974a, pp. 18–34.

Arthur Fink, "The Social Services in America: Early Growth of Voluntary Social Services." In A. Fink, ed., *The Field of Social Work.* Holt, Rinehart and Winston, 1974b, pp. 35–48.

Arthur Fink, "The Social Services in America: From the Almshouse to Social Security." In A. Fink, ed., *The Field of Social Work.* Holt, Rinehart and Winston, 1974c, pp. 49–68.

Robert Fogelson and Robert Hill, "Who Riots?: A Study of Participation in the 1967 Riots." In National Advisory Commission on Civil Disorders, Supplemental Studies. U.S. Government Printing Office, 1968, pp. 217–248.

Henry Ford, "Separation of Powers Necessitates Corruption." in E. Banfield, ed., *Urban Government.* The Free Press, 1969, pp. 238–247.

Douglas Fox, "Federal Aid to the Cities." In D. Fox, ed., *The New Urban Politics: Cities and the Federal Government.* Goodyear, 1972, pp. 29–37.

Linton Freeman, Thomas Fararo, Warner Bloomberg, and Morris Sunshine, "Locating Leaders in Local Communities: A Comparison of Some Alternative Approaches." In W. Hawley and F. Wirt, eds., *The Search for Community Power.* Prentice-Hall, 1968, pp. 189–199.

Robert French, "Change Comes to Cornucopia—Industry and the Community." In R. French, ed., *The Community.* Peacock, 1969, pp. 392–407.

James Geschwender, "Civil Rights Protest and Riots: A Disappearing Distinction." In J. Geschwender, ed., *The Black Revolt.* Prentice-Hall, 1971, pp. 300–311.

Claire Gilbert, "Community Power and Decision-Making: A Quantitative Examination of Previous Research." In T. Clark, ed., *Community Structure and Decision-Making: Comparative Analyses.* Chandler, 1968, pp. 139–159.

Herman Goldstein, "Police Discretion: The Ideal Versus the Real." In A. Niederhoffer and A. Blumberg, eds., *The Ambivalent Force: Perspectives.* Holt, Rinehart and Winston, 1973, pp. 148–155.

Daniel Gordon, "Immigrants and Urban Governmental Form in American Cities, 1933–1960." *American Journal of Sociology,* 1968, 74:158–171.

Daniel Gordon, "Immigrants and Municipal Voting Turnout: Implications for the Changing Ethnic Impact on Urban Politics." In D. Gordon, ed., *Social Change and Urban Politics*. Prentice-Hall, 1973, pp. 167–186.

David J. Greenstone and Paul Peterson, "Reformers, Machines, and the War on Poverty." In J. Wilson, ed., *City Politics and Public Policy*. John Wiley & Sons, 1968, pp. 267–292.

Morton Grodzins, "The Metropolitan Area as a Racial Problem." In D. Bromley and C. Longino, eds., *White Racism and Black Americans*. Schenkman, 1972, pp. 91–99.

Robert Gutman and David Popenoe, "The Field of Urban Sociology: A Review and Assessment." In R. Gutman and D. Popenoe, eds., *Neighborhood, City, and Metropolis*. Random House, 1970, pp. 3–23.

Jeffrey Hadden, Louis Masotti, and Victor Thiessen, "The Making of Negro Mayors—1967." In J. Goodman, ed., *Perspectives on Urban Politics*. Allyn & Bacon, 1970, pp. 297–318.

Harlan Hahn, "The Political Objectives of Ghetto Violence." In D. Gordon, ed., *Social Change and Urban Politics*. Prentice-Hall, 1973., pp. 225–256.

Mark Haller, "Urban Vice and Civic Reform: Chicago in the Early Twentieth Century." In K. Jackson and S. Schultz, eds., *Cities in American History*. Alfred A. Knopf, 1972, pp.290–305.

Oscar Handlin, "The Attachment of the Immigrant to the Boss." In E. Banfield, ed., *Urban Government*. The Free Press, 1969, pp. 195–199.

Amos Hawley, *Human Ecology: A Theory of Community Structure*. Ronald Press, 1950.

Amos Hawley, *The Changing Shape of Metropolitan America: Deconcentration Since 1920*. The Free Press, 1956.

Amos Hawley, "The Incorporation Trend in Metropolitan Areas, 1900–1950." *Journal of the American Institute of Planners*, 1959, 25:41–45.

Amos Hawley, "Community Power and Urban Renewal Success." In W. Hawley and F. Wirt, eds., *The Search for Community Power*. Prentice-Hall, 1968, pp. 343–352.

Samuel Hays, "The Politics of Reform in Municipal Government in the Progressive Era." In D. Gordon, ed., *Social Change and Urban Politics*. Prentice-Hall, 1973, pp. 107–127.

Werner Hirsch, "The Supply of Urban Public Services." In H. Perloff and L. Wingo, eds., *Issues in Urban Economics*. Johns Hopkins Press, 1968, pp. 477–525.

Melvin Holli, "Social and Structural Reform: Mayors and Municipal Government." In K. Jackson and S. Schultz, eds., *Cities in American History*. Alfred A. Knopf, 1972, pp.393–403.

Walter Hugins, "Jacksonian Democracy and the Working Class." In D. Gordon, ed., *Social Change and Urban Politics*. Prentice-Hall, 1973, pp. 102–106.

Floyd Hunter, *Community Power Structure*. Doubleday, 1953.

Floyd Hunter, "Methods of Study: Community Power Structure." In M. Aiken and P. Mott, eds., *The Structure of Community Power*. Random House, 1970a, pp. 228–232.

Floyd Hunter, "Power Structure of a Sub-Community." In M. Aiken and P. Mott, eds., *The Structure of Community Power*. Random House, 1970b, pp. 377–380.

J. Joseph Huthmacher, "Urban Liberalism in the Age of Reform." In A. Wakstein, ed., *The Urbanization of America: An Historical Anthology*. Houghton Mifflin, 1970, pp. 307–314.

Kenneth Jackson and Stanley Schultz, "Bosses, Machines, and Urban Reform: Introduction." In K. Jackson and S. Schultz, eds., *Cities in American History*. Alfred A. Knopf, 1972, pp.357–370.

Philip Jacob and Henry Teune, "The Integrative Process: Guidelines for Analyses of the Bases of Political Community." In P. Jacob and J. Toscano, eds., *The Integration of Political Communities*. Lippincott, 1964, pp. 1–45.

Paul Jacobs, "America's Schizophrenic View of the Poor." In J. Larner and I. Howe, eds., *Poverty: Views from the Left*. William Morrow, 1968, pp. 39–57.

Victor Jones, *Metropolitan Government*. University of Chicago Press, 1942.

Harold Kaufman, "Toward an Interactional Conception of Community." In R. Warren, ed., *Perspectives on the American Community*. Rand McNally, 1966, pp. 69–77.

Herbert Kaufman and Victor Jones, "The Mystery of Power." In M. Aiken and P. Mott, eds., *The Structure of Community Power*. Random House, 1970, pp. 233–240.

Frank Kent, "How the Boss Runs the Organization." In E. Banfield, ed., *Urban Government*. The Free Press, 1969, pp. 200–208.

John Kessel, "Governmental Structure and Political Environment: A Statistical Note About American Cities." In T. Dye and B. Hawkins, eds., *Politics in the Metropolis*. Charles E. Merrill, 1967, pp. 289–297.

Lewis Killian, "Community Structure and the Role of the Negro Leader-Agent." In R. French, ed., *The Community*. Peacock, 1969, pp. 221–232.

Lewis Killian and Charles Smith, "Negro Protest Leaders in a Southern Community." In M. Aiken and P. Mott, eds., *The Structure of Community Power*. Random House, 1970, pp. 389–394.

Orrin Klapp and L. Vincent Padgett, "Power Structure and Decision-Making in a Mexican Border City." In R. French, ed., *The Community: A Comparative Perspective*. Peacock, 1969, pp. 271–280.

Bruce Kovner, "The Resignation of Elgin Crull." In E. Banfield, ed., *Urban Government*. The Free Press, 1969, pp. 316–321.

Jonathan Kozol, "Death at an Early Age." In D. Bromley and C. Longino, eds., *White Racism and Black Americans*. Schenkman, 1972, pp. 326–335.

Roger Lane, "The Expansion of Police Functions." In A. Wakstein, ed., *The Urbanization of America: An Historical Anthology*. Houghton Mifflin, 1970, pp. 151–169.

Kurt Lang and Gladys Lang, "Racial Disturbances as Collective Protest," In J. Geschwender, ed., *The Black Revolt.* Prentice-Hall, 1971, pp. 257–263.

Marvin Lazerson, *Origins of the Urban School: Public Education in Massachusetts, 1870–1915.* Harvard University Press, 1971.

Stanley Lieberson and Arnold Silverman, "The Precipitants and Underlying Conditions of Race Riots." In J. Geschwender, ed., *The Black Revolt.* Prentice-Hall, 1971, pp. 323–331.

Seymour Martin Lipset, "Political Sociology." In R. Merton, L. Broom, and L. Cottrell, eds., *Sociology Today: Problems and Prospects.* Harper & Row, 1959, pp. 81–114.

Michael Lipsky and David Olson, "On the Politics of Riot Commissions." Paper presented at the 1968 annual meeting of the American Political Science Association. Washington, D.C., 1968.

Norton Long, "The Local Community as an Ecology of Games." In J. Goodman, ed., *Perspectives on Urban Politics.* Allyn & Bacon, 1970, pp. 9–26.

Theodore Lowi, "Machine Politics—Old and New." In A. Callow, ed., *American Urban History.* Oxford University Press, 1973, pp. 265–272.

Peter Lupsha, "On Theories of Urban Violence." Paper presented at the 1968 annual meeting of the American Political Science Asssociation. Washington, D.C., 1968.

James McKee, "Community Power and Strategies in Race Relations: Some Critical Observations." In M. Aiken and P. Mott, eds., *The Structure of Community Power.* Random House, 1970, pp. 395–402.

Blake McKelvey, "The Age of the Industrial City." In A. Wakstein, ed., *The Urbanization of America: An Historical Anthology.* Houghton Mifflin, 1970, pp. 203–211.

Jerome Manis, "Annexation: The Process of Reurbanization." *American Journal of Economics and Sociology,* 1959, 18:353–360.

Arthur Mann, "La Guardia Comes to Power, 1933," In K. Jackson and S. Schultz, eds., Cities in American History. Alfred A. Knopf, 1972, pp. 404–419.

Gary Marx, "Report of the National Commission: The Analysis of Disorder or Disorderly Analysis?" Paper presented at the 1968 annual meeting of the American Political Science Association, Washington, D.C., 1968.

Louis Masotti, "Prologue: Surburbia Reconsidered—Myth and Counter Myth." In L. Masotti and J. Hadden, eds., *The Urbanization of the Suburbs.* Sage Publications, 1973, pp. 15–25.

Paul Meadows, "The City, Technology, and History." In P. Meadows and E. Mizruchi, eds., *Urbanism, Urbanization, and Change: Comparative Perspectives.* Addison-Wesley, 1969, pp. 10–18.

Robert Merton, "Latent Functions of the Machine." In A. Callow, ed., *American Urban History.* Oxford University Press, 1973, pp. 220–229.

Martin Meyerson and Edward Banfield, "A Machine at Work." In E. Banfield, ed., *Urban Government.* The Free Press, 1969, pp. 169–179.

Delbert Miller, "Industry and Community Power Structure: A Comparative

Study of an American and an English City." In R. French, ed., *The Community: A Comparative Perspective.* Peacock, 1969, pp. 250–259.

Paul Miller, "The Process of Decision-Making Within the Context of Community Organization." In T. Clark, ed., *Community Structure and Decision-Making: Comparative Analyses.* Chandler, 1968, pp. 307–318.

Zane Miller, "Boss Cox's Cincinnati: A Study in Urbanization and Politics, 1880–1914." In K. Jackson and S. Schultz, eds., *Cities in American History.* Alfred A. Knopf, 1972, pp. 382–392.

Robert Morlan, "The Unorganized Politics of Minneapolis." In E. Banfield, ed., *Urban Government.* The Free Press, 1969, pp. 279–285.

Paul Mott, "Configuration of Power." In M. Aiken and P. Mott, eds., *The Structure of Community Power.* Random House, 1970a, pp. 85–99.

Paul Mott, "The Role of the Absentee-Owned Corporation in the Changing Community." In M. Aiken and P. Mott, eds., *The Structure of Community Power.* Random House, 1970b, pp. 170–180.

Dick Netzer, "Federal, State, and Local Finance in a Metropolitan Context." In H. Perloff and L. Wingo, eds., *Issues in Urban Economics.* Johns Hopkins Press, 1968, pp. 435–476.

Eric Nordlinger, "Political Sociology: Marx and Weber." In E. Nordlinger, ed., *Politics and Society.* Prentice-Hall, 1970, pp. 1–22.

Anthony Oberschall, "The Los Angeles Riot of August, 1965." In J. Geschwender, ed., *The Black Revolt.* Prentice-Hall, 1971, pp. 264–284.

Vincent Ostrom, Charles Tiebout, and Robert Warren, "The Organization of Government in Metropolitan Areas: A Theoretical Inquiry." In P. Coulter, ed., *The Politics of Metropolitan Areas.* Crowell, 1967, pp. 285–306.

Dewey Palmer, "Moving North: Migration of Negroes During World War I." In D. Bromley and C. Longino, eds., *White Racism and Black Americans.* Schenkman, 1972, pp. 29–48.

Roland Pellegrin and Charles Coates, "Absentee-Owned Corporations and Community Power Structure." In D. Gordon, ed., *Social Change and Urban Politics.* Prentice-Hall, 1973, pp. 65–73.

Harold Pfautz, "The Power Structure of the Negro Sub-Community: A Case Study and a Comparative View." In R. French, ed., *The Community.* Peacock, 1969, pp. 209–220.

David Popenoe, "On the Meaning of 'Urban' in Urban Studies." In P. Meadows and E. Mizruchi, eds., *Urbanism, Urbanization, and Change: Comparative Perspectives.* Addison-Wesley, 1969, pp. 64–75.

Edward Power, *Main Currents in the History of Education.* McGraw-Hill, 1962.

Phillip Present, "Defense Contracting and Community Leadership: A Comparative Analysis." In C. Bonjean, T. Clark, and R. Lineberry, eds., *Community Politics.* The Free Press, 1971, pp. 201–209.

Don Price, "The Promotion of the City Manager Plan." In E. Banfield, ed., *Urban Government.* The Free Press, 1969, pp. 286–298.

E. L. Quarantelli and Russell Dynes, "Property Norms and Looting: Their Patterns in Community Crises." In J. Geschwender, ed., *The Black Revolt.* Prentice-Hall, 1971, pp. 285–299.

Leonard Reissman, *The Urban Process: Cities in Industrial Societies.* The Free Press, 1965.

James Richardson, "To Control the City: The New York City Police in Historical Perspective." In K. Jackson and S. Schultz, eds., *Cities in American History.* Alfred A. Knopf, 1972, pp. 272–289.

Arnold Rose, *The Power Structure: Political Process in American Society.* Oxford University Press, 1967.

Charles Rosenberg, "The Nature of Poverty and the Prevention of Disease." In K. Jackson and S. Schultz, eds., *Cities in American History.* Alfred A. Knopf, 1972, pp. 258–271.

Donald Rosenthal and Robert Crain, "Structure and Values in Local Political Systems: The Case of Fluoridation Decisions." In J. Wilson, ed., *City Politics and Public Policy.* John Wiley & Sons, 1968, pp. 217–242.

Peter Rossi, "Power and Community Structure." In T. Clark, ed., *Community Structure and Decision-Making: Comparative Analyses.* Chandler, 1968, pp. 129–138.

Peter Rossi and Alice Rossi, "An Historical Perspective on the Functions of Local Politics." In D. Gordon, ed., *Social Change and Urban Politics.* Prentice-Hall, 1973, pp. 49–60.

Wallace Sayre and Herbert Kaufman, "Governing New York City." In W. Hawley and F. Wirt, eds., *The Search for Community Power.* Prentice-Hall, 1968, pp. 125–133.

Leo Schnore, "Metropolitan Growth and Decentralization." *American Journal of Sociology,* 1957, 63:171–180.

Leo Schnore, "The Timing of Metropolitan Decentralization: A Contribution to the Debate." *Journal of the American Institute of Planners,* 1959, 25:200–206.

Leo Schnore, "Municipal Annexations and the Growth of Metropolitan Suburbs." *American Journal of Sociology,* 1962, 67:406–417.

Leo Schnore, "The Socioeconomic Status of Cities and Suburbs." *American Sociological Review,* 1963, 28:76–85.

Leo Schnore, "Urban Structure and Suburban Selectivity." *Demography,* 1964, 1:164–176.

Leo Schnore, *The Urban Scene.* The Free Press, 1965.

Leo Schnore and Robert Alford, "Forms of Government and Socioeconomic Characteristics of Suburbs." *Administrative Science Quarterly,* 1963, 8:1–17.

Stanley Schultz, "Breaking the Chains of Poverty: Public Education in Boston, 1800–1860. In K. Jackson and S. Schultz, eds., *Cities in American History.* Alfred A. Knopf, 1972, pp. 306–323.

Robert Schulze, "The Role of Economic Dominants in Community Power Structure." In M. Aiken and P. Mott, eds., *The Structure of Community Power.*
Random House, 1970, pp. 60–66.

Robert Schulze and Leonard Blumberg, "The Determination of Local Power
Elites." In M. Aiken and P. Mott, eds., *The Structure of Community
Power.* Random House, 1970, pp. 216–221.

Edwin Schur, *Crimes Without Victims: Deviant Behavior and Public Policy.*
Prentice-Hall, 1965.

Gregory Singleton, "The Genesis of Suburbia: A Complex of Historical Trends."
In L. Masotti and J. Hadden, eds., *The Urbanization of the Suburbs.* Sage
Publications, 1973, pp. 29–50.

Theodore Sizer, "The Schools in the Bad City." In J. Wilson, ed., *The Metropolitan Enigma: Inquiries into the Nature and Dimensions of America's
"Urban Crisis."* Harvard University Press, 1968, pp. 311–334.

Gideon Sjoberg, "Theory and Research in Urban Sociology." In P. Hauser and
L. Schnore, eds., *The Study of Urbanization.* John Wiley & Sons, 1965,
pp. 157–190.

Irving Sloan, "Balance and Imbalance: 'New' History Texts and the Negro."
In D. Bromley and C. Longino, eds., *White Racism and Black Americans.*
Schenkman, 1972, pp. 336–351.

Lee Sloan, "The Black Beater." In E. Banfield, ed., *Urban Government.* The
Free Press, 1969, pp. 422–425.

Bayrd Still, "Establishing a Full Range of Urban Services." In A. Wakstein,
ed., *The Urbanization of America: An Historical Anthology.* Houghton
Mifflin, 1970, pp. 170–183.

John Strange, "The Negro and Philadelphia Politics." In E. Banfield, ed., *Urban
Government.* The Free Press, 1969, pp. 405–421.

George Taylor, "Building an Intra-Urban Transportation System." In A. Wakstein, ed., *The Urbanization of America: An Historical Anthology.*
Houghton Mifflin, 1970, pp. 128–150.

Robert Ulich, *The Education of Nations.* Harvard University Press, 1967.

Richard Wade, "Competition Between Western Cities." In A. Wakstein, ed.,
The Urbanization of America: An Historical Anthology. Houghton Mifflin,
1970, pp. 99–107.

John Walton, "The Vertical Axis of Community Organization and the Structure
of Power." In C. Bonjean, T. Clark, and R. Lineberry, eds., *Community
Politics: A Behavioral Approach.* The Free Press, 1971, pp. 188–197.

Jules Wanderer, "An Index of Riot Severity and Some Correlates." In J. Geschwender, ed., *The Black Revolt.* Prentice-Hall, 1971, pp. 312–319.

Sam Warner, *The Private City: Philadelphia in Three Periods of Growth.* University of Pennsylvania Press, 1968.

Roland Warren, "Toward a Reformulation of Community Theory." In R. French,
ed., *The Community.* Peacock, 1969, pp. 39–48.

Roland Warren, *The Community in America.* Rand McNally, 1972.

William Westley, "Secrecy and the Police." In A. Niederhoffer and A. Blumberg, eds., *The Ambivalent Force: Perspectives.* Rinehart Press, 1973, pp. 129–131.

Raymond Wheeler, "Annexation Law and Annexation Success." *Land Economics,* 1965, 41:354–360.

Brand Whitlock, "The Absurdity of Partisanship." In E. Banfield, ed., *Urban Government.* The Free Press, 1969, pp. 275–278.

Andrew White, "Municipal Affairs Are Not Political." In E. Banfield, ed., *Urban Government.* The Free Pres, 1969, pp. 271–274.

William Whyte, "The Nature of Political Obligations." In E. Banfield, ed., *Urban Government.* The Free Press, 1969, pp. 209–213.

Oliver Williams, "Life-Style Values and Political Decentralization in Metropolitan Areas." In T. Clark, ed., *Community Structure and Decision-Making: Comparative Analyses.* Chandler, 1968, pp.427–440.

Oliver Williams and Charles Adrian, "Community Types and Policy Differences." In J. Wilson, ed., *City Politics and the Public Policy.* John Wiley & Sons, 1968, pp.17–36.

Oliver Williams, Harold Herman, Charles Liebman, and Thomas Dye, *Suburban Differences and Metropolitan Policies.* University of Pennsylvania Press, 1965.

Robin Williams, *American Society: A Sociological Interpretation.* Alfred A. Knopf, 1970.

James Wilson, "Negro Politics in the North." In D. Gordon, ed., *Social Change and Urban Politics.* Prentice-Hall, 1973a, pp. 192–199.

James Wilson, "The Police and Their Problems: A Theory." In A. Niederhoffer and A. Blumberg, eds., *The Ambivalent Force: Perspectives.* Rinehart Press, 1973b, pp. 293–306.

James Wilson and Edward Banfield, "Public Regardingness as a Value Premise in Voting Behavior." In J. Goodman, ed., Perspectives on Urban Politics. Allyn & Bacon, 1970, pp. 333–354.

Raymond Wolfinger and John Field, "Political Ethos and Structure of City Government." In J. Goodman, ed., *Perspectives on Urban Politics.* Allyn & Bacon, 1970, pp. 454–495.

Robert Wood, *1400 Governments: The Political Economy of the New York Metropolitan Region.* Doubleday, 1961.

9.

PLANNING AND AMELIORATION OF URBAN PROBLEMS

William Michelson

Back in the old days, it was an honorable and elevated calling to save men's (and presumably women's) souls. Later on, with the development of medicine, it was equally respectable to save body and soul. In recent years, environment has been added to body and soul on the list of items whose salvation made the basis of an attractive career.

City planning is one of the world's newer professions. It is vigorous and expanding. At a time when more than two-thirds of North Americans live in cities, it is a calling potentially affecting the welfare of most people, directly or indirectly. Spurring enthusiasm for this movement is the assumption that by helping to save urban environment, planners are also saving the bodies and souls of their fellow human beings.

Nonetheless, when planning is viewed under the sociologist's microscope, it becomes readily apparent that city planning is many things to many people. Planners themselves disagree as to what they should be doing, and even men of like mind find themselves set upon widely divergent tasks. Those who utilize what planners produce have still different perspectives on planning, as well as interests of their own that would frequently negate what planners attempt to do.

Another factor compounding the difficulty in presenting a simple picture of planning and its effect on urban problems is that while planners are feverishly busy, not all their efforts are implemented and hence made visible to the public eye. Their "successes" are largely restricted to limited domains of action, and there is some distortion involved when people generalize about the profession from what they "can see with their own eyes."

While the various kinds of planners commonly make assumptions that their work will tend to ameliorate urban problems, there is little point to pretending this field is a homogeneous one; in fact, the differences internal to urban planning are of interest in themselves, paralleling developments over time in other professions and in society more generally.

In the first section of this chapter, then, I shall explore the various kinds of substance with which planners deal. Then I shall explore the temporal trend in the intellectual and methodological approaches used by planners to solve urban problems. Following this, I shall turn to an examination of factors having to do with social structure that affect the working conditions of the planner, as well as the solution of problems pursued. Finally, I shall discuss ways in which the sociologist joins the planner in the common act of pursuing solutions to urban problems.

THE PRODUCT

Roses are red, violets are blue, and planners make plans. Don't they? This would be one of the world's greater tautologies were it in fact completely true. Many people, however, will argue that the job of a planner is *not* to produce plans, but rather to propose and help run a process whereby politicians and members of the public can find solutions to problems which they themselves are capable of carrying out without further assistance. This view of planning as a process, rather than as a product, is a relatively recent one, and it does not characterize the great accumulation of planning work. Nonetheless, even when a plan is the exclusive product of planning, there are very different types of plans pursued. Therefore, I shall identify and discuss in this section several different types of plans created by planners and the relationship of each to urban problems. I shall postpone all discussion of planning as a process until the next section.

Comprehensive Planning and Zoning

Throughout history, architects and engineers serving European nobility have carved out splendid monuments of urban design, which in some cases gave character and direction to whole cities. Castles, cathedrals, and canals lent dignity and identity to cities struggling out of the dark ages. Grand road patterns—like that imposed by Baron Haussmann on the existing fabric of Paris in the nineteenth century—lent order to a city.

Such efforts were neither new nor original. The Greeks and the Romans had left their own legacy, as had earlier groups who were strongly oriented to religion. Nonetheless, when the cities of America were settled and then expanded, their layouts were largely utilitarian and without inspiration [Tunnard & Reed 1956]. Although the occasional capital city (state, provincial, or federal) was granted more explicit design concern, most others grew either along strictly functional lines or along those dictated by surveying techniques. Some cities were characterized largely by buildings and locations dictated by the technologies present during their periods of great growth—large numbers of factories on bodies of water, tenement houses, unsightly wharf areas, or bisecting railroads, for example. Others were highly regular, with few distinctions marking the landscape.

While there were pleasant features such as the New England green, later exported to the midwest, the physical environment of cities was really the business of no individual. In Europe, magnificent urban artifacts crowned the glory of empires; there was pressure for monarchs to translate the grandeur of their realms into civic amenities. North American growth, however, had a very different frame of reference.

The industrial revolution, which underlay great growth in American cities, as well as in cities on other continents, did bring with it, however, the same rise in civic consciousness that occurred elsewhere, particularly in Great Britain. While reform movements were predicated by the observation of hitherto unprecedentedly calamitous living conditions, a fact of the cities in the last half of the nineteenth century was the growing concern for more effective urban management [Alonso 1967]. In North America, though, this did not give rise quickly to explicit planning of the physical environment.

In 1893, however, a single event made men see cities with new eyes. A world's fair, called the Columbian Exposition, was held in Chicago. It was built on an exclusive site along Lake Michigan that was set apart from and in contrast to the rest of Chicago. The buildings were in harmony with one another, and there was a planned movement pattern for pedestrians from building to building around the site. There were open spaces, pools, and fountains. The roads were wide and rationally placed. In short, the Columbian Exposition was a monumental and beautiful reflection of heroic European patterns.

The Columbian Exposition served as an example of what could be done in and to cities. And it triggered what was called the "City Beautiful Movement," which inaugurated the training of planners and the inception of large-scale planning in North American cities.

In the decade and a half that followed the exposition, British planners were imported, and the first domestic planners were trained. Harvard was the first university to commence a formal planning course, and others followed suit. By 1917, over a hundred cities had undertaken the construction of a plan [Hancock 1967].

Several aspects of these plans must be noted.

First, they were comprehensive plans, guiding the growth of the entirety of the city far into the future.

Second, these plans were entirely physical in character. The plans dealt with streets, parks, landscaping, and the location of such major categories of land use as residential, commercial, and industrial. The major criteria underlying most plans were order, beauty, and rational guesses about the future. There was no marked input from the social sciences.

Nonetheless, those behind the City Beautiful Movement were convinced that their plans were of great social consequence. Designers have always been strong supporters of the view that people's surroundings have a strong influence on their morale and well being. According to this view, people surrounded by ugliness and misery could not help but be burdened by it. While architects had historically attempted to improve the well-being of their individual clients, normally wealthy or titled, the impact of the City Beautiful Movement was to extend this reasoning to the city at large. As Hancock put it, they were "convinced that physical order equalled social order" [1967, p. 293]; at a time when great numbers of immigrants were flooding North American cities and living in apparent poverty in high density accommodations, a little social order through means apparently under the control of planners was very much desired.

While some parts of some cities greatly benefited from the grand plans conceived during the years of the City Beautiful Movement, it is nonetheless an unfortunate truth that virtually none of the comprehensive plans were effectively implemented. In reaction to this sorry situation, a major effort was made, influenced to no small extent by the New Deal, to improve the criteria underlying comprehensive city plans. Before and after World War II, plans were formulated that increasingly utilized considerations such as economy and convenience, to go along with beauty and order. These renewed efforts to create comprehensive plans for existing cities were carried forward by a belief in science, rather than common sense or professional training alone, as the basis for the making of plans. What this meant for the "process" of planning will be discussed in the next section, but the preeminence within the planning profession of the comprehensive plan for more than a half-century can be explained by the presence of two successive movements, each of which supported the creation of comprehensive plans.

Whether comprehensive plans did or did not solve urban problems was largely a moot point; it was untested, since most plans were not implemented. The physical bias of these plans makes it likely that they would have been found disappointing in anything but an aesthetic sense had they in fact been implemented. In an analogous situation at a lower level of scale, for example, there was a movement in favor of public housing that originated at about the same time as the City Beautiful Movement. This more limited movement suggested that the lives of people would be drastically changed if their clearly inadequate housing units could be replaced by newly constructed, safe, and sanitary buildings. Although there is no question that the replacement of grossly inadequate living conditions contributed positively to some aspects of health and well-being, it became clear with the years that the same pressures of poverty, which had forced people into their initially inadequate housing units, prevented them from becoming "different people" once parachuted into physically improved premises [Schorr n.d.; Wilner et al. 1962]. In short, it was hardly a proven case that plans with only physical parameters taken into consideration had much to do with urban problems of a social nature.

Nonetheless, comprehensive planning spread rapidly, as it was in tune with both the growing rationality and empiricism of the twentieth century. Although some estimable works had already been completed by architects and engineers working for great men in England and on the continent, city planning growth in Europe was roughly coincident with its growth in North America. One of the most famous comprehensive plans, perhaps because it is so easily visualized, comes from Denmark, for the city of Copenhagen. It is called the "Finger Plan" because its shape resembles a hand, with five fingers coming out from a central mass. Formulated in 1949, this plan concerned itself with a wide range of objectives—order, beauty, economics, and convenience.

According to the Finger Plan, the existing built-up area in the center of the city (i.e., the palm of the hand) would remain its commercial focus. Future growth would be encouraged along the lines of existing railroads by the implementation of fast, frequent electrified suburban train service, and new commuter facilities would be built. A guiding factor was that no one be forced to travel more than 45 minutes to work. The settled area of Copenhagen proper would continue to be served by trollies with possible replacement by buses; trollies were not considered practical outside the central city because of the time factor. The electrified train routes would extend out from the center like fingers.

Basing city form on transportation facilities illustrates a major tenet increasingly acknowledged by planners: transportation patterns and city form are increasingly interdependent.

Apartments were to surround the suburban station, with single homes slightly further from the stations. It was expected that the apartment dwellers would be close enough to the stations to walk to them, while, if necessary, buses could funnel those living in lower density areas into the stations. Nonetheless, the settlements of housing were to be sufficiently compact and coherent that they would not sprawl endlessly over the available land.

Industry was to locate midway between the station developments, on the railroad and at the intersection of these railroads with radial highways, some existing and some new, bypassing the center of the city and adding simultaneously to the beauty and economics involved.

The land between the fingers was to be set aside as parkland. The greater Copenhagen area was one where people could live in pleasant, efficient settlements within easy reach of their work place, but where residents of the new fingers could easily reach open space.

Nonetheless, even this famous plan illustrates the dangers facing those who feel they can successfully implement a comprehensive plan. While the Finger Plan was fortunate enough to be formally adopted and even had its transportation measures implemented, the growth of the Copenhagen area in the long run did not follow the Finger Plan. In 1949, its framers could not conceive the tremendous pressure for expansion that would occur beyond the area covered by the finger plan because of the eventual economic feasibility and popularity of the private automobile. Furthermore, they did not take into consideration the relationship of Copenhagen to other Danish cities, which influenced industry to locate on or near some fingers but not others. As a result, subsequent development was both more diffuse than had been anticipated, creating pressures for more interstitial road networks than had been planned, as well as more focused in the area southwest of the city.

At least two problems with comprehensive plans are illustrated in this one example. The first is that they may be based upon unrealistic assumptions about the future. No matter what the scientific caliber of work going into a plan, it is inevitably based upon some considerations of the future that cannot be substantiated immediately. Second, no matter how comprehensive a plan may be, both in its geographic scope and in the number of factors it takes into consideration, it is highly unlikely that all possibly relevant factors will be covered. Hence, an exogenous variable may nonetheless prove to be a decisive one. In the case of Copenhagen, for example, its relationship to economic and urban growth centers elsewhere in Denmark had not been appreciated.

Surely, though, those responsible for comprehensive plans are not so totally naive that they ignore the question of implementation entirely? Despite failures, there are, in fact, very definite measures in North America with the explicit purpose of implementing comprehensive plans. One of them, zoning, is well-known.

Thus, while the comprehensive plan is both a set of goals and principles, and a map applying these geographically to guide the long range growth of the city, it has no legal force without a corresponding zoning ordinance. The comprehensive plan is a statement of what ought to be and why; zoning is a legal statement defining what is permitted and what is not. Comprehensive plans are always future oriented; zoning concerns the here and now.

Most zoning laws divide a municipality into districts, with regulation in each of these districts as to 1. the use of buildings and land for specified purposes, 2. the maximum density of the population permitted 3. the height and bulk of buildings and other structures, and 4. the percentage of the lot occupied and the amount of open space required.

Legislation concerning restrictions on the use of land must always be stated in the name of health, welfare, and safety, which are legally considered as public considerations that override the normal sanctity of private property in the eyes of the law. Hence, zoning has dealt with the kinds of restrictions that presumably protect people (in their homes, places of recreation, and other highly cherished uses of land) from more obnoxious uses such as heavy industry, warehousing, and the like. Restrictions on the size of buildings, their bulk, and the amount of space around them has to do with the provision of fresh air and sunlight for people's health and welfare. High densities have traditionally been considered deleterious to both health and welfare except in very limited circumstances (although this view may be changing at present, and in any case has been proven invalid in other cultures) [Mitchell 1971].

Ideally, a zoning ordinance is prepared after the creation and adoption of a comprehensive plan to support and enforce what the plan calls for. Since plans are prepared for cities already in existence, which even at present do not normally follow all the provisions of the plan, it is obvious that some, or indeed many, parcels of land violate zoning ordinances at the time they are passed. These exceptions to the law are normally allowed for at least a basic number of years, during which owners can presumably move away or change the land use without hardship to themselves. These exceptions are called "legally nonconforming usages." Needless to say, there is less hardship when zoning laws are made to apply to vacant land.

However, not all zoning ordinances follow upon or are tailored to successfully adopted comprehensive plans. More frequently, zoning ordinances are made without waiting for the adoption of such a plan, and even when a plan is passed, there is always some degree of inexactness between the plan and its zoning bylaws.

Most cities regulate their use of land through zoning. Zoning has had far more influence than the comprehensive plans it presumably supports. The idea of zoning is a fairly straightforward one. The elected officials of the municipality formally pass a set of laws that serve as a guide to all as to where which activities can be located within the city, and by what means. Zoning presumably protects the poor from the unchecked wishes of the rich, and the quiet from the noisy. It is to be run in a public, quasi-judicial manner.

In practice, there are two approaches to zoning. One of them takes as its starting point the assumption that there is a hierarchy of obnoxious land uses. The approach is to zone with respect to particular points in this hierarchy. Everything more obnoxious than any particular point is thereby banned from a given location, while everything lower on the scale is permitted without any specification or elaboration. With this approach, industry is considered the most obnoxious land use, commerce less so, and residence the least so; finer breakdowns are of course made with respect to these categories in most cases. Thus, according to this approach, areas zoned for residence may have only dwelling units, while areas zoned for commerce or industry may also have housing.

The second approach to zoning is considerably more exact. In attempting to overcome the ambiguities of the previous system, with its broadly inclusive categories and its automatic inclusion within an area of all less obnoxious abuses, it seeks to specify exactly what is or is not permitted. According to this approach, anything that was not specified in the zoning ordinance is illegal; the ordinance, however, is very much more detailed and elaborate in this case. More forethought has to go into its preparation.

The first type of zoning is found very much more frequently than the second, although the latter is a more recent development.

Lest zoning be too inflexible, both with respect to the definition of land uses and the practical application of these provisions throughout the city, there is always provision for exceptions to the zoning bylaws. In every municipality, there is a body that hears and rules on arguments for so-called zoning variances. This group is not the same one as that which creates the city's comprehensive plan, although planners are frequently called upon for advice about the desirability of granting particular zoning variances. Although local situations differ, one effect of such bodies is the vitiation of the intent of zoning. It is the rule, rather than the exception, in many cities that variances are granted that go contrary to the spirit of the zoning bylaws and that counteract any plan that the zoning was intended to implement. Liquor stores in areas zoned residential, commerce on parkland, and high rise in low density are typical outcomes of zoning variance hearings. Zoning variances have been a major locus of political bribery and payoffs.

While the practice of granting zoning variances, as compared to the theory behind such practice, has represented a disastrous loophole to the positive intent of planning, there are still additional problems that counteract the positive, universalistic rationale behind zoning. Zoning can be criticized for being both too inexact and too exact.

With respect to the former, suburban neighborhoods are frequently criticized for their dullness. This adjective generally signifies the lack of specific kinds of commerce or activity which people might find desirable to have near their homes in order not to require mechanical means of access. But the same zoning that protects people from what they do not want also protects them from some uses of land that they do want, but that falls into the same general land use categories of more obnoxious uses. Many people have recently urged the creation of day-care facilities on the grounds of their suburban apartment complexes, only to discover that this contravenes the zoning bylaws.

This kind of problem is carried to an extreme when the second type of zoning discussed above, that specifying only permitted land uses, is in effect. No zoning body can think of all contingencies, and this has led to some highly embarrassing court cases, where boys have been prosecuted for building tree houses, and husbands, patios. Although one would expect that variances would be given freely for items supported by common sense and public sentiment, yet the pressures for "adjustment" are of markedly different strength when they come from a developer with strong political and economic influence, as compared with an individual home owner or group of tenants. In Toronto, an uncompleted shell of a high-rise building mars the landscape along one of the more scenic routes into the downtown area; it represents the product of a developer who started building before receiving his variance *and was then stopped.* How many buildings do we see in other cities as faits accomplis that began the same way, and became de facto arguments for zoning variances?

Furthermore, while it is assumed that houses may prosper without factories, the opposite assumption is not contemplated in the typical approach to zoning. Hence, factories, whose technology increasingly requires large amounts of space on one floor, find their expansion possibilities constricted by so-called lower levels of land use (i.e., housing and commerce). The same care that goes into the protection of expensive residential areas is not extended by most zoning ordinances to the particular needs of industry and commerce. In fact, it took the industrial park, a large tract of land appropriately zoned, held by a single private or public organization, to protect the needs of industrial users.

Furthermore, zoning has treated all land uses of this category as if they were alike in their performance. But all manufacturing firms are not equally obnoxious, nor are all commercial operations. Conceivably, some commercial operations, such as shopping centers or drive-in restaurants, could create much more noise and trouble than many modern manufacturing firms. While the second type of zoning is more likely to recognize this distinction, basing its specification of permitted uses on performance standards, this is still a problem in the typical case of zoning.

While the above examples indicate the inexactness of zoning, other problems arise when people try to make zoning overly exact. Many smaller towns and suburbs have attempted to maintain or insure that poor people or members of disadvantaged minority groups be excluded from living within the borders of their municipalities by zoning laws that specify, for example, that building lots have to be a certain large minimum size, such as two acres, or that new houses have to cover a relatively large percentage of these lots, such as 25 percent. Such practices, while in no way referring to the names of particular "undesirables," have nonetheless been effective in pricing these municipalities out of the range of certain groups requiring housing.

A variation on this theme is for an existing municipality to specify a given percentage distribution of the sizes of building lots permitted in the city, of which the smaller ones have long since been built, leaving only expensive lots for the privileged people they desire.

One other problem with the exactness of zoning is that, through specifying where given activities may take place, it narrows the range of areas where these activities may eventually occur. While this is highly desirable in terms of planned, orderly growth, it also has the effect of focusing competition on a more limited pool of available land. Since land is allowed to have a market value in North America, this generally tends to drive the price of land up. If developers could build almost anywhere, it might have an adverse effect on the structure and growth of the city, but it might result in less competition for specific pieces of land and thus lower prices for all parcels.

In theory, then, zoning is a practice designed to fulfill the aims of comprehensive plans and to protect the health, welfare, and safety of individuals; in practice, it has by no means been an unmitigated success. Although single examples are always filled with dangerously idiosyncratic factors, Houston, Texas is nonetheless worthy of considerable attention. Houston, almost alone among major cities, has never had zoning. Yet, it is usually considered one of the more handsome and functional American cities, and its house prices have generally been among the lowest in major North American cities.

Zoning, then, has never been the strongest form of protection for the comprehensive plan. Nonetheless, the problems encountered both in formulating and in implementing comprehensive plans go very much further than the zoning question alone. They are rooted in intellectual, methodological, and contextual difficulties. These problems will be discussed in later sections.

Community Planning and Renewal

Comprehensive planning is not very visible these days. This contrasts sharply with the high profile of those now making plans for local areas within cities. While a legal requirement of those who deal with what is called *community planning* is that their products have to be consistent with an overall city plan, this does not necessarily mean that the larger plan is being implemented elsewhere in the city as actively as in areas for which special plans are being made.

In most North American cities, urban development has long since exceeded the boundaries of the original political entities, spilling over into other political jurisdictions, usually called suburbs. As a result, the creation of plans for communities within these cities is really a matter of *re*planning, rather than planning for original settlement or new growth.

Urban renewal is a generic name for this type of planning. By itself, it does not necessarily imply any given strategy of action or final product. Yet, because it became largely associated in the public mind with indiscriminate physical destruction of the existing buildings and land uses, without adequate consideration for the needs or aspirations of those living in the areas affected, the name itself has been replaced by a number of more recent euphemisms ("community renewal," "neighborhood improvement," etc.).

Until about 1949, changes within existing cities were made largely on a building-for-building basis. The reform movements, which were mentioned earlier, influenced the replacement of badly dilapidated housing units with new housing, usually in the public domain. Outdated stores and factories were replaced by private developers as the need was seen. The housing stock and downtown edifices were not entirely stationary, although large-scale, planned change was largely absent. However, arguments were made about the need to make plans for the coordinated change of land use and buildings in entire neighborhoods, an activity requiring the active participation of planners for the first time.

For legal purposes, the same justifications had to be made as with respect to zoning—health, welfare, and safety. Arguments justifying neighborhood-wide change utilized the imagery of cancer. The kind of factors producing negative effects among slum dwellers were said to reside in the larger characteristics of the neighborhood itself. One could not get rid of this pervasive influence just by updating the quality of housing. Instead it was thought necessary to remove the whole context of disease and destruction. Otherwise, the poor person whose home had been improved would again be engulfed. Surgical removal was felt to be necessary.

While the cancerous effects of neighborhood milieu on individual health, welfare, and safety were the paramount legal arguments for urban renewal, there were many other pressing reasons why cities wanted to replan existing neighborhoods. A highly important factor was the improvement of the tax base. The single most important contribution to municipal budgets is money raised from the taxation of land and buildings. The amount raised on any building or property is dependent on its value. Industries and stores produce more in the way of revenue to cities than do homes. Similarly, expensive homes and apartments return more to cities than do poor homes and apartments. Therefore, any plan that would replace poor, old housing or activities with newer, more expensive substitutes was expected to greatly aid city treasuries. At a time when many of the cities' wealthier residents, together with their commercial and industrial enterprises, were fleeing the boundaries of the city entirely in favor of suburban locations, such an increase in the cities' revenues was seen as extremely welcome.

From the point of view of the comprehensive planner, the replanning of local areas was a way in which the *functioning* of cities could be modernized in line with the thinking going into comprehensive plans.

Certainly, what had been an appropriate location for housing, commerce, or industry as much as a hundred years earlier would not necessarily be the best location for that land use at the present, or in the future. Renewal, therefore, offered the opportunity of placing activities in a more appropriate location in light of the growth of the city as a whole.

Downtown merchants and city politicians, often one and the same, saw urban renewal as a tool to update the size, appearance, and/or vitality of downtown shopping areas, which were starting to suffer in competition with the more recent and modern suburban plazas that were increasingly attracting larger numbers of patrons.

Other segments of opinion, representing established industries, hotel and entertainment establishments, real estate interests, and the like, felt that dramatic improvement in certain parts of town would exercise a "halo effect," which would influence others to make similar improvements, with the face of the whole site exhibiting such dramatic progress that more attention would be paid to the city and more investment would be made in it in the future by outsiders.

Finally, some people in medium-size cities containing only one area deemed a slum, but surrounded by other cities with problems, saw urban renewal as the way of transferring their own problems into surrounding areas. By eradicating their one low-income area, without providing effective replacement housing within city borders, they could effectively remove the pariah group from their municipality. It was reasoning of this sort that gained urban renewal the name "Negro removal" in some cities.

Within the broad concept of urban renewal there were at least two paths to action. While polar, they could be combined, at least theoretically.

The first, most commonly used, is redevelopment. When an area is redeveloped, the various properties making it up are purchased by the developer. He then demolishes all existing buildings, and he frequently removes internal streets as well. Then he starts from scratch in producing a configuration of buildings and spaces deemed appropriate for present or future needs, either constructing them himself or turning the land over to someone who will do it, usually on prearranged terms. Only redevelopment, and only if done correctly, fulfills *all* of the rationales for urban renewal cited above.

On the other hand, many people feel that the existing land uses are appropriate. Hence, the change in neighborhood living conditions, in the tax base, in the resident population, and in the aesthetic appeal of the area can be achieved with less destruction and a lower cost by upgrading the quality of the buildings that are already there. This kind of urban renewal is called rehabilitation.

In both the United States and Canada, there have been many urban renewal projects since the 1940s. At first, they focused almost exclusively on physical changes, with a heavy emphasis on redevelopment. In recent years, with some observation of the effects of the earlier programs, they have become less dependent on redevelopment and more heavily reliant on rehabilitation and on social programs.

In the United States, urban renewal was almost entirely government financed. It was argued that large-scale changes within cities simply could not occur under private initiative because both the expenses and the difficulties of assembling land were so great. Any change, it was felt, depended upon governmental intervention. Funding came largely from the federal government, although states and municipalities were required to pay a smaller percentage of the bill, as an incentive to avoid spending federal money thoughtlessly. Planning, however, was to be done at the local level, under the approval of higher levels of government. The costs that all these levels of government were asked to absorb represented the net difference between what they had to pay to purchase the land and either destroy or improve the buildings, and the ultimate funds they would receive from the eventual developer or consumer.

The early redevelopment programs are not generally considered as having been successful.[1] Large sums of money were spent, but the areas affected were tiny in comparison with the size of major metropolitan areas [Vernon 1966]. Only in smaller cities did an urban renewal project have a chance for very much impact on the urban fabric. Sprucing up a few blocks of the downtown would not have a drastic effect on activity patterns if people did not want to come downtown because they now lived in the suburbs, and if they were increasingly deterred from going downtown by rising crime rates. Although the downtown was a very important symbolic object to downtown merchants (obviously) and to politicians whose jurisdiction was the central city and not the whole metropolitan area, redevelopment could not change the more macroscopic reasons for the metropolitan growth of cities. Even New Haven, Connecticut, with one of the most visible and widely acclaimed downtown

---

1. For many points of view on this subject, see Bellush and Hausknecht [1967], Wilson [1966], and Greer [1965].

redevelopment projects, is starting to follow the path of other cities, albeit with a lag in time purchased by their renewal expenditures.

The benefits from these early programs were not generally for the people living in the areas. Although guaranteed replacement housing on the spot, these people found that the plans were for luxury buildings, designed to induce more affluent people to return to the city center. The original residents could not afford the luxury buildings provided in replacement. Usually with the assistance legally required to be given them, the original residents found replacement housing of equal or better quality, but at considerably higher costs to themselves. Hence, they were forced to leave established settings, without substantial accounting for the personal and financial costs of relocation, and subsequently to face higher housing costs. It is a common opinion that these people were forced to bear a substantial part of the real cost of redevelopment themselves. This was particularly true for home owners, the elderly, and most notably elderly home owners. In many ways, the early urban renewal projects tended to accentuate the very problems they were formally framed to ameliorate.

On the other hand, the more affluent persons that redevelopment plans sought to attract, introducing trends counter to those that led them to move outward, were not effectively attracted to return to the city in great numbers. Conditions of crime and pollution, which had driven them outwards, were not effectively rebutted by the opportunity to live in a small area still surrounded by the conditions they deplored. And many of the people that the new redevelopment plan had sought to remove were now simply relocated across the street in the next neighborhood.

Redevelopment plans calling for industry to replace outdated land uses were not as directly affected by crime and pollution as were residentially based plans. Nonetheless, many smaller cities that had counted on the existence of large tracts of land as the basis for an industrial renaissance found it slow to arrive. The same reasons industries did not choose to come to their towns in the first place—location, labor force, taxation practices, union policies, etc.—were still largely in effect. A good number of cities that had hoped to raise their tax base instead found a very low tax base replaced by little or none at all. In any case, the lag between the destruction of the old tax base and the arrival of the new one cost them money. Furthermore, many of the firms taking advantage of the newly claimed land were already within the city, leading to little net gain.

In addition, many small businesses forced to leave their existing neighborhood settings found themselves unable to reestablish themselves elsewhere without their original clients [Zimmer 1966]. Stores based on a homogeneous clientele (e.g., ethnic groups) find it difficult to operate without the same people as close as before.

Although rehabilitation did not attempt to do as much as redevelopment, it still did not solve some of the more ticklish problems inherent in the public programs pursued in the United States. While it proved less costly than redevelopment, the difference did not turn out to be as great as expected. Furthermore, it proved impractical to assume that the same people could continue to live in the same dwellings after rehabilitation, with the public paying the additional costs. Although the same problems of relocating former residents are relevant, rehabilitated housing appears to be somewhat more favorably received on the part of affluent people wishing to return to the city. Nonetheless, even rehabilitation projects that are considered highly successful, such as Society Hill in Philadelphia, an area largely composed of restored colonial row houses in the center city (although with some new high-rise towers on the site), are still but a tiny segment of areas perplexing leaders of large American cities. They are not the answer to the rather ostrich-like goal of redistributing population through such limited physical means.

Canadian practice, however, represents a considerable contrast. Most of the renewal, despite legislation paralleling the American legislation in many ways, has been done under private auspices. What could not be done in American cities, thus justifying federal legislation on urban renewal, has led to unprecedented changes in the fabric of downtown Montreal, Toronto, and Vancouver. Recent years have seen an inward movement of affluent people in these cities, and the overwhelming pattern in American cities of poor people living in the center and rich people living only in the doughnut surrounding the hole is not a clear reality in Canada. In fact, this patter of concentric zones, described by Chicago sociologists [e.g., Burgess 1925] and established as a universal rule in urban areas, seems to be violated in just about every other country where researchers have investigated "foreign" patterns. Although it is difficult to document precisely the reason for this, it does appear clear that simple physical measures are insufficient to change a situation probably rooted in uniquely American racial and economic contexts.

In Canada, however, there are still problems facing those moving from areas that are privately renewed. Since many of these people are tenants, the decision is not theirs as to whether the properties on which they reside are sold for renewal. Furthermore, while governments, if they desire, can expropriate land for renewal at prices to be established through legal means, private developers can still exert considerable influence to force people to sell. While some owners are eager to sell and pocket attractive prices for their property (sometimes not realizing the cost of buying replacement housing at current market values), others sell only when harrassed, after seeing surrounding dwellings boarded up or turned into rooming houses, or upon seeing definite, deleterious changes in the character of their surrounding neighborhood.

In fact, Canadian cities are potentially facing a problem common to cities in the Third World. With the elite rushing in to live in the centrally located areas of the city, which are usually accessible to good public transportation and to expensive stores, facilities, and services, poor people may be forced to jump over the other established areas of town with currently more costly housing and so land entirely outside the existing built up areas, in areas with poorer housing and few of the external advantages of central city living. In the United States, the affluent are paying the price of inconvenience if they continue to use the center after having moved outward, something they are in a position to do[2] while in Canada, the poor would lack the facilities and still be forced to depend upon meager resources in order to get them.

One early example of urban renewal received considerable attention as a consequence of a detailed research project. Information brought out in this project had a considerable influence in changing renewal practices. The West End of Boston, described most fully in books by Gans [1962] and Fried [1973], was about 50 acres in size. Located just on the fringe of Boston's central business district, it was largely residential in character, consisting mainly of old walk-up apartment houses built right to the sidewalks of narrow streets, a high density, low open-space situation. Some local stores were scattered throughout the area. Although local residents had not categorized the area themselves as a single neighborhood, it was nonetheless a traditional area of first settlement for foreign immigrants. Before demolition of the area about 40 percent of

---

2. One disturbing trend is that affluent people are using the central city to a decreasing degree, taking both jobs and amenities outward with them to the suburbs, forcing the poor to spend more on transportation, as in the potential Canadian case. However, the so-called "Energy Crisis," which is in effect at the time of this writing, may affect all such trends, placing a premium once more on central city residence, particularly if the crisis is as long and severe as some anticipate it will be.

the residents were Italian. The studies conducted largely had to do with the Italian population. These studies brought out the following facts:

1. The area was slated for renewal not because it acted as a cancer to its residents, but because it was in an ideal location in the eyes of merchants, who wanted a more affluent downtown atmosphere. Other areas of town with equally old housing had considerably higher crime rates, and the housing in the West End, while not attractive or well-kept on the outside, belied considerable internal improvements not visible to the planner in his automobile. The presence of large numbers of persons on the street reflected a cultural preference for use of space and social activity, rather than the disorganization planners had imputed to the area [Gans 1959; Fried & Gleicher 1961].

2. Far from being disorganized, the people had their own subculture, which reflected their national background in part and their social class to a great extent. The vitality of this subculture created a divorce between their world and the so-called outside world that kept the people from organizing to fight something they could not believe was going to happen to them [Gans 1962].

3. The housing they found subsequent to forced moves was probably in better structural condition, but it was considerably more expensive. Officials had justified this increase because the people previously had paid a far smaller percentage of their incomes on housing than the 25 to 30 percent expenditure that official formulas legitimize. This was, however, no solace to people with a different set of priorities and whose money was concerned. Furthermore, there was evidence that renewal officials tended to overemphasize the bad qualities of housing they wished to condemn and overemphasize the good qualities of that to which they wished to relocate the very same people [Hartman 1966].

4. The people were emotionally and physically upset from being forced to move, and very real medical consequences lasted a considerable time after their move [Fried 1965].

5. Old neighborhoods such as the West End are in fact important for people to live in after having first entered a new country. While making their entrance into the occupational world, the newcomers still get necessary emotional and cultural supports from others with the same ethnic background [Fried 1967].

After a series of reports from this study was released, federal renewal officials, while publicly treating the West End project as simply a bad example of ongoing programs, nonetheless revised their criteria for subsequent renewal projects. They were henceforth to be centered exclusively on conferring benefits to those people actually living within the neighborhoods to be changed. This was, of course, a drastic change from the original set of physical practices.

Subsequent plans begin to give much more emphasis to removal of only the worst or the least appropriate buildings in an area ("spot redevelopment"). More emphasis was put on rehabilitating existing housing and on improving the social services and amenities available to people living in the area.

The Model Cities legislation in the United States retained this new emphasis, although it stated that the improvements intended were to be made to a large enough part of the city so as to have a significant effect on the city as a whole. This was, of course, a reaction to the relatively small impact of urban renewal projects in some cities. A further addition to the requirements of renewal plans under the new legislation was that they be formulated with the "maximum feasible participation" of the groups affected by them. This was, of course, a considerable change from the situation noted in the West End of Boston, where the people refused to believe that the proposed plan could affect them. While Model Cities programs as a rule never got very far, largely as a consequence of the major political and social upheavals in the mid-1960s, the introduction of citizen participation was a major legacy to the field of planning. As part of "process," citizen participation will be discussed in the next section.

In subsequent programs, so-called community renewal remains the greatest emphasis. It is now no longer certain at all that physical changes will be made in areas seen in need of amelioration, and the determination of what needs to be done is considered unique to the area under treatment. A greater emphasis than before is placed on bringing the various agencies and constituencies relevant to the neighborhood together, so that coordinated solutions may be pursued. Since under this emphasis a result is highly unlikely to take the form of a map or a finite plan for an area, it is perhaps no wonder that planners talk more explicitly about producing a process rather than a plan these days. Community renewal is clearly a process, and if the planners concerned with it justify their existence on the production of plans, they might be out of business.

Thus, in contrast to comprehensive planning, the creation of renewal plans represents quite a paradox. In the case of renewal, planners produced plans that were clearly implemented, and as a consequence they were told to stop. This has had a drastic effect both on the content of attempts to bring about urban amelioration and on the process of what planners do.

New Town Planning

All growth does not occur on the edge of existing cities or suburbs, house by house, street by street. Although it is largely invisible to people living in the middle of existing cities and with no reason to travel off the beaten path, in recent years great numbers of large settlements have been built from scratch according to definitive comprehensive plans. Producing a plan for a new city or community is very different from producing a comprehensive plan for one already in existence, as the internal features of the settlement have to be planned entirely from scratch. "New town" planning, as it is called, thus presents the planner with a situation largely free from the constraints of past practice but filled with the challenge of producing something that will in fact work.

While the mystique of pastoral splendor and planning artistry surrounds the words "new town," new towns are in fact very different from one another in different countries and at different points in time within single countries. As one reviewer noted, new towns differ in size, internal differentiation, predominant form of housing, social class and social class mixtures, their integration to the regions in which they are found, who developed them, and how they are financed [Merlin 1969]. Because new town planning is directly addressed to the amelioration of urban problems, I shall describe many of the variations of new town planning potentially available.

When people think of new towns, they think of Britain, where the new town movement, as we know it now, originated. Nonetheless, the inspiration behind English new town planning was much more diffuse, its origins traceable in no small part to North America. Throughout the preceding centuries, a number of social philosophers designed Utopias, one component of which was normally the *design* for a newly built town, whose form would reflect and support the Utopian activities to be conducted within it [Reiner 1963]. Ebenezer Howard, who was chiefly responsible for elaborating and selling the principles of new town planning in Great Britain, was known to have been greatly influenced by a Utopian novel, *Looking Backward,* by Edward Bellamy, which he read while on a tour of North America in the late nineteenth century. This was a remarkably perceptive work which, even at the time, made a number of accurate predictions, including the radio. It stressed that private property was an anachronism and that the gain to be made from improvements to the community fabric should go back into public coffers, to be used for the public good. The novel itself was centered on the experiences of men from that time who wake up in the future and who not only compare the changes in cities and society from time to time, but who also examine the assumptions behind the practices found at both points of time.

Howard marshalled his energies upon his return to England to rationalize his own ideas for completely new towns in the countryside outside London and to organize for their actual construction. The former task finally took the formal shape of a book now known as *Garden Cities of Tomorrow* [1902]. In it, Howard argued for the construction of cities of up to about 30,000 people. While surrounded on all sides by agricultural lands (called green belts), the cities were nonetheless to be connected by rail to London and to each other. Internally, Howard's garden cities would be built according to a plan, the exact nature of which would depend on the individual location and geography. None - theless, each town would have jobs sufficient to cover the employment requirements of the residents of these towns. All construction would be planned so that, while people would be able to travel very easily and conveniently to their jobs, industrial locations would be situated so as not to interfere with the pleasant enjoyment attached to residential settings. In the same way as jobs and people were to be balanced, the various social classes were to be balanced with one another. Mixtures of different kinds of housing were to reflect differences both in class and family size.

This coordinated plan would be carried out by a nonprofit organization, which would retain ownership in quasi-public fashion. Individuals would have long-term leasehold on the land where they lived, and would participate in civic corporate activity. In fact, back at the turn of the century, Howard called for the citizen participation that only now has become fashionable, proposing that the residents of individual neighborhoods would gradually take over the practical governments of these neighborhoods.[3] Such profits as would be made in the city from rentals of commercial and industrial land, for example, would be utilized for the public good in garden cities. There were many reasons advanced in favor of such new towns:

1. A city where the individual resident could see the sun, escape the crowding, and avoid the air pollution and squalor of London was felt to be highly important for the health and welfare of the common man.

2. The very bigness of the large city was felt to be detrimental to the daily life of the common man, and the accommodation for the "overspill" of the big city into compact, manageable, and efficient smaller cities, still tied with each other by good transportation for flexibility, was felt to be desirable.

3. Building cities at one time in which the buildings, land uses, roads, and utilities were all jointly planned led both to great economies and to better use of space. Howard showed that more people could live in a healthful environment with access to outside space in a planned community than in tenement-like conditions in unplanned settlements.

4. City management would be much more efficient if facilities were integrated. When everything is built together according to a plan, one is at least sure that necessary services are not left to the whim of the market or to private entrepreneurs.

5. The quasi-public ownership of land was designed to demonstrate the benefits to be expected from the end of private ownership of land. Howard's greatest support came from members of the land nationalization society [Buder 1969].

6. Building according to this plan would mean that people were always in contact with nature, while still enjoying the benefits of urban living and industrial society. It was absolutely firm that the cities were not to grow further than their pre-agreed size. The answer to additional overspill from the large cities, or from future generations born within garden cities, would be the creation of additional garden cities in agreed-upon locations, not the destruction of the green belts.

7. The daily balance between a person and his work place and between the various social classes were important goals with respect to human daily activity (i.e., commuting) patterns and social contact patterns, respectively.

---

3. When the first garden city was constructed, however, this aspect of Howard's plan was conveniently forgotten by the men of the world whose cooperation was necessary to translate Howard's ideas into reality.

In short, Howard felt that the construction of garden cities would ameliorate many of the urban problems of the time for those persons moving to them.

Howard's activities finally succeeded in the start of construction of Letchworth in 1908 and Welwyn in 1920. While the plans for these towns were not completely true to Howard's intentions (the ownership and management, for example, were not exactly as envisioned), these towns were honest attempts to realize the benefits of Ebenezer Howard's ideas.

While the rest of the world took note of Letchworth and Welwyn, no new cities of this type were constructed in Great Britain until after World War II. At that time, the "new town," as they called it then, was officially adopted as a major postwar effort by the British government. The postwar situation created several pressing reasons for the construction of new towns: 1. There was a desperate shortage of housing, partly through bomb damage and partly through the lack of construction in the preceding years. 2. Bombs had also damaged industrial establishments, requiring their rebuilding and/or their relocation. 3. The war had demonstrated the vulnerability of placing most people and industrial establishments in very large cities, open to efficient bombing. 4. Pockets of economic depression were anticipated [Buder 1969].

From that time to the present, thirty-four additional new towns were authorized. As the British started to enjoy greater experience with these settlements, they began to alter their concept and form somewhat, although not the overall goals. There have been at least three stages in this process.[4]

In the era after the war the so-called Mark I towns were built along the lines of Letchworth and Welwyn. They emphasized relatively low density housing, much greenery, and the "neighborhood unit plan." This last concept stipulated that the basic divisional units within the city would be neighborhoods of approximately 400 families, sufficient to stock an elementary school with pupils. This unit was felt to be ideal as a basic unit for social intercourse. Local commercial establishments were centered within each neighborhood. Arterial roads were made to run between neighborhood units, and local streets placed within the neighborhood units were designed so as to maximize pedestrian safety. The neighborhood unit plan was justified on every ground from safety through citizenship, and it was adopted elsewhere in the world as one

---

4. See, for example, Eldredge [1967], Evans [1972], Godschalk [1967], Tyrwhitt [1973].

of the basic concepts for the planning of new communities. Although no one could ever prove that it actually did achieve all it set out to, the major criticism of this plan has been along two lines: **1.** that the low densities are uneconomical and uninteresting (certainly not proudly symbolic) to those living there and **2.** that the neighborhood unit is an ideal vehicle for class and/or racial segregation [e.g., Isaacs 1948].

Mark II new towns, characterized most strongly by Cumbernault, outside Glasgow, Scotland, were somewhat greater in overall size (80,000 to 100,000) and had dramatically higher residential densities, centering on a more variegated and vital single city center. While there is still much greenery in Cumbernault, for example, planners felt that people would find it more interesting and fruitful for their daily lives if they lived somewhat closer to other people, with this clustering of consumers supporting more intensive shopping and recreational facilities.

The most recent new towns, however, are again different. Cities such as Milton Keynes are planned for over 200,000 residents living in relatively low-density settings. One of the leading goals underlying the design of these cities is the opportunity for residents to choose from among alternative commercial and recreation facilities, supported by transportation patterns that enable easy movement in all directions (partly by the private automobile, which never received much attention in earlier new towns, and by newly designed public transportation systems).

While a number of problems have arisen in new towns, this experiment is generally viewed as a solid success. Sociologists have discovered that most people have adjusted with the passage of time to these communities, and most report that they are glad they moved [Willmott 1967]. The movement of jobs to new towns has been eminently successful, and there are large registers in the big cities of people desiring to move to new towns should the right match of housing and job needs appear. Furthermore, these cities are proving to be profitable (the current annual return on investment is enviable), and such funds are not, then, the province of the wealthy few.

Nonetheless, some of the problems encountered are worthy of note. First, the balance within these cities has not always been as intended. Some studies, for example, have indicated that within individual towns, there were strong tendencies for professionals and managers to move out and for really poor people not to get in, the latter on grounds of occupational skill deficiencies [Heraud 1968]. While the overall class background of residents of new towns approximates rather closely that of Great Britain as a whole, this tends to hide large amounts of homogeneity within individual towns.

With time and increasing personal transportation flexibility, not all residents of new towns work in these towns, and British authorities have adopted the position of regarding employment possibilities in a more regional perspective. In fact, one recent trend is the designation of development designed to coalesce existing urban settlements into a single new town through the construction of appropriate new artifacts (new housing, new roads, new facilities, etc.).

Another problem has had to do with the physical and social monotony of the earlier new towns, now being counterbalanced by attempts at building transportation facilities, housing densities, and shopping and recreational facilities in ways that correspond with lifestyles. The early attempts simply did not take nonresidential and nonoccupational needs fully into consideration, and the resulting recreational facilities planned were very skimpy and limited. When most new residents were young husbands and wives, with babies, furnishing, and jobs to keep them busy, this was no catastrophe; but as these children grew into teenagers, and as the parents themselves found more time on their hands, new towns received a bad name as boring places to live, however beautiful, efficient, or generally beneficial.

In addition, those services that were provided had to be tied very closely to the particular and relatively homogeneous cohort of people who moved to the town. A day nursery or a grade school, for example, could be completely besieged with customers in one decade and empty the next.

There was also a problem with the degree of inflexibility presented by the comprehensive plan underlying the construction of a new town. In some cases, later observers discovered that a higher population than was allowed by the town plans and the green belt surrounding the town would have been more desirable. The addition of more residents would make facilities already built in the town more economically viable. Yet it was difficult to find appropriate locations for these new residents without violating the beneficial aspects of the plan.

In other countries, new town plans have met particular national needs. In Holland, for example, there is a serious problem of urban overpopulation. Yet, in addition to any of the usual rationales for new towns, the Dutch have used them as basic residential units in the reclamation of areas formerly covered by North Sea waters. The Dutch have also been particularly active in analyzing the success of individual neighborhoods in new towns through sociological research. In this way, each succeeding development would benefit directly from earlier efforts [Godschalk 1967]. This has not been done as explicitly in other countries.

Many of the socialist countries have used new towns as forces for industrial development. Desiring that the new industries they considered necessary should be founded in previously underurbanized regions, both Poland and Hungary, for example, have built new cities to house and provide services for workers in those industries [Merlin 1969; Gorynski 1973].

The building of new cities this way is based on a different rationale from that which underlies the British cities. While the latter are intended to accommodate the overspill from existing metropolitan areas, the new towns of Poland and Hungary were intended to precipitate urban growth in other parts of these countries, pulling persons from elsewhere with the magnetic force of good housing and jobs. This concept, which does not necessarily require industry as its basis, is called the *growth pole* approach to urbanization. Brazil, for example, attempted to introduce urban growth nearer the center of that country through the construction of a new capital, Brasilia.

Swedish new town planning has received considerable attention. Centered largely around Stockholm, Swedish practices have a different focus from those already mentioned. There was little intention for those living in the new communities outside Stockholm to work near home. The intention was rather to channel the growing suburban development in the Stockholm area into a series of thoroughly planned urban concentrations that were integrally tied to downtown Stockholm by fast, inexpensive public transportation. The city of Stockholm was able to carry out such a plan because, several centuries earlier, it had purchased all the land within a reasonable distance of the existing urban settlement and subsequently prohibited unplanned sprawling developments. The private land market played no appreciable role in the development of Stockholm as we know it today.[5]

This type of community, identifiably separate from, but economically dependent upon, the central city, is referred to as a *satellite*. Although itself as new a town and as demanding of comprehensive planning, the satellite is distinct from the new town (which historically assumes as many jobs as wage earners) and the growth pole.

---

5. Buildings themselves have appreciable value, however.

The famous Swedish town of Vällingby, for example, is actually five settlements, each one centered on one station of a subway line to downtown Stockholm. In this respect, Swedish development incorporates some of the conceptual ideas put forward by the Spaniard, Soria y Mata, who argued that urban settlement should be planned in linear fashion along lines of fast transportation, thus contributing to efficiency of travel and allowing easy contact with areas left in their natural or agricultural conditions within close reach of the single line of urban development.[6]

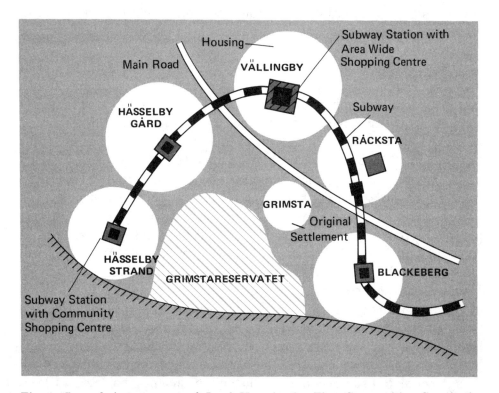

Fig. 1. General Arrangement of Land Uses in the Five Communities Constituting Greater Vällingby, Sweden. (Source: Adapted from Åsvärn 1966, p. 17.)

While an exact equivalent of the neighborhood unit plan was not attempted, the Vällingby development had its own clear-cut conceptual framework [Asvarn 1966]. Each community had a center for local shopping, service, and recreation needs largely surrounding the subway sta-

---

6. For a discussion of this and other concepts of urban form, see Goodman and Goodman [1960].

tion, in a plaza in the center. Then, housing for approximately the number of people thought necessary to support these land uses was sited in relatively low-density settings within walking distance of the station, in a concentric pattern. In practice, this amounted to approximately 10,000 people, living within about 300 yards of each station and plaza.

The five communities did not run into each other physically, as natural surroundings were allowed to remain as a minor green belt around each community. Yet, the five communities were grouped as a family by the placement of those services that demanded more clients than single communities could support into the center of Vällingby, the middle community of the row of five (the other four being Hässelby Strand, Hässelby Gård, Råcksta, and Blakeberg). This arrangement is illustrated in figure 1.

More recent developments in the Stockholm area, such as Farsta and Kärholmen, have tried to group larger numbers of people around larger centers, foregoing lower residential densities in favor of easier access to a wider range of commercial and recreational opportunities, much as was the idea in British Mark II new towns. This has generally been regarded as not as satisfactory with respect to residents' quality of life, although perhaps more practical economically. In any case, even more recent developments have seen building in greater Stockholm following somewhat along the lines of the British Mark III new towns, providing even lower densities and more flexible movement patterns. It must be kept in mind, however, that these concepts have been tried, in the Swedish case, on suburban satellites, rather than on relatively removed, independent entities.

In the United States, there are at present over one hundred new towns under construction, although what constitutes a new town has not been rationalized either by practice or by authoritative public policy. Virtually all new town construction has been under private auspices, although not all has succeeded in producing the earnings expected, at least in the short run.

The neighborhood unit plan was actually written into its most concrete form in America, when Clarence Perry, under contract to a private organization called the New York Regional Plan Association, wrote a volume in 1927 proposing this concept as the major one required for orderly metropolitan growth in that area [1966 ed.]. Shortly afterward, an association was organized to build a new town in what is now part of Fairlawn, New Jersey, along the lines of Welwyn, situated with regard to New York City as Welwyn is to London. While the early stages of this community, Radburn, are still available for inspection (and in fact are highly valued by residents and potential residents because of the clever ways in which people are separated from motor vehicles while situated near green spaces), this enterprise was curtailed by the onset of the Depression, and it never became either large or balanced as was anticipated. During this period, the community of Sunnyside, in Queens, New York, a less independent suburb but one that followed British microscopic planning principles, was completed. It proved most successful. In this tradition Clarence Stein wrote a classic book, *Towards New Towns for America* [1951].

The United States government built two new towns of modest size, keyed to government job needs in Maryland and Wisconsin, calling them Greenbelt and Greendale.

Following World War II, most activity was channeled into the construction of new suburban areas. While much of the national development effort consisted of relatively uncoordinated small developments, located all over the map, wherever developers could purchase available land (a phenomenon referred to as suburban sprawl), some development could be appropriately referred to as new town planning. In 1946, Levitt and Sons, a New York development corporation, built a city for about 100,000 people, all living in single-family homes, arranged strictly according to the principles of the neighborhood unit plan and with a major shopping center for the use of people in all neighborhoods. Levitt, through his several subsequent "Levittowns," represented a major break in traditional building patterns, inasmuch as homes were mass-produced, constructed in a carefully choreographed, logical sequence, and sold in a package with complete landscaping, appliances, and legal fees included in already low prices. Contrary to initial predictions, the owners of these mass-produced homes took good care of them, and the planned community generally seemed to receive good marks from its occupants.[7]

Much to his credit, the developer constructed the major community facilities he felt were necessary, such as schools and swimming pools, with the same economics of scale, presenting them to the local communities at the time new residents arrived, rather than forcing calamitous and expensive construction thereafter. He also reserved prime land for

---

7. For a penetrating analysis of Levittown, New Jersey, showing how it successfully met most resident needs while at the same time receiving criticism directed to most such developments, see Gans [1967].

churches. He reportedly made little money on the sale of houses, but reaped considerable economic benefits from continued ownership of the shopping facilities in his community.

Equivalent communities were built outside several other large American cities, such as Chicago and San Francisco.

In the years following the initial Levittowns, the price of suburban land escalated appreciably, and it became more difficult for building corporations such as Levitt and Sons to assemble the land necessary to build such new communities ensuite. They turned instead to smaller developments where the price of housing rose somewhat to match the higher cost of land (a correlation carefully followed by the real estate sector).

The construction of new towns was taken up instead by very much larger investment corporations, attempting to build communities stressing quality of environment rather than the satisfaction of a housing shortage. These towns were also to be economically balanced, in contrast to the Levittowns, which were exclusively satellites. While these large corporations usually acknowledged the desirability of balancing the communities socially and racially as well, they were above all to earn money for the investors, including such organizations as Goodyear, Westinghouse, Gulf Oil, and ITT.

Two of the better known of these communities are Reston, Virginia, and Columbia, Maryland, both in the Washington, D.C. area. Reston was built on the premise that building in the United States had ignored environmental and aesthetic values, not to speak of other aspects normally enhanced by planning. Hence the developers isolated an attractive rural area about 25 miles from the center of Washington, with many trees and a varied topography. They designed a town consisting of seven villages and town centers. There were also to be two industrial areas that would provide employment for local residents. All of the homes were designed by famous architects, whether multiple units or single, detached units. The developers felt that there were surely 24,000 families in the Washington area who would appreciate what Reston offered that other suburbs did not, and who, as a result, would be willing to pay the rather steep cost of housing developed with such inordinate care.

No one seriously quibbles with Reston's beauty. But in the crucial years after the developers of Reston had bought the land and committed their capital to construction, fewer residents appeared than had been anticipated, and the investors, Gulf Oil, were forced to take over active managerial control of the later development of this town, illustrating the crucial importance in the development of American new towns of profits or losses on private investment.

One general problem associated with new town planning in America is that these investors feel they must maintain control over town development until very late stages in the process of city growth, lest changes be made that would hurt their very real position with respect to their town. Ordinary residents of these towns may wish greater control over what happens to their communities, in true democratic civic tradition, but their wishes may conflict with the strong interests of these developers. Normally, there are tensions between town residents and town developers at about the middle stages of town development, perhaps like adolescents within a family [cf. Whyte 1956].

Columbia, Maryland represents a somewhat different emphasis. From the beginning, the developers, the Rouse Corporation, called in a number of experts in social science for counsel about the most desirable emphases both in housing and in land-use arrangement in the proposed new town. Armed with these recommendations, considerable care was taken to provide for a complex hierarchy of centers, ranging from neighborhood centers with 7–11 grocery stores, snack bars, meeting rooms, and other facilities, to village centers emphasizing normal weekly shopping needs, and large-scale recreational facilities, to a major regional shopping center. Great efforts were also made for the provision of organizational life in the community, and housing was designed to be friendly and inviting, rather than imposing. Some effort was made as well to secure housing for disadvantaged minorities within the community through a government aid program. Indirect suggestions were made that while it might be one's "duty" to live in Reston, it would be fun to live in Columbia.

Columbia represents an answer to another type of problem facing American new towns. Since these towns are developed privately, there is no formal relationship necessary between developers of new towns and the governments of preexisting municipalities. New towns seldom coincide with the boundaries of existing municipalities. In some cases, a whole new town will occupy only part of an existing jurisdiction, usually rural and governed on the country level. In other cases, it might be spread over several jurisdictions. This matters to a new town developer, since the existing population (i.e., those who have not sold to the developer) is seldom sympathetic and may try to block either the development as a whole, or some of the innovations the developer hopes to introduce.

When a development is spread over several municipalities, diverse constraints may be put on the very same community, and different political and fiscal policies may affect different parts of the very same new development. Typically, disputes break out between the existing residents, who are likely to be older, without young children, and interested in the maintenance of low taxes, and the newcomers, with growing young families and the desire to impose civilization where they presume it is lacking.

What Rouse did in Columbia was to locate his entire planned development within a single county, and then, before construction, to persuade the county fathers that his plan was the only desirable future alternative for the county, gaining their cooperation and their assistance in the legalities of uniform city building.

The general problem of building innovative, workable communities in political jurisdictions with existing, usually old, zoning and other regulations resulted in a recent American plan, implemented by a number of states, called "Planned Unit Development" (or PUD). This acknowledges that it may be fruitful, in order to attain modern, well-designed housing and new, revenue-producing commercial and industrial land uses, to ignore existing land-use regulations and, hence, the costly and slow process of becoming exceptions to them. Under the PUD program, a developer will present a firm proposal for both housing and other land uses to a local political jurisdiction. If they are convinced that the proposal is both economically and socially beneficial, they may give the one and only approval necessary for the developer to proceed to completion. The latter, on his part, is required, then, to complete the whole development within about four-to-eight years, producing definite and speedy results [Burchell 1972; U.S. Department of Housing and Urban Development 1970].

While new towns in America differ widely from one another, they have been the scene of some use of a more recently articulated planning concept—the *cluster concept* [Whyte 1967]. Really harking back to Howard's idea of the garden city, the cluster concept suggests that if individual housing units are clustered next to one another, very much more space is made available for parks, playgrounds, sports facilities, and other amenities for which common land is necessary. When individual entrepreneurs built small numbers of homes without reference to any overall urban plan, there was really little way that they could provide for such common acreage. People, in any case, seem to insist on as much land around their own homes and under their own care as possible. Many people, however, consider that dividing all the available land among individual resident families is not only wasteful, but ultimately less than desirable. While the cluster concept does not necessarily call for the abolition of all privately controlled open space, as some family functions such as infant care, gardening, and many forms of lounging and small-scale sport are feasible only in private open space, it does strongly urge a balance between private and public open space, to allow the benefits of both. And this is ultimately arranged most feasibly when the planning of large areas of residential settlement is carried out in a comprehensive fashion, as happened in new town planning.

Although only several of the American new towns have been mentioned, the more than 100 under construction are located in all corners of the United States, and they range in size from suburbs of several thousand families to one planned by ITT in Florida of 600,000 residents. New town planning has also proceeded apace within Canada, with mineral exploitation cities such as Elliott Lake and Kitimat in remote regions coexisting with relatively balanced suburban settlements under private auspices, such as Don Mills and Erin Mills near Toronto and Nun's Island outside Montreal; with government-supported satellites such as Malvern near Toronto and Saltfleet near Hamilton; and with newly proposed balanced cities of around 200,000, such as the Ontario government proposes to build in North Pickering, Ontario.

Public evaluations of American new towns have been generally favorable, although it has yet to be proved that a wide cross-section of the population has been carried away by enthusiasm. Some studies have indicated, however, that the primary benefits that residents see in such overall planning represent only a very small sample of those intended by planners.

A team from the University of Michigan, for example, discovered that residents of several eastern planned communities were in fact happier with their communities than residents of comparable unplanned suburban communities. It was true that the new town residents were more highly educated than their counterparts and they had paid more money for their new homes, perhaps leading them to feel obligated to express satisfaction; nonetheless, this satisfaction was made evident in interviews with them. Specifically, the reasons they cited for their satisfaction at the neighborhood scale centered on its level of maintenance. At the community scale, they were most pleased with their accessibility to their jobs and to local facilities [Lansing, Marans, & Zehner 1970; Zehner 1971]. While planners would undoubtedly be pleased that these objectives were successfully fulfilled, the extent to which people notice or tend to appreciate other intentions in new town planning is open to discussion.

In a somewhat earlier study of new California communities, the single aspect of planning clearly appreciated by residents of planned communities was certainty in predicting future land-use trends. One could be certain in his planned community that a gas station or glue factory would not be built across the street from a dream home, nor would the view from the veranda be blocked by a smoke stack [Werthman, Mandel, & Dienstfray 1965].

Some of the major complaints parallel complaints in English communities, concerning the boredom of early new communities. When young children grow into teenagers, for example, it is difficult to meet other young people, or do anything interesting without the need to travel a considerable distance, placing great pressure in the American scene on the acquisition of "wheels," legally or illegally. Housewives stuck at home without a second car, or even with one and the need then to use it, have parallel problems, though their expression is different.

Since later American new towns were built for corporate profit-making, requiring relatively affluent resident populations on the whole, the major solution to the problem may be appropriate. Home owner groups are formed, with annual dues, to build and run nonprofit-making recreational facilities. Membership in such groups is either mandatory for all residents or else semimandatory (as the basis for getting any benefit out of the desired new environment). Of course, when home owners are charged with the task of building and organizing their own facilities, those facilities chosen are likely to represent a basic common denominator of enjoyment, rather than the solution to social needs on the part of restricted segments of the population, such as health centers, day-care centers, and the like. While developers continue to control the profit-making areas of town, people and/or local governments are left to their own devices for nonprofit-making facilities, benefitting only from such tax support as they can manage to win (a very roundabout and partial way of realizing the profits made in their community).

While this division in the control of community facilities may not be a calamity among affluent people willing and able to support their own local, nonprofit-making facilities, it is much more problematic when contemplating planned communities for poorer people. In this case, people are simply unable to pay for these facilities themselves (indeed, these are usually cases where the cost of their housing is already subsidized), while at the same time municipalities are reluctant to support any semblance of the needed recreational or social facilities. When provided at all, their extent is normally only a fraction of that actually required. Yet, at the same time, in line with "acceptable" practice, the planned commercial areas are handed over to commercial developers who realize continued profits, without the burden of supporting the complementary, profitless activities. More consideration might be given to the "Robin Hood" principle present, in theory at least, in British new towns.

The second major problem in American new towns is that, with predominant.y private initiative and its understandable profit motive, little housing has been provided for poor people. The Lee County Rural New Town, a black cooperative in the southern United States, is a clear exception to the usual emphasis on building for affluent populations. Most new towns must be profitable, and this requires that the developers receive market values for their creations. The market value of new housing is currently so high that poor people simply cannot afford them without substantial subsidy. While new towns that are tightly controlled and/or subsidized by levels of government are certainly possible (for example, one variation of this theme has taken place in Ontario), it has certainly not been the rule up to this time in North America. What social integration has taken place has been on a very small scale, and it has in no way been an integral element in the life of the new towns. If the new town were to become a major instrument of housing for the poor, different forms of initiative and rationale for this initiative would have to appear.

One hint of this possible reorientation is the introduction of the so-called *new town in town* [Perloff 1966]. This refers to the placement of a large balanced community of people on land near the center of existing cities, large tracts assembled because their existing use was archaic (for example, downtown railway yards, penal institutions, etc.) or otherwise newly found. New towns in such locations are claimed as ideal for poorer people, due to their proximity to already established transportation lines, community services, and jobs in the central city. At least two projects along this line have already been initiated, in Minneapolis (Cedar-Riverside) and in New York (Welfare Island). Although these communities are in no way removed from the existing metropolis in distance (although the East River helps in New York's case), their large size leads to their designation as "new towns." Since this concept is, in any case, viewed in public favor, its assignment in this situation does not hurt the effort.

According to one's point of view, the construction of suburban satellites and new towns in town are more relevant for the American scene than the construction of new towns built according to the British policy of considerable distance between the new town and existing large cities. Alonso [1970] claims that American growth has occurred dramatically in major cities for reasons having to do with the economics of scale inherent in the metropolis. This would prevent major decentralization of jobs to possible new towns, particularly those suitable to poorer people needing both jobs and housing most drastically. Any new towns that Americans could build in the traditional sense would be highly unlikely to have much effect on the total needs they might be expected to meet. Alonso states that even in Britain only 1 percent of the population lived in new towns after 20 years of explicit national new town construction.

What he would rather see are specific policies to match people and jobs, to break up exclusionary suburban bylaws, and to deal with pollution and other pressing matters. To Alonso, the major benefit one might expect from new towns in America is *experimentation* in town building, something not as readily available elsewhere. In this regard, it is worth noting that one major American new town, in Minnesota, is planned expressly as an experiment.

Hence, our enthusiasm about the successes of new towns, even in the face of the specific problems mentioned, is tempered by Alonso's caution that "even if new towns turned out to be wonderful places, this would be almost irrelevant to our present urban problems, and that as sirens of Utopia they might distract us from our path" [p. 54].

One more general comment on new town planning must be noted. The essence of new towns is that they are planned comprehensively and settled over a shorter period of time than were existing cities, which continue to grow in increments. The challenge in their design is to produce a city that will immediately accommodate the needs of large numbers of residents. Living, of course, is more than bed, board, and job. It is recreation, commerce, citizenship, and much more. All of these various functions must be physically situated in some relation to people's places of residence so that they can be reached sufficiently easily. Planning for living is something very different than planning for sleeping. To turn a phrase, a dwelling unit is not necessarily a home.

In the existing large cities, many parts of town we have come to appreciate have been established incrementally over a long period of time, as population needs have been observed by large and small entrepreneurs. Such neighborhoods reach their current condition in a long evolutionary process, and they continue to change as people in their neighborhoods change. We frequently refer to this process as "organic" growth, a luxury not possible when large numbers of newcomers or underhoused persons require housing in short order.

The new town by definition does not have the benefit of organic growth in its life at the time of its inception. Badly managed new towns may have only housing at the outset, although governments have come to recognize the necessity of assuring services from the beginning, sometimes with a subsidy. But if space in a new area is entirely planned, even along the most rational lines, it may *plan out* organic growth in the future. It may *plan in* many real benefits seen to be essential, but it runs the risk of closing the door on the future. The real challenge in new town planning on the microscopic level may lie in not only creating an environment that is satisfactory at the time, but also one that has allowed enough flexibility for future changes (substitutions, additions) so as to approximate the organic growth present in older, unplanned areas.[8]

Other Planning Activities

The major planning activities discussed so far are at the citywide and neighborhood levels. Considerable planning of relevance to cities takes place at a higher scale. Before the Polish and Hungarian new towns were planned in detail, for example, someone had to decide what the pattern of urbanization should be for those nations taken as a whole. National strategies of urbanization are of considerable concern, as nations must decide where they want their growth, whether older cities should be allowed to grow indefinitely, and where national industrial aspirations should be satisfied, with the resulting implications for large numbers of persons in those nations [Rodwin 1970]. In Britain, for example, national urban planning has an honorable history, although in North America, in contrast, relatively little concerted effort has been devoted to this task.

Similarly, cities are part of a regional context since urban areas stand in a symbiotic relationship with small towns and agricultural areas

8. For a brilliantly worded but more technical statement of this basic question, see Alexander [1973]. A very persuasive but theoretically lacking statement of this problem is found in Jacobs. [1961].

even considerable distances from their borders. The channeling of metropolitan growth and the location of large-scale facilities, such as recreation areas, airports, and wilderness areas, not to speak of the maintenance of vital agricultural and mineral resource activities, are a potential
source of considerable planning attention, increasingly so in recent
years.

These larger scale concerns, however, will receive short shrift in
this discussion, as the planning activities involved are relatively less connected with the amelioration of urban problems. Although planners
themselves are hardly a homogeneous bunch at any level of the scale,
national planners and regional planners nonetheless tend to have different enough backgrounds and orientations that a report on their activities would take one or two additional units, however crucial their work.

Nonetheless, if we focus our attention on city and community planning, we discover that planners by no means devote their time exclusively to the three specific types of planning discussed above. A recent survey of planners, for example, indicated that while the three most intensive uses of the time of planners are zoning, comprehensive planning,
and the technical studies that go into comprehensive planning, planners
also perform a number of other tasks requiring much time and effort
[Wright 1970]. For example, cities generally have 6-year capital improvement budgets. Every year, they look ahead 6 years toward what
their needs will be with respect to construction and repair of public facilities. This enables the next budget to reflect activities scheduled for the
next 5 years, so that their progression will be logical and orderly. Each
year activities are reviewed, possibly rearranged, and inevitably brought
closer to the present. Planning advice and studies are important in making good decisions about capital improvements.

Street and highway location occupies a considerable part of the time
of planners. Although this is but one aspect of city structure, it is certainly an important one and one on which the public places considerable
attention. Federal highway trust funds in the United States have been
earmarked in part for research on transportation planning (traditionally
spelled highway planning). Transportation studies have been among the
most sophisticated within the planning field, due in no small way to the
generous level of funding behind them. Consequently, many planners
specialize in transportation, and much time is spent on pragmatic questions of street and highway locations. Urban renewal and public housing
then fall at the bottom of the list, in terms of the time planners spend
on them.

These findings tend to suggest that although some of the main planning activities, which justify the field in most people's minds, have led to limited results, dubious results, or no results at all, planners nonetheless fill a number of useful pragmatic roles. In fact, the proliferation of federal, state and provincial, and local programs makes the need for planners greater all the time. As both the preceding and the following discussions indicate, planners may not have overwhelming influence in either the final formulation or the implementation of these plans or programs, but their technical input is essential to these programs. Someone, for example, has to have the technical expertise to put together a physical plan, even if the plan is destined to sit on the shelf; frequently, the existence of a plan is simply a necessary qualification for a city to receive a grant from a higher level of government. In other cases, applications for grants-in-aid, whether to build schools, old age homes, public housing, or day nurseries require specific information that a planner is the best-equipped person to deliver, even if the product of his efforts is not necessarily a community plan. At other times, the routine management of a city, whether for budgeting or for the operation of normal facilities, such as transit or sewage, requires the continued and expert contribution of the planner. These activities are unsung, but they contribute to the current strength of the profession, even if they are, ironically, not the factors that might attract great numbers of idealistic people to the profession. The strain between the ideal and the actual within planning offices, and within the profession more generally, is a modern fact of life.

Planning is also a lucrative business. While many municipalities may require the services of a planner in the context of their daily business and in their relationships with other levels of government, not all of them are financially able or willing to hire their own full-time staff. Large business and industrial organizations are also ready clients for planning expertise, as they must plan their own futures in and around urban areas. Only about 60 percent of planners in the United States and Canada work in official planning agencies [Hodge 1968]. The rest are employed within universities (teaching new planners, doing research, and engaging in consultation) or in private consultation. While the provision of planning expertise on a consultation basis is suitably flexible for the client and frequently fruitful for the consultants, who are not bound permanently to a single bureaucracy of nonplanners and who can earn what the market will bear, there is nonetheless an inherent danger to the client in getting his planning advice from an outsider. The outsider

may simply not have the time or desire to understand the client's idiosyncratic planning context, and may produce a product ill-suited to the
client's real needs. At the worst, some consultants cheerfully sell the
same master plan to all municipal clients requiring them, with virtually
only the names changed. On the other hand, at their best, consultants
produce the very most appropriate and innovative suggestions, through
economic incentives and wider ranging bases of experience than within
a single bureaucracy.

In any case, planning products are diverse, certainly greater than
the production of plans, however important and stimulating the latter.
Let us now turn to the intellectual and methodological end of planning.

THE PROCESS

Planning has undergone a metamorphosis intellectually and methodologically. The closer one comes to the present in this and analogous fields,
the more diverse and complex is the picture, for older approaches remain
as a residue, joined but not totally abolished by more modern ways of
thinking and acting. It is sometimes difficult to banish earlier assumptions and approaches from the mind, and all previous wisdom does not
automatically turn into idiocy with time.

Therefore, while I shall enumerate what I see as the major trends
in the planning process over time in apparently simple, serial form, one
must remember that the presence of new ideas and methods by no
means automatically implies that a majority in the field take that or any
other single approach.

The Legacy of Architecture and Reform

Most early planners either were architects or nondesigners applying the
principles of civic reform to the structure and growth of the city.

Carried over from traditional architectural practices were several
intellectual and methodological approaches. The architect was seen as
a dynamic, creative individual, assessing the needs his design was to
fit, and then, alone, creating a unique solution that, at the same time,
would be aesthetically superior. While architects work within broad
styles of tradition, the intellectual emphasis had been upon the architect's personal ability to invent appropriate solutions to the problems

posed. Scientific values on experimentation and the accumulation of verified knowledge were not a part of this tradition, other than with respect
to engineering aspects.

When the architect worked for an individual client, he would take
great care to spend time with him, to learn as much as possible of what
his client was like, and what his client wanted from the new building.
The assessment of what architects call "user needs" was done on a one-
to-one basis. However, there was no formal mechanism, beyond personal
communication, for the architect to learn after construction whether the
user was pleased or displeased with the architect's "solution" to his
needs.

However, the one-to-one relationship disappeared by definition
when architects started to plan for larger aggregates of people. While
both architects and the public assumed that the former took the needs
of the latter into consideration, communication, at best, became indirect,
mediated by third persons, those who commissioned or sponsored the
designs or plans on behalf of the actual users.

While today's architects have adopted a number of mechanisms in
an attempt to overcome blocked communication with their clients, this
was not the case when architects first turned their attention to community and city planning. It is no wonder, then, that the City Beautiful
Movement was primarily an aesthetic movement. While there is no question but that design-oriented city planners felt that they were socially
relevant, what they lacked was the specification of a definite process
whereby their actions in the physical realm would have clear and specific
behavioral effects upon those exposed to their plans.

This dynamic causal chain was also missing in the reasoning of the
nondesign-oriented reformers who entered city planning. While rational
universalistic procedures, if applied to the growth of cities, could not
help but make the process of growth less painful (just as the introduction
of the civil service would rationalize city government), it was another
matter to set forth a set of procedures whereby city plans would become
implemented according to both the spirit and the form intended and,
even then, it remained unknown in what ways this would affect the life
of the common man.

The early plans, then, were ingenious intellectual documents based
on people's assumptions as to what would be good for people and for
urban growth, but remote from the way this would actually happen. It
is perhaps this legacy that led to the failure of most plans to be implemented (at the least, their framers seldom had a strategy to ensure later

implementation) and that brought forward the need for great changes in the later application of those types of plans which were implemented.

Value-free Empiricism

Into this situation stepped science. As suggested earlier, the onset of the New Deal in the United States brought forward the application of scientific principles to large-scale problems of urban and social development.

An early attempt to introduce objective criteria about human welfare into city planning was the utilization of *standards* devised by organizations such as the American Public Health Association. These had to do with the amount of exposure to precious resources, such as light and air, which might be necessary for the individual dwelling unit on grounds of health. They had to do with the density of persons who might be expected to live decently both within individual dwelling units and also in the same buildings, plots, and neighborhoods. They had to do with the number and size of parks that *had* to be provided for every 1,000 inhabitants.

The derivation of these standards is not entirely clear. To some extent they are based on practices considered good in the judgement of people at the time the standards were made. To some extent they are based on the observation of situations exhibiting clearly negative consequences. Yet, the clarity of numbers, against which new plans could be measured, was an important step in taking planning out of the realm of good intentions by beneficent people.

Planners increasingly came to the conclusion, however, that such standards had to be supplemented in large part by their own careful studies of the particular circumstances and prospects of the cities for which they were making comprehensive plans. Hence, a thorough-going planning process took shape in which planners would inventory the initial status of their city, make projections about the future, assess the goals of the citizens, and then decide what would have to be done to account for all of these variables in optimal fashion. Due to the need for a planning study to investigate so much so carefully, and due to the necessity of figuring out *how* to get from here to there after discovering the characteristics of "there," plans were normally based on a future 20 to 30 years ahead, the realism of which could only be assessed as time passed and once the plan was formulated. Plans thus were conceived as flexible and open to evolutionary change consistently through time, however carefully specified at the outset.

The planning process was conceived roughly as follows [cf. International City Managers Association 1941; Chapin 1957]:

Goals

The goals for planning operations could come from many sources. Planners were cautioned to start by thoroughly understanding the past development of the city, as these held cues to action. Goals were imposed on the one hand by elected political representatives, and on the other hand by the planning profession itself, which had adopted certain notions as to generally desirable practices. Particularly relevant as goals were explicit standards, such as those described above, as well as those from such other organizations as the National Recreation Association, the National Board of Realtors, and other commercial, civil rights, and interest groups. The goals of individuals in the area were also thought relevant, but these were usually easier to assess by suggestion (usually by established leaders or those with strong economic positions) than to discover directly.

While these goals were usually made explicit in the first section of the eventual plan, they were not always as explicit at the beginning of the planning process, contributing to less than optimal focus during the time in which planning occurred.

Inventories of the Status Quo

In any planning activity, it is essential to know the nature of the beast under consideration. Characteristics of the current economy, employment, and population, must be known. Maps must be drawn of the physical properties of the area, property ownership lines, and location of all structures. A land-use survey must be made simply to find out the current distribution of uses of land, with particular attention to vacant land and its characteristics.

Evaluation of both structures and the more macroscopic environment may require yet more surveys, and such evaluation must take into account the goals articulated for the plan.

Still additional studies must be made to determine the costs of municipal services and who is bearing them, the variation of land values, and the presence or absence of aesthetically important sites.

Studies of the transportation network are particularly important. Roads, railroads, and other types of transportation not only fill a demand, but create one as well. Both people and goods require efficient transportation, and, if permitted by legal strictures, both will locate near the most satisfactory network compatible with their other needs, regardless of the fact that an area had not been settled prior to the establishment of new transportation facilities. It must always be questioned whether projected changes should be a function of current demands or future desires, as it is highly likely that whatever pattern of settlement the system is designed to meet will be cemented by it. But in any case, it is highly important to know the nature of the current system and the use given it.

Studies of the Future

One series of studies would project the socioeconomic characteristics of cities at the specified future date. Economic studies, for example, were conducted in a number of different ways, from the sophisticated input-output analysis attempting to estimate eventual repercussions of certain assumed policies, events, or trends on specific industries and institutions, to the economic base approach that measures projected shifts in the more general categories of occupation. Related, but separate predictions were considered necessary concerning the extent and distribution of employment and concerning such characteristics of the population as age, sex, size of family, and, not least, total numbers.

Given the socioeconomic forecasts, it was then necessary to project what future needs would be in both the required amounts and qualitative nature of residential dwellings, commercial and industrial structures, municipal services and open space.

Making the Plan

Having in hand knowledge of municipal goals, hard facts on the present, and scientific predictions of the future, planners could then make their plans. Such a plan would in no way differ from the status quo situation in the unlikely event that the studies conducted were ever to demonstrate the following situation: 1. Current land use and municipal services meet every standard set for the present and projected future. 2. No changes in economy, employment, or population are foreseen. 3. The present transportation network is adequate and thought to remain so despite any impending technological innovations. 4. The city's residents are not opposed to the current situation.

Since this ideal is almost inevitably lacking, plans are then to be drawn up. Greatly simplified, it is necessary to decide how much more or less land is needed for any particular land use in the future than is used at present, specifying just which locations should be reserved for which uses, specifying the fiscal arrangements under which this could be carried out, and detailing the transportation network that would both serve it and insure the other aspects of the plan.

Where the amount of land, money, or flexibility simply do not permit satisfying all criteria, it is necessary to order goals according to explicit priorities.

Programming

Once a plan had been drawn, the next step would be to outline the order in which its provisions should be carried out. Successive steps assume each other, and their logical order is important in the plan; since major projects may involve many forms of preparation, such as site clearance, work is clearly expedited by their anticipation. Such "programming" is also essential to the rational handling of costs, and must be drawn up with costs in mind. The advance budgeting procedures discussed earlier are no less relevant to the implementation of comprehensive plans than to city management in general.

Implementation

There are at least two steps to implementation. The first is "selling" the plan. Before it can have any force or effect, it must be accepted and adopted. It took many years before planners realized that the same degree of conscientious effort that was put into the creation of plans was also necessary to communicate them to other people and to help the latter understand and appreciate the product of their efforts. Even then, as the next section will indicate, there is no guarantee of acceptance. This part of the process is potentially open to empirical study from a sociopolitical perspective; it is entirely possible, and in many cases desirable, for planners to study the structure and functioning of those organizations and groups of people who have to adopt and later implement their plan. But this was not part of the scientific effort that accompanied the bulk of work going into the comprehensive plan.

Still necessary, though, even beyond adoption of the plan, is its practical implementation. Such measures as zoning and the distribution of development and building permits are the ones that essentially decide whether a plan will have any effect or not. Yet these are normally administered by bodies independent of planning authorities. As a result, planners must prepare documents introducing their products to other regulatory bodies if they expect the latter to cooperate fully in implementing the comprehensive plan.

While the general steps of the process of comprehensive planning have remained more or less the same since the onset of the scientific approach to comprehensive planning, what has changed dramatically has been the methodological inputs to the various steps. Very much more effort from a social science perspective is being placed on the steps of goal formulation and plan implementation. Very much more sophisticated techniques, utilizing the computer and mathematical simulation of reality, have been introduced to the steps of projection and plan formulation, with a recent emphasis on the creation of alternative plans and some assessment of the consequences potentially accompanying the adoption of the various alternatives [e.g., McLoughlin 1969].

Even in its heyday, comprehensive planning had its outspoken critics. They felt that the scientific aura surrounding this operation disguised some overwhelming obstacles to the success of comprehensive planning. They felt that the long-range projections were based on essentially unverifiable assumptions. Both technology and society are changing so quickly, they argued, that it is folly to make plans based on a future very likely to be different from our assumptions of it. On the other hand, we know what our problems are now and should concentrate on taking steps to ameliorate these real, pressing problems. They argued also that the structure of politics makes it much more realistic to expect support for plans that attack specific pragmatic problems, rather than a remote and diffuse set of needs. They felt the future should be approached step-by-step as it arises, rather than with such intensive effort to reach a goal state likely to change.

This opposite approach, highly pragmatic and down to earth in its character, was called "incrementalism." Planning according to the incremental approach was concerned with creating the physical solutions for the here and now, rather than with getting from here to there. The foremost practical exponent of this approach was Robert Moses, who, in the New York City area was responsible for enormous feats of civic engineering, in the construction of numbers of transportation facilities, long praised for their innovative content (as well as for the fact that Moses simply managed to get them done so quickly and so dramatically) and now condemned because of the long-range consequences these "solutions" are having for New York City (i.e., traffic strangulation and urban sprawl).

Nonetheless, if one were to characterize the planning process from the 1930s through the 1950s, it would be in terms of comprehensive planning, based on what was presumed to be value-free empirical research.

Pragmatism: Decentralization and Citizen Participation

Urban renewal assumed conprehensive planning. It also assumed that specific neighborhood conditions required "dynamite" force if they were ever to change. Required change at the neighborhood level had to be consistent with the urban long-range growth plan.

Other forces tended to shift interest away from a fixation on the comprehensive and in the direction of specific problems in local areas. Politicians, for example, traditionally had difficulty in understanding the practice of comprehensive planning. For one thing, they did not share the background, training, and assumptions of professionally trained city planners, and the plans created thus were not always intelligible to them; in addition, they did not always see how plans solved immediate problems. Second, since political leaders tended to be reelected for short terms, evaluated on what they did in the short run, their interests were not well-served by plans whose effects could be imperceptible at any given point in time. Immediate problems that went unsolved, even at the same time that long-range plans were in preparation, created untenable situations for local political leaders. Partly in order to narrow this gap, planners began to adopt the notion of "middle-range planning," in which political leaders supplied goals for action and planners supplied the physical means to achieve these goals. The middle range applied generally to neighborhood applications.

In addition, planners began to see that their long-range assumptions and predictions were simply not on solid ground, given the many changes and upheavals occurring in accelerated fashion. The extent of adoption and use of the private automobile, for example, was seldom, if ever, gauged accurately, nor were the events in the fall of 1973 that heralded the end of an age of promiscuous use of the automobile. Planners even began to notice that societal values, one of the most basic elements in long-range plan formulation, were subject to change. The most basic premise in a long-range plan might become untenable even at the time that a plan was finally realized [Dakin 1973].

The public also tended to focus the activity of planners onto more local and pragmatic situations. Urban renewal, highway planning, and other planning practices presented problems people did not have prior to "successful" (i.e., implemented) urban planning. There were at least two results. From the Model Cities program onward, plans had to be made, as stated earlier, with the "maximum feasible participation" of the populations involved. Results had to be demonstrably clear, both to the ordinary person, whose hopes were pinned upon such programs, and to politicians, who hoped for positive feedback within election cycles. To fulfill these requirements, planning became very much more a process of working with people on questions of their general well-being, as compared to the spatial arrangement of bricks and roads; and the focus of planning effort turned to pragmatic changes in small areas within shorter time frames.

Decentralization in planning began to occur on two fronts. First, in facing the responsibility of producing sensitive and beneficial action for the people resident in local areas, planners had to be very much more knowledgeable about the residents and the physical details of specific neighborhoods. The planners' time-tested "windshield survey," assessing the characteristics of an area while driving through it slowly in an automobile, was now grossly inadequate. Planning heads, where able, began to assign full-time responsiblity for individual neighborhoods to specific members of their planning staffs.

Second, once residents began to make an input of their own about the future of their neighborhoods, they began to wonder whether the many tasks of urban government should be managed at the neighborhood level, rather than at a more remote, metropolitan or city-wide level. Neighborhood groups argued that they knew their own needs better than the leaders of several million people. They could both determine and articulate their priorities better than an outsider looking on them as one of very many segments of his jurisdiction.

While these arguments are extremely cogent, they do raise some problems for planning and municipal management. Many urban services are grossly inefficient unless procured and coordinated at a high level. Second, what is good for a local community may on occasion be disastrous for the rest of the city, just as what is good for the rest of the city may on occasion be disastrous to a local area. Planning decisions somehow have to maximize the greatest good for the greatest number, without, on the other hand, seriously endangering the rights of minorities. Third, since tax money is not raised exclusively on a neighborhood basis and then allocated directly to those neighborhoods, at the very least, since residential neighborhoods normally require more in tax-supported city services than they themselves produce in tax revenue, bodies larger than local neighborhood groups must sit in judgement on expenditures from the public purse. Observers have also pointed out that decisions made within neighborhoods are not necessarily more democratic or broad-based than decisions made at higher levels, but this is a question that will receive further attention in this unit.

Planning now has advanced to the point where there are clear tensions to be reconciled from strongly articulated local desires and from diffuse, more comprehensive considerations. Logic, of course, calls for the reconciliation of differential demands according to some fair middle ground, but when people finally become involved in a position, this is easier said than done. While the most attention has been focused on this phenomenon with respect to school decentralization, the same issue is relevant to city-planning phenomena more generally.

Faced with the explicit need to account for the welfare of identifiable groups of people, planners have adopted many strategies.

An early strategy, consistent with the scientific approach of comprehensive planning, is the empirical study of people in areas to be planned. A basic assumption of this approach is that planners are needed to plan *for* people but require good information about their clients—the lives of these people, their social and economic characteristics, and their opinions. It is assumed that the most efficient way to represent the needs and desires of the population is to survey them with questions providing exactly and only that information that the planner believes relevant, so that the latter can merge it with his own planning experience, expected to be more broadly inclusive and more flexibly relevant to the situation than whatever limited knowledge of planning practice may be held by the clients themselves.

In fact, much extremely helpful information can be gathered in this and in no other way, since the findings of good empirical studies are transmittable evidence from which generalizations can be made. A planning group, for example, from Harvard and M.I.T. were planning a new city, Ciudad Guayana, Venezuela. After three years' effort, they were still not certain as to whether or not they were serving the needs of their target population. Their answer to this problem was to conduct a survey that emphasized perception and indicated under what circumstances some of the newly planned sections of the city were in fact being used as intended [Appleyard 1968]. Other studies may be done in advance of the formulation of plans, to use as a basis for their formulation.

Many planners have come to feel, however, that such studies, while of potential interest and value are not sufficient. These studies may either assume or ignore whatever priorities people hold. Furthermore, a careful study of people's habits and desires may not be adequately indicative either of the practical design or social problems that have to be resolved, or of the constraints surrounding their solution. Another approach, then, to citizen participation is to hold preliminary meetings in neighborhoods to be effected by plans, in advance of plan formulation. These are designed to ascertain public viewpoints and priorities.

The dangers in this approach reflect the difficulty in attracting previously uninterested people to attend such meetings, the possibility of selected attendance along lines such as education or economic interests, the possibility that meetings may be "packed" (that only several among many community views may be represented), and the lack of required follow-up, once planners leave these meetings with the views expressed.

Still another approach, used either alone or in combination with the foregoing one, is the holding of public forums once preliminary plans are formulated, with the intention of receiving opinions and information to either confirm or modify these plans. An early attempt at this process was the creation of a museum exhibit of a proposed plan in Philadelphia (not a neighborhood plan), where citizens viewing proposals, either in person or on television, were invited to respond. In Toronto, specific plans are created with the assistance of public meetings for individual areas of the city, and then hearings are held in various schools within these districts to receive more public opinion.

A more direct approach to citizen participation and planning is to take citizens onto committees directly charged with formulating local plans. This does not necessarily give the citizens ultimate control over the creation of the plans, but it does allow their views to enter the planning context at exactly the time when they can affect the outcome, not after something is on paper that professional personnel may feel prone to defend. In Toronto again, for example, local neighborhood plans now benefit from so-called "working committees," where citizens are selected for participation by local residents' associations.

A final approach, which is receiving considerably more attention over time, is the grant of power to create plans directly to local citizen groups. In this case, professional planners act only as technical advisers in the formulation of plans. While, according to this arrangement, local committees have complete control over the formulation of plans, the extent that external, formal and legal activity is subsequently required of other parties (politicians, planning boards, etc.) for the actual implementation of these plans is extremely variable. An even more recent phenomenon in Toronto is the creation of neighborhood traffic plans by local citizen groups. For example, an area called Moore Park felt threatened by the increasing incidence of heavy traffic on their local residential streets, generated by new commercial development near them. In an effort to keep all through traffic on several arterial roads crossing the area and off residential streets that were previously used as short cuts, they created plans that turned many residential streets into cul de sacs, and introduced additional restrictions on left and right turns during rush hours. The city planning board and city politicians then accepted and implemented the plan that the citizens had made themselves. Reactions to it illustrate the possible divergence of interests between neighborhood groups working on their own behalf and the mood of the greater public. While it would appear that most residents of Moore Park may be satisfied with the consequences of their plan, commuters from other parts of town, including devotees of public transportation operating on main arteries (which gained in traffic), vigorously protested the ability of residents in a single neighborhood to force apparent changes in their commuting habits and/or commuting time. The issue may even become more pronounced, as groups in other centrally located neighborhoods rush to complete their own defensive plans.

Citizen participation thus takes many forms and serves many purposes. Some of them have more effect on plans and their implementation than others. One writer for example, suggests that citizen participation may **1.** provide citizens with education in planning matters, **2.** represent therapy, in draining off their emotions about planning matters,

3. induce change in their use of and attitudes toward local artifacts and spaces, 4. help to supplement planning staff in the completion of necessary planning tasks, 5. co-opt local support for professionally drawn plans, and/or 6. represent a locus of genuine community power [Burke 1968].

A second writer analyzes some of the existing practices and classifies them as 1. actual *non*participation, and hence deceiving, 2. participation representing various degrees of tokenism, in which citizens actually participate but with no requirement that their input be treated seriously, and 3. power and control, where participation ranges from partnership to delegated power to final control [Arnstein 1969].

Now that one or another form of citizen participation is considered a major requirement in the formulation of plans, there is pressure for it to be part of the making of all types of plans. One must note, however, that citizen participation must necessarily take very different forms when planning a totally new area than when "replanning" an existing area. In the former case, the greatest number of eventual clients are not on the spot; in fact, the planner may only be able to guess their identity, unless there are waiting lists available for the housing to be constructed. Meeting with those actually present in the area to be planned may be helpful in accounting for their particular problems and interests, but it may be counterproductive in terms of soliciting information about the plan for the new community, as the characteristics and interests of the newcomers are likely to be different. One approach to participation in this situation is for the planner to form proxy groups—persons with characteristics *similar* to those expected to reside in the new town, who might speak for an otherwise unformed collection of persons. Only after the initial stages of a new community are constructed will there be residents who can speak directly for the community being built.

All of this has greatly changed the process of planning. Even in the most nonparticipatory type of citizen participation, the planner of local areas is forced to act as a broker for citizen needs, whether physical or social. He must deal not only with the people who are affected as recipients of the various facilities and services potentially available within neighborhoods, but with the agencies and organizations providing them. And in the case of social services, there is usually a wide variety of organizations having no necessary contact with one another. Planning, in this context, has turned, in the words of Herbert Gans, "From Urbanism to Policy-Planning" [1970]. According to the editor of a recent review on *The Future of Planning* [Cowan 1973], planning education should increasingly produce personnel skilled in urban management. Planners are producing "plans" much less than before, as their role increasingly turns to the coordination of citizen inputs, with technical directives issued by experts, toward the creation of strategies to solve urban problems for continued public airing. The planner is, then, a middleman working with many other people to produce processes by which problems are solved, rather than single optimum plans.

Ira Robinson summarizes this trend succinctly: "The focus of planning is shifting from the preparation of a single product, the master plan—a single document that presents a tidy blueprint for the sometime future—to a process- and program-oriented activity" [1972, p. 21]. It is "basically a set of procedures for making decisions about the future in accordance with certain established goals. . . " [p. 26].

The intellectual and methodological tools utilized when planning this way diverge from the emphasis on science and the scientific methods that characterized comprehensive planning. While scientific criteria and procedures are no less welcome than before, the main activities of the planner in the planning process are very much more interpersonal, intermediary, and negotiative, than overtly value free and empirical.

Advocacy

Despite this reorientation of planning activity, many planners feel that this still does not represent the public interest adequately. Even if the planner is genuinely concerned with local needs and citizen input, he cannot change the fact that he is employed and paid by a larger organization, whose concern and focus is more comprehensive than the welfare of individual neighborhoods. It is therefore difficult for the planner to give the most effective defense of the plea of his neighborhood area if the nature of his employment requires that he also reconcile this with the more comprehensive and universalistic concerns of his employer. Using the analogy of the legal system, these planners argue that the planner is expected to be both the prosecuter and the defense attorney in presenting a case to the jury. This, it is felt, may not be fair to either side.

These planners also ask why planning practice normally calls for the preparation of only one plan, eventually issued by the official planning organization. In fact, should there not be a variety of preliminary plans drawn by parties with particular interests in the planning of an area before settling on a given plan of attack? If so, the official planning organization should be the source of only one set of preliminary ideas, with the groups directly involved producing their own.

The consequence of such reasoning is the establishment of what has been called "advocacy planning." Planners would work with specific local groups involved in planning decisions or proposed plans, and they would prepare proposals reflecting *exclusively* the opinions and desires of these "clients." These proposals could well be in opposition to other plans already created or in preparation by official planning bodies, but they would represent a professionally adequate "defense" of the interests of these local groups, who previously could not expect to receive the crucial *technical* input of the planner in representing their point of view. It is one thing for a local group to organize and say what they think; it is another thing to have it presented in a way that is as competent technically as the official plan and, hence, credible to others involved in decision-making.

Planners serving in an advocacy capacity normally have to do so either on their own time and at their own expense, or else with a grant from a foundation or (in behalf of local citizen groups) from a higher level of government. Quite apart from normal professional positions in planning, advocacy planning "is basically defined as technical assistance to public and private groups premised on *articulated commitment* to the urban core" [Kaplan 1969, p.101, emphasis supplied].

Those promoting advocacy planning go so far as to suggest that this form of planning should be undertaken even without the necessity of a client. Thus, some planners advocate challenge to and change in suburban plans and regulatory measures so as to open suburban areas more fully to poor people and minority groups. Surely few suburbanites would be clients for such alternatives to existing plans. Advocacy planners in this case speak for an assumed group of people living elsewhere. The requirements of these people for sufficiently numerous and decent housing units are currently being denied [Davidoff, Davidoff, & Gold 1970].

One must stress that advocate planners retain, perhaps even more strongly than conventional planners working with citizen groups, the professionalism of their craft. They are not just middlemen organizing divergent points of view; rather they are persons with specialized skills coming to the assistance of disadvantaged persons in an otherwise technologically complex world.

Nonetheless, the act of advocacy is not an easy one to fulfill for a number of reasons that vary from situation to situation.

First, residents, businessmen, and others with interests in local areas may not be aware of or interested in events that could objectively be shown to be of extremely high relevance to them in the future. Although researchers were easily able, for example, to create an alternative plan for the development of the West End in Boston, which took into account the interests of its residents, it is very unlikely that such a plan would have been successful at the time of redevelopment, because no one could convince the residents at that time that the proposed urban renewal was something to take seriously [Brolin & Zeisel 1968].

Second, local neighborhoods are seldom completely homogeneous, and there is little likelihood that a single group of citizens will faithfully represent all the interests within even that neighborhood, leaving aside completely the interests of the majority in the metropolitan area. It is not unusual for different organizations, each speaking for the neighborhood, to appear in areas facing change as representing residents opposed to change, residents welcoming change (as a way of realizing capital gain in some cases, or changes in the physical and social facade of their areas in others), and local merchants.

The second problem is easier for the advocate planner to solve than the first. Since by definition he defends only one interest, he generally tends to choose that interest his own values support most fully. After all, belief in finding a single scientifically supported truth in city planning declined with the onset of increased focus on short-range, neighborhood-level problems.

The first problem, a lack of community interest or involvement, has been the subject of various remedies, predating the onset of advocacy and planning.

The late Saul Alinsky, for example, made a considerable reputation in forging vigorous activity within neighborhoods for the solution of common problems, through the creation of adversary relationships between local citizens and some other person or group [1969]. He felt that there was no better way of achieving common activity among neighbors than to actively oppose someone or something on a matter of interest. Hence, when called to enhance the force of a local group from the nonprofit, foundation-supported, Chicago-based organization he founded, Alinsky would have to find an emotionally intense problem or else create one. Once the group was large and united in opposition, the job then was to channel their energies into the achievement of common goals. While this procedure has been extremely effective in many circumstances, in fact creating considerable resentment and opposition to it on the part of establishment figures, its major difficulty was continuing the level of community solidarity once the initial problem was settled.

Another approach is to create a rational coalition of existing citizen organizations, representing both well-entrenched and beleaguered interests, by presenting them with reputable goals they may share, and that require common action. This coalition is then channeled to help achieve universally defensible changes for the beleaguered members of the coalition.

Others try to achieve action and unity in local areas through the use of communications devices, such as film. One excellent example of its use was on Fogo Island, Newfoundland, where fishing, the economic base of the community, was falling on hard times. The extension service of Memorial University in Newfoundland, in conjunction with the National Film Board of Canada, interviewed individual residents of the island with the aid of a movie camera. They then played back the results of the various interviews to other individuals, who discovered that many of their ideas and their thoughts of solutions were quite similar. In a situation where people do not in everyday life discuss their problems or solutions, the film medium served as a mode of communication from people to people, until the point was reached where they felt they had enough in common with each other that they could actively work in unison to ameliorate their problems. The consequence on Fogo Island was the creation of a fishing cooperative, to replace external ownership and control of the fishing industry. Videotape recordings are now commonly used for the same purpose elsewhere, because they are more easily handled.

While widespread participation in newly active groups is normally considered desirable, it may not be necessary for the success of local groups. Lisa R. Peattie, for example, suggests that to most effectively promote and achieve neighborhood intentions, "what the organization needed to be effective as a political force was the following: a limited number of leaders; enough supporters to fill a hall at occasional public meetings; and the absence of active local opposition" [1970, p. 406]. According to this argument, citizen participation under the assistance of an advocate planner resembles more a dramatic performance, designed to communicate a point indelibly before the eyes of those whose job it is to make decisions, rather than a widespread or continuous operation.

According to a very recent statement [Friedmann 1973], the process of planning is ideally a situation of mutual learning on the part of planners and the planned, transactive in nature and removed entirely from official structures such as traditionally conducted planning operations. According to this view, the really important decisions in planning are made by politicians in any case, and a united, convinced population is the only way of achieving the changes that are thought necessary. The planner in this scheme has the lowest possible profile, one where gentle counsel and mutually beneficial interchange diffuse outward through the population into eventual effect.

While advocate planners commonly stress independence from practice with official planning organizations, it is clear that the approaches they take and the methods they use vary greatly, as might be expected in the infancy of any new movement.

As our attention has come increasingly close to the present, more and more mention has been made of the relationship of planning products and processes to political structures and functions. In fact, the success or failure of planning cannot be understood without reference to a much wider societal context.

SOCIETAL CONTEXT

I have thus far painted a picture that is far from pretty. It shows some products that were lovingly created but hardly used, and others rushed into use only to create new problems, which then require an increasing rate of change in programs, and in both intellectual and methodological processes. While one can point to occasionally stellar products of planning around the world, it is a matter of serious debate within the United States as to whether, on balance, cities have really benefited from the practice of city planning.

Since there is no reason to suppose that planners are any more evil or stupid than the rest of us, one must look to specific details in the society around them in order to discover why the very rational products and processes of this profession have not produced concrete results which are up to potential expectations.

There are at least three nonmutually exclusive, potential explanations: 1. the structure of employment, 2. the structure of urban decision-making, and 3. the scope of planning in regard to the source of urban problems.

Employment Structure

In the United States, municipal affairs is legally a state power, and in Canada, it is a provincial responsibility. In both cases, legislation enables municipalities to have planning staffs, to create plans, and to implement them, although in some cases with residual rights of approval or review held by the more senior level of government. The major context of planning activity, however, is at the municipal level, in concert with other aspects of municipal government.

There are very few cases in which local planning authorities or quasi-planning authorities are constituted in such a way as to be able to do anything they want to *without* approval by elected officials and their financial support.[9]

Regardless of where the formal planning function is located in municipal government, its internal structure is usually bifurcated. While there is usually a planning "staff" charged with conducting the technical studies and other ongoing work, there is also usually a planning "commission" (or board), which formulates official policies about planning. No plans or planning reports are official, let alone adopted by elected representatives, without the approval of the commission. Consequently, there is a division between the planning professionals and a group of lay people in the planning process, and it is the latter who decide what goes forward for adoption and implementation. The chief planner from the planning staff normally sits on the planning commission, in a position such as executive secretary. The other members of the commission, however, are generally civic leaders, often unpaid, with a background either in law, real estate, engineering, or business. Aldermen may also sit on the commission, but this is not typical.

Planning commissions are normally seen as "blue ribbon" organizations, representing a literate community elite. They seldom include representatives of disadvantaged groups affected by city plans or persons highly knowledgeable about actual day-to-day political processes. The work of planning professionals, then, has had to go through a body primarily lacking in professional expertise, in knowledge of their primary

---

9. One well-known exception is the Port of New York Authority, set up to build and administer all forms of transportation facilities within a 30-mile radius of the tip of Manhattan. With its own borrowing power and with board members enjoying long, staggered periods of appointments by the governors of New York and New Jersey, this organization worked for years in virtual autonomy, concentrating on transportation projects that would earn money for future reinvestment. Only in recent years have the practices of this authority been put so strongly into the public spotlight, that what are considered its abuses of power have been curtailed to a greater degree.

clientele (at least in numbers), and in the realpolitik necessary for plan implementation. Nonetheless, planning commissions have normally been benign, and the forceful chief planner has been able to see his own and his department's suggestions adopted by his commission.

Although this may be a satisfactory situation for the morale of the planning staff in the short run, it is not necessarily as satisfactory if one were to expect planning commissions to improve upon the quality of plans submitted or to help to insure their implementation.

One of the frustrations in the early days of comprehensive planning was the wide gulf between blue-ribbon planning commissions and elected representatives. A consequence of this gulf was that planning commissions did not succeed in selling these plans to political leaders, leading to the lack of implementation of plans representing considerable investments of time and money. It is only in fairly recent years that sociologists and political scientists have been conducting studies outlining the structure of community power,[10] and neither planners nor planning commissions without extraordinary powers of observation were able to utilize this information in the course of attempting to put their plans into operation.

The commission and staff may report directly to the mayor. In this case, personal rapport and political sophistication are highly important, and planning has the important advantage of a direct link to a powerful person with the potential to help implement their suggestions. A recent study, for example, indicates that the support of the local mayor is still a vital factor in the success of community projects [Kuo 1973].

Planning may also be a governmental division or section, like the recreation department or the public health department, in a line of hierarchy and with formal equality in comparison with other departments. In this case, an effort must be made to balance the demands of higher authorities with the professional judgement of the planning staff, while at the same time settling interdepartmental jealousies over what functions the planners will perform as one among equals. Planning, in this situation, also lacks the direct ear of decision-makers in a formal sense, although astute planners may arrange this informally.

In those unusual occurrences when planning is in fact an independent authority, completely outside of political control, the balance between effective activity and regard for the public interest must be closely scrutinized. In the case of the Port of New York Authority, for exam-

---

10. See, for example, the wide range of contributions to this subject in Hawley and Wirt [1968].

ple, no one would ever accuse this organization of a lack of effective activity, but their practice of pursuing projects that would be money-makers, selecting only these from a very much larger number of possible activities of more considerable social relevance to the community, raised some questions about how well they fulfilled their potential of serving the public interest.

Structurally, then, the planner works in an employment setting where he not only has to deal with great amounts of information, and with a wide variety of interests relevant to the formulation of plans, but where the output of his work must filter through a special stratum of laymen and/or formal channels of government. Since planning is also governed by legal structures, planning output may also require judgement from judicial structures.

While innovation, scientific vigor, and sound municipal management practices may all be part of the planning process, the acceptance of any or all of these is almost exclusively dependent on others. While the planner is generally proud of having the skills of a professional, and usually some degree of insulation from direct political or civil service operations, this same structural situation also is in part responsible for his ultimate frustration.

According to one view, the wise planner, wishing to optimize his "success," will work as closely as possible with political leaders, he will adopt their goals (since he has no power of his own with which to succeed in defeating them), and then he will try to insure that these goals are carried out with the very best planning solutions. According to this view, politicians are much more likely to give heed to planners who support their own objectives.

This particular view was derived by Meyerson and Banfield [1955] after a study partly based on the experience of the senior author in the planning of public housing in Chicago. Their work indicates the great difference that can occur at times between the criteria arising from professional planning standards for the location and construction of a facility like public housing and the requirements held by formally elected political leaders. The former, for example, may emphasize the placement of public housing away from slums and near middle-class housing, in an attempt to help the residents of the new housing avoid problems attributable to poorly serviced neighborhoods. Politicians, on the other hand, may make their ultimate decisions on the basis of criteria such as the avoidance of public housing in the wards of powerful aldermen. Ultimately, Meyerson and Banfield claim, it is the elected political leaders who have formally been given the power to make decisions under existing civic structures, so that one should acknowledge this de facto situation. Regardless of how vigorously one might disagree with the activities and decisions of some political leaders, they must in some way represent their constituents or face defeat at the polls. In thus accepting the goals of political leaders and in grafting the very best planning practices to these goals, the planner, according to this view, is acting in the role of "handmaiden" to the politician.

This very situation, however, is that which has turned some planners to the pursuit of advocacy. If their only hope of success within their formal employment structure lies in the adoption of the goals of their superiors, helping to serve whatever particular interests these people wish to pursue (interests assumed to be different from those of great numbers in the population, despite the threat of elections), then some planners feel the need to make alternative plans from a different place in the social structure. What hinders the advocacy effort is that the source of support to pay the fees or salaries of planners still lies predominantly within official planning structures.

According to Martin Rein [1969], there are three possible forms of legitimation underlying planning: **1.** the need for consensus among elite institutional interests, **2.** the reverence for science and fact, and **3.** the validation of pluralism, diversity, and conflict on which democracy depends for its vitality. Rein feels that within normal planning structures, these forms of legitimation are mutually exclusive. Planning according to one or another of these criteria, depending on the specific setting, must either be abandoned within official structures, or taken elsewhere.

There is a general opinion that the typical planner in an official municipal planning position is in fact a government bureaucrat, pursuing specific technical tasks and with limitations to his own power. This is, of course, in conflict with the view that the planner gains from his training: that he is a comprehensive professional, whose judgment should be well regarded and heeded. The public, on the other hand, is thought to view the planner as an artist, capable of innovative and potentially useful flights of the imagination, but one to keep an eye on [Barr 1972].

As the preceding discussion suggests, the planner copes with these contextual paradoxes by concentrating on only one of several different styles available to him. He may emphasize his role as a "technician," not worrying about goals or implementation; as a "broker," worrying most about effectiveness in the political world that eventually decides the fate of plans and planners; or as a "mobilizer," going to and making active the public that in reality serves as clientele for the planning process [Rabinovitz 1969].

While the aforementioned discussion focuses on the difficulties inherent to most planners' structures of employment with respect to the adoption or acceptance of planning output, there is also a problem concerning eventual implementation. Even if plans and processes are fully accepted by the formal decision-makers, they are in fact carried out by a separate body of personnel. I referred earlier, for example, to the history of zoning, where committees deciding on zoning variances were able in practice to defeat any semblance of the implementation of the comprehensive plans that the zoning ordinances under their administration had been intended to achieve. While this is a clear and regular occurrence with respect to zoning issues, it is potentially applicable to any planning practice. In fact, when people are acting on behalf of other people because it is the job of the former and not the latter, there is always the possibility that the actual needs of the client may not be served. Much of this may be totally inadvertent, with the "servant" unaware of the actual consequences of his activity, because of differences in social class and/or personal experience. This problem of implementation might be thought of as the "many a slip twixt the cup and lip" phenomenon.

One solution may be the conscious selection, wherever possible, of people who are actually going to be involved as clients in jobs dealing with the implementation of plans. While public housing, for example, might not expect to have architects or planners as tenants, some workmen, superintendents, clerical workers concerned with tenant selection and rental payments, and the like, may well be drawn from among the constituency to live in the public housing. With them on the job from start to finish, there is much less likelihood that project planners and managers, not to speak of politicians, will be unaware of practices or conditions altering in midstream the positive intent behind the creation of a project. A second positive consequence of this practice, in return, would almost surely be a greater feeling of loyalty to such a project on the part of more "clients."

Therefore, while planners might hope to have more influence than they do in the implementation of their plans, the ultimate success of implementation may well depend on the extent to which ordinary people can be recruited without sacrificing the technical considerations in the implementation of the plans effecting them.

The Structure of Urban Decision-Making

It is one thing to explore the place of the planner with respect to decision-making *inside* his structure of employment. It is a much more complex question to explore the place of plans and planning operations vis-à-vis the many other forces in society that also have an effect in fact, if not in explicit intention, on planning decisions and their implementation. The burgeoning literature on community decision-making indicates that the concentration of power is in the hands of very few people with specific interests to be served, or in the hands of many people who represent a variety of interests (as well as all shades in between these extremes). Of course, the nature of the decision-making process tends to vary considerably between cities. It depends in large part on various other characteristics of these cities and their social and economic conditions. A common theme that emerges is that many persons and interest groups outside the realm of formal political decision-making are in fact overwhelmingly important in the resolution of urban problems and issues. While planners, planning commissions, planning directors, and politicians are themselves "actors" in the unfolding drama of urban legislation and management, they are part of a much larger cast, many of whose names never appear either in programs or reviews.

This situation is but another application of the distinction between formal and informal structures in society. The formal "blueprint" as to how decisions are made includes far fewer people and interests than the informal structure, which focuses on how things actually happen, whether or not sanctioned by laws or norms.

Some of the actors are those in positions where formal power may be wielded to control a situation, even if no one expected them to take part as *principal* actors in a planning decision. In a careful study, for example, of a large suburban housing project in Oslo, Norway, researchers aimed to discover the basis for satisfaction or dissatisfaction of the residents of this project. They felt it was necessary to go back to the period before construction in this study so as to see what motives the planners and architects of this project had in mind and whether these ideas were even incorporated in the implementation of the project. They discovered that the process of decision-making about the project took considerable time and that many different interest groups were involved in this process. Municipal politicians, planners, citizens groups, labor groups, and financial institutions were among the interested actors. On the basis of their observations, the authors concluded that the major design constraints on the project were exercised not by the planners and architects, or even by representatives of the potential residents, but by the lending institution involved [Norwegian Institute for Building Research 1969]. When one group has the power to say you may build it any way you want, but we will only give you the money if you build it this way, this group has the ability to wield considerable power in planning decisions.

A study of a renewal scheme affecting one segment of the black population of Halifax, Nova Scotia, indicated that once again there were a variety of actors affecting the choice of action to be taken [Clairmont & Magill 1974]. In a setting of considerable concern and uncertainty as to the most desirable path of action, the crucial actor turned out to be an outside consultant, brought in at a time of deadlock and with highly regarded professional credentials, whose advice after two days of exposure to the local situation was accepted. The point is not that this consultant may have been capable of being right or wrong after two days, but rather that the cruciality of his input would not have been expected from an inspection of the "normal" planning process and its relationship to how municipal decisions *should* be made. Outside professional reputations are frequently a source of additional power.

Altshuler [1965a] indicates in several illustrations in the Minneapolis-St. Paul area how the planner is but one of a number of forces, many of them legitimate, affecting planning decisions. In framing a decision on the construction of an urban freeway, for example, highway engineers were given considerably more credence than were planners, even though highway location has a considerable bearing on the future of urban neighborhoods and problems among the residents of these neighborhoods. The size and apparent exactness (because everything they produced came out in the form of numbers) of the corps of highway engineers underlay the strength of their influence.

This mixture of potential influences on planning decisions, all legitimate and powerful, although not part of the formal *planning* picture, is thought to dramatically weaken the planning function, since the constant input of formally external voices jeopardizes the possibility of ever moving very far in one direction. As one observer summarizes it, "money and programs would probably help a lot, but not unless accompanied by fundamental changes in the politics and management of cities" [Rogers 1971, p. 9]. The many ways in which legitimate and powerful groups or persons from outside the formal decision-making apparatus on planning questions can excercise an influence on the outcome of issues "contribute tremendously to the cities' lack of implementation power."

Participation in planning decisions by citizen groups is more recent. Although the reasons for such participation are clearly justifiable, with their absence in the past contributing to some of the difficulties in making acceptable plans, this presence is not unaccompanied by difficulties. If the planner was already hindered by the presence of "too many cooks" in preparing his broth, at a time when his fellow cooks spoke with quiet (though decisive) voices, his concern turns to fluster when these cooks have loud voices. As pointed out in an earlier section, local areas are seldom homogeneous, and citizens' groups are frequently in opposition to other citizen groups, to other interests of an economic or political nature, or to concerns held by *larger* numbers of people throughout the metropolitan area. Yet, there is a general tendency for groups of people, whether on planning issues or on any other issues, to think that they are the only ones on the side of sense and truth. According to Mack [1969], what is called "ethnocentrism" when applied to national groups of people is equally operable as a basis for *community* sentiment and conflict. When a group thinks that it's way is the only way, compromise is more difficult.

Coleman [1957] suggested that community conflicts may begin from a very minor and pragmatic issue to be settled. However, once any group takes serious exception to the proposed solution, there is usually a vast reservoir of uncommitted people available for them to win over. In an effort to win the day through the support of these uncommitted persons, the forces in opposition escalate the battle by generalizing the issues into those of a more emotional and all-encompassing nature, so that their "opponents" are now made to appear as people who are all bad. A typical controversy of the 1950s, for example, centered around fluoridation of drinking water, and the issue typically escalated into one of mass poisoning by big government, rather than dealing with the pros and cons of the particular actions suggested.

The planner, of course, stands in the middle of such controversy. While he may have encouraged citizen participation, its outcome may have a determinative effect on his plans, based on criteria quite apart from the terms of reference, because political leaders eager to benefit from clear statements of public sentiment are highly likely to seek out the largest and loudest of the public voices and then follow it to its logical conclusion. Planners are seldom a significant portion of a politician's constituency.

Although citizen group expressions commonly arise in response to a relevant planning issue, possibly escalating beyond it, one additional frustration of the planner arises from groups whose concern is directly with the political process and not with the planning process. Although formed in response to a planning issue, the purpose of the groups is to acquire a measure of political power, and not to work rationally to create a solution to the planning issue. One study, for example, indicates that this contribution of citizens groups was common in the Model Cities program in the United States. When the battle is raging for political control, no one is really in control of the planning decision (least of all the planner, who is never given formal control over it), the result being further delays and/or obstacles to the achievement of any consistent program [Warren 1969]. As Rein put it, "involvement, although it facilitates legitimation, impedes innovation" [p. 237].

Some actors in the planning process seldom appear explicitly, even in the informal situation. These are persons served by the assumptions generally adopted by existing levels of government, as well as by some of the general principles underlying acceptable professional planning practices. These are persons benefiting, for example, from institutions such as free enterprise, the market for land, and economic growth, in favor of which most existing bodies quite clearly and purposefully operate. Yet, as some commentators have observed, planning is inherently a matter involving the distribution of resources [Pahl 1970; Kravitz 1970; Grabow & Heskin 1973], and the ways in which such resources as land, location, and enterprise can be distributed are much more varied than the ways supported by most current practices. According to this argument, even advocate planners, when encouraging local groups to put forward plans reflecting the best arrangement of land with respect to their interests, are overly conservative, because they encourage continuing to play in a game with a set of rules based upon overly restricted premises. It is not clear what would then be necessary other than a revolution, either of goals or of state (although Friedmann, [1973] makes this revolution incredibly gentle and pleasant, calling it "learning"), but the point here is that there *are* nonuser actors being actively served by most planning decisions, since they commonly reaffirm land value (as an important determinant of location and land use), private ownership of land (hence profits on land accruing to private or corporate individuals), and the continual growth of cities (profiting existing enterprises).

The multiplicity of actors involved in planning decisions represents a situation brilliantly described by Norton E. Long. In an article entitled

"The Local Community as an Ecology of Games" [1958], he demonstrated that within the city there are many groups with focused, limited interests. The pursuit of each interest involves a minor sphere of all city life, but within this sphere there are distinct rules to be followed, as in games. You attack each problem that arises by playing a long-established game according to its rules. In the aggregate, though, there are a lot of people playing a lot of games, each with a separate set of rules. The game of urban management, and hence planning, is to achieve some order from the many divergent interest group outputs. For any one group, the rest of the world is an external environment. The environment of the planner, however, is a mosaic of interest groups, not in cooperative contact with one another. This is a most hostile environment for concerted, effective planning.

One partial test of this influence was made by Hawley [1968], who assessed whether effective action with respect to urban renewal was related to the number of interests participating in these decisions. His analyses confirmed his expectations that urban renewal programs were implemented most quickly when *fewer* groups were involved in the process.

Another analysis was concerned with environmental decision-making in Sweden. Seizing upon a case of citizen protest against a proposed housing project, the author concludes that even when sustaining an unusual display of protest, plans are implemented as efficiently and as expertly as they are in Sweden because virtually the only forum for such decision making is a surprisingly vast but nonetheless homogenous and technically expert body of designers, predominantly trained in planning and architecture [Anton 1969].[11] The absence of widely divergent interests in the Swedish case is therefore thought more permissive of concerted planning and its implementation, however "wrong" in the eyes of someone representing interests unrealized in the products of planning.

Therefore, in addition to whatever misgivings planners may have in their formal relationship with municipal decision-makers, their jobs are made considerably more complex by the fact that planners and politicians together share the world with many others.

---

11. It is perhaps the combination of monolithism and proven effectiveness that has provoked the degree of organizational competence and outspoken ideology characteristic of Swedish environmental protest groups since about 1971.

The Scope of Planning in Regard to the Source of Urban Problems

A final point may be made much more briefly. Despite formidable difficulties, planners do the best they can to create a better city. Yet, no matter how widely the field of planning has been expanded in order to include the consideration and the coordination of nonphysical factors, there are certain problems that inevitably pervade the planners' province.

The racial problem, for example, is so deep-seated and multiply based that it is overly optimistic to expect the kinds of recommendations with which planners deal to have much effect on anything with the exception of scattered symptoms of the problem. Yet, this kind of problem has an affect on almost anything the planner might choose to do in American cities.

The same is true, for example, of land values. While the planners' activities may greatly *affect* the value of individual parcels of land, the fact that land has value and that this value influences land use is something beyond the scope of their activities. If desired, something can obviously be done about land value. Czechoslovakians have done it through nationalization, and Swedes have done it through taxation. But it is not the planner whose voice is crucial in a decision as monumental as abolishing the possibility of increases in land value.

None of us, of course, are omnipotent, fun though it might be. What represents a considerable limitation, however, on professional efforts upon which many people pin such high hopes, is that the effects of these efforts are limited by phenomena that those responsible are powerless to control.

Furthermore, some persons through the years have expected city planners to ameliorate many of the more purely "social problems," such as delinquency, addiction, prostitution, gambling, etc., despite the lack of clearly related causal factors under their control. Surely, the scope of planning does not go as far as all this.

SOCIOLOGY IN PLANNING

In a unit written as part of an urban sociology series, some mention of where the working sociologist fits into the planning process is relevant. Although it is hardly unsociological to investigate the products of planning from a social perspective, to examine planning processes as they increasingly take into consideration, and interact directly with, urban residential groups, and to examine the success, failure, and potential of planning with respect to the societal context in which planners are found, it is also appropriate to ask whether sociologists are capable of doing anything besides *dissecting* this field.

Since sociology is a discipline focused on the behavior of people with reference to their membership in groups and aggregates (not the least of these being the kinds of groups and aggregates found in cities), a field such as planning, which has been forced to turn its attention to the amelioration of urban problems having a local and social content, is forced to admit its dependence on sociology. What is far less certain is *how* the two pursuits interact. In practice, considerable malaise often accompanies attempts at interaction between planners and sociologists, despite the best of intentions on the part of the two groups. They seem unable to communicate.

One immediate reason for this difficulty is that neither side necessarily has an a priori vision of the needs and talents of the other. Much sociology, for example, is not directly related to urban development, and most sociologists are capable of remaining on the exciting frontiers of their field for a lifetime without considering the kinds of questions relevant to planners.

Furthermore, there is an attitude, among many nonsociologists working in areas in which sociological input is now considered relevant, that sociological concerns are a "black box" in outlines of their own subject matter. Planners, for example, would continue to emphasize, as strongly as before many extremely detailed physical and economic factors impinging upon the planning decision, while reducing the sociological to a single category, which an outsider should be thought capable of handling.

What the participants in these "interdisciplinary" encounters fail to realize is that much of planning is *inherently* sociological. What they had been doing already was already sociological, but simply developed far less than the potential for it and far less than comparable inputs that were a more traditional part of the recognized system.

According to this perspective, planning is sociology. Planning is also political science. It is economics. It is civil engineering. It is geography. It is social work. It is much more again.

Each of these is not an exotic input to something definite and concrete called the planning process but is intrinsically present at many points in the various processes involved in the creation and implementation of plans.[12]

Someone, too, has to put the diverse factors together, but this itself may be a specialty within the planning process rather than the process itself. In fact, as earlier discussions have suggested, citizens may increasingly be the ones to fit the elements together in the creation of operating programs, under the guidance of an urban manager (originally spelled "planner").

It is for this reason that a formal degree in city planning no longer appears as exclusively necessary as it once might have been as qualification for a job in planning. Persons with training in sociology, geography, economics, and the other backgrounds may be just as useful, if not more so, through the necessarily greater depth of knowledge in a single field, for most jobs in planning offices.

All specialists need not necessarily speak each others' languages if they are free and responsible to produce what is required in the context of planning. Their reduction to a single common denominator is unnecessary, if their output is complementary and complete.

So the major question of this section is not "what can sociologists do for the planners?" but "what can sociologists do in planning?"

The answer to this question is in fact found throughout the first three sections of the unit. The sociological content of planning is scattered among the various concerns of planning and its processes. At this point, only some summarizing observations are required.

1. It is basic, for plans to have any effect for the planning group or agency, to understand the societal context in which it is operating and, hence, the kind of program that might eventually suceed in the amelioration of urban problems. Studies of the political process, both formal and informal, in which a planning operation will unfold, as well as the nature of the urban problems to be attacked, are essential as prerequisites to the choice of a mode of proceeding.

2. Sociologists can gather much factual data, documenting the people and places to which a planning operation is oriented.

3. Sociologists are unquestionably involved in the assessment of goals and specific opinions and judgments, whether by indirect or direct means of assessing these in the relevant publics.

---

12. The reader may note that the definition and practice of a discipline may vary from nation to nation. In Eastern Europe, a great deal of *all* work done by sociologists is what we refer to as social and physical planning.

4. Sociological understanding of group and political processes may dictate the most fruitful ways in which public participation might be harnessed in any particular situation.

5. Sociologists can measure the experience that people have with elements already in existence and that are being considered for future plans. These include some of the major concepts used in planning, as well as specific social programs.

6. Sociologists can aid the actual process of design through their knowledge gained from previous studies of what social implications have arisen under specific contextual conditions.

7. Sociologists are obligated to join others in the planning process in evaluating such plans as are implemented, so that future planning may benefit from the consequences of existing plans. This is nothing more than the research and development process employed in other sectors of science and technology.

In order to work satisfactorily in this context, sociologists require few tools additional to those already in the repertoire of the methodologically competent sociologist. While it is true that some techniques, which are underutilized within the field of sociology more generally, are particularly useful in environmental contexts, and that others may be utilized in somewhat differing fashions when applied to environmental questions,[13] this does not require a totally different curriculum to train the sociologist in planning.

What is required is a deep sensitivity to the widest ranges of the context relevant to planning. This is the same attention, however, increasingly forced upon even the most traditional planner not versed in any single *substantive* discipline. It is this attention that not only puts planning in the sociologist but also puts sociology, together with some hope of overcoming current obstacles and frustrations, into planning.

---

13. For more discussion of this, see Dolven [1970], Michelson [1970], and Michelson [1974].

Bibliography

Christopher Alexander, "A City Is Not a Tree." In John Gabree, ed., *Surviving the City.* Ballantine, 1973, pp. 106–136.

Saul D. Alinsky, *Reveille for Radicals,* Vintage Books, 1969.

William Alonso, "Cities and City Planners." In H. Wentworth Eldredge, ed., *Taming Megalopolis.* Doubleday Anchor Books, 1967, 2:580–596.

William Alonso, "What Are New Towns For." *Urban Studies,* 1970, 7:37–55.

Alan A. Altshuler, *The City Planning Process: A Political Analysis.* Cornell University Press, 1965a.

Alan A. Altshuler, "The Goals of Comprehensive Planning." *Journal of the American Institute of Planners,* 1965b, 31:186–195.

Alan A. Altshuler, "New Institutions to Serve the Individual." In William R. Ewalt, Jr., ed., *Environment and Policy: The Next Fifty Years.* Indiana University Press, 1968, pp. 423–444.

Thomas J. Anton, "Politics and Planning in a Swedish Suburb." *Journal of the American Institute of Planners,* 1969, 35:253–263.

Donald Appleyard, "City Designers and the Pluralistic City." In Lloyd Rodwin and Associates, eds., *Planning Urban Growth and Regional Development.* M.I.T. Press, 1969, chapter 23.

Sherry R. Arnstein, "A Ladder of Citizen Participation." *Journal of the American Institute of Planners,* 1969, 35:216–224.

Donald A. Barr, "The Professional Urban Planner." *Journal of the American Institute of Planners,* 1972, 38:55–159.

Jewell Bellush and Murray Hausknecht, *Urban Renewal: People, Politics, and Planning.* Doubleday Anchor Books, 1967.

Thad L. Beyle and George T. Lathrop, "Planning and Politics: On Grounds of Incompatibility?" In Beyle & Lathrop, eds., *Planning and Politics.* Odyssey Press, 1970, pp. 1–12.

Walter Bor, "Designing for New and Expanding Communities in Britain, 1946-1971." *Ekistics,* 1973, 36:8–13.

Brent Brolin and John Zeisel, "Mass Housing: Social Research and Design." *Architectural Forum,* July/August 1968, pp. 66–71.

Stanley Buder, "Ebenezer Howard: The Genesis of a Town Planning Movement." *Journal of the American Institute of Planners,* 1969, 35:390–398.

Robert W. Burchell, *Planned Unit Development: New Communities American Style.* Rutgers University, Center for Urban Policy Research, 1972.

Ernest Burgess, "The Growth of the City." In Robert E. Park, Ernest W. Burgess, and Roderick McKenzie, *The City.* University of Chicago Press, 1925, chapter 2.

Edmund M. Burke, "Citizen Participation Strategies." *Journal of the American Institute of Planners,* 1968, 34:287–294.

F. Stuart Chapin, Jr., *Urban Land Use Planning.* Harper, 1957.

Donald Clairmont and Dennis Magill, *Africville: The Life and Death of a Canadian Black Community.* McClelland & Stewart, 1974.

James Coleman, *Community Conflict.* The Free Press, 1957.

Peter Cowan, ed., *The Future of Planning.* London: Heinemann, 1973.

Fred M. Cox et al., *Strategies of Community Organization.* Itasca, Ill., F. E. Peacock, 1970.

John Dakin, "The Evaluation of Plans." *Town Planning Review,* 1973, 44:3–30.

Paul Davidoff, "Advocacy and Pluralism in Planning." *Journal of the American Institute of Planners,* 1965, 31:331–338.

Paul Davidoff, Linda Davidoff, and Neil N. Gold, "Suburban Action: Advocate Planning for an Open Society." *Journal of the American Institute of Planners,* 1970, 36:12–21.

Arne S. Dolven, "Sociologi i by-og regionplanlegning." Unpublished paper. Oslo: Norsk Institutt for By-og Regionforskning, 1970.

H. Wentworth Eldredge, "Lessons Learned from the British New Towns Program." In Eldredge, ed., *Taming Megalopolis.* Doubleday Anchor Books, 1967, 2:823–829.

Hazel Evans, ed., *New Towns: The British Experience.* London: Charles Knight, 1972.

Henry Fagin, "The Evolving Philosophy of Urban Planning." In Leo F. Schnore and Henry Fagin, eds., *Urban Research and Policy Planning,* Sage, 1967, pp. 309–328.

Gordon Fellman, "Neighborhood Protest of an Urban Highway." *Journal of the American Institute of Planners,* 1969, 35:118-122.

James Marston Fitch, *American Building.* 2nd ed. Houghton Mifflin, 1972.

Marc Fried, "Transitional Functions of Working-Class Communities: Implications for Forced Relocation." In Mildred B. Kantor, ed., *Mobility and Mental Health.* Charles C. Thomas, 1965, pp. 123-165.

Marc Fried, "Functions of the Working Class Community in Modern Urban Society; Implications for Forced Relocation." *Journal of the American Institute of Planners,* 1967, 33:317-323.

Marc Fried, *The World of The Urban Working Class.* Harvard University Press, 1973.

Marc Fried & Peggy Gleicher, "Some Sources of Residential Satisfaction in an Urban Slum." *Journal of the American Institute of Planners,* 1961, 27:305-315.

John Friedmann, *Retracking America.* Anchor Press/Doubleday, 1973.

Herbert J. Gans, "From Urbanism to Policy Planning." *Journal of the American Institute of Planners,* 1970, 36:223–225.

Herbert J. Gans, "The Human Implications of Current Redevelopment and Relocation Planning." *Journal of American Institute of Planners,* 1959, 25: 15–25.

Herbert J. Gans, *The Urban Villagers.* The Free Press of Glencoe, 1962.

Herbert J. Gans, *The Levittowners.* Pantheon, 1968.

Herbert J. Gans, *People and Plans.* Basic Books, 1968.

David R. Godschalk, "The Circle of Urban Participation." In H. Wentworth Eldredge, ed., *Taming Megalopolis.* Doubleday Anchor Books, 1967, 2: 971–979.

David R. Godschalk, "Comparative New Community Design." *Journal of the American Institute of Planners,* 1967, 33:371–387.

David R. Godschalk, "Reforming New Community Planning." *Journal of the American Institute of Planners,* 1973, 39:306–315.

Paul Goodman and Percival Goodman, *Communitas.* Vintage Books, rev. ed., 1960.

Julius Gorynski, "The Problem of Participation in New Town Development: Nowa Huta, Poland." *Ekistics,* 1973, 36:40–41.

Stephen Grabow and Allan Heskin, "Foundations for a Radical Concept of Planning." *Journal of the American Institute of Planners,* 1973, 39:106, 108–114.

Scott Greer, *Urban Renewal and American Cities.* Bobbs-Merrill, 1965.

John L. Hancock, "Planners in the Changing American City, 1900–1940." *Journal of the American Institute of Planners,* 1967, 33:290–303.

Chester Hartman, "The Housing of Relocated Families." In James Q. Wilson, ed., *Urban Renewal: The Record and the Controversy.* M.I.T. Press, 1966, pp. 293–335.

Amos H. Hawley, "Community Power and Urban Renewal Success." In Terry N. Clark, ed., *Community Structure and Decision-making: Comparative Analysis.* Chandler Publishing, 1968. (Originally published in *American Journal of Sociology,* 1963.)

Willis D. Hawley and Frederick M. Wirt, *The Search for Community Power.* Prentice-Hall, 1968.

Wilson A. Head, "The Ideology and Practice of Citizen Participation." In James A. Draper, ed., *Citizen Participation: Canada.* New Press, 1971, pp. 14–29.

B. J. Heraud, "Social Classes and the New Towns." *Urban Studies,* 1968, 5:33–58.

Gerald Hodge, "Who Are the Planners—Where Do They Plan." Paper presented to the Annual Meeting of the Town Planning Institute of Canada, 1968.

Ebenezer Howard, *Garden Cities of Tomorrow.* London, S. Sonnenschein, 1902, M.I.T. Press, 1965.

International City Managers' Association, *Local Planning Administration.* Chicago, 1941.

Reginald Isaacs, "The Neighborhood Theory, An Analysis of Its Adequacy," *Journal of the American Institute of Planners,* 1948, 14:15–23.

Jane Jacobs, *The Death and Life of Great American Cities.* Random House, 1961.

Marshall Kaplan, "Advocacy and the Urban Poor." *Journal of the American Institute of Planners,* 1969, 35:96–101.

Alan S. Kravitz, "Mandarinism: Planning as Handmaiden to Conservative Politics." In T. L. Beyle and G. T. Lathrop, eds., *Planning and Politics.* Odyssey Press, 1970, pp. 240–267.

Wen H. Kuo, "Mayoral Influence in Urban Policy Making." *American Journal of Sociology,* 1973, 79:620–638.

John B. Lansing, Robert W. Marans, and Robert B. Zehner, *Planned Residential Environments.* Ann Arbor: Institute for Social Research, Survey Research Center, 1970.

Norton E. Long, "The Local Community as an Ecology of Games." *American Journal of Sociology,* 1958, 64:251–261.

Raymond Mack, "The Components of Social Conflict." In Ralph M. Kramer and Harry Specht, eds., *Readings in Community Organization Practice.* Prentice-Hall, 1969, pp. 327–337.

J. Brian McLoughlin, *Urban and Regional Planning: A Systems Approach.* Praeger, 1969.

Pierre Merlin, *Les Villes Nouvelles.* Paris, Presses Universitaires de France, 1969.

Martin Meyerson and Edward Banfield, *Politics, Planning, and the Public Interest.* Free Press, 1955.

William Michelson, *Man and His Urban Environment: A Sociological Approach.* Addison-Wesley, 1970.

William Michelson, ed., *Behavioral Research Methods in Environmental Design.* Dowden, Hutchinson, & Ross, 1974.

Robert E. Mitchell, "Some Social Implications of High Density Housing." *American Sociological Review,* 1971, 36:18–29.

Simon Nicholson and Barbara K. Schreiner, *Community Participation in City Decision Making.* Milton Keynes: The Open University, 1973.

Norwegian Institute for Building Research, *Ammerud 1.* Oslo, 1969.

R. E. Pahl, *Whose City? and Other Essays on Sociology and Planning.* Longman, 1970.

Lisa R. Peattie, "Drama and Advocacy Planning." *Journal of the American Institute of Planners,* 1970, 36:405–410.

Lisa R. Peattie, "Reflections on Advocacy Planning." *Journal of the American Institute of Planners,* 1968, 34:80–88.

Harvey S. Perloff, "New Towns Intown." *Journal of the American Institute of Planners,* 1966, 32:155–161.

Clarence Perry, "The Neighborhood Unit Formula." In William L. C. Wheaton et al., eds., *Urban Housing.* The Free Press of Glencoe, 1966, pp. 94–109.

Norman Pressman, "French Urbanization Policy and the New Towns Program." *Ekistics,* 1973, 36:17–22.

Francine Rabinovitz, *City Politics and Planning.* Atherton, 1969.

Francine Rabinovitz and J. Stanley Pottinger, "Organization for Local Planning: The Attitudes of Directors." *Journal of the American Institute of Planners,* 1967, 33:27–32.

Lee Rainwater, "The Lessons of Pruitt-Igoe." In John Pynoos et al., eds., *Housing Urban America.* Aldine, 1973, pp. 548-555.

Martin Rein, "Social Planning: The Search for Legitimacy." *Journal of the American Institute of Planners,* 1969, 35:233–244.

Thomas Reiner, *The Place of the Ideal Community in Urban Planning.* University of Pennsylvania Press, 1963.

Ira M. Robinson, "Beyond the Middle-Range Planning Bridge." *Journal of the American Institute of Planners,* 1965, 31:304–312.

Ira M. Robinson, ed., *Decision-Making in Urban Planning.* Sage Publications, 1972.

Lloyd Rodwin, *Nations and Cities.* Houghton-Mifflin, 1970.

David Rogers, *The Management of Big Cities.* Sage Publications, 1971.

Frank Schaffer, *The New Town Story.* Paladin, 1970.

Alvin L. Schorr, *Slums and Social Insecurity.* U.S. Department of Health, Education and Welfare, Social Security Administration, Division of Research and Statistics, Research Report No. 1.

Robert Sommer, *Design Awareness,* Rinehart, 1972.

Clarence S. Stein, *Towards New Towns for America.* Reinhold, 1951.

Christopher Tunnard and Henry H. Reed, *American Skyline.* Mentor Books, 1956.

Jacqueline Tyrwhitt, "Changes in New Town Policies in Britain 1946–1971." *Ekistics,* 1973, 36:14–16.

U.S. Department of Housing and Urban Development, *Planned-Unit Development with a Homes Association.* Government Printing Office, 1970.

U.S. Department of Housing and Urban Development, "General Observations on British New Town Planning." Mimeographed report, 1973.

Raymond Vernon, *The Myth and Reality of Our Urban Problems.* M.I.T. Press, 1966.

Roland L. Warren, "Model Cities First Round: Politics, Planning, and Participation." *Journal of the American Institute of Planners,* 1969, 35:245–252.

Carl Werthman, Jerry S. Mandel, and Ted Dienstfray, "Planning and the Purchase Decision: Why People Buy in Planned Communities." A prepublication of the Community Development Project. University of California, Berkeley: Institute of Regional Development, Center for Planning and Development Research. Reprint No. 10, July 1965.

William H. Whyte, Jr., *The Organization Man.* Anchor Books, 1956.

William H. Whyte, Jr., "Cluster Development." In H. W. Eldredge, ed., *Taming Megalopolis.* Anchor Books, 1967, pp. 462–477.

Peter Willmott, "Social Research and New Communities." *Journal of the American Institute of Planners,* 1967, 33:387–398.

D. M. Wilner and R. P. Walkley, "Effects of Housing on Health and Performance." In Leonard J. Duhl, ed., *The Urban Condition*. Basic Books, 1962, pp. 215–228.

James Q. Wilson, ed., *Urban Renewal: The Record and the Controversy*. M.I.T. Press, 1966.

Deil S. Wright, "Governmental Forms and Planning Functions: The Relation of Organizational Structures to Planning Practice." In T. L. Beyle and G. T. Lathrop, eds., *Planning and Politics*. Odyssey Press, 1970, pp. 68–105.

Robert B. Zehner, "Neighborhood and Community Satisfaction in New Towns and Less Planned Suburbs." *Journal of the American Institute of Planners*, 1971, 37:379–385.

Robert B. Zehner and Robert Marans, "Residential Density, Planning Objectives and Life in Planned Communities." *Journal of the American Institute of Planners*, 1973, 39:337–345.

Basil Zimmer, "The Small Businessman and Relocation." In James W. Wilson, ed., *Urban Renewal: The Record and the Controversy*, M.I.T. Press, 1966, pp. 380–403.

Gunnar Åsvärn, *Servicestudier i Vallingbyområdet*, Stockholm: Generalplaneberedningen, 1966.

Index